TRANSPORTATION
Economics and Public Policy

THE IRWIN SERIES IN ECONOMICS

Consulting Editor
LLOYD G. REYNOLDS
YALE UNIVERSITY

AMES   *Soviet Economic Processes*

ANDERSON, GITLOW, & DIAMOND (Editors)   *General Economics: A Book of Readings*   rev. ed.

BALASSA   *The Theory of Economic Integration*

BEAL & WICKERSHAM   *The Practice of Collective Bargaining*   3d ed.

BLAUG   *Economic Theory in Retrospect*   rev. ed.

BORNSTEIN (Editor)   *Comparative Economic Systems: Models and Cases*

BORNSTEIN & FUSFELD (Editors)   *The Soviet Economy: A Book of Readings*   rev. ed.

BUCHANAN   *The Public Finances*   rev. ed.

CARTTER   *Theory of Wages and Employment*

CARTTER & MARSHALL   *Labor Economics: Wages, Employment, and Trade Unionism*

DAVIDSON, SMITH, & WILEY   *Economics: An Analytical Approach*   rev. ed.

DAVIS, HUGHES, & McDOUGALL   *American Economic History: The Development of a National Economy*   rev. ed.

DOLL, RHODES, & WEST   *Economics of Agricultural Production, Markets, and Policy*

DRUMMOND   *The Canadian Economy: Organization and Development*

DUE   *Government Finance: An Economic Analysis*   3d ed.

DUE & CLOWER   *Intermediate Economic Analysis*   5th ed.

DUNLOP & HEALY   *Collective Bargaining: Principles and Cases*   rev. ed.

FELLNER   *Probability and Profit: A Study of Economic Behavior along Bayesian Lines*

FERGUSON   *Microeconomic Theory*

GAMBS & KOMISAR   *Economics and Man*   3d ed.

GORDON   *The Investment Financing and Valuation of the Corporation*

GRAMPP & WEILER (Editors)   *Economic Policy: Readings in Political Economy*
   3d ed.

GROSSMAN, HANSEN, HENDRIKSEN, MCALLISTER, OKUDA, & WOLMAN (Editors)
   Readings in Current Economics   rev. ed.

GUTHRIE   *Statistical Methods in Economics*

GUTHRIE & WALLACE   *Economics*   3d ed.

HALM   *Economics of Money and Banking*   rev. ed.

HARRISS   *The American Economy: Principles, Practices and Policies*   6th ed.

HIGGINS   *United Nations and U.S. Foreign Economic Policy*

HERBER   *Modern Public Finance*

JOME   *Principles of Money and Banking*

KINDLEBERGER   *International Economics*   4th ed.

KUHLMAN & SKINNER   *The Economic System*   rev. ed.

LEE   *Macroeconomics: Fluctuations, Growth, and Stability*   4th ed.

LLOYD   *Microeconomic Analysis*

LOCKLIN   *Economics of Transportation*   6th ed.

MEYERS   *Economics of Labor Relations*

PEGRUM   *Public Regulation of Business*   rev. ed.

PEGRUM   *Transportation: Economics and Public Policy*   rev. ed.

PHILLIPS   *The Economics of Regulation: Theory and Practice in the Transportation and Public Utility Industries*

REYNOLDS   *Economics: A General Introduction*   rev. ed.

RIMA   *Development of Economic Analysis*

SCITOVSKY   *Welfare and Competition: The Economics of a Fully Employed Economy*

SIEGEL   *Aggregate Economics and Public Policy*   rev. ed.

SIRKIN   *Introduction to Macroeconomic Theory*   rev. ed.

SMITH & TEIGEN (Editors)   *Readings in Money, National Income, and Stabilization Policy*

SNIDER   *Introduction to International Economics*   4th ed.

SPENCER, CLARK, & HOGUET   *Business and Economic Forecasting: An Econometric Approach*

SPENCER   *Managerial Economics: Text, Problems, and Short Cases*   3d ed.

VANEK   *International Trade: Theory and Economic Policy*

WILCOX   *Public Policies toward Business*   3d ed.

TRANSPORTATION
Economics and Public Policy

DUDLEY F. PEGRUM, Ph.D.

Professor of Economics, Emeritus
University of California at Los Angeles

Revised Edition · 1968

RICHARD D. IRWIN, INC.   Homewood, Illinois

IRWIN–DORSEY LIMITED   Nobleton, Ontario

REVISED EDITION

First Printing, March, 1968

Library of Congress Catalog Card No. 67–30243
PRINTED IN THE UNITED STATES OF AMERICA

To

Douglas and Nancy

and

their irrepressible three:

Phyllis Elaine

Pamela Elise

Patrice Eileen

PREFACE to the First Edition

Transportation is an activity that involves the movement of people and goods from one place to another. As a consequence, it is one of the most significant aspects of the spatial phases of man's everyday life. To perform its functions, transportation must utilize the mechanical and physical equipment developed by the physical scientists and engineers. It requires huge capital expenditures to provide the necessary facilities and a large labor force to operate them. The technical problems of business organization and traffic management require specialists in this area of the activity. The necessity of transportation for defense and for organized community life has led government through the ages to participate extensively, and in various ways, in the supplying of the services. In all countries, therefore, transportation is a matter of prime concern to the governments. In countries where private enterprise renders transportation services for others, specialized forms of public control have grown up, and a large body of transport law has emerged. Finally, transportation, with its huge demands on economic resources, has been of special interest to the economist because of the unique place it occupies in the economic activity of society, and because of the unique institutional setting in which it discharges its functions.

It is clear, therefore, that one can scarcely discuss transportation as such. It must be dealt with primarily from the standpoint of the particular discipline involved. Furthermore, in many respects each one may be self-contained in its treatment. However, it is necessary to be aware of the interrelationships. The economist is concerned with the problem of the economical allocation and utilization of resources as this relates to transportation. He cannot deal with it, however, in a vacuum. He must recognize the impact of technical developments and the implications of the political, legal, and institutional arrangements under which the services are rendered. It is necessary, therefore, to present a considerable array of factual information derived from these other fields in order to deal with the specific economic questions that arise. Nevertheless, this information is not significant for its own sake; it is important only as it provides the empirical basis for the development of the economic analysis. A mere recitation of the rulings of courts and commissions, of traffic movements, of technical developments, or of the techniques of shipping goods or moving persons is significant only as it provides the necessary facts upon which the economic analysis can be built or from which it may be derived. It is upon this basis that the factual information in this book has been developed. Finally, it may be noted that the treatment was purposely confined to less than 600 pages. This necessitated the elimination or compression of much detail that might be of interest to many readers.

The book is divided into five main parts, each of which is designed to be more or less self-contained. Each part, however, is built upon the preceding one with the endeavor to avoid as much repetition as possible. Part I deals with transportation as an economic activity and its place in the economy. The development of transportation is set forth so as to emphasize the way in which the present problems of business operation and public policy have emerged. The description of the transport system of the country is designed to give the reader a comprehensive picture of the means utilized in supplying the services today.

Part II sets forth the basic economic principles that bear upon transportation and its problems. These are then applied to an analysis of the economic structure of the agencies that make up the transport system of the country and the significance of this to competition, monopoly, and organization. Attention is centered on the pricing process and the factors that have to be considered in the making of decisions, because these are the focal points of an efficient allocation and utilization of economic resources, and the subject matter of most of the discussion and controversy in transportation today.

Part III deals with the regulation of transportation in the United States. This has been presented in the framework of the historical approach, because present arrangements and policies constitute a continuous development from the beginning of regulation with surprisingly little discarding of what has been done in the past. Every attempt has been made to keep the details of legislation and its administration to a minimum. The emphasis has been on key issues and the steps that have been taken to deal with them as they have arisen.

Part IV on national transportation policy discusses what, in my opinion, are the key issues of the present time as they affect the conduct of private enterprise in transport, and as they affect public policy which is presumed to be directed to achieve an efficient allocation and utilization of economic resources. Every attempt has been made to deal with the problems in an objective fashion by a consistent application of the economic principles developed earlier in the book. That the evaluations will lead to sharp differences of opinion is unavoidable, but I hope that I have succeeded in laying a foundation of sound economic analysis that will generate more light than heat as the questions are debated.

Part V on urban transportation endeavors to set forth the basic problems of transportation that face the large metropolitan areas today. These problems vary from one center to another, but they have the common threads of a close relation to national transport policies and basic changes in the structure of the urban region as affected by the developments in modern transportation. Solutions to the issues that have arisen will have to give consideration to many similar factors, at the same time that they will differ in many fundamental respects. This has made it necessary to discuss suggested solutions in general terms with a limited number of illustrations of proposals for meeting some of the situations.

This book is a deliberate attempt to develop the economic principles of transportation. Therefore, the emphasis on economic theory calls for no apology. I believe that the underlying theory needs to be explained to the reader for, although it may be assumed that the latter has some acquaintance with elementary economics, few are likely to possess more than this. Unfortunately, too much that goes under the name of transport economics either ignores the theory or is in conflict with it. Sound transportation policies cannot be derived from unsound economic principles or from a lack of principles altogether. If the theory of efficient allocation and utilization of economic resources is established, then the grounds for differences of opinion on transport policies will have been narrowed to an application of the theory and to whatever other considerations may be relevant.

I also offer no apology for expressing my appraisal of the economical approach to the resolution of contemporary transport problems. No meaningful discussion of the issues can be undertaken outside of a clear-cut framework of economic theory. If this is established, it should be applied rigidly even though it runs counter to past policies and thinking, and to many current preconceptions. This does not mean that there are not wide areas for debate, but it does mean that if students of transport economics do not approach it through the accepted corpus of theory, or that they feel that what we have is inadequate or inapplicable, then they should develop new theory that is relevant.

The decision to limit the length of the book compelled a compression of the factual material, the analytical framework, the application of the principles, and much of the discussion of problems. It was thus not possible to present lengthy arguments on both sides of policy questions. For those who wish to pursue the study of various topics at greater length, a selected and annotated bibliography will be found in Appendix II.

I wish to acknowledge my indebtedness to the numerous scholars and writers who have made contributions to the subject matter covered by this book. I have drawn so heavily on them that it is often difficult for me to know which ideas are theirs and which are mine. I have given extensive recognition to them in footnotes and in the bibliography. Many, however, will not find their names in either place and for this I offer my apologies. Only the names of those whose works were directly and specifically drawn upon or whose writings constitute a convenient starting point for those who wish to pursue further the study of any particular topic have been included.

I also wish to accord recognition to colleagues and friends in economics and transportation in many universities throughout the country. My discussions with them on many of the topics have served to clarify issues to me and to shed new light on many of the problems. My association with a large number of persons in government and in private industry, both as a consultant for all the agencies of transport, except water, and as a participant in numerous conferences, forums, and personal discussions have served to keep me keenly aware of the practical issues with which these men have to deal and with the forces that help to shape their points of view. I hope that they will recognize my endeavor to maintain an objective position in the field of transportation as a whole.

Finally, special recognition must be given to my research assistants: Mrs. Gratia C. Bell, who worked untiringly in collecting materials on the law and its administration; and to Mr. Anthony C. Sutton for his aid on urban transportation, especially in the Los Angeles area. The selection of the material and its evaluation, however, are entirely my responsibility. Finally, to my wife must go that recognition for assistance, encouragement, and self-denial too often taken for granted, without which this book would never have been completed.

PREFACE to the Revised Edition

Transportation, particularly as the result of the impact of the spectacular development of recent technology, has emerged as one of the most important areas of economics and public policy at the present time. The enormous investment requirements, the emergence of many modes, and the changing relations among them have given rise to issues that are among the most complex faced by government today at all levels—local, state, and federal. Under the impact of huge governmental expenditures we are witnessing the phenomenon of technology running wild with little attention to, or responsibility for, the costs involved, and the impact of these on the public treasury or the public at large. It is especially imperative, therefore, that the economic issues of resource allocation and utilization be subject to critical evaluation and that economizing in transport become a matter of prime public consideration. This requires the development and application of market criteria, with all their complexities, to the control and operation of the transport system, even though private ownership may not be of universal application. If economics and economic principles are to play a significant role in transport operations and policy, then economists must take a stand on the issues that are at stake. If they do not do so, somebody else will do it for them.

The first edition of this book endeavored to examine the various problems of transportation, particularly as they related to public policy, from the standpoint of economics. The revision adheres to the same theme. Economics does not involve all the technical conditions of private management, nor, for that matter, all the technical considerations of regulation and administration; but it does establish the economic criteria upon which these must be based, if an economical and efficient system of transportation is to be developed for the future.

Every endeavor has been made to bring factual material up to date, although this is not intended to be a statistical, technical, or legal encyclopedia. There has been some reorganization of material in the section on National Policy with regard to Competition, Consolidation, and Administration. The Department of Transportation, recommended in the first edition, is discussed fully. Urban transportation has been given more comprehensive treatment and some new programs are included. Finally, the author has endeavored to clarify some of the economic analysis as a result of comments of colleagues in the field.

New editions always seem to suffer from expansion, and apparently this one is no exception, although the addition is not very large because of some excisions of the previous book. Authors find it difficult to discard very many of their previous "pearls of wisdom."

DUDLEY F. PEGRUM

University of California,
Los Angeles
February, 1968

TABLE OF CONTENTS

PART I. THE TRANSPORT SYSTEM

1 Transportation and the Economy   **3**
Scope of Transport Economics: *Nature of Transportation. Function of Transportation. Scope of Transport Economics.* Transport and the Location of Industry: *Factors in the Location of Industry. Transport and Regional Development. Development of Metropolitan Areas. Transport Location.* Transport and Prices: *Price Policies. Significance of Price Policies in Transport. The Unique Problem of Discrimination.* Effects of Improved Transportation: *Development of Technology in Transport. Transport and Production. Political and Social Effects. Measuring the Gains of Improved Transport.* The Political Basis of Transport: *Political Unity. National Defense. Eminent Domain. Common Carrier Obligations.* An Economical System of Transport: *Need for Cheap Transport. Meaning of Cheap Transport.* Reasons for Separate Treatment of Transport: *Unique Position of Transport. A Group of Industries. Limitation on the Forces of Competition. Public Investment. Antitrust Inadequate.*

2 Elements of a Modern Transport System   **24**
Introduction: *Purpose of the Description. Multiplicity of Agencies. Principal Groupings of Agencies. Relative Importance of the Agencies.* Railroads: *The Railroad Plant. Organization of Rail Transport. The Role of the Rail System in Modern Transport.* Motor Transport: *The Motor Transport Plant. The Role of Motor Transport.* Domestic Water Transport. The Domestic Waterways System: *Inland Waterway Transportation. The Role of Water Transport.* Air Transport: *The Air Transport Plant. The Role of Air Transport.* Pipe–Line Transport: *Oil Pipe Lines. Natural Gas Pipe–Line Companies.* Summary.

3 Development of Transportation in the United States   **47**
Introduction: *Significance of the History of Transport. Early Transport.* Rise of Modern Transportation: *Domestic Water Transport. Development of Rail Transport.* Rise of the New Transport Structure: *Inland Waterways. Motor Transport. Air Transport. Pipe Lines.* Effects of Changing Technology. Public Ownership and Public Aid: *Public Ownership. Public Aid. Public Aid versus Subsidy.*

4 Transport Geography   **77**
Introduction. Geographic Considerations: *Topography of the United States. Resources for Traffic Flows.* Basis of Transport Routes: *Physical Factors. Political Considerations.* Transport Routes of the United States: *Railroad Routes. Water Routes. Highway Routes. Air Routes. Pipe–Line Routes.* Commodity Flows.

5 Transport Services   104

Introduction. The Common Carrier: *Nature of the Common Carrier. Duties of Common Carriers. Freight Forwarders. Express and Package Service.* The Role of the Common Carrier: *The Common Carrier in the Transport System. Historical Nature of the Common Carrier.* Other Carriers for Hire: *Contract Carriers. Private Carriers.* Control of Service: *Sanctions for Regulated Carriers. Rail Passenger Service. Car Supply and Car Service. Extra Services.* Terminal Services: *Carload Freight. Less-than-Carload Freight.* Co-ordination of Services: *Joint Action of Independent Agencies. Methods of Traffic Interchange.*

PART II. ECONOMICS OF TRANSPORT PRICING

6 The Economic Structure of Transport   127

Transport as a Group of Industries: *Nature of an Industry. The Products of Transportation. Differences in Economic Structures.* Economies of Scale: *The Law of Diminishing Returns. Nature of Economies of Scale. Returns to Scale. Large-Scale Production.* Economies of Scale in Transport: *Economies of Scale in Rail Transport. Economies of Scale in Motor Transport. Other Agencies.* Competition versus Monopoly in Transport: *Nature of Railroad Monopoly. Ruinous Competition.* Organization of Transport.

7 The Theory of Pricing   149

Introduction. Classification and Characteristics of Markets: *Competition. Monopoly. Monopolistic Competition. Oligopoly.* Pricing for the Different Market Structures: *Pricing under Competition. Pricing under Monopoly. Pricing under Oligopoly. Pricing under Monopolistic Competition.* The Competitive Model as a Standard for Public Policy. Costs and the Pricing Process: *Costs and the Rate of Output. Traceability of Costs. Costs and Decision Making.* Price Discrimination: *The Idea of Discrimination. Costs and Price Discrimination. Hard versus Soft Competition.*

8 Theory of Pricing for Transport   174

Introduction. Pricing on the Basis of Costs: *Economical Pricing Reflects Costs. Difficulty of Ascertaining Precise Costs. Meaning of Pricing on the Basis of Cost for Transport.* Theory of Railroad Rate Making: *Railroad Costs. Cost Allocation. Discrimination and Differential Pricing. Ruinous Competition.* The Theory of Motor Carrier Rates: *Competitive Features of Motor Transport. Fixed and Variable Costs. Joint and Common Costs. Absence of Ruinous Competition.* Other Agencies: *Pipe Lines. Water Transport. Air Transport.* Theory of Interagency Pricing: *A Multiple Pricing Problem. Interagency Competition. Differential Pricing and Efficiency. Ruinous Competition.*

9 The General Level of Rates   198

Introduction. Principles of Price Regulation: *The Problem of Fair Prices. Regulation of Minimum Prices. Regulation of Maximum Prices. The Regulation of Precise Prices.* Theory of the General Level of Rates: *Cost-Plus Pricing.* Fair Value and Fair Return: *Valuation for Rate*

Making. Fair Value and the Courts. Fair Return. The General Level of Rates for Railroads: *The Legal Basis. Record of Railroad Earnings.* The General Level for Other Carriers. The General Level in a Competitive Setting.

10   Rate Making in Practice   227
      Introduction. Principles Underlying Particular Rates: *Cost of Service. Value of Service. Standards of Public Policy. The Problem of Discrimination.* Passenger Fares. Freight Classification: *Development of Classification. Commodity Rates. Classification for Other Carriers.* Rate Systems: *Freight Tariffs. Railroad Rate Systems. Motor Carriers. Other Carriers.* Long and Short Haul. Co-operation among Carriers: *Railroad Co-operation. Other Carriers. Through Routes and Joint Rates. Rate Bureaus.*

PART III. THE REGULATION OF TRANSPORT

11   The Agencies of Regulation   255
      Introduction: *Law and Economic Life. The Meaning of Regulation.* The Common-Law Basis of Regulation: *Nature of the Common Law. Emergence of Common-Law Control. The Right to Regulate.* Regulation under Federal Government: *The Federal Form of Government. The Constitution and Regulation. Powers of the National Government.* The Role of the Courts in Regulation: *Judicial Review. Functions of the Courts.* The Independent Regulatory Commission: *Development of Commission Regulation. The Nature of the Regulatory Commission. Courts versus Commissions in Regulation. Criticism of the Independent Regulatory Commission.* The Interstate Commerce Commission: *Membership and Appointment. Scope of Authority. Internal Organization.* The Civil Aeronautics Board: *Membership and Appointment. Scope of Authority.*

12   The Foundations of Transport Regulation   287
      Introduction: *The Basis of Regulation. Early Regulation. Reasons for the Development of Regulation.* State Regulation: *The Granger Laws. Court Interpretation of the Granger Laws. State versus Federal Authority.* The Act to Regulate Commerce, 1887: *Provisions of the Act of 1887. Judicial Interpretation. Results of the Act.* The Elkins Act, 1903. The Hepburn Act, 1906: *Provisions of the Act. Judicial Interpretation.* The Mann-Elkins Act, 1910: *Provisions of the Law. Application of the Law.* The Panama Canal Act, 1912. The Valuation Act, 1913. Appraisal of Regulation to 1920.

13   Railroad Regulation since World War I   312
      Introduction. The Basis of the New Policy. The Transportation Act of 1920: *Transitional Provisions. Control over Rates. Intercorporate Relations. Regulation of Securities. Control of Service.* Reasons for Legislation after 1920. The Emergency Transportation Act, 1933: *Amendments to the Interstate Commerce Act.* The Transportation Act of 1940: *The Declaration of National Policy. Rate Making. Land-Grant Rates.*

Consolidation. Board of Investigation and Research. The Transportation Act of 1958: *Reasons for the Legislation. Provisions of the Law.*

14　The Regulation of Motor Transport　　　334

Introduction. State Regulation: *Limitation on Powers of Regulation. State versus Federal Authority. Nature of State Regulation.* Federal Regulation: *Reasons for Federal Regulation. The Motor Carrier Act of 1935. Contract Carriers. Private Carriers and Brokers. Exempt Carriers.* Administration of the Motor Carrier Act: *Control of Entry. Consolidation and Mergers. Rate Regulation. Agricultural Exemptions. The Gray Area.* Conclusion.

15　Regulation of Air, Water, and Pipe-Line Transportation　　　361

REGULATION OF AIR TRANSPORTATION: Introduction. The Agencies of Control: *Early Legislation. The Civil Aeronautics Act of 1938. The Federal Aviation Act of 1958: The Civil Aeronautics Board. The Federal Aviation Agency.* State Regulation. Regulation by the Civil Aeronautics Board: *Certification of Carriers. Rates and Fares. Airmail Compensation. Regulation of Service. Consolidations and Mergers. Appraisal of Civil Aeronautics Board Policy.* REGULATION OF WATER TRANSPORTATION: Regulation to 1940. Reasons for the Act of 1940. The Transportation Act of 1940: *Provisions of the Act. Conclusions on the Legislation.* REGULATION OF PETROLEUM PIPE LINES: The Pipe-Line Problem. Federal Regulation.

PART IV. NATIONAL TRANSPORTATION POLICY

16　Transportation as a National Problem　　　395

Introduction. Transportation—A Perennial Problem: *Uniqueness of the Transport Problem. The Changing Nature of the Problem. The Formulation of Public Policy. General Objectives of Public Policy.* Public Investment and Public Aid: *Public Aid and Subsidy. Criteria for Public Investment. User Charges and Resource Allocation.* Competition, Co-ordination, and Integration: *Competition in Transport. Co-ordination of Transport. Consolidation and Integration.* Terminal Problems. The Labor Problem: *Labor Legislation. The Uniqueness of the Labor Problem. Transport Technology and the Labor Problem.* Agencies of Public Policy: *Regulation of Transport. Administration and Promotion. Federal, State, and Local Responsibilities.* Conclusion.

17　Competition and Regulation in Transportation　　　422

Introduction. Intra-agency Competition: *Competition in Rail Transport. Competition in Motor Transport. Competition in Other Modes.* Interagency Competition: *The Problem of Interagency Competition. Inherent Advantages. Commission Policy on Interagency Competition.* The Common Carrier Problem. Equalizing Competition. The President's Message: *A Basic National Transportation Policy. Equal Competitive Opportunity under Diminished Regulation. Consistent Policies of Taxation and User Charges. Evenhanded Government Promotion of Intercity Transportation. Protection of the Public Interest. Conclusion.*

18   Consolidation and Integration   446
     Meaning and Problem. Railroad Consolidation: *The Problem of Con-
     solidation. History of Consolidation. Public Policy on Consolidation.
     The Recent Merger Movement. A Program for Consolidation.* Other
     Agencies. INTEGRATION AND DIVERSIFICATION: The Nature of the
     Issue. Integration for Ancillary Purposes. Transportation Companies.
     Diversification.

19   Financing Transportation   467
     Introduction: *The Allocation of Economic Resources. The Unique
     Problem in Transport. The Equalization of Competition.* History of
     Public Aid: *The Early Period. The Railroad Era. The Modern Period.*
     Financing the Railroads: *Nature of the Problem. Capital Requirements.
     The Passenger Deficit Problem. Conclusion.* Financing Motor Trans-
     port: *Introduction. Equalizing Competition.* Development of the High-
     way Program: *Federal Highway Legislation.* Financing the Highway
     System: *Extent of Public Investment. Sources of Highway Funds.
     Highway Cost Allocation. The Allocation of User Costs.* Financing
     Air Transport: *Introduction. Airway Investment. Airport Investment.
     Subsidy to Air Transport. Financing the Air Lines.* Financing Do-
     mestic Water Transport. Taxation of Way and Imputed Interest.
     Conclusion.

20   The Special Problem of Labor   501
     Introduction: *Uniqueness of the Labor Problem.* The Railroad Labor
     Problem to 1926: *Railroad Labor Organizations. Railroad Labor Legis-
     lation to 1926. The Railway Labor Act of 1926. The National Rail-
     road Adjustment Board. National Board of Mediation. Arbitration.
     Emergency Boards. Results of the Railway Labor Act.* The Coordinator's
     Report. The Presidential Railroad Commission. Railway Social Se-
     curity: *Railroad Retirement Act, 1936. The Railroad Labor Unemploy-
     ment Insurance Act, 1938. Extension of Benefits.* The Labor Problem
     in Air Transportation: *The Railway Labor Act. Labor Organizations.
     Labor Problems. Mutual-Aid Pact. Results of the Legislation.* Other
     Transport Industries. Conclusion: *Areas of Conflict. Effects of Chang-
     ing Technology. National Transportation Study.*

21   Regulation and Administration in Transport Policy   522
     Introduction. THE ROLE OF REGULATION: The Independent Regula-
     tory Commission: *The Role of Regulation in Transport. Inadequacy
     of Antitrust. Criticism of Commission Regulation. Reorganization of
     Transport Regulation.* THE ROLE OF ADMINISTRATION: Executive
     Responsibilities. Administrative Organization. Proposals for Reorgani-
     zation. The Department of Transportation: *President Johnson's Mes-
     sage, March 2, 1966. Congressional Action. The Department of Trans-
     portation Act, 1966.* Conclusion.

PART V. URBAN TRANSPORT

22   The Urban Transportation Problem   547
     Introduction. Emergence of the Problem: *The Rise of the City. In-
     dustrialization and Transport. Revolution by the Automobile. The*

Inertia of the Past. Transport and the Urban Structure: *Transport and Urban Development. The Changing Economic Function of the Central City. The Los Angeles Industrial Structure. The Los Angeles Residential Structure. The Pattern of Traffic Movements.* The Commuter Problem: *The Rail Commutation Problem. Revenue and Expense Squeeze. Action to Keep Commuter Trains Running.* The Pricing Problem: *Rationing of Service. Possible Devices.* The Problem of Organization: *The Nature of the Problem. Multiplicity of Jurisdictions.* Problems of Finance.

23 Transport Terminals   578
Introduction. The General Nature of the Terminal Problem. Railroad Terminals: *Passenger Terminals. Freight Terminals. Traffic Interchange. Produce Terminals. Authority over Terminals. Conclusion.* Airports: *The Air Terminal Network. Ownership and Management. Airport Location.* Motor Terminals: *Passenger Terminals. Freight Terminals.* Water Terminals. The Port of New York Authority: *The Interstate Compact. Powers and Jurisdiction. Terminal Unification. Rail Transportation. World Trade Center. Investment. Conclusion.*

24 Proposed Solutions to the Urban Transport Problem   601
Introduction. The Doyle Report: *The Urban Transport Problem. Suggested Plan for Federal Legislative Aid. Conclusion.* The Washington Program: *The Mass Transportation Survey Report, 1959. Joint Committee on Washington Metropolitan Problems. Proposals for Action.* The Chicago Area Transportation Study. The Los Angeles Metropolitan Transit Program: *Background of the Problem. The Los Angeles Metropolitan Transit Authority.* The San Francisco Bay Area Rapid Transit District (BART): *Geographical Setting. Formation of the Rapid Transit District. The Rapid Transit System. Financing the System. Cost Estimates.* President Kennedy's Message: *Long-Range Program. Emergency Aid. Role of the Highways. Relocation Assistance. Mass Transit Research and Demonstrations. Interstate Compacts.* Urban Mass Transportation Act, 1964. The Problem of Planning.

APPENDIXES

I The Transportation System of Our Nation   635
II Selected References for Further Reading   651

INDEX

Index   665

PART I

The Transport System

TRANSPORTATION AND
THE ECONOMY

SCOPE OF TRANSPORT ECONOMICS

Nature of Transportation

Transportation is that aspect of economic activity which provides for the carriage of persons or things from one place to another. In its broadest sense, this encompasses all such transfers, whether within plants, factories, or even buildings, as well as between plants or places. Literally all productive activity entails the movement of persons or things from one location to another, but much of this is simply an integral part of any process of production. Transport, however, may be an independent affair consisting merely of the carriage from place to place. Even this may be within a given plant or factory, as illustrated by the transfer of pig iron from the blast furnace to the open hearth. This aspect of transportation is significant for the organization of the plant, but it can scarcely be distinguished from the other aspects of the immediate process. When, on the other hand, the conveyance takes place between plants, places, or firms, the use of public facilities in some form or another is usually involved, and the transport becomes an independent activity of itself. This is the aspect of transportation that forms the subject matter of separate inquiry.

This phase of transport generally partakes of both public and private interest in some way or another, and it may relate to either production or consumption. The economics of transportation therefore deals with associated effort engaged in the movement of persons and goods from place to place. Strictly speaking, this should include even the transmission of electricity and the transport of water. Because of the closely integrated nature of the production of the energy itself and the water with the transportation and distribution of them to the ultimate users, and because of the unique problems connected with these processes, those industries usually classified as public utilities will not be dealt with in this treatise.

Function of Transportation

One of the most important features of transport is that it is one of the processes in the production of goods and services. The high degree of specialization of production in the modern world is the result of two main factors, namely, the division of labor and the extent of the market. The division of labor may manifest itself as specialization in particular processes, as in the case of factory workers, or in the completion of an entire product such as custom-made shoes. Even in the latter illustration, however, the materials and tools used by the tradesman will be made by others. Division of labor also occurs on a geographic basis where particular areas specialize in particular products. Agriculture and iron ore mining are illustrations.

The opportunity to realize the advantages of the division of labor depends upon the markets which can be reached. The larger the market for a product, the more is it feasible to specialize on it. There is consequently a continuous pressure for the reduction of costs so that new markets can be tapped, as well as the constant urge to search for new outlets. The possibilities for expansion and the opportunities to make new products which industrial research is constantly uncovering lead to intensive efforts to develop new tastes and new markets. The extent of the latter is intimately related to the availability of transport facilities.

It is the function of transport to supply the means to bring together the resources used in the productive processes and to provide access to the markets for the resulting products. In other words, it is the function of transport to bridge the time and space gaps separating buyers and sellers. In its economic aspect this means diminishing the effects of spatial factors of time and distance between producers and users. Efficient transport reduces this combination of time and distance costs to the minimum, that is, with the most economical combination of resources that will accomplish the given object.

Scope of Transport Economics

As has already been noted, transportation consists of the mere movement of persons and goods from one place to another. It therefore involves considerations of both time and place, and is a creator of time and place utilities. In the process of creating these utilities, it is an integral part of production. It is also of itself an object of consumption. Travel may be undertaken by people for the sheer enjoyment it affords, an activity which has reached enormous proportions in this country.

The economic problems of transport are concerned with the efficient allocation of resources to the provision of transportation services and facilities as compared to other uses to which these resources might be put, with efficient allocation among the various agencies which supply transportation today, and with the efficient utilization of the resources already allocated. These phases involve complex problems of public policy, and they are intimately related to the institutional arrangements through which public policy is implemented. Thus, for example, in this country a "mixed" system of public and private ownership is inescapable, and policy decisions must be made by both business and government in full recognition of this fact. This is significant not only for the development of criteria for an efficient transport system but also in connection with considerations of national defense.

At this point it may be instructive to call attention to the difference between the engineering and the economic aspects of transport. Engineering is concerned with the mechanical phases of the construction and operation of transport facilities. The engineer must design and build the equipment, roadway facilities, communications, and so forth. He must construct the highways to handle the estimated traffic and the bridges to carry the assumed loads, and it is he who will calculate the costs of these undertakings. However, it is the economist who will have to tell him what the constructions are to be for, and what the traffic requirements and prospects are. These will depend upon the resources that are to be devoted to transport and the conditions—that is, the prices and the pricing alternatives—under which the facilities are to be used. Transport services and the means of supplying them are economic goods and are therefore scarce. They have to be rationed like all other economic goods. This means, for example, that such a thing as highway traffic congestion can never be solved economically so long as the use of a particular route is literally a free good to the individual user.

TRANSPORT AND THE LOCATION OF INDUSTRY

Factors in the Location of Industry

The location of industry and economic activity is determined by many factors, some of them clearly ascertainable in measurable and objective terms, some of them apparently the result of historical accident. There seems, however, to be general agreement that the principal factors are markets, raw materials, fuel or power, labor, and transportation. All of these, and also others not included in the list, are of varying importance depending on the nature of the undertaking. In addition, the mobility of factors and the way in which they are distributed geographically is significant. Labor and raw materials may be essential at all times, but those that are widely distributed or are mobile may exert little direct influence, thereby leaving the decisive role to other forces.

Transportation is one of the major factors which influence the location of industry; some even regard it as the most important. Whatever the correct verdict as to the weighting may be, transport is not merely one of the decisive factors; at times it may of itself be an independent factor. Thus the location of the city of New York is primarily, if not entirely, the result of transport considerations. Its site at the meeting of the ocean and the Hudson River makes it the focal point for transatlantic traffic and that of the continental United States which is able to reach the seaboard by the easy land route through the mountains to the west to the Great Lakes and the great plains areas. Chicago's location can be explained in a similar way, as can that of other great metropolitan centers of the world. Similar remarks apply to Los Angeles, but development of the ability economically to transport water and power over long distances has been an additional significant factor that has made the phenomenal growth of the latter city possible.

Transport and Regional Development

The influence of transportation on location and regional development stems from the function of transport to lessen the costs of the barriers of time and space which arise in connection with the processes of production. No economic purpose will be served in developing transport facilities if the involved costs cannot be reduced to the point that the interchange of commodities and persons will take place. In short, the differences of regions and areas which lead to the interchange must be such as to make the incurrence of the transport costs worthwhile. By the same token the prices which are charged for the transport services are of vital significance to the development of areas. This is particularly true with regard to the effects of freight rates and privileges—for example, milling in transit—that are accorded by transportation companies, especially railroads.

Freight rates and, more specifically, the relative rates on different commodities and for varying distances can thus be decisive on location. Because freight rates are based on price policies through which the decisions of management can play such a vital role in the functioning of transportation, because competition operates unevenly in the field of transport, and because arbitrary decisions can literally make or break industries, firms, or areas, rate making and the control of rate policies have been of major concern to public authority from time immemorial. The impact of freight rates on different commodities and on commodities produced in different places is such that changes in rate levels cannot, as a practical matter, be made by uniform horizontal increases or decreases, either in percentage terms or in absolute amounts.

Development of Metropolitan Areas

The rapid growth of metropolitan areas and the urbanization accompanying the development of modern industrial society have been the result, in no small measure, of the rise of contemporary transport facilities. The increase in industry and commerce, to which the application of modern technology to agriculture has contributed so much, has increased the role of transport in present-day society and also has been the result of the spectacular development in the means of moving people and goods. Urban concentration is not a new phenomenon, but its twentieth-century manifestation has given transport a new significance. Down to the end of the first quarter of this century, railways provided the principal means of transportation between and within metropolitan centers. This brought about concentration of people in both working and residential areas of cities. The rapid rise of the newer means of transport, especially the motor vehicle, after 1920 ushered in the decline of mass rapid transit by rail, with the resulting decentralization, particularly of residential patterns. Hence, at the present time we are witnessing increased concentration in urban centers and a marked decentralization within them. The new geographical structure of city life is being shaped by the new and individualized means of transportation, as was the old by the mass means of movement by rail.

Transport Location

While transport is a basic factor in the location of economic activity, the location of transport facilities is conditioned by factors which are independent of that transport. Traffic routes develop as the shortest and most feasible connecting links between areas and places of unlike economic interests. They will be affected by conditions of terrain but will be found to connect, as circumstances permit, one center with another between which the traffic movements take place. This accounts for the fact that the rail, highway, air, and water routes of this country parallel each other over such a wide area. Indeed, a map for the major railroad routes is almost completely identifiable with the primary routes of highway and air. In urban centers, rail lines have created the framework of the geographic structure, particularly of industrial activity, these lines being dictated to a large extent by topography, points of access to the urban centers, and connections with water transport where the latter is present. Even the growth of motor transport does not seem to have changed this pattern in any fundamental way, at least as far as the location of heavy industry is concerned.

TRANSPORT AND PRICES

Price Policies

The pricing of the products or services of modern industry is rarely determined solely by the impersonal operation of the market. Instead, the seller participates directly in the process of pricing because of the general practice of quoting prices at which goods will be sold and because of the departure from pure competition in a great many market situations. When a producer is able to exercise, to his own advantage, some influence on the market for the product he sells, he has the choice of fixing his price and then adjusting his supply to it, or of determining the supply and letting price take its course. In other words, the seller will have a price policy as well as a production policy.

When an enterprise determines its prices in advance, the management must decide what kind of a pricing policy it will adopt and set its prices accordingly. This operation will entail decisions as to the price relationships of the various commodities or services that are to be produced and the prices that are to be charged to different classes of customers and in different geographic areas. Decisions will also have to be made regarding frequency of price changes.

Price policies perform two major functions in modern business. In the first place, they are part of the mechanics of the pricing process. Prices over a wide range of economic activity do not emerge immediately and automatically as the result of auctions under totally impersonal procedures. The seller has to state the price at which he is willing to sell, and the buyer expects him to do so. The determination of what the prices are to be for a large modern business is a highly complex and technical task. The enormity of this in the making of prices and the influence of those engaged in the sheer mechanics of it have a strong tendency to introduce price inertia. Customary procedures come to play an important part in the process. Prices and price structures, therefore, are largely the result of relatively slow growth and experimentation. They do not emerge overnight; it would be literally impossible for a modern industry to start from scratch and to construct a workable price structure all at once.

The second main function of price policies relates to the strategy and tactics of business. Management may prefer to protect its price structure to prevent spoiling the market. The reaction of competitors to price changes may have to be taken into consideration. The raising of prices may mean the loss of business to competitors who do not follow suit, whereas the lowering of them may result in a price war. Price policies may be used as part of the strategy to effect a stabilization of prices or to assist in securing or maintaining monopoly. They may also be employed as one of the effective tactics for eliminating rivals or for forcing them to conform to the policies of the leaders in an industry. Finally, price policies in this connection are important as they affect price relationships among commodities or services, among customers, and among firms. It is here that price discrimination is an especially important issue. Minimum prices as a part of the question of price discrimination and minimum prices as a weapon of economic warfare enter the picture here, too. This second aspect of price policies frequently calls for direct intervention in the pricing process by public authority through limitations placed on price differentials that may be granted or the minima below which particular prices may be prohibited from going.

Significance of Price Policies in Transport

Price policies play a particularly important role in transport economics because common carrier rates in this country are the result of considered action by the carriers themselves as well as governmental agencies. This does not mean that competition plays no part in the determination of the rates; competition always, directly or indirectly, imposes some restrictions on price policies, but the scope accorded to competitive considerations and the influence the market is permitted to exercise on price making in transport are severely circumscribed by private and public decisions. Common carrier rate schedules are developed by carriers acting alone, or in concert with other carriers, and with shippers, as well as by sanction or by order of public authority. In fact, in no other area except public utilities do price policies develop under such deliberate and comprehensive action.

Limitations of some form or another on competition have always characterized transportation. These, together with the essential nature of transport to community and political life have led to the development of common carrier obligations which, among other things, require the charging of reasonable rates without undue preference. This has led to a thoroughgoing formalization of published rates, strict adherence to which is required by law; to the systematization of classification of commodities into a limited number of groupings; and to the application of uniform distance scales to these classes over wide areas, in many instances to the entire country. This formalization of the price structures of common carriers, especially the railroads, and what is just as important, the attempts to force conformity to it as nearly as possible when circumstances compel exceptions, mean that the decisions of private carriers and public authority combined are of vital significance to the movement of commodities and the location of economic activity.

The Unique Problem of Discrimination

An analysis of discrimination and the part it plays in transport pricing will be found in Chapters 7 and 8. It may be noted here, however, that the problems of discrimination have played a larger role in transport pricing than in any other area of industry. Historically, this is the result of the development of common carrier obligations, limitations on competition in transport, and the monopoly features of railroads. Currently, it is becoming a critical issue in connection with user charges for publicly supplied facilities, especially highways.

Theoretically, discrimination presents the same kinds of problems in transportation as in other industries. Practically, however, it is much more complex in transport, and it is here that its uniqueness lies. The difficulty of defining a "commodity," in other words the unit of measurement or the output unit, in transport, the presence of heavy fixed costs in some phases, together with the influences of monopoly and joint costs, make the detection of discrimination very difficult. At the same time, the unavoidability of differential charging and unused capacity, coupled with limitations on common carrier practices involving undue preference, has given rise to continuous public concern with and supervision of transport charges.

The significance of transportation in the economy and the strategic monopoly occupied by railroads, at least down to the end of the first quarter of the present century, made the incidence of freight rates a matter of major public concern. This led many to regard these rates in a category similar to that of taxes, and even to consider freight rates a form of taxation. The burden of freight rates on commodities and on production has thus been given special attention that would not have

been accorded it had transportation been subject to the over-all influences of competition characteristic of industry in general. Freight
rates quite commonly bear a higher ratio to the price of commodities at
destination on such things as gravel, sand, and coal than they do on
cotton, cigarettes, or airplanes and parts, even though the charges for
transporting the lower valued commodities may be less per hundred
pounds than those for the higher valued ones. Weight, distance, and
other cost factors turn out to be only some of the considerations that
enter into the complex problem of rate making. Orientation of transport prices to market influences independent of the total costs involved
in producing the particular services has consequently come to be recognized as an inescapable feature of pricing for many transport services,
especially of railroads, despite the departure from strictly competitive
price theory which this entails, and despite the basic assumption of regulation that rates should be based on costs.

EFFECTS OF IMPROVED TRANSPORTATION

Development of Technology in Transport

Improved technology in manufacture that formed the basis of
what has come to be known as the Industrial Revolution, and subsequent developments down into the twentieth century, created continuous pressure for improvements in transportation and the reduction
of costs of transport so that the advantages of the newer processes and
techniques could be realized and new markets obtained. New and improved technology in transport was also forthcoming, but it is interesting to note that the most outstanding changes in transportation really
followed those in manufacturing. That is, the revolution in transportation followed that which took place in industry.[1] This may be ascribed
in part to the fact that the major technological achievements in transport grow out of those of manufacturing, and in part to the fact that the
improvements in transport grow out of pressure for wider markets. The
forces are interacting, but the immediate sequence seems to be that
transport follows rather than leads the course of events. In any case,
advancing technology has created the need for improved transport and
has provided the opportunity for it.

The real break-through for modern transportation came with the
application of mechanical power to land transport. The principal development in this direction was that of the steam railroad, which made

[1] See N. S. B. Gras, *An Introduction to Economic History* (New York: Harper &
Bros., 1922), p. 219.

possible the penetration of the large land masses of the world and the opening-up of them to the cheapest, most rapid, and safest land transportation yet known. By the beginning of the twentieth century the railroad had become the means par excellence for efficient land transport throughout the entire industrial world. Railroads in more ways than one enjoyed a veritable monopoly.

This unique position, however, was relatively short-lived. The emergence of new sources of power, especially petroleum, resulted in the reduction in size of the practical power unit so that it was no longer necessary to rely solely on the giant steam locomotive or even on mass movement for the efficient transfer of goods and people. The railroads themselves were able to introduce major improvements that enhanced their efficiency, but the most significant changes came with the rise of the automobile, which has individualized so much traffic, and with the development of the airplane, which is free from the limitations imposed on land routes. Today the automobile has become the principal means of moving people, both in urban and interurban travel, while air travel, measured by intercity passenger-miles, now exceeds that by rail in this country. Even in freight traffic the motor carrier has superseded the railroad in urban movements, and has made major inroads on the longer hauls of a great deal of freight. Petroleum and natural gas pipelines have become almost the exclusive carriers of the bulk movement of these products, thereby depriving the railroads of their petroleum traffic and also of much of their haulage of coal. As a consequence of this, inland transport today is no longer a railroad monopoly. Instead, it is characterized by what has been described as pervasive competition. This is competition among the agencies or modes, thereby giving the user of services alternative means, and competition among the suppliers in particular modes, notably motor transport. In addition to this, changing technology has also compelled government participation in the supplying of transport facilities on a much greater scale than heretofore and in a way that appears to be unavoidable. The provision of streets and highways is scarcely feasible on a private basis to any great extent.

Transport and Production

Transport is an integral part of the process of production, and any developments which lead to a reduction in the costs of providing the services of transportation result in an increase in the efficiency of utilizing economic resources. This does not mean that improvements in transportation lead necessarily to a diminution in the total resources devoted to the movement of goods and people. Indeed, the reverse has commonly been true, but as a result of improvements the costs of the final product may be reduced. This may be true even though the proportion of resources devoted to transportation is greater than heretofore, and even though transport costs may be a larger percentage of the price of the final product than previously. For coal at the mine mouth, transport costs may be considered virtually nil, but in faraway markets they often are more than the cost of the coal at the mine. Yet transportation which makes it possible to sell the coal in distant markets lowers the cost of fuel in those markets, probably makes it possible to lower the costs at the mine, and releases other economic resources to more efficient uses. This promotes division of labor, regional specialization, and the growth of large-scale production. Promotion of economic growth of countries and communities has been one of the most significant results of improved transportation, and much aid to underdeveloped countries has gone into it in order to open up their resources to the markets of the world and to make the goods of the industrial countries available to them.[2]

Transportation is itself an object of consumption. It is undertaken not merely to reach a destination but also for the enjoyment which travel affords. This is not limited to the carriers for hire which people use. In the United States, travel by automobile in particular is a major source of recreation.[3] Provision of facilities which make possible the use of the motor vehicle for pleasure purposes falls in many respects into the same category as public support of parks and recreational facilities. Thus, as a consumption service, transportation must be evaluated as part of the economic goods available to satisfy consumer wants, whereas as part of the productive process it must be evaluated in terms of its contribution to economic output.

Political and Social Effects

Although this is a treatise on the economics of transport, the political and social effects of improved transportation cannot be ignored because the need for improved transportation may go beyond purely economic considerations. One of the earliest requirements of this country immediately after the attaining of independence was a system

[2] For a summary of the literature on transportation and economic development, see John B. Lansing, *Transportation and Economic Policy* (New York: The Free Press, 1966), Part II.

[3] See *Final Report of the Highway Cost Allocation Study,* Part VI, House Document No. 72, 87th Cong., 1st sess. (Washington, D.C.: C.S. Government Printing Office, 1961), p. 70.

of transportation that would make a unified political life possible through adequate communication and interchange among the members of the new nation. The construction of the transcontinental railroads after the middle of the nineteenth century was a necessity if the territories of the west to the Pacific coast were to be incorporated into the union and made an integral part of the United States. Similarly, the construction of the Canadian Pacific Railway with the aid and blessing of the Dominion government was one of the main considerations that brought British Columbia in as a province—a condition that had to be met in order that members from that province could have a feasible means of getting to the meetings of Parliament.

On a more restricted geographic scale, modern city life would be impossible without adequate transport to bring to it the very needs for its existence, as well as to provide for the movement of people and goods within its boundaries. Provision of the means for transporting people in our large metropolitan areas has become one of the most pressing problems of the present day. The solutions that are developed will have a vital effect on the political and economic structures of the cities of the future in this country.

Considerations of national defense bear heavily on the organization of all productive resources in a country. In the event of national emergency arising out of disputes with other countries, our transport facilities must be able to assemble the matériel for defense, convey goods to areas of production that may not be precisely the same as those of peace times, and speed the supplies and armed forces to the areas of conflict. This requires transport facilities that would not be forthcoming under purely commercial considerations. The government must therefore take into account the transportation requirements of possible conflict, and modify or supplement the transport system which has been developed to meet economic needs. The railroad network of Germany before World War I was developed with military factors as primary, and shipping throughout the world has always been heavily influenced by this consideration.

The social effects of improved transportation are manifest at the local, national, and international levels. Community life has been able to develop on a more expansive scale. Rural living today is much more closely associated with urban activity than heretofore; and rural communities, through more widespread travel and marketing facilities, enjoy the benefits of urban developments previously denied them. Life in urban communities has become more mobile, with the resulting growth of "suburbia." This greater mobility has led to a wider diffusion of urban culture and has accentuated, as well as created, social problems that are of the gravest import.

At the national level, improved transportation has led to a diffusion of cultural patterns that has diminished in a marked degree much of the local distinction that characterized earlier periods. This has been accompanied by an increased mobility of population, and a rapid shift of it and industry to newer areas of the country. Similar changes have been taking place throughout the world as a whole, with the consequent difficulties of adjustment that are proving to be so puzzling and even terrifying to the "new era" of the twentieth century.

Measuring the Gains of Improved Transport

Despite the many attempts that have been made to measure the gains from improved transportation, no satisfactory quantitative gauge has been developed. If all transport services were disposed of through the market process, and especially if competition were fully effective, one could ascertain the total expenditures made by the recipients of those services, and assume with a tolerable degree of accuracy that these expenditures represented the share of the total national product contributed by transport.[4] The total output of transportation cannot be measured through the market, because all of the services which are rendered cannot be sold directly. Nonusers as well as users have to contribute some of the costs. This is not unique to transport; similar situations arise in connection with flood control, education, and so forth. The problem is particularly difficult in transport, however, because of the mixture of commercial and noncommercial features, and the inescapability of both public and private investment. This is especially the case in highway transport. No satisfactory measuring rod has yet been devised by which we can gauge the amount of investment that should be made economically in highways. This is one of the most pressing needs at the present time. We shall return to a more detailed discussion of this problem in Chapter 19.

THE POLITICAL BASIS OF TRANSPORT

Political Unity

Transport is differentiated from much of the rest of our economic activity because of its immediate connection with the political life of a

---

[4] See Stuart Daggett, *Principles of Inland Transportation* (4th ed.; New York: Harper & Bros., 1955), pp. 19–23, for a discussion of attempts to measure the benefits from improved transportation.

country. Government in one way or another is always called upon to assist in the process of supplying transport facilities to the territories it encompasses. This is not necessarily the result of the inability of private enterprise to meet the requirements, although this is frequently the case; it arises from the fact that governmental powers have to be exercised in order to secure feasible routes, to provide streets and roads where organization under private ownership is not practicable, to develop waterways and harbors, adequate navigation aids, and so forth. In addition to the economic considerations that seem to make government participation in supplying transport unavoidable, adequate transportation is essential to national unity. The centers of government must have continuous and relatively rapid communication with the people and the territories they govern. In the absence of economic inducements that are adequate for private enterprise to supply the necessary transportation, government must fill the gap.

National Defense

Closely connected with political unity is the problem of national defense. This relationship has long been recognized by all governments. In ancient times it was the reason for the great system of roads throughout the Roman Empire. In some countries, military considerations were more important than economic ones in designing the system of railroads. In the United States, one of the most important arguments used to support public investment in inland waterways has been the needs of national defense. This consideration carried a good deal of weight in the decision to participate in the building of the St. Lawrence Seaway, and during World War II the national government constructed the Big Inch and Little Inch pipe lines to assist in carrying liquid petroleum products from the Southwest to the eastern states. Recently, the requirements of national defense have been advanced as a major reason for the construction of a system of nationwide, interconnected superhighways. Similarly, the large current expenditures on air transport are based more on military and political considerations than on economic ones.

Thus, while it seems safe to say that the American transportation system has been shaped primarily by economic factors, political and military developments have played an important role. For this reason, transport policy cannot be examined in a purely economic setting. In fact, it can be examined in such a setting considerably less than much of the rest of economic enterprise. Public participation in the economic aspects of transport development and supply is unavoidable because all of the decisions regarding them cannot be made on a purely economic basis, at least within the framework of the requirements of a private enterprise system. The economic features of transport preclude that possibility, and the political considerations that transportation entails likewise compel active and direct public participation.

Eminent Domain

Government may acquire property for public use by the exercise of the power of eminent domain. This is the right to appropriate property for public uses on payment of compensation. When the power of eminent domain is exercised, the owner of the property is compelled to sell it even though he does not wish to do so. However, the taking of the property must be for a public purpose, the ascertainment of which is ultimately a judicial question in the United States.[5] In the event that the parties involved fail to reach agreement on the price to be paid, condemnation proceedings may be undertaken. The courts will be called upon to fix the fair or reasonable transfer price. The owner is thus protected against "unfair" dispossession at the same time the government is safeguarded against obstruction of its projects.

Transport enterprises need to be assured of the ability to acquire routes and terminal facilities that are feasible for their undertakings. Therefore, they have been accorded the right of eminent domain. This sanction of the exercise of the power of eminent domain arises from the theory that the construction of highway and other necessary facilities for public purposes carries with it the exercise of powers that are essentially governmental in nature.[6]

Common Carrier Obligations

A common carrier is a supplier of transport services which holds itself ready, either expressly or by a clearly implied course of conduct, to serve all who seek the service offered for sale. The duty of a common carrier to render service without discrimination is a common-law obligation derived from the guild system arrangements known as common callings. The responsibilities which were derived from common law have been greatly extended by statute. The first step taken at the federal level in this country was under the Interstate Commerce Act of

[5] See Ernest Freund, "Eminent Domain," *Encyclopedia of the Social Sciences* (New York: The Macmillan Co., 1931), Vol. V, pp. 493–97.

[6] Public utilities can exercise eminent domain in constructing power, water, or gas lines. Petroleum pipe lines are commonly accorded this privilege, but this is not so everywhere. See D. P. Locklin, *Economics of Transportation* (6th ed.; Homewood, Ill.: Richard D. Irwin, Inc., 1966), p. 612.

1887, by which all railroads offering service for hire in interstate commerce were declared to be common carriers. The concept has since been extended to motor, water, and air carriers, and pipe lines for hire, although all of the companies in these agencies do not fall into the category of common carriers. Since many of them perform special services on a contract basis and do not hold themselves out as ready to serve the public in general, they do not fall into the classification of common carriers under the present state of the law.

The development of common carrier obligations has been the result of the dependence of the public on the services of particular transport firms. What the situation would have been had transportation grown up under freely competitive enterprises not requiring any particular type of public privilege or assistance, it is impossible to say. However, inroads on the position of the common carrier today by private carriers and those which are for hire but are not compelled to assume the responsibilities of common carriers have given rise to serious discussion of the question of whether the common carrier needs special protection. The answer to this turns in part upon economic considerations which will be discussed later, and in part upon political ones.

AN ECONOMICAL SYSTEM OF TRANSPORT

Need for Cheap Transport

It is almost axiomatic to say that a country needs cheap transportation and that it needs the cheapest possible transport that will adequately meet the requirements of the country. This statement, however, literally means all things to all people and does not indicate what the essence of a cheap system of transport in the economic sense implies.

The need for the cheapest possible transport system arises from three considerations. First of all, as has already been pointed out, transportation is one of the large items quantitatively in the production process. Improvements in transport efficiency aid in increasing the productivity of industry and are one of the essential ingredients of it. In this respect, transport is in the same category as all other phases of productive activity; there is a constant striving to reduce the relative costs of the various processes of production. Second, the enormous total investment in transport facilities and the relatively large amount of our wealth devoted to transport require that careful attention be given to ways and means of assuring that the investment is wisely made and that overexpansion is avoided as much as possible. This is once more becoming an acute problem because of the heavy demands that are being made for public investment in highways, and the difficult problems of traffic congestion to which the automobile has given rise. Third, if transport is to be cheap, the allocation of economic resources to it must be in keeping with the efficiency principle, which means that those resources are being devoted to their most valuable uses. The absolute amount of investment and expenditure in transportation is a significant matter in the final analysis only insofar as it relates to the problem of an economical allocation of resources. If the amount of resources in transport is the result of a rational allocation, a country has an economical system because, by economic criteria at least, it cannot afford any more, and it has all it needs.

Cheap transport for a country and cheap transport for an individual or a firm are not necessarily the same thing. When an individual, or a firm, seeks cheap transportation or the cheapest means of transportation, he typically counts only the immediate prices or rates he has to pay. These rates do not necessarily cover even all the direct costs that are involved in supplying that transportation. The difference may be made up by subsidies, disguised costs, and taxes that are borne in large measure by others. Under such circumstances, cheap transport for the individual may actually be very expensive for the country. Whether this is so will depend upon whether the service that is being supplied is worth the total costs that are being incurred. Modern transport presents some very severe obstacles to ascertaining the full cost and even severer ones to gauging whether it is worthwhile. It is in part because of this difficulty that a good deal of confusion exists in public thinking, with the result that cheap transport to the individual and cheap transport to the country are too frequently regarded as being the same thing.

Meaning of Cheap Transport

If a country is to have the cheapest transport commensurate with its needs or, in the words of Congress, "an adequate, economical and efficient" transport system, it must measure its investment and costs of operation in terms of an efficient allocation of its economic resources. This means that consumers must be free to select the type of transport service they wish to employ on the basis of the price they are willing to pay for it. That is, they must be permitted to select among the alternatives on the basis of the lowest relative rates or costs. The various transport agencies which offer the alternatives will have to be allowed to seek the traffic on a competitive basis, so that the one that can profitably take the traffic at the lowest price is the one that will get it. This is the only way to secure an economical allocation of traffic whether the transport system is in private hands or is entirely owned by the state. Furthermore, for economical price-cost relationships to exist among the agencies, it is necessary to see that all of them cover similar costs of supplying the transport services. If there are reasons for differentiating among the agencies with regard to the cost burdens they must bear, those reasons will be of a political or some other nature, not economic.

An economical transport system means that there must be an economical allocation of traffic among the agencies and an economical investment in each mode. That is, the total investment in transportation should be such that the investment would not be worth more if made elsewhere, and the investment made in one agency would not be worth more if it was made in another. This means that the benefits received from investment made in each agency of transportation should be worth more than if it were made in any other economic activity. This carries us back to the utilization of consumers' freedom of choice and the price mechanism as the gauge for economical investment. In other words, whether a transport system is economical depends on whether it can meet the competitive standards. If it cannot do so, it will not be economical, whatever else it may be.

The application of competitive standards to transportation is one of the most difficult tasks in economics. This is because of the technological structure of transport, the "mixed" system of ownership, and the political and social aspects. Unfortunately, too frequently this has been used as an excuse for justifying policies and expenditures that cannot meet the economic tests that are available, and as a basis for contentions that the diffused benefits of transport are such as to warrant abandoning the economic tests. The fact is that all costs of transport can be obtained with workable accuracy and that they can be assessed on users in the aggregate if that is desired. It is the failure to use the measuring rods that are available that has led to the present transport dilemma in this country with its railroad "crisis," highway "inadequacy," and metropolitan "congestion."

REASONS FOR SEPARATE TREATMENT OF TRANSPORT

Unique Position of Transport

The unique position which transportation occupies in economic activity arises from the reduction by it of the resistances of time and space to the production of economic goods and services. The significance of this in terms of the allocation of economic resources is indicated by the fact that probably at least one third of our national wealth is directly devoted to transportation. So important is it that without it organized human activity would be impossible; complete stoppage of a community's transport services is the quickest way to assure complete paralysis of co-operative effort, economic, political, and social.

It is because of these features that the provision of transportation has always been a concern of government. Governmental authority is necessary to supply the routes and to safeguard the use of them. If commercial considerations prove to be inadequate to induce the investment necessary to provide the facilities considered essential to political life, social life, and national defense, government will take steps to fill the gap. Furthermore, transportation is an activity to which the allocation of economic resources has never been sufficient without some sort of government inducement. This is because of the noneconomic contributions of transport to human endeavor, and also because it is not possible to subject all of the services rendered to the calculus of the market. This is probably truer today than ever before. Because of the enormous demands of modern transport on economic resources, and the difficulties of relating directly the costs of providing the services with the use of them, the economic problems connected with transport rank with some of the most complex in the whole body of economic analysis and policy.

A Group of Industries

As will be explained more fully later on, transport service is supplied by a group of industries, some of which are structurally in the category of natural monopolies and others thoroughly competitive in nature. Moreover, a large amount of transport service is not for hire; it is supplied by the owners of the vehicles for themselves. Much of it is readily substitutable for services which are offered for hire, and much of the for-hire traffic can move into the private category if for any reason the service of the former is unsatisfactory. The regulation of railroads developed in the same pattern as the regulation of public utilities. Water, air, and motor transport lack the critical economic characteristics of public utilities. Even when they operate for hire, they do not fit the latter category economically; and when they serve only their owners, they cannot be brought under public regulation.

Limitation on the Forces of Competition

Transportation does not yield as readily or as completely to the forces of competition as do manufacturing and many other economic activities. Even though part of the facilities respond with ease, others succumb to monopoly. Harbors are key points of entry for water transport; railway routes and highways are subject to limitations of terrain; even the seemingly limitless sky is already presenting serious problems of control at key points. The great cost of providing transport facilities, most particularly the harbors or ports and routes for inland transport, has imposed severe limitations on the effectiveness of competition. As a consequence, regulation in some form has been characteristic of transport at all times, and literally throughout its history it has been subject to more public surveillance than any other of our productive activities. In fact, it is in this field that our most comprehensive and varied experience in public regulation has been obtained.

Public Investment

Public investment in transportation today is unavoidable, in that the investment decisions for the supply of "right of way" and the terminal facilities for motor, water, and air transport must be made largely by public authority. Quantitatively, the most significant problem relates to highways, and this is precisely where the economic issues are the most difficult. Reasonably adequate gauges for the proper amount of investment to be made are lacking, partly because all highway costs cannot very well be assessed directly on the users. Even if they could be, there would still be the problem of deciding what amount of costs should be imposed on the various kinds of users, and what differentials should be charged for the different highways and facilities that are used. These problems, of course, have to be resolved in a workable way; but the solutions that are adopted affect the total resources allocated to transportation and the distribution of them among the various agencies. The management of the public investment in transport, therefore, is an integral part of the national transport problem and program. To date, no attempt has been made to unify public investment policy in transportation, let alone integrate it with the private sector in the transport field.

Antitrust Inadequate

Transport cannot be put into the category of industry in general, subject only to the control of the antitrust laws and similar statutes. The pricing of transportation for hire, even with competition as pervasive as it is today, is more complex and of necessity has to be more systematized than industrial pricing. It is difficult to see how published rates, classification, and many other rules could be dispensed with, even under the most ideal conditions that could be obtained with present technology. Railroads need to be regulated to prevent ruinous competition among them, unless they are permitted to enter into rate agreements which would be contrary to the antitrust laws in the absence of special exemption. Even if they were consolidated on a regional basis regulation could not be dispensed with. The Robinson-Patman Act could scarcely be applied to transport, yet this would be necessary in the absence of special regulation. The problems of interagency ownership cannot well be left to antitrust, because each situation is so individualized that separate regulation is called for, no matter whether one assumes complete separation in principle, or widespread integration. In other words the special requirements of transport regulation today do not fit into the category of public utility control or of antitrust. The uniqueness of the transport problem demands separate treatment.

Chapter
2

ELEMENTS OF A MODERN
TRANSPORT SYSTEM

INTRODUCTION

Purpose of the Description

A description of the principal components of a modern transport system and the role that each plays in supplying transport services is essential to understanding transport economics, and the problems of private management and public policy that emerge therefrom. This is because transportation today is provided by a variety of agencies of markedly different economic characteristics that offer services for which each is peculiarly fitted, at the same time that each is able to provide some transportation that is readily substitutable for that of another mode. In other words, transportation in the modern world is supplied by different agencies or modes, each of which performs unique functions beyond the scope of the other modes, while each is able to offer services that are readily substitutable for those of others within a reasonable range of price alternatives. That is, modern transport agencies offer services that, on the one hand, differ from one agency to another in an absolute sense and, on the other, are really differentiated products. The distinction of the services of the various modes is not merely a matter of large or small differences in the services which are available; it is also a distinction arising from the conditions under which they are supplied with regard to the economic and organizational features of the agencies themselves.

Thus, while transportation may be described as a mere movement of persons and things from one place to another,[1] and in this broad sense the agencies may be regarded as constituting an industry, they exhibit such distinct characteristics and perform such distinct functions that it only adds to confusion to treat them as though they formed even a reasonably homogeneous group. The fact that transportation under-

[1] A. Marshall, *Industry and Trade* (3d ed.; London: Macmillan & Co., 1921), p. 423.

takes merely to move persons and things from one place to another, but accomplishes the task through a variety of instrumentalities which perform their functions under such diverse conditions, is what makes for the complexity of transport problems and policies today.

Multiplicity of Agencies

The tasks of transportation today are performed by a variety of carriers from the standpoint of the conditions under which they render the services and the obligations they assume. Private carriers service only their owners. They do not offer themselves for hire although their activities may be of a commercial as well as a noncommercial nature. Carriers may also be organized as business enterprises operating for hire seeking to market their product. Some firms fall into the category of common carriers, subject to varying degrees of public regulation; others, known as contract carriers, are less completely regulated than common carriers; while other carriers for hire may be completely exempt from the unique provisions of transport control. There are other agencies such as brokers and freight forwarders who perform transport services by employing carriers for hire to carry out the actual movement of goods, and still others such as the Post Office or REA Express that do both.

The complexity of the transport system is also illustrated by the multiplicity of ownership within the various agencies, by the extreme variations in size of the ownership unit, by the different types of business organization they employ, and by the mixture of private and public investment. There were 78 Class I[2] railroads in the United States in 1966, of which the largest have an investment of over $2 billion each, all privately owned and organized as corporations. At the other extreme is motor transport with millions of owners, supplying both commercial and noncommercial services, and owned by individuals, partnerships, and corporations.

There is only a relatively small amount of ownership integration or diversification among the agencies, especially among common carriers. Many railroads operate trucking companies to a limited degree, and a few of them also operate petroleum pipe lines,[3] but separate and independent ownership of the various modes characterizes the organizational pattern in this country at the present time.

---

[2] As of January 1, 1965, Class I railroads were defined as those railroads with annual operating revenues of $5 million or more. Class I railroads in 1964 and prior years were defined as those with annual operating revenues of $3 million or more. There were 103 such reporting carriers in 1964 and 78 in 1965.

[3] The Southern Pacific Co. is an illustration.

Finally, investment in the transport system is supplied through both private and public sources. Rail and pipe-line transport is financed by private capital;[4] but the public has a large investment in air, water, and motor transport, the federal government being the largest single investor, private or public, in transportation in the United States.

Principal Groupings of Agencies

The suppliers of transport services may be grouped in a number of different ways depending upon the purposes of the classification. From the standpoint of their economic characteristics they may be put into two categories: Railroads and pipe lines have the basic economic characteristics of public utilities and are what economists call natural monopolies; motor, water, and air transportation exhibit the features of competitive industries. If the instrumentalities of transport are classified according to the various types of services they perform, which services are also related to the mechanical devices used to render those services, they make up a rather large number. One author lists 41 types under 15 major groupings.[5] Such a listing may be convenient for some purposes, but it is not very useful for economic analysis or public policy. The Interstate Commerce Commission employs five groupings for statistical purposes, and these same groupings are also the basis of regulatory policies. These are railroads, motor vehicles, water transport, pipe lines, and airplanes. Each of these agencies or modes differs from the others by the mechanical devices used to provide the transport services, and each one may conveniently be said to comprise a separate industry. The distinctions among them arise not merely from the differences of the mechanical means used for transport; they are the result of different economic characteristics. In other words, public policy and the organization of the supply of transport facilities are derived primarily not from the types of machinery or the methods used but from the different economic features of the various modes and the organizational arrangements resulting therefrom.

Relative Importance of the Agencies

The volume of intercity traffic by both private and public means is set forth in Table 2–1, which indicates clearly the dominant position

---

[4] There is some public ownership of street railways, and the city of Cincinnati still owns the Cincinnati Southern Railway, which is leased to and operated by the Cincinnati, New Orleans and Texas Pacific Railway. The federal government owns the Alaskan Railroad.

[5] G. Lloyd Wilson, *Transportation and Communications* (New York: Appleton-Century-Crofts, Inc., 1954), pp. 53–54.

TABLE 2–1
VOLUME OF INTERCITY TRAFFIC, PUBLIC AND PRIVATE, BY
KINDS OF TRANSPORTATION *

| | Ton-Miles | | | | | Passenger-Miles | | | | |
| | 1963 | 1964 | Per cent In- | Percentage of Grand Total | | 1963 | 1964 | Per cent In- | Percentage of Grand Total | |
Agency	(Millions)	(Millions)	crease	1963	1964	(Millions)	(Millions)	crease	1963	1964
1. Railroads and electric railways, including express and mail ...	629,337	666,207	5.86	43.40	43.51	18,632	18,374	d1.38	2.19	2.05
2. Motor vehicles:† Motor carriers of passengers.	....	....	.....	......	......	21,917	22,700	3.57	2.57	2.54
Private automobiles.....	....	....	.....	......	......	765,887	801,796	4.69	89.90	89.57
Motor transportation of property....	331,800	347,470	6.50	22.88	22.69	....	....	.....	......	......
Total motor vehicle.	331,800	347,470	6.50	22.88	22.69	787,794	824,496	4.66	92.47	92.11
3. Inland waterways, including Great Lakes....	234,172	250,165	6.83	16.15	16.34	2,763	2,838	2.71	.32	.32
4. Pipe lines (oil)‡..	253,431	265,826	4.89	17.48	17.36	....	....	.....	......	......
5. Airways (domestic revenue, pleasure and business flying, including express, excess baggage, and mail).........	1,296	1,504	16.05	.089	.098	42,765	49,500	15.75	5.02	5.53
Grand total..	1,450,036	1,531,172	5.60	100.00	100.00	851,954	895,208	5.08	100.00	100.00

d Decrease.
* Some revisions have been made in the data presented in the *78th Annual Report*, and parts of the 1963 and 1964 data are still preliminary. Alaska and Hawaii are included.
† Schoolbus data are excluded.
‡ Includes refined products and crude oil, with an allowance for gathering lines.
SOURCE: Reproduced from Interstate Commerce Commission, *79th Annual Report, June 30, 1965* (Washington, D.C.: U.S. Government Printing Office, 1965), p. 59.

of the railroads in the volume of freight transported and of motor vehicles in passenger traffic. If the ton-miles of deep-sea coastwise and intercoastal water traffic, however, were included in the tabulation, the percentage of domestic water transport would be increased considerably and that of the other agencies decreased accordingly. The ton-miles of coastwise and intercoastal water transport were approximately 247 billion in 1963.

Although the same absolute standing of the carriers for hire is maintained if the comparison is in terms of operating revenues, the percentage relationships are somewhat different, especially as between rail and motor transport of freight. In 1964, Class I railroads had total operating revenues of $10.3 billion, while regulated motor carriers of property had $9.2 billion. In other words, regulated motor carriers of property earned over 90 percent of the railroad freight revenues although they had less than 20 percent of the ton-mileage.[6] This emphasizes the greater revenue-producing capacity of motor freight. The motor carriers are moving more of the higher grade traffic. If to this the estimated revenue equivalent of motor carriers that were not for hire were added, the absolute superiority of the railroads would be eliminated. One estimate places the total revenue of all intercity motor carriers of property even in 1955 at $13,551 million as against $8,538 million for railroad freight revenues.[7]

RAILROADS

Facilities for railway transport include the railroads with their plant and equipment, terminal and industrial rail lines, interurban railways, and street railways. These various types perform different functions and offer different services. Some are used exclusively for the movement of freight, some for passengers only, but most of them do both. The railroads and the terminal facilities connected immediately with them constitute the principal means of rail transport, especially for intercity purposes. Street and interurban railways are part of the urban transport structure of the country; these will be discussed later in that connection. It should be noted, however, that the railroads play a significant role in commuter transportation in many of our large cities.

The Railroad Plant

The railroad plant of the United States consists of the roadbed and rails over which the rolling stock is moved, terminals such as freight yards and depots for both passenger and freight traffic, the locomotives, passenger, mail, and express cars, cars of various kinds for hauling the wide variety of freight presented for shipment, as well as roundhouses and other facilities for servicing and operating the trains.

The estimated net investment in railroads in the United States in 1964 was approximately $26.4 billion, covering a mileage of about 214,000 miles of line or 350,000 miles of trackage. The operating revenues for the same year were $9.9 billion, of which $8.4 billion was derived from freight and only $578 million from passenger traffic, the remainder being from mail, express, and other services. The

---

[6] Table 2–1 shows that motor transportation of property was 22.69 per cent of the total ton-miles of intercity traffic in 1964. Of this, however, only about 8.2 per cent, or a little over one third of the total, was subject to federal regulation.

[7] J. C. Nelson, *Railroad Transportation and Public Policy* (Washington, D.C.: The Brookings Institution, 1959), p. 445.

total number of employees was 665,017; these received a compensation of approximately $4.7 billion.

It is significant to note that farm, marine, forest, and mineral products accounted for 58 per cent of revenue freight carload tonnage originated by railroads in 1964 and only 32 per cent of total carload freight revenue. Manufactured commodities comprised 42 per cent of total tonnage and 68 per cent of total revenue. The average load in each car for the first-mentioned group was 61.7 tons; revenue per car, $217; and revenue per ton, $3.52. This compares with 36.3 tons per car, $391 revenue per car, and $10.77 revenue per ton originated for manufactured commodities. In other words, railroad freight traffic is comprised primarily of low-rated freight which produces lower revenue in proportion to tonnage than lower volume higher rated manufactured goods. This is further illustrated by the fact that 49 per cent of freight cars in service in 1964 were gondolas and hoppers, and these provided 55 per cent of the freight-carrying capacity in that year.

Railroad transportation in the United States is provided primarily by private companies operating on an intercity basis, utilizing their own road, terminal, and equipment facilities. However, there are some terminal and switching companies as well as industrial railways which serve the manufacturing plants which own them and which also perform terminal services for the common carrier railroads for the freight these manufacturing firms originate and receive. A relatively small amount of the rolling stock handled by the railroads is also owned by other companies. Thus, in 1963 the railroads owned an estimated total of 1.5 million freight cars of all types; in addition, 257,000 were owned by nonrailroad companies, 160,000 of these being tank cars, 75,000 refrigerator, and 32,000 others. Similarly, the railroads operated a total of 24,602 passenger-train cars, of which 12,500 were passenger-carrying, owned by the railroads, 2,073 owned by the Pullman Company, and 10,600 head-end cars owned by the railroads.[8]

Organization of Rail Transport

The railroad transport system of this country, with the exception of the facilities provided by manufacturing companies, is made up entirely of common carriers. That is, the railroads stand ready to serve all who seek transportation on publicly announced terms at reasonable prices. Furthermore, they are complete common carriers in the sense of

---

[8] The above figures were gathered from reports of the Association of American Railroads, the *Annual Report* of the Interstate Commerce Commission, and the Transportation Association of America. The Pullman Company is owned jointly by the railroads.

the term that they perform only common carrier services and, with the exception of lumber and its products, transport only the goods of others. In this respect, they differ from the other modes of transport in which the various enterprises may be common carriers, contract carriers, private carriers for hire, or private carriers for the firms which own them. The railroads are the only mode operating in the complete category of common carriers and, with the exception already noted, as transport undertakings only. Even when they provide the motive services for private-car lines or plans for piggyback, they act as common carriers standing ready to serve all alike under similar circumstances.

The status of the railroads as common carriers emerges primarily, if not entirely, from the technological conditions of railroad transport. The technical features of railroad operations are such that particular lines must be operated as units. Individual utilization of motive units is not possible, as in motor or water transport, because of the fixity of rail lines over which the vehicles must move. The rail highway cannot be open to all who wish to drive on it. The specialized facilities and the large investment connected therewith preclude over-all competition among rival suppliers of service.

The need for feasible routes between places led at the outset of railroad development to granting to railroads the right of eminent domain to acquire rights of way and terminal facilities. The resulting limitations on competition, together with the privileges that had to be accorded to railroad companies, carried with them the ancient concept that railroads were common callings subject to the common-law idea of common carriage. With the growth of railroads into the only extensive system of land transport after the middle of the nineteenth century, dependence of the user on the services of particular railroads, together with lack of the ability of the shipper to seek alternative sources of supply, became so obvious that comprehensive regulation was instituted. Common carrier obligations became a matter of public concern. The resulting legislative action led to the extremely detailed regulation surrounding common carriage, especially by rail, today. It is thus significant to note that common carriers as we now know them emerged from the technological conditions connected with the development of land transport, and the institutional response to that technology.

The Role of the Rail System in Modern Transport

For the one hundred years from the middle of the nineteenth century to the middle of the twentieth, the railroads were by almost any standard the most important agency of inland transport in this country, and down to 1920 practically the exclusive means of land transport for intercity purposes. Even within cities, rail lines were the principal type except for short distances. In 1920 the total volume of intercity freight traffic, excluding coastwise and intercoastal shipping, was 500 billion ton-miles. The railroads hauled 84 per cent of this, or about 420 billion ton-miles; inland waterways, 15 per cent, or 75 billion; and motor vehicles, less than 1 per cent. In the same year the total volume of intercity passenger traffic was approximately 65 billion passenger-miles. It was estimated that 89 per cent of this was by public carrier, the railroads providing about 57 billion passenger-miles, or 85 per cent of the total. Intercity automobile and air transport was virtually nonexistent.

At the present time, in contrast, the railroads transport only about 43.5 per cent of the intercity ton-miles of freight and 2.05 per cent of the intercity passenger-miles. The total volume of rail freight increased from 420 billion ton-miles in 1920 to 666 billion in 1964, but the percentage of the total handled by all carriers decreased from 84 to 43.5. The passenger traffic, on the other hand, showed a drastic percentage decrease and also an absolute decrease from 57 billion passenger-miles to 18.4 billion and from 85 per cent to 2.05 per cent of the total intercity passenger movement. Nevertheless the railroads still maintain their primacy as the haulers of the long-distance freight traffic with an average haul per ton of 466 miles in 1964 as against 256 miles per ton for Class I common carriers by motor and 136 miles per ton for contract motor carriers. By 1964, however, the railroads had dropped to third place in for-hire intercity passenger traffic, but they remained the second most important long-distance carrier. The average passenger journey for Class I railroads (excluding commutation) was 122.4 miles—in coaches, 106.1 miles; in parlor and sleeping cars, 467.9 miles. Passengers on Class I motor carriers on intercity schedules traveled an average of 94 miles per trip, while for scheduled domestic airline operations the distance was 605 miles.[9]

Thus the position of the railroads in the nation's transport structure has changed drastically over the last forty years. As the suppliers of

[9] Figures derived from Association of American Railroads, and Transportation Association of America. An exhaustive presentation of transport statistics will be found in the presentation of President James Symes of the Pennsylvania Railroad in *Adequacy of Transportation Systems in Support of the National Defense Effort in the Event of Mobilization* (Kilday Report), Hearings of Subcommittee on Armed Services, House of Representatives, 86th Congress, 1st session, October, 1959 (Washington, D.C.: U.S. Government Printing Office, 1959), pp. 445–562.

long-distance transport service by land the railroads are the principal mode for the country and perhaps in this sense may be said to be the core of the transport system. They are still the principal common carriers of freight for intercity movements, and "they are our most pervasive form of mass transportation."[10] It seems reasonable to assume that they will continue to occupy this position for some time to come. However, the impacts of changing technology and governmental policies make generalizations difficult.

MOTOR TRANSPORT

Motor transport is different in so many respects from the other agencies that it falls into an almost totally independent category with regard to its technical characteristics, ownership, operation, public and private use, financing, and even the relationship of the market to output considerations. In its technical aspects, motor transport is characterized first of all by a separation of the vehicle from the highway over which it operates in such a way that the motive equipment can go literally wherever its operator wishes to take it independently of other vehicles. Thus, individual control is possible, and carriers of all kinds may mingle indiscriminately on the highways provided for them.

The technique of motive equipment makes the individual vehicle the operating unit, and this may vary from the smallest passenger car to the largest trucks. Similarly, ownership of the units may be from one vehicle to large fleets of cars or trucks. The roadways are predominantly publicly owned and supplied by public funds; terminal (and parking) facilities may be in private or public hands; and the motive equipment is characteristically privately owned. Hence, motor transport is financed principally by public investment in the roadway and private investment in the vehicles. The latter may be operated for commercial or noncommercial purposes, or both; they may serve as carriers for hire or as private carriers; and they may be common carriers or noncommon carriers. Furthermore, these distinctions apply to both passenger and freight services. Finally, motor transport, especially the private passenger car, provides a very significant proportion of its service for consumption purposes only.

[10] *National Transportation Policy* (Doyle Report), Preliminary Draft of a Report to the Senate Committee on Interstate and Foreign Commerce, 87th Congress, 1st session (Washington, D.C.: U.S. Government Printing Office, 1961), p. 43. It is instructive to note that the railroads transported over 90 per cent of all military freight in World War II and over 97 per cent of all organized military travel. They also transported 71.3 per cent of all intercity freight traffic in 1943 and 74 per cent of intercity passenger traffic. See *Adequacy of Transportation Systems in Support of the National Defense Effort*, pp. 311–13.

These characteristics, together with our current inability to assess motor transport costs directly on the users in proportion to the costs incurred, and for the specific services rendered, eliminates the precise gauges and controls of the market that can be applied to the other modes. Thus, it is possible to speak of motor transport as constituting a "mixed" system from almost every point of view.

The Motor Transport Plant

The motor transport facilities of the country consist of the various automotive vehicles that use the streets and highways provided for them, the streets and highways over which the vehicles move and which also in effect provide a large proportion of the terminal and station services, and the passenger and freight terminals specially constructed for motor traffic. Strictly speaking, one ought also to include gasoline filling stations and even garages, both of which are used directly in the provision of highway transport.

The highway system of the United States consists of some 3.6 million miles of road, of which about 490,000 consist of municipal roads and city streets, the remainder making up the rural highways. Of the 3.6 million miles, 2.1 million are surfaced, and 680,514 are of the high-surfaced type. The main structure of the highway system of the country is comprised of the state highway systems and the national system of interstate highways. These roads are financed by both state and federal governments. For this purpose they are divided into four groups: the federal-aid primary system, which includes the most important highways in each state; the urban extensions of this system; the federal-aid secondary system, consisting of the principal secondary and feeder roads; and the national system of interstate and defense highways, commonly known as the interstate system. As of December 31, 1964, the federal-aid primary system, including the interstate system, totaled 267,774 miles. The federal-aid secondary system amounted to 633,346 miles. The urban portions of the primary and secondary systems amounted to 47,451 miles.[11]

Accurate figures for the total net investment in the motor transport plant of the United States are not available and at best can be estimated only roughly. The net investment in highways and streets is probably of the order of $80 billion.[12] The Doyle Report states that $13

---

[11] U.S. Department of Commerce, *Highway Progress, 1965,* Annual Report of the Bureau of Public Roads (Washington, D.C.: U.S. Government Printing Office, 1965), pp. 110–11.

[12] Mr. Symes estimated the gross investment as of 1958 at $63 billion (*Adequacy of Transportation Systems in Support of the National Defense Effort, op. cit.,* p. 422).

billion were appropriated by the federal government from 1946 to 1959 for highways,[13] while the National Highway Users Conference reported that the total congressional authorizations in regular federal-aid grants from 1916 to the end of 1958 amounted to $38.7 billion.[14] Federal-aid funds programmed during the fiscal year ended June 30, 1965, alone, were as shown in Table 2–2.[15] Publicly and privately

TABLE 2–2

	Total Cost	Federal Funds	Miles
Primary	$ 796,077,754	$ 418,075,398	3,842.2
Secondary	566,837,096	301,421,696	8,730.6
Urban	527,251,865	266,741,045	432.1
Interstate	3,185,592,396	2,854,337,132	3,793.0
Total	$5,075,759,111	$3,840,575,271	$16,797.9

owned motor vehicles in the United States in 1964 were 71.9 million passenger cars and 14.4 million buses and trucks, for a total of 86.3 million vehicles, excluding the military. If one assumes a net investment of $1,000 per motor vehicle, the total investment in motor transport, including highways, would give a figure of about $166 billion.[16] Thus, it appears that the total investment in the motor transport plant is about six times that of the comparable figure for the railroads. No such comparison is possible for motor and railroad revenues because much of the traffic, especially passengers, is not reducible to a revenue basis. It has been noted, however, that one attempt to derive an equivalent estimates all intercity freight revenues, of both private and public motor carriers, at $13.5 billion for 1955 as compared with $8.5 for Class I railroads.[17]

The Role of Motor Transport

The foregoing description of motor transportation in this country indicates that automotive transport in the aggregate constitutes the most important single means of transportation today, a least in a quan-

[13] *National Transportation Policy, op. cit.,* p. 68.

[14] National Highway Users Conference, *Federal Aid for Highways* (rev. ed.; Washington, D.C., 1959), p. 3.

[15] *Highway Progress, 1965, op. cit.,* p. 82.

[16] The Transportation Association of America estimates the investment in privately owned vehicles, only, at $84.2 billion for 1963.

[17] Nelson, *op. cit.,* p. 445.

titative sense. It is the largest conveyor of passengers at all levels, and if a revenue equivalent for passenger miles could be derived, it would be the largest producer of passenger revenue. Just what the total ton-miles of freight would be if all local and intercity freight movements were included, it is impossible to say, but estimates indicate that if a revenue equivalent were obtainable, motor freight would exceed that of the railroads by a considerable margin. In other words, motor transport seems to be the largest element in total transport movement in the national system from the standpoint of volume of business, total investment, and revenue produced.

At the same time, motor transport is primarily local and relatively short distance. For a considerable amount of the traffic involved, it is a substitute for rail, but for a large portion it is an independent means, supplying services heretofore unavailable by other modes.

It is also from the standpoint of ownership, organization, and the services offered the most complex form. As already noted, it ranges all the way from a strictly private and personal means to the common carrier; the services may be rendered on a completely private basis or by corporate entities of considerable size operating on a national scale.[18] A major part of the investment in plant is supplied by government, but the services are offered primarily on a private basis. Finally, the present technological state of the industry makes it impossible, even on a relatively moderate scale, to employ the market mechanism to recover the costs of supplying the services from the users of the services which they specifically receive.

DOMESTIC WATER TRANSPORT

Water transport possesses many of the features of motor transport and thus stands in sharp contrast to the railroads in much the same way. It is characterized by a separation of the vehicle from the highway over which it moves such that the operator may go literally wherever he wishes independent of other vessels. The individual boat is the operating unit, and this may vary all the way from small motor launches and ferries to the huge iron ore freighters of the Great Lakes, cargo-passenger ships, or the 8,500-horsepower towboat, the "United States"

---

[18] There were 1,175 trucking companies in the United States in 1963 with annual operating revenues of $1 million or more. Of the 5,902 motor carriers of property reporting to the ICC in 1963, 1.83 per cent had annual operating revenues of over $10 million and received 50.58 per cent of the total revenues, while 25.37 per cent had revenues of $25,000 or less, and received only 0.33 per cent of the total.

on the Mississippi, which can handle 40,000 tons of freight at a time. The ownership of the units may be from one small vessel to relatively large fleets.

The waterways over which the traffiic moves are public highways, the investment in them where navigational improvements are necessary being supplied by public funds. Terminal facilities, consisting of harbors and the docks themselves, are financed from both public and private sources, but the waterway improvements in the harbor and navigational aids represent public investment. The vessels which provide transport service in domestic trade are predominantly in private hands. They may serve as carriers for hire or as private carriers, and the carriers for hire may be common or noncommon. It is estimated that about 90 per cent of domestic water transport is not regulated, which means that considerably less than 10 per cent of the total is of a common carrier nature.[19]

Water transport differs from motor in certain respects which are important from the standpoint of public policy. The use of harbor facilities, canals, locks, and improved waterways can be controlled directly and restricted in accordance with the policy of the government. Thus, if it is so desired, charges may be levied on the users in accordance with the use, and for the specific use. In other words, the pricing of the services provided by public investment can be established on the same basis as other services amenable to the direct operations of the market. Secondly, public investment in water transport is primarily for commercial purposes. None of the complexities presented by the private automobile are present in water transport.[20]

THE DOMESTIC WATERWAYS SYSTEM

The United States has the most extensive domestic water transport system of any country in the world. This is the result of geographic features that have given it the Great Lakes, which penetrate nearly to the middle of the continent; the Atlantic, Gulf of Mexico, and Pacific coasts; and the vast Mississippi river system that embraces the great central plain from the Gulf of Mexico to the Canadian border and from the Appalachians to the Rocky Mountains. Water transport on this

[19] Interstate Commerce Commission, *79th Annual Report* (Washington, D.C.: U.S. Government Printing Office, 1965), p. 61.

[20] This does not ignore public expenditures for recreational purposes, nor the existence of 7.8 million (*National Transportation Policy* [Doyle Report], p. 168) pleasure craft. These, however, do not enter the transport picture in any meaningful way.

domestic system for descriptive and statistical purposes is commonly divided into two groups, namely, domestic deep-sea shipping and inland waterways.

Domestic deep-sea transportation is made up of the coastal shipping between the ports of the Pacific coast, and between the ports on the continuous coastline of the Gulf of Mexico and the Atlantic seaboard. Intercoastal shipping is that which plies between Pacific coast ports and those of the Gulf of Mexico and the Atlantic coast. Intercoastal traffic as measured by domestic traffic passing through the Panama Canal amounted to a total of 4,692,000 tons in the year ended June, 1963, about 60 per cent of this being eastbound.[21] As of March, 1960, there were 39 private vessels in the intercoastal trade operating as carriers of 294,000 gross tons register. They transported 3,625,828 short tons of dry cargo.[22] Coastwise traffic is much greater than intercoastal, the coastwise tonnage being 15 times that of the intercoastal in 1965.[23] Common carriers in coastwise trade carried 27,512,000 long tons for the year ended March, 1960, in 235 vessels of 1,187,000 deadweight tons. However, only four common carriers remained in the coastwise and intercoastal services in 1960, and all of these reported a loss for that year.[24]

Inland Waterway Transportation

The inland waterway system of the United States, exclusive of the Great Lakes, on which traffic actually moved during the three-year period 1956–58, inclusive, amounted to 20,153 miles. Of this, 13,576 miles consisted of channels of 9 feet or over in depth, 12,216 miles of which had been provided by the federal government, the remainder being from state and local agencies. The total mileage improved by the federal government was made up of the Atlantic coastal canals from Trenton, New Jersey, to Key West, Florida, 5,270 miles; the Gulf coast canals from Carabelle, Florida, to Brownsville, Texas, 4,334 miles; the Mississippi basin from Minneapolis–St. Paul to the Gulf of Mexico, together with the tributary streams of the Ohio, the Illinois to Chicago, the Tennessee to Knoxville, and the Missouri to

[21] D. P. Locklin, *Economics of Transportation* (6th ed.; Homewood, Ill.: Richard D. Irwin, Inc., 1966), p. 712.

[22] *Decline of Coastwise and Intercoastal Shipping,* Merchant Marine Subcommittee of Committee on Interstate and Foreign Commerce, U.S. Senate, 86th Cong., 2d sess. (Washington, D.C.: U.S. Government Printing Office, August, 1960), p. 3.

[23] *Transport Economics,* June, 1966, p. 12.

[24] *Decline of Coastwise and Intercoastal Shipping, op. cit.,* p. 3.

Sioux City, Iowa, 7,443 miles; and the Columbia-Snake and Sacramento rivers on the Pacific coast, 1,913 miles.[25]

The Great Lakes comprise the greatest system of inland waterways in the world. With the locks of 31 feet at Sault Sainte Marie and 29 feet at the Welland Canal, a controlling depth of 21 feet upbound and 25 feet downbound is now available on traffic from Duluth to Lake Erie, and 27 feet from Lake Ontario to Montreal. Thus, there is a minimum channel of 21 feet from Duluth to Ogdensburg, New York, a distance of 1,340 miles, over 1,000 miles of which is open-water navigation.

The New York State Barge Canal is really an integral part of the Great Lakes system, since it connects Lakes Erie and Ontario directly with the Hudson River and the Atlantic Ocean. It was built by the state of New York in 1918 at a cost of $176 million. It deepened and widened the main routes of the old Erie Canal to a depth of 12 feet and a width of approximately 100 feet.

The St. Lawrence Seaway, which was opened in 1959, provides a 27-foot channel from Lake Ontario to Montreal, a distance of 160 miles, thereby accommodating deep-sea traffic from the lake ports to the open sea.[26] The seaway's principal importance is in foreign trade and the direct water access of that trade to the lake ports. This is of considerable significance for domestic transport policy, however, because of the diversion of rail-haul traffic from the Great Lakes ports to the Atlantic seaboard. This traffic is now subject to shipping competition which the railroads will have to meet.

In 1963 the intercity traffic on inland waterways, including the Great Lakes, amounted to 234.2 billion ton-miles. The inland waterways, exclusive of the Great Lakes, moved 138.9 billion ton-miles. Of this 138.9 billion the Mississippi system transported approximately 82.3 billion.

The total investment in the domestic water transport plant can only be estimated. The Transportation Association of America places the figure for net private investment in inland and coastal water carriers at $838 million and for Great Lakes carriers at $235 million. Investment in ocean carriers engaged in foreign as well as domestic

---

[25] *Water Resources Activities in the United States,* Committee Report No. 11, Select Committee on National Water Resources, U.S. Senate, 86th Cong., 2d sess. (Washington, D.C.: U.S. Government Printing Office, 1960), p. 3. For a description of inland water transport, see American Waterway Operators, Inc., *Big Load Afloat* (Washington, D.C., 1965), p. 38. According to this publication there were 15,228 miles of inland waterways with a depth of 9 feet or more in 1964.

[26] It is approximately 2,400 miles from Chicago to the Atlantic Ocean.

trade is $1,800 million. American Waterways Operators, Inc. estimates that investment of all for-hire carriers operating on inland waterways (exclusive of the Great Lakes) in carrier equipment only, in 1965, was $1.65 billion.[27] Thus, it would appear that the total investment in domestic water carriers is somewhere in the neighborhood of $2 billion.

Figures for net investment in waterway facilities and harbors are likewise unavailable. The Doyle Report[28] states that $7.1 billion in federal funds were spent on aid to navigation from 1917 to 1960. This sum includes about $5.7 billion for navigation improvements by the Corps of Army Engineers, $219 million for similar work by the Tennessee Valley Authority, some $1.7 billion for U.S. Coast Guard work relating to navigation, and $158 million for charts and other aids by the Coast and Geodetic Survey. The bulk of these expenditures were made in aid of domestic commerce, but it should be noted that they include maintenance and operation as well as investment. The Committee on National Water Resources states that the total cost to the federal government of constructing, operating, and maintaining the inland waterway system as it existed in 1959, for the 135-year period from 1824, was $2.8 billion, of which about 38 per cent was expended for operation and maintenance.[29] From these various figures it would appear that the total investment in domestic water transport in this country at the present time is somewhat in excess of $5 billion.

The Role of Water Transport

Water transportation suffers from certain distinct disadvantages which limit its scope. First of all, it depends upon waterways which are available for navigation without improvement or upon those which are susceptible to practical improvement. Even these waterways for much of the country are subject to the severe limitations of weather conditions. Then, too, water transport is limited to the places located on the waterways and cannot be extended beyond them. In this respect it is a much less flexible agency than the other means of inland transport.

[27] *Big Load Afloat, op. cit.,* p. 3.

[28] *National Transportation Policy, op. cit.,* p. 167 and p. 68.

[29] *Water Resources Activities in the United States, op. cit.,* p. 10. The Association of American Railroads in *Government Expenditures on Transport Facilities* (Washington, D.C.: 1966), estimates that total federal expenditures down to 1965 amounted to $6.8 billion, and state expenditures $4 billion. If 40 percent of these were for maintainance and operation, the total investment would amount to about $6 billion. However, a considerable portion of this would have to be written off to obtain present net investment.

On the other hand, water transport has the great advantage of less resistance to traction at moderate speeds than does land transportation. This makes it possible for iron ore boats to move up to 21,000 tons of ore in a single trip on the Great Lakes and for a towboat on the Mississippi to move 40,000 tons of freight in a single tow. Whether such transport is more economical than land movements depends upon all the costs necessary to make it possible. The economic feasibility of the Great Lakes for the bulk of traffic which moves on them is scarcely open to question. That of the other water routes, including the St. Lawrence Seaway, is by no means so evident.

Most of the traffic which moves on the domestic waterways of this country consists of bulk commodities. The traffic of the Great Lakes is comprised of iron ore, coal, stone, gravel, cement, petroleum, forest products, and grain. On the inland waterways, 34.9 per cent of the total tonnage for 1957 was petroleum and petroleum products; coal, 25.3 per cent; sand, gravel, and crushed rock, 12.2 per cent; unmanufactured sea shells, 5.4 per cent; and logs, 4.8 per cent. These five groups made up 82.6 per cent of the total tonnage.[30]

AIR TRANSPORT

The airplane forms the newest means of transport in literally every respect. With its development a vehicle became available for effective use over land or water, unhampered by the obstacles of terrain that restrict the scope of operations of other agencies. In many respects, air transport partakes of the nature of water transportation; the individual aircraft is the operating unit, and this may vary from the smallest pleasure plane to the latest jet transport; the air through which the plane moves is free and literally boundless; origin and destination of journeys are airports constructed to accommodate the motive equipment. The journey must be navigated in the real sense of the word.

In this country the airplanes are, with the exception of the defense forces, privately owned and operated. They may serve as common carriers, contract carriers, or private for business and pleasure purposes. At the present time, air transport as part of our national transportation system is supplied by a relatively small number of companies operating under strict supervision with regard to routes, technical operations, and

---

[30] *Water Resources Activities in the United States, op. cit.,* p. 7. Apparently, no substantial change in these percentages has taken place in the last nine years.

conditions of service. The facilities used by the suppliers of transportation by air, apart from the planes and the means of servicing them, are
provided mostly by public funds. These consist of airways and airports.

The Air Transport Plant

Domestic air transportation for the continental United States is
provided by 11 domestic trunk lines, 13 local service lines, 3 helicopter airways, 3 all-cargo lines, and 12 supplemental air carriers. In
addition to this, some 69,000 planes are employed in what the Federal
Aviation Agency classifies as general aviation flying. The domestic
trunk lines consist of those carriers which have permanent operating
rights within the country. Most of these fly high-density traffic routes
between the principal traffic centers. Eight of them also ply between
the United States and foreign nations, excluding Canada. The local
service lines supply air service to routes of lesser traffic density between
the smaller traffic centers and between these centers and the principal
ones. Helicopter airways fly between airports, central post offices, and
suburbs in New York City, Chicago, and Los Angeles. The all-cargo
lines render freight service under temporary certificates between designated areas in the United States. The supplemental carriers are authorized to conduct unlimited charter operations and the right to charter
aircraft to tour operators who in turn sell package tours to individual
members of the general public. General aviation flying consists of all
civil flying except that which is covered by the categories already noted.
It includes business flying, transportation for hire, aerial application
(dissemination of seeds, crop dusting, etc.), instructional flying, and
pleasure flying.

The total net investment in the domestic airlines of this country
at the end of 1964 was approximately $3 billion. They transported
approximately 80 million passengers for a total of 47 billion passenger-miles in intercity service, 186 million ton-miles of mail,[31] 75
million ton-miles of express, and some 662 million ton-miles of freight.
About 1,839 aircraft were used in supplying these services, for which
operating revenues of approximately $3.1 billion were received. In gen-
eral aviation, 88,742 aircraft were employed in 1964, 76 per cent of
this fleet being used for pleasure flying and business.

---

[31] Comparable figures for railroad haulage are not available because no count is
made of mail movement by rail. Only space transportation is purchased from the railroads. A comprehensive analysis of air transportation will be found in *Airlines,* Report
of the Antitrust Subcommittee, Committee of the Judiciary, House of Representatives,
85th Cong., 1st sess. (Washington, D.C.: U.S. Government Printing Office, 1957).

The airways are aerial "highways," under the control of the Federal Aviation Agency, which link the various population centers. Each airway is ten miles wide and includes all the navigable space above this area; each airway is divided into thousand-foot levels up to 24,000 feet. These airways are key elements of the nation's air traffic control system. Above 24,000 feet the continental control area begins, where flight under FAA control is optional in clear weather but is compulsory during restricted visibility. On January 1, 1965, the FAA operated a total of 158,512 miles of airways. The total capital expenditure on these by the federal government from 1935 to 1965 was approximately $550 million (net cost).

Airports and airfields on record with the Federal Aviation Agency at the end of 1964 numbered 9,490. Of these, 2,773 were lighted, and 2,620 had paved runways; 466 had runways of 7,000 feet or more in length. As of December 31, 1964, 2,020 airports were included in the federal-aid airport program, which has as its objective the planning and development of a national system of airports. From 1947, when this was undertaken, through 1964, the total programmed investment amounted to $1.8 billion, of which the federal government supplied $888 million. From 1962 through 1966, $75 million per annum have been appropriated for federal grants-in-aid for airports.

Accurate figures of the total net investment in domestic air transportation in this country are not available. However, it is probably close to $7 billion at the present time; and because of the expansion in airport construction and the introduction of jet transports, it is rising at a rather rapid rate.

The Role of Air Transport

Modern air transportation is a young industry with its role in the transport system of the country not yet clearly defined. Its growth into an integral part of the national transport system may conveniently be said to date from the end of World War II. Its primary commercial function at the present time is in supplying high-speed service for passengers and airmail. The domestic trunk lines in 1964 provided 44.6 billion passenger-miles of the domestic total of approximately 47 billion, and 181 million ton-miles of mail out of about 186 million transported by air for the entire country; they also carried about two thirds of the domestic air freight.

It is frequently stated that air transportation has come of age with the utilization of jet propulsion. This may be true in terms of specialized long-distance traffic. It is not, however, a self-sustaining industry in the sense that the railroads or other totally private enterprises are, and the prospects of its being so are not promising for some time to come. Short-distance air transport, such as that which is supplied by the local service lines, occupies a dubious role in the transport system of the country, to say the least; it promises to constitute a burden on the national treasury for the indefinite future. The movement of a substantial volume of air freight on an economical basis is not in prospect at the present time.

PIPE-LINE TRANSPORT

Pipe lines constitute a highly specialized form of transportation for the movement of products in liquid or gaseous form. These products are composed mostly of crude oil, gasoline, and other liquid petroleum products, water, natural gas, and natural gas in liquid form.[32] The commodities are transported in bulk, and the movement is in one direction, thereby eliminating back-haul and similar problems. For the most part the products which move by pipe line do not constitute a diversion of business from the other agencies, but rather have facilitated the development of traffic which would have been extremely limited had it not been for the pipe lines.[32a] This means of transport is of major importance not merely in the volume of movement; in the case of petroleum products and natural gas, it offers substitutes for traffic moved by other modes which have had severe effects on the composition of the traffic of these other modes and their earnings.

Oil Pipe Lines

Petroleum pipe lines are of two major types, namely, crude-oil lines and the products or refined-oil lines. In 1964 the oil pipe line system of the country consisted of 159,583 miles, of which 110,106 were crude-oil lines and 49,477 refined-oil or products lines. These

[32] Small amounts of coal and gilsonite are also moved by pipe line. To accomplish this, they are transported in a liquid medium. This development is largely in an experimental stage. Pipe-line transport of water is one of the most important transportation activities in the country. It is, however, more conveniently treated as a public utility undertaking than as transport. Nevertheless, if one were endeavoring to obtain the total cost of transport for production and consumption, he would have to include the cost of conveying water to the consumer. Similar remarks apply to sewage, electricity, telephone, and even television and radio.

[32a] It is true that the railroads lost a good deal of petroleum traffic and that their haulage of it is now relatively small, but the development of the petroleum industry and the movement of the product over long distances by land in this country is dependent on pipe lines.

lines were used principally in transportation beween the oil fields of the Southwest and the large consuming areas in other parts of the country east of the Rocky Mountains and in California.[33] Lines are now being built out of Wyoming and even between Texas and California. The Interstate Commerce Commission reported that oil pipe lines transported 214.4 billion ton-miles in 1964 which, in terms of barrels, amounted to 1,045 billion barrel-miles of crude oil and 449 billion barrel-miles of refined oils. The pipe lines carried 75 per cent of the crude oil moving in domestic commerce and about 45 per cent of the refined products.

Investment in the 85 pipe line companies reporting to the Interstate Commerce Commission in 1964, which constituted most of the investment in oil pipe lines, amounted to approximately $2.4 billion. These pipe lines are classified as common carriers and are controlled principally by the large oil companies. The major exception to this is the Southern Pacific Pipe Line Company, owned by the railroad of that name and built on its right of way to Arizona from California and Texas; the Great Northern, Northern Pacific, Union Pacific, and Pennsylvania railroads also have pipe line interests. Pipe line transportation of petroleum in this country is thus closely associated with production and refining in the oil industry. The desirability from the standpoint of public policy of this association has given rise to much discussion; but so far, no acceptable arrangement other than to make the interstate lines operate as common carriers has been obtained.[34]

Natural Gas Pipe-Line Companies

Natural gas pipe-line companies are engaged primarily in the business of transportation. They transport natural gas in interstate commerce from the major fields, which extend from the Gulf of Mexico to the Canadian border along the eastern shelf of the Rocky Mountains. These companies transport the gas mostly at wholesale for resale, although they sell at wholesale for large users. Unlike the petroleum pipe lines, they own the entire product which they ship and therefore do not act as common carriers. Instead, they fall into the category of public utilities and are regulated accordingly. The total investment in these

---

[33] Mid-America Pipe Line Company completed a 2,180-mile liquefied petroleum gas pipe line from Eunice, New Mexico, to the Minneapolis–St. Paul area which began operations in December, 1960.

[34] See Leslie Cookenboo, Jr., *Crude Oil Pipe Lines and Competition in the Oil Industry* (Cambridge, Mass.: Harvard University Press, 1955).

lines amounted to $11.3 billion as of the end of 1963. Although they are basically transportation enterprises and therefore enter into the total transport system of the country, they will not be dealt with further in this treatise because of their essentially public utility features.

SUMMARY

The total investment in the five agencies of transport that have been described above amounts to somewhere around $210 billion, exclusive of natural gas pipelines. Approximately $91 billion of the total has been supplied by public funds. Of the $210 billion, $166 billion is accounted for by motor transport, $44 billion being the investment in the other agencies.[35] The Transportation Association of America estimates that the total freight bill of the nation for 1963 was $60 billion, of which $36.5 billion was for highway freight transport. The estimated passenger bill for the same year was $64.7, of which $56 was for private automobile transportation. Motor transport thus accounted for about 77 percent of the total national transport bill for domestic services in 1963. The total operating revenues of carriers subject to the jurisdiction of the Interstate Commerce Commission were estimated to be approximately $21.8 billion for 1964 of which $9.9 billion were for motor carriers.

These statistics indicate the overwhelming significance of the motor vehicle in the transport system of the country today, and a similar position for private and nonregulated transportation. Furthermore the private and nonregulated portion is the part that accounts for the bulk of the public investment. This is also the area, as will be shown later, in which the agencies are the most competitive within themselves and which have given rise to the pervasiveness of competition for transport as a whole.

The diversity of the conditions of supply of transport services involving inescapable public as well as private investment provides a transport system for the country that can no longer be comprehended within the earlier concept of monopoly and big business enterprise. Because of the necessity for large public investment in facilities such as streets and highways, however, the direct market gauge for total resource allocation to transport and for utilization of the resources that are allocated to it is not available nor adequate to resolve all of the

[35] The Transportation Association of America estimated this to be about $42 billion in 1963.

economic problems that have emerged. On the other hand, careful economic evaluation is more urgent than at any previous time because of the magnitude of the resources that are required, and the elusiveness of the means for measuring the requirements and for rationing the services that are being produced.

DEVELOPMENT OF TRANSPORTATION IN THE UNITED STATES

Chapter 3

INTRODUCTION

Significance of the History of Transport

Transportation and transportation problems are as old as the history of mankind. The story of the development of the means of transport and the influence of them on man's political, social, and economic evolution are the province of the historian. Nevertheless, it is necessary to give a brief account of the growth of modern transport and transport facilities because of the relationship of this growth to present-day policies. The organization of transport supply, the law relating to obligations and rights of transportation companies, and the assumptions underlying present-day regulation are all the result of historical development and the sequence of emergence of the different agencies during the past one hundred and fifty years.

For the greater part of its history to date, mankind has had to depend on human and animal energy, the currents of streams, and the wind for motive power. Perhaps the greatest and certainly the most spectacular achievement in the history of transportation came with the utilization of mechanical forces to provide locomotion. This development in the evolution of man's endeavors to overcome the obstacles of time and space is so strikingly modern that it is hard to realize that in its practical application it is scarcely more than 150 years old.

The five major modes or agencies that are presently available for moving goods and people have emerged at different times. The steamboat was the first mode to supply transport services by the application of mechanical power. This made possible the effective use of natural inland waterways, especially the Mississippi and Ohio rivers. This was followed in a relatively short time by the steam locomotive that led to the development of railroads, which were able to overcome the limitations of topography and climate, thereby paving the way to the opening

47

of the whole of the continental United States to settlement and commerce. These two methods of transportation were the only ones of importance in the country for anything but the shortest distances until after World War I. In the succeeding fifty years, railways and waterways have undergone significant technological improvements. But the real evolution of the twentieth century in transport has come about as the result of the development of automobiles, airplanes, and pipe lines. Although the different agencies have grown up at different times, they all form an integral part of the current transport system. While their relative positions have changed, each is of greater absolute importance than in any previous period.

The history of transportation in the United States for the last three quarters of the nineteenth century, particularly the last half, and the first quarter of the twentieth century, was the history of railroads. From 1860 to 1920 the railroad was literally the sole supplier of inland transport except for the limited and restricted role of water. Public policy, especially with regard to regulation, was confined almost exclusively to the railroads, while transport economics and railroad economics were practically synonymous terms. The development of the program of regulation around the idea of railroads as natural monopolies led to the belief that all transport needed to be regulated in this fashion, with the result that the extension of regulation to the other agencies after 1920 was patterned in this mold. Thus the history of transportation in the modern industrial world has been until very recently the history of railroads, and the shaping of public policy with regard to transport for the past 150 years has been the result of the problems connected with the railroads.

Early Transport

Transportation in colonial America was relatively primitive and was confined largely to the Atlantic seacoast and the navigable inlets and bays. This, among other reasons, led colonists to establish their settlements along the coast and the navigable streams because this gave them the only access to markets of consequence. For example, it cost less to transport a ton of iron ore across the Atlantic Ocean than it did for the seventy-mile land journey from Lancaster to Philadelphia. As the settlers moved inland, roads were built to connect the different settlements, but they were inadequate for any significant amount of travel or commerce. By 1760, it was possible to journey from Boston to New York in four days and thence to Philadelphia in three days more.

In the period following the Revolution, water traffic on the navigable streams assumed considerable importance, especially downstream. As early as 1790, it was estimated that about 150,000 bushels of grain were floated down the Susquehanna River from Pennsylvania and southern New York State to Philadelphia. It was on the Mississippi, however, that the greatest movement of freight took place. Despite obstacles and navigational handicaps, as early as 1817, according to estimates, 1,500 flatboats and 500 barges went down the Mississippi to New Orleans annually. The value of the cargoes, mostly agricultural products, was over $3.6 million in 1801 and about $5.37 million in 1807. Because of lack of mechanical motive power, only about 10 per cent of the traffic was upstream. It was customary to sell the flatboats for lumber in New Orleans. As late as 1847, nearly 2,800 flatboats arrived at New Orleans. They continued to be used until the outbreak of the Civil War.

Land transport down to the beginning of the nineteenth century was supplied largely by pack horses. Many thousands of persons were employed in this business throughout the country. The cost of this means of moving goods was prohibitive, however, except for the most valuable articles, the cost from Philadelphia to Erie, for example, being $249 per ton. The need for more practicable land transport led to the construction of turnpikes, which were either toll roads or public roads that could be used without charge. A few turnpikes were built about 1789, but the Philadelphia and Lancaster Turnpike, completed in 1794, was the first one of importance. The financial success of this venture led to a rapid growth of road construction. Within the next few years, Pennsylvania chartered eighty-six turnpike companies which built about 2,200 miles of road. New York chartered 135 companies which had constructed about 1,500 miles by 1811, and New England had chartered 180 companies by 1810. Some states gave subsidies to turnpike companies, and some of the companies were profitable. The costs of transport were still very high, however, apparently being about $10 per ton per hundred miles. Probably the most famous of the turnpikes was the Cumberland Road or "National Pike." It was begun in 1806 and constructed by the federal government. By 1818, it extended to Wheeling, West Virginia, and finally in 1838 was completed to Vandalia, Illinois. For a while it was an important thoroughfare from Cumberland to Wheeling, but cheaper means of transport provided by the development of canals and railroads put an end to highway building as a means of providing significant intercity transport routes until the coming of the automobile in the second quarter of the twentieth century.

RISE OF MODERN TRANSPORTATION

Domestic Water Transport

At the same time that the toll roads were being constructed, two major developments in water transport were taking place which opened up the Middle West and greatly reduced the cost of inland transportation. The first of these was the successful application of steam to the propulsion of water-borne craft, and the second was the construction of canals connecting important bodies of water, thereby providing for through traffic.

Efforts to apply steam power to boats had been tried in this country as early as 1783, but the first practicable steamboat was the "Clermont," constructed by Robert Fulton. In 1807, it steamed up the Hudson River from New York to Albany, a distance of 150 miles, in 32 hours and returned in 30 hours. Steamboats were soon being built for general use. In 1811 the steamboat made its first appearance on the Ohio when the "New Orleans" went downstream from Pittsburgh to New Orleans. In 1815 the same vessel made the trip upstream to Pittsburgh; and in 1817, regular service was established on the Ohio and Mississippi rivers. The value of commerce carried on the rivers grew rapidly, the value of the produce received at New Orleans alone expanding from $5.4 million in 1807 to $50 million in 1840 and to $185 million in 1860. The development of the railroads and the Civil War brought this traffic to a standstill. It did not undergo any substantial revival until after World War I.

Coastwise shipping played an important role in domestic commerce from 1815 to the Civil War period. With the acquisition of Louisiana and the port of New Orleans in 1803, a considerable part of the goods which went down the Mississippi moved to northeastern ports in coastwise vessels. The California gold rush gave great impetus to the building of the famous clipper ships, and a lucrative intercoastal trade flourished until the construction of the transcontinental railroads. This trade did not revive until the opening of the Panama Canal in 1914. The bulk of the coastwise and intercoastal traffic was transported in wooden vessels down to the beginning of the twentieth century and consisted principally of commodities such as coal, lumber, and cotton. The failure to modernize this fleet left the domestic merchant marine in a very unsatisfactory condition at the outbreak of World War I.

The second important factor in nineteenth-century growth of domestic water transport was the building of an extensive system of canals. The era of canal construction was ushered in by the completion of the Erie Canal connecting Lake Erie with the Hudson River at Albany by the state of New York in 1825. The cost of the canal was about $7 million, but the revenues from the tolls in the first nine years more than covered this sum; by 1841, tolls amounted to $2 million for the year.

The immediate effect of the Erie Canal was to reduce the cost of freighting from Buffalo to New York to $5.00 a ton and the time of transit to five days. Previously, the cost had been $100 a ton and transit time twenty days. The traffic from the region around the Great Lakes soon came to be focused on New York City, thereby establishing its position as the most important seaport on the Atlantic Coast. A second effect of the Erie Canal was a veritable orgy of canal building, especially in Pennsylvania, Massachusetts, Maryland, Virginia, Ohio, Indiana, and Michigan, resulting in the construction of 4,468 miles of canals, principally before 1850. Most of these were state undertakings that led to a rapid rise in state debts between 1820 and 1840. Many of the works were ill-conceived, and a number of the states repudiated their obligations in the economic crisis of 1837. Nevertheless, the canals proved to be the first feasible means of providing relatively cheap inland freight transport. However, the limitations imposed upon them by geography, and the successful development of the railroad, led to the decline of their importance after 1860 even in the areas where they had the greatest relative advantage. By the beginning of the present century the old canal system had literally disappeared.

The major exception during the nineteenth century to the rise and decline of domestic water transport was the Great Lakes. The Erie Canal opened up the area along the shores of this vast series of inland seas to settlement. Buffalo had 42,000 inhabitants by 1850, and by 1860 Chicago had 109,000. Statistics covering the movement of traffic upon the whole lake system were not collected until 1899. However, information is available on commerce passing through the St. Mary's Falls Canal (the Soo Canal), constructed in 1855, and the Detroit River.[1]

The registered tonnage passing through the Soo Canal in 1855

[1] For an account of this, see George Tunell, "Transportation on the Great Lakes of North America," *Journal of Political Economy*, Vol. IV (December, 1895–September, 1896), pp. 332–51. See also Vol. IV, pp. 243–45; and Vol. V (December, 1896–September, 1897), pp. 23–39 and 340–75.

amounted to 106,296 tons. By 1881, this had risen to 2,092,757, with total net freight tons of 1,567,741. These amounts had increased by 1895 to 16,806,781 tons and 15,062,580 tons, respectively. Movements through the Detroit River were larger in amount, although the growth was less rapid than that of the Soo Canal. In 1895, 25 million tons of freight passed through the Detroit River. The traffic on the Great Lakes was predominantly eastbound and consisted of long-distance shipments in bulk of the products of mines, grainfields, and forests. Iron ore traffic increased rapidly after 1880, the amount shipped from Lake Superior being 677,073 net tons in that year and increasing to over 8 million net tons in 1895. In 1896, coal constituted almost five sixths of the westbound traffic through the Detroit River. The total freight movement on the Great Lakes has continued to increase to the present time.

Development of Rail Transport

The growth of railroad transportation from its beginnings in 1825 to the position of complete pre-eminence in inland transportation in a period of forty years constitutes what is probably the most significant and far-reaching phase of transport improvement in the history of mankind and one of man's greatest and most influential achievements. In this country it opened up the vast reaches of the continent to settlement and economic development as well as providing the means of communication essential to political unity. It freed the country from the severe geographic and weather limitations of water routes, and it provided a means of urban transportation that made possible the rise of the modern metropolis with its enormous concentration of population. The latter was the result of rail transport which could supply the people with the products needed as well as the means of transportation within the city itself.

Growth of the Railroad System. Railroads as highways with tracks over which vehicles were made to run were developed in the latter part of the eighteenth century. It was the invention of the steam locomotive, however, that made possible the rise of the railroad to its position of eminence in land transport. The first practicable locomotive was George Stephenson's "Rocket," which made its successful trial run in 1829 in England. Successful developments followed quickly in this country. The Baltimore and Ohio was chartered in 1827 as a railroad to be constructed for general transportation purposes. It commenced steam operations in 1830. The Charleston and Hamburg Railroad of South Carolina was completed in 1833. This road, 135 miles long, for two decades held the distinction of being the longest railroad in America.

The first ten years of railroad development were largely ones of experimentation. The lines were built primarily as feeders to waterways and radiated out from the important centers of water transport like the spokes of a wheel. In 1840, there were 2,818 miles of railway line in this country. Much of this was of 4-foot, 8½-inch gauge, this being the width between rails required for the first engine imported from England. In 1842 a series of lines were connected end to end between Buffalo and New York, all having the 4-foot, 8½-inch gauge. This soon became the standard for most of the country, thereby laying the basis for a national network on which equipment could be interchanged readily.

The technical success of the railroad was firmly established by 1850. It had become clear that it could compete successfully with the waterways. Of much greater importance was the demonstration that it could provide economical transportation throughout the country where water transport was not available. The period from 1850 to 1900 was one of phenomenal expansion and rapid technological improvement. In 1850 the railroad mileage was 9,021 miles; by 1860, it had grown to 30,626 miles and had taken on the basic pattern in the area east of the Mississippi which it exhibits today. (See Figure 3–1.) The most significant development in the next decade was the establishing of the first all-rail route to the Pacific coast at San Francisco in 1869. In the next twenty years, that is, from 1870 to 1890, the railroad net grew from 52,922 miles to 163,597, and the present structure was so completely established that a map of 1890 would serve as the basic outline map even for today, although total railroad mileage continued to grow until 1915, at which time it reached the high point of 264,378 miles. Since then, it has undergone a steady though somewhat slow decline to just over 212,000 miles in 1965. On the other hand, technical efficiency and intensity of use of facilities have shown continuous improvement throughout the railroad history.

Although the railroad industry began as private enterprise and has continued primarily in that category, a number of earlier roads were constructed by states and some even by municipalities. Opposition of vested interests such as canals, and even farmers, and difficulties of raising venture capital, on the one hand, coupled with the desire of many localities for improved transportation, on the other, led a number of states to embark upon railroad construction. Pennsylvania, Illinois, Indiana, Michigan, Virginia, and Georgia all built lines. In addition,

FIGURE 3-1

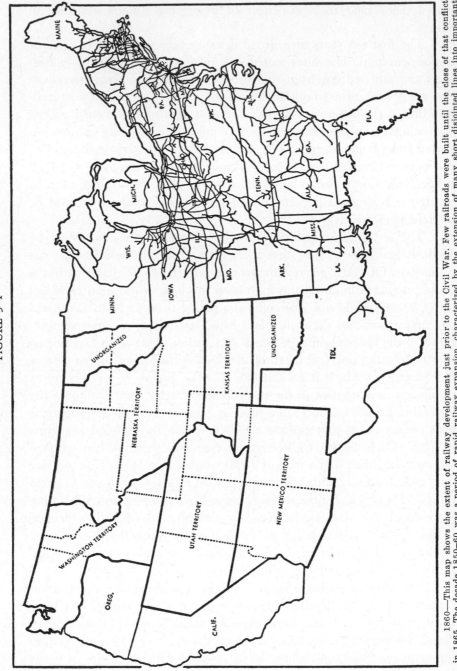

1860—This map shows the extent of railway development just prior to the Civil War. Few railroads were built until the close of that conflict in 1865. The decade 1850–60 was a period of rapid railway expansion, characterized by the extension of many short disjointed lines into important rail routes. This decade marked the beginning of the railway development in the region west of the Mississippi River. By 1860 the "iron horse" had penetrated westward to the Missouri River and was beginning to make itself felt in Iowa, Arkansas, Texas, and California.

some railroads came into the hands of states like Massachusetts, North Carolina, and Missouri as a result of the failure of private corporations. The results of the state ventures were quite disappointing, and these governments disposed of the enterprises before the railroad boom started in the 1850's.[2] By that time the federal government and the states had withdrawn from direct participation in internal improvements, thereby leaving railroad building to private corporations. Some municipalities continued to undertake railway projects, the most ambitious being that of the city of Cincinnati, which built the Cincinnati Southern, a railway of over 300 miles in length connecting Cincinnati with Chattanooga. It was leased to the Cincinnati, New Orleans and Texas Pacific in 1881.

As has already been mentioned, railroads began as disconnected independent lines radiating out of the more important centers. Extension of them led to end-to-end combinations in a relatively short time to establish through routes and unified operation. In 1853 the New York Central Railroad was formed by the combination of a number of end-to-end lines connecting Albany and Buffalo. This example was followed by numerous other railroads so that by 1873 there were sixty-nine such combinations with lines in excess of 200 miles each. The Erie Railroad was the longest, with 959 miles. From 1873 to 1893 the short through lines were transformed into a number of large railroad systems. At the same time the long through lines, particularly in the territory west of the Mississippi, were being built, with the result that the pattern of railroad grouping of today was established before the turn of the century.

The combination and consolidation movement which developed after 1893 was largely centered on uniting in some way or another competing systems. The main purpose was evidently that of limiting competition, although some attempts were made to establish true transcontinental railroad enterprises. Many of these endeavors ran counter to the antitrust laws. The result, among other things, was that no railroad system was established which extended from coast to coast. Instead, the systems were confined largely to each of the major territorial regions, namely, north of the Ohio and east of the Mississippi, south of the Ohio and east of the Mississippi, and the territory west of the Mississippi. In the latter, only two lines, the Atchison, Topeka and Santa Fe and the Chicago, Milwaukee, St. Paul and Pacific have a through

---

[2] The state of Georgia still owns the Western and Atlantic, although it was leased to the Nashville, Chattanooga and St. Louis Railroad in 1890. North Carolina owns a majority of the stock of the North Carolina Railroad Company.

route under their own jurisdiction between Chicago and the Pacific coast, although the term *transcontinental* is applied to those railroads which reach the Pacific coast and have connections east to the Missouri River.

Factors in Railroad Development. A number of factors influenced the tremendous growth of railroad transportation in this country during the period from 1850 to 1910. Many of these were of prime significance in shaping public policy and in conditioning the attitude toward the railroads which persists even today. Large amounts of private capital became available during this period. This, coupled with the westward movement of population and a speculative fever largely uninhibited by business scruples and public control, led to abuses that resulted in a very unfavorable public reaction when the inevitable day of reckoning arrived. To these pressures for expansion must be added the encouragement given by state and local governments through various kinds of local aid. Probably the greatest impetus in public aid came in the form of land grants from the federal government, most of which were made to a few railroads west of the Mississippi. A final factor which is too frequently overlooked, especially in its impact on public policy, is the unique nature of railroad economics. The railroads were the first industry in which large "overhead" costs became of prime importance. Public policy did not recognize that competition could not be relied upon to act as a satisfactory regulator of prices and resource utilization. The inescapably unsatisfactory results of following a competitive policy developed antagonisms and attitudes for which the railroads were by no means completely to blame.

In the nineteenth century the countries of Europe were heavy exporters of capital to the new and developing areas of other continents. The rapid growth and promise of the United States aroused the interest of investors, railroads being one of the most attractive ventures. State bonds issued to aid the railroads, as well as corporate stocks and bonds, were sold to European interests. As late as 1899, nearly $3 billion were in railroad stocks and bonds; European stock interest in large American railroads ranged all the way from 86 per cent in the Illinois Central to 21 per cent in the Chicago, Milwaukee, and St. Paul.

Local and state aid to railroads took a number of forms. Counties and municipalities purchased stocks and bonds of railroads, donated land for right-of-way and station facilities, guaranteed bonds, and in some cases even granted tax exemptions. State aid, particularly in the South and West, took much the same form. These aid programs led to overexpansion, speculation, and fraud, which resulted in the inevitable disillusionment and resentment. The outright gifts to the railroads were

relatively small, while investments in railroad securities were made
with the expectation of success. The fact that a considerable amount of
the latter was lost, however, does not seem to justify labeling it as subsidy any more than the investment of private persons in the railroad
securities.

The chief public contribution to the railroads came in the form of
land grants made by the federal government during the period from
1850 to 1871. The purpose was to encourage the building of railroads
into the unsettled and largely unchartered West. For political reasons, in particular, the national government was anxious to secure railroad transport into the area before it was economically justified. The
first of the land grants was made to the Illinois Central in 1850, the
federal government granting the land to the state of Illinois, which in
turn granted it to the railroad. This policy was changed in 1862, when
the federal government undertook to make the grants directly to the
railroad corporations themselves. A railroad received the strip of land
for its right-of-way and for a distance of six miles on either side. The
total acreage deeded under this arrangement amounted to just over
131 million acres. (See Figure 3–2.) In return the recipient railroads

FIGURE 3–2

UNITED STATES LAND GRANTS TO RAILROADS

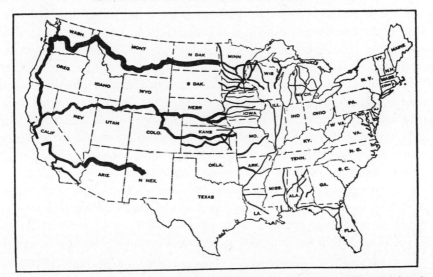

The federal government granted lands to railroads in alternate sections, retaining the
sections between. It is impossible to present this "cheekerboard" pattern on so small a map, but
the shaded areas show the approximate locations of the land grants, and are in proportion to the
amounts actually received by railroads.

Reproduced from Robert S. Henry, "The Railroad Land Grant Legend in American
History Texts," *Mississippi Valley Historical Review*, Vol. XXXII, No. 2 (September, 1945),
p. 180.

were required to give reduced transportation charges on mail, troops, and government property. The mail rates came to be 80 per cent of the regular rates for mail, and the other rates 50 per cent of the regular charges. This arrangement continued until Congress modified it in 1940 and then ended all land-grant reductions in 1945. In this connection it should be noted that competing lines which did not receive land grants nevertheless had to accord the same charges in order to get government traffic.

Public aid to railroad development resulted in a very rapid expansion of the railroad network, which probably assisted in opening up the country more rapidly than would have been the case otherwise. At the same time, it gave rise to abuses that were to have serious repercussions later on. The inevitable overbuilding and the extensive duplication of competitive lines created excess capacity that resulted in unsatisfactory earnings and financial failures that still plague the industry. Financial abuses flourished under public aid and the totally inadequate standards of financial responsibility of the period.[3] Among the most notorious of these were the frauds practiced through the use of the construction company. This was a corporation organized to take over the work of construction at so much on a contract basis, payment being made usually in railroad land and securities. Honestly carried out, this was a thoroughly sound business procedure. Unfortunately, however, it was often used as a device by insiders to milk the railroad completely. One of the most famous of these organizations was the Credit Mobilier established in connection with the Union Pacific. The insiders were the interests that controlled the Union Pacific. Through the Credit Mobilier they awarded themselves the construction contracts that greatly inflated the prices paid for the property. The money for this was obtained from securities sold to the general public, and from bonds secured by the facilities which were constructed. When the inevitable bankruptcy came, the same insiders held control of the property through foreclosure on the bonds and retained their construction profits, too.[4]

Emergence of the Railroad Problem. The particular problems of railroads which have persisted in various forms to the present day began to emerge in their modern aspects shortly after the end of the Civil War. With the onset of distressed economic conditions in the

[3] For a detailed account of railroad financing, see W. Z. Ripley, *Railroads: Finance and Organization* (New York: Longmans, Green & Co., 1915).

[4] For a somewhat unique appraisal of public policy and the influence of the railroads on economic development, see R. W. Fogel, *The Union Pacific Railroad* (Baltimore, Md.: The Johns Hopkins Press, 1960) and *Railroads and American Economic Growth* (Baltimore, Md.: The Johns Hopkins Press, 1964).

postwar period, particularly in the Middle West, the railroads became the focus of a great deal of public resentment, some of which was deserved and some of which was not. Nevertheless the railroads had achieved a position in the economy of the country which was to make them a particular object of attention henceforth.

Judged by most standards, the supplying of the vast continental area of the United States with the most efficient type of mass land transport that has yet been made available was a phenomenal business and engineering accomplishment. This, however, was not without its accompanying problems. First of all, there were the excesses and abuses that seem invariably to emerge with the rise of a new industry in a new country. The extreme concept of *laissez faire* that prevailed at the time and the lack of grasp of many of the problems of the modern corporation led to financial excesses, fraud, and speculation that resulted in failures, heavy losses to investors, and an aroused public. The lavish aid of various kinds extended by the different governments—local, state, and federal—to encourage construction led to overexpansion, in addition to giving unscrupulous financiers and promoters almost unlimited opportunity to fleece the public and reap personal fortunes. These and other abuses, together with the emergence of the railroad monopoly of inland transport, soon led to the demand for public regulation, first of all at the state level and then at the federal.

The second problem connected with the development of the railroad arose from the nature of railroad economics. The railroad was the first of the modern industries that came to be characterized as a "natural" monopoly. This meant that competition alone was a totally inadequate means of securing reasonable prices and of protecting the consumer. In addition, over-all competition was ruinous to competitors and inevitably resulted either in agreements to control it or in the emergence of a single firm without competitors. The monopoly position, heavy fixed costs, and unused capacity led to discrimination as an exercise of monopoly power and as a necessity for an economical pricing policy. These problems were an inescapable part of the economics of rail transport and would have required regulation, at least as long as private ownership existed, without any of the abuses. Unfortunately, this was not understood, and the chief reason advanced in support of railroad regulation was the necessity of curbing the abuses and the excesses.[5] This seems to be the attitude even today.

[5] But see Gabriel Kolko, *Railroads and Regulation 1877–1916* (Princeton, N.J.: Princeton University Press, 1965). Kolko contends that the purpose of the Act of 1887 was to lend stability to the railroad cartels which the expansion of the industry had

RISE OF THE NEW TRANSPORT STRUCTURE

The position of the railroad as the sole supplier of inland transport services, except for the somewhat limited role of water transport, came to an abrupt end with the new technological developments following World War I. This resulted in a revival of interest in inland waterways, the restoration of the highway to a new prominence with the growth of automotive transport, the rapid development of pipe lines, and the emergence of a completely new means, namely, the airplane. The effect of these changes was to turn transportation from a monopolistic structure into one of the most competitive areas of economic activity in our whole system of production, at least as far as the consumer is concerned.

Inland Waterways

The revival of attention to inland waterways at the turn of the century was the result of a number of factors. The awakened public interest in the development and conservation of our natural resources included domestic waterways in the program. There was also the widespread notion that waterways provided a means of natural transport that was cheaper than the railroads. This was reinforced by the memories of, and a nostalgia for, the steamboat days on the Mississippi, coupled with the desire to secure federal aid for local advantage. The resentment against the railroads, together with their inability to supply transport to much of the country as cheaply as had been expected, led to support for alternative means. Finally, it was felt that water competition would be a way of bringing about a lowering of railroad rates and a method for measuring the reasonableness of them. President Herbert Hoover openly advocated the development of the vast Mississippi as one way of providing a yardstick for railroad charges.

The revival was marked by the establishment by Congress of the Board of Engineers for Rivers and Harbors in the War Department to serve as the federal agency charged with investigating the feasibility of proposals for waterway improvement, a task it still performs. In 1903 the state of New York undertook to transform the old Erie Canal into the present-day New York State Barge Canal. In 1911, Congress authorized improvements on the Ohio designed to give it a 9-foot chan-

rendered chronically unstable. Subsequent legislation was designed to strengthen the Interstate Commerce Commission's efforts at cartelization. The legislation certainly had its shortcomings, but Kolko supplies no alternative approach, nor does he describe what he frequently refers to as the "railroad problem."

nel to the Mississippi. Probably the greatest impetus to the revival came with the plan advanced by Herbert Hoover when he was Secretary of Commerce. This called for a north-south trunk line 1,500 miles in length, reaching from Chicago to New Orleans, and a great east-west trunk line from Pittsburgh through Cairo to Kansas City. The minimum depth was to be 9 feet. To encourage inland waterway developments still further, the federal government set up the Inland Waterways Corporation in 1924. This took over the federal barge line that had been set up on the Mississippi and Warrior rivers during World War I. The purpose of this corporation was to demonstrate the practicability of barge operations. The undertaking was not financially successful, and in 1953 it was sold to the Federal Waterways Corporation of Delaware for $9 million.

Mention should also be made of the opening of the Panama Canal in 1914. Although this is an international waterway, it is an integral part of the domestic waterway facilities of the United States. It provided an effective water route for domestic trade between the three seacoasts of this country.

The last major step in the development of inland waterways came with the opening of the St. Lawrence Seaway in 1959. Because the Great Lakes–St. Lawrence system is an international waterway with both navigation and power aspects, joint development by Canada and the United States was under consideration from 1909 to 1954. In the latter year, Congress passed the Seaway Act creating the St. Lawrence Seaway Development Corporation, which was placed under the supervision of the Department of Commerce. This Corporation was authorized in conjunction with the St. Lawrence Authority of Canada to construct, operate, and maintain the single-stage navigation project in the International Rapids section and do the necessary dredging in the Thousand Islands section. It was also to co-operate with the New York Power Authority for power development, but all the joint costs of the dual project were to be allocated to the power phase of the undertaking. The Corporation was instructed to establish tolls that would make its activities self-liquidating. The investment by the Corporation as of December 31, 1965, was $141.7 million, of which approximately $19 million was from deficit from operations incurred since 1959.

Motor Transport

The automobile did not become a significant factor in transportation until after World War I. By that time, Henry Ford had demonstrated the potentialities of mass production of automobiles, such that the output of the Ford Company alone in 1920 was 1,074,366 cars. It was the development of the automobile that brought about the revival of interest in highways. Even as late as 1900, one distinguished student of transportation stated that the road system as a matter of national importance was a thing of the past. Moreover, a mere $2,997 was spent by the federal government in 1894 on highways, and only $662,785 was spent as late as 1916.

A renewed local and state interest in roads emerged at the beginning of the century, and a number of states had established highway departments by the outbreak of World War I. It was the federal government, however, that really promulgated the development of the modern highway system. In 1916, Congress passed the Federal Aid Road Act, which marked the beginning of federal grants-in-aid to the states. Each state receiving a grant-in-aid was required to set up a highway department together with management and construction standards acceptable to the controlling federal agency. The Federal Highway Act of 1921 provided that the Secretary of Agriculture should designate a system of interstate highways on which a state in any year might receive federal aid on mileage not to exceed 7 per cent of its existing system of improved state highways. The states had to match the amount they received from the federal government. The Federal Aid Highway Act of 1944 extended this primary system to 40,000 miles to connect all major centers and to join with continental routes at the nation's borders. It also extended aid to streets of urban centers of over 5,000 population, to secondary rural roads, and to grade-crossing eliminations. In 1949 the Bureau of Public Roads was created and placed in the Department of Commerce.

The Federal Aid Highway Act of 1956 marked a substantial departure in federal policy. It authorized a federal expenditure of $46.2 billion extending over a period of thirteen years. Of this amount, $25 billion were to be spent on the national system of interstate and defense highways of 41,000 miles, the remainder on the other federal-aid highways. On the interstate system the federal government was to bear 90 per cent of the cost. For the first time, specific tax revenues were recognized as applicable to highway work. These were to be placed in a highway trust fund, out of which the authorized expenditures were to be made. This was known as the "pay as you go" plan. Trying to speed up highway construction faster than the acquisition of funds permitted has resulted in additional appropriations by Congress; also, aid to the primary system has now been increased to 60 per cent.

The biggest relative impact of the automobile on passenger traffic took place between 1920 and 1930, for by the latter year out of 196.3 billion intercity passenger-miles, private cars and busses accounted for 168 billion, or 85 per cent of the total. It was during the same period also that the automobile came to the front in urban passenger transport, with the consequent difficulties for urban commercial facilities, especially street and interurban railways. The major impact on freight traffic came between 1930 and 1940. By the end of that period, motor freight traffic had increased from about 5 billion ton-miles, or less than 1 per cent of the total intercity ton-miles in 1920, to 62 billion ton-miles, or 10 per cent of the total.

Air Transport

Air transport, like that of the motor vehicle, emerged after World War I; but unlike highway transport, its technical development has been focused primarily on military and national defense considerations, while its traffic has been confined almost entirely to passengers and mail.

The first practicable air transportation was undertaken by lighter-than-air craft, as a result of the work of Count Ferdinand von Zeppelin of Germany. By 1911, regular commercial operations had begun in Europe. It was not until the disastrous explosion of the "Hindenburg" in New York in 1937 that it was evident that the airship would have to give way to the airplane. The latter means of flight came into existence with the first sustained power flight by man at Kitty Hawk, North Carolina, on December 17, 1903, when the Wright brothers covered 120 feet in twelve seconds. Technical improvements followed rapidly such that airplanes became a practicable weapon of war in World War I. In 1919, two Britishers, Alcock and Brown, made the first transoceanic crossing when they flew from Newfoundland to Ireland in just over sixteen hours. By the outbreak of World War II in 1939 the airplane had established its position as a major weapon of warfare and as a rapidly growing device for long-distance mail and passenger transport. The present position of the airplane as the principal supplier of common carrier intercity passenger transportation is due largely to the policy of public aid and subsidy and the enormous government expenditures in the aircraft industry for military purposes.

Government participation in the development of air transportation came in 1919 when the Post Office Department established the first regular air-mail route between New York and Washington. In 1919, transcontinental service was undertaken, and this was extended to continuous day and night service in 1924. The early air-mail routes were operated by the government, but with the Kelly Act of 1925 the Post Office began contracting with private companies. This stimulated the development of commercial aviation because the carriers were required to provide facilities for the transportation of passengers. In 1926 the Air Commerce Act empowered the Secretary of Commerce to designate and establish civil airways and to establish, operate, and maintain along these airways all necessary air navigation facilities except airports. As a result of this legislation the federal government has developed airway facilities open to all who wish to use them. The present elaborate system of air navigation and control, known as the federal airways system, is under the direction of the Federal Aviation Agency, which took over the functions of the Civil Aeronautics Administration in 1958.

Federal encouragement to air transport was also afforded by federal aid to airport construction. Prior to 1933, airports were financed largely by local governments, although a number of important privately owned ones were in operation. The Civil Aeronautics Act of 1938 removed limitations on federal participation in airport development and specifically empowered the Civil Aeronautics Administrator to engage in a plan of airport development and improvement. Congress embarked upon a program of financial assistance in 1940, and in 1946 enacted the Federal Airport Act, the legislation providing for an expenditure of $520 million under which the federal government's share of improvement costs to the larger airports was not to exceed 50 per cent. For an airport to be eligible for aid, it had to be included in the national airport plan, which was under the direction of the Civil Aeronautics Administration, but is now under its successor, the Federal Aviation Agency.

Federal policy with regard to aviation differs from that which has been applied to the other agencies. Federal aid has been afforded to airways and airports; and so far, no charges have been levied in return for the use of the facilities provided by the federal government. Instead, air transport has also been subsidized directly by payments to the air transport companies for the purpose of supporting them, without any requirement for subsequent repayment. This had much to do with the shaping of the pattern of the air transport system and of public policy toward it. Routes and companies grew up under the conditions established by air-mail contracts. Even today the legislative mandate to the Civil Aeronautics Board to provide subsidy where needed is a factor for consideration in the awarding of certificates for routes. This direct participation, from the beginning of air transport development, also resulted in federal regulation and control from the start of the industry.

Brief mention should be made here of federal encouragement to the development of local air transportation. In 1944 the Civil Aeronautics Board issued a report on the question of local and feeder airline service. The Board concluded that it was desirable to encourage this type of transportation and so decided to issue temporary certificates covering a three-year period only. At the same time, it discouraged competition between trunk and feeder lines. The feeder service has become firmly established as part of the air transport system. There are now thirteen such lines in operation in addition to three helicopter airways which serve the cities of New York, Chicago, and Los Angeles. All of the direct subsidies disbursed by the Civil Aeronautics Board to domestic air lines at the present time are paid to the feeder lines and the helicopter airways.[6]

Pipe Lines

Petroleum pipe-line transportation in the United States began with the development of the first oil fields at Titusville, Pennsylvania, in 1872. As the industry developed, gathering lines became a part of every oil field operation. In 1879 the Tidewater Pipeline Company completed a trunk line from the Pennsylvania fields to the Reading Railroad, which then transported the oil to the New York City area. The old Standard Oil Trust soon stepped into the picture to build long-distance pipe lines from the oil fields to the Atlantic coast and the Great Lakes region. By the turn of the century, Standard Oil of New Jersey controlled about 40,000 miles of pipe lines as compared with 550 miles of its largest competitor. The dissolution of the Standard Oil Trust in 1911 and the discovery of the vast oil resources of the Southwest and California shortly thereafter led to a rapid expansion of pipe-line transportation, especially after the end of World War I. These lines were owned and operated principally by the major oil companies. They extended from the southwest oil fields to the Midwest and the Atlantic seaboard. On the Pacific Coast they were confined to California, and as late as 1948 there were no pipe-line connections between the area east of the Rocky Mountains and the Pacific Coast. California, Oregon, and Washington, however, are now connected with fields east of the mountains and a pipe line also connects the latter state with the oil fields of Alberta and British Columbia. The pipe line is today the principal means of transporting crude petroleum from the oil fields to

---

[6] Northeast Airlines classified as a trunk line, still receives a subsidy, but it occupies an anomalous position in the trunk-line system.

the refineries, 76 percent of the crude oil moving in domestic commerce using this means in 1959.

Some considerable development of products lines has also taken place. The transportation of gasoline by pipe line began in 1930 when the Tuscarora Pipeline Company, controlled by the Standard Oil Company of New Jersey, began using an old crude-oil pipe line for transporting gasoline. Technical improvements led to a fairly rapid expansion of this development, such that by 1949 there were 14,133 miles of products lines. By 1965, these had grown to 53,000 miles. In December, 1960, the Mid-America Pipeline Company had completed a 2,180-mile pipe line for liquefied petroleum gas from Eunice, New Mexico, to the Minneapolis–St. Paul area. In 1965, products lines carried 45 percent of the refined oils moving in domestic commerce.[7] As noted in the previous chapter, one outstanding feature of petroleum pipe-line development has been its close association with the oil industry and the consequent predominance of ownership by the large refining companies.

EFFECTS OF CHANGING TECHNOLOGY

The most obvious effect of changing technology in transport is improved transportation. It has rendered the movement of people and goods more regular and calculable, safer, more rapid, and cheaper. This has reduced impediments in space relationships, thereby making it easier for people to cooperate in activities involving spatial factors. The improvement in speed has reduced the cost of the time factor in the movement of people as well as goods. Improved transport has also widened the market and encouraged the division of labor and geographic specialization, thereby bringing about increased competition and a reduction of prices. These consequences of improved transport differ from those arising from technological advances in other areas of production, principally because of the bearing they have on spatial and time factors in the production process.

There are other effects which relate more directly to transport itself. One of these concerns the structure of transport. Only in the very generalized sense of a production activity that provides for the movement of people and goods can the various transport agencies be grouped together in the category of an industry. For firms to be so classified, it is necessary that there be a rather high degree of homogeneity of product

---

[7] U.S. Department of the Interior, *An Appraisal of the Petroleum Industry of the United States* (Washington, D.C.: U.S. Government Printing Office, January, 1965).

and similarity of economic structure or conditions of production.[8] Thus, railroads may be classified as an industry because they have similar economic characteristics and offer essentially similar types of services. By the same token the other agencies may be considered as separate industries. Over a considerable range, there is a good deal of ready, indeed almost complete, substitutability of services among the different modes of transport; but they also offer services that are very distinct from each other, some of them being scarcely substitutable at all. In other words, the suppliers of transportation manifest diverse economic characteristics with regard to costs, supply of services and facilities, and organizational structure. Prior to 1920, because of the predominant position of the railroads, it was possible to treat land transport as an industry. The impact of the new technology, however, has converted it into a group of industries with such markedly different characteristics as to have profound implications for national transportation policy.

The second effect of changing technology on transport itself has been periodically to alter the position of the dominant type of carrier. At first the dominant type was road transport with turnpike and slow-moving animal power. This was almost completely superseded by canals and inland waterways. From the middle of the nineteenth century down to 1920 the railroads took over, and water carriage was relegated to a minor role except in special instances, particularly the Great Lakes. Developments after World War I revived the old types of carriers, giving them new roles, brought the pipe lines into prominence, and established air transport. The railroads are probably still the most important carrier for hire, but they are no longer able to supply all the types of transport we need. They are now faced with ready substitutes for many of the services they alone used to provide. In 1930 the railroads carried approximately 74 per cent of the total of domestic intercity freight traffic, while motor carriers carried less than 4 per cent of the total, oil pipe lines about 5 per cent, and inland waterways 15 per cent. In 1964, the railroads hauled only 43.5 per cent of the intercity freight traffic, only a small amount greater than that which was moved in 1956. In the same year the motor carriers had increased their share to 22.7 per cent. Changes in the distribution of commercial passenger traffic have been even more striking. From 1930 to 1964 the railroads' share of total commercial passenger-miles dropped from 68.5 per cent to 20 per cent, while buses increased their share from 18 per cent to 25 per cent, and airways raised theirs from a fraction of 1 per

---

[8] E. A. G. Robinson, *The Structure of Competitive Industry* (New York: Harcourt, Brace & Co., 1932), pp. 6–14.

cent to nearly 55 per cent. Furthermore, railroad passenger traffic has declined steadily in absolute terms since 1951. Finally, the impact of these changes on the railroads' financial position has been heavier than the traffic figures themselves indicate. The freight traffic lost to other agencies includes some of the most profitable traffic—high-rated commodities which competitors have taken away from them. Thus the revenue losses have been even more significant than those of tonnage. (See Figures 3–3 and 3–4.)

FIGURE 3–3

INTERCITY TON-MILES, PUBLIC AND PRIVATE, BY KINDS
OF TRANSPORTATION, 1939–1964

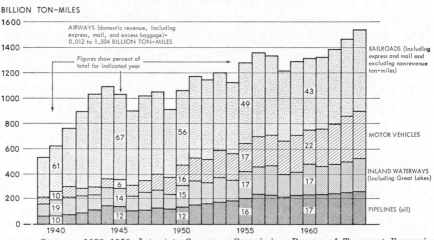

SOURCE: 1939–1959, Interstate Commerce Commission, Bureau of Transport Economics and Statistics, *Intercity Ton-Miles, 1939–1959*, Statement No. 6103; 1960–1963, *Annual Reports* of the Interstate Commerce Commission; 1964, staff estimates.

Reproduced from Interstate Commerce Commission, *76th Annual Report* (Washington, D.C.: U.S. Government Printing Office, 1965), p. 141.

A third effect is that "the transportation industry operates today in the general atmosphere of pervasive competition."[9] As far as the buyer of transport services is concerned, transportation over a wide range has few features of monopoly or even oligopoly. In fact, these are literally nonexistent in motor carriage and little in evidence in water transport. The structural characteristics of railroads have not changed, but on the supply side of transport the monopoly features have been so severely reduced as to render obsolete much of the regulation that was erected on the premise of monopoly. The rapid technological advances since World War II in all of the modes of transport have

[9] *Revision of Federal Transportation Policy* (Weeks Report), Report of Presidential Advisory Committee on Transport Policy and Organization (Washington, D.C.: U.S. Government Printing Office, 1955), p. 2.

FIGURE 3–4

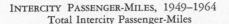

INTERCITY PASSENGER-MILES, 1949–1964
Total Intercity Passenger-Miles

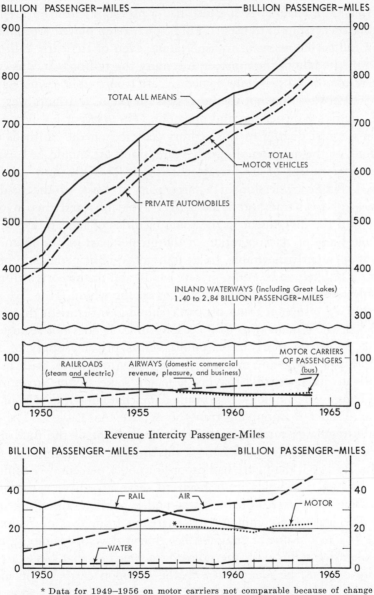

Revenue Intercity Passenger-Miles

* Data for 1949–1956 on motor carriers not comparable because of change in base.

SOURCE: 1949–1956, Interstate Commerce Commission, Bureau of Transport Economics and Statistics, *Intercity Passenger-Miles, 1949–1956*, Statement No. 580; 1957–1963 *Annual Reports* of the Interstate Commerce Commission; 1964, staff estimates.

Reproduced from Interstate Commerce Commission, *76th Annual Report* (Washington, D.C.: U.S. Government Printing Office, 1965), p. 142.

intensified competition among them, and within each mode. The present rate of change is likely to continue for the foreseeable future, posing problems of adjustment, the outcome of which is difficult to predict.

Changing technology has also had a profound effect on the issue of public ownership in transport. Public ownership played a prominent role in the development of transportation, even of the early railroads, but by the middle of the nineteenth century the railroads in this country were almost all privately owned. Apart from public ownership of inland waterways, but not of the vessels on them, transport was provided by private ownership and operation. The issue of public ownership in the first quarter of this century centered on the railroads and, therefore, on the question of whether land transport should be supplied by the government or by private enterprise. This has now all been changed. Public ownership of a large part, at least, of the roadway facilities for road transport is no longer avoidable, and this involves the bulk of the investment in the route facilities of land transport. At the same time, private operation of the greater part of the motor vehicles is apparently inevitable. In air transport, public ownership of the airways is unlikely to be put in private hands, and the airports will most probably remain under public ownership on the whole. Thus, we now have a mixed system of transport ownership and investment that in all likelihood will remain with us for a long time. It does not seem to be possible to debate the issue of public versus private supply of land transport as a whole any more. Both are likely to remain, with public and private interests alike having a major stake in the investment.

Changing technology has resulted in changing the role of the common carrier in supplying transport service. As Table 3–1 shows, federally regulated carriers transported 79 per cent of the total intercity freight traffic in 1946. In 1958, this amount had dropped to 67.5 percent. By 1963, the figure had dropped to 60.1 percent.[10] A common carrier is one that holds itself ready to serve all alike, without discrimination, and at reasonable rates under publicly specified conditions. The idea of a common carrier, arising from that of "common calling," is an old one at common law, but it developed into its most comprehensive status with the railroad, so much so that land carriage for hire came to be identified with the common carrier. The motor vehicle in particular has presented a new problem because a great deal of its use is in private carriage and a considerable part is conducted

---

[10] The railroads are completely common carriers; inland waterways and motor carriers for hire, even when regulated, are only partially so, a considerable amount of their traffic being hauled by contract carriers. If these tonnages were separated from each other, the trend would be even more pronounced.

TABLE 3–1

COMPARISON OF TOTAL INTERCITY TRAFFIC BY CARRIER TYPE WITH INTERCITY TRAFFIC BY FEDERALLY REGULATED CARRIERS
(Billions of Ton-Miles)

Calendar Year	Airways* (Total Ton-Miles)	Railroads* (Total Ton-Miles)	Inland Waterways† Total Ton-Miles	Inland Waterways† Federally Regulated Ton-Miles	Inland Waterways† Per Cent	Motor Carriers Total Ton-Miles	Motor Carriers Federally Regulated Ton-Miles	Motor Carriers Per Cent	Oil Pipe Lines Total Ton-Miles	Oil Pipe Lines Federally Regulated Ton-Miles	Oil Pipe Lines Per Cent
1946	0.1	502.1	124.0	7.44	6	82.0	30.4	37	92.5	73.1	79.0
1947	0.2	564.4	146.7	8.80	6	102.1	37.7	37	104.2	82.3	79.0
1948	0.2	547.3	150.5	9.03	6	116.1	46.7	40	119.6	94.5	79.0
1949	0.2	534.7	139.4	8.36	6	126.6	47.9	38	114.9	91.4	79.5
1950	0.3	596.9	163.3	9.80	6	172.9	65.6	38	129.2	102.1	79.0
1951	0.4	555.4	182.2	10.93	6	188.0	72.3	38	152.1	120.2	79.0
1952	0.4	523.4	168.4	10.10	6	194.6	70.8	36	157.5	124.4	79.0
1953	0.4	514.2	202.4	12.14	6	217.2	76.5	35	169.9	134.2	79.0
1954	0.4	556.6	173.7	10.42	6	214.6	72.3	34	179.2	141.6	79.0
1955	0.5	631.4	216.5	12.99	6	226.2	82.9	37	203.2	160.6	79.0
1956	0.6	655.9	220.0	13.20	6	253.8	83.0	33	230.0	179.8	78.0
1957	0.6	626.2	231.8	13.90	6	244.9	78.3	32	222.7	173.7	78.0
1958	0.6	558.7	189.0	11.30	6	247.0	79.1	32	211.3	167.8	78.0
1959	0.8	582.0	195.0	....	....	275.0	....	....	225.0	....	....

* One hundred per cent regulated.

† Percentage is derived from information obtained from sample study of annual waterway carrier reports to Interstate Commerce Commission.

NOTE: The Bureau of Economics of the Interstate Commerce Commission reports, as of 1963, that 33.6 per cent of intercity motor freight was federally regulated; 10.6 per cent of the water traffic; and 85.7 per cent of the oil pipe line traffic.

SOURCE: Compiled from data obtained from Interstate Commerce Commission, Civil Aeronautics Board, and Bureau of Public Roads. Reproduced from *National Transportation Policy* (Doyle Report), *Preliminary Draft of a Report to the Senate Committee on Interstate and Foreign Commerce*, 87th Cong., 1st sess. (Washington, D.C.; U.S. Government Printing Office. 1961), p. 50.

under specific contract. Water transport lends itself only partly to common carriage. Air transport is mostly in the common carrier category; whether it will remain so depends upon technological developments. Thus the effect of the technological changes has been to remove permanently a great deal of transport from the category of common carriage. This has altered materially the position of common carriers, and it may be doubted that protection can be given them by extending the idea more completely to the noncommon carriers. Indeed, it may be doubted that the concept even fits the bulk of motor carriage. A re-examination of this aspect of regulation is urgently needed because it is by no means evident that the rules which applied in the days when the railroad was supreme are useful in the same way today.[11]

PUBLIC OWNERSHIP AND PUBLIC AID

Public Ownership

Transport service is so important that providing for it has always been regarded as a responsibility, in some way or another, of the state. The urgent need for improved transport, together with the insufficient supply of private capital in the early days of the United States as a nation, led to proposals for extensive federal participation in the work of internal improvements. This gave rise to the famous Gallatin Report of 1808, which recommended that the federal government embark on an extensive scheme of highway and waterway developments. For the most part, however, public ownership and investment in these early facilities were confined to state and local governments. The transport vehicles were almost entirely privately owned.

As has already been pointed out, there was some public ownership of railroads, too, at first. The state of Pennsylvania constructed two railroads; Illinois completed one; and Michigan, Georgia, and Virginia also undertook construction. State participation led to overexpansion and serious financial difficulties that brought about a collapse of state credit in many instances. This, together with the influence of the philosophy of *laissez faire,* brought an early end to practically all public ownership in railroads. Not until after World War I did public ownership again become a prominent issue. At first, this took the form of debate on the question of government ownership of rail-

---

[11] Changing technology has also had a profound effect on urban transport. To the end of the first quarter of the present century, at least, cities were dependent upon street railways, interurban lines, and railroads for all but the very shortest movements of people. Today the situation has changed so radically that mass transportation of the bulk of city passenger movements is a thing of the past almost everywhere. The effects of changing technology on urban transport will be dealt with in the last section of the book.

roads, which had spread rapidly throughout a large part of the world. Public ownership of this agency has meant ownership and operation of its entire transport plant.

In the period since 1920 the role of public ownership in the national transport system has taken on a different turn. The major change has been brought about by the development of motor transport. This is the result of a number of factors: (1) The ownership and operation of the motive equipment may readily be separated from the highway facilities—so much so, in fact, that it is literally impossible to combine them in any very extensive way. (2) Public ownership of the highways is unavoidable, for the most part. (3) From the standpoint of technology the vehicles can move indiscriminately on the highways and on the routes. This is also true of water and air transport. This has important implications in pricing for transport services. In rail and pipe-line transport, pricing is used to control specific use of service, which means that prices can reflect both the quantity and the quality of the service supplied. This can be done for water transport and possibly also for air, although it is not the practice at the present time. Motor transport so far has been brought within this pattern only in a very limited way, and the prospects of extending it are not very great as yet. The problem of precise pricing of the highway service to the operators of motor vehicles is one of the most difficult ones that has yet emerged in the field of transport because of the indiscriminate and largely undifferentiated use of the highway. A motor vehicle, with relatively few exceptions, pays as much per mile for the use of a dirt road as for a superhighway. The intermingling of private for-hire freight and passenger traffic on roadway facilities, and the utilization of the facilities for both production and consumption purposes, have presented problems of measuring need for investment, pricing for the use of the services the investment provides, and assessing the cost of the transport burden, which are the most complex that transport policy has ever faced. In addition, the individualization of transportation that characterizes highway traffic has undermined a significant part of our mass transport facilities, with the consequence that much of the transport supply has become more expensive than is commonly realized. This is because price, as the direct measuring rod of alternatives and as a rationing device, has been dispensed with to a large extent in motor transport.

Public Aid

Public aid is now inextricably mixed with public ownership. When public aid to transportation was first undertaken on an extensive scale in this country, it was used to assist and encourage railroad development. The ownership and operation of the railroads, however, were left in private hands with the result that aid and ownership were two different things. In addition, most of the aid was granted on the assumption that repayment, or its equivalent, would be made to those giving the aid. The most important of the public aids was the land grants to the railroads. The latter, in return, granted the government special rates known as "land-grant rates." These were not terminated until 1945. Estimates of the total public aid vary rather widely, but the consensus is that the railroads, through *quid pro quo*'s, repaid the value which they realized.[12] Professor Daggett points out that the present value of past public aid to railroads is negligible, either as a source of revenue or as a help in competition with other forms of transport.

Public aid to air, water, and highway transport, however, is in a different category. This is partly because aid to the railroads, at the time it was given, did not seriously affect other forms of transport or competition with them, since the other forms were virtually nonexistent, and partly because of the fact that aid to the other forms today takes place through the medium of public ownership of the fixed route and terminal facilities, which are then used by the many and varied private operators. Governments supply inland waterways through river improvements and canalization. In addition, large amounts of public funds are spent on harbors. Practically all of the highway and street facilities are provided by public funds, and the same remarks are true for airways and airports. This relieves the users from assuming the risks involved in the large investment in the fixed facilities, the obligation to meet interest chargers, and so forth, and, in addition, gives them the benefit of lower interest costs resulting from reliance on government credit.

The method of providing public aid which obtains today raises many new and important questions, such as (1) the amount of public investment that should be made and how the requirements should be measured, (2) the bases of charging for the use of publicly provided facilities, (3) the items which should be included in calculating the full economic costs entailed in providing public transport facilities, (4) the effect of public aid on transport supply, and (5) the effect of public aid on railroads and the economical allocation of traffic. It is not possible to discuss these issues at length at this point; they will be dealt with later on. It should be noted, however, that they have arisen

[12] See Stuart Daggett, *Principles of Inland Transportation* (4th ed.; New York: Harper & Bros., 1955), pp. 740–41.

out of the breakdown of the mechanism of pricing as an effective guide to total necessary investment in transport because of (1) the way in which public aid is administered, (2) the difficulties accompanying the use of the pricing system as an effective rationing device in transport because of the technology of motor transport, and (3) the failure of public policy to require the various modes of transport to bear similar types of costs.

At the present time, except for the St. Lawrence Seaway, no tolls are charged for the use of inland waterways or canals. Public aid excuses the users from meeting the costs of the investment and maintenance in these facilities. The same remarks apply to the air routes and, to a considerable extent, to airports. Available information indicates that motor vehicle operators have not paid sums equal to the cost of public aid and that the deficit has been considerable.[13] The biggest deficiencies incurred on this score are in receipts of local rural units and urban areas for highways where general property taxes make up a significant portion of the total expenditures.[14]

So long as the total costs are not assessed on the users, the pricing mechanism is by-passed as a measure of economical investment allocation. Waterways and air routes could be constructed on the usual capitalistic basis, if we so desired, because control of use can be effected. Highway transport is another matter, however. It may be possible to assess aggregate road-route costs on the users; but even if this were so, there would still be the difficulty of charging the users on the basis of the costs incurred for each. So far, we have made little progress in arriving at those individual costs. Furthermore, we have not developed any workable device of general applicability whereby the user can be charged according to the quality of the facility he uses. Toll roads are an exception to this, but they are not in wide use and offer little prospect for urban traffic.

Public Aid versus Subsidy

At the present time, public aid to air, water, and motor transport is of such magnitude that a significant shift in the allocation of traffic among the various agencies of transport would very likely take place if the users were required to cover the costs of each mode in the same way. Whether this means that air, water, and motor transport are

[13] *Ibid.*, p. 745.

[14] D. P. Locklin, *Economics of Transportation* (6th ed.; Homewood, Ill.: Richard D. Irwin, Inc., 1966), pp. 627–28. See, however, the discussion of this problem in Part V on Urban Transport below.

subsidized depends upon how one defines the term *subsidy*. If it means direct payments to make up deficiences in revenues so as to bring the latter up to a stipulated amount, then the only subsidized transport in this country today is air, where direct payments are made by the federal government to support it. Operators in water and motor transport are not subsidized—in this sense, at least—but they do get aid in the form of facilities for which they do not pay in full. Nevertheless, these publicly supplied facilities are all subsidized in the sense that support for them comes, in part at least, from the general taxpayer. In view of the enormous investment being made in transportation in the United States today, this is a problem that needs to be given much more study and objective analysis than it has received to date.[15]

[15] A more extensive discussion of this problem is given in Chapter 19 in the discussion on financing the transport system.

Chapter
4
TRANSPORT GEOGRAPHY

INTRODUCTION

Geography has two important implications for transport economics. In the first place, it provides the physical and natural resource bases upon which the flow of commodity and passenger traffic is founded. Secondly, it exercises a decisive influence on the routes over which the traffic moves and, in this country, has been an important factor in ownership groupings of carriers, especially the railroads. The continental United States probably presents the most complex transportation problems faced by any country in the world. Its size, location, diversity of climate, and location of natural resources have made transportation the principal physical factor in the attainment of the political unity which characterizes the nation and its present industrial and economic stature. Conversely, these same conditions have shaped the arteries of the country's transport system and have determined the direction and volume of the traffic flows on it.

The economic patterns of this country have been molded more by the railroads than by any other transportation agency, although the key and unique position occupied by the Great Lakes must not be underrated. The position of overwhelming dominance occupied by the railroads for the last half of the nineteenth century and the first quarter of the twentieth was the most significant single transportation factor in the development of the present industrial structure of the United States. The other agencies have played their principal role within the framework developed by the railroads, such that a map of the major railroad traffic routes and traffic centers literally suffices as a map for the other agencies except that the railroad map is more coextensive with the country as a whole than are those for pipe lines and waterways.

Finally, it should be noted that physical geography has so conditioned the development of the railroad routes that they are clearly definable in terms of major regions. This in turn has had such a strong influence on operating and ownership arrangements as to confine the railroad systems to each of these regions with little overlapping. Thus, for example, there is no true transcontinental railroad in the United States in the sense of a line under single ownership and management stretching from the Atlantic coast to the Pacific. This regional grouping is a factor of prime importance when policies regarding railroad consolidation and interagency ownership are being given consideration.

GEOGRAPHIC CONSIDERATIONS

Topography of the United States

A land relief map of the United States emphasizes one of the most striking features of its geographical structure, namely, that from a physical point of view the lines of communication are in a north-south direction, which accounts for the direction of traffic movements in the days before the development of the railroad. The Appalachian Mountains parallel the east coast and, until the Erie Canal was built, imposed an almost impassable barrier to the great central plain. In the Far West the Rocky Mountains, extending over nearly a third of the continental United States, offer only a limited number of gaps through which surface land transport conveniently may be undertaken. On either side of these two mountain ranges lie the coastal plains of the Pacific and Atlantic with north-south water communication and relatively easy land routes, although the Pacific coast is more impeded in this respect than the Atlantic.

In between the mountain barriers of the East and the West lies the great central plain, with a literally unobstructed sweep from the Canadian border to the Gulf of Mexico, and drained by the Mississippi system, which over the major portion of its route is unobstructed by serious obstacles such as waterfalls and rapids. The vast Great Lakes system, which lies in the great central plain and penetrates to the heart of the continent, offers an east-west route for traffic, its outlet being the Atlantic Ocean down the St. Lawrence River. American traffic on the Great Lakes has been confined largely to Lakes Erie, Huron, Michigan, and Superior. The severe barrier of Niagara Falls and the restricted navigability of the St. Lawrence between Lake Ontario and Montreal have provided one limitation. The greater proximity of coal to the shores of Lakes Erie and Michigan have created

another. Finally, connection of Lake Erie by canal with the Atlantic
Ocean through the gap in the eastern mountains afforded by the Hudson and Mohawk rivers made an all-American traffic route possible.
It was not until the railroads became the prime agency of land transport that the potential of the Great Lakes came to be realized and
that the east-west nature of the traffic route afforded by them became
apparent. (See Figure 4–1.)

FIGURE 4–1

LAND RELIEF MAP

The coast lines of this country are another important factor in the
geographic structure of its transport routes. On the Pacific coast only
four places offer ready access to significant hinterlands and feasible
connections with the rest of the country. These are Seattle on Puget
Sound; Portland at the tidewater of the Columbia River; San Francisco at the gateway to the great central valley of California; and Los
Angeles, with the wealthy although somewhat limited hinterland of
southern California, but with the easiest land connections of any of the
Pacific coast ports to the rest of the country. The Atlantic coast abounds
in harbor facilities, particularly north of Cape Hatteras. The significant
ones from the standpoint of transport geography are those that provide
the meeting point of the overland rail routes and ocean shipping. The
superior position of New York over the other Atlantic ports, achieved
with the building of the Erie Canal, has already been pointed out. On

the Gulf of Mexico, New Orleans, at the mouth of the Mississippi, enjoyed the early advantage of water connections with the great plains to the north.

Resources for Traffic Flows

One of the outstanding features of the geographic structure of the United States, particularly as it relates to transport, is the concen-

FIGURE 4–2

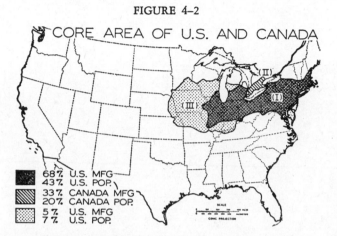

CORE AREA OF U.S. AND CANADA

68% U.S. MFG
43% U.S. POP.
33% CANADA MFG
20% CANADA POP.
5% U.S. MFG
7% U.S. POP.

Additional data for these regions: Area I: 7.7 per cent U.S. area; 52 per cent U.S. income; 70 per cent of persons listed in *Who's Who*. Area III: 6.9 per cent U.S. area; 7.3 per cent U.S. income. Areas I and III combined: 14.6 per cent U.S. area; 50.3 per cent U.S. population; 59.3 per cent U.S. income; 73.3 per cent U.S. industrial employment. Area II: 0.4 per cent Canada area; 19.8 per cent Canada population; 33 per cent Canada industrial employment. Areas I and II combined: 3.7 per cent U.S. and Canada area; 41.2 per cent U.S. and Canada population; 65.9 per cent U.S. and Canada industrial employment. Areas I, II, and III combined: 6.9 per cent U.S. and Canada area; 47.7 per cent U.S. and Canada population; 70.8 per cent U.S. and Canada industrial employment.

Reprinted from E. L. Ullman, *American Commodity Flow* (Seattle: University of Washington Press, 1957), p. 7, by courtesy of the publishers.

tration of industry, population, and consequently traffic in the area bounded on the north by the Great Lakes, on the south by the Ohio River and a line extending to Baltimore, on the east by the Atlantic Ocean, and on the west by a line from Chicago to the Mississippi, thence to the junction of it with the Ohio. This is the heart of what has been called the "core area" by Professor Ullman.[1] This region comprises 7.7 per cent of the area of the United States and 52 per cent of the income of the country; it contains 68 per cent of the manufacturing and is one of most readily identifiable traffic and transport

[1] E. L. Ullman, *American Commodity Flow* (Seattle: University of Washington Press, 1957), p. 7.

regions in the country. It corresponds to one of the three districts into which the Interstate Commerce Commission groups the railroads for statistical and regulation purposes. It is known as the Eastern District. The other two are the Southern and the Western. The Southern District consists of the area south of the Eastern District and east of the Mississippi River. This grouping has both a geographic and a historical

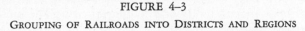

FIGURE 4–3

GROUPING OF RAILROADS INTO DISTRICTS AND REGIONS

SOURCE: Interstate Commerce Commission, *Statistics of Railways in the United States* (annual).

basis, it being practically identifiable with the Old South. The third district is the Western, which lies west of the other two. Except for that territory in it which comprises only 6.9 per cent of the country, the Western District, like the Southern, contains none of the core area. These facts have obviously been of major importance in limiting railroad ownership and operating grouping to the respective territories, with minor exceptions resulting from overlapping, especially in Illinois.

It is also important to note that Chicago is the focal point of the land transport area of the country, because it is the geographic meeting point of the rail routes in the three districts, with its strategic location on the lower end of Lake Michigan. It is thus the key point of the east-west route of the Great Lakes, the north-south route of the Mississippi valley, the east-west rail route of the core area, the three east-west transcontinental routes to the Pacific coast, and the south-east route via the Ohio River crossings to Birmingham, Alabama.

Almost 70 per cent of the ton-miles of transportation in this country is of bulk raw materials. The most important in terms of ton-miles are coal, petroleum, iron ore, and grain, followed by cotton, lumber, livestock, and perishable fruit and vegetables. Coal accounted for almost one third of the American rail tonnage up until World War II and even today makes up about one quarter of it. The bulk of this is mined in the central Appalachians of Pennsylvania, West Virginia, and Kentucky, and in the interior fields of southern Illinois. Appalachian coal is all-important to the American economy; it is in or near the center of the industrial belt. The petroleum resources at the present time are concentrated primarily in the southwestern states of Texas, Louisiana, and Oklahoma, and in the Far West in California. At present, these states account for over 70 per cent of the output of the country. The development of other fields, especially on the eastern slopes of the Rocky Mountains, may alter this distribution in the course of time; it is already changing the pattern somewhat of the pipe-line routes. The iron ore resources of the country are located principally around Lake Superior, especially in the great Mesabi Range. The principal agricultural regions for the production of grain and livestock are the fertile corn belt, adjacent to the western part of the industrial belt, and the wheat-growing areas stretching west into Kansas, Nebraska, Minnesota, the Dakotas, and Montana, and south into Oklahoma and Texas. The same great plains areas are the source of most of the livestock of the country. Lumber, which forms one of the major items of traffic, is produced in the Pacific Northwest, especially in Oregon and Washington, and in the southeastern states along the Gulf and Atlantic seaboards. Cotton is grown mostly in the southern states, although California has become one of the leading producers in the period commencing with World War II. Perishable fruits and vegetables that enter into the long-distance traffic flows are produced principally in California, the Rio Grande area of Texas, and central Florida.

It is evident that the raw materials that make up the traffic flows are rather highly localized. None of the regions are self-contained, and it is the function of transportation to bring these materials together for further processing and for consumption. They may also be moved to seaports for shipment to foreign countries. These same seaports are the principal points of origin for domestic traffic in raw materials and products imported from overseas. Sugar is a good illustration of this.[2]

Finally, mention should be made of the enormous volume of traffic generated by travel for business and for personal reasons. As will be seen later, the principal routes utilized by it are the same as those exhibited by the commodity flows.

BASIS OF TRANSPORT ROUTES

Physical Factors

Physical features largely determine the exact path followed to connect trade centers. Waterways have always formed important routes because of the relative cheapness of water transport, and river valleys have been important guides for railroads and highways. They provide the break through terrain, routes through mountain barriers typically following river valleys and connecting them, and they commonly provide the harbor facilities that connect land and sea transport. However, the waterways themselves are not necessarily significant transport routes, even though they may be readily navigable, and in this country the major routes have an east-west direction despite the fact that the land relief generally runs north and south.

While physical features largely dictate the precise course of the transport way, the foremost factor in establishing transport routes is the traffic potential. Transportation results from areal differentiation, which makes for a demand in one area for the commodities or services that are produced in another. It is the function of efficient transport to bring these together in a way that, and in places where, they can be most efficiently turned to the uses for which they are required. Thus the Pacific coast was long deficient in iron ore and coal, yet this did not result in the movement of these two raw materials from the eastern areas for processing at the points where steel was required. Instead, the raw materials are brought together to be processed in the industrial area, and then the finished products are shipped to the regions needing them. In other words, the routes over which traffic flows, and the type of traffic which flows over those routes, depend upon the cost factors of the various ingredients entering into production, of which the costs of transportation are significant and often controlling.

The major routes over which traffic moves are those which con-

[2] See Stuart Daggett, *Principles of Inland Transportation* (4th ed.; New York: Harper & Bros., 1955), pp. 217–52.

nect the important centers of trade and commerce between which the exchange of goods and services takes place. These centers will be the focal points of the business activity in the areas surrounding them and are typically located where they are because they are the meeting points of the natural surface routes. Thus, for example, Salt Lake City is at the western end of the gap through the Rocky Mountains from which rail and highway lines can radiate to the Pacific Northwest, to San Francisco, and to the Pacific Southwest at Los Angeles. Those centers which are the meeting point of major land and water routes, thereby becoming gateways to important market areas, owe their pre-eminence to transport conditions more than to any other factor.

Finally, it should be noted that the transport routes will afford the shortest distance which surface conditions permit between the centers through which, or to and from which, the traffic takes place. This explains the extremely close conformity of the principal air, rail, and highway routes of this country to each other. There will be some differences, especially on long-distance through traffic, because of physical conditions and intervening points. Thus the air route on through traffic from Los Angeles to New York will deviate somewhat from the rail route because the latter is forced to pass through Chicago, but even here the deviation is surprisingly small.

Political Considerations

The route structure of the transport system of a country may also be influenced by political considerations. These have not played a particularly significant role in the United States. It is true that the transcontinental lines were first undertaken more for political than for economic reasons, but the routes followed were those which trade and commerce would have dictated in the course of time. Similar remarks apply to the Panama Canal. Political factors influenced the timing of the development of the St. Lawrence Seaway, but it is doubtful that the pattern of transport routes to the Atlantic seaboard would have been appreciably different from what it is because of weather and technical conditions that influence the use of the St. Lawrence outlet to the sea.

The pattern of highway and air routes has been determined almost entirely by economic considerations. Even the demands of national defense have been of little importance. This is because of the geographic position of the United States. To the north and the south, the land frontiers are without need of important military establishments, with the result that land communication to a large part of these frontiers is not of great consequence. The seaports which constitute the

principal gateways to the outside world have achieved their present
position as commercial centers because of their role in the economic
development of the country.

TRANSPORT ROUTES OF THE UNITED STATES

Railroad Routes

There are ten major railroad routes in the United States. These
form the main lines of communication between the principal regions
of the country and between the principal centers of those regions. The
following presentation does not indicate the relative importance of the
routes in terms of traffic flows, nor does it deal with ownership groupings; these will be discussed in subsequent sections.

1. *The Trunk-Line Route.*   The rail lines which comprise this
route run from Chicago and St. Louis in the Middle West to the
Atlantic seaboard at Norfolk on the south and Boston and Portland
on the north. Thus, this route lies between the Ohio River on the
south and the Great Lakes on the north, and parallels these two lines
of water communication.

2. *The Atlantic Coast Route.*   This route extends from New
York on the north along the Atlantic coast east of the Appalachians to
Florida. It also moves to the southwest through Atlanta to Birming-
ham and New Orleans.

3. *The Chicago-Southeast Route.*   This is sometimes referred to
as the Chicago-Atlanta route. This route extends from Chicago on
the north to Atlanta in the south and then divides to serve the Gulf
and the south Atlantic coast. It connects the western trunk-line territory with the Southeast by way of the Ohio River crossings such as
Louisville and Cincinnati. None of the roads serving the area handle
traffic over their own rails all the way from Chicago to Atlanta and
the Southeast. Most of the interchange takes place at the Ohio River
crossings. However, the Illinois Central does have a line from Chicago
to Birmingham.

4. *The Mississippi Valley Route.*   This route, as its name indicates, parallels the Mississippi River, extending from Chicago through
St. Louis to New Orleans.

5. *The Granger Route.*   This route is made up of the railroad
lines extending from Chicago and St. Louis into the grain-growing
states of Minnesota, North Dakota, South Dakota, Kansas, Nebraska,
and Iowa. Many of the lines of this route form the bridge between
Chicago and the Missouri River with what are commonly known as
the transcontinental lines. These Granger lines are classified as a

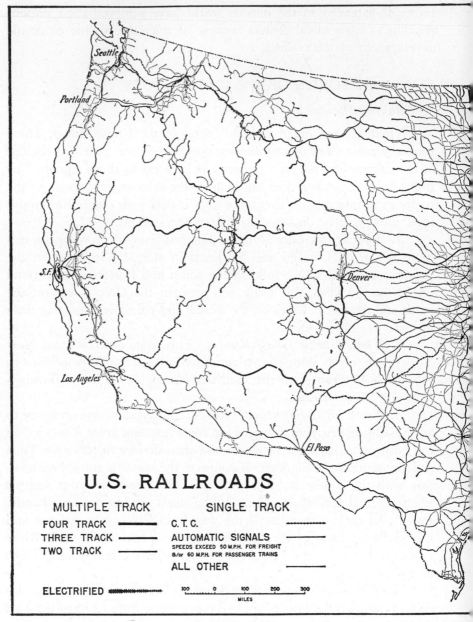

FIGURE 4–4

separate route because of the function they perform in transporting grain from the great agricultural belt to trunk-line territory. (See Figure 4–4.)

6. *The Southwestern-Gulf Route.* This route extends principally from Kansas City and St. Louis into the territory of the Southwest

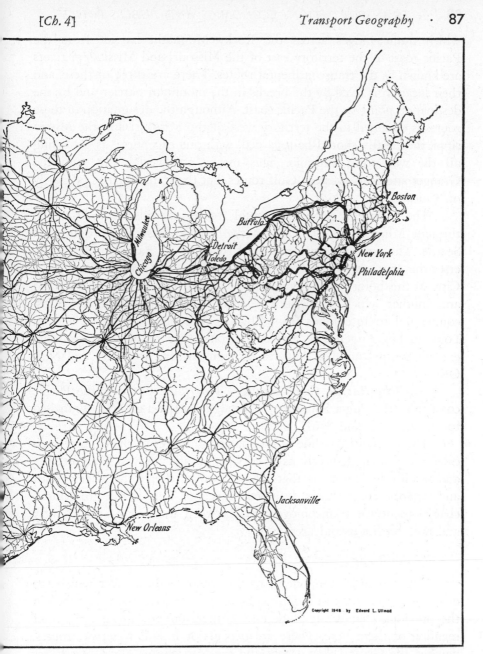

SOURCE: E. L. Ullman, *American Commodity Flow* (Seattle: University of Washington Press, 1957).

from New Orleans to El Paso, Texas. Although this route may be regarded as originating in Kansas City and St. Louis, much of the traffic is destined to or originates in Chicago. Some prefer to designate it as the Chicago-Southwest route.

7, 8, and 9. *The Transcontinental Routes.*   The routes over which traffic moves across the Rocky Mountain barrier from the Pacific coast to the territory east of the Missouri and Mississippi rivers are known as the transcontinental routes. There are three of these, and their location is fixed by the breaks in the mountain barrier and by the destination point on the Pacific coast. Although the designation of these routes is confined to the territory west of the Missouri and the Mississippi, they really should be regarded, with one exception, as extending all the way from Chicago. This means an overlapping with the Granger and Southwestern-Gulf routes, but the traffic focuses primarily on Chicago.

The northern transcontinental route extends from Chicago through Minneapolis–St. Paul to the Pacific coast at Portland and Seattle. The central transcontinental route, as its name implies, traverses the continent from Chicago to San Francisco through Salt Lake City. At this point it also divides into one which goes north to Portland and another which goes south to Los Angeles. The southern transcontinental route extends from Chicago through Kansas City and St. Louis to Los Angeles by way of Arizona. One branch of this route extends south from Los Angeles through Arizona to Texas and New Orleans.

10. *The Pacific Coast Route.* This route parallels the Pacific coast from the Puget Sound ports through Portland and San Francisco to Los Angeles and San Diego.

The foregoing outline of the major rail routes of the country indicates the principal directions over which traffic moves. One striking and significant feature is that all but two of them, the Pacific coast and Atlantic coast routes, lead into Chicago. This is the great interchange point for traffic movements between the rest of the country and the core industrial area.

Water Routes

The principal components of the water facilities over which the domestic commerce of the United States moves have been described in the previous chapter. It is necessary, therefore, to make only brief mention of them here. There are two major inland waterway routes, namely, the Great Lakes system and the Mississippi. The Great Lakes system now may be said to extend from the upper end of Lake Superior to the Atlantic seaboard via the New York State Barge Canal. The St. Lawrence Seaway extension to the Atlantic Ocean is important primarily in connection with foreign trade, but the diversion of export and import traffic from the Atlantic seaport to the ports of the Great

Lakes is of great concern to the railroads of the trunk-line route. (See Figure 4–5.)

The second important inland waterway route is provided by the Mississippi system. At the present time, this extends from St. Paul and Chicago in the north, Sioux City, Iowa, in the west, and Pittsburgh in the east, to New Orleans in the south. It is therefore primarily a north-south route which taps both the Granger and the trunk-line territories but is principally a competitor of the Mississippi Valley railroad route. (See Figure 4–6.)

The Atlantic, Gulf, and Pacific coasts provide the other major water routes for domestic commerce. These really constitute three distinct lanes of traffic. In order of importance to domestic trade, they are the Atlantic coast–Gulf route from Maine to Texas, the Pacific coast route from Puget Sound to San Diego, and the inter-coastal route connecting the Atlantic and Pacific through the Panama Canal.

Highway Routes

The national system of interstate and defense highways forms the basic framework of the principal highway routes of the country. A comparison of the map of this system with that of the major railroad routes indicates how closely they follow each other all over the continent. (See Figures 4–7 and 4–8.) If the federal-aid primary highway system is added to this, the rail and highway routes become even more closely identifiable.

Air Routes

The basic air route pattern of the country is formed by the federal airway system, which is constructed and maintained by the national government. As in the case of the highways, this route pattern conforms to that established by the railroads. The air routes are not identifiable with the air lines which operate over them in the same way that the individual rail lines are identifiable with particular routes and regions. This is because the certified trunk-line carriers for the most part operate over wider areas than do the rail systems. (See Figures 4–9 and 4–10.)

Pipe-Line Routes

The major pipe-line routes of the United States extend from the great oil-producing area of the Southwest into the Midwest and the industrial region of the Great Lakes. The general pattern of these routes therefore is to follow the Southwestern-Gulf route to Kansas

FIGURE 4-5

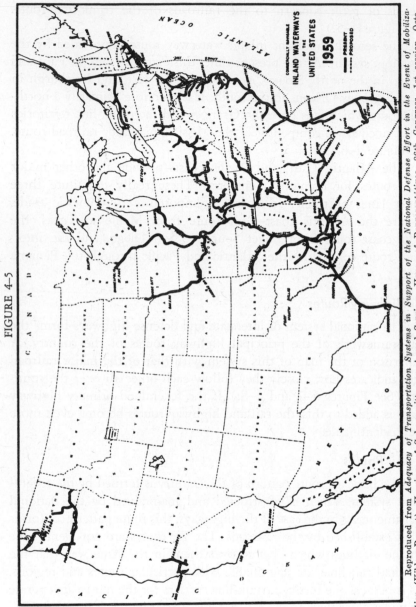

Reproduced from *Adequacy of Transportation Systems in Support of the National Defense Effort in the Event of Mobilization* (Kilday Report), Hearings of Subcommittee on Armed Services, House of Representatives, 86th Congress, 1st session, October, 1959 (Washington, D.C.: U.S. Government Printing Office, 1959), p. 524.

FIGURE 4-6

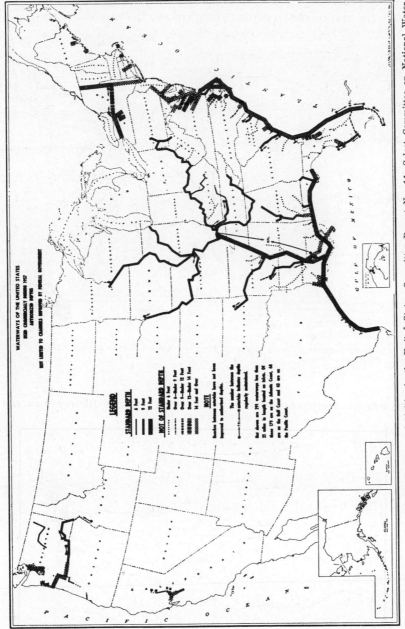
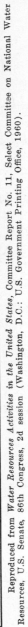

Reproduced from *Water Resources Activities in the United States*, Committee Report No. 11, Select Committee on National Water Resources, U.S. Senate, 86th Congress, 2d session (Washington, D.C.: U.S. Government Printing Office, 1960).

FIGURE 4–7

THE NATIONAL SYSTEM OF INTERSTATE AND DEFENSE HIGHWAYS

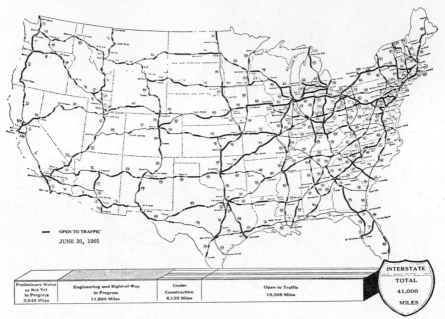

SOURCE: Reproduced from *Highway Progress,* Annual Report of the Bureau of Public Roads (1965), pp. 58–59.

FIGURE 4–8

HIGH-SPEED, LIMITED-ACCESS MULTILANE SYSTEM OF TOLL HIGHWAYS IN THE UNITED STATES, 1959

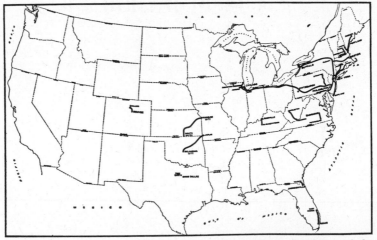

Reproduced from *Adequacy of Transportation Systems in Support of the National Defense Effort in the Event of Mobilization* (Kilday Report), Hearings of Subcommittee on Armed Services, House of Representatives, 86th Congress, 1st session, October, 1959 (Washington, D.C.: U.S. Government Printing Office, 1959), p. 520.

FIGURE 4-9

THE FEDERAL AIRWAY SYSTEM

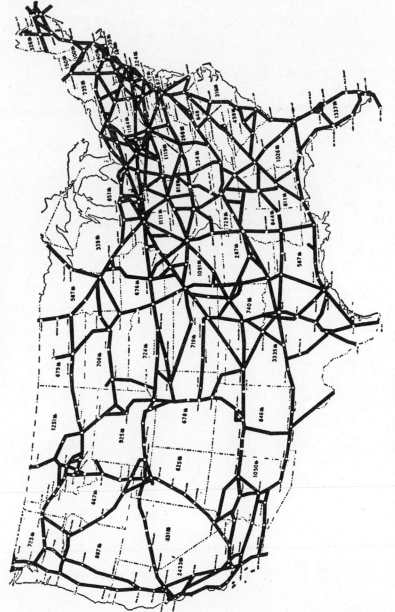

Reproduced from *C.A.A. Journal*, Vol. VII (1946). p. 63.

FIGURE 4-10. UNITED STATES AIR TRANSPORT SYSTEM ROUTES CERTIFIED TO TRUNK-LINE CARRIERS (June 30, 1965)

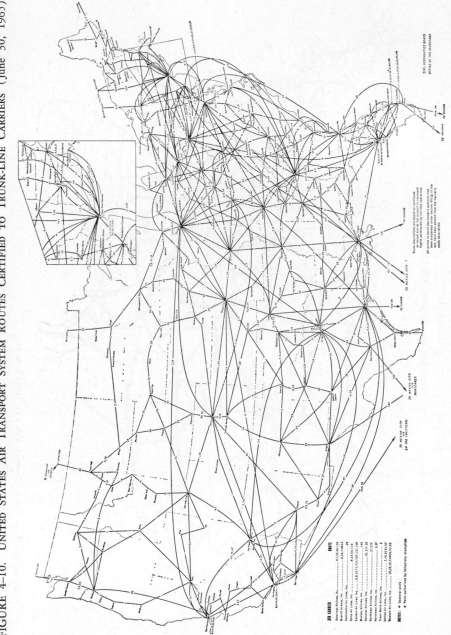

Reproduced from *Report* of the Civil Aeronautics Board for fiscal 1965, p. 108.

FIGURE 4-11

LOCAL AIRLINE SERVICE . . . THE VITAL LINK

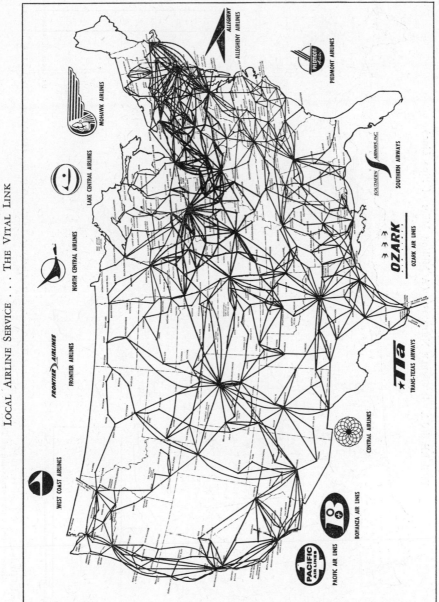

Reproduced from *Air Transport Association of America 1967.*

FIGURE 4–12. INVISIBLE NETWORK (A Million Miles of Pipe Line)

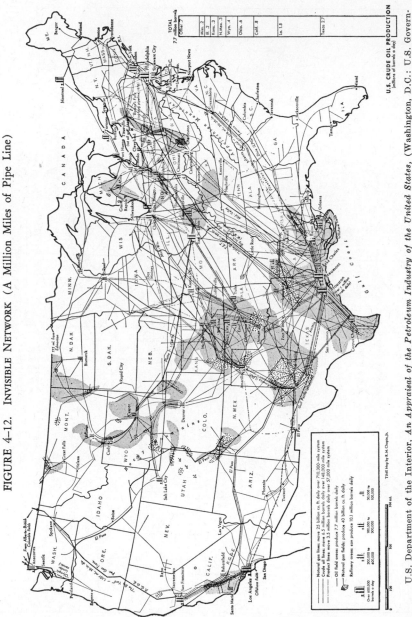

U.S. Department of the Interior, *An Appraisal of the Petroleum Industry of the United States*, (Washington, D.C.: U.S. Government Printing Office, January, 1965). Reproduced with permission of Time, Inc., New York, 1962.

FIGURE 4-13. MOST OF THE NATION'S CRUDE OIL IS CONSUMED OUTSIDE OF THE MAJOR PRODUCTION AREAS (1703-Thousand Barrels per Day)

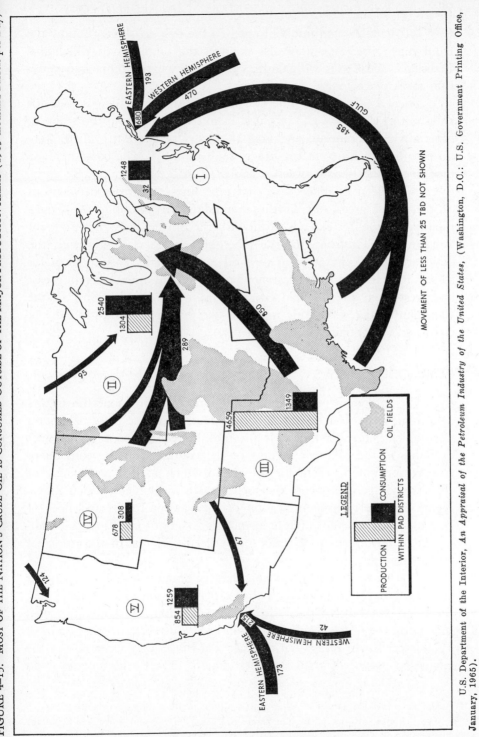

MOVEMENT OF LESS THAN 25 TBD NOT SHOWN

LEGEND

PRODUCTION   CONSUMPTION

WITHIN PAD DISTRICTS

CONSUMPTION

OIL FIELDS

U.S. Department of the Interior, *An Appraisal of the Petroleum Industry of the United States*, (Washington, D.C.: U.S. Government Printing Office, January, 1965).

City and St. Louis and into Chicago. To the east coast they follow the trunk-line route. Pipe lines also connect the oil fields of Oklahoma, Louisiana, and Texas with Gulf ports, from which points transportation takes place to the Atlantic coast.

There is also a pipe-line system in California which is used for transporting crude oil and products from the oil fields to the seaports, especially San Francisco and Los Angeles. Until recently, there were no pipe-line facilities in the other states of the Pacific coast nor any pipe-line connections between it and the rest of the country. Recently, these have been established so that pipe lines now exist between all of them and areas east of the mountains. In addition, the Trans-mountain Pipeline extends from Alberta oil fields to the state of Washington. The shape of the pipe-line map is changing with the discovery and exploitation of new oil fields, but its basic pattern for some time into the future is bound to be that of lines extending east and west from the oil field belt that ranges from the Gulf to the Canadian border. California lines are likely to remain mostly local in character. (See Figures 4–12 and 4–13.)[3]

COMMODITY FLOWS

The foregoing presentation is designed to bring out the factors determining the flow of traffic in the country and the principal routes over which that traffic moves. It also indicates the transport alternatives available in the different regions of the country and the consequent competition among them for the traffic which may move by any of the various agencies where the facilities are available for such movement. However, the identification of the various routes and lines of communication of the different agencies does not of itself give any indication of the intensity of traffic over the routes nor in the principal traffic regions.

One of the most significant features about traffic movements is that the bulk of them occur within a given region. Thus, in the year 1950, 87 per cent of the railroad carload shipments both originated and terminated in a single traffic district. Furthermore the study of Professor Ullman brings out the fact that the flows concentrate in the region of state of origin and destination.[4] These observations hold

---

[3] The Colonial pipeline from Texas to New Jersey was completed in 1965. It has a total length of 2,900 miles with a capacity of 960,000 barrels a day. Nine oil companies have invested a total of about $400 million in the Colonial system.

[4] Ullman, *op. cit.*, p. 28. This study is focused on rail and water traffic, but the point would be emphasized even more if motor freight traffic were included. For a more

even if the state is located in a sparsely populated, relatively un-productive region. However, if the volume of the flows is measured by value instead of weight, the localization of traffic is not so pro-nounced. In other words, the long-distance interstate traffic takes on much greater importance when measured in terms of value rather than of weight.

The trunk-line region is the most intense area of railroad traffic in the country. This reflects the traffic density within the region and the flow of traffic to it, through it, and from it to the various parts of the

FIGURE 4–14

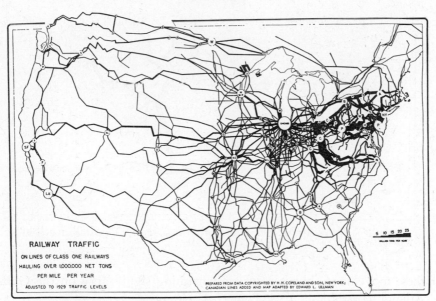

RAILWAY TRAFFIC

ON LINES OF CLASS ONE RAILWAYS
HAULING OVER 1,000,000 NET TONS
PER MILE PER YEAR
ADJUSTED TO 1929 TRAFFIC LEVELS

PREPARED FROM DATA COPYRIGHTED BY H. H. COPELAND AND SON, NEW YORK;
CANADIAN LINES ADDED AND MAP ADAPTED BY EDWARD L. ULLMAN

Reproduced from E. L. Ullman, *American Commodity Flow* (Seattle: University of Washington Press, 1957), by courtesy of the publishers.

country. This is influenced by the tremendous flow of raw materials within it and the immediately adjacent area, and from various parts of the United States to it, of those commodities in which it is deficient. In addition, it reflects the heavy movement of manufactured goods within the same area and to other parts of the nation. (See Figure 4–14.)

The commodity flow of traffic by water is confined to the three major routes. The Great Lakes form the major one for iron ore and

recent confirmation of this, see U.S. Department of Commerce, *Commodity Transportation Survey, Area 25,* 1963 Census of Transportation (Washington, D.C.: U.S. Government Printing Office, 1963).

grain on the eastward movement, and for coal on the westward movement. Barge and raft traffic is concentrated on the Mississippi system, with the most significant part of that freight moving upstream. (See Figure 4–15.) Coastwise traffic is dominated by the heavy movements between the Gulf and Atlantic coasts. Pacific coastwise traffic ranks second and intercoastal third. Tanker traffic makes up the bulk of

FIGURE 4–15

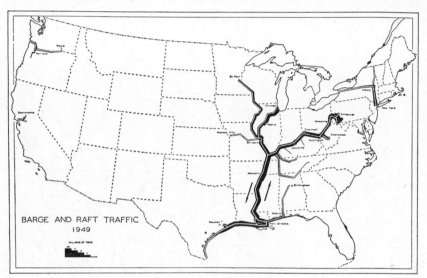

Reproduced from E. L. Ullman, *American Commodity Flow* (Seattle: University of Washington Press, 1957), by courtesy of the publishers.

these movements, but it is of overwhelming significance on the Gulf-Atlantic coast route. (See Figures 4–16 and 4–17.)

The traffic flow of passengers for air lines is indicative of the major movements of people by commercial carriers. Here again, the bulk of the traffic is in the intensely developed area of the Great Lakes and trunk-line territory. The routes from New York to Florida, and from the Atlantic coast to San Francisco and Los Angeles, are also important generators of passenger traffic. One striking feature of traffic flows by air is the intensity of use of the route between Los Angeles and San Francisco.[5] (See Figure 4–18.)

[5] The most detailed discussions of traffic movements in the United States will be found in Ullman, *op. cit.;* and in Daggett, *op. cit.,* Part III. According to an article in *Aviation Week* (September 14, 1964), p. 3, total passenger traffic between the Los Angeles and San Francisco airports ranks first in the nation.

FIGURE 4–16

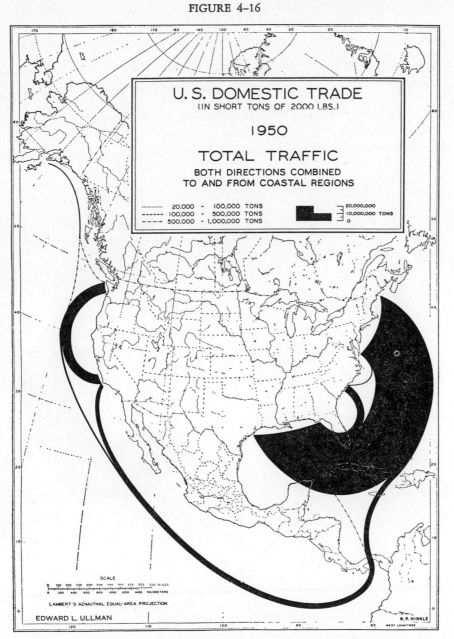

Reproduced from E. L. Ullman, *American Commodity Flow* (Seattle: University of Washington Press, 1957), by courtesy of the publishers.

FIGURE 4–17

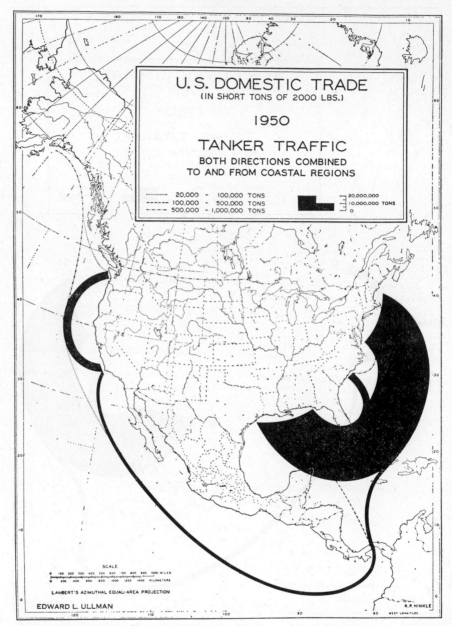

Reproduced from E. L. Ullman, *American Commodity Flow* (Seattle: University of Washington Press, 1957), by courtesy of the publishers.

FIGURE 4–18

PASSENGER ORIGINATIONS AND DESTINATIONS BETWEEN THE 100 TOP-RANKING
PAIRS OF STATIONS, 1948

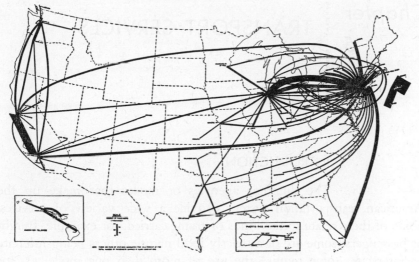

Bureau of Economic Regulation, Civil Aeronautics Board.

Chapter 5 | TRANSPORT SERVICES

INTRODUCTION

The different agencies or modes that make up the American transportation system provide a wide variety of services. Some of these relate to the kinds of traffic carried, for example, freight or passengers; some are of a strictly local nature, others being intercity or interstate; some require the use of more than one mode, as, for instance, air travel that normally involves the air lines and some other means for the terminal services; and some are highly specialized services which only a particular mode or a particular firm can deal with. Transport service may also be viewed from the standpoint of the obligations assumed by the carriers and the institutional arrangements under which the transportation takes place. Thus, there may be common carriers, contract carriers, private carriers for hire, private carriers which engage in commercial transport but do not offer themselves for hire at all, and private noncommercial or nonbusiness carriers, such as private automobiles.

Apart from those industrial lines that are utilized only for plant facilities, railroads are the only mode of carriage which falls totally into the category of a common carrier. All of the other agencies may supply transport services of the various types mentioned, although as a general rule a particular firm which acts as a common carrier does not engage in other types of transport; some, however, may haul traffic which is exempt from regulation. In other words, firms can generally be classified into common, contract, and private carriers, even though the agencies, with the exception of the railroads, cannot be so grouped. Just what types of transport activities fall within these three categories depends upon federal and state laws and on occasion even on local ordinances.

From the standpoint of public policy, carriers may be grouped as

104

regulated and private. Regulation in this context refers to public control to which the carrier must conform if it wishes, legally, to be able to continue to do business. Carriers subject to this control or regulation can perform only those services which the public authority—local, state, or federal, as the case may be—authorizes them to undertake. Violation of the conditions attached to the permission may result in penalties even to the point of loss of the privilege to continue in business. The regulation commonly involves some type of price control by the public authority of minimum, maximum, or precise rates. Generally speaking, numerous other restrictions on the freedom of action of the particular enterprise are also imposed. The conditions of operation laid down by government for the regulated carriers are in addition to those imposed upon nonregulated private business and constitute the *quid pro quo* for the privilege of rendering the approved services. At the same time, these carriers may be exempt from some of the laws governing the conduct of what is often called purely private business, if legislation specifically excludes them from the application of these laws. Thus, railroads and motor carriers may enter into rate agreements with each other under the provisions of the Reed-Bulwinkle Act, but the Interstate Commerce Commission must sanction the rates agreed upon.

Private carriers in this country are those transport undertakings which are not regulated in the sense just discussed above. They are confined primarily to motor, water, and air transportation. They may operate for hire where the services they perform or the goods they haul are exempt from regulation, or they may supply transport only for the owner. This may be commercial or noncommercial in nature. For the most part, private freight transport is commercial, while private passenger carriage is largely noncommercial. A large amount of the private traffic is a substitute for common and contract service, but a considerable portion would not exist if private movement were eliminated. Motor and domestic water transportation are preponderantly in the private, nonregulated, category, while air is overwhelmingly in the common carrier field. The dominance of private activity in motor and water arises from the technical conditions of operation that characterize these two modes and from the nature of the services performed. For example, the motor vehicle is an individualized means of passenger travel, while vessels engaged in bulk movement go from port to port in response to available cargo.

The private carrier, within the limits of safety and traffic rules, may undertake any transportation not forbidden to it. When operating for hire, it may supply only those services that are specifically exempt from regulation, although the border line between what is exempt and what is not is a matter of some controversy in motor, water, and air traffic. What constitutes private carriage that is not for hire has also given rise to some dispute in motor freight transport. The Interstate Commerce Commission has taken the position that such transportation cannot be used as a subterfuge to escape regulation but must be organically a part of the business that owns it. Transport can in no sense be the principal activity of such a business.[1]

THE COMMON CARRIER

Nature of the Common Carrier

A common carrier is a transport company that holds itself out as ready to serve the general public for hire at reasonable rates, without discrimination, up to the limit of the facilities of the carrier. The concept of the common carrier is derived from common law, and the duty to render service without discrimination is old and well established. The real test of whether a firm is a common carrier is whether it holds itself out, either expressly or by a course of conduct, to carry for hire without discrimination the goods of all persons who send it goods to be transported. The courts and commissions have held that a carrier must accept a shipment of any commodity tendered if that commodity is included in the category of goods which the carrier, through its published tariffs or otherwise, holds itself out to carry.

The common-law concept of what constitutes a common carrier and the duties that such carriage entails has been embodied and extended in the statutes of the various states and in federal regulation relating to transportation. These laws do not define common carriers; instead, they name them specifically. The agencies thus enumerated become subject to all the statutory rules governing common carriers in addition to common-law obligations. Although common carriage could be subject to legal obligations without legislation in the various states, such legislation is necessary for federal regulation and control because in the absence of it the federal government would be unable to exercise adequate jurisdiction. However, legislation of itself is an insuf-

[1] See for example, *Woitishek Common Carrier Application*, 42 M.C.C. 193 (1943); *Lenoir Chair Company Contract Carrier Application*, 51 M.C.C. 65 (1949); *Brooks Transportation Company* v. *United States*, 93 F. Supp. 517 (1950), 340 U.S. 925 (1951,); and *Red Ball Motor Freight* v. *Shannon*, 377 U.S. 311 (1964). The issue has been confused, however, by the Commission's decision in *Winter Garden Freezer Co., Inc. Investigation of Operations*, 103 M.C.C. 513 (1967).

ficient basis for establishing common carrier obligations. The Supreme Court of the United States has held that the state cannot make a private carrier into a public one by decree because that would be taking private property for public use without just compensation, which would be in violation of the Fourteenth Amendment.[2] Nor can the state require an individual to assume the responsibilities of a common carrier as the price of the privilege of doing business upon the highway.[3] This laid the basis of distinction for regulatory purposes between common and contract carriers.

Transport companies may act as common carriers of persons or property. The fact that they are common carriers, however, does not necessarily mean that they must carry all kinds of goods that may be offered. Permission to act as common carriers may be limited to certain types of commodities, as, for example, common carriers of household goods by truck. As a general rule, they operate over fixed routes and between fixed termini on publicly announced schedules, but these are not necessarily characteristic of all common carriers. Nevertheless the public normally expects certainty and regularity of service by them. The comprehensive legislation which governs common carriers, especially at the federal level, has resulted in restricting this type of service to those who are specifically authorized to offer it, by the appropriate federal authority. The Interstate Commerce Commission has followed the general rule that it will not allow a carrier to operate in the common and contract category at the same time. This would be permissible under common law because the latter imposed the common carrier obligation only on the service which the transport agency stood ready to perform for all comers.

Duties of Common Carriers

The duties of common carriers are embodied in a mass of both state and federal enactments. They constitute an extremely elaborate and detailed extension of the traditional status and responsibilities of carriers at common law and have grown up very largely through legislation which was enacted to regulate the railroads. How far these common-law duties can be extended by statute rests with the courts. It should be noted, however, that although a firm may fall into the category of a common carrier under common law, it does not necessarily take on that status under statute law because it may for some reason

---

[2] *Michigan Public Utilities Commission* v. *Duke*, 266 U.S. 570 (1925).

[3] *Frost and Frost Trucking Company* v. *Railroad Commission of California*, 271 U.S. 583 (1926).

or other be exempt by legislative action from the application of a particular law. However, there is little doubt that all transport which is common under the common law can be regulated as such under statute law and subject to the rules which the legislatures are empowered to impose.

The traditional obligations of the common carrier are basically four in number, namely, (1) the duty of service, (2) the responsibility for the safe delivery of that which is entrusted to the carrier's charge, (3) the duty to treat all customers without discrimination, and (4) the duty to charge a reasonable and only a reasonable price for the service that is performed.

The duty of service of the common carrier has already been mentioned in connection with the concept of such an undertaking. This has been expressed as follows:

It is the common-law duty of a common carrier, on being tendered a reasonable compensation, to receive at reasonable times and carry all goods offered to it for transportation, within the line of its business or of the kind which it undertakes to transport. Having room or the facilities for transporting the goods, and holding itself to the public as ready and willing to carry goods for all persons indifferently, the law imposes upon it the duty of receiving and carrying them over its established route.[4]

Thus, common carriers do not have the privileges normally accorded to business not falling into such a category of selecting their own customers or deciding when to sell and when not to sell. Such carriers are required to supply facilities which are sufficient to accommodate a normal volume of traffic.

The carrier, however, may limit the public which it undertakes to serve. An enterprise that is set up for transporting people is not obligated to carry freight, nor is it required to supply facilities that are not for transportation purposes. The goods that are to be carried must be offered at reasonable times and under reasonable conditions. Furthermore the carrier is required to offer service only on its established routes.[5] Where the undertaking operates under a franchise, or in the case of a corporation under a charter, it cannot at common law withdraw from service without public consent unless it gives up all of its privileges. Partial abandonments are therefore not possible without public sanction.

[4] D. C. Moore, *A Treatise on the Law of Carriers* (2d ed.; Albany: Matthew Bender & Co., Inc., 1914), pp. 116–17. These conditions presumably apply whether the undertaking is in private or public hands.

[5] The extent to which this can be modified by statute is an open question. See Stuart Daggett, *Principles of Inland Transportation* (4th ed.; New York: Harper & Bros., 1955), pp. 240–41.

The second duty of the common carrier is to deliver safely the goods entrusted to its care. This means that the carrier is liable with certain exceptions for any loss or damage to the goods even though such loss does not arise from an act or from negligence of the carrier. Where loss or injury occurs, the presumption is that the carrier is at fault. The reason for this unusual liability is that shippers are unable to determine in most cases the cause of loss or damage to goods when it occurs. There are, however, certain exceptions to this sweeping rule. These include (1) an act of God, (2) an act of the public enemy, (3) an act or default of the shipper, (4) an act of public authority, and (5) an inherent defect or nature of the goods. An act of God refers to some extraordinary or unavoidable event but does not cover those which would be expected to occur in the ordinary course of operations. Acts of the public enemy refer to acts of organized and armed forces, and not to strikes or riots. An act or default of the shipper covers failure of the latter to mark accurately or to pack or load according to accepted standards and regulations. An act of public authority applies to such things as attachment for debt or other seizure by legal process. Inherent nature or defect of the goods includes diseases of plants or animals and damage to merchandise occurring before shipment; it also includes injury to livestock resulting from goring or kicking. Liability for damage which is the result of delay is confined to negligent delay or to that which is not reasonably necessary under the existing conditions.

The common-law exemptions apply to all types of common carriers, whether they be by land, water, or air. Common carriers by water have some additional exemptions, however, as a result of the unusual hazards of navigation that have been recognized over the centuries. The common-law status of the air carrier is that, as a bailee, it is liable for damage or loss resulting from gross negligence or action of the carrier or its employees. The gist of the cause of action is the carrier's negligence, and the burden of proving the negligence and that it was the proximate cause of injury or damage rests upon the plaintiff who alleges it. As far as loss or damage to property transported is concerned, the exact liability status of air carriers in the United States cannot be stated since there is no federal statute or Supreme Court decision defining it.[6]

The third duty of the common carrier, namely, that of treating

[6] For a discussion of liability of carriers by aircraft, see G. L. Wilson and L. A. Bryan, *Air Transportation* (Englewood Cliffs, N.J.: Prentice-Hall, Inc., 1949), chap. xxi; M. L. Fair and E. W. Williams, Jr., *Economics of Transportation* (rev. ed.; New York: Harper & Bros., 1959), pp. 184–88.

all customers without discrimination, means little more than that it must stand ready to supply all who seek the service which the enterprise as a common carrier holds itself out to provide. This means that all must be treated alike who seek identical services under identical conditions. It does not, however, offer a practicable basis for establishing appropriate relationships among commodities, among commodities shipped under different conditions nor for services for the same persons, or commodities between different places or at different times. In consequence, limitations on common carrier discretion with regard to undue preference or various kinds of discrimination are a matter of statutory development at both state and federal levels. Similar remarks apply to the obligation of common carriers to charge only reasonable rates. Despite the indefinite nature of this idea, it was used, as will be pointed out later, to sustain the constitutionality of state legislation which undertook to regulate the prices charged by railroads and ancillary agencies against the contention that such regulation violated the Fourteenth Amendment.[7]

Freight Forwarders

A freight forwarder is an enterprise that assembles and consolidates shipments and distributes them; it assumes the responsibility for the transportation of goods from the point of receipt to the point of delivery and utilizes the services of common carriers. Its function is to solicit and assemble traffic, but it does not undertake the actual movement itself except perhaps for the terminal services. Freight forwarders are common carriers under the Interstate Commerce Act as amended in 1950 if they hold themselves out to serve the general public. They perform their services without charge to the shipper, their revenues being derived from the difference between the contract rates they are permitted to make with the carriers that move the goods and the rate the shipper pays, which is the same as that which would apply if he dealt with the carrier directly.

The primary function of the freight forwarder is to assemble and consolidate small shipments for various shippers into carload or truckload amounts which move at lower rates; the shippers pay the less-than-carload rates, or sometimes lower ones. Forwarders may deal with rail, motor, or air common carriers.[8]

In 1965, there were 61 Class A freight forwarders (annual gross

---

[7] For a more extensive discussion of the duties of common carriers, see Daggett, *op. cit.,* chaps. xii–xv; and Fair and Williams, *op. cit.,* chap. x.

[8] For a careful discussion of the freight forwarder, see Daggett, *op. cit.,* pp. 678–83.

revenue of $100,000 or more) reporting to the Interstate Commerce Commission. In 1964, total annual revenues amounted to $487 million as compared to forwarder revenue of $170.1 million in 1945. In 1964, the investment of freight forwarders amounted to $73.4 million, of which $59.7 was in current assets, and only $6.1 in transportation property.[9]

Express and Package Service

Express and package service throughout the country is provided largely by the REA Express, the United Parcel Service and the Post Office. The Railway Express Agency Inc. was established in 1929. At that time it was owned entirely by the railroads with profits over operating expenses to be paid to them. Under new contracts, as revised in 1959, REA was authorized to route traffic over the various modes of transportation, with compensation for railroad movement based on service used. The sale of 20 per cent of REA's stock to Greyhound was authorized by the Interstate Commerce Commission in 1965. Complications arising from litigation led Greyhound to dispose of this stock (June, 1967). Since 1959, REA has been diversifying into containerized and palletized shipments and in 1964 it was authorized by the Interstate Commerce Commission to haul large-volume containers holding up to 3,000 pounds of straight and mixed shipments when loaded by the shipper. REA conducts air express under uniform contracts with the 39 scheduled air lines; it also provides water carrier service on shipments to Alaska and foreign overseas destinations by contracts with water carriers. The REA Express is still a common carrier under Part I of the Interstate Commerce Act, and it also operates motor vehicles as a common carrier subject to Part II of the Act. Its vigorous expansion program is arousing much opposition on the part of other carriers.[10]

Intercity bus lines also offer express services. These include interline services and service to all stations operated by the company. This business increased from 1.1 per cent of bus revenues, ICC Class I in 1947, to 5.8 per cent in 1958.[11]

[9] Interstate Commerce Commission, *Transport Economics*, Monthly by Bureau of Economics, August, 1966.

[10] See: *Civil Aeronautics Board, Federal Maritime Commission, Interstate Commerce Commission*, Staff Liaison group, *Study of REA Express* (Washington, D.C., U.S. Government Printing Office, August, 1965).

[11] *National Transportation Policy* (Doyle Report), Preliminary Draft of a Report to the Senate Committee on Interstate and Foreign Commerce, 87th Cong., 1st sess. (Washington, D.C.: U.S. Government Printing Office, 1961), p. 360.

Parcel delivery service, arising from the efforts of city department stores to reduce delivery costs through pooling arrangements, has expanded into extensive transportation systems providing small-shipment delivery in multistate areas. According to the Doyle Report,[12] the United Parcel Service is the largest of the firms supplying this sort of transportation. It has received several interstate service authorizations from the Interstate Commerce Commission, and has established extensive distribution networks in New York, the Midwest, and California. It operates both as a contract and as a common carrier. The contract operations serve department stores and specialty shops, and the carrier undertakes to deliver or dispatch via other means all the stores' outgoing parcels within the agreed weight limit, usually 50 pounds. The common carrier operations of United Parcel Service involve services for manufacturers and wholesale distributors. This service was undertaken in 1956 with the authorization of the Interstate Commerce Commission because of United's desire to hold its parcel distribution services open to all shippers, other than retail stores, who could use such services. This offered direct competition to the parcel post system of the Post Office.

Mention should also be made of the Post Office Department of the United States. The Post Office purchases transportation for intercity movements but supplies much of its own urban pickup and delivery service. In rural areas, delivery is made by star route contracts with private firms, the contracts being awarded the lowest responsible bidder. The Post Office also operates the parcel post service, through which shipments weighing up to twenty pounds may be made.

THE ROLE OF THE COMMON CARRIER

The Common Carrier in the Transport System

Until quite recently, especially down to the end of World War II, the common carrier was the most important means of transport for intercity traffic; and even within cities, except for local deliveries, it occupied much the same role. With the rise of the new transport structure under the changed technological conditions since World War I, the relative position of the common carrier has been altered radically, although in absolute terms the common carrier transports more goods and people than at any previous time. This is, of course, an aggregative picture and does not indicate the changing roles of the various modes or agencies which perform common carrier services. The issues concern-

[12] *Ibid.*, p. 361.

ing common carriage versus other types of carriage are analytically quite distinct from those of the relative roles of the various modes in the transport system, although, because of existing policies for transportation, these two questions have frequently come to be regarded as one and the same thing. Common carriers of all the agencies (with the possible exception of pipe lines) find common cause in demanding the restriction of transport provided by other carriers, even though this seems to be almost the only ground upon which they can find basis for agreement. The common carriers of each agency insist on the privilege to compete with those of the other agencies, but all appear to be desirous of limiting or eliminating the competition which the noncommon carriers present. The insistence upon such limitation is usually based on the contention that common carriage must be preserved because it is essential to national welfare and national defense. Furthermore, it appears that the demand for the preservation and protection of the common carrier assumes the continuation of existing rules and regulations surrounding common carriage, although the arguments for this are not carried through with any marked consistency.

Historical Nature of the Common Carrier

The idea of the common carrier is associated with that of common callings. This grew up at common law under the guild system in England and related to activities considered essential to community life which were undertaken only by those who were given specific authorization to do so. These activities were said to be clothed with a public interest, and those who performed them were not only subject to special obligations but also could be regulated by public authority even though a special grant of monopoly privilege had been afforded by the Crown. Undertakings connected with transportation, such as inns and wharves, were placed in this category because of the special need for protecting the public and because of the limitation on alternatives faced by the buyer. This designation of certain activities as common callings or industries affected with a public interest has carried down to modern times even though many services once included have long since passed out of that category. The common carrier concept in transportation, however, has remained but has been greatly extended by legislation in this country.

Railroads were subject to common carrier obligations from the very beginning, but they did not necessarily fall into the common carrier category for all of their activities, nor were they restricted solely to common carrier traffic. It was the development of regulation, particularly at the federal level, that resulted in placing all of the transport services of railroads in the common carrier category and subjected them to the extremely comprehensive controls that are in effect today. This regulation may have been necessary when the railroads possessed a virtual monopoly of domestic land transport.

The recent growth of the newer agencies, especially motor, water, and air, has resulted in over half of the total transportation of the country being undertaken by other than common carriers, much of it even by nonregulated carriers, as well as by private carriers. The law has been forced to recognize this, and even the fact that all transport for hire cannot successfully be regulated as common carriage.

The concept of the common carrier grew up because of the necessity of protecting the shipper and the general public. During the era of railroad pre-eminence the regulations that developed were also the results of the unique characteristics of railroad economics. With the development of the new transport structure, this situation has been altered so radically that it is well-nigh reversed, and much of the discussion today which concerns the common carrier revolves around the question of protecting the latter rather than protecting the consumer. It is possible that these two may turn out to mean the same thing, but it is by no means self-evident. Nor is it self-evident that the common carrier needs protection for its own preservation or for the public interest. At the present itme, convincing evidence is lacking to support the position that whatever common carriage is essential to public needs cannot survive under conditions of fair competition and under regulation of sufficient flexibility to meet modern conditions. It seems to be clear that the type of regulation designed to control a transport system based on railroads alone is totally outmoded. Further discussion of this question will have to await the analysis of transport economics and public regulation in the next two parts of this book.

OTHER CARRIERS FOR HIRE

Under common law there are two kinds of carriers for hire, the common carrier and the contract carrier. Those that are not for hire fall into the category of private carriers. However, the extensive legislation that has grown up around transportation in this country has created a somewhat different distinction, namely, regulated and nonregulated carriage. State laws vary considerably as to the dividing line, but federal legislation regulates in some way all carriers for hire in interstate commerce unless they are exempt. The exemptions may apply to the commodities transported, such as agricultural products, or to the type of carriage performed, such as bulk carriers by water. Private carriage is that which is not for hire, but instead is used only for the supplier of the transport. As a general rule, carriers are confined to one of the three categories by law, although motor carriers are permitted to haul exempt agricultural commodities even though they are also common or contract carriers, provided that the motor vehicles while used in carrying the exempt agricultural commodities are not at the same time used in carrying any other property or passengers for compensation.[13]

Contract Carriers

Contract carriers are those for-hire carriers which do not hold themselves ready to serve the general public but instead serve one or a few shippers under specific contracts with them. Quite commonly, they are specialized as to the commodities hauled, the character of the service rendered, and perhaps even as to the equipment used. They are not subject to regulation as to precise rates although contract motor carriers have to publish the actual rates they charge and the Interstate Commerce Commission does have the power to prescribe the minimum rates. The Commission may also fix reasonable minimum rates for contract water carriers. Moreover, contract carriers are not subject to the duties imposed upon common carriers which were discussed in the previous section. Presumably, it would be possible for Congress to impose stricter liability requirements for loss and damage as a matter of law if it deemed this to be necessary for the protection of the public.

Private Carriers

There are many private carriers for hire that are not subject to regulation at the federal level. Most of the tonnage moving in domestic shipping is not subject to regulation since it does not fall within the statutory definition of common or contract carriage. Motor carriers of agricultural products fall into the same category. Only common carriers by air are subject to federal control. However, many of the carriers that are not under federal jurisdiction may be covered by state regulation

[13] C. C. Linnenberg, Jr., "The Agricultural Exemptions in Interstate Trucking: Mend Them or End Them?" *Law and Contemporary Problems*, "Transportation," Part II, Vol. XXV, No. 1 (Winter, 1960), pp. 139–83. Agricultural cooperatives may now transport nonfarm-related commodities for nonmembers on backhauls, provided that the transportation of these products is small in proportion to the overall transportation operation. *I.C.C.* v. *Northwest Agricultural Coop. Assn. Inc.*, 350 F.2d 252 (1965); certiorari denied by the U.S. Supreme Court, 382 U.S. 1011 (1966).

if they are engaged in intrastate commerce and the state law so provides. Very extensive control exists in California, for example, where even taxicabs are treated as common carriers. Thus the distinction between regulated and nonregulated carriers varies from one jurisdiction to another. What enterprises may as a matter of constitutional law, however, be treated as common carriers is uniform for the country as a whole. Whether all the statutory restrictions that are characteristically imposed upon them today are necessary in the public interest is a matter that will be given further consideration.

CONTROL OF SERVICE

The control over service offered by the different types of carriers is confined almost completely to those of the common carriers, although control is exercised over the entry of contract carriers. The latter are limited to the kinds of services they offer, but apart from matters of public health and safety, they are free to perform as they see fit.

Sanctions for Regulated Carriers

All common carriers in interstate commerce operate under the permission of the federal government in offering their services to the public. Railroads receive their sanction through charter grants which originally were specifically given, but later were obtained under general incorporation laws. Prior to the Transportation Act of 1920 the Interstate Commerce Commission did not exercise any authority over extension or abandonment of railroad lines or services. Within very broad limits the railroads could use their own discretion, although the common law prevented whimsical behavior, but abandonment of service that was not being operated at a loss presented legal difficulties.[14] With the passage of the Act of 1920, however, thoroughgoing federal control was established. Railroad lines may not now be extended or abandoned without the sanction of the Interstate Commerce Commission. The same remarks apply to service, except for that which is strictly local in nature. New service offerings such as those afforded by trailers on flatcars (piggyback) can be introduced only with public sanction and then only after the opposition has been given the opportunity to voice its objections. This is true also for the abandonment of service.

The procedure with regard to common carriers by highway, water,

[14] See D. P. Locklin, *Economics of Transportation* (6th ed.; Homewood, Ill.: Richard D. Irwin, Inc., 1966), p. 575 ff.

and air is to require them to secure a certificate of public convenience and necessity as a condition of operation. To secure a certificate, it is necessary for the applicant to prove that he is fit, willing, and able to render adequate service, and furthermore that public convenience and necessity demand the issuance. If an existing common carrier is already providing what in the judgment of the Commission is adequate service, a certificate permitting the entry of a competitor will be denied. The opposition of existing holders of certificates to new entrants is usually so vigorous that entry is severely limited.[15] In fact, the underlying theory which governs the granting of these certificates is that they are a grant of monopoly privilege and that, on condition of good behavior of the recipient, competition by a rival of the same mode will not be sanctioned. Where the regulated carrier does not fall into the common carrier category, permits instead of certificates are required. The permits are to be issued only if the public interest is served thereby, but the assumption seems to be that obtaining permits is faced with a less vigorous test than securing certificates. Commission reluctance in administering the law to recognize the force of competition among carriers under its control has made it difficult to see wherein there is any real difference in the proof necessary to convince the Commission that the service of a new contract carrier is warranted.

The Civil Aeronautics Board to date has not been as severe in restricting entry as has the Interstate Commerce Commission. Instead, it has recognized competition as a significant factor in air transport and therefore has permitted a good deal of competition over the same routes, particularly between trunk-line carriers. However, recent developments seem to indicate that the route structure has been pretty well stabilized and that control over entry and rates has imposed effective limitations on competition in air transport. Competition has shifted, therefore, more and more to considerations of matters of service, concerning which the Civil Aeronautics Board seems to be embarking upon more positive action designed to upgrade service even though this may be contrary to the carrier's financial interest.

The raw root of the adequacy of service question is whether the air transportation needs of the public will be satisfied by dependence on profit incentive in a competitive market, unrestricted by government control, or whether the regulatory structure within which this competition is to operate to satisfy transporta-

---

[15] See D. F. Pegrum, "Effects of Regulation on Small Business in Motor Transport," *I.C.C. Administration of the Motor Carrier Act*, Hearings before Select Committee on Small Business, U.S. Senate, 84th Congress, 1st session, November, 1955 (Washington, D.C.: U.S. Government Printing Office, 1956), pp. 465–70.

tion needs is so designed that the profit incentive will not do the job, requiring, therefore, further government control, resulting ultimately in government assumption of managerial reins as well as regulation.[16]

Rail Passenger Service

The heavy deficit that has been sustained annually in recent years in rail passenger service as a whole has resulted in an examination of ways to lighten the burden resulting from this. One of the steps taken in this direction has been to make it easier for the railroads to escape local resistance and impediments to abandoning unprofitable services. This was one of the purposes of the Transportation Act of 1958, which permitted railroads to discontinue or change interstate passenger train service upon thirty days' notice to the Interstate Commerce Commission, and to the governor of each state involved, unless the Commission intervened to prevent the discontinuance. If the operations are intrastate in nature, a petition may be filed with the Commission if the state authorities refuse permission to discontinuance or abandonment. After holding hearings in the state where the operations occur, the Commission may sanction discontinuance if it finds that public convenience and necessity will permit it, and if it finds that continuance will constitute an undue or unjust burden on the interstate carrier. This puts federal authority over both freight and passenger service in practically the same category.

Car Supply and Car Service

Car supply and car service of railroads for interstate commerce is under the control of the Interstate Commerce Commission. The latter has ruled that it is the legal duty of a carrier to provide reasonably adequate and suitable equipment for all of the traffic it holds itself out to transport. This obligation extends to special types of equipment if there is a sufficient amount of traffic to justify the requirement. However, the carrier is not liable for failure to supply cars when there is an unexpected demand for them.

Car shortages arising from various situations are of special concern to shippers, especially where heavy seasonal movement of traffic occurs. Because of the extensive interchange of freight cars among railroads the Interstate Commerce Commission finds it necessary to

[16] *National Transportation Policy* (Doyle Report), *op. cit.*, p. 720. Support to this evaluation is afforded by recommendation of the CAB examiner in Docket 16984 (July, 1966), awarded the through route to Vancouver, British Columbia, to United Air Lines. See Examiner Brown's report for a full discussion of the case. However, the CAB did not follow the examiner's recommendation. Instead it awarded the route to Western Airlines. See chap. 15.

take special measures at times to deal with the situation. The Interstate Commerce Act authorizes the Commission, when necessary, to invoke the following steps: (1) suspend car service rules of the carriers; (2) require the pooling of equipment; (3) require joint use of terminals; (4) establish embargoes, require certain commodities to be given priority, or require that traffic may move only under a permit system; and (5) route traffic to relieve congestion. In addition, the Commission establishes the per diem charge to be paid by one railroad for the use of the cars of another and fixes the charge, known as "demurrage," to be levied on a shipper for retention of a car beyond a stipulated period of free time for loading or unloading.

Extra Services

Railroads also provide a number of special services, many of which are required as a result of the particular commodities shipped or the conditions under which shipments are made. Some of these are the result of competition for traffic; others, such as refrigeration service or special treatment of livestock, derive from the necessity of satisfactory shipment. Two services in particular are of great importance to the manufacture, sale, and distribution of commodities, namely, diversion and reconsignment, and transit privileges.

Diversion and reconsignment permit change in the destination or billing of a shipment either before or after it reaches its original destination, with possibly a small charge for the reconsignment privilege. Commodity brokers, in particular, make extensive use of the service.

The transit privilege makes it possible to stop a shipment en route for processing at some intermediate point. "Milling in transit," as this privilege is known when applied to grain, permits the processing of the grain before the final destination of the shipment is reached. A large number of other commodities are accorded similar treatment. The processed commodities move on the through rate for the original product from point of origin to destination, and because the through rate is normally less than the sum of the local rate in and the local rate out, the privilege is a valuable one to the shipper.[17]

TERMINAL SERVICES

Terminal services are performed at all points of origin or destination of passenger or freight traffic, whether the movement takes

[17] See Locklin, *op. cit.*, pp. 581–84 for a full discussion.

place by rail, motor, water, or air, or any combination of these. The services performed by the carrier will vary with the nature of the terminal area. Large cities, especially where there is considerable interchange of traffic, offer the most varied services and present the most complex problems. Prior to the development of motor transport, it was possible to make a rather clear-cut distinction between line-haul and terminal traffic movement. The motor vehicle has obliterated a good deal of this distinction. The growth of air transportation has also altered the picture radically. The terminal problem has now become so intimately related to urban transport that it needs to be given separate treatment in this connection. The present discussion, therefore, will deal only with some of the services offered by the carriers.

Passengers load and unload themselves and usually have the responsibility of getting to and from the point of embarkation by means separate from the carrier which takes them on their intercity journeys. These intercity carriers may provide means of transferring the passengers from one company to another when interline movements are involved, but most of this service is confined to railroads. They may operate through unified passenger depots, as in Los Angeles, or provide other means of interconnection between depots, as is done in Chicago. Apart from situations like this the passengers have to take care of the interchange themselves.

Most of the terminal services provided by transport companies relate to freight, and here the most extensive development has been by the railroads. The bulk of railroad freight traffic moves in carloads, and the major terminal problems relate to the handling of such traffic. For this the railroads normally provide facilities whereby shipper and consignee do the loading and unloading. The railroads typically perform this task for less-than-carload (l.c.l.) traffic.

Carload Freight

Terminal handling of carload traffic is carried out in a number of different ways. The railroad may supply "team tracks" from which loading and unloading takes place; it may provide spur tracks to warehouses; or it may connect with the industrial or tap line of a firm, movement within the plant facilities being undertaken by the manufacturer. In any case the railroad must provide the switching connections, the appropriate charges for which are set by the Interstate Commerce Commission. It is customary for the railroad to switch freight cars to and from the convenient point of access to the shipper and consignee without any charge above the regular line-haul rate.

Railroads are required to provide proper facilities for the interchange of traffic with each other at terminals. This is a problem only where a center is served by more than one rail line. This service may entail an extra charge, but frequently it results in the absorption of the switching cost by one carrier, or in what is known as reciprocal switching, under which the line-haul charge to the shipper covers the interchange service.

Reciprocal switching is really only one form of joint use of terminals. The most important commercial centers of this country are served by a number of railroads, each of which has developed its own terminal facilities. Because of the complexities of interchange that have resulted from this, and because of the inconvenience to shippers that frequently arose from competitive rivalries, means have been devised for joint use of terminals. One method is to put the terminals of a center under joint ownership, with member railroads having equal access to the facilities; another is to provide for "belt" lines, which are frequently under municipal ownership; a third procedure is to establish "open" terminals by which the owning carrier permits use to all other carriers alike. The Interstate Commerce Commission may under appropriate circumstances require the joint use of terminals. If widespread consolidation of railroads into a limited number of systems should take place, this aspect of the terminal problem will decline, except for key interchange centers, which will still be served by separate roads.

Less-than-Carload Freight

The bulk of carload traffic is handled on a "door-to-door" basis, but until 1932 for most less-than-carload (l.c.l.) shipments, railroads provided only station-to-station transportation. There had been some door-to-door service in what were known as trap or ferry cars. These were freight cars placed at an industrial or commercial warehouse which was on a private siding. The l.c.l. shipments were loaded in them, and the cars were then moved to the regular freight sheds for reloading by the railroad. As a result of motor carrier competition, railroads turned to the general establishment of pickup and delivery service in the 1930's. The railroad undertakes to provide pickup and delivery service under regular tariffs filed with the Interstate Commerce Commission. The service is available only on shipper's application, and is rendered only for commodities and at stations specified in the published tariffs. The consignor or consignee may supply its own transport, in which case the railroad will make it an allowance for the local carriage. The service supplied by the railroads may be in their own trucks or in those of firms operating under contract with them.

CO-ORDINATION OF SERVICES

Co-ordination in transportation is a term that may be used to designate two essentially different things. It may be used to describe the means by which the various modes of transport are made to perform the transport functions they are economically most fitted to carry out. In this setting they may be competitive or complementary. Co-ordination may also refer to the complementary use of the same or different modes in providing for what is essentially a single movement by firms of the same mode or by firms of a different mode. For example, a freight shipment from Chicago to San Francisco may travel over the lines of more than one railroad company. The collection and delivery of the freight may be made by truck. The shipment, however, may be made as a single movement as far as the shipper is concerned. Various arrangements have been worked out to accommodate this type of traffic. It is in this second sense that co-ordination is discussed here, the first type being dealt with later in connection with competition among the agencies and interagency ownership.

Joint Action of Independent Agencies

A great deal of railroad traffic, passenger or freight, must move over the lines of different companies from origin to destination. Some of the arrangements to facilitate this have already been discussed in connection with terminal services. In addition, the co-operating railroads interchange freight and passenger cars to provide for through movement of traffic. They do this by what is known as through billing and through tickets. As far as the user of the services is concerned, he will be treated as though he were dealing with a single carrier and in many instances may not even know the difference.

Through routes and joint rates may also be established by carriers of different types.[18] Railroads frequently provide such traffic facilities with water carriers. The Interstate Commerce Commission is empowered to require railroads to enter into joint arrangements with water carriers. It has no authority to do so, however, for railroads and motor carriers, or water carriers and motor carriers. Such transport

___

[18] Through routes constitute a continuous haul by connecting carriers from origin to destination. The rates on such hauls may be a "through rate" which is a combination of the rates of the separate carriers, or it may be a "joint rate" which is a single rate that is usually less than the "through" or combination rate.

may be provided on a voluntary basis, with the sanction of the Commission. Similar arrangements may be worked out through the Interstate Commerce Commission and the Civil Aeronautics Board for air carriers and surface carriers. Co-ordination by through routes and through rates is ordinarily not difficult to achieve when the movements are complementary. When they involve some sort of division of haulage among competing carriers, co-operation is not so likely to be forthcoming readily. The extent to which it should be compelled under present-day conditions by public authority offers considerable ground for differences of opinion. The bases for decision require among other things an understanding of transport economics; discussion of the question, therefore, will be deferred until this has been dealt with.

Methods of Traffic Interchange

Transfer of freight from one agency or mode of transport to another may be expected in a number of different ways. Car floats or car ferries are extensively used in many parts of the country; this makes joint use of rail and water facilities possible without unloading and reloading the freight cars. Seatrain Lines uses specially designed ships to move freight cars between ports in Gulf and Atlantic coastwise service. Recently, the possibilities of cheaper and more expeditious transfer of freight from one mode of transport to another by the use of containers adapted to special uses have come under extensive examination. SeaLand now offers a service between Atlantic and Pacific ports, on container ships. The trailers are assembled and distributed at the ports by SeaLand.

The severe loss of freight traffic to the highway carriers in recent years has led the railroads to embark aggressively upon securing means to reverse the trend. One of the devices that is undergoing extensive experimentation on the technical side for equipment, and on the economic side for pricing, is the transporting of motor trailers on flatcars, commonly known as piggyback or T.O.F.C.

At the present time, five different plans are in use. Under Plan I the railroad transports the loaded trailers of the motor carriers, the shipments moving on motor carrier rates. The railroad either receives a division of the rates or makes a flat charge per trailer. Under Plan II the freight moves on railroad billing at railroad rates in railroad-owned trailers. The rate includes pickup and delivery. Under Plan III the railroad furnishes the flatcars; the shipper or freight forwarder furnishes the trailers, providing his own pickup and delivery service. The railroad usually loads the trailers on the flatcars and unloads them. In 1964, the

Interstate Commerce Commission ruled that this service should also be available to for-hire motor and water carriers. This ruling was upheld by the Supreme Court. Plan IV requires the shipper or forwarder to provide both the flatcars and the trailers. The railroad merely hauls them loaded or empty from point to point. Plan V provides for the movement of commodities in T.O.F.C. service on through routes and joint rail-truck rates. Under this plan the railroads publish tariffs for joint motor-rail rates for complete door-to-door piggyback service.[19]

Piggyback transport has grown rapidly in the last ten years. Some 65 railroads now offer piggyback service as compared with 19 at the start of 1955. In 1954, 44,102 flatcars loaded with truck trailers were handled by the railroads. In 1955, piggyback loadings increased to 168,150; they reached 415,156 in 1959 and 1,216,900 in 1964.[20] It should be noted that this service constitutes a substitution of rail line haulage for motor line haulage by special equipment adapted to rail transport. It is not, therefore, a form of interagency ownership for line-haul traffic. Nevertheless, because of the competitive threat which it poses to motor transport, it is the subject of vigorous opposition by the American Trucking Association and the Teamsters' Union.[21]

[19] The rules governing the various plans are a matter of considerable dispute at the present time. The ICC made an extensive investigation of piggyback in *Ex Parte 230*, 322 I.C.C. 301 (1964) and prescribed rules governing trailer-on-flatcar, (T.O.F.C.) service. It is still in the process of implementing these rules.

[20] *Transport Economics, op. cit.*, October, 1965.

[21] See *National Transportation Policy* (Doyle Report), *op. cit.*, pp. 655–68, for discussion of piggyback service.

PART II

Economics of Transport Pricing

THE ECONOMIC STRUCTURE
OF TRANSPORT

TRANSPORT AS A GROUP OF INDUSTRIES

Nature of an Industry

Some of the most important questions that arise today in connection with transport economics center on the issue of whether transportation constitutes an industry or a group of industries. If it is an industry, essentially uniform treatment may be accorded to all the firms that comprise it. If it consists of a group of industries with significantly divergent economic characteristics, this may necessitate policies that are fundamentally different for some of the agencies as compared with others.

An industry in the strictest sense consists of a group of firms producing the same commodity for the same market. This is too rigid a concept upon which to build a usable classification in the real world. However, practical groupings can be set up which, while not conforming to the strictest theoretical definition, may nevertheless approximate it. Thus, one may conveniently speak of the coal industry, of the wheat-growing industry, or of the steel industry. In each of these cases the products of the firms in the industry have a high degree of substitutability for each other, that is, there is a high degree of cross-elasticity of demand within each group. Moreover, production takes place under quite similar technological conditions with the result that the cost structures of the firms exhibit similar characteristics and behavior.

A further point to be recognized is that the grouping of firms into an industry for analytic purposes will be influenced by the purpose of the grouping. This is not unique to economics. For example, we may distinguish animals from human beings by putting the latter into a single classification. When we turn to examine the latter group, however, we may find it necessary to recognize that the members of it are

127

quite distinct from the standpoint of age, sex, color, and so forth. Similar remarks apply to the groupings of firms into industries.

The Products of Transportation

The products of transportation are the services supplied in moving goods or people from one place to another at the time the movement is desired. In other words, transportation produces time and place utilities. This production may be divided into the two main categories of passenger and freight service. Of the five agencies that make up the transport system of the country, four supply both types of services; the fifth, namely, pipe lines, moves commodities only. From the point of view of these functions, transportation can be divided into two industries, one handling freight traffic, the other passengers. This classification is useful and significant for some purposes. There is still the question, however, whether the suppliers of passenger service fall into a single industry, and whether a similar grouping is appropriate for freight. Because the same general considerations are involved in answering the question regarding each of these, it will be unnecessary to deal with them separately.

The various agencies of transport offer a wide range of services that are quite readily substitutable for each other. Railroads are capable of transporting much of the freight that goes by motor carrier, and vice versa. The possibility of substitution alone is not sufficient reason for classifying the agencies as a single industry, however. Timber may be substituted for steel, yet the differences between the two are sufficiently great that the sources of supply may be labeled as two distinct industries. The transport agencies produce ton-miles of freight, but these are heterogeneous rather than homogeneous services even within the same firm. As among agencies, they may be even more heterogeneous. Motor carriers can frequently offer services that railroads are unable to supply literally at any practicable price, and railroads move traffic that motor carriers are technically unable to take care of. Shipping companies supply services between points that railroads and motor carriers cannot even reach. Air lines offer services for which other agencies may provide reasonably ready alternatives, but they also offer some for which there is no substitute. If a person needs to go from Los Angeles to New York in less than twelve hours, an air line is his only choice. In short, the different modes of transportation offer services which are so readily substitutable for each other that these services may be regarded as differentiated products and therefore as being derived from a single industry. On the other hand, they also create outputs that differ so completely in quality and service as to make them quite distinct from each other and in some instances not substitutable by any standard.[1]

Differences in Economic Structures

Another aspect of the question of whether the agencies of transport constitute a single industry or a group of industries arises in connection with the economic structures of these different agencies. Railroads and pipe lines possess those economic characteristics that put them into the category of natural or technological, monopolies. Motor, water, and air carriers do not exhibit the features that warrant putting them into such a classification. Thus, these two groups operate under quite different conditions of production and from this point of view constitute distinct industries. The fact that railroads and pipelines are natural monopolies does not make them an industry, of course, any more than electricity and natural gas form a single industry. Similarly, grouping motor, water, and air carriers into a single category because of common characteristics of cost behavior does not make them a single industry. The differences of conditions of production, however, between natural monopolies and other industries are such as to have brought about recognition of the fact that they fall into distinct economic categories.

The differences in the economic structure of the agencies of transport have been recognized, in part at least, by the Interstate Commerce Commission and the Civil Aeronautics Board even where the law did not call for such recognition. The Interstate Commerce Commission considers the operating ratio as a more satisfactory gauge of the reasonableness of the rate level of a motor carrier than fair return on fair value, which is the basis of measurement for railroads when one is used. The Civil Aeronautics Board has taken a somewhat similar position with regard to air lines. The unsatisfactory nature of the public utility basis of fair return on fair value as the measure of the reasonableness of rate levels for motor and air carriers arises from the competitive nature of their structures.[2] Finally, it should be noted that in the case of motor and water transport, competition among suppliers within

---

[1] For discussion of problems of homogeneity and substitutability in transport, see George L. Wilson, "On the Output Unit in Transportation," *Land Economics,* Vol. XXXV, No. 3 (August, 1959), pp. 267–76.

[2] It may be urged that fair return on fair value is not a practicable device for gauging the reasonableness of the general level of railroad rates today. This, however, is the result of (a) regulatory policies with regard to railroads and (b) the alternative sources of supply of transport offered by the other modes. It is not the result of the economic structure of the railroads. This matter will be dealt with more fully in later chapters.

each of them cannot be avoided, at least under existing institutional arrangements of private ownership. If technology permits individualized operation of air facilities and such wide variations in size and type of the supply unit as exists in motor transport, then thoroughgoing competition in air transportation will be unavoidable, too. No such possibilities are at present in sight for rail and pipe-line transport.

ECONOMIES OF SCALE

The production of goods and services takes place under widely varying technical conditions. Many industries require large amounts of capital investment and can operate successfully only when large units of equipment are employed. Others require much less capital investment, and the equipment which is used may be obtained in smaller units. The size of the enterprise in each instance will depend upon a number of different factors: technical, managerial, financial, and market. Size may also be influenced by organizational possibilities, which create the opportunity of expansion for the purpose of limiting or eliminating competition.

Discussion of the scale of enterprise in the economy calls for an analysis of some of the significant aspects of the theory of production. This area of economic theory comprises some of the most elusive and unsettled topics of economic analysis. Because of the critical organizational and public policy questions connected with scale of enterprise in transport, it is desirable to present a few of the economic principles that bear upon the size of plants and firms in general. Unfortunately, we are as yet unable to supply much quantitative information that will tell us whether the scale of operations of firms in particular industries is too large or too small, or how much bigger they may be able to grow and still be economically or socially desirable.

The Law of Diminishing Returns

The production process requires the utilization of many different agents or resources. When these productive services are combined in varying proportions, the output also varies. This is the result of the operation of what is frequently called the "law of diminishing returns." This law states that if, with a fixed agent of production, successive increments of variable agents are employed, a point is reached where the increase in the output of the variable agents is less than proportional to their input. If the variables are added indefinitely, the additions to total output attributable to an additional variable unit ultimately will become zero.[3] Between these two limits is the stage which is significant in economic problems, known as the "stage of diminishing returns." This law assumes a given state of technology and relates only to the proportion of the factors used in production, not to their absolute amount.

Figure 6–1 illustrates graphically the behavior of output as the input of one factor is increased, with the other remaining constant. As additional units of the variable factor are added, the total output rises

FIGURE 6–1

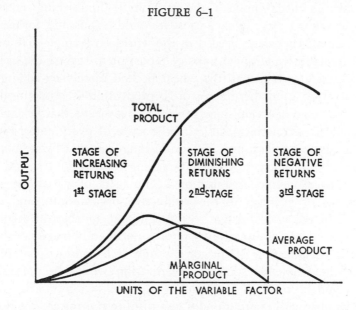

more than proportionally to the input. For example, if the variable factor is increased from one to two units, the total output more than doubles, and the additional (or marginal) output or product increases; the average product also increases. As this process continues, a stage will be reached, sooner or later depending on conditions of production, when the marginal product will commence to decline. This will result, at a later stage, in a decline in the average product per unit of input of the variable factor, at which time the total product will cease to in-

---

[3] See F. H. Knight, *Risk, Uncertainty, and Profit,* London School of Economics Reprints, No. 16 (London, 1935), chap. iv, pp. 98–106, for a careful discussion of this; also F. M. Taylor, *Principles of Economics* (9th ed.; New York: Ronald Press Co., 1925), chap. ix. Diminishing returns may also be defined in terms of diminishing marginal productivity. The statement of the law in terms of diminishing average product seems preferable because it is when average product begins to decline that the "stage of diminishing returns" sets in.

crease proportionately,[4] although it will still increase. Finally, the marginal product will be reduced to zero—that is, there will be no additional output from an additional unit of the variable. When this point is reached, total output will commence to decline.

It is the second stage of variation in returns that is the economically significant one. A producer would not continue to expand his output into the third stage because the total output would diminish. He would not stop expanding until the end of the first stage because he is not only increasing his total output, he is also getting more than proportional returns on the inputs of the variable. If diminishing returns did not set in at some stage of expansion, it would be possible, for example, to produce all the wheat needed in the world on a single acre of land merely by adding additional units of labor; or to reverse the example, one man could produce all the wheat needed merely by adding additional acres of land. In other words, production is economical only within the stage of diminishing returns. This means that at any given time there are economical limits to the scale of every enterprise, and these limits are established by diminishing returns. Even more important is the fact that without diminishing returns there would be no problem of economic organization. "The facts of variability in the proportions of agencies in the productive organization, and of the variation of the yield relative to the different agencies in accordance with the principle of diminishing returns not merely make possible the economic organization of society through free contract, but in their absence the whole question of organization would be meaningless; there would be no such problem."[5]

The changes in output under diminishing returns are the result of varying the proportions of the productive factors which are being used. A producer therefore must decide what combination of factors he will employ. The combination he selects will determine where in the stage of diminishing returns his output will be. This will depend upon the relative costs of the factors which are employed. When a producer uses that combination which gives him the lowest average total cost per unit for a given output, the factors are combined in their most economical proportions for that output. That is, there is an optimum combination of factors of production. Under these circumstances, the firm obtains

---

[4] This is also the point beyond which the "actual" increase of output resulting from additional units of the variables is less than the "proportional" increase. For an arithmetic and tabular exposition of this, see Taylor, *op. cit.*, p. 127.

[5] Knight, *op. cit.*, pp. 102–3.

the maximum product from a given cost of outlay, or the minimum average unit cost for a given output.

Where the optimum combination will lie, will depend upon the relative costs of the fixed and variable agents. If the fixed agent is relatively high-cost, expansion conceivably may continue until additional increments of the variables add nothing to the total product. If the variables are relatively high-cost, expansion may cease as soon as the marginal output of the variables is equal to their average output. Between these two extremes lies the most economical scale of operations. The reason for this is the unutilized or excess capacity of the fixed agents. If they are relatively expensive, that is, expensive as compared with the cost of the variables, it will pay to utilize them intensively. If the reverse is true, the variables will be used more intensively and may not even be added beyond the point where diminishing returns set in.

Nature of Economies of Scale

At the outset it is necessary to distinguish between the law of diminishing returns and the concept of economies of scale. Diminishing returns lays the foundation for the economic limits on the amount of output or the size of firms under given conditions. It does not give an indication of the absolute economical size a given enterprise may achieve, even under the assumption of fixed technology, because it deals only with proportions. What the most economical size of an enterprise may be depends upon the economies of scale.

Economies of scale refer to the increased efficiency or lower unit costs of production that are realized from the expansion in the size of a firm as a result of increasing all of the factors of production. Economies of scale therefore reflect the effects of changes in the total quantities of factors of production used by the firm on the cost per unit of output, economies of scale being realized when an increase in the size of operations yields a lower cost per unit of output. Thus a farmer may double the amount of land he owns, increase the number of his employees, and take someone into partnership with him, thereby lowering the unit cost of his output. His larger scale of operations is more economical than the smaller one.

There appear to be three principal reasons for the economies of scale. First, economies of scale are related to the size of the market. For example, an electric light and power plant may be serving a small community. Its generating and distribution facilities will be adapted to that market, and if it is operating most economically, it will be organized on the basis of the least cost combination. If the market expands, the firm will increase its productive capacity and will be able to lower its costs per unit of output. Again, it may operate at the least cost combination, but the increase in size will result in economies of scale. There will be a new least cost combination and a lower unit cost of output. Economies of scale may therefore arise as the market for a product expands.

Second, economies of scale may be the result of the indivisibility of some of the factors of production. Units of productive resources are not completely divisible. Some of them, like hydroelectric dams and blast furnaces, are obtainable only in relatively large units and are cheaper to obtain per unit of output capacity than technically possible smaller units. Larger outputs can therefore be obtained at a lower cost per unit of output than with the smaller plants. Indivisibilities also apply to labor and management. In the case of a hydroelectric undertaking a very large generating establishment can be operated with nearly the same amount of labor and management as a small one. In other words, the economies of scale in this instance arise from the change in the proportion of the factors which is the result of indivisibility. Some economists contend that indivisibility in management is ultimately the most important single factor making for economies of scale. These economists also assert that without indivisibility there could be no economies of scale. Whatever may be the merits of the controversy, it is clear that indivisibility of factors is a very important influence on economies of scale.[6]

Third, economies of scale also may arise from increased specialization in the use of factors. As a business expands, it may be able to take advantage of the specialization of labor and managerial activities in addition to being able to secure the services of more highly specialized and superior abilities. Specialization of processes and machines may also be possible with increases in size.

Returns to Scale

There are three stages to the economies of scale, and a firm may be in any one of them. It is also possible that an enterprise may never pass beyond the first one. These stages are the result of the operation of the forces discussed in the previous section. The first of these stages is

---

[6] For a discussion of this whole issue, see E. H. Chamberlin, "Proportionality, Divisibility and Economies of Scale," *Quarterly Journal of Economics,* Vol. LXII (February, 1948), pp. 229–57.

that of increasing returns to scale. In this stage an increase in the scale of operations, that is, an increase in the inputs or quantities of factors used, leads to an increase in output at a faster rate than the increase of inputs. The limit to increasing returns for any firm will depend upon the extent to which the influences of indivisibility and specialization create increased resistance to expansion. Indivisibilities are very important in the case of capital goods, especially in modern industry—as, for example, railroads, the steel industry, or electric light and power. Indivisibilities may also appear in connection with marketing, finance, and research activities. All of these indivisibilities encounter limitations, and although the latter may not be reached for all of them at the same time, when the resultant effect is that output ceases to increase more than proportionately to input, increasing returns arising from indivisibilities have come to an end.

Many economists are of the opinion that the most significant limitations on scale arise in connection with specialization in labor and management. Increases in labor force create problems of supervision and co-ordination as well as the need for an increase in managerial requirements. Specialization obviously encounters limitations, and expansion leads to growing complications in co-ordination and decision making. In other words, the limitations on increasing returns arise primarily from the complexities of organization, impersonal relations, divided responsibility, and so forth. In fact, if genuine economies could be obtained without limit from such aspects of a firm's activities as finance, research, and management, particularly the latter, there seems to be no reason why a firm should encounter an end to increasing returns. "It is the economies of large-scale government rather than of large-scale technique which dictate the size of the modern business unit. . . . As in manufacture, it is the limit to the economies of large-scale government and not of large-scale technique which dictates the size of the producing unit: but unlike manufacture, agriculture runs its head into the former barrier first."[7] This is the reason why economies of the firm may exceed the economies of the plant and why multiple-plant firms may therefore be more economical than single-plant firms.[8]

Economies arising from indivisibilities may be limited, but it does not follow that further expansion promptly leads to diseconomies.

[7] D. H. Robertson, *The Control of Industry* (New York: Harcourt, Brace & Co., 1923), pp. 24–25.

[8] See, however, F. A. Fetter, *The Fundamental Principle of Efficiency in Mass Production,* Temporary National Economic Committee, Monograph No. 13 (Washington, D.C.: U.S. Government Printing Office, 1941), Appendix D, pp. 398–415; and G. J. Stigler, *The Theory of Price* (New York: Macmillan Co., 1946), chap. 11.

When expansion has exhausted increasing returns, the firm enters the stage of constant returns, that is, output increases in the same proportion as input. This stage will be the result of counteracting influences being in balance. There seems to be considerable evidence that this stage holds for a substantial range of output in many types of business and that many of our large manufacturing firms are in this stage.

The third stage, that of decreasing returns to scale, arises when the balance resulting in constant returns has been upset so that further expansion can be effected only by an increase of inputs that yield a less than proportionate increase of output. Total output, of course, may still be increasing. It is very probable that many electric light and power companies operate in this stage. They find it impossible to increase the regularity and intensity of the use of their facilities, but continue to experience growth by market or territorial expansion.

Perhaps it should be pointed out that economies of scale differ from the economies, or lower costs, that result from the more complete utilization of a given plant. When a plant is suffering from underutilization of existing facilities, it will be able to lower its unit costs if it increases its output. This is not a matter of economies of scale because the scale remains the same. It is the result of "spreading the overhead" connected with fixed costs and the production of goods or services derived from joint or common costs. Many of the difficult problems presented by present-day rail transport are the result of unused capacity.

Large-Scale Production

The consequences flowing from the law of diminishing returns and the influence of the forces making for economies of scale provide us with concepts that explain why there are economical limits to the size of firms at any particular time or, to put it another way, under given conditions. They also explain why firms may grow and, over a range of output, experience economies that make the larger scale more economical than the smaller one. These principles apply to all types of production and productive activity, the economical scale of operations being determined by the same forces in each case. There still remains, however, the task of applying these principles to various industries or types of industries in order to explain the differences in scale that appear among them—for example, the difference in the scale of operations typically found in agriculture from that in the manufacture of farm machinery, or that in motor transport from that in rail transport. There is even the problem of deciding what we mean by large-scale production and the usual distinction between it and economies of scale.

The term *large-scale production,* which is frequently used to designate certain characteristics of modern industry, actually has a number of different meanings and implications. Although most of these have certain factors in common, some of them are also derived from quite different sources which require separate consideration. For example, large-scale production and giant enterprise are not necessarily synonymous terms. A holding company may own corporations engaged in many different lines of production, its own size, however, being determined merely by the amount of control it exercises. It may exhibit none of the economies and none of the economic advantages that may derive from large size.

Large-scale production commonly refers to the contrast in size between the giant business enterprises which characterize such industries as steel, automobile manufacturing, railroad transportation, and the generation and distribution of electrical energy, on the one hand, and the multiplicity of small businesses which make up such undertakings as agriculture, the service trades, much of the building industry, and a large part of retailing, on the other hand. The term may also refer, however, to the scale of production or the size of enterprise within a particular industry. Thus, large-scale farming may be contrasted or compared with small-scale farming. Probably the most generally accepted connotation is that which comprehends both large-scale operation and large-scale organization, thereby including economies of scale of both the plant and the firm.

When expansion of enterprise into fields of activity having little or no technological connection with each other takes place, large-scale production is succeeded by large-scale ownership. Frequently, large-scale ownership has emerged under the impetus of economies of large-scale production, but much of it is to be explained by endeavors to secure control of markets and to get insulation from the disturbing effects of competition, that is, disturbing to those seeking control. Large-scale ownership under the influence of the holding company and the privileges of intercorporate stock ownership led to large-scale control. This was a purely financial and managerial development, arising out of the existing legal status of the corporate device.

The distinction between large-scale production as descriptive of certain industries, and large-scale production as applied to the size of operations within particular industries, has an important bearing on public policy. Certain industries lend themselves to a scale of operations which would be characterized as large by almost any measuring rod, whereas others are typically small by similar standards. In each instance the question may arise as to the proper public policy required to make possible the achievement of the most economical size. When public policy turns its attention to increasing productive efficiency, the scale of production is a relative matter which must be considered in the light of each particular industry. This makes it especially difficult to impose a workable minimum or maximum size for any enterprise. However, this does not preclude the possibilities of devising practicable limitations on large-scale ownership and large-scale control. This has been done in commercial banking and in transportation. The issues arising in this connection in the field of transportation are dealt with in a later section of this book.

ECONOMIES OF SCALE IN TRANSPORT

Economies of scale as they relate to the various modes of transport are no different than for other industries. The principles of the returns to scale are the same here as elsewhere. However, the economies of scale manifest themselves in somewhat different ways among the modes because of the varied economic characteristics of those modes. It is not a question of whether there are economies of scale in the organization of each of the agencies but rather a question of how the economies of scale influence the most economical size of the different undertakings. Issues connected with large-scale production and the appropriate size of the firm must be examined from within each mode as well as among them.

Economies of Scale in Rail Transport

The technology of railroad transport necessitates a relatively large investment in plant and equipment which is also quite highly specialized. When it is stated that investment is large in railroad enterprises, it is implied that the absolute amount is large. This may be true, but it does not convey much meaning, for there are many enterprises that are a great deal bigger than many railroads in terms of total investment. It is not the absolute amount of investment which is of prime importance but rather the total investment in relation to the income it produces. This may be expressed in terms of the annual turnover of the capital, or the ratio of gross revenues from operations to total investment. The turnover is about once every three years; or to put it in another way, the gross revenues from railroad operations typically constitute annually about one third of the capital investment. For electric light and power the turnover is about once in five years, although for purely hydroelectric establishments it is even as low as once in ten years. For the steel industry the turnover is about once every one and one-half years, while for petroleum it is about once a year. Thus, railroads fall into that rather limited group of industries that has a very slow capital turnover, and this is true regardless of the size of the particular railroad.

The relative significance of capital investment in rail transport is also emphasized by the operating ratio. This is the relationship of operating expenses to operating revenues expressed in percentage terms. The operating expenses exclude taxes and return on investment, while operating revenues exclude nonoperating income. The operating ratios for various railroads will differ considerably depending on their relative efficiencies, and they will also differ for the railroads as a whole from year to year, particularly when there are wide variations in traffic volume. The ratio has ranged from 61.6 per cent in 1942 to 83.4 per cent in 1946; in 1964 it was 78.5 per cent. The high percentage in the postwar years reflects a low rate of return on investment. The operating ratio for railroads has to be lower than for most industries because of the relatively large investment.

A railroad has to make large initial outlays to build a single-track line and acquire the necessary terminal facilities and rolling stock to operate it. When that plant is utilized to capacity, double-tracking will require a large additional investment which cannot profitably be made unless there is a prospect of a large proportionate increase in traffic. Expansion of this type entails difficult problems of market anticipation because the facilities have to be built well in advance of market opportunities. Meanwhile the traffic which is available will have to bear the burden of keeping the railroad in operation until the new traffic has been built up. If, instead of double-tracking, a new railroad were to be built, a complete duplication of the facilities of the existing road would be necessary, and the immediately available traffic would be inadequate to give either road a profit. The building of the second road would cost more than double-tracking the first, although doing this would give the two railroads only the same capacity as the double-tracked one, or perhaps even less.

This brings out two important points. The first is that a second track will not be added until the operation of the first one is in the stage of decreasing returns to scale. The second is that the expansion by the building of the second track again puts the railroad back to the stage of increasing returns to scale. It is not correct to say that railroads are subject to the law of increasing returns with the implication that they are always in the stage of decreasing costs or increasing returns to scale. This would mean that there were no economical limitations to expansion. It is the persistence of unused capacity that is the real problem, not the matter of absolute size.

Just what are the economical limits to the size of a railroad enterprise is a matter of debate. It seems to be clear, however, at the present time that more economical railroad transportation is not likely to result from consolidation into a single national system, nor even from the establishment of three great regional systems. The limits of economy and efficiency seem to fall considerably short of this. Professor Kent T. Healy, after a careful study of scale in the railroad industry, comes to two conclusions: (1) For roads of low traffic density, consolidation which transforms low-density systems into a single system with traffic density in the higher ranges will offer economic benefit if the resultant system scale does not get so large that scale losses offset density gains; and (2) where density is already high, enlargement of scale above a level of some 10,000 employees will most likely be accompanied by real diseconomies.[9] Whatever the merits of the more or less precise limits to scale that Professor Healy's study establishes, it is clear that railroads, like other enterprises, are subject to economic limitations with regard to size. However, this should not be interpreted to mean that direct and over-all competition among them should be encouraged. There is another factor which must be considered; this will be dealt with after the other agencies have been examined.

Economies of Scale in Motor Transport

Economies of scale manifest themselves to a much smaller extent in motor transport than they do in rail. That is to say, the economies of scale available to motor carriers are such that opportunity to expand under the influence of lowering costs of production are of far less importance than in the case of railroads. The technical operating units are relatively small and may be very small. Operations may be started with a very small investment, and expansion may be undertaken with very small increments of investment in direct and almost immediate response to growth in traffic. Most of the facilities are not highly specialized or unalterably committed to a particular geographic area, and they can readily be shifted to any other market. Physically, the highways or

---

[9] Kent T. Healy, *The Effects of Scale in the Railroad Industry* (New Haven, Conn.: Committee on Transportation, Yale University, 1961). *Traffic World,* January 7, 1961, p. 28, reports the issuance of a white paper by the British Ministry of Transport calling for the reorganization of the British railways into three regions in order to reduce the scale of organization to a more economical basis. This appears to be additional evidence supporting Professor Healy's position, although not necessarily the limits which he imposes.

routes are available to all who wish to use them, and no carrier is committed to the investment in them. Investment in terminal facilities by motor carriers is relatively small and much of the time is almost non-existent. Economic limitations on the additions to plant are very slight because small increases in traffic increase the need for additional equipment, at least above very narrow limits, and these additions may be made in small units. This will not result in an appreciable lowering of the average total unit cost of output, because this additional output comes in response to the incurrence of added costs that are largely proportionate to output. Emphasis is given to this by the fact that the capital turnover of motor carriers of freight reporting to the Interstate Commerce Commission is almost five times a year, and the average operating ratio was 95.8 percent in 1963.[10]

The economical scale of operation for motor carriers will vary with the market that is to be served. The California Public Utilities Commission estimated that 55 per cent of the carriers reporting to it in 1946 earned less than $5,000 each per year in gross revenues from carrier operations. Even as late as 1958, 31 per cent had gross revenues of less than $5,000. On the other hand, 1.5 per cent had gross revenues of over $500,000. In 1963, only 1,175 motor carriers of freight had revenues of $1 million or more out of 15,618 reporting to the Interstate Commerce Commission while 11,910 had revenues of under $200,000 in that year.[11] Extensive operations for intercity and interstate carriage require larger enterprises than for purely local contract transport. The smaller carriers seem to be able to compete without difficulty with the larger ones on short hauls. Larger carriers, however, are evident in the intercity and interterritorial traffic. Even though, according to Professor Roberts' findings, these larger interterritorial carriers do not exhibit economies of scale as measured by vehicle-mile costs, these being essentially the same for the interterritorial carriers as for the intraterritorial ones, a certain minimum size for interterritorial business greater than that for the intraterritorial seems necessary.[12] Nevertheless a wide range of size appears to be possible within these market areas;

[10] American Trucking Associations, Inc., *American Trucking Trends* (Washington, D.C., 1964), pp. 16–17.

[11] *Ibid.,* p. 13.

[12] Merrill J. Roberts, "Some Aspects of Motor Carrier Costs: Firm Size, Efficiency and Financial Health," *Land Economics,* Vol. XXXII, No. 3 (August, 1956), pp. 228–38. See also Edward W. Smykay, "An Appraisal of the Economies of Scale in the Motor Carrier Industry," *Land Economics,* Vol. XXXIV, No. 2 (May, 1958), pp. 143–48; and Michael Chisholm, "Economies of Scale in Road Goods Transport? Off-Farm Milk Collection in England and Wales," *Oxford Economic Papers,* Series 2, Vol. XI (1959), pp. 282–90; J. R. Meyer, M. J. Peck, J. Stenason, and C. Zwick, *The Economics of Competition in the Transportation Industries* (Cambridge: Harvard University Press, 1959), p. 97.

and to date, evidence is lacking that economies of scale can lead to a monopolistic position or, for that matter, even an oligopolistic one in motor transport today.

Other Agencies

Economies of scale for pipe-line transportation are so similar to those of the railroads that no further discussion is necessary here. Shipping follows the pattern of motor transport, and no further development will be undertaken. Air transport possibly possesses sufficiently different features to warrant brief treatment.

Air-line transport, to date, has not been given the careful examination with regard to economies of scale that has been true of rail and motor transportation. The evidence seems to suggest that the pattern is quite similar to that of motor transport. The introduction of the very expensive jet airplanes does not appear to have resulted in any significant change in the situation. At present air lines have a rate of capital turnover of about once a year, which is lower than for motor carriers but higher than for industries like steel and petroleum.[13] Furthermore the operating ratios are characteristically high, like those of motor carriers.[14] However, the total investment necessary for the successful undertaking of domestic trunk-line service is much larger than that required for motor carriers. In other words, economies of scale are present at least to the extent that a moderately large enterprise seems to be essential to an assurance of success. One group of authors concludes that scale economies in air transportation stem from the decline in operating costs per available ton-mile or seat-mile with increases in the size of the plane, and from the decrease in costs per available ton-mile or seat-mile with the lengthened journey between plant stops. These economies seem to be realized to the full by medium-sized domestic trunk lines.[15]

[13] See Nelson Lee Smith, "Regulation of Returns to Transportation Agencies," *Law and Contemporary Problems,* "Transportation," Part I, Vol. XXIV, No. 4 (Autumn, 1959), p. 719.

[14] The position of the domestic trunk lines at the present time is somewhat anomalous. The rate of capital turnover is slower than it was in earlier years, but the operating ratio remains at about 90 per cent. At the same time, debt in 1964 comprised more than 60 per cent of the industry's total invested capital as compared with 28 per cent in 1954. Air Transport Association, *Air Transport Advisory* (Washington, D.C., April, 1965), p. 3. The relatively slow capital turnover, the high operating ratio, and the high debt ratio would seem to indicate some difficult problems of adjustment for air transport.

[15] Meyer *et al., op. cit.,* pp. 135–36. See also H. D. Koontz, "Domestic Air Line Self-Sufficiency: A Problem of Route Structure," *American Economic Review,* Vol. XLII, No. 1 (March, 1952), pp. 104–25. In his comment on this article, Professor J. P. Carter (*American Economic Review,* Vol. XLIII, No. 3 [June, 1953], pp. 368–73, and rejoinder by Koontz, pp. 373–77) points out the importance of the relationship of the size of the productive unit to the size of the market and emphasizes the failure of aircraft manufacturers

No studies of this sort are available for feeder-line service, but similar remarks would seem to hold true, although the size would be much smaller than for trunk lines.

COMPETITION VERSUS MONOPOLY IN TRANSPORT

The foregoing discussion of economies of scale in transportation has brought out the fact that evidence is lacking to warrant the judgment that a single enterprise for any one of the modes for the entire country can be supported on the grounds of economy of operations. All studies lead to the conclusion that the economies of scale are exhausted long before a size sufficient to encompass the entire market for the type of transport services supplied by a particular mode is reached. In other words, for transport services to be supplied economically, a number of separate undertakings are essential in each agency. In each case, they may vary in size and scope. Thus the minimum economical size for interterritorial motor freight carriers is larger than that required for intraterritorial operators; but beyond these minima, economies of scale do not seem to be important, as a result of which a number of carriers or firms may serve the same markets without ruinous effects. That is to say, markets can be shared by the competing firms just as in noncarrier industries. Similar remarks apply to water and air transport, although the larger minimum economical size for air trunk lines may restrict the number of competitors in such a way that oligopoly is the most likely market pattern. Railroads and pipe lines, however, fall into a different category.

Nature of Railroad Monopoly

During the railroad era it came to be recognized that unregulated competition among railroads was an unworkable means of establishing satisfactory prices and that monopoly in some form or another was bound to emerge in the end. Monopoly and monopoly pricing were inescapable features of railroad transport because of the economic structure of the railroads. In other words, they were what has come to be known as "natural" monopolies.

The word *natural,* as it is used in this connection, refers to the fact that monopoly emerges from the economic characteristics of the industry in question and that competition is forced to play a very

---

to make the adaptation satisfactorily. The resulting unused capacity leads easily to financial difficulties. This problem may be rearing its head in serious fashion for the trunk lines with their emphasis on the giant jets.

subordinate role in the fixation of prices to be charged for the particular type of services offered. As one economist puts it, with reference to railroads: "Competition fails to establish a normal level of rates sufficiently remunerative to attract the additional investments of capital that recurrently become necessary."[16]

There are several reasons why monopoly is natural to certain industries. Capital has to be invested in amounts which are large relative to the market opportunities available for the goods or services that are to be produced. Capital costs, therefore, form a relatively large part of the total costs of production; addition to the plant will involve a large proportionate increase in capital investment and will necessitate a large prospective increase in the market. As has already been pointed out, a railroad has to make large initial outlays to build a single-track line and acquire the necessary terminal facilities to operate it. When that plant is utilized to capacity, double-tracking will require a large additional investment, which cannot profitably be made unless there is a prospect of a large increase in traffic. Expansion of this type entails difficult problems of market anticipation because the facilities will have to be built well in advance of market opportunities. In the meantime the traffic which is available will have to bear the burden of keeping the railroad in operation until the new traffic has been built up. If, instead of double-tracking, a new railroad were to be built, an almost complete duplication of facilities would be necessary, and the immediately available traffic would be inadequate to give either road a profit. In addition, the economies of scale which could be obtained by a fuller utilization of facilities by more continuous movement of traffic in both directions would be unavailable. Similarly, withdrawal of facilities to adjust to a declining market is a slow and expensive process. In other words, adaptation to changing markets takes place in a decidedly discontinuous fashion.

Then there is the fact that much of the investment that has been made is specialized, both as to functions and as to markets. Railroad tracks are only useful where they are laid and cannot readily be turned to other areas if the markets shift. In addition, they have little use except for supplying railroad transportation to a geographically fixed area.

Natural monopolies are also characterized by a concomitance of production and consumption. That is, the services must be consumed in direct conjunction with the production facilities. This results in the absence of what is known as "shopper's technique." The consumer

---

[16] Eliot Jones, *Principles of Railway Transportation* (New York: the Macmillan Co., 1925), p. 91.

cannot shop around, because no other supply is readily available to him. He is forced to take the services offered by a particular supplier; otherwise, he must go without or move. The facilities of two suppliers are not available to him because it is too costly for both to supply the equipment necessary to be ready to serve. At the same time, producers can serve only those whom they are able to contact with their production facilities. The physical area served by the plant constitutes the limits of its market, and it cannot readily change those limits because of the extreme immobility of the plant.

This situation is most completely illustrated by public utilities such as electricity and natural gas. Technology necessitates the connection of the consumer's facilities with those of the producer, thereby depriving the former of any choice between one producer of a given service and another. This would not be altered even though two different companies were allowed to operate in the same area, because the consumer could not be connected to more than one of them at the same time. The result is that each buyer, in fact, constitutes a separate market for the utility, and in the absence of restriction such a utility could have a separate basis of charges for each and every buyer. In addition, with possibly minor exceptions, the commodities or services supplied cannot be stored by the consumer, as a consequence of which the supplier may be able to divide up even the market of an individual buyer into time segments; each buyer may, in fact, constitute a number of markets.

In other words, concomitance of production and consumption, together with relatively large amounts of investment in plant that is specialized both geographically and functionally, makes the presence of more than one producer in most markets economically wasteful. Thus, direct competition is absent in most of the markets, and readily available alternatives or substitutes are not usually present. For these reasons, it has long been recognized that direct competition over the entire range of output of natural monopolies is an unsatisfactory way of trying to secure reasonable prices. As a consequence, monopoly in particular markets has been accorded public sanction and even protection.

Railroads do not offer as complete an illustration of natural monopoly as do public utilities because the buyer of the services can, within limits, shift from one railroad to another without too much inconvenience to himself, although this is not so, even in a center served by more than one railroad, if his plant is located on a spur line. On the other hand, public utilities can easily be prevented from invading each others' markets by the refusal of public authorities to permit them to serve beyond designated boundaries. A limitation of this nature cannot be as completely imposed on railroads because, short of a single system for an entire region, competition at terminal points is unavoidable. Thus the natural monopoly features of railroads are harder to control than are those of public utilities; and with the extensive competitive groupings resulting from earlier policies, railroads have always presented a serious problem of reconciling natural monopoly with direct competition in the same industry.

The foregoing characteristics of rail transport have not changed under the impact of the growth of the newer agencies. What has changed is the alternatives that are available to consumers. Uncontrolled or over-all competition among railroads today would be as uneconomical as it ever was. The question of competition among railroads rests on very different grounds from the question of competition among motor carriers, water carriers, or air carriers. Whether these agencies should be dealt with in the same way as railroads will be discussed later.

Ruinous Competition

One of the consequences of natural monopoly is that over-all competition among those of the same type is ruinous. For example, if two or more electrical utilities were allowed to compete for the business of every customer, it would be necessary for them to duplicate their distribution systems at least, and this is the most expensive part of the supply facilities. This would result in continuous excess capacity, because all of the productive capacity of all of the companies could never be utilized at the same time. Because of the high proportion of fixed costs, each would endeavor to utilize its unused capacity by sales at prices that would cover only the extra or out-of-pocket costs. This would drive all prices down, so that none of the competitors would be able to cover their full costs. The end result of this would be the emergence of a single firm. It was the recognition of this fact that led to regulation under which public utilities came to be recognized as natural monopolies and competition was deliberately restricted by public authority. It should be noted, however, that competition between gas and electrical utilities is not ruinous. Over a wide range the services are not readily substitutable. Where substitution is possible on a price basis, either one may be allowed to lower its rates so as to obtain business and thereby utilize its unused capacity. Many off-peak rates are sanctioned for the purpose of meeting competition.

Railroads are faced with the threat of ruinous competition among themselves because they are natural monopolies. The problem has been more difficult to control in the railroad field, as already noted, because of the early competitive construction of railroads and also because of competing routes, competing markets, and competing areas of production. Certainly at the present time, freedom of entry of railroads into the market areas of other railroads would not be conducive to economical rail transport, nor would it be in the public interest.

The essence of ruinous competition is that over-all competition between two or more firms, so that each endeavors to serve the same markets, cannot survive because of the continued and unavoidable presence of excess capacity. Capacity cannot be adapted to the market because of the fixed and specialized nature of the facilities. In this manner ruinous competition differs from predatory competition, which is designed to drive competitors out of business by tactics that are inimical to competition and which are not necessary to the practice of competition on an economical basis. This does not mean that healthy and economical competition will never drive out competitors or be injurious to any of them. All competition is injurious to competitors or threatens to be so, in the sense that it eliminates the inefficient and limits the rewards the successful firms can receive. This is the heart of competition—the incentive to strive for profits, and the compulsion to go somewhere else if they are not forthcoming. This procedure may be hard on competitors since they win only if they can stay in the race. The fact that they may lose, however, is not indicative of ruinous competition. The latter emerges only when competition cannot economically survive regardless of the size of the market.

ORGANIZATION OF TRANSPORT

The foregoing discussion of the economies of scale as they affect the various modes of transport indicates that economical organization within the modes calls for many different firms in each. At the same time, the different economic characteristics exhibited by the separate modes point up the need for different organizational arrangements among them—railroads, for example, requiring a pattern that must give recognition to the natural monopoly features of them. Thus the evidence indicates that there must be a number of railroad systems—a large number if Professor Healy's evaluation is correct—if there is to be economical rail transport. These, however, should be established so that each system has a monopoly of rail transport of the region it serves, insofar as this can be done; otherwise the difficulties of competition among natural monopolies will persist. Competition may be pervasive for the transport system as a whole; it cannot be so among railroads. The economic structure of them prevents this today just as it did before the rise of the new modes of transportation.

This also has important implications for the problem of inter-agency ownership and operation. If the economies of scale limit the economical size of railroads, then economies arising from the extension of ownership by this mode into another are very unlikely to emerge. This is not a conclusive argument against interagency ownership, that is, ownership of one mode by another, but it does seem clear that the reason for permitting it will have to be based on grounds other than the economies of scale. Transport companies may be in the public interest as a means for providing more economical service, but it is by no means self-evident that this is so. More extensive discussion of this problem will be presented in a later chapter.

THE THEORY OF PRICING

INTRODUCTION

Price theory as it relates to the economy and to public welfare deals with the economic principles that bear upon the most efficient utilization of economic resources. In the broadest sense, all economic analysis is concerned with pricing problems. Price theory is the focal point because it is through prices and the price system that, in some way or another, economic resources are mobilized and utilized. The reason for this is that prices measure the basis upon which alternatives are offered, and through them the rationing of scarce goods takes place. A systematic and thorough presentation would pursue price theory through many varied ramifications. Thus, it would deal with the reactions of the individual firm under varying situations and assumptions, with the problems of the price level, with employment, and with the distribution of economic resources, together with the implications of these for economic welfare.

Price theory as it relates to the firm may endeavor to analyze the forces at work in the pricing of products, on the assumption that a firm seeks to maximize its profits under the circumstances with which it is faced, or describe how it would behave if it tried to achieve this end. This same analysis may describe and appraise the processes by which a firm undertakes to price its products where the pricing of them is one of the tasks which, by necessity, the firm must perform.

Pricing and prices are also tools of public regulation. An analysis of the processes in this setting is somewhat more circumscribed in its purpose and potentialities than either of the aspects mentioned above. Public welfare is the general focus of interest, but this also means that the policies which are adopted must be in keeping with the assumptions of private enterprise. It is the function of public regulation to establish the conditions within which private management may exericse discretion in the conduct of its affairs, and it is therefore necessary for public authority to recognize the basic requirements for the survival of private enterprise. Consequently, price theory as it is applied to public regulation must endeavor to develop standards or gauges which can be utilized to set the limits within which private management may be allowed to pursue its own interests and to establish the economic criteria for the legal framework of an acceptable private enterprise system.

CLASSIFICATION AND CHARACTERISTICS OF MARKETS

Market situations fall into a number of different categories that lie between the limits of perfect competition at the one extreme and complete monopoly at the other. These limits and the intermediate market patterns are economic rather than legal and are set up for purposes of analysis. For this reason, they do not necessarily establish a classification into which particular industries or firms may fit, although some may do so. More often the market structures in which firms conduct their activities embrace more than one analytic category. As a result, it becomes impossible to describe the behavior of these firms by any one descriptive title; and as will be shown later, it is usually not possible to speak of an industry as falling completely within any category, even though it may be primarily in one of them. These groupings or categories, then, provide an analytic framework with which the behavior of a firm may be examined to the extent that its activities fall within the particular classification.

Competition

Competition has a number of different meanings; but in whatever way it is used, it refers to the market situation in which no producer is able to control the supply of a commodity so as to be able to influence price to his own advantage. Thus, competition always denotes complete substitutability of one seller's commodity for that of another seller, together with the inability of any one seller acting separately to influence the price of the commodity he is offering for sale so as to enhance his revenue. There are varying degrees of competition, however. These may be classified as perfect, pure, and imperfect.

Perfect competition is a strictly analytic concept and can never exist in fact. Nevertheless, it provides the standard or gauge for the most economical allocation of resources because it assumes the conditions under which alternatives can be precisely evaluated and instantaneously realized. That is, perfect competition assumes that there are no obstacles of any kind to the allocation of economic resources to their most important uses. Therefore a number of assumptions underlie the model of perfect competition.

First, it is assumed that the products which are being offered for sale are homogeneous, so that there is perfect substitutability among them. Second, buyers and sellers possess complete knowledge of the conditions of the market at all times. Third, there is a sufficient number of buyers and sellers, so that no one buyer or seller can exercise a significant influence on the market or by his behavior influence the market in such a way that he gains an advantage by his actions. Fourth, no kinds of restraints are imposed upon the operation of economic forces, either by law or by the actions of buyers and sellers. Fifth, there is complete mobility of all economic resources, so that there can be complete and immediate transfer from one type of production to another and from one area of production to another.

The competitive requirement of mobility of economic resources has its legal as well as its economic aspects. For resources to be legally mobile, it must be possible, as far as the law is concerned, that they be free to move from one use to another and from one market to another. There must be freedom to move the physical facilities according to the wishes of the producers, or to convert them or divert them to other uses. Similarly, the decision for investment or disinvestment must be left to the enterprisers. In other words, what is called freedom of entry, which also carries with it freedom of exit, is one of the fundamental requirements of a truly competitive structure. Economic mobility of resources requires that they be readily transferable to uses other than those in which they are presently engaged. This may be accomplished by the physical adaptation of facilities to new markets, either by technological changes resulting in the production of new or different commodities and services, or by a geographic shift of plant or facilities to tap other markets.

Pure competition is a less restrictive category than perfect competition, in that it does not assume that the forces of competition are able to work without impediments. For example, it recognizes that perfect knowledge of markets is not possible and that instantaneous mobility can never be achieved. It does assume, however, that buyers and sellers cannot influence the market to their advantage; that is, they must accept the market as they find it and act accordingly. Furthermore, buyers and sellers are supposed to act independently and not in collusion for the purpose of exercising control. Pure competition may be said to characterize all market situations where both buyers and sellers act independently and where each takes the market as something to which he must adapt himself.

The third category of competition, namely, imperfect competition, does not have a universally accepted meaning. To some, it represents a condition of competition that involves more serious departures from perfect competition than does pure competition; these arise from rigidities in the economic system which are the result of technological conditions or institutional arrangements. The position of buyers or sellers is still the same, however, in that they must take the market and prices as data. Thus, agriculture, according to this view, would be characterized as operating under imperfect competition because of the conditions of immobility that seem to be ever present.

Some prefer to regard imperfect competition as arising from various kinds of restrictions that may be imposed by agreements, price leadership, differentiated products, and so forth. According to this view, imperfect competition means that producers, by deliberate action of some kind on their part, influence the behavior of the market in their favor. If imperfect competition is regarded in this light, it partakes of some of the characteristics of monopoly and should be viewed as a subcategory of it. If imperfect competition is used to characterize departures from competition which still leave buyers and sellers in the position of having to take the market as datum, then it is very similar to pure competition.

Monopoly

Monopoly may conveniently be defined as that market situation in which a seller has sufficient control over the supply of a commodity to enable him to exercise influence on the behavior of the market to his advantage; that is, he can control supply so as to be able to influence the price of the product to his own advantage. This does not mean that the seller can control the market without regard to the effect of his actions on the consumer, or without regard to the effect of his actions on the price he receives or the quantity of the commodity he can sell. The discretion he is able to exercise will depend on the elasticity of the demand for the product. However, insofar as a seller can act so as to influence the price of the product in his favor, he behaves as a monopolist and is able to exercise monopoly power; this may be very great or very small, depending upon the circumstances.

The most complete form of monopoly arises in the case of a commodity or service for which there is no ready substitute. Possibly the leading illustrations of this in the United States today are to be found in urban water supply, electricity, natural gas, and telephone service. The buyer of the commodities or services of these industries is typically dependent upon one supplier, and there are no readily available substitutes for them. Monopoly may also be the result of collusion or agreement among sellers, and if the commodity involved does not permit ready substitutability, it will be possible for the supplier to exercise appreciable monopoly power. More frequently, monopoly power arises from control over supply for which substitutability is, for various reasons, only somewhat limited. In this sense, monopoly characterizes the markets of a wide variety of commodities and services.

Monopolistic Competition

This is a term which has come to be applied to markets in which the products that are offered for sale are of essentially the same type but differ slightly from each other by virtue of trade-mark, brand, type of wrapping, color, style, or some other distinguishable feature. This means that the products are quite readily and directly substitutable for one another. The differentiation gives a uniqueness to each product which makes it possible for each producer to enjoy some distinction for his product, thereby being able to exercise some control over the conditions of sale. To the extent that he is able to do so, the producer enjoys monopoly power. To the extent that the buyer finds ready substitutes, competition prevails. Monopolistic competition commonly refers, therefore, to market situations in which sellers would not be able to exercise control over the market for their product if it were not for the differentiation they are able to introduce. Monopolistic competition represents a departure from pure competition as a result of the uniqueness which a producer is able to give to a product or service that would otherwise be the same as that of his competitors.

Oligopoly

When sellers in a market are few, the market is classified as an oligopoly. Under conditions of oligopoly, no firm in an industry is likely to ignore its rivals' reactions to the policies it adopts. The importance of each seller in the market is such that any one of them, acting alone, can influence it in a significant way. In other words, each seller must recognize the fact that his own behavior will have a positive effect on the market when he is deciding upon the course of action to pursue. Oligopoly assumes independence of decision on the part of each of the sellers as well as homogeneity of product. If there is collusion or agreement, oligopoly becomes monopoly. Fewness of sellers does not refer to absolute numbers but rather to the situation in which a seller must recognize that his actions will affect competitors and the market. Oligopoly resembles competition is that no producer can act independently of the market; it resembles monopoly in that there is no market for the producer that is independent of his actions.

PRICING FOR THE DIFFERENT MARKET STRUCTURES

It was pointed out in the previous section that the analytic categories of markets do not necessarily establish a classification into which particular industries or firms may fit. In fact, most firms in modern industry fall into more than one group, and this is certainly true for transportation. It is necessary, nevertheless, to deal with price theory as it applies to the "pure" market categories because theory cannot comprehend them all at once. Examination of the prevailing conditions, however, may indicate the dominant situation. For example, one firm may be able to differentiate its product from that of another, thereby introducing an element of monopoly. The differentiation may be so slight, however, that the customer is more price- than product-conscious, with the result that the competitive forces exert much greater influence than the monopoly ones.

Pricing under Competition

Under conditions of competition, no seller is able to do anything about the prices he receives. He either takes them or leaves them; in other words, the market prices are data to him. His problem, therefore, is to adapt himself and his production policies to the market. The market prices themselves are the result of the interaction of demand and supply, each being determined by the independent decisions of all buyers and sellers. As already noted, competition is never perfect, but to the extent that competition is effective in any market, the principles that govern pricing under perfect competition are operative.

Under perfect competition, costs and prices will always equal each other because of the ability of producers to adapt their outputs to the market, because of the inducements to do so, and because of the necessity of doing so. A producer will expand his output as long as his marginal cost is less than the price he can obtain for the additional unit because of the extra profit he can secure. Similarly, he will contract his output when marginal cost exceeds the price that he gets for the last unit, because it is unprofitable for him to produce that unit. Price will be equal to marginal cost, or vice versa.

For the individual producer, marginal cost and average cost of output are equal when average cost is at the minimum. The reason for this is that when marginal cost is below average cost, as expansion of output takes place, rising marginal cost approaches average cost, while the latter falls. When marginal cost begins to exceed average cost, the latter will commence to rise. The most efficient level of output, therefore, is when average cost is at the minimum. No firm can continue to operate indefinitely if average cost exceeds price, because it would then be operating at a loss. Under perfect competition the adjustment would take place instantaneously. Similarly, no firm can continue to operate

FIGURE 7–1

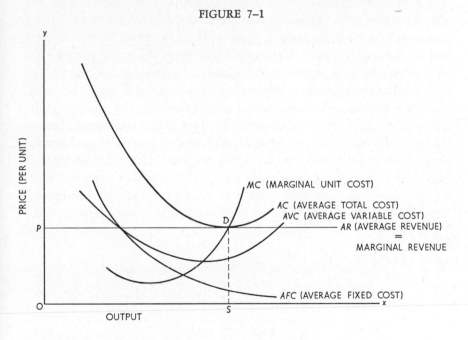

with price exceeding average costs, because the extra profits would induce the supply of additional output until average cost and price equalized. Because marginal cost equals price and price is the same for all competitors, and because marginal cost and average cost are equal under competition, it follows that marginal cost and average cost under competition are the same for all competitors, and each firm is of the optimum size and is producing its optimum output. (See Figure 7–1.)

The term *cost,* as used in the foregoing discussion, means all the inducements that are necessary to attract resources into a particular line of production. It thus has a different meaning from what it has in accounting and also is broader in scope, in that it includes the entrepreneurial income and earnings on proprietary capital that are necessary to maintain the enterprise. Average cost refers to the average cost of a homogeneous output; the assumption is that the firm is a single-product enterprise. The concept does not apply, therefore, to a multiple-product firm. Indeed, average cost for the entire output has little, if any, meaning when applied to different products of a firm. Unfortunately, this is too infrequently recognized in business practice and in the administration of public policy.

Pricing under Monopoly

Monopoly pricing differs from competitive pricing in that the seller does not take prices as given. Instead, he is an active and direct participant in the price-making process. If he increases his output of a product for a given market, the effect will be to lower the price of the total which he sells in the market; and if he reduces his output, the price for the entire amount he puts on the market will rise. Therefore, when the monopolist considers the question of expanding output, he will look to the relation of his marginal cost to the additional revenue which he will receive from an additional unit of output, the additional revenue being known as the "marginal revenue." He will therefore adjust his output to that point where marginal cost equals marginal revenue. By this procedure, profits are maximized, or losses are minimized, depending upon whether price is high enough to cover all costs. (See Table 7–1.)

TABLE 7–1

Units of Output	Marginal Unit Cost	Selling Price per Unit	Total Revenue	Marginal Revenue
100	$80	$100.00	$10,000.00	. . . . .
101	81	99.90	10.089.90	$89.90
102	82	99.80	10,179.60	89.70
103	83	99.00	10,197.00	17.40

Under monopoly, price will exceed marginal cost because the marginal revenue curve, which is derived from the average revenue or demand curve, must lie below the demand curve. That is, the point of intersection of the marginal cost curve and the marginal revenue curve will be below the average revenue curve. It follows that price will never be equal to minimum average cost for the plant or the firm. This does not mean that monopoly pricing always results in profits. It may also result in losses because it is possible that the average revenue curve may fall below the average cost curve. The monopolist, nevertheless, by adjusting his output to the amount set by the intersection of the marginal revenue and marginal cost curves, will be able to maximize his profits or minimize his losses. (See Figure 7–2.)

FIGURE 7–2

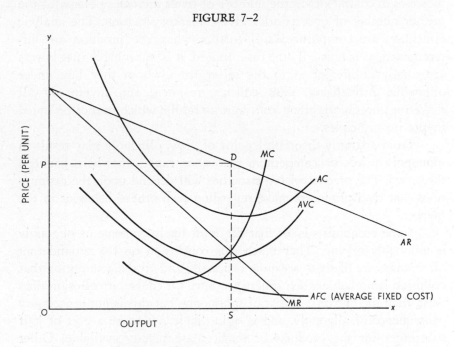

Pricing under Oligopoly

Pricing under oligopoly does not lend itself to the precise formulation that is possible with competition and monopoly. The determination of marginal revenue depends upon the unknown reactions of rivals, and the determination of marginal cost depends on the producer's assumptions regarding those unknown reactions. It is not possible, therefore, to formulate a general theory of oligopoly pricing. Professor Stigler points out that not even all of the important situations can be enumerated.[1] "There is no stated body of economic opinion as to the pattern that market behavior can be expected to take among oligopolists."[2] Even if one assumes the complete standardization of products among rivals, the solution to the problem of pricing in markets

[1] G. J. Stigler, *The Theory of Price* (New York: Macmillan Co., 1946), p. 269.

[2] Alex Hunter, "The Control of Monopoly," *Lloyds Bank Review* (London), October, 1956, p. 23.

supplied by a few large sellers depends upon the assumptions each makes regarding the reactions of others to his moves. The observer can tell what the actual particular pricing situation will be only if he knows the assumptions upon which the sellers are proceeding. Even the sellers may not know what assumptions to make or may not even be clear on the ones that are implicit in their decisions. The problem increases in complexity as the number of rivals increases because of the greater number of uncertainties in the market situation. The analytic difficulties are complicated still further when the products are differentiated, as is normally the case. Indeed, it is improbable that buyers are totally indifferent as to the seller from whom they buy under oligopoly. Advertising, sales policies, research, and investment all make for uncertainties that contribute to results which cannot be stated in precise principles.

From a strictly theoretical point of view, oligopoly may result in monopoly prices or competitive prices, or range anywhere between these two. The precise pricing structure will depend upon the assumptions that rival producers make regarding each others' behavior in the market.[3]

Some economists insist that the most likely outcome of oligopoly is monopoly pricing. They reach this conclusion on the ground that oligopolists are likely to act quite rationally and on the assumption that collusion is probable when sellers are few.[4] Of course, if collusion does exist, then the outcome is that of monopoly, but this is not a necessary consequence of oligopoly, and is quite likely not to be a part of it if substitutes for the products or services are readily available. Other economists maintain that no one can predict market behavior under oligopoly and that existing theory provides few norms for evaluating the effects of oligopoly on public interest. Perhaps all that can be said is that the most significant feature of oligopoly is uncertainty, which can well mean that prices deviate from competitive ones no more than they do under imperfect competition.

The foregoing discussion is based upon the assumption of a complete standardization of rivals' products, which, strictly speaking, must eliminate even trade names. Consequently, when fewness of sellers also involves differentiated products, evaluation of pricing results is even

[3] For an exposition of this, see E. H. Chamberlin, *The Theory of Monopolistic Competition* (6th ed.; Cambridge: Harvard University Press, 1950), chaps. ii and v. For a general summary of the theory, see John F. Due, *Intermediate Economic Analysis* (rev. ed.; Homewood, Ill.: Richard D. Irwin, Inc., 1953), chap. x.

[4] See G. W. Stocking and M. W. Watkins, *Monopoly and Free Enterprise* (New York: Twentieth Century Fund, Inc., 1951), chap. iv.

more difficult. Differentiated products introduce an element of monopoly for each seller, and to the extent that the differentiation is really effective, the seller will be able to charge a monopoly price because the market under such circumstances is really not an oligopoly but a monopoly instead. The fact that the products are only differentiated, however, must mean that the monopoly power is very tenuous; therefore the oligopoly influence will predominate. Obviously, the outcome can be predicted with even less certainty than when the products are standardized, but it would not be correct to assume that the results will be socially disadvantageous.

Pricing under Monopolistic Competition

When sellers are fairly large in number and the products are differentiated, then, as already noted, the market is described as one of monopolistic competition. The resulting price, theoretically, will be higher than it would be if perfect competition prevailed. Selling costs, advertising, and so forth add to the cost of production, and these would not be present under perfect competition. On the other hand, markets may be broadened by such activities, and competition may become keener, with the result that the actual price, as distinct from the theoretical one, may be lower than it would be under perfect or pure competition. Neither of the latter are even possible, in fact, over a wide range of products with which the consumer is faced today. How great a departure from the strictly theoretical competitive price will occur depends upon the extent of the monopoly power enjoyed by the producer. If his product is significantly unique or unusual, he may enjoy such market advantages as to gain, temporarily at least, profits well above the competitive level. Just how much this may be in any situation is difficult to measure because the costs included in making the measurement have to be the alternative ones, which cannot be ascertained with any certainty.

THE COMPETITIVE MODEL AS A STANDARD FOR PUBLIC POLICY

Markets in the real world, in contrast to the analytic classification of them, quite commonly display the characteristics of some or almost all of the different kinds at the same time. No real market exhibits or can exhibit all the necessary features of perfect competition. A considerable range of production falls within the category of pure competition, especially if this be extended to include imperfect competition.

Departures from pure competition, however, seem to be more prevalent than strict adherence to it, so that the equilibrium of perfect competition is unlikely to be achieved in practice.

Despite this, the foundation of public policy in establishing the rules for the conduct of private enterprise must be the competitive model. The model for monopoly or any variation of it cannot serve as the basis of an economical public policy because it lacks the standards by which to gauge the economical allocation of resources. Even the model for an economically efficient system of socialist production will be based on competitive principles.[5] Moreover, a private enterprise system assumes the possibility of establishing rules and procedures of public policy that will make competition workable.

One of the major problems of public policy is to establish rules for pricing within which private enterprise is permitted to make its own decisions. Where pure competition prevails, it is not necessary to set up pricing rules for producers or sellers; the market takes care of that, because there is no inducement for a seller to deviate from the market, and no harm would be done even if he attempted to do so. As has already been noted, however, pure competition does not obtain over a wide range of economic activity. Individual producers may be able to behave in such a way as to injure other producers and competition by uneconomical and/or predatory action; they may also be able to exploit the buyer because of the inability of the latter to obtain satisfactory substitutes within a reasonable price range. Public authority intervenes in order to achieve as much as possible the advantages of competition by reducing the disadvantages that may arise as a result of the departures from it. For this purpose, no set of rules can be devised that is uniformly applicable to the widely varying market situations the modern industrial structure presents.

In devising rules, public authority must therefore give recognition to the different situations that are encountered. For industry in general this usually entails endeavors to eliminate practices designed to impede or limit competition. Sometimes it involves the determination of minimum prices below which sellers may not be permitted to go in offering their products for sale. On other occasions, it may be the relationship of the prices charged to different buyers that comes under scrutiny. In any case, competitive standards and competitive cost-price relationships will be used for evaluating the behavior of the firms. In the field of public utilities, where monopoly is virtually complete, the problem is

[5] See B. E. Lippincott (ed.), *On the Economic Theory of Socialism* (Minneapolis: University of Minnesota Press, 1938).

to limit prices, so that only fair profits are received, while efficiency is being maintained. Here again, the concepts are competitive ones, even though the application of them to markets where competition is so thoroughly lacking presents great complexities. In transport, both of the foregoing situations are encountered, with the result that definite monopoly features are mixed with highly competitive ones in a way that requires the application of both monopoly and competitive controls at the same time. Yet, again, the starting point for a formulation of public policy, if it is to achieve an economical transport system, must be the competitive model. The application of competitive principles to transport pricing and policy is a difficult task, however, because of the diverse economic characteristics of the industries supplying the services, and because of the diverse and complex cost features exhibited by them. Nevertheless the cost considerations in the pricing and production policies of transport are of the same types that are faced by industry in general, and an economical transport policy must take the competitive norm as its point of departure.

The problems of deviation of economic activity from the competitive model arise principally from the complexities of costs of production. Competition assumes an adaptability of costs to market situations, such that marginal costs and price are equal for the units of the various products. This supposes that the cost of each unit of output is readily identifiable and ascertainable, and that marginal cost times the total output equals total cost. Costs of production for a wide range of industry, however, are not readily adjusted to changing rates of output, nor are all of them traceable to particular products or services. It is to the identification of costs that we now turn our attention.

COSTS AND THE PRICING PROCESS

The relationship of costs to output and prices is one of the most important factors affecting the behavior of business and the formulation and administration of public policy, and is one of the most significant aspects of price theory. Management must constantly keep costs in mind in making its decisions, because it is the margin between costs and income which constitutes the profit which business seeks to obtain. Regulatory agencies, whether they are engaged directly or indirectly in the control of prices, have to resort to cost as a guide to many of their decisions, because the deviations of prices from relevant costs are indications of the imperfections in the operation of competitive forces. Costs, especially under modern conditions of production, are an extremely complex phenomenon, however. They vary widely under differing circumstances; all of them cannot be attributed specifically to each of the many products turned out by modern plants; and they cannot even be calculated precisely for a given plant or firm for a given period of operations. Moreover, the cost considerations which are significant for one situation may be different from those which must be taken into account in another instance.

Costs and the Rate of Output

Costs of production may be placed into two broad categories according to the way they are related to varying rates of output, or to different units or groups of commodities or services that are produced. In the first category the costs are classified as fixed and variable; in the second, they are specific, and joint or common. The first group will be discussed in this section, the second in the following one.

Fixed costs are those costs which, for a given plant and given production period, are unaffected by the rate of output. A change in the scale of operations will bring about a change in the total of the fixed costs; but if this change in scale does not take place, the fixed costs will remain the same for the period. As a consequence, the average fixed cost per unit of output will vary with the number of units produced and will decrease as the output for the period increases. Interest on the funds invested in capital equipment is a fixed cost. Obsolescence of plant and equipment is largely unrelated to volume of production. Fixed assets wear out through use; but they also deteriorate as a result of the passage of time, the effects of weather, and other factors not related to rate of output. A considerable part of depreciation is, therefore, a fixed cost.[6]

Fixed costs must be calculated for a particular period of time, because in the long run all costs are variable. Once costs are incurred and can be recovered only by the sale of the products that are derived from the services acquired by those costs and are not influenced by the rate of use of the services, they are fixed until the time arrives for the decision to renew the costs or not to renew them. It is not possible to say whether the cost of a particular type of service represents a fixed cost without examination of the particular situation. Payment for labor

[6] Fixed costs are frequently called "overhead costs," especially by economists. The use of the term in this way causes some confusion, however, because of its use by accountants to mean a different thing. Accountants use the term *overhead* to cover all expenses which are not directly attributable to output; thus, overhead costs in accounting are the indirect costs. As such, however, they include both fixed and variable expenses, because accounting classification does not typically separate the fixed from the variable expenses.

may be a fixed cost for a particular contract, if the contract calls for a monthly wage, for example, and must be paid for the month, regardless of the amount of time of the employee that is utilized. The investment in Hoover Dam is a fixed cost for the useful life of the dam, which may be a hundred years or more. Thus the fixed costs of a firm will vary, depending upon the time period which is assumed, the fixed costs for a month being different from the fixed costs for a year or five years. Ascertaining what they are for a particular period also involves estimates of the prospective output of the investment in question. If equipment is estimated to be usable at full capacity for five years, the fixed cost may be calculated on that basis; but if obsolescence occurs in three years, the fixed cost per year and per unit of output will turn out to be greater than the estimate. Uncertainties such as this make precise cost calculations impossible. Under the most favorable circumstances, average fixed cost per unit of output can be obtained for a given period of time only when the period has ended, because it depends upon the total output for the period. When the period of time used for making the calculation is shorter than the life of the assets which give rise to the fixed costs, precise calculation is impossible. Reliance will have to be placed on estimates made on assumptions regarding the future. Because fixed costs are unaffected by the rate of output, they do not enter into economic calculations for output or for prices. They are therefore called "noneconomic" costs.

Variable costs constitute the second type that is related to the rate of output. These are the costs that fluctuate directly with the rate of output. When the rate of output is increased, the total variable cost increases; and when that rate is decreased, the total variable cost diminishes. The variable costs for a given period of production are those which arise during that period as the result of utilizing resources. If resources are not used, there are no variable costs. A large part of the costs of labor, raw materials, selling, and advertising, for example are variable costs. Depreciation that is the result of use is also a variable. A large part of maintenance and repairs falls into the same category. For a given production period the variable costs constitute the controllable part of the costs of production, for they can be discontinued with shutdowns, or increased with increased rate of output.

Although fixed and variable costs can readily be differentiated by definition, it is frequently very difficult to make an accurate distinction between them in practice. For example, the amount of depreciation which arises from use and the amount which is independent of the rate of output do not seem to be determinable except within wide limits. Quantitative relationships between fixed and variable costs in industry have been the subject of considerable study, but the results obtained so far have been somewhat inconclusive. Railroads were one of the first industries to be analyzed in quantitative terms. It is frequently stated that two thirds of the costs of a railroad operating at normal capacity are fixed, and one third is variable. This means that the controllable element of costs for any railroad plant, for any particular period of time, is small relative to the total costs. The reliability of these estimates is a matter of considerable dispute, and at best they would be valid only for an assumed rate of output. This problem will be discussed at greater length in the next chapter.

The quantitative relationship of fixed to variable costs in manufacturing industries varies widely. The proportion of fixed costs is considerably less, however, than it is for railroads. The United States Steel Corporation estimated that fixed costs were 25 per cent of the total in February, 1939, when the plants were operating at nearly 55 per cent of capacity. This means that fixed costs are somewhat less than 20 per cent of the total costs when operations are at 90 per cent of capacity. If this is a reasonably accurate estimate, then fixed costs at capacity operation are a relatively small part of the total.[7]

This estimate seems to be at variance with the common belief that fixed costs are a significant part of the total costs when a steel plant is operating at capacity. It also contradicts the contention, frequently advanced by management, that sizable price concessions are made to obtain large orders because of the opportunity thereby afforded to spread the fixed costs. It seems probable that in the past, business has tended to overestimate the relative importance of fixed costs for a particular production period. The rather common practice of using the "straight-line" method of depreciation is an illustration of this. To the extent that fixed costs are overestimated, differential pricing based on the distinction between fixed and variable costs may be overdone. The element of judgment, however, especially in allocating costs among accounting periods, looms so large in the picture that a precise separation of fixed and variable costs is not possible.

Traceability of Costs

Just as some costs are related to the rate of output while others are independent of it, so some costs are attributable to specific units of

[7] Temporary National Economic Committee, Monograph No. 41, *Price Discrimination in Steel* (Washington, D.C.: U.S. Government Printing Office, 1941), pp. 31–32.

output, while others are not. Most firms produce more than one product. When this is the case, there will be costs which will be incurred specifically for each of the products and therefore are directly traceable to those products. These are known as specific costs. Under such circumstances, however, many of the costs of production are not specifically incurred for a particular product. These are known as "joint" and "common" costs. Costs are joint when the creation of one product unavoidably results in the output of another one. The familiar example is beef and hides. The raising of an animal for beef inevitably results in the production of a hide, and most of the costs incurred in rearing the animal cannot be traced to either product. The prices at which each of the two products will sell cannot be related to its costs of production, because the joint costs are attributable to both, not to either one specifically.

True joint costs, by definition, require that the joint products be forthcoming in fixed proportions and that there cannot be variations in the proportions resulting from variations in the costs. To the extent that the variability in proportions is impossible, there is no way the joint costs can be traced to the separate products. It is frequently held that true joint costs are rare and that some variability in proportions is nearly always possible. When that is so, the marginal costs of each product are ascertainable; and therefore, within the range of variability, the total cost attributable to each can be calculated.[8] It is more probable that variability over the total range of output is not possible, and to the extent that this is so, the costs outside the range of variability are joint. A calf is always born with a hide, and at that point the carcass and the hide are joint products.

Common costs are similar to joint costs in that they are incurred for the production of a number of different products, but the use of the resources to create one commodity does not unavoidably result in the production of a different one. The proportions of the different kinds of commodities turned out by a plant may be varied, frequently over a wide range. Changes in the proportions in which these are produced may result in variations in the common costs. Careful examination of these variations and experimentation with different proportions of outputs may make it possible to trace a part of these common costs to a particular type of product. Practically, however, there are serious limitations to this procedure. A considerable portion of the common costs

[8] Stigler, *op. cit.*, p. 306; see also Jacob Viner, "Cost," *Encyclopedia of the Social Sciences* (New York: The Macmillan Co., 1931) Vol. IV, pp. 466–75.

cannot be traced directly to the product. These costs are therefore non-traceable and give rise to the same problem of cost allocation as joint costs.

Whatever the actual situation may be with regard to joint costs, common costs are prevalent in almost every line of production. Variations in the proportions of the output may be practicable in the short run, although frequently this is not feasible. Plant facilities may be established such that variations in the proportions of the output of the various products may not affect the total costs of the facilities that are used in common. Electricity supplied before midnight is, economically, a different product from that which is supplied after midnight. The proportions of output of the two may vary, yet the same plant produces both; the capacity that is created to produce the premidnight supply inevitably results in the capacity to produce after midnight. The plant is used in common for both products, but the allocation of the plant costs between the two is not possible on the basis of traceability. Similarly, when a railroad supplies transportation in one direction, it unavoidably supplies it in the other direction. Over a wide range of production, common costs that are not joint in the strictest sense are not distributable among the products in any traceable way, and the average cost of each of the various products cannot be ascertained.[9]

In this connection, and adding to the complications of ascertaining actual costs, it should be borne in mind that fixed and variable costs, on the one hand, and joint and common costs, on the other, are not mutually exclusive categories. Fixed costs may be specific, or they may be joint and common. The same remarks apply to variable costs. It is often stated that fixed costs belong to the business as a whole and that all variable costs are traceable to particular outputs. This is not true. The fixed costs of railroad passenger cars belong to the passenger service, not to the freight. Variable costs incurred in moving a train in one direction and bringing it back are partially joint to both movements.

Costs and Decision Making

Under perfect competition, costs always equal prices, marginal cost and minimum average cost being equal and the same as price. All of the costs are directly identifiable with the products; costs and output of the individual firm are immediately adjustable to the price which the firm must accept as datum. These precise relationships between particular products and costs will not obtain, however, where competition departs from the model of perfect competition.

[9] Due, *op. cit.,* chap. xi. See n. 6, Chap. 8, below.

Fixed costs, because the amount of them is invariable for a given period of production, will be incurred whether there is any output or not. They will not, therefore, enter into the decision of management on how much to produce, because they are independent of that decision. The problem is to recover as much of the fixed costs as possible from the sale of the products. In other words, the economical thing for a firm to do is to ignore its fixed costs when deciding on its production and pricing policies. If it can recover only part of them, it will be better off than to refuse to take this course of action; if it can more than recover them, so much the better for the firm.

A firm can exercise control over its variable costs, and it is on these costs that its decisions for a given production period will have to rest. If sales will only just cover the variable costs, the decision whether to produce is really a matter of indifference; but if sales will more than cover variable costs, then the economical decision will be to undertake production, because the difference between the sales price and the variable costs will contribute toward covering the fixed costs. In other words, if the firm acts economically, it will not consider average total cost in making its decisions. Average total unit costs are not, therefore, a bench mark for policy decisions, because for a given period the variable costs are the only controllable element in them; the fixed costs are unavoidable for the period, regardless of the volume of output.

Average variable costs and average total costs can be ascertained for the units of a homogeneous output. These averages, however, are not obtainable when joint and common costs are present. To the extent that these are part of the fixed costs of a firm, it is not possible to ascertain the precise fixed cost per unit of output; and to the extent that they are part of the variable costs, it is not possible to obtain the precise variable unit cost. The only precise cost that can be ascertained for a particular product is the specific variable cost. This sets the minimum price below which the firm cannot afford to sell, but it may also be true that production of a particular product may be warranted if it can be sold at any price above this minimum.

It follows from this that pricing on the basis of average costs is not the appropriate basis for decision making. First of all, such pricing includes fixed costs in the calculation. To refuse sales because they will not cover some arbitrary share of fixed costs results in a loss of net revenue if there is unused capacity. In the second place, for multiproduct firms, price and output decisions based on average cost require an arbitrary allocation of joint and common costs. If the price which can be obtained is higher than this average of "full" cost, revenue will be lost if this higher price is not realized. If the higher price is accepted, the arbitrary allocations have served no purpose. If the market will not take the product or service at the average cost, then either the sale will not be made, resulting in a loss in net revenue and in unused capacity; or if it is made, it will be below the cost calculation, which means again that this will not have served any rational decision-making purpose.

When a decision is to be made on the addition to, or replacement of existing capacity, all of the prospective costs involved will have to be equated against the estimated revenues. At the time of the decision all of the costs are prospective and variable. They may be lower than the average full cost of existing facilities. If they are not lower than the variable costs of the present production they should not be undertaken. In other words, the "long-run" marginal costs should be lower than the "short-run" if the expansion or addition is to be made. If these "long-run" costs are equal to or higher than the present full costs and prices will not cover the latter, then the expansion or replacement is not economically feasible. It is the relation of present variables (which exclude fixed costs) to the perspective total costs of replacements that sets the basis for the decision on output and pricing; whichever is the lower should govern.

PRICE DISCRIMINATION

The Idea of Discrimination

One of the most controversial issues in transport pricing arises in connection with what is called price discrimination. The term *price discrimination* carries the implication of arbitrary action, and it generally means unfair treatment among buyers by a particular seller. Thus, it connotes a deviation from the competitive norm. When prices are determined solely by the forces of competition, no producer is able to exercise any control over the prices he charges or the conditions of sale. He adapts himself to the market as he finds it. Hence, he is unable to practice price discrimination.

If a producer has sufficient control of the supply of his product to influence the market, he may be able to practice discrimination. Control over supply, however, does not always, or necessarily, give rise to discrimination or permit it. A monopolist, offering a single product for sale and marketing it under uniform conditions, may charge the same price to all customers. His is a monopoly price, but it is not usually regarded as discriminatory. On the other hand, if a firm sells different kinds of products under competitive conditions—that is, without the ability to control the market for the product—it is not usually regarded as practicing discrimination, even though the prices of the different products are not proportionate to their cost. This will be the situation where joint costs are present, and it will also be the case where the total costs are traceable to each different product.

The concept of price discrimination, therefore, implies two things: (1) There is discrimination when the prices a seller charges the various buyers of similar products differ by more than the differences in the cost of the commodities or services, and (2) these price differences are possible because of the control the seller is able to exercise over his sales by the separation of his markets. That is, discrimination arises as the result of departure from the competitive norm brought about by the exercise of monopoly power.[10] Sometimes the concept is defined in such broad terms as to cover all differences in prices not matched by differences in costs.[11] This presumably would include all prices that deviated from cost, as that term is used in connection with perfect competition. Under such circumstances, all prices that did not conform to the standard of perfect competition would be discriminatory. The most widely accepted concept, however, seems to be that of differences in prices charged by a single seller that are not matched by differences in costs. Unfortunately, this concept is not as simple as it sounds.[12]

Costs and Price Discrimination

A satisfactory definition of price discrimination that will adequately fit modern conditions is difficult to formulate.[13] If it is defined in terms of cost, it assumes a simplicity of costs that does not exist in fact. The complexities of costs and their calculation was pointed out in

[10] For an extensive theoretical treatment of price discrimination, see Joan Robinson, *Economics of Imperfect Competition* (London: Macmillan & Co., Ltd., 1934), Book V. Mrs. Robinson's theory is restricted to homogeneous output. She defines discrimination as "the act of selling the same article, produced under single control, at different prices to different buyers . . ." (p. 179.)

[11] See M. W. Watkins, "Price Discrimination," *Encyclopedia of the Social Sciences* (New York: The Macmillan Co., 1931), Vol. XII, pp. 350–55.

[12] Section 2 of the Clayton Act forbids, with qualifications, a person to discriminate in price between different purchases of commodities of like grade and quality. For an analysis of the problem of like grade and quality, see Ralph Cassady, Jr., and E. T. Grether, "The Proper Interpretation of 'Like Trade and Quality' within the Meaning of Section 2(a) of the Robinson-Patman Act," *Southern California Law Review*, Vol. 30, No. 3 (1957), pp. 241–79.

[13] See Ralph Cassady, Jr., "Some Economic Aspects of Price Discrimination under Non-perfect Market Conditions," *Journal of Marketing*, Vol. XI, No. 1 (July, 1946), pp. 7–20.

an earlier section of this chapter. Precise costs can rarely be ascertained, and the commodities and services a firm offers for sale are rarely homogeneous. The cost concept of discrimination does not cover the case of products produced under conditions of joint cost, and does not apply to essentially different products produced by the same firm. Furthermore, there is the additional complication of deciding what are essentially the same or different products. For example, a motion-picture house may exhibit the same film in the afternoon and in the evening. It is the same picture, but it is not the same service. The products which are being offered are joint; how much each should share of the total cost burden is for the market to decide; cost cannot be the arbiter. Similarly, the seats in the theater differ markedly; yet the cost of each may be the same. If price is to perform its rationing function, the market will have to decide what is to be paid for the various seats, not cost. What is more, if the same price were charged for all seats on the assumption that they all cost the same, discrimination could be said to exist, because services of differing qualities were being sold at the same price.

Average cost is not a satisfactory basis by which to measure discrimination, especially where the most difficult and controversial public questions arise, because average cost in a multiproduct firm is not a meaningful concept. Marginal or incremental cost is not satisfactory as a guide, because there is no necessary relation between marginal cost and common or joint costs. If there are joint costs and the products are sold under competitive conditions, the total price will just cover the total costs. There is no discrimination in such a case, even though the prices of the products cannot be related to their respective total costs. When pricing falls into this category, it would seem to be preferable to refer to it as differential pricing. Unfortunately, it is usually very difficult, if not impossible, to distinguish between differential and discriminatory pricing in the real world. Because discrimination in common usage covers both types of pricing, it ought not necessarily to imply reprehensible practices nor practices which in some way or another constitute an undesirable deviation from the competitive norm.

Where there are joint costs, the pricing of the main product in a monopoly market and the by-product, or a second one, in a competitive one would not involve discrimination. Each would be carrying its own specific costs, and in addition the by-product would be making as much contribution to the joint or common costs as the market would permit. If the sale of the by-product yielded "profits" such that an expansion of total output resulted in increasing by-product "profits" more than the decrease in the monopoly "profit" from the main product resulting from the increase in the main output, then the sale of the by-product would bring about the reduction in the monopoly price and lead to an increase in the total output of the firm. This would not be the result of discrimination; it would, however, involve pricing policies as far as the monopoly output was concerned. The result would be a greater total utilization of resources, by virtue of sale of the second product, and either the same monopoly output as before or a larger one, but never a smaller one. If monopoly is inescapable in the main product, then pricing on the basis of average costs will be uneconomical. The implications of this for transport pricing, particularly for railroads, is that an average cost approach is not conducive to an efficient transport system.

The foregoing may be illustrated effectively by electricity, where the monopoly situation is clearly in evidence, and where also the total profits permitted to the firm are restricted by public action. The sale of electricity after midnight (a by-product or a secondary product) is made under monopoly conditions, although the price discretion of the seller may be severely circumscribed. Nevertheless the seller may equate marginal cost (i.e., the additional cost of the by-product) and marginal revenue; and moreover, he can vary the output of the by-product. The seller would be recovering common costs from the market in accordance with the competitive principle, but he would also be a part of the market. This of itself does not involve discrimination in the prices charged before and after midnight. The fact that the prices of the two services are not proportionate to their respective marginal costs is not controlling; they are not so in the case of beef and hides. The situation is not altered by the fact that monopoly may exist for one or both of the products.

However, there is one other factor in the case of public utilities which must be recognized, namely, if there is any discrimination, it is against those who purchase the by-product if the price for the latter is set at the point that will produce the maximum net revenue from it. This is the result of the fact that public authority limits the total profits which may be earned. From the standpoint of resource utilization, off-peak sales should be permitted as long as the additional cost equals price; in fact, the greatest utilization will ensue when this cost is equal to the price. This, however, would make no contribution to the common costs. On the other hand, if off-peak prices are being kept up by public edict above the point where the net revenues would be maximized, the peak users are being required to bear a larger share of joint costs than would be the case if output were such that $MC = MR$;

at the same time, the nonpeak users are being denied service for which they are willing to pay. If this is the case, then if there is any discrimination under these circumstances, it is against the peak users because they are being compelled to carry all the common costs, some of which could be recovered from lower off-peak rates. If off-peak output is permitted to the point where the marginal cost equals marginal revenue then discrimination is not being practiced in favor of off-peak users even though they enjoy a lower price in terms of kilowatt-hours.

Hard versus Soft Competition

Discrimination, if differential pricing is included in the term, is an inherent and inevitable part of the structure of modern industry. The unavoidable presence of varying degrees of monopoly, oligopoly, and monopolistic competition means that departures from the competitive norm of pricing are the rule rather than the exception. Product differentiation is an integral part of the competitive structure, although at the same time it also entails departure from the ideal of competition and leads to discrimination or to differential pricing. Fixed costs give rise to more or less immobility in the utilization of resources, frequently provide the basis for the exercise of a certain amount of discretionary power, and frequently entail the continuous existence of some unused capacity. The influence of geography on markets means that they are often imperfectly connected with each other; and if impediments such as tariffs or other restrictions are present, the resulting variations in the effectiveness of competition can give rise to discrimination, even though a producer has not sought to acquire monopoly power. Thus the producer of a heavy commodity, in which transportation charges loom large, may be able to obtain high profits from his product in his immediate area. Cost considerations may dictate a capacity larger than can profitably be utilized for that particular region. If contributions to the cost of this extra capacity can be obtained by reaching out into other markets that are unable to bear the full share of costs but can contribute something more than the variables incurred, it not only will pay the producer to take such business but also may mean that the average unit costs of production are lowered, so that all the buyers receive lower prices than they otherwise would. Even the monopoly price in the restricted area may be lower than it would be if the producer were unable to reach out into other markets. This factor has played an important part in the recognition of discrimination as unavoidable in railroad transportation. Time considerations may play a similar part in the pricing policy. This is exemplified in public utility pricing and may warrant more attention in the future than it has here-tofore received in railroad rate making. It also should be given much more thought as a means of dealing with peak loads in urban mass transport than has been the case to date.

If differential or discriminatory pricing were always a manifesta-tion of monopoly, and if at the same time the monopoly was used for the purpose of driving out competitors, there would be few differences of opinion on the need for eliminating discrimination. As has already been pointed out, the matter is not that simple. Discrimination is not necessarily a question of undesirable monopoly pricing. "The firm that does not discriminate in its pricing policy or differentiate in its product line, or invade new markets dies in the competitive struggle."[14] If pri-vate enterprise is to be preserved, so must competition. Preservation of competition and preservation of competitors, however, are two differ-ent things. All competition is injurious to competitors that cannot survive. The essence of competition is that it drives out the inefficient and limits the rewards that the successful competitors can receive. Policy which prevents competition based on an economical utilization of resources is a denial of the principles of competition. Admittedly, it is not always easy to discern when discrimination is being used for predatory purposes and when it is not; but this is no reason for not endeavoring to do so, or for espousing a public policy based on the opposite theory.

[14] Eli W. Clemens, "Price Discrimination and the Multiproduct Firm," *Review of Economic Studies,* Vol. XIX (1), No. 48 (1950–51), p. 11. Professor Clemens takes the position that multiproduct production and price discrimination are more or less universal means to the same end and differ only in degree, even where there are no joint or common costs.

<table>
<tr>
<td>

Chapter

8

</td>
<td>

THEORY OF PRICING
FOR TRANSPORT

</td>
</tr>
</table>

INTRODUCTION

The economic principles applicable to the pricing of transport services are no different from those which apply to the pricing of the outputs of other industries. These principles have already been dealt with, and it is not necessary to repeat what was covered previously. The reason for separate treatment of the pricing of transport services arises from the complex problems that are connected with the application of these principles to transport.

At the outset it should be recalled that transportation is supplied by a group of industries that have diverse economic characteristics. Some of the agencies, as we shall see, are only partially competitive, at least within themselves, as the result of their economic structures; the others are capable of a high degree of competition. At the same time, the different modes of transport, over a rather wide range, offer services that are readily substitutable for each other, while each also has its own field of specialization.

Public policy to date has imposed limitations on competition in transportation by direct and continuous price fixing for common carriers, and by limiting the number of enterprises in the various agencies that can offer services to the public. Thus, common carriers, be they railroad, motor, or any other, must secure certificates of public convenience and necessity which serve to protect the existing carrier, unless it can be shown to the satisfaction of the appropriate public authority that an additional carrier is called for on the basis of public interest.[1] This means that a convincing demonstration must be made on the part of the new applicant that public convenience will be served by the new addition and that it is necessary. In air, water, and motor

---

[1] Railroads have been required to obtain certificates of convenience and necessity only for construction of new lines, extensions, or abandonments since 1920.

transport, there are also contract carriers. Water and motor contract carriers must secure permits, but the restrictions on entry are, in principle at least, less severe than for common carriers. All of this is complicated by the fact that there is also a great deal of transport for hire in the same fields that is not regulated at all either because of the nature of the transport or because of the commodities that are moved. Finally, there is a large amount of transportation by these modes, as well as by pipe lines, that is private in nature, that is, it is not for hire. The movement of passengers by private car and freight by private truck are illustrations. Thus the transport agencies supply public transport, private commercial transport, and private noncommercial transport, with a mixed use of public and private facilities in a way that embraces public obligation, private discretion, competition, and monopoly found nowhere else in our industrial structure.

The regulation of transport has proceeded on the theory that it is in the public interest for public authority to fix the prices of an essential service supplied under monopolistic conditions, or at least supplied by enterprises that enjoy a wide range of monopoly power. There is also the prevalent idea that public interest requires that competition among the carriers of a particular mode, as well as among the carriers of the different modes, should be limited, and that the rates charged by all common carriers should be regulated by public authority. This puts transportation in a category apart from industry in general. This calls for an examination of the economic structure of transportation upon which the theory was erected, but even more, especially today, of the economic structures of the various agencies to discern whether the theory fits the present situation or whether changed conditions have rendered obsolete the elaborate program of regulation that has developed over the past 100 years.

The regulation of monopoly price poses special and difficult issues even in the simplest of situations. This is manifest in the public utility industries, where the problem can be dealt with in literally isolated form because each firm can be treated separately. Railroad transport exhibits many of the characteristics of those industries and is subject to essentially the same legal rules that are applied to them. As a problem in monopoly, however, rail transport is considerably more complex because, first of all, monopoly has been less complete by virtue of competition among the railroads. Railroad rate regulation has therefore presented more difficult issues of monopoly price control than has public utility rate regulation. Second, with the rise of the newer modes of transport, application of the theory of monopoly price control to it can no longer be undertaken on the assumption that it can be made to work by severely limiting competition or even eliminating it over a wide range. At the same time, the type of regulation that is imposed by the antitrust laws would, without any supplement, be inadequate. Here is an area that falls between antitrust and public utility control in such a way as to give it a unique status in public policy.

Analysis of price policies and price control in transport in the United States has to be made in light of the ownership operation of transport facilities and also with recognition of the technical differences connected with the rendition of service. It has already been pointed out that railroads own all the facilities they use and hence have to carry directly the burden of investment which this entails. Motor vehicles, even though they may pay for the highways they use, do not pay for them if they do not use them. This makes for a difference in the cost characteristics of the operating companies and therefore in the impact of the costs which are the basis for decision making in the price policies of each. From a social point of view the total cost considerations are essentially the same in each case because of the public investment in highways; from the point of view of the private user, they are radically different.

PRICING ON THE BASIS OF COSTS

Economical Pricing Reflects Costs

The theory of pricing presented in the previous chapter brought out the fact that insofar as competition is effective, prices reflect costs. This is because alternative uses to which resources may be put are known and available. As a consequence, if competition is not restrained for various reasons, that is, if it is operating perfectly, costs and prices are equal—marginal cost equals average total cost—the latter is at a minimum, and costs cover all the inducements necessary to attract resources to the particular product that is being turned out, or to retain the resources used in that activity. These are the economic costs which affect prices. They are the ones that must be covered if production is to continue. Deliberate restraint of production so that prices exceed these costs means that economic resources are not being put to their most effective use and buyers are being deprived of the economic benefits which competition will yield to them.

Fixed costs, that is, costs that are embodied in resources committed to a particular use for a particular period of time, are not price-determining, and rational calculation should omit them in decisions on price and production policies. They therefore play no part in the economic calculation of precise or minimum prices. In the case of public utilities, which are regulated by public authority, fixed costs do enter into the calculations of what constitutes the appropriate amount of total revenue the firm is permitted to receive. This is because of policy that deems it necessary to impose limitations on monopoly exploitation of the consumer so as to bring the total revenue of the firm into conformity with an assumed competitive standard. The fixed costs, however, should have no direct influence on the minimum or maximum prices for the particular services. Maximum prices as a whole, however, may be held down by restriction of monopoly profits by public authority. The application of this to particular maximum rates would require the exercise of judgment.

Difficulty of Ascertaining Precise Costs

Although it may be desirable to base prices on precise and total economic costs, the realities of modern transport are such that this is not possible. The fact that fixed costs are not price-determining, at least as far as the resources already committed are concerned, does not eliminate the need for revenue that will cover the cost of replacing them when they are used up, if service is to continue. This cost is included in economic costs but may be extremely difficult if not impossible to calculate at the time the service is being rendered. The "noneconomic" costs do not have to be covered; but at the time the investment is made, the suppliers of capital expect that a return will be forthcoming, and public policy that denied this after the investment was made would soon lead to a refusal of investors to participate in undertakings controlled in this fashion. Consequently, prices will have to cover noneconomic costs if such prices can be obtained. What is more, they will be obtained if law and the market permit, but they cannot economically enter into the determination of particular prices.

The problem of ascertaining precise costs is further complicated by joint and common costs. These cannot be allocated rationally to a particular product or service, and as a consequence, precise cost calculation for output produced where they are present is impossible. Furthermore, both fixed and variable costs may be joint or common. In other words, the only costs that can be precisely ascertained at a particular time are the variable ones that are specific. These, however, form only the minimum basis upon which decisions can be made. Because total revenue will have to cover more than these costs, the price for any service in transport cannot be related to any precise cost except as the absolute minimum below which economical pricing should not be permitted to go.

Meaning of Pricing on the Basis of Cost for Transport

As far as the pricing of the particular services which the various agencies of transport supply is concerned, pricing on the basis of costs must mean that the minimum rate that may be charged for a service is the relevant cost of performing that service. The actual amount that is charged above this cost will depend upon the market. Economical pricing therefore calls for charging what the traffic will bear on the different services. As pointed out in the previous chapter, this means minimum prices that will maximize the margin between the relevant costs of performing a particular service and the marginal revenue it will yield. The same remarks apply to maximum individual rates. If public authority decides to impose a limit on these, it will have to be cognizant of the fact that by so doing it will be limiting the total net revenue the carrier receives. This may jeopardize the financial position of the firm or firms whose rates are controlled.

Recently, there has been a good deal of discussion on value of service versus cost of service in rate making, the burden of the argument being that rates should be based on costs. This point of view stems from the fact that a good deal of rate making for railroads has been based on the value of the commodity, it being assumed that more valuable commodities can and should bear higher rates than the lower valued ones. If these two terms are taken to mean the same thing, then criticism of this method of rate making is valid. There is no necessary relationship between the value of a commodity and the freight rate it will bear, especially under present-day competitive conditions. If, however, value of service means what the service is worth to the shipper, then the rate becomes a market-determined one and, as already pointed out, will be synonymous with what the traffic will bear, especially on competitive traffic. The fact that the traffic is in low-grade commodities will not of itself warrant lower rates than those on high-grade traffic. It is only in this sense that basing rates on cost of service can have meaning for railroad rate making.[2]

---

[2] The broader and extremely complex problem of appropriate tests for allocation of economic resources among the agencies so as to provide for an economical transport system as a whole is not covered by this discussion of costs as a basis of pricing. The costs included in the above presentation are those which the various carriers have to bear. They do not include all the costs of transport which in one way or another make up the transport bill of the country. Factors which have to be considered in this connection will be discussed in a later chapter.

THEORY OF RAILROAD RATE MAKING

The economic principles applicable to railroad rate making are no different from those which apply to the other agencies of transport. Nevertheless, separate treatment is necessary because of the differences in the cost structures of the agencies. These differences raise questions of policy as applied to the various modes, whether there should be a uniform policy for all modes, or whether there should be separate ones and, if so, what sort of distinctions should be made. This calls, therefore, for an analysis of the cost characteristics of each agency and the impact of these on competition among the firms of a particular mode, as well as among the firms of the various modes—in other words, intra-agency and interagency competition.

Railroad Costs

Railroad costs, like those of any other business, may be analyzed from the point of view of rate of output or from the point of view of traceability. Fixed and variable costs relate to the rate of output, joint or common costs to traceability.

Fixed Costs. One of the distinguishing features of railroad costs is that a relatively large proportion of them are fixed for a particular period of time. Although it is axiomatic that all costs are variable in the long run and that the impact of fixed costs is only for the short run, the short run in railroad transportation may be for a considerable period of time. Rights of way, roadbeds, and bridges may have a life of half a century or more; locomotives, passenger cars, and freight cars are subject more to obsolescence than depreciation, which means that the investment in them is not a function of the rate of output; instead, it is a function of time. The dieselization of American railroads forced the retirement of a very large number of steam locomotives that showed little effect of wear when they were replaced. In other words, the plant facilities of railroads which give rise to a large part of the fixed costs last for a longer period of time than is true for most industries. Adjustments of total costs to output respond much more slowly to output than is the case for industry in general. Public utilities are the only other ones characterized by such a large amount of fixed and specialized investment. Fixed costs for railroads are also large relative to total costs at any time. This is because the investment in the railroad plant is large relative to output for a given period. As was pointed out in an earlier chapter, this relationship may be expressed in terms of capital turnover per annum. This is the ratio of capital investment to annual gross revenues from railroad services. The average annual turnover for railroad investment is about once every three years; that is, for an investment of $600 million the average annual gross revenue will be about $200 million. By way of contrast, for the steel industry the turnover is about once every one and one-half years, for petroleum about once a year, and for large merchandising establishments from two to three times a year. In fact, the only other industries that have a slow turnover like railroads are public utilities, for which it may range from 3 years for telephone utilities to 10 years for hydroelectric plants.

It is difficult to state the precise proportion of total costs that is made up of fixed costs. In the first place, it will depend upon the rate of operations. Assuming the "normal" or average rate of operations that is used to calculate the rate of turnover, fixed costs have rather commonly been estimated to constitute two thirds of the total. On the other hand, a study by the Cost-Finding Section of the Interstate Commerce Commission[3] estimated that long-run rail operating costs were 20 per cent to 30 per cent fixed if investment was excluded. However, it concluded that only 50 to 70 per cent of rail investment was variable. Whatever the precise facts may be, it is obvious that fixed costs are a large part of railroad costs and therefore occupy a very prominent role in price-making decisions. As was pointed out in the chapter on pricing, fixed costs are not "economic" costs in terms of price determination and therefore should not be taken into consideration when decisions are being made on the rate of output or on the prices which should be charged for specific units of the output.

The relatively high fixed costs in railroad transport are the result of a number of factors that are characteristic of the industry. Investment is large relative to annual output. This means that cost of capital is a larger element of cost than for industries where the capital turnover is more rapid. Railroads must be able to retain and attract capital if they are to continue to serve, as well as to improve their service in competition with other agencies. A considerable part of railroad depreciation, especially if obsolescence is included under this heading, is independent of the volume of traffic. Much of the rolling stock becomes obsolete instead of wearing out, and a good deal of the railroad plant wears out because of weather and other factors rather than

---

[3] *Rail Freight Service Costs in the Various Rate Territories of the United States,* Senate Document No. 63, 78th Congress, 1st session (Washington, D.C.: U.S. Government Printing Office. 1943), p. 75.

because of use. Transportation expenses do not vary directly with the traffic. Minimum train crews and station and yard forces must be maintained even though traffic varies widely, and motive equipment can be adapted only within limits with changing traffic volumes. Property taxes are a fixed cost, and state and local taxes based on the assessed valuation of the property are a significant item of railroad expense. Finally, as common carriers, railroads are required by law to maintain minimum train schedules on a regular basis even though the traffic may not warrant them. Maintenance of unprofitable passenger service at the present time is a genuine source of difficulty for the railroads.

Variable Costs. Variable costs for railroads, as an average, are probably somewhat less than 50 per cent of total costs for the short run. These are the costs that are important at any particular time when pricing decisions are being made. Furthermore, this short run covers a considerable period of time, somewhat over five years. Thus, for railroads the total costs which must be covered over time, if they are to continue in business successfully, are much greater than those above which it may pay to take traffic at any particular time rather than decline to do so. It is this rather wide range between total costs which must be covered over time if operations are to continue and the minimum to which prices may fall before traffic should be refused that makes it economically possible for railroad rates to fluctuate widely with varying volumes of traffic. In other words, the "economic" costs to be considered in railroad rate making for a given period are relatively less than those of enterprises with lower relative fixed costs. Unfortunately, it is not easy to ascertain with precision the range between the total costs that need to be covered and the minimum that must form the basis of decision for rate making.[4] Whatever the facts may be, it is clear that railroad pricing is subject to a wider range of variation over a considerable period of time with changing rates of output than is the case for most other industries.

Joint and Common Costs. Cost-price relationships in railroad transport are also complicated by the presence of joint and common costs. The role that these play in this industry has been the subject of much debate.[5] On one point, at least, there seems to be complete

---

[4] See D. P. Locklin, *Economics of Transportation* (6th ed.; Homewood, Ill.: Richard D. Irwin, Inc., 1966), chap. 8; and A. M. Milne, *The Economics of Inland Transport* (London: Sir Isaac Pitman & Sons, Ltd., 1955), chap. v.

[5] For a careful review of the literature on this subject and an extensive bibliography, see D. P. Locklin, "A Review of the Literature on Railway Rate Theory," *Quarterly Journal of Economics,* Vol. XLVII (February, 1933), pp. 167 ff.

agreement: When rail transport is supplied in one direction, it inevitably is supplied for the back haul. This is a case of true jointness. Professor A. C. Pigou contended that this was the only example of joint cost in rail transport, and many agree with him. Whether this is so depends partly on the definition of what constitutes a unit of railroad service. Pigou took the ton-mile as the unit and then insisted that the output was homogeneous. This, however, seems to be an oversimplification. If a railroad supplies service from *A* to *C* through *B,* it inescapably supplies service to *B.* The service to *B* is a different one from that which is rendered to *C.* Similarly, traffic may move at different times of the year. In other words, railroads are multiple-product firms in which provision of facilities for some places and at some times in one direction provides services for other places at other times as well as in the opposite direction. Furthermore a ton-mile of freight of one commodity is not the same service as a ton-mile for another commodity, as evidenced by the differences in costs which may be incurred in supplying each. How much of railroad transport involves joint and common costs is not readily ascertainable, but they appear to loom larger than is commonly assumed by the regulatory authorities.[6]

Cost Allocation

It is not possible to calculate the precise costs of performing each of the many services which railroads provide. In the first place, railroads are multiple-product enterprises. This means that there are joint and/or common costs, and there is no rational method of allocating these, as has already been pointed out. Any allocation that may be undertaken is arbitrary[7] and serves no useful purpose in price making.

[6] It may be that common costs are more important than joint costs for railroads. However, if the backhaul is conceded as involving true joint costs, then investment costs in terminal and line facilities would have to fall into this category, and these are always a large element in railroad costs. The common costs arise in connection with the movement of the different types of traffic. These may vary in their proportion to each other and therefore do not meet the strict definition of joint costs; but as was pointed out in Chapter 7, electricity before and after midnight falls into the same category. Furthermore, what constitutes fixed proportions as required by the strict definition of joint costs is largely a matter of market determination. There may be one hide on a cow, but whether it is a product depends on whether there is a market for it. Moreover, apart from the market there is no fixed proportion between the edible and the nonedible part of the animal. This general lack of fixed proportions may mean that the term *joint costs* should be discarded in place of *common costs.* This does not avoid the problem of traceability, however, because, as was pointed out in Chapter 7, many of these are not traceable theoretically or practically. For a discussion of this issue in transport, see G. W. Wilson, "On the Output Unit in Transportation," *Land Economics,* Vol. XXXV, No. 3 (August, 1959), pp. 266–76.

[7] The Cost-Finding Section of the Interstate Commerce Commission has recognized this fully. See n. 3 above. However, its findings and evaluations have not been given official recognition by the Commission, nor have they been accorded much support in the

In the second place, railroads have large fixed costs. Insofar as these are not joint, they could be allocated on an average basis among the units of output, but this would have meaning only after the volume of traffic had been ascertained, not before it had been moved. In other words, the fixed expense per unit of homogeneous traffic can be discovered only after the traffic has been obtained. What this means in terms of pricing has already been discussed, namely, that fixed costs are not "economic" costs for price-making decisions. As a consequence of these fixed and joint costs of railroads, "average" cost is a meaningless term, and as a basis for decisions on the rates that should be charged, it is positively deceptive.

Cost determination is an essential part of railroad rate-making procedure. Much remains to be done by way of more precise cost finding for railroad traffic movements, however. The amount of joint costs in all probability can be obtained with considerably greater accuracy than is now the case, and the same remarks apply to fixed costs. Nevertheless, no matter how "scientific" cost accounting becomes, it cannot allocate joint costs scientifically nor fixed costs in advance. What is urgently needed at the present time is better information on the minimum economic costs below which rates on particular items of traffic should not be permitted to go. The relationships of the rates above those minima should be based on market and policy considerations, not on cost.[8]

---

decisions of the Commission. See Howard Freas, *Aspects of Transportation Based on Regulatory Experience in the United States*, a paper delivered to the High Authority European Coal and Steel Community, Luxembourg, October 10, 1958, p. 130 and especially pp. 61–69 (mimeographed).

[8] See W. J. Baumol and Associates, "The Role of Cost in the Minimum Pricing of Railroad Services," *The Journal of Business of the University of Chicago*, Vol. XXXV, No. 4 (October, 1962), pp. 1–10; M. J. Roberts, "Transport Costs, Pricing and Regulation," *Transportation Economics* (New York: National Bureau of Economic Research, 1965), pp. 1–42; Bureau of Railway Economics, Association of American Railroads *A Guide to Railroad Cost Analysis* (Washington, D.C., 1964); Interstate Commerce Commission *Rules to Govern the Assembling and Presenting of Cost Evidence*, Docket No. 34013, Report and Order Recommended by J. S. Kaplan, Hearing Examiner, September 20, 1966. Examiner Kaplan undertakes to ascertain transportation costs for the purpose of cost finding. He rejects the development of a formula in favor of a more flexible approach. He takes the position that all costs must be assigned. He insists that this is a separate question from costing for rate-making purposes but he constantly confuses the two statements to the contrary notwithstanding. He states that variable costs should be used to determine the minimum compensatory level of rates, and that fully allocated costs should be used to determine the low-cost or rate-setting carrier. Incremental costs should be rejected for either of these two purposes. "Inherent cost advantages should generally be protected through the approval or prescription of rate differentials, measured by the difference between the respective fully allocated cost levels of competing modes of transportation, when the involved rates are shown to be below such levels." (p. 123.) The

Discrimination and Differential Pricing

The complexity of railroad costs, together with the monopoly features of railroad transportation, have created the exceedingly difficult problem of price discrimination. If all railroad costs were variable and directly associated with output, discrimination would be easy to detect. If railroads possessed no element of monopoly, they would be unable to practice price discrimination as defined in economics. However, railroads are multiple-product enterprises, as a consequence of which it is not possible to ascertain precise unit costs. At best, it is only possible to find the minimum "economic" cost below which a rate should not be permitted to go. In earlier years the railroads enjoyed a good deal of monopoly power and hence were able to discriminate, no matter how that word is defined. At the present time, they do and must engage in differential charging in the sense that rates will deviate from directly ascertainable costs and from average costs. How much this represents discrimination in the economic sense is a matter of conjecture. Whatever the facts may be, it is clear that railroads do engage in differential pricing, if that term can be applied to multiple-product pricing, and it is to this that the term *discrimination* commonly refers.

Discriminatory pricing in railroad rate making today is of three types, namely, discrimination among commodities, discrimination between places, or local discrimination, and discrimination at different periods of time. There is a wide range in the rates that are charged for transporting different commodities or offering different types of services. The rate for hauling a ton of coal one mile is different from that for hauling a ton of steel, and both are less than that which is charged for hauling a ton of furniture. These differences may be explained on three grounds. First of all, there are differences in the directly ascertainable costs of service. Some articles require special and more expensive types of equipment than others, some are bulkier than others, and some entail greater liability and risk to the carrier. Rate differentials based on these cost differences do not constitute

---

report confuses incremental cost with marginal cost, and the latter is rejected. (p. 111.) There is no recognition that fixed costs are "noneconomic." There is also a lack of understanding of competitive adjustments to joint costs involved in the backhaul. (pp. 100–105.) It is unlikely that this report will assist the ICC in clarifying its cost analysis or its application of costs to rate making.

For a critical examination of the report, see also Docket No. 34013, "Rules to Govern the Assembling and Presenting of Cost Evidence," Exceptions of the Railroads to the Report and Order Recommended by Hearing Examiner Jair S. Kaplan, March 1, 1967.

discrimination. Second, there is the element of joint and common costs. These must be covered by the traffic as a whole, and they cannot be attributed to any particular item of traffic. The market will have to be the gauge of the amount which the various commodities can contribute to these, and insofar as the market has competitive alternatives, the resulting differential pricing will not be descriminatory, at least in any monopoly sense. Third, railroad pricing may also be based upon monopoly powers. To the extent that this is so, some commodities may be required to bear charges that can be explained neither by assignable costs nor by joint costs. This will be true discrimination. How much of this exists in fact cannot be readily ascertained, and so long as a railroad is not making unreasonable profits in total, it is difficult to see how genuine discrimination exists. If the competitive alternatives to the buyers of transport services are such that the railroads can earn only a reasonable profit, then the differential charging will have to be explained on the basis of recouping unassignable costs in accordance with what the market will pay, and not on the basis of discrimination emerging from monopoly.[9]

Local or place discrimination refers to differences in rates on a particular commodity that are unrelated to the distance the commodity is hauled. If rates are based on cost, they will not be proportionate to distance for two reasons. First, the terminal costs at each end will be the same regardless of distance; and second, it costs more per mile to haul a commodity a short distance than a longer one, although the difference will diminish rather rapidly as the length of the haul increases and will disappear altogether over longer distances, assuming similar terrain and other relevant conditions. Apart from these two qualifications, however, it is generally held that rates should vary with distance, and when this is not so, local or place discrimination is said to exist. This may take the form of equal rates for unequal distances, rates increasing with distance less rapidly than the cost of service justifies, or the charging of higher rates for shorter than for longer hauls over the same line in the same direction.

[9] This assumes that the railroad does not have "excess" capacity as distinct from "unused" capacity. If it has excess capacity, then all of its charges might be reduced if that excess capacity were eliminated. Probably, however, under the pervasive competition which exists today, elimination of the excess capacity would improve the position of the railroad without affecting the rates it could afford to charge. In any case, it would be unlikely to affect the economical minimum rates. There is probably considerable excess railroad capacity, at least under present conditions. This adds support to the argument that railroads should not be protected against competition. It also supports the contention that other agencies should not be protected against the railroads. In other words, "umbrella rate making" should be eliminated from regulatory policy.

The problem of ascertaining whether place discrimination is being practiced is essentially the same as for any other form of discrimination. A railroad may haul freight from *A* to *B* and similar freight from *A* to *C* through *B*. If *C* is a place where there is water competition, the railroad may be forced to offer lower rates to *C* in order to get that traffic, and it will pay the railroad to take the traffic as long as the rate is higher than the costs that are directly attributable to that traffic if unused capacity exists without the additional traffic. If the railroad is to stay in business, places like *B* will have to pay a higher relative rate under such circumstances and may even pay a higher absolute rate. Whether this is discrimination, in the monopoly sense at least, can be a matter of debate; the critical question really is whether such pricing is so harmful that it should be limited or prohibited. If the railroad has unused capacity, if the lower rates to the more distant point make for more complete use of that capacity, and if the lower rates are compelled by another carrier that is carrying the traffic profitably, then the pricing is economical. This is the situation that is commonly met at seaports, which have the natural advantage of location and which as a consequence are able to secure more favorable rates on some commodities. The intermediate point is not placed at a disadvantage by the pricing policy of the railroad because the more distant point will get the favorable rates whether the railroad meets the competition or not. If, as a result of the practice, the railroad receives more than a fair profit in total, the remedy is to lower the higher intermediate rates, since these would be the source of the monopoly profit, not to raise the longer haul rates. In other words, if unreasonable discrimination, or undue preference, exists, the remedy is to lower the higher rates, not vice versa, and this is the corrective for any form of discriminatory pricing because it is only from the higher prices that monopoly profits, if there are any, can be obtained. If, instead, public authority follows the policy of raising the lower rates, it is then protecting competitors, not protecting competition, which is presumably the objective of national policy; it is also not assisting in a greater utilization of capacity, which is the economical thing to do.

Temporal or time discrimination arises when rates are varied according to the time at which the service is performed. Excursion and seasonal passenger fares are illustrations of this. Higher rates on seasonal traffic movements which create unbalanced haulage and unused capacity in off seasons should be permitted if the market will accept them. This applies to water competition, which may exist in summertime but which disappears with winter weather. Economical pricing would allow railroads to compete for the traffic in the summer and charge higher rates on similar traffic in the wintertime, or employ some equivalent arrangement. The difference in the charges would depend upon the market and the financial requirements of the railroads.

Ruinous Competition

In a previous chapter it was pointed out that complete competition among natural monopolies is ruinous. Complete competition among railroads will therefore be ruinous. It is not apparent, however, that this affects the pricing theory for railroads that has just been discussed. The effect of ruinous competition is to eliminate excess capacity that is inescapable if there is more than one firm; in other words, only one firm can survive. If the competition to which one railroad is subjected by another applies only to a relatively small portion of its total traffic, the competition will be no more ruinous than that between an electric and a gas utility. If it ranges over a wider area, however, the solution is to bring about a consolidation of the competing railroads that will eliminate much of the excess capacity and competition, thus giving recognition to the natural monopoly characteristics. This issue will be dealt with more extensively in a later chapter.

THE THEORY OF MOTOR CARRIER RATES

Competitive Features of Motor Transport

The development of the internal-combustion engine has radically altered the technical and economic structure of transportation. It is no longer composed largely of natural monopolies. On the contrary, the economic features which characterize natural monopolies are almost completely lacking in the field of motor transport. This is why economics of scale are much more circumscribed than in rail transportation. The technical units are relatively small and may be very small. Operations may be started with a very small investment, and expansion may be achieved with very small increments of investment in direct and almost immediate response to the growth in traffic. Most of the facilities are not highly specialized or unalterably committed to a particular market or geographic area, and they can readily be shifted to any other market if the law permits this. Physically, the highways or routes are available to all who wish to use them. Alternative sources of supply can readily be made available to the buyer or consumer. There is no absence of shopper's technique; consumers may even supply their own equipment and do so a great deal of the time. Economic limitations on the additions to facilities are very slight because small increases in traffic increase the need for additional equipment, at least outside of narrow limits, and these additions may be made in small units. Existing facilities can be completely utilized except within narrow limits, and additional traffic can be accommodated only by acquiring additional operating units. This will not result in an appreciable lowering of the average total unit costs of output, since the additional output comes as a result of the incurrence of additional costs that are largely proportionate to output. Mr. Bonavia expresses this by saying: "When the internal combustion engine was sufficiently developed it became possible to enter the business of carrying goods with a very small initial investment, building up the business by reinvesting profits. The qualities necessary for success were largely similar to those required in the tramp shipping industry. The lorry, like the tramp steamer, often competes for freight under, it has been said, 'conditions of almost classical simplicity.' "[10]

Fixed and Variable Costs

Evidence supporting the foregoing evaluation of the economics of motor transport is afforded by studies which have been made of the costs characteristic of motor carrier operations. The Cost Section of the Bureau of Transport Economics and Statistics of the Interstate Commerce Commission has made some elaborate studies of cost behavior for both railroads and motor carriers.[11] These were undertaken for the purpose of examining the relationships of fixed to variable costs for different carriers and for varying conditions of operations. They endeavored to portray the basic principles underlying transportation costs and the relation of those costs to rate making.

The study on motor transport involved a wide sampling of the statistics available and an extensive analysis of operating costs under varying lengths of haul in different traffic densities. One analysis, based on data of Class I common carriers of general freight in the central region in 1943, involving an average haul of 300 to 349 miles, showed that on the average 93.6 per cent of the costs varied directly and proportionately with the traffic, while the remaining 6.4 per cent

[10] M. R. Bonavia, *The Economics of Transport* (New York: Pitman Publishing Corp., 1947), p. 66.

[11] Bureau of Transport Economics and Statistics, Interstate Commerce Commission, *Explanation of the Development of Motor Carrier Costs,* Statement No. 4725 (Washington, D.C., 1949), p. 103.

did not vary with the traffic; that is, they were fixed regardless of traffic.[12]

The conclusion drawn for the study as a whole was that for Class I general commodity carriers, between 90 and 100 per cent of the operating expenses were directly proportional to output. This contrasted with long-run rail operating costs, which were estimated to be between 70 and 80 per cent variable if investment was excluded. But only 50 to 70 per cent of rail investment is variable, according to this study, which means that the variable expenses of railroads are a much lower proportion of total expenses, since railroads have a very heavy investment.

The contrast in the variability of costs between rail and motor carriers is explained partly by the fact that fixed costs are present in rail maintenance-of-way expenses and in the capital costs resulting from the investment in road property. The corresponding roadway costs for motor carriers are distributed on a "use" basis through gas taxes and license fees, and insofar as the motor carriers are concerned, they tend to be proportional to the traffic carried.[13]

The operating ratios of rail and motor carriers reflect the same situation. Where fixed costs are high and the costs of capital a large part of the total, the operating ratio must be relatively low if the operations are to be profitable. If the fixed costs are low, the reverse will be true. In 1946 the operating ratio for Class I railroads was 83.4 per cent; in 1964 it was 78.5 per cent, while in 1942 it was only 61.6 per cent. The operating ratio for Class I motor carriers of property was 95.1 per cent in 1948 and 93.2 per cent in 1947. It averaged 96.4 per cent for the eight-year period from 1940 to 1947 and was 95.8 per cent in 1963.

Another test, which supports the two which have just been given, is afforded by the ratio of gross revenues from operations to the total capital investment, or the turnover of capital. The turnover of capital for railroads is about once every three years; or to put it another way, the gross revenues from operations of railroads typically constitute annually about one third of the capital investment. The turnover for Class I motor carriers of freight reporting to the Interstate Commerce Commission was approximately five times in 1963. Although indi-

[12] Bureau of Accounts and Cost Finding, Interstate Commerce Commission, *Explanation of Rail Cost Finding Principles and Procedures,* Statement No. 2–48 (Washington, D.C., 1948), p. 88.

[13] Ford K. Edwards, "Cost Analysis in Transportation," *American Economic Review,* Vol. XXXVII, No. 2 (May, 1947), p. 453.

vidual carriers necessarily varied somewhat from this overall picture, the variations from the average do not seem to have any correlation with the size of the individual carriers.

The precise relationship of costs to the rate of output in motor transport cannot be obtained, but it is evident that fixed costs play a much less significant role than they do in rail transport. Motor carrier equipment is relatively short-lived as compared with that of the railroads, and obsolescence is a much less important factor. Depreciation is closely associated with amount of use. Variable costs are high, therefore, even for the short run, and noneconomic costs are not of great importance. The margin between economic costs and total costs is so small that the range of variation between the total costs that need to be covered and the minimum that must form the basis of decisions for rate making is of little consequence, even over a short period of time. In other words, controllable variable costs are the ones that govern motor carrier pricing.

Joint and Common Costs

Joint and common costs are present in motor carrier operations, but they are also relatively small as compared with railroads. The operating unit is small, never legally equaling that of a single railroad freight car of one hundred tons capacity, which is a rather common unit in this country. Hence, it is not difficult to have "homogeneous" loads for a single conveyance. The motor carrier, like the rail carrier, has the problem of the back haul, but even here the joint costs are relatively much less important because of the size of the operating unit and because joint costs in the fixed and specialized highway and terminal facilities are largely absent. Therefore the specific variable or relevant costs for motor transport are such a large proportion of the total costs that pricing based upon costs comes about as close to the competitive norm as can be obtained in real life. It follows from this that differential pricing based on cost considerations is not very significant and that price discrimination is not a problem unless a particular carrier enjoys a monopoly position in some or all of its markets, as a result of legal restrictions on entry.

Absence of Ruinous Competition

Competition among motor carriers cannot be ruinous. Ruinous competition, it should be emphasized, can arise only when fixed costs are a large part of the total costs of a firm, and when, as a consequence of the techniques of production, the consumer is unable to shop around.

The essence of competition is that it provides the incentive to strive for profits and the compulsion to go somewhere else if they are not forthcoming. Reliance on competition keeps costs to the consuming public at the minimum necessary to attract the services for which it is willing to pay. There is no danger of rates rising above that level if competition is not restricted by public action. In other words, the cost structure of motor transport is such as to make it possible for competition to function as a fully effective force for establishing economical prices. In fact, obstacles placed in the way of such competitive pricing will redound only to the benefit of the protected carriers. It will be to the disadvantage of the consuming public and the carriers that are precluded from competing.[14] This does not mean that there is no place for the common carriers in motor transport. What it means is that the economic basis for imposing limitations on competition among common carriers is lacking. This problem will be dealt with at greater length in the section on national policy.

OTHER AGENCIES

It is not necessary to discuss price theory as applied to the other agencies of transportation in the same detail that was accorded rail and motor carriers. This is because the latter exhibit the two major categories of market and economic structures into which the other agencies fall, namely, monopolistic and competitive. Pipe lines are in the monopoly group, while water and air carriers are in the competitive one.

Pipe Lines

Pipe lines have cost characteristics similar to railroads although the fixed costs are even more important in relative terms. Pipe lines are natural monopolies as a result of high relative fixed costs and a concomitance of production and consumption. In addition, they have a highly specialized plant without the problem of a back haul. The traffic carried by the respective lines is also quite homogeneous in character. Thus the joint and common cost features are considerably less significant and more readily identifiable than is the case for railroads. This is especially true of petroleum and other pipe-line prod-

[14] See D. F. Pegrum, "The Economic Basis of Public Policy for Motor Transport," *Land Economics*, Vol. XXVIII, No. 3 (August, 1952), pp. 244–63; J. C. Nelson, "New Concepts in Transportation Regulation," *Transportation and National Policy* (Washington, D.C.: U.S. Government Printing Office, 1942), pp. 197–243.

ucts, although it is less so for natural gas.[15] Thus the relevant costs upon which price decisions may be made are much closer to the average costs than they are in railroad transport. On the other hand, discrimination in the monopoly sense can be practiced much more easily because of the lack of readily alternative means of transportation for producers in many of the oil fields. There is little pricing incentive for the pipe lines to charge rates designed to attract traffic from other transport firms. There is also the fact that the bulk of pipe-line transportation is for the owners of those lines.

Water Transport

The cost characteristics of domestic water transport are essentially the same as those of motor carriers, and for the same reasons. Ownership of the vessels can be separated from that of the waterways, canals, and terminals. Shipping costs are mostly variable, and the industry is therefore highly competitive in its structure. The plant, that is, the vessel, may follow the traffic to whatever place it may be obtained and take it anywhere else. Cargo may move in many different ways: in bulk, on tramp ships, on liners, or through forwarders. The result is that rates are highly volatile and commonly fluctuate widely. When shipping is scarce, the rates may rise to high levels; at other times they may sink to out-of-pocket costs which can be very low at any particular time or for any particular shipment. Thus, for example, if a ship is moving from one port to another to pick up cargo, it may take on freight at a very low price in order to get some revenue between the two ports. The prices, however, are in direct response to the market situation, which is what competition means.

It has been urged from time to time that competition has resulted in suicidal rate cutting, especially in the years since 1930. This seems, however, to be a case of excess capacity which cannot survive such competition and which it is the function of competition to eliminate. The carriers which cannot survive such competition have no economic justification to continue. In fact, the principal matter of concern in domestic water transportation has been to protect it against competition from the railroads. This is certainly not a basis for price control in water transport, and the economics of water transport do not disclose why it is more necessary there than for industry in general. If there are reasons for imposing price controls, they do not stem from the economic characteristics of the industry.

[15] See D. F. Pegrum, *Public Regulation of Business* (rev. ed.; Homewood, Ill.: Richard D. Irwin, Inc., 1965), pp. 689–93.

Air Transport

Air transport is very similar to shipping in its economic characteristics. From a strictly economic point of view, air transport supply can be provided in a thoroughly competitive atmosphere. It might turn out to be oligopolistic in some markets if public control were not exercised, but even in these cases the governing factors would be so indeterminate that competitive pricing would probably result.

Because of technical problems of air safety and air traffic control at the present time, strict government supervision seems to be necessary, and limitations on the use of airways may have to be maintained. This, however, does not necessitate limitations on the competition among carriers, and it probably does not require even the restriction on the number of carriers. Mail pay and subsidies, however, raise another issue. It does not seem to be reasonable to support the carriers through the public treasury and then allow unlimited entry. Public aid, nevertheless, does not require control of maximum prices as an arm of its policy, even though minimum rate control may have to be invoked as a means of protecting the public purse. If maximum rate control is necessary, then either public aid should be reduced, or more competition should be allowed.[16]

THEORY OF INTERAGENCY PRICING

A Multiple Pricing Problem

The pricing problems of the various agencies of transport are not one, but many. Each mode has its own particular product and service which may be priced more or less independently of the other agencies. The prices for these services will depend on the amount of intra-agency competition. In motor, water, and air transport, they will not, if market forces are permitted to operate freely, deviate significantly from fully allocated costs. In other words, differential pricing or price discrimination is not a serious problem in these areas of transport. In fact, apart from predatory practices, it will not exist except over a narrow range and for the short run. Nor does monopoly pricing pose a problem for public policy.

[16] See Walter Adams (ed.), *The Structure of American Industry* (3d ed.; New York: Macmillan Co., 1961), chap. xiii, "The Airlines Industry," by Horace M. Gray. Belief in the effectiveness of competition in air transport and the desirability of it even when that competition is with government-owned corporations was the basis of the decision of the Air Licensing Transport Board in Great Britain when it granted a license to the Cunard Eagle Airways to fly the North Atlantic route from London to New York in competition with BOAC (*Manchester Guardian*, June 29, 1961).

In railroad transport, intra-agency competition is necessarily limited, with the consequence that differential or discriminatory pricing can and should be practiced if unused capacity exists and revenue requirements necessitate it. This may require some controls to prevent competition among railroads from becoming ruinous, as well as to prevent possible exploitation of the consumer.

Interagency Competition

If the different agencies were totally distinct from each other in the services they offered, or if they competed with each other only incidentally, no significant problem of interagency competition and pricing would emerge. This is not the case, however, and very extensive competition between rail carriers, on the one hand, and motor, water, and air carriers, on the other, has developed. Because of the different cost considerations that enter into price decisions for railroads and for these other carriers, there arises the question of the economical basis of competition among them. Only the railroads can resort to differential pricing to any significant extent in this competition. The question is whether they should be permitted to do so, and if they are, to what extent it should be sanctioned.

If traffic is to be shared by the different modes of transport according to their relative efficiencies for moving that traffic, then the apportioning of it must be made upon the basis of relative costs. Economical transport means that the agency which can move the traffic at the lowest cost should be allowed to take the business if it wishes to do so. The costs which are the decisive ones in this connection are those that will be incurred if the traffic is taken and will not be incurred if it is refused. There is no difference *in principle* with regard to the costs which each agency should consider. All of the different modes of transport have costs which are independent of the volume of traffic they haul, and all have costs which vary with it. In other words, all of them can engage, economically, in differential pricing, but it is only with the railroads that this takes on any great importance. Public policy which fails to give recognition to this fact is denying the public the use of the most economical type of transport. It is always in the interest of the economy to use the cheapest means for achieving a given objective. This is a cardinal principle of economics. Minimum rates, which attract traffic that increases the net revenue of the carrier that can get it, are in the public interest and are a necessary part of public policy which relies on competition. These rates are also a necessary part of public policy which aims at the most efficient utilization of economic resources. The fact that the minimum rates may be based on costs which are below "average" is not a relevant consideration. The important question is: Will the net revenue of the firm be increased by obtaining the traffic?

If this is to be the basis of public policy in transportation, competition among the agencies must be free and fair. If the competition is to be free and fair, then the carriers of the different agencies must be allowed to compete for the traffic which may be moved by any of them on the basis of charging prices for the services that will maximize the revenue that can be obtained from them. That is, as long as the carrier can take the traffic at rates which will better the carrier's net revenue position as compared with what it would be if the business were not obtained, that carrier should be permitted to take it. To prevent it from doing this results in unused capacity, a misuse of economic resources, and an allocation of traffic contrary to relative efficiencies as evidenced by cost considerations. What this means is that the pricing structure for transport services should be developed in accordance with market considerations. The minimum prices which should be permitted are those below which the carrier would be worse off if it took the traffic than it would be if it did not do so.[17]

Differential Pricing and Efficiency

It is frequently urged that differential pricing by a carrier, with regard either to commodities or to places, results in prejudicial treatment to those commodities or places which are not accorded the lower rates. The fact is, however, that when this differential charging is the result of competition, it is because the carrier which grants the differential rates does so in order to get the traffic. If the carrier is not permitted to do this, the traffic will move by the carrier of another agency and so will get the benefits of the lower rates in any case. Thus, no matter what restrictions are placed upon the carrier which tries to get the traffic by economical differential pricing, it is not possible to protect the commodities or the communities against such charges. The only beneficiary of the policy which prevents carriers from engaging in this differential pricing is the carrier which is protected against losing the business to its more competent rival.

The objective of the transportation policy of this country, as stated

[17] For agreement with this position, see Milne, *op. cit.,* chap. vi; and J. R. Meyer *et al., The Economics of Competition in the Transportation Industries* (Cambridge: Harvard University Press, 1959), chap. ix. For a contrary view which presumably represented the position of the Interstate Commerce Commission, at least in 1958 when Mr. Howard Freas was Chairman, see Freas, *op. cit.,* especially p. 66.

by Congress, is to provide an adequate transport system at the lowest possible cost. The economic basis for achieving this is to permit and encourage traffic to move by the means which can haul it most efficiently. The measure of efficiency for this purpose is the relative cost of haulage, the carrier which can afford to move the traffic at the lowest relative cost being the most efficient one. The costs which are relevant in this case are the "economic" costs. That is, they are those which will be incurred if traffic is taken and will not be there if the traffic is not taken. It is these costs which should set the minimum rates for any of the agencies. Any other basis for the allocation of traffic will impair the economic efficiency of the transport system of the country.[18]

Ruinous Competition

The point is frequently made that "unrestricted competition between the different modes of transportation, like unrestricted competition between railroads, may be ruinous in character."[19] This position rests on the assumption that competitive rates would be reduced to an out-of-pocket cost basis. However, as has already been emphasized, this does not apply to competition among the carriers of those agencies whose cost structures are of the strictly competitive type. It also would not apply to the traffic of one agency that is not subject to the competition of other agencies. In the case of motor or water carriers, nevertheless, all of the traffic still will be subject to competitive pricing because of the nature of these carriers. Furthermore, motor or water carrier competition cannot be ruinous to the railroads in the economic sense. Therefore the issue that is raised is whether railroad competition can be ruinous to the other carriers. Even this concerns only the traffic that each mode can accommodate. The answer to this issue is that the competition will not be ruinous so long as railroad pricing is based on relevant costs. It has already been pointed out that such pricing is economical. If public policy prevents it, then the result will be to inhibit the efficient utilization of the economic resources allocated to railroad transport in order to protect the resources in motor or water transport. The effect is to deny the shipper the opportunity to patronize

[18] See D. F. Pegrum, "The Special Problem of Inter-Agency Competition in Transport," *I.C.C. Practitioners' Journal* (December, 1956), pp. 307–14. An interesting discussion of the problem of cost equalization is given in J. R. Sargent, *British Transport Policy* (Oxford: Clarendon Press, 1958).

[19] Locklin, *Economics of Transportation, op. cit.,* p. 858; also *National Transportation Policy* (Doyle Report), Preliminary Draft of a Report to the Senate Committee on Interstate and Foreign Commerce, 87th Congress, 1st session (Washington, D.C.: U.S. Government Printing Office, 1961), Part VI, chaps. iv–vi. For a contrary point of view, see Meyer *et al., op. cit.,* chap. ix; and Milne, *op. cit.,* chap. vi.

the most efficient supplier available to him. This is protecting competitors against competition from suppliers of transport services whose resources are in the industry, which resources will go unutilized if the limitations are imposed.

The complex problems of interagency rate competition have led some to espouse the position that the low-cost modes should determine the minimum rate for competitive purposes. (See footnote 8, above.) This rate would be based on the fully allocated costs of the low-cost carrier. Other carriers might be permitted to meet this rate but not go below it. The difficulty with this approach is that it necessitates the averaging of all costs, which must assume a homogeneity of output. This requires averaging the costs of competitive and noncompetitive traffic. The objections to this have already been dealt with. There is the additional fact that much of the problem arises from competition between regulated and unregulated carriers, and the latter cannot be made to conform. Furthermore, there do not seem to be good reasons why the nonregulated carriers should be protected from competition by the regulated ones. Use of this low-cost approach by regulatory authorities to limit competition among the regulated modes encourages escape from regulation into the unregulated area, and constitutes cartelization of them by public authority, a policy which is encountering increased resistance because of changing technology.[20]

This problem of interagency competition and the economic basis of rate policy for such competition is not the result of private ownership of railroads, nor is it related to the problem of competition among railroads. It is independent of both. Even if the railroads were owned and operated as a single national system, thereby eliminating any intra-agency competition among them, the interagency problem would remain precisely the same as it is now. The cost structure of railroad transport would not be affected, and the basis for economical differential pricing would still be the same. The argument, therefore, that if policies for interagency pricing are to be developed on the basis of free and unhampered price competition, they should be extended throughout all the agencies on an intra-agency basis, is quite spurious. It is simply unrelated to the interagency problem. The policies for intra-agency competition in service and pricing should be dealt with on an individual agency basis.

[20] See D. F. Pegrum, "Is Minimum Rate Regulation Necessary in the Public Interest?" Papers, Fourth Annual Meeting. Transportation Research Forum (Boston, 1963), pp. 41–45.

Chapter

9

THE GENERAL LEVEL
OF RATES

INTRODUCTION

Price regulation in a private enterprise economy arises as a result of the inability, real or alleged, of competition, without any public intervention with regard to specific prices, to perform adequately the task of bringing about the most economical allocation and utilization of resources. Institutional and technological conditions of themselves necessitate some public participation in the determination of relative prices over a rather wide range of economic activity. For industry in general, this commonly takes the form of steps to insure conditions that will make competition workable and normally does not involve public determination of specific prices. Transportation and public utilities constitute a large exception to this general rule.

Direct regulation of various kinds of the prices charged by public utilities and common carriers has been the rule in this country for nearly a hundred years, although its complete manifestation has been confined to the present century. During this time the general theory has been that the prices of the enterprises in these industries have to be regulated to protect the public against monopolistic practices that are characteristic of the industries. It has also been assumed that the buyer is unable to obtain suitable alternative services. These conditions still obtain in public utilities; it was true for a good deal of railroad service at least down to 1920. The development of the new conditions in transport since that year, with the rise of the new agencies, has brought about thoroughgoing competition within some of them and widespread competition among the modes. This has led to the injection of a new note in transport regulation, namely, that it is necessary to control prices to protect the carriers from competition among themselves, and from others who may wish to intrude.

As has already been pointed out, transport supply ranges all the

198

way from that rendered by natural monopolies to highly competitive industries, with the additional complication of keen interagency rivalry in readily substitutable services. It is therefore pertinent to give a brief analysis of problems of price regulation that arise in connection with the fixing of minimum, maximum, and precise prices before turning to them as applied to transport. This is because transportation presents all the complexities of price regulation that are encountered in any market situation.

PRINCIPLES OF PRICE REGULATION

The principles of price control that are appropriate to any economy must be examined in the light of the underlying institutional assumptions and conditions of the economy. The problem is quite different if competition is severely restricted, or if there is no competition in production at all, from what it is if private enterprise and predominantly competitive conditions prevail. The basic objective of price regulation in the United States, presumably, is to bring about the allocation and utilization of economic resources that competition would yield under existing concepts of social desirability of particular lines of activity. The need for price regulation arises from the inability of public authority to establish rules apart from price controls which will make it possible for competition within those rules to achieve the desired results. Whether price controls do or can serve this purpose will depend upon circumstances; but frequently, they are a device that is ill-suited to the task imposed upon them. This is particularly the case when, instead of being utilized to promote competition or to substitute for it where it is absent, they are used to restrain it on either the supply or the demand side.

The regulation of minimum prices may have one of two main objectives. The first one is to impose limitations on minimum prices where lower prices would offend public standards or result in some form of undesirable exploitation. This is one of the purposes of minimum wage laws. In some states the alleged purpose, at least of minimum wellhead prices for natural gas, is to prevent wasteful exploitation of this natural resource. Most minimum price controls, however, are to protect producers against some of the effects of competition, either to aid the industry or to make competition workable.

Maximum prices are generally imposed as a means of protecting the consumer. Here, the theory is that the seller may be able to exploit the consumer beyond what seems to be reasonable where the commodity or service is a necessity. Maximum prices may also be imposed where limitations of supply prevent adjustments to the demand other than through prices which seem to be unreasonably high. In addition, maximum prices may be utilized for the purpose of limiting the production of some commodity or service when it is desired to divert economic resources into other channels of activity.

In addition to fixing minimum or maximum prices, regulation may fix the precise price at which commodities or services may be sold. This type of price regulation usually involves the determination of the profits which the firm is permitted to receive as well as the prices of the various commodities or services it sells. The regulatory agency, as a consequence, is engaged in deciding what the total income of the firm should be as well as the relationship among the prices of the products it sells. Although the basic purpose of this type of price regulation is to protect the buyer against exploitation because of the lack of adequate market alternatives, it also imposes upon public authority the responsibility of sanctioning prices that are adequate for the successful functioning of the firm. The objective of such regulation, therefore, is to permit the continuation of private production where competition is unable to perform the task of establishing reasonable prices, either to the producer or to the consumer. In this situation, public regulation is supposed to act as a substitute for competition in those aspects of a firm's activities that lack the incentives or restraining pressures of competition.

The Problem of Fair Prices

Price regulation necessarily raises the question of fair prices, because regulation presupposes that the market is unable to determine the prices that are fair to both consumers and producers. What constitutes fair prices involves ethical, legal, and economic considerations. From the standpoint of economics a fair price is one which would be established by full and free competition. The economic standard of a fair price is a competitive price, and the most precise form is that which would obtain under the model of perfect competition. It includes, therefore, normal profits for a business or "reasonable" payment for services. The problem for public regulation which fair prices present arises, first of all, from the fact that competition does not work perfectly, and substitutes have to be invoked to remedy some of the deficiencies. Ethical concepts may dictate a departure from purely competitive pricing even when the latter could be used. Minimum wage requirements are based, in part at least, on ideas of social justice.

Legal limitations may be imposed upon purely economic criteria either by statutes which may embody political and ethical considerations or by constitutional restrictions on regulation. Ethical considerations also play a part in the legal limitations that may be imposed by public authority. For example, prices do not have to cover noneconomic costs arising from sunk and specialized investment since there is no alternative use for the resources. Refusal by public authority to permit prices to recover these costs, at least in the case of public utilities, would meet with judicial disapproval because this would involve unfair treatment of the property owners.[1]

The fair price that is sought by public authority will present different problems, depending on whether it is a minimum price, a maximum price, or a precise one. In any event, it involves the matter of effecting ways and means of equilibrating demand and supply, because the fact that prices are being fixed means that the market processes that would operate without such price fixing are being interfered with. The interference is not that of affecting demand and supply directly by changing the rules and conditions of competition and allowing prices to work out the adjustments. Price fixing, in its various forms, prescribes the prices to which demand and supply must adjust themselves. The problem of public policy, therefore, is to determine the standards by which the appropriate prices are to be fixed.

Regulation of Minimum Prices

Minimum prices may be established for at least three different purposes. First of all, they may be used as a means of dealing with the problem of price discrimination. This may take the form of limiting or eliminating such practices as quantity discounts, freight absorption, and so forth. In these situations, regulation does not usually take the form of setting the minimum price; rather, it lays down the conditions of relative pricing. For example, the range and terms of quantity discounts may be prescribed; but the actual or base price on which the discounts are calculated will not be fixed by public authority. Similarly, freight absorption by the selling firm may be limited or permitted, under certain conditions, without determination of the base price which absorbs the freight. However, the question of the appropriate minimum does emerge, in that the basis of the differential may be questioned if predatory pricing is involved. When public authority is called upon to prevent pricing that is being used for the purpose of eliminating rivals, one of the issues that will arise is whether the differential or discrimi-

[1] See *Yakus* v. *United States,* 321 U.S. 414 (1944).

natory prices that are being charged are warranted by the costs of the price discriminator.

Second, minimum price regulation is used in the field of transport, where public authority is usually called upon to authorize all rate minima for regulated carriers. This is also true in public utility regulation. In transport, minimum price fixing was first applied to railroad rate regulation in order to deal with the problem of "ruinous" competition. Subsequently, as new agencies appeared, it was extended to them; and as interagency competition grew, it was extended to the control of competitive rates among the agencies. In other words, minimum prices have been set in transportation as a device for restricting interagency competition. In the case of public utilities the control of minimum rates is an integral part of the overall control of rates and the fixing of the precise rates.

Third, outside of the fields of transport and public utilities, where control has been developed on the theory of monopoly markets, the principal application of minimum price fixing has been in industries where the government has endeavored to put a bottom under prices for the purpose of relieving distressed conditions or as a means of establishing a predetermined status for an industry. The use of agricultural price supports based on a parity formula is an illustration of minimum price fixing for maintaining the economic status of agriculture at the relative level of a previous period that is used as a standard. The minimum price arrangements that were adopted before World War II for the bituminous coal industry were designed to afford relief to a distressed industry. The National Industrial Recovery Act embodied the minimum price device to assist in bringing about recovery from the depression of the thirties.

The fixing of minimum prices for these purposes necessitates, first of all, the determination of the required minimum. This may be based on a parity concept such as is used in connection with some agricultural commodities, by average costs for an industry, by some formula device such as is used for milk price controls, or by average costs as defined in the California Unfair Practices Act. Under this legislation a person engaged in business in California is prohibited from selling any article or product below cost. Cost of production is defined as including the cost of raw materials, labor (including salaries of executives and officers), and all overhead expenses of the producer. The law also prohibits the sale of any article or product as a "loss leader."[2] The

[2] Statutes of California, 1913, as amended in 1937, Chap. 860, Sec. 3.

problems connected with the administration of such a law, the totally uneconomic nature of it when applied to multiproduct firms, and the unrealistic concept of costs contained in it are too obvious to require further examination after the earlier analysis in this text of costs.

Effective minimum price fixing necessitates some form of production controls for the purpose of limiting supply in industries where there is more than one producer. This is the result of the fact that the minimum is imposed because supply under existing conditions will drive prices below the level which is desired. The imposition of the minimum conditions will result in unused capacity, which must be taken care of in some way. This may be accomplished by pooling arrangements, by cartelization, or by restriction of entry by requiring permits or certificates of public convenience and necessity. It may also be achieved by having an agency stand ready to buy whatever surplus emerges. The price support policy for agricultural products in this country is made to work by the government's readiness to acquire agricultural products at the minimum prices stipulated, by its surplus crop controls, and by its soil bank payments. Whatever the device used, it is a means of restricting competition to protect a particular group of producers.

Effective minimum price fixing also involves issues concerning the determination of costs and the role which costs play in the pricing process. When minimum price fixing is based on a parity formula, it assumes, first of all, that the price relationship existing between the industry whose prices are being fixed and the general level of prices for a particular period are to be maintained in future periods. Thus, it assumes that the cost relationships of the industry for the base period as compared with other industries are the "correct" ones which are to be maintained for those future periods. For industries where minimum price fixing is not based on a parity formula but instead on the direct basis of costs, the problem of what and whose costs are to be used emerges. Apart from the difficulty of ascertaining the precise minimum cost basis for the products of multiproduct firms, there is the question of the proper minimum to be used, because all firms will not have the same minimum. If minimum prices are to be set on the basis of the costs of the most efficient producer, they obviously can serve no real purpose, because prices will ordinarily be above those costs. If they are to be set on the basis of average cost for the industry, they meet the same objections, since they can offer no protection to the higher cost producers. If they are set on the basis of the highest cost or most inefficient producer, no gauge is available for the amount of production that should be forthcoming, and no standard is left whereby to judge or to compel efficiency.

The basic objection to minimum price control where competition is the dominating factor is that it is based upon false assumptions with regard to the nature of costs and the role of costs in the pricing process. It assumes that the costs which are to be used for the purpose are un-equivocal in nature and are readily ascertainable. The incorrectness of this viewpoint has already been discussed. In the second place, it assumes that prices are cost-determined and that the relationship is a one-way affair from cost to price. The fact is, of course, that the costs and prices are interrelated; they equal each other under competitive conditions only because of the adjustments on both sides of the relationship of demand and supply that competition compels. Competition dictates the adjustment of costs to prices as much as it does prices to costs. The setting of minimum prices by public authority in competitive industry ignores the effect of prices on costs and ignores the compelling pressure of competition on efficiency. In other words, it dispenses with two of the most significant economic bases for decision making and replaces them by purely arbitrary action.

Regulation of Maximum Prices

The prime purpose of imposing maximum limits on prices is to protect the consumer, although it may be employed as a device for limiting output. In transport and public utilities, maximum rate regulation theoretically is used to impose limitations on the power of monopoly to exploit the consumer of the commodities or services, and to limit the range of the relative prices charged by the companies. The policy here is related to the over-all price regulation problem in these industries and is therefore a phase of the question of fair return or fair profit. These issues will be dealt with later; but it may be noted in passing that transport under contemporary conditions presents a peculiarly difficult problem because of the breakdown of the fair return or fair profit concept under the intense competition that has emerged.

Maximum price fixing in competitive industry means that the maximum prices must apply to all of the producers of the commodities or services that are being controlled. This destroys part of the rationing function of prices, because the prices must be fixed for the industry. They cannot be fixed for a single firm, since such a procedure would make that firm's prices lower than the market price and lower than the prices of some competitors. This would force the latter to reduce their prices if they wished to continue to sell; and this, in turn, would force the high-cost producers to curtail production or go out of business. The result would be to limit supply and raise the problem of rationing, because consumers would be willing to pay higher prices than are permitted. This is the consequence of dispensing with the price mechanism as a means of deciding who shall get the product.

The same remarks apply if maximum ceilings are imposed for the purpose of restraining price advances while supply is catching up with the demand situation. Such maxima do not necessarily curtail production, because they may not be severe enough to do that; but they will necessitate some other means than price for rationing the product which is being sold at a price lower than that which could equilibrate demand and supply. In the case of rentals, for example, if controls are imposed, some means of protecting existing occupants must be found; eviction at will cannot be permitted. At the same time, those without dwellings are deprived of means of acquiring them; and in any case, they are prevented from getting what they want, even though they can afford to pay for it. In other words, maximum price fixing disequilibrates demand and supply, either by restricting output or by compelling the sale of products at a price that will leave some willing buyers unable to make purchases. This gives rise to "black" markets, "gray" markets, and under-the-counter "premiums" in the absence of other effective rationing devices. Maximum price fixing, in the absence of other arrangements than the mere control of the prices themselves, is an uneconomical and ineffective procedure for channeling the allocation and utilization of a country's economic resources.

The Regulation of Precise Prices

The fixing of the precise prices a firm may be permitted to charge embraces all the complexities of both minimum and maximum price fixing, because it combines them into one. It involves the additional problem of "fair" prices, that is, prices which yield to a firm the revenue it needs to attract economic resources to its employ, so that it can supply consumers with the services they desire at prices that will cover the costs of those services, but no more. To put it another way, total revenues must be such as to approximate the sort of equilibrium that would obtain under competition.

The starting point for fixing precise prices, therefore, is that of estimating the total revenue required by the firm to cover the costs of production plus the necessary fair profit. The determination of the fair profit necessitates a standard against which to measure the fairness. The gauge may be the profits being earned by similar types of industries (if there are any), or it may be the profit needed to attract the amount of capital required to produce the quantity of goods demanded at the "fair" prices. This means that some measure of the amount of capital, as well as the amount already being used, must be obtained. The standard commonly adopted in this connection is prudent investment. Having calculated the amount of profit the firm should be allowed to earn, public authority must then ascertain the costs of doing business. This means that it must not only be able to find out what the actual costs are; it means, in addition, that it must be able to exercise control over those costs and decide whether they are reasonable; otherwise, uncontrolled costs would provide an avenue of escape that would nullify the objective of controlling profits. When the total revenue requirements have been calculated, the burden of providing them has then to be assessed on the various commodities or services being sold.

This very general outline describes the method employed in fixing public utility rates, and it works with tolerable acceptability. The problem is simplified in this situation, however, because regulation may be applied to each firm separately. Public utility regulation is not usually complicated by any appreciable amount of competition among the firms. The difficulties which are encountered when competition is significant are thoroughly illustrated by the breakdown of this approach in the field of transport, especially since the rise of the newer agencies.

Industry in general is even less amenable to this type of control than is transport. In any industry where there are a number of competing firms, it would be unworkable to try to establish different individual prices for each firm. If the attempt were made to set prices for the industry as a whole, the immediate question that would arise would be what firm should be used as the standard. If the most efficient were selected, the others would earn inadequate revenues; if the least efficient were chosen, the regulation would fail of its purpose. If an average were used, the disadvantages of both of these would be encountered. In short, if precise price fixing is to be adopted for industry in general, it will be necessary to create monopolies by consolidation and restrict entry, or resort to a program of cartelization.

THEORY OF THE GENERAL LEVEL OF RATES

The theory and practice of regulation of the prices charged by transportation and public utility enterprises is most clearly exemplified in the case of public utilities, although, as previously pointed out, the distinction between rail transport and public utilities is not easy to draw. The difference between them lies not in their economic characteristics but rather in the market conditions under which they dispose of their services.

Cost-Plus Pricing

Theoretically, the objective of public utility regulation is to achieve the results that competition would yield; and theoretically, the cost-price relationships of competition are the ones that should be used. Unfortunately, the conditions that are necessary to the functioning of the competitive market are well-nigh totally absent. The consumer has literally no alternatives for the services. Regulation therefore turns to the cost side for the gauge for reasonable prices. However, the costs, which for competitive business are competitively determined, are only partially so for public utilities. The basing of rates on costs proceeds on the assumption that costs are readily and almost unequivocally ascertainable, whereas in fact this is not so. For example, in competitive industry the presence of a relatively high or relatively low return is taken to indicate either under- or overinvestment; but in public utilities, such a return suggests that rates need to be adjusted so as to bring the return into line. In competitive industry, prices cannot be forced to adjust themselves to committed costs. In public utility regulation, this is what is done, and there seems to be little possibility of avoiding it.

As a basis for economical pricing the cost-plus method has serious disadvantages, but if pricing by or for a monopoly is to be restricted below the full possibilities of exploitation, then the cost-plus approach must occupy a dominant role. This means that all phases of costs must be thoroughly supervised and controlled, and that standards of adequacy and quality of service must be established. The control of costs presents a particularly difficult problem, because many of them are not subject to market determination at any particular time. Capital costs, including depreciation and return on investment, loom large in the public utility pricing process; yet once they are committed, they are not subject to the forces of the market in a cost-plus approach. They are not economic costs to be considered in pricing, yet they are treated that way in cost-plus pricing.

The monopolist, whose prices are not regulated, resolves these problems by resort to the market and so preserves the same interplay of costs and prices, supply and demand, that obtain under competition, even though the compelling pressures for efficiency which competition imposes are lacking. Monopoly theory resolves the problem of cost-price relationships and price equilibrium by resort to the market—by equating marginal cost and marginal revenue. But economic theory is able to resolve the problem of economical allocation of resources which monopoly presents only by introducing competitive concepts. That is to say, in establishing standards for limiting monopoly profits, it endeavors to resort to the cost-price relationships which competition would compel. This is the standard which, theoretically at least, public authority uses in determining reasonable rates for public utilities. In so doing, it tries to resort to competitive standards in a situation in which the principal ingredients of market competition are lacking. This problem exists, however, wherever monopoly is present, be it under public or private ownership, unless full exploitation of monopoly power is permitted, in which case the adjustment of costs and prices will be worked out by the monopolist to his advantage.

The regulation of railroad rates developed on the theory that railroad transportation was an industry characterized by monopoly, which necessitated control of prices in the public interest. The original purpose was to protect the shipper against unreasonable rate differentials and exorbitant prices. Experience in imposing upper limits on railroad rates soon disclosed the fact that some measuring rod was necessary by which to gauge what the upper limit should be. The fixing of maxima on prices meant that the profits a firm could earn were also limited. If private operation was to be successful, the profits had to be adequate for that purpose. In addition, the law of the land prevented public authority from limiting profits below what was fair and reasonable.

Before particular prices can be set, therefore, it becomes necessary in some way to decide what the general level of rates shall be. That is, it is necessary to ascertain or assume the total revenue that is required before the specific prices which will yield that total revenue can be established. To do this means that total costs must be calculated, as well as the amount of the fair profit. To prevent profits from being siphoned off through costs, public authority must exercise control over the costs which are to be covered and over the quality of the service which the costs are supposed to provide. Finally, a measuring rod must be developed as the basis for deciding what constitutes a fair profit.

The most difficult questions connected with establishing the appropriate general level of rates arise in connection with the amount of income to which the enterprise is entitled because of its capital investment. The costs arising from this source are an important part of the total revenue requirements, although the proportion varies from one type of activity to another. For example, the proportions for a somewhat typical electrical utility will be as follows. Assume that the utility has an investment of $100 million, on which a return of 6 per cent is permitted, a capital turnover of once in five years, and a depreciation rate of 4 per cent per annum. The total revenue would be $20 million, the return on the investment $6 million, and the depreciation $4 million. The profit and the depreciation, both derived from the capital costs, would absorb 50 per cent of the gross revenues. The proportion for railroads may be somewhat less because of a higher capital turnover, but the rapid rate of obsolescence of railroad equipment in the last fifteen years has made the depreciation higher than the 4 per cent assumed above, which probably means that a similar ratio would hold for railroads today.

Most of the remaining costs are market-determined in that they are not dependent upon the monopoly position of the enterprise but will have to be met by it and covered in the revenues. Items like fuel, wages, and property taxes are in this category. They are not subject to control by the regulatory authority except that the latter is supposed to see that they are genuinely incurred and properly accounted for. Statutes providing for regulation therefore commonly empower the public authority to establish uniform accounting systems and procedures, supervise service standards and performance, and often exercise authority over corporate affiliations and security issues. Where public utility regulation is thoroughly comprehensive, the extent of control exercised by the regulatory agency is very great, covering almost every detail of operations. The situation varies widely in the case of the transport industries, regulation of railroads being extremely detailed and embracing all of them, whereas regulation of the other carriers is much less comprehensive and restrictive.

FAIR VALUE AND FAIR RETURN

The theory of fair value and fair return as applied to transportation is largely a matter of historic and academic interest. Historically, it is significant because of the attempt, subsequently abandoned, to apply it to the railroads in the period following 1920. Academically, it merits consideration because of the possibility that it might be revived if the railroads should be consolidated into a limited number of systems, or if regional consolidation should emerge. It also illustrates the nature of the problem of determining what the appropriate gauge should be if the general level of rates, for any mode of transport, is to be fixed by public authority. The most important developments to date connected with fair return on fair value have taken place in the field of public utilities, but the interpretation by the courts in the litigation in which the utilities have been involved is applicable to transport.

Valuation for Rate Making

Three theories of valuation have been advanced for determining the rate base upon which the calculation of reasonable rates is to be made, namely, market value, cost of reproduction, and what has come to be called prudent investment. The first two are really variants of the same thing, although they are arrived at in different ways.

Market Value. The market value of an income-producing property is dependent upon the net income that property can be expected to yield. That is, it is the capitalized value of the expected net income. One method of ascertaining this value at any time is to find the market value of the outstanding securities. This will depend upon the income the buyers expect to receive from these securities and the rate of return at which these buyers appraise that income. For example, if a security has a prospective earning of $10 a year and the rate of capitalization is 5 per cent, the capital value of the security will be $200. Another way of finding the value of a firm is to capitalize the net earnings at the going rate of return for such a business. If the total expected earnings are $10,000 a year and the rate is 5 per cent, the value of the firm will be $200,000. Whatever may be the precise technique that is used for ascertaining the value, the principle is the same, namely, capitalizing the expected net income at the appropriate rate of return.

This method, which is the correct way to ascertain economic value, cannot be used to determine what the base upon which fair profits are to be calculated should be, because it must assume that the earnings which are the object of control are known. Until these have been received, however, the economic value of the enterprise cannot be ascertained, and therefore the economic or market value cannot be used to prescribe the fair profit that may be earned. In addition, net earnings are not a matter of revelation; they are the difference between the gross income and the costs of producing it. But these costs include, among other things, the costs arising from using up the capital, particularly depreciation and obsolescence. Some basis for calculating the proper amounts of these items must also be found; and obviously, that basis cannot be market value. In other words, market value is deficient on two counts: It fails to give a gauge for measuring fair profit which is independent of the earnings, and it fails to give a basis for calculating some of the most important items of cost, which must be known before net earnings can be discovered. Any firm must use some basis from which it calculates depreciation and obsolescence, and market value alone cannot serve as that base. There is the additional fact that some property has no alternative use which might be employed as a gauge. This makes it impossible to obtain an economic value apart from the use to which it is being put. A structure such as Hoover Dam is an illustration of this.

Cost of Reproduction. Cost of reproduction, as a method of determining the rate base, may mean one of a number of different things. It may mean what it would cost to reproduce an existing plant under original conditions, what it would cost to reproduce it under present conditions, or what it would cost to produce a substitute plant with the advantages of changed technology which would afford the most modern services. The problem of prices also enters in, but it is usually assumed that current prices are to be used.

Calculating the cost to reproduce an existing plant under original conditions means primarily making an engineering estimate of what it would cost, under present-day prices, to reproduce the present facilities under the conditions which obtained at the time the plant was built. Such an estimate could have no possible relationship to reality in any way, because reproduction would not take place under such conditions. It would be ridiculous to assume the use of techniques as of the original time of construction, and to calculate the cost of reproducing nearly obsolete machinery would necessitate estimating what it would cost to produce the facilities to make that machinery. It would be like calculating what it would cost to produce a Model T Ford in a modern plant. Apart from creating a museum piece, nothing would be accomplished in doing it, and nothing would be accomplished in making the estimate. Much of the time, the estimate would involve calculating the reproduction cost of something that would not be reproduced. It would scarcely make sense to calculate the cost of reproducing many of the passenger coaches and railway stations still used by the railroads. In addition, nearly all of the facilities that are being "valued" are partially worn out. This may be accounted for by deducting depreciation, but depreciation calculated on the cost of reproduction would be as artificial as the initial evaluation.

Cost of reproduction of the existing plant under current conditions is subject to even more criticism, in that much of the reproduction might not take place under existing conditions. For example, gas or water mains may be laid under streets now paved; if new rail facilities were to be constructed today, they would be quite different with regard to grades, curves, and tunnels than they are now; and many of the huge passenger terminals would not even be thought of.

The third meaning of cost of reproduction refers to the estimated cost of replacing an existing plant with the most up-to-date one that could be constructed under present conditions, with the needs of the future carefully in mind. Under strictly competitive conditions, this variant of cost of reproduction would be the equivalent of market value. It could be used as a measure of value because it would equal the capitalized value of the prospective income. But it would not be independent of the prospective income, and so this would get us right back to the original problem. Market value and cost of reproduction are equal under strictly competitive conditions, because the forces on both sides of the market are freely adjustable to changing circumstances. Public utility property cannot be valued in terms of its alternative use, however, because most of it does not have an alternate use. It is the lack of this attribute that creates the problem in the first place. Even when there is an alternate use, it may not be possible to calculate the value. For example, the land values of railroad freight terminals cannot logically be ascertained on the basis of the value of adjacent lands. If the terminals were not there, the land values would be different, and what they would be may be impossible to calculate.

Finally, cost of reproduction at any particular time may not reflect value, even in nonpublic utility enterprises. For example, during the war the value of houses was not reflected in what it would cost to reproduce them, in any of the three meanings of that term, because they could not be reproduced. Similarly, in times of severe depression, houses may be worth less than cost of reproduction because of the surplus. Cost of reproduction cannot reflect value in public utility enterprises at any time and consequently fails as a means of providing equitable treatment both to the consumer and to the enterprise. The public is scarcely likely to sanction profits on modern equipment not in existence when the prices necessary to yield those profits may be coming from inferior property and inferior services from which the prices may be obtained because of the presence of monopoly.

Apart from these considerations, cost of reproduction is impracticable. In other words, it fails to meet the test of expediency. It can be obtained only by extensive engineering appraisals, which are costly and time-consuming. They require years to complete in the case of large properties and lead to marked differences of opinion on amounts, because of the imponderables which must be evaluated. As a practical matter, they cannot be kept up to date; a new valuation is needed every time an adjustment of the general level of rates is in order, but the process of making it is so slow that it would be far out of date every time it is used.

Prudent Investment. The essence of the prudent investment method of determining the rate base is that it is derived from the amount of investment, wisely made, and used and useful in rendering the public utility service. What this means is that the investment must be bona fide and made in accordance with the judgment of prospective market conditions that sound business practice would dictate. The qualification of "prudent" is introduced to eliminate speculation and fraud, and to compel the exercise of good judgment. Thus, if the investment a utility proposes to make is fully disclosed to a commission and receives the sanction of that body, it is regarded as being prudently and wisely made, even though subsequently it should be discovered that the initial estimates were in error because of unforeseen circumstances. The requirement that the investment be in property that is used and useful is designed to prevent property from entering into the rate base that performs no function in rendering public utility service. However, stand-by facilities that are not being used, but are useful and necessary, would be included in the investment.

Investment in property, whether tangible or intangible, can readily be ascertained if the accounts of the enterprise are maintained on that basis. When property is retired, the amount of investment that is thereby dispensed with, or written off, is a matter of record. When new property is acquired, that becomes a matter of record, too. For example, if a piece of property that cost $2,000 is retired and sold for $1,000, and a new item is acquired in its place for $4,000, this replacement will require $2,000 of new investment, the other $2,000 being derived from depreciation of $1,000 and sale of the original equipment for $1,000. Assuming that the transaction is properly carried out, the $4,000 will represent prudent investment, and it will also represent cost of reproduction new of the property at the time the transaction takes place. Because public utilities are continuously engaged in replacement, even prudent investment will reflect a considerable amount of current prices. These, however, will not be the result of artificial estimates but of actual transactions.

A great deal of the property of public utilities, excluding land, is in a state of being used up. The investment originally made in it has partially disappeared. It is the function of depreciation accounting to record this fact. At any particular time, the amount of depreciation that has actually taken place can only be estimated, and therefore the calculation of the amount of the investment in any particular piece of property that has been used up can only be estimated. It may be understated, or it may be overstated; but this will not affect the rate base as a whole, because accounting for depreciation serves the purpose of maintaining the investment by deductions from earnings, which are thereby retained in some form or other assets in the business.[3]

If prudent investment is used as the basis for evaluation for rate-making purposes, the determination of the rate base becomes a matter of accounting. Ascertaining prudence, used and useful property, integrity of transactions, adequacy of service, and so forth are not solved by it. In fact, for prudent investment to be effective, these aspects of public utility operation must be carefully supervised. However, this is true under the other proposals for valuation. Prudent investment has the advantage, among others, of eliminating the valuation costs, delays, and controversies, without adding to any of the other aspects of supervision which any method of control entails. The question of adequacy of earnings under it will be discussed later.

Prudent investment as a method of determining the rate base sometimes goes under the name of original cost to date, original cost plus additions, and betterments or historical cost. These are not necessarily the same thing; but in practice, that is what they amount to. Original cost to date means the amount actually invested in the property from the beginning. This takes into account property which has been retired as worn out or obsolete, new investment made through the sale of securities, and earnings which have been retained in the business. If the records have been kept properly and the present property is used and useful, the amount shown will be the same as prudent investment. Because a good deal of utility investment was made before adequate regulation and control of accounting took place, it was necessary to make physical appraisals to determine the investment at the time of valuation. No matter how carefully it was done, it was still only

---

[3] This does not deal with the intricacies of depreciation policy with regard to adequacy of service or replacement. These are quite different matters, which involve other considerations. The effect of excessive depreciation charges at any time would be to make the cost of serving the public at that time higher to that extent. This would not alter the prudent investment of the firm as shown by the books, however. Therefore the rate base and the net return would be unaffected. When the property was totally depreciated on the books, there would be no depreciation to enter into the cost of service, and the total revenue requirements would diminish accordingly; but the total investment in the firm would still be the same. Similarly, these remarks would apply, vice versa, to underdepreciation. The writing off of intangibles is handled in an analogous fashion.

an estimate. The California Commission dealt with the difficulty by what it called the historical cost method.[4] It established the estimated prudent investment as of the date of the appraisal; and then, with this as a starting point, it kept the valuation up to date through the accounting record of the changes in the property. It was necessary at all times, however, to include land in the rate base at market value because of the decision of the Supreme Court of the United States in the second Minnesota rate case.[5] The market value of land under this ruling was to be based upon the value of similar lands in the community. The method used by the California Commission is also sometimes called the split inventory method because of the necessity of starting with an appraisal of the property before accurate accounting for maintaining the rate base could be introduced.

Fair Value and the Courts

Relatively early in the development of regulation the Supreme Court of the United States took the position that it would afford relief from unreasonably low rates prescribed by legislatures or commissions.[6] The result was to make the courts an immediate and integral part of the rate-making process. In theory, it was the function of the courts to see that rates were not set so low as to result in the taking of property without due process of law, or confiscation, as it came to be called. Unfortunately, what the Court did, in fact, was to intervene in such a way that the judicial measure of confiscation became the Commission's measure of reasonableness, because the Court, in establishing the minimum below which rates could not legally be compelled to go, embraced both equitable and economic considerations. Unfortunately also, the Court set no precise means for determining what the minimum should be, with the result that long-drawn-out litigation has occupied the center of the regulatory stage. Fair value and fair return became the focal points of the controversy, the Court apparently believing that fair value and fair rate of return were independent variables for the determination of fair profit, and that each could be discovered by the application of principles derived from competitive economics.

The first decision of the Supreme Court to establish a judicial

---

[4] For a detailed discussion of this, see D. F. Pegrum, *Rate Theories and the California Railroad Commission* (Berkeley, Calif.: University of California Press, 1932).

[5] *Simpson* v. *Shepard*, 230 U.S. 352 (1913).

[6] See *Stone* v. *Farmers' Loan and Trust Company*, 116 U.S. 307 (1886); *Chicago, Milwaukee and St. Paul Railway Company* v. *Minnesota*, 134 U.S. 418 (1890). These reversed the original position taken in *Munn* v. *Illinois*, 94 U.S. 113 (1877).

standard for public utility rate making was rendered in *Smyth* v. *Ames* (1898).[7] The standard, the Court stated, was to be a fair return on a fair value which was to be derived from a number of considerations that were set forth in the opinion. The case arose from an order issued by the Board of Transportation of Nebraska, fixing maximum railroad freight rates. William Jennings Bryan, counsel for Nebraska, in defending the order, argued (1) that the states had a right to fix maximum rates, which should be interfered with by the courts only if such rates yielded an income so small as to leave nothing above operating expenses; and (2) that if the Court should pass upon the reasonableness of the profit allowed the railroads, the present value of the roads, as measured by the cost of reproduction, should be the basis upon which the profit should be computed. The cost-of-reproduction argument was advanced because the price level at the time much of the railroad property was constructed was considerably higher than it was in 1898, the price level then being only slightly above what it was in 1896, which was the low point in the history of the United States. In addition, cost of reproduction was urged as a means of checking against the excesses that had frequently taken place in the earlier periods of construction and were manifest in the financial structures of the companies. In dealing with the arguments, Mr. Justice Harlan stated:

> The corporation may not be required to use its property for the benefit of the public without receiving just compensation for the services rendered by it. How such compensation may be ascertained, and what are the necessary elements in such an inquiry, will always be an embarrassing question. . . .
>
> We hold, however, that the basis of all calculations as to the basis of the reasonableness of rates to be charged by a corporation . . . must be the fair value of the property being used by it for the convenience of the public. And in order to ascertain that value, the original cost of construction, the amount expended in permanent improvements, the amount and market value of its bonds and stock, the present as compared with the original cost of construction, the probable earning capacity of the property under particular rates prescribed by statute and the sum required to meet operating expenses, are all matters for consideration, and are to be given such weight as may be just and right in each case. We do not say that there may not be other matters to be regarded in estimating the value of the property. What the company is entitled to ask is a fair return on the value of that which it employs for the public convenience. On the other hand, what the public is entitled to demand is that no more be exacted from it . . . than the services rendered by it are reasonably worth.[8]

Because of the facts of the case the rates would have been invalid under any standard of reasonableness. It was not necessary, therefore, for the Court to make any definite finding on the fair value of the railroads

[7] 169 U.S. 466.
[8] *Ibid.*, pp. 546 and 547.

involved in the case or even to give any intimation as to how the pot-
pourri of irreconcilable and incommensurate statistical computations
could be made to yield a single meaningful figure.

Litigation down to the end of World War I served to focus the
whole controversy sharply on fair value. Operating costs dropped from
the picture as an item to be considered in ascertaining fair value; earning capacity and value of stocks and bonds were rejected as valid
factors.[9] Considerable weight came to be given to cost of reproduction
as a means of arriving at the "reasonable value" of property, and the
Court seemed to feel that cost of reproduction was a better measure
than original cost, because it eliminated excesses that often had accompanied much of the original construction.[10] However, because property was not to be protected in its actual investment, recognition had to
be given to the fair value, if this was more than its cost.[11] The results,
at the time, were probably not far from a workable prudent investment
figure; but the skyrocketing of prices as a result of World War I removed any relation that cost of reproduction might have had to prudent
investment. In litigation that followed the end of World War I, the
Court soon came to reflect the point of view expressed in the Minnesota
rate cases. In *Southwestern Bell Telephone Company* v. *Public Service
Commission of Missouri* (1923),[12] the Court unanimously agreed that
the rates prescribed by the Missouri Commission were far too low by
any standards, in that they did not accord any weight to the marked
increases in costs of material, labor, and supplies. The majority held
that weight should be given to cost of reproduction because of the
greatly enhanced costs of construction of the post-World War I period
over those of the prewar years. How much weight was to be given cost
of reproduction was not indicated. In a minority opinion which concurred in the results but dissented from the reasoning, Mr. Justice
Brandeis, supported by Mr. Justice Holmes, developed his famous presentation on behalf of prudent investment. And so the issue within the
Court and before the commissions became sharply drawn.

Cost of reproduction as the most important factor to be considered
in arriving at the rate base reached its highest point in the *McCardle et
al.* v. *Indianapolis Water Company* (1926),[13] where the Court, recog-

---

[9] *Simpson* v. *Shepard* (second Minnesota rate case), 230 U.S. 352 (1913); *Knoxville* v. *Knoxville Water Company*, 212 U.S. 1 (1909).

[10] *San Diego Land and Town Company* v. *Jasper*, 189 U.S. 439 (1903).

[11] Minnesota rate cases, 230 U.S. 352 (1913). See also *Willcox* v. *Consolidated Gas
Company*, 212 U.S. 19 (1909).

[12] 262 U.S. 276; see also *Bluefield Water Works and Improvement Company* v.
Public Service Commission of West Virginia, 262 U.S. 679 (1923).

[13] 272 U.S. 400.

nizing the higher level of prices prevailing at that time, held that fair value should be based on "the present cost of constructing the plant, less depreciation, if any." This position was given additional support in the Baltimore street railway case in which the Court ruled that the allowance for depreciation should also be based on present value.[14]

The turning point in emphasis upon cost of reproduction or upon any particular formula, for that matter, in determining the rate base for measuring confiscation came in *Los Angeles Gas and Electric Corporation* v. *Railroad Commission of California* (1933),[15] which upheld the California Commission in the first forthright test of historical cost, the practical equivalent of prudent investment. This development may be attributed to four things: (1) The California Commission had established itself over a period of twenty years as one of the leading state commissions, and its rulings had not been challenged theretofore; (2) the Commission had been generous in its rate of return, so that it was difficult to contest the over-all result of fair return; (3) there was a growing tendency on the part of the Court to look with more favor on well-considered commission regulation; and (4) the price level was declining rapidly, and this dampened enthusiasm for cost of reproduction. The opinion of the Court foreshadowed developments that were to take place during World War II.

The Court pointed out that it did not sit as a board of revision but rather as an agency to enforce constitutional rights. It held that in determining the weight to be ascribed in this case to historical cost, the outstanding fact was that the development of the property had for the most part taken place in a recent period. Furthermore the prices for labor and materials which were reflected in historical cost were higher than those which obtained in the later period to which the rates applied.

It is the appropriate task of the Commission to determine the value of the property affected by the rate it fixes, as that of an integrated, operating enterprise, and it is the function of the Court in deciding whether rates are confiscatory not to lay down a formula, much less to prescribe an arbitrary allowance, but to examine the result of the legislative action in order to determine whether its total effect is to deny to the owner of the property a fair return for its use.[16]

[14] *United Railways and Electric Company of Baltimore* v. *H. E. West et al.*, 280 U.S. 234 (1930) 254. For a similar interpretation by state courts, see *Waukesha Gas and Electric Company* v. *Railroad Commission of Wisconsin*, 191 Wis. 565 (1927).

[15] 289 U.S. 287.

[16] *Ibid.*, p. 314. See also *Natural Gas Pipeline Company* v. *Federal Power Commission*, 315 U.S. 575 (1942). In the opinion of three justices this decision laid the ghost of *Smyth* v. *Ames* to rest.

The issue of original versus reproduction cost came squarely before the Court in *Federal Power Commission* v. *Hope Natural Gas Company* (1944).[17] The company argued for reproduction cost, while the Federal Power Commission stood by the prudent investment basis of determining the rate base. The Court sustained the commission's decision, but it did not espouse any particular basis of fair value. Mr. Justice Douglas, speaking for the Court, said:

> It is not the theory but the impact of the rate order which counts. If the total effect of the rate order cannot be said to be unjust and unreasonable, judicial inquiry . . . is at an end. The fact that the method employed to reach the result may contain infirmities is not then important. . . . Rates which enable the company to operate successfully, to maintain its financial integrity, to attract capital and to compensate its investors for the risks assumed [may be taken as a guide to reasonableness as far as the courts are concerned].[18]

It appears, under this doctrine of the "end result," that legislatures and commissions are now free to employ whatever method they see fit to determine the general level of rates. They are not bound by any formula or any prescribed set of rules. It is therefore more difficult for utilities to challenge commission decisions in the courts; but by the same token, it may be more difficult for commissions to be sure of their ground. The Court did not lay down a gauge by which confiscation could be measured, but quite possibly a distinction can now be made between rates which are confiscatory and those which are reasonable from an economic point of view. It is with the latter that commissions must be concerned, especially in times of uncertainty. Severe economic stress might well bring the whole matter to the fore again.[19] Furthermore, commissions cannot avoid the problem of valuation because of the issues arising from "used and useful" property, depreciation, and financial structure. In addition, if the courts are to serve as a safeguard against taking property without due process of law they will have to face up to the issue in some way or another.

Fair Return

The problem of fair return has always been an integral part of the problem of reasonable rates; yet, curiously enough, it has never been

[17] 320 U.S. 591.

[18] *Ibid.*, p. 602. Three justices dissented from the majority that the new "rule" was too indefinite.

[19] See also *Market Street Railway Company* v. *Railroad Commission of California*, 324 U.S. 548 (1945); *Colorado Interstate Gas Company* v. *Federal Power Commission*, 324 U.S. 581 (1945); *Panhandle Eastern Pipe Line Company* v. *Federal Power Commission*, 324 U.S. 625 (1945). For a more extended discussion of the rate base, see C. F. Phillips, Jr., *The Economics of Regulation* (Homewood, Ill.: Richard D. Irwin, Inc., 1965), chap. 8.

given the attention or promoted the controversy that has accompanied fair value. Slight reflection, however, will indicate that a change from a return of 6 per cent on a given base to 8 per cent is the equivalent of increasing the rate base by 33⅓ per cent. The indifferent treatment that has been accorded fair return may be accounted for on three assumptions: (1) that it is upon the value of property that firms are entitled to earn a reasonable profit, and the alternatives for investment are what determine the profit of competitive firms; (2) that returns on comparable business activities can be readily ascertained by observation; and (3) that the profits which a utility is permitted to earn are for it to disburse in accordance with its own judgment. In other words, financial structure is a matter of indifference in determining fair return and fair value. As a matter of fact, financial structure could not be given any serious consideration until cost of reproduction was dispensed with, because the two have no relation to each other.

It has become standard practice for commissions and courts alike to regard fair return as the income which is to be used as the payment to all of those who contribute capital to the enterprise. This fair return, therefore, is supposed to cover all interest costs, dividends, and whatever may be left over to go to surplus. Under the rulings of the courts, this fair return is what the firm is entitled to after corporate income taxes. The latter, for the purpose of calculating fair return, is an expense, just like all other taxes, to be covered before the return is ascertained. In addition, depreciation to the amount necessary to maintain the capital intact must also be provided for before the fair return is calculated. How the fair return is distributed among the suppliers of the firm's capital will depend upon the contractual arrangements with the security holders. Bondholders will be paid the interest specified in the indenture; preferred stockholders, the dividends stipulated in their stock certificates; and the common stockholders, the amount which is allotted by management from what is left over after the other claims have been satisfied. Incidentally, it may be noted that bonuses to management are commonly an item which must be provided out of fair return, because they are not chargeable to expense.

Over the years the courts have sustained fair rates of return varying from 5.5 to 8 per cent, depending on circumstances. Companies having well-established credit positions have frequently been accorded lower rates than others, and lower rates were upheld in the 1930's than were permitted earlier.

The Supreme Court gave its most authoritative statement on fair return in *Bluefield Water Works and Improvement Company* v. *Public Service Commission of West Virginia* (1923):[20]

> What annual rate will constitute just compensation depends upon many circumstances and must be determined by the exercise of a fair and enlightened judgment, having regard to all relevant facts. A public utility is entitled to such rates as will permit it to earn a return on the value of the property which it employs for the convenience of the public equal to that generally being made at the same time and in the same general part of the country on investments and in other business undertakings which are attended by corresponding risks and uncertainties. . . . [It] has no constitutional right to profits such as are realized or anticipated in highly profitable enterprises or speculative ventures. The return should be reasonably sufficient to assure confidence in the financial soundness of the utility and should be adequate, under efficient and economical management, to maintain and support its credit and enable it to raise the money necessary for the proper discharge of its public duties. A rate of return may be reasonable at one time and become too high or too low by changes affecting opportunities for investment, the money market, and business conditions generally.[21]

This merely states the problem and does not identify any of the crucial measurements in concrete fashion. If it means what it says, it ignores either the problem of financial structure or the rate base. A rate of return based on this "formula" would have to be very high if the cost-of-reproduction rate base were much lower than the security obligations outstanding, or very low if the reverse were the case. The right amount would have to be ascertained by revelation, not by analysis.

Mr. Justice Douglas, in the Hope Natural Gas case, emphasized the ability of a company to attract new capital as the test:

> From the investor or company point of view it is important that there be enough revenue not only for operating expenses, but also for the capital costs of the business. These include service on the debt and dividends on the stock. By that standard the return to the equity owner should be commensurate with returns on investments in other enterprises having corresponding risks. That return, moreover, should be sufficient to assure confidence in the financial integrity of the enterprise, so as to maintain its credit and to attract capital. The condition under which more or less might be allowed is not important here. Nor is it important to this case to determine the various permissible ways in which any rate base on which the return is computed might be arrived at. For

[20] 262 U.S. 679.
[21] *Ibid.*, p. 692 and 693.

we are of the view that the end result in this case cannot be condemned under the act as unjust and unreasonable from the investor or Company point of view.[22]

A comparison of these two statements, which were made twenty years apart by two judges having markedly different points of view, discloses the fact that as far as fair return is concerned, they both said the same thing. The difference lies in the concept of the rate base. This probably would make a difference in the end result, because Mr. Justice Butler was inclined to view some rate of return independent of the rate base as the correct one, while Mr. Justice Douglas would be more likely to support the judgment of commissions. Nevertheless, apparently having dispensed with the rate base controversy, the Court has shifted its position to financial requirements as the basis for measuring the legality of the fair return. If this is a correct interpretation of the position of the Court, it is necessary to establish what constitutes a sound financial structure before proceeding to deal with the fair return.

THE GENERAL LEVEL OF RATES FOR RAILROADS

The Legal Basis

The Interstate Commerce Commission did not obtain the power to establish maximum rates for railroads until the passage of the Hepburn Act in 1906. Although this in effect gave the Commission authority to control the general level of rates, there was no standard in federal legislation to guide it. Rising prices after 1896 and the moves of the railroads for higher rates led to a recognition of the need for some gauge. Congress responded in part with the Valuation Act of 1913, which embodied the criteria set forth in *Smyth* v. *Ames* and instructed the Commission to make a valuation of the railroads accordingly. There was no stipulation regarding the use to which the valuation was to be put, but the Transportation Act of 1920 filled the gap. This legislation embodied a rule of rate making that instructed the Commission to prescribe just and reasonable rates that would yield a fair return on the aggregate value of the railway property. The fair return was to be between 5.5 and 6 per cent at the discretion of the Commission. The statute also provided for the recapture by the government of one half of the earnings of any particular carrier that exceeded 6 per cent of the value of the property of that carrier.

[22] 320 U.S. 591 (1944), 603. For an up-to-date treatment of the problem of fair return, see M. G. Glaeser, *Public Utilities in American Capitalism* (New York: The Macmillan Co., 1957), chap. xxiii. For a more sophisticated treatment of the problem, see M. J. Peck and J. R. Meyer, "The Determination of a Fair Return on Investment for Regulated Industries," National Bureau of Economic Research, *Transportation Economics* (New York: Columbia University Press, 1965).

The Commission proceeded to exercise the authority given it by the legislation, although it did not permit an upward adjustment of rates that would have yielded the statutory standard. The endeavor to apply the provisions of the law relating to the recapture of excess earnings was challenged by the railroads in *St. Louis and O'Fallon Railway Company* v. *United States* (1929).[23] The government sought to recapture from the St. Louis and O'Fallon Railway the excess earnings as measured by the valuation made by the Commission. The Supreme Court held that the Commission had not given appropriate consideration to the cost of reproduction in arriving at the final figures. Thus, as late as 1929, no basis had been established by which valuation for general rate level and recapture purposes could be ascertained. It is possible that, had the case been brought before the Court four years later, a different verdict would have been rendered. In 1933, however, Congress repealed the rule of rate making and the recapture clause, substituting in their place the general provision that among other things the Commission must give due consideration to the need of sufficient revenues to enable the carriers, under honest, economical, and efficient management, to provide adequate and efficient railway transportation service. This is the law as it stands today. The Commission has control of the general level of rates, but after nearly seventy-five years of regulation, no meaningful measuring rod has emerged by which the reasonableness of the general level can be tested. This is a particularly serious shortcoming because of the requirement that carriers prove the reasonableness of new rates when increases are requested, and because of the opportunity for all interested parties to oppose such increases.

Record of Railroad Earnings

The record of railroad earnings under the limitations imposed upon the general rate level by the Interstate Commerce Commission since 1920 has been anything but satisfactory. In only two years have the railroads as a whole earned 5.75 per cent on the investment in their property—in 1942, when the return was 6.58 per cent, and 1943, when it was 6.08 per cent—according to the Commission's computations. Since 1945 it has never exceeded 4.5 per cent, and for 1965 it was 3.69 per cent. These percentages, of course, cover a wide range among the individual roads, many of whom have been reasonably prosperous. The situation as a whole, however, indicates that adjustment of rates to any theory of a reasonable general level can serve only as an impediment to realistic rate making at the present

[23] 279 U.S. 461.

time. Whatever may be the difficulties besetting the railroads, it seems to be clear that control of the rate level on the monopoly theory upon which it is based is unworkable today.

THE GENERAL LEVEL FOR OTHER CARRIERS

The provisions of the law with regard to the general level of rates for other carriers under the jurisdiction of the Interstate Commerce Commission are essentially the same as for the railroads. No effort has been made to apply the principle of fair return on fair value to the general level of rates for motor carriers. Instead, the Commission has used the operating ratio as a gauge for the adequacy of the rate level in this industry. This has been done on the theory that:

> [On the other hand] where the amount of investment is relatively small in relation to total costs, investment is not the primary factor in determining revenue needs. . . . The owners of motor carriers can hardly be expected to look to the return on the amount of their investment as an incentive where the principal risk is attached to the substantially greater amount of expense.[24]

This appears to concede the fact that the motor carrier industry is essentially a competitive one for which the attempt to control maximum prices and the general level of earnings is subject to the difficulties discussed in the section on regulating maximum prices under conditions of competition. Excessive profits are not a problem with motor carriers unless, perhaps, entry is severely restricted; even when this is done, competition from nonregulated carriers will prevent it. Moreover, it is hardly logical to control the upper limit to motor carrier rates and then restrict the competition which railroads can offer in order to protect it.

The Interstate Commerce Commission enjoys only very limited jurisdiction over water carriers in domestic commerce, although its rate authority over common carriers by water is essentially the same as over railroads. Because of the competition between rail and water carriers the principal interest of the Commission has been to protect the latter against rail competition. Limiting the general level of rates, therefore, has not been a matter of concern.

[24] *Middle West General Increases,* 48 M.C.C. 541, 552–53 (1948). The ICC refused the request for increased rates by motor carriers in *Increased Class and Commodity Rates, Transcontinental,* 326 I.C.C. 397 (1966), but on appeal the district court remanded the case to the Commission on the ground that the latter had failed to state in what respect the carriers' cost evidence was inadequate to support the increase. After reconsideration by the Commission, the issue has again been carried to the courts by the motor carriers.

Most of the pipe lines operating in interstate commerce are common carriers subject to the jurisdiction of the Interstate Commerce Commission. They are also natural monopolies and as a consequence are amenable to the type of regulation applicable to such enterprises. The relationship of the pipe lines to the oil companies and the fact that transportation for their owners constitutes the bulk of the business make for a different problem from that which would obtain if they were independent transportation undertakings. Nevertheless, it has been considered necessary to protect those who rely on the common carrier status against unreasonable charges. In the few cases that have come before it, the Commission has used fair return on fair value to determine the general level of rates. It has been more generous to the pipe lines in both valuation and rate of return than to railroads, presumably because it feels that there is more uncertainty connected with the common carrier business of pipe lines.

The Civil Aeronautics Board has the authority to control the general level of rates for common carriers by air. Administration of the law, however, has been complicated by a number of factors. Air transport, as was pointed out earlier, has the structure of a competitive industry. Even with restricted entry, competition is keen in most of the markets. This alone makes for serious difficulties in arriving at a workable basis for a general rate level, just as it does with motor carriers.[25] The use of air-mail payments and direct subsidies to assist in the development of air transportation precluded the necessity of considering limitations on the general level of rates. The Board has, however, used the investment base in the determination of air-mail rates. It has used 7 per cent as the measure of fair return for past periods and 8 per cent to 9.5 per cent for the future. It has also used 7 per cent as the basis for measuring the need for subsidy.

The first general investigation to be carried somewhat to a conclusion of the level of passenger fares and the guiding principles for the determination of the appropriate level was initiated by the Board in 1956.[26] All the carriers urged the use of the operating ratio, and some suggested combining it with fair return on fair value. The examiner relied upon the fair return approach and stated that the operating ratio could not be taken as the measure of reasonableness independently of

[25] For a careful discussion of the regulation of return to transportation agencies, with special attention to air carriers, see Nelson Lee Smith, "Regulation of Returns to Transportation Agencies," *Law and Contemporary Problems,* "Transportation," Part I, Vol. XXIV, No. 4 (Autumn, 1959), pp. 702–32.

[26] *General Passenger Fare Investigation,* Civil Aeronautics Board, Docket No. 8008, Order No. E–10279, May 10, 1956.

the return on investment, although it was a useful tool in appraising variations in earnings. He found that 10.6 per cent was an appropriate return for the domestic truck-line industry as a whole, some modifications being made for different groupings. The Board in its order decided that the trunk lines should be able to receive average earnings of about 10.5 per cent over a period of years.[27] In so doing, the Board emphasized the fact that it was breaking away from the traditional public utility rate standards because of the general risk position of the industry. Just what all this means in practice may be a matter of conjecture, but the reasons for recognizing the differences between air transport and public utilities might well have led the Board to abandon the policy of limiting maximum fares and the general level of rates in favor of relaxing restrictions on entry.

THE GENERAL LEVEL IN A COMPETITIVE SETTING

This somewhat lengthy discourse on the problem of regulating the general level of rates in transportation brings out the fact that there is no concept of an appropriate general rate level for transport as a whole. Attempts to apply it have been confined to the separate industries in the field. It has not been used as a guide for rate making in interagency competition. Control of the general level for the different modes has achieved literally no success. It must be regarded as a failure in railroad transport, and whatever blame for the present plight of the railroads may be attached to the attempt to utilize it, it cannot be credited with aiding in the resolution of their revenue problems. The evidence is lacking that it has had any use in water and motor transport. It may have had some limited value in the case of pipe lines, where the conditions for applying it more closely approach those necessary for success. It has had very limited applicability to the air lines, but experience with its operation is still lacking. The prospects for success, however, seem to be very meager.

The unsatisfactory record of regulation of the general level of rates in transport stems from the absence of the necessary conditions for success. Difficult problems are present even when it can be applied to individual firms that can be controlled in almost complete isolation, as is possible with public utilities. Where competition is as pervasive as it is in transportation, control of the general level is bound to be abortive, and the need for it is anything but evident. Whether it may be or could be applicable to individual railroads under certain circumstances is a matter which will be dealt with later.

[27] CAB Economic Order No. 16068, June, 1960.

Chapter 10

RATE MAKING IN PRACTICE

INTRODUCTION

The determination of the charges which should be made for the particular services performed by transportation enterprises is a task that involves an enormous amount of sheer mechanics in price making and price regulation. Thousands of different commodities move between innumerable places within the country, and millions of people traveling under various circumstances do the same thing. Prices for the services which are readily ascertainable by the employees of the transport companies, the shippers, and passengers must be established. The pricing structure, particularly of the common carriers, has grown up over a long period of time and has been subject to rather continuous although somewhat gradual modification. It reflects the general considerations that have been discussed in connection with the theory of pricing, and the general level of rates, and has become highly formalized in a number of different ways, especially for the railroads. A certain amount of this formalization for common carriers is inescapable because of the nature of the services performed and the wide geographic coverage of transport movements, but the comprehensive and detailed regulation, particularly by the Interstate Commerce Commission, has resulted in the placing of rate making for freight by railroad in a strait jacket that is now a matter of vigorous controversy.

Rate making for transportation is the counterpart of the pricing procedures followed in other segments of the economy. The prices to be charged for the various services have to be arrived at by evaluating cost and market considerations. A great many of the prices charged for transport services are not regulated, and the pricing procedures of the firms supplying these are similar to those of industry in general. Many of the rates of these firms are not published, or at least they are given no more publication than is usual for prices in manufacturing and retail distribution; nor are they less subject to change from time to time. The charges made by contract carriers are not regulated as a general rule, although these undertakings may be required to file minimum or actual rates. In interstate commerce, contract carriers by motor must now file their actual rates, but these may be changed by the carrier in accordance with the conditions of the contract and at any time, provided that 30 days' notice is given the Interstate Commerce Commission which may invoke the suspension provisions of the law if it sees fit to do so.

Common carrier rates by rail, motor, and water are subject to precise control by the Interstate Commerce Commission, as well as by most of the states through their appropriate commissions. The Civil Aeronautics Board has the same powers over common carriers by air. Thus, pricing for common carriers is subject to strict supervision in the formulation of rates; furthermore, these cannot be changed at will by the carriers. Other transport undertakings, both regulated and non-regulated, may contest the proposed alterations, and so can shippers and communities. The proposals for rate adjustments may constitute a request for general revenue increases or decreases, or for changes in rates on specific services between certain points or in certain areas; they may also involve the filing of new tariffs for services to be offered for the first time.

Rate making in transportation today, therefore, entails a complicated procedure of pricing for the services of regulated and non-regulated carriers, with the common carriers alone facing the requirement of full scrutiny of the prices they are charging, the necessity of justifying them, and the task of convincing public authority of the reasonableness of the proposals they are making. It is safe to say that this is the most complicated problem of pricing that is faced in any area of economic activity.

Transport has long been recognized as one of the most important factors in the location of industry. This is why rates are such a significant consideration. If one were to assume that transport pricing was based on thoroughly competitive conditions among the suppliers of the services, there would be no need for rate regulation because competition would embrace all the relevant conditions that would secure to each location its competitive or "natural" advantages. In point of fact, this is the situation today for a large part of the supply of transport services, particularly if one includes that which is not for hire.[1] Until

[1] Some estimates credit unregulated transportation with 60 to 70 per cent of the total intercity freight movements. The ICC estimated that 40 per cent of the intercity freight

the rise of the modern transport structure, however, the monopoly features of the railroad were such that discrimination in the monopoly sense was a pressing problem. The influence of transportation on location, therefore, was not merely that which was inescapable under competitive conditions; it also involved the pricing decisions of railroad management. In other words, the latter helped to make or mar the markets which the railroads served. In a similar way, they were able to affect competitive relationships among individuals, firms, and commodities. These conditions led to the comprehensive and detailed regulation we have today, and the formalized procedures of pricing that will be discussed in the ensuing sections. It must be emphasized, however, that this applies only to common carriers. It covers, consequently, only a part, albeit a significant part, of carriage for hire, and a smaller part of the total supply of transport services being produced at the present time. An analysis of the problems presented by this complex situation will be undertaken in a later section of this book.

PRINCIPLES UNDERLYING PARTICULAR RATES

On the assumption that the question of what constitutes the appropriate general level of rates has been resolved, the task of rate making then becomes that of determining the charge to be made for hauling the various commodities and transporting passengers so as to provide, or endeavor to provide, the total revenue the carrier needs. In deciding what these rates should be, public authority must give consideration to cost of service, demand for service, and standards of public policy.

Cost of Service

The basic assumption of price regulation is that the price for the services or commodities for regulated enterprises shall, as nearly as possible, be the same as they would be if thoroughgoing competition obtained. Cost of service therefore plays a primary role in the deliberations of public authority. The Interstate Commerce Commission proceeds on the initial assumption that each item of traffic should bear its fully allocated or fully distributed costs. This is what would happen if perfect competition obtained. First of all, therefore, each item of traffic is assessed with all the costs that are directly traceable to it. To these

---

ton-miles was not federally regulated in 1963; 63.7 per cent of the motor traffic was not regulated. Commissioner Tucker has stated recently that about 50 per cent of the intercity freight ton-mileage is not regulated.

directly ascertainable costs is added a predetermined percentage of the nonallocable costs, which percentage may be arrived at on the assumption that each kind of traffic should contribute its proportionate share to the nonallocable costs, although this may be modified to account for some differences in conditions of haulage that are not reflected in the direct costs. The latter will differ for various shipments as a result of the influence of such things as space occupied in proportion to weight; risks and hazards of handling; special services like icing, ventilation, and so forth; and handling costs incident to methods of packing, and volume, regularity, and direction of movement. These are the cost factors which are considered in arriving at the appropriate rate relationships among commodities moving between the same points.

It will be noted that the foregoing cost factors do not include the distance over which the traffic will move. The length of haul or distance factor is concerned with the relationship of the rates for moving the same commodities different distances. Thus, there are two aspects of cost of service in rate determination. The one relates to the costs of handling different commodities for the same distances, and the other relates to the costs of handling the same commodities for different distances.

Even though one were to assume that all traffic should be priced on the basis of fully allocated costs, it is clear that it is impossible to give this term any meaning other than an arbitrary one. There is no means whereby nonallocable joint, common, and fixed costs can be traced to particular items of traffic; and no formula, by the very nature of the problem, can be developed which can result in "scientific" rate making on a cost basis.

A strictly full-cost formula for rate making for transport, even though perchance it yielded adequate total revenues, would nevertheless be arbitrary and would not, for this reason, result in the most economical utilization of transport facilities. If costs are to be used for rate making, with the latter purpose in view, traffic should be assessed with the costs that can be traced to it directly. The remaining costs should be recovered on the basis of what the market will yield, with due regard to limitation of monopoly profits if that should be necessary. The deviations of costs from precise prices differ with the different modes of transport, as was pointed out in a previous chapter, railroads and motor carriers being literally at opposite poles. Nevertheless the principles are the same in both cases; it is in the quantitative consideration only that the differences occur.

Value of Service

Cost of service as the sole determinant of transport prices, especially railroad rates, breaks down because of the difficulties connected with ascertaining costs and because of the market situation which prevents the full utilization of the plant when price making ignores demand. Regulatory authorities recognize the influence of demand under the names of value of service, value of the commodity, or what the traffic will bear. In rate-making administration, at least, these three terms do not always mean precisely the same thing. Value of service is used as a means of apportioning nonallocable costs on the basis of what the market is willing to contribute, except that the limitation on such pricing is the total to which the carrier is entitled. As a consequence, the amount that each item is required to bear may be tempered by the judgment of the Commission rather than by the limitations of the market. Value of the commodity is supposed to reflect, in part at least, differences in value of service, based on differences in the value of commodities, on the theory that commodites of higher value can and ought to pay higher rates than lower valued commodities. Apart from the fact that commodities of higher value may entail higher costs of transport because of considerations such as greater carrier liability, there is no economic reason, at least, why they should bear a higher rate, and there is no a priori reason why they always can. "What the traffic will bear" is commonly taken to mean charging for each item of traffic what the market will pay. In this extreme form, it may lead to unreasonable monopoly profits. Pricing practices of the railroads before comprehensive regulation was introduced led to widespread public opposition with the result that the idea of pricing on the basis of "what the traffic will bear" became charged with a good deal of emotional content. Today, where transport pricing is severely limited by competitive conditions, and where the profits of the suppliers of transport services are not unreasonable, the demand for the service, the value of the service, or what the traffic will bear, all of which amount to the same thing, will have to be used as the upper limit for rates. In any case, commissions must give full recognition to demand as the upper limit for transport prices today. The result may be the same as the cost of rendering the service. This is unlikely to be the case most of the time, especially in railroad transport. If fully distributed costs are used as the gauge, much traffic will go to other agencies, with the resulting unused capacity for the railroads. If relevant costs are used, then they can set only the minimum, and—again for railroads—rates will typically be above these.[2]

Standards of Public Policy

In fixing particular rates, commissions may also take into consideration the effect of rates on military policy, foreign trade, utilization of natural resources, industrial location, and so forth. These factors have had considerable influence on the distribution of the burden of covering the nonallocable costs and, therefore, on the shaping of the rate structures of the country. As long as it is assumed that total carrier revenues have to be limited, considerations of social policy have a role in rate making. They can have little or no place, however, in a competitive industry like motor transport; and their validity in rail transport today is very dubious indeed, especially if the railroads are compelled to bear the burden which they may entail.[3]

The Problem of Discrimination

Transportation enterprises are usually engaged in producing a heterogeneous group of services for each of which the precise cost cannot be ascertained. This is true for all modes, although railroads are the most outstanding illustration. Because of the position the latter occupied in the transport structure of this country until recent years, discrimination in some form or another has attracted much of the attention of regulatory bodies. Legislation down to 1920 was primarily for the purpose of dealing with this problem. Public authority has always been forced to recognize the fact, however, that railroad rates cannot be based on costs alone, and so it has directed its attention to the reasonableness of rate practices, controlling undue preference,

---

[2] For a comprehensive coverage of value of service as used by the Interstate Commerce Commission, see "Value of Service in Rate-Making," Interstate Commerce Commission, Bureau of Transport Economics and Statistics, *Statement No. 5912,* November, 1959.

[3] "Theoretically the reasonableness of rates should be determined by ascertaining the direct expenses involved in moving a certain commodity. Then, after a study of the various demand factors . . . , the overhead costs should be distributed with careful regard to the principle of what the traffic will bear. But as a matter of fact, the reasonableness of rates is not determined exactly in this way, although the results are often approximately the same. The regulating body, as we have seen, uses the comparative method. Rates on the commodities in question are compared with rates on similar commodities. Cost factors and ability to pay factors are compared, and the Commission arrives at a conclusion. The weight accorded to the various factors is not usually stated and the process by which the conclusion was reached is often not revealed. This gives a mysterious appearance to rate decisions." D. P. Locklin, *Economics of Transportation* (6th ed.; Homewood, Ill.: Richard D. Irwin, Inc., 1966), p. 430. This same theory should apply to intermodal rate competition.

eliminating personal favoritism, and dealing with the problem of distance, especially the long and short haul.

If a transport undertaking produced a homogeneous output, discrimination could be detected readily because any difference in charges per unit of service would indicate its existence. The lack of homogeneity and the presence of joint and common costs, however, eliminate any such simple test. Prices or rates will not conform to the costs of particular services because the costs cannot be ascertained. Discriminatory pricing, or what is sometimes called differential pricing, may therefore contain both competitive and monopoly elements. Unfortunately, it is generally impossible to separate the two and very difficult to give them a quantitative content. Even if this were not so, it does not follow that all discrimination would be undesirable; indeed, as was pointed out earlier, it may be necessary for survival. Where discrimination, however, leads to unreasonable profits for transport companies, curbing the practice is in the public interest.

There are four principal kinds of discrimination in transportation. These are personal, commodity, place, and temporal. Personal discrimination refers to the practice of charging different rates to different persons for the same services. This will be possible only when the carrier is able to separate the buyers into distinct markets, thereby making it possible to charge different prices to each. This may be the result of different elasticities of demand, or because of personal favoritism. The law, by various provisions, seeks to prevent personal discrimination, but it cannot be eliminated entirely. Thus, rates may be adjusted to the volume of shipments, larger shippers alone being able to take advantage of the reductions. The difficulty of scaling the rates precisely in accordance with the differences in costs is such that discrimination, in the generally used sense of the term, will be there; but whether discrimination in the monopoly sense is present cannot very well be ascertained. An arbitrary dividing line for the differences in charges is inescapable.

Discrimination among commodities is the result of charging different rates on different commodities moving between the same places, where the rates are not proportional to the differences in costs. The reasons for this may be the same as for personal discrimination, but the objections to it are usually not so forceful. Market conditions are a much more compelling factor to be reckoned with in commodity discrimination than in personal. Under present competitive conditions in particular, different commodities will have to bear rates that are not proportionate to their relevant costs, especially in the case of railroads.

That is to say, the various commodities will contribute differently to the nonallocable costs.

The issue of place discrimination arises in connection with rate relationships on the same commodity or for the same services between different points. Again, the same problems of monopoly and competition emerge. Rates will vary with the mileage a commodity is moved as a result of cost factors such as length of haul, density of traffic, nature of the terrain, and direction of haul. However, the different places between which the services are offered constitute different markets that are clearly separable from each other. The competitive conditions in these markets may vary widely. Some have the advantage of competition among the different modes of transport, others have more limited opportunities. The major centers of the country commonly enjoy competition among carriers of the same mode from other markets and to other markets, yet the distances and conditions of transport are frequently quite different. For example, California and Florida citrus fruits compete in the Chicago market, although the distance from California is over twice that from Florida. If California is to be able to enter that market and the western railroads are to get the traffic, rates from California must be such as to make it possible to market the fruit in Chicago. Intermediate points, however, may not have the same competitive advantages. These may have to pay more per ton-mile for their service than the more distant points. It is also possible that more distant points may have to bear higher rates per ton-mile on a given commodity than the intermediate points if competition compels it. Thus the distance factor becomes distorted because of the variety of competitive conditions that prevail. Railroads may even find it necessary to charge proportionately less on short-haul traffic than on long-haul traffic of the same kind because of motor competition if they wish to compete.

Temporal discrimination arises because of variations in the seasonal movement of traffic. This has not been a significant consideration in freight movement of particular commodities to date. It offers prospects, however, of becoming an important issue in connection with the competition presented by the St. Lawrence Seaway. If the seaway diverts considerable freight from the railroads during the season when it is open, the railroads will be forced to recognize this if they wish to compete. During the season when the seaway is closed, they may need to raise their rates in order to secure adequate revenues. This is sound economic and business procedure. It is a special illustration of peak and off-peak rate making.

PASSENGER FARES

Passenger fares are relatively simple in structure. They are constructed primarily on a uniform mileage basis, that is, a uniform rate per mile traveled, although the same rate per mile does not necessarily hold for all of the carriers. Most railroads offer two types of service, namely, coach and first class, for which differential rates are charged. In addition, differential charges are added for sleeping accommodations when these are supplied. Intermediate points are not charged more than distant points, but where two railroads are competing between the same points, the same fare will be in effect for each. Thus a person may travel to Chicago from Los Angeles by the Santa Fe or via San Francisco by the Southern Pacific, the distance in the latter case being over five hundred miles more than by Santa Fe. The equalization is the result of competition between the routes. Some railroads may also run extra-fare trains which their competitors do not have. Railroads generally offer reduced fares for round trips, and frequently rate reductions for special events. The construction of passenger fares does not contain the same separation of terminal and line-haul costs that characterize railroad freight rates.[4]

Fares for motor buses are much less uniform throughout the country than are those for railroads. This reflects highly competitive conditions, especially with the private automobile. Bus fares typically follow the "tapering" principle in contrast to the uniform mileage arrangements of the railroads, that is, the rate per mile diminishes with the distance traveled. Reduced fares are also given for round-trip tickets.[5]

Air-line fares vary widely with the type of service offered. Passenger fares between two particular points are usually constructed by the application of a constant rate per mile of the shortest route carrier operating by way of all the certificated intermediate points on the route. Other competing carriers then meet this fare between the two

---

[4] At the present time the railroad deficit for the country as a whole on passenger traffic is about $400 million according to the ICC calculations which assigns to passenger service the expenses solely incurred for it, together with some of the common expenses. Since 1953, revenues from passenger-train services have failed to cover even the solely related passenger-train costs. It is not possible to say what the situation would be if passenger service were abandoned entirely, but some railroads still find it worthwhile to continue passenger operations.

[5] For a detailed description of motor carrier passenger operations, see C. A. Taff, *Commercial Motor Transportation* (3rd ed.: Homewood, Ill.: Richard D. Irwin, Inc., 1961), chaps. 24 and 25.

points. This fare thereby becomes the maximum charged between any other pair of intermediate points on the competing segments. A carrier operating on a circuitous route therefore could have intermediate points on its route for which it would offer the same fare as that which was charged between the competitive points. All of the fares between Chicago and the Pacific Coast terminals are the same despite the difference in distances. Passengers from Chicago to intermediate points between Los Angeles and San Francisco may travel through either gateway for the same fare and also enjoy stopover privileges at either city.[6] The differentials between coach and passenger fares are set by the Civil Aeronautics Board.

FREIGHT CLASSIFICATION

Development of Classification

Freight classification as it exists today developed primarily through the railroads. The movement of thousands of commodities between innumerable points led to the placing of commodities into a limited number of groups, known as classifications, for the purpose of simplifying the pricing and price quotation processes. The rates or charges for shipment between any two points were applied to the grouping or class and therefore became known as class rates. All commodities falling into a particular class took the same rate between two given points. The classification or grouping of the commodities depended upon common characteristics of shipment, value, risk, market conditions, and so forth. The rate applied to the class between any two points was determined by the factors affecting distance that have already been mentioned. The relationship of the rates for the various classes to each other remained the same regardless of the points between which the traffic moved, as long as the classes were part of the same classification. The difference in charges per one hundred pounds for shipment arose from the difference in the classification of the commodities.

Early classifications were developed by the individual railroads; but by 1889, three classification territories had been established, with a uniform classification for each. (See Figure 10–1.) These became known as the Official, Southern, and Western classifications. These classifications were drawn up by committees representing the carriers, there being a separate committee for each territory. During World

[6] For a description of this, see J. H. Frederick, *Commercial Air Transportation* (4th ed.; Homewood, Ill.: Richard D. Irwin, Inc., 1955), pp. 280–94.

War I, attempts were made to unify the wide divergencies in the classification ratings of the various territories, with the result that what came to be known as the *Consolidated Freight Classification* was published. This simplified matters somewhat by eliminating a great many differences and by combining the classifications for the three territories into one publication, the rating for each territory being given in one of the three columns appearing after each item.

Further efforts to unify classification resulted in the *Uniform Freight Classification,* which established a uniform classification of freight for the entire country and became effective on May 30, 1952, for the territory east of the Rocky Mountains. In 1956, it was extended to the entire United States. This new classification contains 31 classes,

FIGURE 10–1

FREIGHT CLASSIFICATION TERRITORIES

eight above Class 100 and 22 below. Class 100 is the base class, the others being stated as percentages of it; the highest is Class 400, and the lowest is Class 13. The *Uniform Freight Classification* also contains rules governing the classification of commodities and the conditions under which a particular shipment may be made.[7] The commodities are always listed alphabetically in the classification. The Uniform Classification Committee, which is composed of railroad representatives

---

[7] See Stuart Daggett, *Principles of Inland Transportation* (4th ed.; New York: Harper & Bros., 1955), pp. 328–36, for illustrations of these rules.

replaced the other classification committees in 1964. Its headquarters are in Chicago. It has the task of dealing with all of the problems of classification arising from putting the new system into effect, as well as with new issues that arise. Final approval of its actions rests with the Interstate Commerce Commission.

Although the *Uniform Freight Classification* is the result of a long period of development and a great deal of effort, it actually covers only a small amount of the tonnage moved by the railroads. Most of the less-than-carload (l.c.l.) freight is shipped under classification rating, but less than 5 per cent of carload shipments are governed by it. This is the result of exceptions which are granted. If the exceptions are made in the classification, then the exception rates are those which prevailed under the previous *Consolidated Freight Classification.* In addition to these exceptions, there are also what are known as commodity rates.

Commodity Rates

The widespread divergence of market conditions for transport services in the United States makes it impossible to have a uniform pricing structure for the entire country, especially on bulk movement of freight, which constitutes the overwhelming proportion of railroad traffic. Commodity rates have developed in response to this situation. A commodity rate is one which is quoted on a specific commodity without reference to classification. It may be a stated percentage of a class rate applicable between the two points between which the shipment takes place, or it may be a special point-to-point rate made for a particular situation, or to meet the pressures of competition. About 80 per cent of the railroad freight traffic of the country moves on commodity rates; in Mountain-Pacific territory it is about 95 per cent. Thus, despite efforts at simplification and unification, railroad pricing as a whole is becoming less rather than more formalized. The same remarks apply to the distance factor, as will be pointed out below. This is to be expected with the growth of competition among the agencies.

Classification for Other Carriers

Common carriers by motor are required to file just and reasonable classifications of freight with the Interstate Commerce Commission. Outside of the New England area the *National Motor Freight Classification* was adopted by most of the carriers after the passage of the Motor Carrier Act in 1935. This followed closely the classification ratings made by the railroads. When the *Uniform Freight Classification* was established by the railroads in 1952, the *National Motor Freight*

Classification was modified to provide for a single set of ratings also. A large number of motor carriers have adopted railroad classifications, and so they may use the *Consolidated Freight Classification* or the *Uniform Freight Classification.* In addition, motor carriers also quote commodity rates and exceptions, but class rates cover a much larger proportion of the traffic of the common carrier by motor than is the case with railroads. This is because motor carriers haul a larger proportion of small shipments. Classification details are dealt with by the National Classification Board which is responsible to the National Classification Committee. This is composed of 100 representatives from the common carriers, with at least 1 member from each state.[8]

A separate system of classification grew up in New England and became known as the *Co-ordinated Motor Freight Classification.* This was the result of the desire of the New England carriers to group all articles into five classes based on a formula which combined weight and space occupied. They felt that this arrangement was more in accordance with conditions peculiar to the motor carrier industry.

Air lines use a very simple system of freight classification. The air express service provided by the REA Express takes nearly all commodities at one basic rate, 250 cubic inches being counted as one pound regardless of actual weight. The air-freight service of the air lines is on a one-class basis, but the lines also publish commodity rates for specific commodities, and employ a system of graduated rates based upon the weight of the shipment to be handled.

RATE SYSTEMS

In the previous section the discussion centered on the classification of freight as one of the steps toward ascertaining the freight rate which is applicable to particular shipments. The price paid by the shipper for the movement of his freight between two given points will be determined by the weight of the shipment multiplied by the cents per one hundred pounds for that type of traffic between the two points. To this amount any extra charges for special services may be added.

Freight Tariffs

The actual rates to be charged for transporting commodities are published in what are known as freight tariffs. A tariff may also contain applicable ratings, rules and regulations governing service, routings available under the given tariff, special service charges, demur-

[8] See Taff, *op. cit.,* chap. 17 for a presentation of motor freight classification.

rage, transit privileges, and so forth. Class tariffs contain the rates on the various classes shown in the classification. Commodity tariffs may be published in the same tariffs with class rates, but usually they are published separately because of their particular application.

Individual railroads usually publish the tariffs, both class and commodity, for traffic which moves between points on their own lines. These are known as local tariffs. The rates between points on different lines are known as joint rates, and they are usually published by an agent acting for the co-operating carriers. These are called agency tariffs. Most of the tariff formation for joint rates is undertaken by rate bureaus and associations, and when traffic moves between rate-making territories, several of them will act together.

Railroad Rate Systems

Railroad freight rates constitute an extremely complicated system of pricing which, in many respects, may be characterized as being quite haphazard. This is because of the wide variety of competitive and cost considerations that enter into the formation of the pricing. A certain amount of uniformity has emerged, however, as a result of efforts both by the railroads and by the Interstate Commerce Commission. Three general types of freight rate structures may be distinguished as they relate to distance. They are distance scales, group rate structures, and what are called basing-point or base rate systems. There are five major freight rate territories in the United States. They are shown in the map in Figure 10–2. These territories have been important in the development of rate structures because of the tendency for a degree of uniformity to prevail within them, and because of their influence on rate making between them even today, especially for commodity rates.

The adoption of the *Uniform Freight Classification* in 1952 led the Interstate Commerce Commission to prescribe a single uniform class rate structure for the entire United States, although the level of the scale was higher for the Mountain-Pacific territory than for the rest of the country. Commodity rate structures and levels, however, are different for the different rate territories, and many of them disregard the territorial boundaries entirely. The class rates are on a distance basis, increases in rates with the growing distance being made in mileage blocks rather than for single miles. The rates also do not increase in proportion to distance; instead, the increase per mileage block decreases gradually as the distance increases. This is known as the tapering principle. One reason for this is that the terminal costs at each end of the haul are the same regardless of the length of the haul.

It is not possible for every railroad to adhere to the strict application of the distance scale because two competing lines operating between the same points may actually have different lengths of haul. The Commission has met this situation by establishing the rule that distance should be computed over the "shortest possible route over which carload traffic can be interchanged without transfer of lading." Obviously, it is necessary to modify the distance scales on some railroads to meet this condition. The distance scales may also be applied to commodity rates, but there is relatively little uniformity for these because of the factors which lead to the establishment of commodity rates in place of class rates.

Group rate systems are characterized by the grouping of points of

FIGURE 10–2

THE FIVE MAJOR FREIGHT RATE TERRITORIES

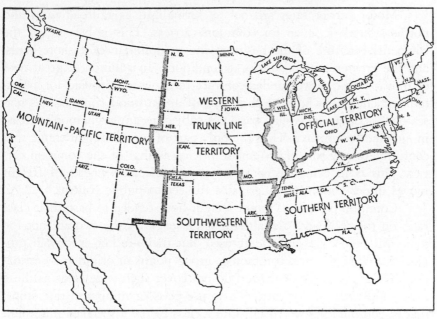

origin and destination, or both, frequently over a wide area. All points included in the group where the traffic originates will take the same rate for the same shipments to a given destination, and all points in a destination group will take the same rate from a given point of origin. Thus, for example, carload rates on dried fruits and vegetables from Fresno, California, take the same rate to all points outside the Mountain-Pacific territory, except New York, which gets a lower rate. The rates on wine from Fresno cover an even larger blanket territory.[9] Many other similar examples on traffic moving in both directions could be given.

Where base rates or basing-point rates are used, the practice is to establish a rate between two points and then relate the rates to other relevant points in some fixed manner. Thus, for example, Baltimore and Philadelphia were given a fixed differential below New York on import and export traffic. This was to equalize the competition between the ports because of the advantage enjoyed by New York in ocean-shipping rates. Efforts of the railroads serving Boston, New York City, and Philadelphia to do away with these differentials and to equalize the rates with those prevailing at Baltimore were denied by the Interstate Commerce Commission, but the latter was overruled by the courts.[10] The situation at the present time is in a state of uncertainty.

Motor Carriers

Motor carrier rates are not as formalized as railroad rates and not as systematic, even for common carriers. This is because of the competitive nature of the business, the predominance of short hauls, and the greater response to local conditions. In addition, a great deal of motor traffic moves under contract rates which provide for point-to-point charges, while the shipment of agricultural commodities and seafoods is on an individual basis not subject to any regulation, at least in interstate commerce. Thus the only part of motor freight traffic that conforms to any sort of systematic pricing is that of the common carrier. This is in complete contrast to the railroads, where all freight moves under common carrier rates subject to public control.

Common carriers of motor freight have tended to base their class rates on the railroad scale, although the levels of the two are not the same. Mileage scales are widely used, but they are not exactly in proportion to distance. It is common to group points of origin and destination. These groupings, however, do not cover such wide areas as those of the railroads. Motor carriers also use class or minimum rate stops; that is, commodities which fall into a class below a specified minimum will be classified at that minimum. What this means is that motor carriers utilize a smaller spread of classes for traffic than the rail carriers. Motor carriers also employ volume minimum weights for traffic

[9] See S. Daggett and J. P. Carter, *Structure of Railroad Rates* (Berkeley, Calif.: University of California Press, 1947), chap. iv.

[10] *Equalization of Rates at North Atlantic Ports,* 311 I.C.C. 689 (1960); 314 I.C.C. 185 (1961); *Boston and Maine Railroad* v. *U.S.,* 202 F. Supp. 830 (1962); affirmed 373 U.S. 372 (1963). For a history of the port differentials and an evaluation of the arrangements, see Daggett, *op. cit.,* pp. 374–78.

moving on class rates. These volume minima may be accorded a shipper even though the weight of the shipment exceeds a truckload. Commodity rates for common carriers by motor cannot be described in any systematic way.

Other Carriers

Only a small fraction of water transportation is subject to common carrier regulation by the Interstate Commerce Commission. The remainder moves under contract rates or is exempt from control. Class rates for common carriers by water are patterned somewhat on railroad class rates but are usually lower, for competitive reasons. Most of the traffic moves on commodity rates. In general, distance rates by water employ the tapering principle; but in coastwise and intercoastal service, port-to-port rates are quite common. The carriers often disregard distance by the practice of charging similar rates to ports quite far apart; that is, blanket rates may apply over a wide area, but the long- and short-haul restriction applies to water carriers.

Rates for freight by air are based on air mileage with the application of the tapering principle. The schedule air lines have a one-class system for class rates, but they also publish commodity rates. Rates are not graduated for volume up to 16,000 pounds for these lines. The all-cargo carriers, however, vary their rates according to the size of the shipment. The air lines also employ what are known as directional rates because of unbalanced freight movements. Rates in one direction may be lower on a mileage basis for some commodities than for others in the opposite direction. This is essentially the same as the rate arrangements made by railroads for back-haul movements. Finally, the air lines offer a "deferred air freight service" by which they give reduced rates on traffic accepted on a "space available basis." The air lines use a consolidated freight tariff, but the Civil Aeronautics Board does not permit competing carriers to receive advance notice of each other's tariff changes. This is designed to promote competition for air freight.

Pipe-line rates are primarily on a distance basis. Minimum tender requirements have to be met by independent shippers. These may vary all the way from 100,000 barrels to the Texas rule of 500 barrels.

LONG AND SHORT HAUL

Distance as a factor in rate making is a particularly controversial issue with regard to railroad rates. Class rates, as already noted, are constructed on the basis of distance scales and the Interstate Commerce Commission, with what Professor Daggett calls its "weakness for mileage rates," in principle favors this for all rate making. Nevertheless, commodity rates as a whole show little conformity to distance scales. Competition in its various forms compels modification of, and marked departures from rates between various points based on mileage alone. This accounts for rates on the same commodity that do not increase in porportion to distance, mileage scales that vary for different routes, and the blanketing of rates over wide areas.

A special case of the relation of distance to rate making for freight is presented in the perennial problem of the long and short haul. This is the practice of making a greater total charge for a given transportation service for a shorter haul than for a longer one when the shorter is included in the longer and both are in the same direction. Such a practice is known as long-and-short-haul discrimination. It is prohibited by Section 4 (long-and-short-haul clause) of the Interstate Commerce Act unless exceptions are made by the Commission in special cases. This clause is applicable to railroads, pipe lines, and common carriers by water. Motor carriers are not subject to it, and there is no such provision in the Civil Aeronautics Act. The principal application of the rule has been to rail carriers.

The reasons why carriers violate the long-and-short-haul principle are essentially the same as those leading to departures from distance scales. As a matter of pure monopoly pricing, such violation would take place if the elasticities of demand were different at the nearer and more distant points, even though costs were all direct and variable. In such cases, pricing would be discriminatory in the monopoly sense. The existence of large fixed and common or joint costs for railroads complicates the problem because of the impossibility of allocating all costs except arbitrarily. If a railroad serving point B passes through C in providing transportation from A to B, then there will be costs that will be common or joint to the traffic for both B and C. This is analogous to electricity before and after midnight. The explanation for violation of the long-and-short-haul principle, therefore, is not to be found entirely in monopoly pricing. It is usually a combination of both common (joint) cost and monopoly pricing. This complicates the control of it because of the difficulty of separating the monopoly and cost elements.

The competitive situations connected with long-and-short-haul violations are basically of two kinds, namely, competition between railroads and competition from other sources. Competition between two railroads which serve the same terminal points will usually compel the long-haul line to compete for the through traffic with the short-haul line by charging the same rate as the latter. If this means that the long-haul line cannot recover fully distributed costs on this competitive traffic, it will endeavor to recoup them by charging higher rates at intermediate points, thereby violating the long-and-short-haul principle. If the shorter road has the capacity to transport more of the through traffic than it is getting, it will be likely to lower its charges on such traffic, thus cutting the other railroad's share. It may also charge higher rates to intermediate points if it is permitted to do so. The Interstate Commerce Commission has endeavored to limit this sort of competition by preventing the short-haul line from departing from the long-and-short-haul prohibition. This serves to permit the longer haul line to compete. Whether this is an economical policy may be open to question, since it denies to the most efficient carrier traffic that it can move at lower costs, and it therefore denies to the terminal points the lower rates which full utilization of the more efficient carrier would give them. In other words, the real question is whether the rates on such traffic should be governed by the high-cost or by the low-cost carrier. The low-cost carrier in this case is the one with the short haul, and the economical thing to do would be to permit it to set competitive rates so as to maximize revenue, allowing the other carriers to meet these as long as their rates were above the relevant costs. This is the way the traffic would move if both lines were combined under one ownership because the road, under such circumstances, would use the most inexpensive route.

Where the competition arises from other sources, the same principles apply. The Interstate Commerce Commission, however, has recognized the reasons for permitting violations of the long-and-short-haul principle more readily where competition has arisen from situations over which it has no control. It has limited railroad competition with water carriers because of the provisions in the law designed to protect the latter. Nevertheless, exemption from Section 4 may be granted to meet actual water competition. The rates that are charged must be reasonably compensatory, by which is meant that they must yield something more than out-of-pocket costs.

Prohibitions against violation of the long-and-short-haul principle grew up as a means of preventing what seemed to be patently discriminatory practices. They were also designed to preserve to communities their so-called "natural" advantage of location. This meant that places nearer the point of origin of traffic had a natural advantage of location over more distant ones. This is true only on the assumption of other things being equal. Thus, interior points in the United States assume that they have an advantage in location, with regard to traffic from the industrial East, over west coast seaports, whereas in point of fact, seaports throughout history have enjoyed natural advantages in transport. As far as economics is concerned, natural advantage lies in cost terms and not in mere mileage. What is more, there is no basic difference in a tariff which applies the same rate to more distant points and to less distant ones than there is to the one which violates the long-and-short-haul provision. Nor does violation of the long-and-short-haul principle promote economic waste if the rates are based on the principles of pricing discussed in an earlier chapter. If it involves monopolistic exploitation, and if this needs to be curbed, then the remedy is to lower the higher rates (intermediate), not to raise the more distant ones. In light of present-day competitive conditions, the long-and-short-haul prohibition appears to have little valid application, if it has any at all.[11]

CO-OPERATION AMONG CARRIERS

The large number of separate carriers in the United States and the fact that no carrier serves all points necessitate arrangements for co-operation among carriers for the interchange of traffic, by carriers of the same mode as well as to a more limited extent by carriers of the different modes. As is to be expected from the nature of their operations, the railroads have developed co-operation to a greater extent than have the other carriers.

Railroad Co-operation

Although the railroad network of the United States is made up of a large number of independent companies, these operate in many respects as a single system. This is the result of arrangements for the movement of traffic throughout the country that make it possible for the shipper to deal with a single firm. Thus a passenger may buy a ticket at the point of departure for a journey that may entail travel over

[11] For a thorough discussion of regulation of particular rates of railroads by the Interstate Commerce Commission, see Locklin, *op. cit.*, chap. 19–23. For a strictly legal presentation, see Edgar Watkins, *Shippers and Carriers, Interstate Commerce*, by Burton Fuller (5th ed.; Atlanta, Ga.: The Harrison Co., 1962), 2 vols. In recent years a great deal of court litigation has resulted from Commission decisions. *Traffic World*, February 11, 1967, p. 77, reports that the volume of ICC cases requiring three-judge federal district courts to review Commission action almost equaled, and in 1963 surpassed, the number of all other types of cases heard before such courts in the last few years.

a number of different lines, and frequently he is able to do this in the same passenger car. Similar arrangements obtain for the movement of freight.

Railroads co-operate in the transportating of freight over different lines (interline traffic) by issuing interline waybills. These are documents covering the freight and the method of shipment from point of origin to destination. Shipping on an interline bill is known as through billing. Generally speaking, the originating carrier quotes a through rate to destination on such billing. The division of the revenue among the railroads participating in the carriage is determined by agreements sanctioned by the Interstate Commerce Commission.

Railroads also provide for the free interchange of freight cars, with little or no regard for ownership. Apart from a relatively small amount of narrow-gauge equipment, all freight and passenger cars in the United States are built to certain general specifications which make complete interchange among all the carriers possible. The interchange of equipment is governed by rules published by the Association of American Railroads.[12] The code of car service rules defines the conditions under which the railroads may refuse to receive cars at interchange points, locates the responsibility between the owning and using companies for making repairs, and gives a detailed list of the charges to be made for the repairs.

The purpose of the car service rules is to insure the return of cars to the owning roads without undue delay. The Car Service Division of the Association may issue relocation orders if shortages develop on occasion in certain regions. In addition, a code of per diem rules is published which provides for a stipulated rental to be paid to the owner of the freight car while it is on other lines. This is designed to prevent delays in the return of empty cars. The Interstate Commerce Commission also has the power to issue orders for relocation of freight cars, as well as the authority over per diem charges which must be sanctioned by it.

Railroads co-operate on interchange in other ways. The Pullman Company was acquired by the fifty-seven leading passenger roads in 1948. This company, as the agent of the owning roads, services them for all or part of their sleeping and parlor cars from its pool of equipment. The Company maintains the cars and, when they are in opera-

[12] The membership of this organization consists of most of the railroads of the United States, as well as the Canadian Pacific Railway, the Canadian National Railway, and the National Railways of Mexico. It carries on an elaborate program of work covering the technical problems of railroad operations, business problems common to all the railroads, and statistical and economic fact finding.

tion, provides personnel, laundry and linen service, and collects the tickets, the costs of the services being charged against the railroad which uses them. Somewhat similar arrangements characterize the Fruit-Growers' Express, which is owned by twenty-three railroads. It provides refrigerator service for perishable commodities for them, as well as by contract with some other lines. Some railroads make agreements whereby they obtain running rights over certain portions of the tracks of another line, operating their own trains over these tracks. Finally, co-operative arrangements have to be worked out at the terminals served by more than one road. The problems connected with this are so closely related to other modes of transport and modern urban transportation that discussion of this is deferred to a separate chapter.

Other Carriers

Co-operation among the carriers of the other modes is not nearly so extensive as that which takes place among the railroads. Common carriers of property by motor are not required by law to enter into through route and joint rate arrangements, but they may do so, and there are many agreements for this throughout the country. They also engage in a certain amount of interchange of equipment; but lack of standardization, together with a wide variety of size and weight limitations in state laws, imposes severe restrictions on this. When such interchange takes place, the Interstate Commerce Commission requires specific and detailed agreements. The carriers which participate in the interchange must also have the operating authority to carry the goods being transported in the through movement. The traffic thus carried moves on through bills of lading issued by the originating carrier. Bus companies make some provision for through passenger tickets, and most of the larger intercity bus operators are associated in one way or another with one of the transcontinental systems.

The air-line companies co-operate with each other by providing for the interchange of passengers on through tickets. They are willing to book passengers one way on their own lines and return on a competitor's. They also have interchange arrangements whereby equipment of connecting lines can be interchanged so that through service may be provided over the routes of more than one carrier without the necessity of transference of the traffic. The Civil Aeronautics Board has taken the position that it has the authority to stipulate the terms and conditions of such operations, as well as the power to compel them when it deems it to be in the public interest.

Through Routes and Joint Rates

Through routes and joint rates may be established between carriers of the same mode, as has already been noted. The railroads are required to do this on a very extensive basis by the Interstate Commerce Commission. The latter's powers are limited only by the provision that it cannot compel a railroad to short-haul itself by requiring it to "embrace in such route substantially less than the entire length of its railroad . . . which lies between the termini of such proposed route." Even then, if observance of the rule results in a route that is unreasonably long as compared with a practicable through route, if the through route is needed for more efficient and economical transportation, or if a carrier has voluntarily short-hauled itself, the Commission may require interchange.

Through routes and joint rates may also be established among the carriers of the different modes. Most of this has been undertaken in connection with water carriers. As a result of the passage of the Dennison Act in 1928 the Interstate Commerce Commission developed an extensive system of joint rail-barge routes and rates on the Mississippi and its tributaries. Under the present law[13] the Commission is required to order common carriers by railroad and water to establish through rates and joint rates whenever it is in the public interest to do so. The Commission has even gone so far as to refuse to recognize diversion of traffic from existing railroads and displacement of tonnage from producing districts as constituting valid reason for refusing to require through rates and joint rates by rail and barge.[14]

The Commission has no authority to compel through routes and joint rates between rail and motor carriers or between motor and water carriers. There has been some voluntary action, however, for trailer-on-flatcar service (T.O.F.C.) under Plans I and V.[15] In 1964, the Commission issued new rules in Ex Parte 230 in which it stated that motor or water common and contract carriers could use rail T.O.F.C. service offered to all other shippers. The "open tariff provisions" extended Plans III and IV service to all for-hire carriers as well as private shippers at the same rates and under the same conditions that

---

[13] Part III of the Transportation Act of 1940 was simply a reenactment on a broader basis of the provisions of the Dennison Act, which was repealed.

[14] *Through Routes and Joint Rates between Ohio and Mississippi Transit Company and Other Common Carriers.* 156 I.C.C. 724 (1929). Also see Daggett, *op. cit.,* pp. 701 f.

[15] For a description of these plans, see Chapter 5 above.

are available to the latter. The Commission's order was reversed by a three-judge district court but was sustained on review by the Supreme Court.[16] Freight forwarders were previously accorded this privilege. Means of interchange have been worked out with water lines. For example, Seatrain operates a fleet of ships between New Orleans and the Atlantic Coast. The vessels carry loaded freight cars that have arrived at port by railroad and proceed to final destination from port of unloading the same way. Recent developments are now providing for through rail-water shipments by containers to European ports.[17]

The Civil Aeronautics Act does not give the Civil Aeronautics Board the authority to require through routes and joint rates between air lines and other carriers. However, such routes may be established. If controversies arise concerning them, they may be referred to a joint board consisting of an equal number of members from the Interstate Commerce Commission and the Civil Aeronautics Board.

Co-ordination of the transport services afforded by the different modes may also be accomplished through the common ownership of one mode by another. This method presents so many complex issues of public policy that full discussion of it is deferred to a separate chapter.

Rate Bureaus

Completely independent rate making by carriers of the various modes is not feasible because of the problems of interchange of traffic. It is also necessary for shippers to be able to obtain the rates on shipments to various parts of the country. Consequently, transportation has a pricing problem on a national basis that does not characterize most other undertakings. Co-operative action is obtained through the utilization of rate bureaus and traffic associations.

The earliest and most comprehensive development of rate bureaus grew up with the railroads. Rate making and prescription of the rules applicable to the various rates are undertaken, although not necessarily initiated, by rate bureaus representing the different carriers involved. Carrier committees consider carefully all rate proposals submitted to them after hearings at which shippers and other interested parties are given an opportunity to present their views.

This arrangement is clearly a method of price making by agreement. The early agreements were declared illegal under the Sherman

[16] *American Trucking Associations, Inc.* v. *Atchison, Topeka and Santa Fe Railway Co.,* 387 U.S. 397 (1967).

[17] See The Port of New York Authority, *Via Port of New York,* Vol. 17, Nos. 10–11 (October–November, 1965).

Act.[18] Nevertheless, such rate making continued to be practiced. The strengthening of the authority of the Interstate Commerce Commission after 1906 led to a rather widespread assumption that such procedures would not be prosecuted so long as the carriers had the right to act independently and the rates agreed upon had the sanction of the Commission. However, the state of Georgia filed suit against the Pennsylvania Railroad, charging it with violating the antitrust laws; and shortly afterwards, in 1944, the Department of Justice did the same thing against the Association of American Railroads.[19] The Supreme Court ruled in the Georgia case that the railroads were subject to the antitrust laws and that Congress had not given the Interstate Commerce Commission the authority to remove rate-fixing combinations from the prohibitions contained in the antitrust laws. Congress responded to this situation by passing the Reed-Bulwinkle Act in 1948.

This legislation made rate bureaus and their operations lawful. At present there are 13 rate bureaus for railroads and 12 for motor carriers.[20] The rules and procedures are under the control of the Interstate Commerce Commission. The Act specifically requires that the bureaus recognize the right of individual carriers to take independent action in making rates if they do not wish to follow the recommendations of the carrier committees. However, there is little room for doubt that rate bureaus exercise extensive control over the rate making of their members, thereby restricting severely price competition among them. Professor Taff says: "Many people feel that the motor-carrier rate bureaus exercise more influence on member carrier actions regarding rates than is the case with the rail rate bureaus," which is saying a lot.[21]

[18] *United States* v. *Trans-Missouri Freight Association,* 166 U.S. 290 (1897); *United States* v. *Joint Traffic Association,* 171 U.S. 505 (1898).

[19] *State of Georgia* v. *Pennsylvania Railroad Company,* 324 U.S. 439 (1945); *United States* v. *Association of American Railroads,* United States District Court, Lincoln, Nebraska, 4 F.R.D. 510 (suit filed in 1944).

[20] R. C. Colton and E. S. Ward, *Industrial Traffic Management* (Washington, D.C.: Traffic Service Corp., 1965), pp. 83–86.

[21] Taff, *op. cit.,* p. 468. See also G. E. Lowe, *Practice and Procedure before Rate-Making Associations* (Washington, D.C.: The Traffic Service Corp., 1967).

PART III
The Regulation of Transport

Chapter
11

THE AGENCIES OF REGULATION

INTRODUCTION

This chapter discusses the agencies of regulation that government in the United States uses to deal with the complex problems that arise in connection with the control of the activities of transport undertakings under private enterprise. It will not discuss, therefore, other aspects of public policy such as the promotion of transportation, public aid, governmental construction of transport facilities, and many technical matters of supervision that may be necessary. Issues concerning these will be dealt with in subsequent chapters relating to national transportation policy. A delimitation such as this is not as simple as it may seem on the surface because the Interstate Commerce Commission is charged with a great deal of responsibility for the supervision of many of the technical aspects of transport operations of those carriers under its jurisdiction and has had a very considerable influence on the development of public policy in transportation. The question regarding the duties which a regulatory commission should be called upon to exercise in the field of transportation today, its role in the formulation of public policy, and the proper repository for the myriad of strictly administrative or executive functions connected with transport are matters of sharp debate. This chapter will be confined to the means by which the regulation of the economic aspects is carried on.

Law and Economic Life

It is the task of law, as it is concerned with economic policy for private business, to develop formal controls or rules that will set the limits within which private enterprise can be left free to use its own discretion. Law is that body of rules of conduct which is backed up by the coercive power of the state or the body politic. It consists of those rules which are recognized, interpreted, and applied to particular situa-

255

tions by the courts of the land. In the final analysis, the law at any given time is what the courts say it is, but to have effect, it must be supported by the power of the state to require compliance with the decrees of the courts. Thus, law constitutes those rules of behavior prescribed by the courts and enforced or supported by the agencies established for that purpose. Finally, law is coercive; obedience is required, or penalties are suffered accordingly.

Although the law ultimately is coercive and implies compulsion, it is not a purely negative arrangement. It not only prescribes rules of conduct by saying what must not be done, but it also may set forth what may be done. It is both prohibitive and permissive, and although it embodies rules of behavior, it does not encompass all of them. Custom plays a major role in our social behavior, and when this custom is incorporated into legislative acts or is given sanction by the courts under common-law procedure, it becomes law. Thus, law is really social policy expressed in legal rules.

Although from a strictly legalistic point of view the state is the supreme authority, the law through which it acts is faced with definite limitations. It cannot persistently flout customary patterns of behavior because, to maintain the continuity which is characteristic of law, it must be deeply rooted in those customs. Furthermore, successful enforcement depends upon the voluntary compliance of the majority of those to whom the law applies. This is especially true of constitutional law, where custom, more than being a support, is an integral part of it. Legislative acts may deal with temporary situations and at times may even do violence to established modes of conduct, but if legislation is to become an integral part of the body of law, it must rest upon widespread custom and upon generally accepted ideals. Even then, the law may be faced with limitations as a result of conflicting interests or objectives, because the attaining of some ideals may involve the sacrifice of others.

The political institutions of the United States are characterized by the rule or supremacy of law. Government in all its actions is bound by rules, fixed and announced beforehand. Everyone is free to pursue his own personal ends and desires, within the law, assured that the powers of government will not be used arbitrarily against him. The rule of law, as contrasted to the rule of men, means that those who govern are also answerable to the law. Equality before the law not only entails impartial administration but also intends that administrators must govern by law and not by personal whim.[1]

[1] See *Youngstown Sheet and Tube Company* v. *Sawyer*, 343 U.S. 579 (1952).

It means, in the first place, the absolute supremacy or predominance of regular law as opposed to the influence of arbitrary power and excludes the existence of arbitrariness, or prerogatives, or even of wide discretionary authority on the part of the government. . . .

It means again, equality before the law or the equal subjection of all classes to the ordinary law of the land as administered by the Law Courts. . . .[2]

Wherever the rule of law characterizes political institutions, the courts play a major role in the development of public policy. They not only interpret the Constitution and legislative acts, but also legalize custom. The very nature of the judicial process, however, makes for a somewhat gradual development of the law. Legislative action may speed it up, but even this is likely to be a more or less gradual procedure. Legislation typically uses language that already has an established meaning, and it is a principle of law that a term used in a legislative act has an accepted meaning, unless it is specifically defined otherwise in statute. In any case the meaning of legislation will be developed by the courts in light of existing law.

The Meaning of Regulation

The term *regulation of business* has three different meanings. In the broadest sense it covers all of the laws which govern the activities of business. From this point of view, all business is regulated, since it is subject to rules of conduct prescribed by the state. This, however, is no different from any other aspect of human behavior which is subject to the law. The second meaning arises from the imposition of rules of conduct by legislative action designed to limit the freedom of activity of business enterprise. These regulations arise because competition is not perfect and because economic forces, working without legislative guidance or restriction, are an independent means of achieving social objectives. Such regulations are designed to channel economic motivation by establishing conditions designed to maintain competition and to eliminate monopoly power as far as is feasible. The third and narrowest meaning is used to describe the controls which have been developed to deal with industries such as transportation, public utilities, and communication. Regulation in this sense means the positive direction of business practices through control of the prices which are charged for the services, possible limitation of profits, restriction of the right of entry and withdrawal, and other devices considered necessary to imple-

[2] A. V. Dicey, *Law of the Constitution* (London: Macmillan & Co., Ltd., 1920), p. 198. For a more extended discussion, see D. F. Pegrum, *Public Regulation of Business* (rev. ed.; Homewood, Ill.: Richard D. Irwin, Inc., 1965), chap. 11.

ment the primary objectives of public policy. It is this restricted definition of regulation that gives rise to the distinction commonly made
between transportation which is regulated and that which is not.

Regulation presupposes private business and economic activity
independent of the government. It assumes the decentralization of the
responsibility for the guidance of economic life and the allocation of
economic resources to various uses. It prescribes rules of conduct, under
which, however, enforcement agencies are allowed considerable discretion. Regulation also frequently involves an element of deliberate
direction which, at times, creates the problem of distinguishing between
regulating and managing. This is particularly true in the case of transportation and public utilities.

The laws governing the regulation of transportation impose many
more duties on the commissions than are encompassed by the control of
competition, the pricing process, regulation of securities, service, and
so forth, all of which may be considered as an essential part of public
policy that provides a substitute for competition or limits it. Public
service commissions are also charged with the duty of setting technical
standards of performance and of supervising innumerable technical
aspects of operations. Thus, for example, the Interstate Commerce
Commission is required to supervise railroad car service and formerly
safety activities; it was also authorized to prescribe rules and regulations
on matters of operating safety of common, contract, and private carriers
engaged in interstate commerce, including qualifications and maximum
hours of service of employees of these carriers.[3]

THE COMMON-LAW BASIS OF REGULATION

Nature of the Common Law

The origins and basis of regulation in this country are to be found
in the common law under which certain rules governing the conduct of
business in general, and the obligations of common carriers, grew up.
The common law is the foundation of the legal system of the United
States. It is one of the two great legal systems of the Western world and
prevails in England and most English-speaking lands.

There are two aspects of the common law which are important in
regulation. The first of these is the common law as a body of rules.
Common law refers to that part of the law of the land which has
grown up without benefit of legislation and which can be found only in
court decisions. As a body of rules it designates that part of the law, in

[3] These and other administrative functions have been transferred to the new Department of Transportation which is discussed in Chapter 21.

countries having the common-law system, which is traditional in form. Substantively, it embraces those rules of law which developed out of customs that have been incorporated into court precedent. In this respect, common law is distinct from statute law and may be referred to as the traditional part of the law of the land. When one wishes to ascertain what the law is on a particular topic, he must search through court decisions to determine what the courts have said the law is. Their interpretation depends upon the issues in the particular case or the customs which have prevailed under such circumstances in the past. When a court decision establishes a rule for a new situation, that rule becomes part of the law of the land, which governs subsequent acts that are of the same nature. Changing conditions and changing ideas over periods of time have introduced new concepts into the interpretation of legal relationships and modified the old ones. As a consequence of this development by interpretation the common law has grown and changed in substance over the centuries and is still in a process of change.

The second aspect of common law is that which relates to the way the law takes form. The common-law system involves a distinct method of procedure in developing the law of the land. This is accomplished by the continuous process of court interpretation in specific cases of the legal issues which arise, the accumulation of decisions giving meaning to the law. It is the function of the courts to give the authoritative interpretation of the law. When this is done for a particular legal issue, the ruling becomes a precedent for subsequent court rulings. It is by adherence to precedent that the law gains its continuity and stability. This method of developing the law is so deeply ingrained in our political and legal structure that it will probably persist in the United States for the indefinite future. "Two things are likely to make the common law, as a system, an enduring basis for American law . . . ; its technique of finding the law through judicial experience and its conception of rights and duties as involved in or incident to relations."[4]

The common law is frequently contrasted with statute law. The contrast is largely that of the way the formal part of the law comes into being. Statute law is that which is enacted by legislative bodies, whereas common law has no such basis. The courts develop the common law out of custom, but statute law is the result of specific enactment by legislatures. Thus, we go to court decisions to see what the common law is, but on statutory matters we first look to the statutes.

However, the contrast is more apparent than real. Where the

[4] Roscoe Pound, "Common Law," *Encyclopedia of the Social Sciences,* Vol. IV, p. 56.

common-law system prevails, statutes must be interpreted by the courts, and the meaning of statutory—or for that matter, even constitutional—provisions depends upon the construction placed upon them by the courts. Furthermore the interpretation of statutory enactments is made in the light of existing law. Unless legal arrangements already in force are specifically set aside, they are presumed to continue, and statutes will be interpreted accordingly. Thus, common-law concepts permeate all of our statutory law in both substance and procedure.

Emergence of Common-Law Control

Until comparatively recent times the regulation of private business practices was a matter of common law. Indeed, down to the latter part of the nineteenth century the use of statute law for this purpose was comparatively rare. Although the common law antedates the development of private business by many centuries, the development of common-law principles relating to the regulation of business came with the breakdown of the medieval system. In medieval England the regulation of business activity was carried on largely by the towns and the guilds. The establishment of a strong national monarchy under the Tudors in the sixteenth century led to the rapid disappearance of the power of the towns and the guilds. With their breakup, private enterprise as we know it now gradually emerged, although the activities were largely local in nature. Statutory regulations, upon which we rely heavily today, did not emerge until very recent times. It was the common law which bridged the gap between the breakup of the medieval system and modern methods of control. During the period of the decline of the guilds, this common law developed as a means of protecting and expanding the rights of individuals. Thus the first manifestations of common-law regulation of business arose in connection with the freeing of labor from the restrictions imposed upon it by the guilds.

The relatively simple business conditions that obtained down to the Industrial Revolution and the acceptance of the principles of *laissez faire* in the nineteenth century resulted in very limited development of statutory regulation. Instead, the legal foundations of private enterprise evolved under common law. Gradually, there grew up a few fairly well-established principles designed basically to protect private rights and to prevent public injury. With the acceptance of *laissez faire* the public injury aspect declined in importance because of the belief in the beneficence of competition. When it became necessary to impose statutory controls, however, these were interpreted in the light of the common law. There were two reasons for this. In the first place, common-law doctrines were frequently incorporated into the statutes, which were interpreted in accordance with legal precedents. In the second place, the principle developed that statutes in derogation of the common law must be strictly construed. Hence, common-law doctrines tended to survive even where legislation provided for comprehensive regulation.

In the evolution of the common-law basis of control of business, four principles, or doctrines, emerged. These were (1) restraint of trade, (2) conspiracy to monopolize, (3) unfair competition, and (4) the right to regulate. The first three furnished the legal rules of conduct for competitive business. The fourth provided the legal basis in the United States for the regulation of prices as well as other aspects of what came to be known as industries "affected with a public interest."

Control of business through the common law was totally inadequate for the structure that grew up in this country in the period following the Civil War. Although it provided the bases upon which foundations of regulation were erected, the common law was too simple in structure and lacked adequate means of application to meet the new situations which arose. Apart from other limitations the common law was confined to the states. Regulation by the federal government of practices that might be dealt with at the state level through the common law could be carried out only by means of federal statutes. The Sherman Act of 1890 was the response of Congress to demands for a basis of federal action. It embodied the first two principles of common-law control. It was supplemented in 1914 by the Clayton Act and the Federal Trade Commission Act, the latter prohibiting unfair methods of competition in interstate commerce.

This antitrust legislation is applicable to all business activity in interstate commerce unless Congress specifically exempts certain types from it. Exemption may be in the form of special legislative provisions such as those contained in the Interstate Commerce Act, or in particular clauses in the Clayton and Federal Trade Commission acts which exclude common carriers or assign the enforcement to the Interstate Commerce Commission. However, it should be noted that the responsibility for enforcing the Sherman Act is in the hands of the Antitrust Division of the Department of Justice entirely, and that this agency has equal authority with other agencies to enforce the Clayton Act and may act independently of them. The scope of the antitrust laws and the powers accorded the Antitrust Division by them explain the actions which gave rise to the need for passing the Reed-Bulwinkle Act and the current interest of the Division in railroad mergers. If special regulation of transportation were discontinued, as some people propose, the Sherman, Clayton, and Federal Trade Commission acts, in the absence of new legislation, would become the only basis of federal control.

The Right to Regulate

The fourth common doctrine which was to become of prime importance in the regulation of business was the right of the state to regulate, regulation in this setting referring to the restricted idea of price and profit controls and accompanying limitations on the scope of private discretion. Since the Civil War, this has become one of the most significant controversies in the constitutional history of the United States.

In medieval times the guilds gave local monopoly to trades and crafts, and because of the importance of these in the local economy, they became common callings requiring close regulation. The term *common* in medieval law indicated that employment was public in the sense of being available to all who might want to be served. With the breakdown of the medieval economy the control of the guilds gradually disappeared. In the succeeding development the process by which certain occupations or callings became subject to special regulation is not clear. Lord Hale, in his treatise *De Portibus Maris,* written about 1670, distinguished between callings affected with a public interest and those which were matters of private concern only. This distinction seems to have been based on the idea that the individual customer required protection against the seller because of the monopoly of the latter over some common necessity. These monopolies were the result of some special grant of privilege but could not escape their responsibility to the public by charging unreasonable prices. With the development of private enterprise in trade and commerce, the concept of the right to regulate became particularly applicable to means of transportation. It was not used in England, however, as a means of limiting the power of Parliament to regulate business; rather, it was a statement that monopolies obtained by special grant, especially by letters patent from the Crown, could not escape the authority of the common law.

When, after the Civil War, the Granger states enacted laws to control the prices and services of railroads and certain other enterprises immediately associated with transportation, the power of the legislative branch of the government to fix the prices charged by any private enterprise was challenged.[5] The courts, harking back to Lord Hale's

[5] See *Munn* v. *Illinois.* 94 U.S. 113 (1877).

treatise, held that it had been customary from time immemorial to regulate property "affected with a public interest." Therefore, legislatures possessed the power to fix the prices of enterprises in those industries which fell into this category. Curiously enough, the idea embodied in the common-law precedent which was used to support regulation by the state was given a reverse meaning by limitations that the courts imposed upon legislative action. The Supreme Court refused to sanction legislation designed to regulate businesses such as theater ticket brokers, employment agencies, and ice manufacture and distribution on the grounds that these were not "affected with a public interest."[6] Moreover, until the mid-1930's the concept of industries affected with a public interest was so narrowly construed as to be almost synonymous with transportation and public utilities. However, the recognition that the state did have the right to regulate under appropriate circumstances laid the constitutional foundation for the expansion of the regulatory powers of legislatures into the much broader sphere which they enjoy today.

The accumulation of legislative pressure, the force of dissenting opinions of the Supreme Court, and the depression which began in 1929 resulted in a thoroughgoing relaxation of the Court's restrictions on the right of the legislature to regulate. In *Nebbia* v. *New York* (1934),[7] the Supreme Court upheld a New York statute which declared that the production, distribution, and sale of milk was a business affecting the public interest and health. Under this law the Milk Control Board established minimum prices for milk sold at wholesale and retail. In upholding the act, Mr. Justice Roberts took the position that it was entirely a matter of judgment when property was used in a manner to make it a public consequence and affect the community at large. Price control was simply one branch of the general police power, but legislation enacted under this power could not be "arbitrary, discriminatory, or demonstrably irrelevant to the policy the legislature is free to adopt"; subject to these conditions, "there can be no doubt that upon proper occasion and by appropriate measures the state may regulate a business in any of its aspects, including the prices to be charged for the product or commodities it sells, and that so far as the requirement of due process is concerned, and in the absence of other constitutional restrictions, a state is free to adopt whatever economic policy

---

[6] See *Wolff Packing Company* v. *Industrial Court of Kansas,* 262 U.S. 522 (1923); *Tyson* v. *Banton,* 273 U.S. 418 (1927); *Ribnik* v. *McBride,* 277 U.S. 350 (1928); and *New State Ice Company* v. *Liebman,* 285 U.S. 262 (1932).

[7] 291 U.S. 502.

may reasonably be deemed necessary to promote public welfare and to enforce that policy by legislation."[8]

In cases antedating *Nebbia* v. *New York,* the Supreme Court had refused to permit the states to regulate contract carriers by motor vehicle as common carriers. In other words, a legislature could not compel a contract carrier to assume the status of a common carrier.[9] Whether this meant that a state could not regulate the precise rates of contract carriers is another matter. So far, this has not been done, and there may be good economic reasons for not doing so. It is constitutional, however, to prescribe minimum rates for contract carriers, and on the basis of the Nebbia decision it may be possible to fix their precise rates.[10] Whether these carriers could be compelled to accept the position of a common carrier by legislative action would have to be settled by further litigation.

REGULATION UNDER FEDERAL GOVERNMENT

The Federal Form of Government

The United States is governed by what is known as the federal form of government. It is the result of the uniting of a number of more or less independent states into a union in which each member retains a large degree of sovereignty. For the purpose of forming the union, the states give up those powers which are considered to be of significance to the union as a whole and which require unity of action of the members. Thus, there emerges a central government with control over those matters that relate to the well-being of the country as a whole and a number of state governments, with the latter enjoying sovereign powers within the limits of the arrangements for federation. Because of its origin, this form of government requires a written constitution. This establishes the basic framework of government for the federal union. It sets forth the respective powers of the central and local governments, and provides means whereby the general framework may be modified to meet the needs arising from changing conditions.

The Constitution and Regulation

There are two distinct features of the Constitution of the United States which are important in the regulation of industry. The first of

---

[8] *Ibid.,* p. 570. See also *United States* v. *Rock Royal Co-operative, Inc.,* 307 U.S. 533 (1939); and *Sunshine Anthracite Coal Company* v. *Adkins,* 310 U.S. 381 (1940).

[9] *Michigan Public Utilities Commission* v. *Duke,* 266 U.S. 570 (1925); *Frost and Frost Trucking Company* v. *Railroad Commission of California,* 271 U.S. 583 (1926); and *Smith* v. *Cahoon,* 283 U.S. 553 (1931).

[10] See *Sunshine Anthracite Coal Company* v. *Adkins,* 310 U.S. 381 (1940).

these relates to the location of the authority for regulation. The Constitution sets forth the respective powers of the state and federal governments. Under it, the powers which the federal government enjoys are delegated and enumerated. All others, except those expressly prohibited, are reserved to the states and the people. In addition to this, the Constitution provides for the separation of powers among the executive, judicial, and legislative branches of government, each of which exercises its own distinct authority. Governmental action, therefore, requires the sanction and co-operation of all three parts. This means that in the matter of regulation of industry the legislative, executive, and judicial viewpoints must function together, but that each division must act strictly within its own sphere of competence. Because of constantly changing conditions, adjustments among these three divisions is a continuous process, often very delicately balanced.

The second distinct and unique feature of the Constitution of the United States which is important from the standpoint of regulation is the Bill of Rights. The Constitution places a special emphasis on the importance of property and individual freedom on economic matters as the basis of liberty. It therefore contains guarantees for the protection of life, liberty, and property. These guarantees are not necessarily an inherent part of a written constitution or of the federal form of government. The Canadian Constitution, for example, does not include them. Since they are, however, a specific part of the Constitution of the United States, they have become interwoven with the other aspects of our constitutional development. This is the reason why the functions of the courts as an integral part of the federal form of government and of the courts as the protector of liberty and property are so frequently confused.

Powers of the National Government

As already noted, the Constitution sets forth the respective powers of the state and national governments. It also contains a provision which gives Congress the authority "to make all laws which shall be necessary and proper for carrying into execution"[11] all powers vested by the Constitution in the government of the United States. This constitutional provision, known as the "doctrine of implied powers," together with the broad terms setting forth federal powers, laid the basis for expanding the scope of the national government to meet changing circumstances far beyond any possible conception which the founders of the Constitution had. Thus, although the Constitution is a written

[11] Article I, Section 8, Clause 18.

document, its meaning and scope continue to change with altering circumstances.

While the general principles dividing the powers between the state and federal governments have remained the same over our history, the application of them has wrought fundamental changes in our constitutional structure and has posed continously the question of state versus federal authority. The enormous growth of economic activity far beyond the boundaries of the states, since the United States became a nation, has led to a great expansion of federal authority. This has brought about an increase of federal functions that has presented a continual constitutional challenge. National and local economic issues have become intermingled on such a broad scale that the division of powers is not as simple a question as it was at the time the Constitution was framed. The division still exists, however, and the effective ways and means of implementing it are even more pertinent considerations today than they were at the time when the nation was founded. The power and prestige of the national government too frequently obscure the immense importance and vital necessity of the states to our constitutional, political, and economic life.

Under the Constitution, all powers not delegated to the federal government are reserved to the states. This division between the state and federal jurisdictions is a matter of constitutional law. Within the limitations set by the federal Constitution, as its meaning is interpreted by the Supreme Court of the United States, Congress is supreme. Whether the powers thus permitted to Congress should be exercised is a political, not a legal question. The Court decides what powers Congress possesses, but the latter decides whether it should use them. Political and legal questions are frequently badly mixed up when constitutional issues are at stake. Once the constitutional question is settled, however, the matter then becomes one of policy.

Neither a state nor the federal government can delegate to the other powers which it possesses exclusively, but it is interesting to note that the courts have shown considerable willingness to sanction cooperation and that this may bring about a further diminution of strict lines of demarcation of authority. Moreover, the Supreme Court has held that the powers of Congress may be exclusive, paramount, or concurrent. If Congressional powers are exclusive, the states cannot exercise any control, even though Congress might be willing to allow them to do so.[12] If, on the other hand, Congressional powers are held to

---

[12] Nevertheless, Congress did almost this when it passed the Walter-McCarran Act of 1945 to take care of the situation facing insurance companies after the decision in *United*

be paramount, the states may exercise jurisdiction in the absence of federal action. When Congressional powers are held to be concurrent, both the state and the federal governments may act at the same time in the same manner.[13]

Section 8 of Article I of the Constitution gives, among other things, extensive powers to Congress to control the economic life of the nation. One of the most significant provisions is that which places control over interstate commerce in the hands of Congress. It stipulates that Congress shall have the power to regulate commerce with foreign nations and among the several states. This clause gives Congress its most comprehensive direct power for the regulation of business (1) because of the broad way in which the Supreme Court has construed the provision and (2) because of the use of this provision in conjunction with others, thereby giving it a wider application than otherwise might have been accorded.

The scope of Congressional authority over interstate commerce is by no means self-evident or unequivocal, for there is no explanation of what constitutes "commerce," or "among the states." The meaning of these words and the validity of federal policies involving them has resulted in an almost continuous process of judicial interpretations.

Early in the nation's history the scope of federal powers was given a very broad interpretation. In *Gibbons* v. *Ogden* (1824),[14] the first case coming before the Supreme Court involving the federal powers over interstate commerce, Chief Justice Marshall said:

> Commerce undoubtedly is traffic, but it is something more; it is intercourse. . . . The subject to which the power is next applied is to commerce "among the several states." The word "among" means intermingled with. A thing which is among others is intermingled with them. Commerce among the states cannot stop at the external boundary line of each state, but it may be introduced into the interior. . . . If, as has always been understood, the sovereignty of Congress, though limited to specified objects, is plenary as to those objects, the power over commerce with foreign nations and among the several states is vested in Congress as absolutely as it would be in a single government having in its constitution the same restrictions on the exercise of the power as are found in the Constitution of the United States. The wisdom and the discretion of Congress, their identity with the people, and the influence which their con-

---

States v. *South-Eastern Underwriters Association,* 322 U.S. 533 (1944). This legislation was designed to take care of a confused situation arising out of the absence of federal legislation on insurance.

[13] For a thorough discussion, see J. E. Kallenbach, *Federal Co-operation with the States* (Ann Arbor: University of Michigan Press, 1942).

[14] 9 Wheat (U.S.) 1.

stituents possess at the election are in this, as in many other instances, as that, for example, of declaring war, the sole restraint on which they have relied to secure them from its abuse. They are the restraints on which the people must often rely solely in all representative governments.[15]

It seems clear that all of the activities controlled by Congress at the present time under the heading of interstate commerce could be completely supported by this decision. Nevertheless, it was not until near the end of World War II that Congress was able fully to assert the powers which *Gibbons* v. *Ogden* seemed to imply. In the years subsequent to this decision the Supreme Court often found occasion to impose restrictions on the federal government. This may be explained, in part at least, by the difficulties involved in analyzing the effects of the growth of the country on a national basis. In any event, the Court held that mining, manufacturing, farming, the generation of electricity, and insurance were not commerce. Furthermore, Congressional authority was limited by a strict construction of the idea of "interstate" that required actual movement across state boundaries. On the other hand, the courts restricted state activity affecting such movements. In *Wabash, St. Louis and Pacific Railway Company* v. *Illinois* (1886)[16] the Supreme Court held that the transportation of grain from the state of Illinois to New York constituted commerce among the states and that the states were powerless to act even when the federal government had not done so.

The rapid expansion of federal regulation of business came in the field of transportation with the passage of the Interstate Commerce Act of 1887. In the years since then, federal power has been extended so far in transportation as to comprehend all the agencies that directly or indirectly affect interstate commerce. Any local medium through which traffic moves in the course of interstate commerce may be subject to federal regulation. It is on this basis that federal control of grain elevators and stockyards has been upheld.[17] Similarly, railroad rates on purely local traffic may be subject to the authority of the Interstate Commerce Commission if the latter considers them sufficiently important in the rate structure to warrant their regulation.[18]

If the courts decide that jurisdiction over a certain matter belongs exclusively to Congress, the states cannot act even though the federal

---

[15] *Ibid.*, pp. 189 ff.

[16] 118 U.S. 557.

[17] *Munn* v. *Illinois*, 94 U.S. 113 (1877); *Lemke* v. *Farmer's Grain Company*, 258 U.S. 50 (1922).

[18] *Railroad Commission of Wisconsin* v. *Chicago, Burlington and Quincy Railway Company*, 257 U.S. 563 (1922).

government would be willing for them to do so. However, there is a wide range of concurrent powers in the concept of interstate commerce, and the interstate commerce which is reserved exclusively to Congress is quite narrowly construed. As a consequence, Congress may permit the states to regulate a wide range of activities which it could appropriate unto itself if it saw fit. It is on this basis that the states have been allowed to exercise very extensive powers over motor transport and public utilities and at times even over rail transport.

THE ROLE OF THE COURTS IN REGULATION

Judicial Review

One of the distinguishing characteristics of the American system of government is the position occupied by the judiciary. In no other country is the power of the judiciary so pronounced or evident. Indeed, this has developed to such an extent in the United States that on matters of social policy the question frequently asked is: "Is the procedure legal?" not "Is it socially sound?" If the answer to the legal aspect is a negative one, there is the tendency to drop the issue. If it is positive, there is an equal tendency to assume that the other aspects of the program are necessarily sound.

The position which the courts have come to occupy in this country has given rise to what has been called the American doctrine of judicial review. In its technical sense this doctrine refers to the procedure whereby the courts review the legislation of the various governments of the country in the light of the constitutions of those governments. When the courts find that the actions of the various parts of the governmental structure violate the written constitutions, they declare those actions invalid. The power to declare legislation unconstitutional has been developed more extensively here than in any other country.

In its broader aspects the idea of judicial review refers to the power of the courts to interpret laws. Although the courts, for example, in Great Britain do not have the right to set acts of Parliament aside, they nevertheless do have the duty of interpreting whatever legislation Parliament enacts; and the law at any particular time in England, as in this country, means what the courts say it means. The difference lies in the power of the judiciary in the United States to declare legislation invalid; this cannot be done in Great Britain. But in both countries the courts do interpret and enforce the law. Both countries adhere to the common-law tradition of the rule of the law and the development of its meaning by court precedent. In this respect, judicial review has a definite historical basis, for through the interpretation of law by the courts there has developed a continuity of process and principle that could scarcely have been attained in any other way.

The most important reason, probably, for the rise of judicial review to its supreme significance in this country was the adoption of the federal form of government, which presupposes agreement by equal parties, in the formation of a government, with contractual rights in that government. Various procedures might have been adopted to interpret these rights, but the most obvious one was to leave to the courts the matter of giving content to the Constitution and of interpreting legislation in the light of the Constitution. It is difficult to see how the federal form of government could have been successful without the courts occupying a key position.

Contrary to widespread belief, review by the courts is not unique to the United States; a similar situation exists in Canada and the other British dominions. There is one fundamental difference, however, which has colored the whole process of judicial review in the United States and which arose from the incorporation of the Bill of Rights into our Constitution. The courts here, as with other federal governments, occupy a key position in the federal system of government; but in addition, in the United States, they also play a rather decisive role in the protection of life, liberty, and property. Which of the two functions has been the most important in American constitutional history may be a matter of debate. It is, however, highly essential to remember that the protection of life and property has given the courts a sense of importance that has made their place in the government decidedly more prominent than it would have been otherwise.

The position of the courts in this country as powerful agencies of public policy has given rise to much criticism and has created the feeling that the country is being ruled by judicial rather than by legislative processes. There is some basis of support for this position, and economists are prone to be impatient when court decisions exhibit economic reasoning of very dubious validity. The possibility of other arrangements is not inviting, however. The long tradition of procedure and the deep-rooted practice of judicial review indicate that changes in our present methods will come about only gradually and more or less imperceptibly as a result of new problems. The dangers that lurk in proposals to exempt the decisions of administrative commissions, for example, from judicial scrutiny are too great to warrant the experiment.

Functions of the Courts

It is the function of the courts in every country where there is orderly government to interpret the laws and to settle litigation arising thereunder. The role occupied by the courts in the regulation of business in this country, however, is greater than that which is exercised by the judiciary of any other. This position is the result of two things. First, the doctrine of judicial supremacy which has grown up as a result of certain unique features of the Constitution of the United States has given a leading role to the Supreme Court in the determination of public policy. Second, Congress has seen fit, notably in the Sherman Act, to give the courts the direct and immediate responsibility of interpreting very broad legislation relating to regulation in general and of developing public policy under it.[19] The courts in this country have, therefore, four major functions in regulation: (1) the interpretation of the Constitution in terms of the framework of government, (2) the interpretation of the Constitution as it applies to the protection of personal and property rights, (3) the direct enforcement of regulatory legislation, and (4) the adjudication of disputes arising from enforcement by commissions.

As has already been pointed out, the federal form of government requires an authority that can decide where powers are located as between federal and state governments in the event of disputes. The Constitution itself appears to be silent on that matter. The issue was settled, however, by Chief Justice Marshall in *Marbury* v. *Madison* (1803),[20] when he ruled that under written constitutions "an act of the legislature repugnant to the constitution is void." This established the supremacy of the judiciary for the interpretation of the Constitution and also the fact that the Supreme Court would be the arbiter of the division of powers between the state and federal governments.

A parallel situation arises in connection with the separation of powers. The Constitution provides for the division of authority in the federal government among three departments: the legislative, the executive, and the judicial. They are co-ordinate branches, and each one must perform all the duties which come within its scope, and only such duties. In the event of conflict, there must be some means of deciding who may exercise the powers in question. Once again, the courts are the authority to which appeal is made.

Numerous legal problems have arisen in connection with the separation of powers. One important constitutional rule prevents Congress from delegating legislative power. No other governmental agency may exercise that legislative power, nor can any agency other

[19] These remarks also apply to the Clayton Act. However, other agencies such as the Interstate Commerce Commission and the Federal Trade Commission are given independent responsibility for interpretation and enforcement of it, whereas only the courts are available for discharging these functions under the Sherman Act.

[20] 1 Cranch 137.

than the courts be given judicial functions. The position of the administrative commissions, whose functions partake both of legislative and of judicial nature, has consequently given rise to considerable constitutional difficulty. The law, however, has accommodated itself by legislative action and judicial sanction, so that many regard the administrative commissions today as a fourth branch of the government.[21] This has come about by court recognition of the legislative right to prescribe general rules, to be administered in detail by the regulatory commission. At the same time, the courts retain the right to hear appeals from the decisions of these commissions.

Congress does not have the right to delegate its lawful powers to the executive, even though it may feel that an emergency exists sufficient to warrant such action. Perhaps the most important peacetime application of this principle arose when the Supreme Court of the United States, by unanimous decision in *Schechter Poultry Corporation* v. *United States* (1935),[22] held that the National Industrial Recovery Act was unconstitutional because it, among other things, constituted a delegation of legislative authority by Congress to the President of the United States without providing legislative standards to limit the exercise of the power which was delegated.

The second function of the courts with regard to regulation is to interpret the provisions of the Constitution as they relate to property rights. With the development of regulation of business by administrative commission in the period following the Civil War, this matter rapidly came to the fore. The extension of regulatory powers to include price fixing met with the contention that this violated the Fifth or Fourteenth amendments of the federal Constitution, which provided that no person should be deprived of life, liberty, or property without due process of law. The challenge to the right of the state to regulate centered around the controversy over the powers of government to fix the prices of private business. The first case coming before the Supreme Court was that of *Munn* v. *Illinois* (1877),[23] which contested the right of the state of Illinois to fix the maximum charges to be exacted by grain elevators on the ground that this violated the Fourteenth Amendment of the federal Constitution. The Court upheld the statute on the

[21] Whether it is desirable for regulatory commissions to be as independent of the executive branch of the government as they are today is a matter on which there may be a considerable difference of opinion. See M. H. Bernstein, *Regulating Business by Independent Commission* (Princeton: Princeton University Press, 1955).

[22] 295 U.S. 495.

[23] 94 U.S. 113.

premise that the property was affected with a public interest and therefore could be controlled by the public for the common good. On the basis of this decision the legislative power to regulate the prices charged by railroads and public utilities was upheld. At the same time, the Court declared that price fixing was a matter of legislative discretion, once the right to regulate was established, and that the courts would offer no protection against legislative action on this score.

Doubts on the validity of this position, however, were expressed by the Court in *Stone* v. *Farmers' Loan and Trust Company* (1886),[24] when it said: "This power to regulate is not a power to destroy, and limitation is not the equivalent of confiscation. Under pretense of regulating fares and rates, the state cannot require a railroad corporation to carry persons or property without reward."[25] The hint contained in this opinion was erected into law in *Chicago, Milwaukee and St. Paul Railway Company* v. *Minnesota* (1890).[26] In its decision the Court said: "The question of reasonableness of a rate of charge for transportation by a railroad company involving, as it does, the element of reasonableness, both as regards the company and as regards the public, is eminently a question for judicial investigation requiring due process of law for its determination."[27] A few years later the Court gave formal effect to this position by prescribing the so-called "rule of rate making" in *Smyth* v. *Ames* (1898).[28] This case and the developments thereafter have already been discussed.

The third function of the courts in regulation is that of directly enforcing some of the statutes, particularly the Sherman and Clayton acts. One authority characterizes this by saying that "in the antitrust field the courts have been accorded, by common consent, an authority they have in no other branch of enacted law."[29] This authority applies to transport the same as to other industries, except where it is specifically excluded from the operation of it by statute.

The fourth function of the courts is to deal with litigation arising out of the enforcement of the laws by the independent regulatory commission. We shall now turn our attention to this agency of regulation.

---

[24] 116 U.S. 307.
[25] *Ibid.*, p. 331.
[26] 134 U.S. 418.
[27] *Ibid.*, p. 458.
[28] 169 U.S. 466.
[29] *United States* v. *United Shoe Machinery Corporation,* 110 Fed. Supp. 295, 348 (1953).

THE INDEPENDENT REGULATORY COMMISSION

Development of Commission Regulation

The independent regulatory commission is literally an "invention" of the United States and one of this country's unique contributions to the regulation of private industry. It may be said to have begun with the laws enacted in 1873 and 1874 by the states of Illinois, Iowa, Wisconsin, and Minnesota to control the rates charged by railroads and ancillary agencies. The Interstate Commerce Commission was the first one to be established by the federal government. This was done in 1887. The Commission was given only limited powers over rates and services at first, but during the present century its scope and authority have been extended, so that today it stands as the most powerful commission in the country. The commission form of regulation has been extended into other spheres of federal control during the last half century with the establishing of the Federal Trade Commission in 1914, the Federal Power Commission in 1930, the Federal Communications Commission in 1934, the Securities and Exchange Commission in 1934, and the Civil Aeronautics Board in 1938.

The Nature of the Regulatory Commission

The theory underlying the functions and organization of the independent regulatory commission is that it is an expert body composed of individuals appointed for the purpose of providing a continuity of business regulation that neither the courts nor the legislatures can supply. The courts are unable to do it because they can act only on the basis of litigation and only on the issues brought before them. They cannot act on their own initiative. Legislatures, by their very nature, are unable to act in an administrative capacity and are unable to supply the day-to-day and individualized regulations that modern business conditions require.

The regulatory commission is supposed to be a nonpolitical agency administering the law, within the framework of the Constitution, according to the intent of Congress, as expressed in the governing statutes. It is for this reason that it is considered essential that such a commission enjoy independent status. Accordingly, commissioners are appointed by the President and approved by the Senate for a fixed term of office. They are removable during their terms only for substantially the same reasons as judges. They may not engage in any other business, vocation, or employment while they are in office.

The regulatory commission is regarded as an arm of the legislative and judicial branches of the government, and is free from control of the executive. In other words, it occupies a dual position, which has been characterized as quasi-legislative and quasi-judicial.[30] This means that it acts in a legislative capacity when it fills out legislation by promulgating rules or enumerating details envisaged in the legislation. Congress may prescribe broad standards to carry out its purposes, such as requiring that rates be just and reasonable, or prohibiting unfair methods of competition. Congress, however, can seldom lay down detailed rules to carry out these standards, because this would be too rigid for effective regulation. The commission takes over this task. When it interprets the law and issues orders for compliance with the rules it has established, it then acts in a judicial capacity. In this capacity, it is predominantly a fact-finding body, by which activity it provides the basis upon which detailed regulations may be issued and public policy developed. Most of the statutes under which the commissions operate specify that commission findings as to the facts shall be conclusive if supported by adequate evidence.

The quasi-judicial, quasi-legislative functions of commissions put them in the position of assuming the tasks of legislator, prosecutor, and judge, all at the same time. Within their statutory power, they promulgate rules and regulations, take the necessary steps to enforce them, and sit in judgment upon those who fail to comply. In performing these tasks, however, they are primarily engaged in prescribing and defining the future privileges and duties of persons subject to regulation. In large measure, this involves making and applying policies to carry out the objectives and standards of the governing statutes. In the strict sense of the word, commissions do not act as prosecutors. They may hail alleged violators before them, but they do not impose penalties. Instead, they issue orders designed to prevent future violations or to secure compliance with announced rules of conduct.

In its formal proceedings a commission functions in much the same way as a court. The commissioners sit as judges on the presentations of the commission's attorneys and those of the interested private parties. Evidence is read into the record by the usual procedure of direct examination and cross-examination, just as in a court trial, except that the rules of evidence are not as strict. As a consequence, matters may be introduced into the record for the information of the commission that would be ruled out in a court case. A commission may also request

[30] (For an extended discussion of these functions, see dissenting opinion of Mr. Justice Jackson in *Federal Trade Commission* v. *Ruberoid Company,* 343 U.S. 470 (1952).

testimony on matters not called for in the proceedings when they started, on the grounds that such information is pertinent to the question at hand. A commission may take its own initiative in this regard, just as it may do in instituting a case. A court cannot take such initiative under either circumstance. When the trial is concluded, the commission may issue an opinion and order which may be embodied in a written document very similar to a court decision. The orders are usually self-enforcing, in the sense that they are binding upon respondents unless set aside by court order arising from an appeal.

In addition to performing their functions as regulatory agencies, commissions may also act as fact-finding bodies for the purpose of securing information that may be used as a basis for the formulation of public policy toward business and for recommendations to Congress for legislative action. The investigations may be made by the staff under commission direction, or they may be made by the members of the commission holding hearings like a Congressional committee. Investigations are usually confined to the field over which the commission has regulatory authority, but the Federal Trade Commission has been asked to undertake them in areas quite outside of those covered by its enforcement responsibilities.

Commissions may also exercise functions that can properly be assigned to the executive branch of the government. Thus the Interstate Commerce Commission prescribes car service rules, supervises safety of rail and motor carrier operations, and even has the authority to set the maximum hours of service for employees of private motor carriers of property in interstate commerce.[31] The Civil Aeronautics Board has functioned as a promotional agency for air transport. In addition, both agencies undertake investigations to see that the carriers under their jurisdiction are complying with their orders. Many of these functions have been given to the commissions because they are so closely related to the primary responsibilities of control over prices and competition. On the other hand, many have been added from time to time as a matter of convenience or expedience. As a result, the Interstate Commerce Commission, in particular, has become so burdened with detailed supervision that its capacity to carry out its principal tasks has been impaired, perhaps seriously so. Just where the line should be drawn is difficult to say.

[31] All of these functions except car service rules have been transferred to the new Department of Transportation, which is dealt with in Chapter 21. The Department began to function officially on April 1, 1967.

Courts versus Commissions in Regulation

When, as in the case of the Sherman Act, the courts alone are given the responsibility for enforcement, the regulatory commission plays no part. If, however, a commission is assigned the responsibility for initial enforcement, as in the Interstate Commerce Act, the courts still have a function to perform.[32] The courts are really the sole judges of the law, and only court decisions act as legal precedents. The courts alone can try criminal cases, assess penalties, and award damages. Finally, only the courts can compel observance of a commission order if a respondent refuses to comply.

On the other hand, the commission is the expert body on policy to the extent that it is embodied in the legislation, the authority on matters of fact, and the agency through which the regulatory program is carried out. Over the years the courts have come to recognize this status of the commission and have gradually placed limitations upon their restriction of commission authority. They now confine their review of commission deliberations to three main considerations:[33]

1. The courts will review the proceedings of the commission to assure that they have been conducted in accordance with procedures required by the statute and by due process of law. This insures that interested parties have a fair opportunity to present their evidence and arguments.
2. The courts may also review the activities and orders of commissions to make sure that they do not exceed the powers conferred by the legislation. This serves to keep the commissions within the statutory bounds prescribed by Congress.
3. Where action of a commission depends upon a factual record, the courts can review a decision or order to determine whether it was supported by substantial evidence in the record. Where substantial evidence does exist, the action of the commission will be sustained, even though the court might of itself have come to a different conclusion.

Thus, judicial review of commission decisions is a safeguard against arbitrary or capricious actions, or actions which do not conform to statutory standards or authority, or actions which are not in accordance with fair procedure or substantial evidence. Finally, court review of commission decisions is in keeping with our legal procedure,

[32] For a discussion of primary administrative jurisdiction as related to the Interstate Commerce Commission, see John Guandolo, *Transportation Law* (Dubuque, Ia.: William C. Brown Co., Publishers, 1965), chap. 37.

[33] Commission on the Organization of the Executive Branch of the Government, *Task Force Report on Regulatory Commissions* (Washington, D.C.: U.S. Government Printing Office, 1949), p. 15.

whereby, upon appeal, a higher court is able to review the decisions of a lower one.

The grounds for court interference in the decisions of the Interstate Commerce Commission were carefully summarized in *Interstate Commerce Commission* v. *Union Pacific Railroad Company* (1912).[34] In its opinion the Court said:

> In cases thus far decided, it has been settled that the orders of the Commission are final unless (1) beyond the power which it could constitutionally exercise; or (2) beyond its statutory power; or (3) based upon a mistake of law. But questions of fact may be involved in the determination of questions of law, so that an order, regular on its face may be set aside if it appears that (4) the rate is so low as to be confiscatory and in violation of the constitutional prohibition against taking property without due process of law; or (5) if the Commission acted so arbitrarily and unjustly as to fix rates contrary to evidence, or without evidence to support it; or (6) if the authority therein involved has been exercised in such an unreasonable manner as to cause it to be within the elementary rule that the substance, and not the shadow determines the validity of the exercise of the power. . . . In determining these mixed questions of law and fact, the court confines itself to the ultimate question as to whether the Commission acted within its power. It will not consider the expediency or wisdom of the order, or whether, on like testimony, it would have made a similar ruling.[35]

Criticism of the Independent Regulatory Commission

Recently, the independent regulatory commission has come under severe criticism from many quarters. One of the sources of criticism springs from the political nature of the agency. Despite the theory that commissions are supposed to be neutral and to enjoy a standing not unlike that of the courts, the fact is that a number of them have failed to measure up to these criteria. Appointments have been made too frequently as political rewards without regard to competence. Subsequent commission decisions have reflected this fact. Appointees are somewhat rarely qualified for the task at hand, and too often they regard the appointment as a steppingstone to another position rather than as a career in itself, apparently because of their ambitions for financial or other rewards. In other words, the position of commissioner has lacked the prestige necessary to encourage continuity of service, at least for the type that too frequently is selected. As to be expected, such appointees have an axe to grind, which often has led them to become

---

[34] 222 U.S. 541.

[35] *Ibid.*, p. 547. A mistake of law would occur if the Commission failed to apply some general rule or principle which the courts consider to be generally applicable and which should control the disposition of the case in question.

apostles for a particular political or economic philosophy, rather than to be expert and judicious members of a regulatory body. This attitude of commission members is aggravated by the fact that too frequently they must keep a weather eye on the political situation if they wish to be reappointed. As a consequence, the development of an independent and objective position becomes somewhat difficult.

Many other criticisms have emerged, such as the tendency of commissions to fall under the control of the industries they are supposed to regulate, undue delay in arriving at and announcing decisions, too much attention to insignificant details and routine matters to the detriment of the basic duties which the commissions are supposed to discharge, a strong tendency toward opportunism with the consequent lack of consistency in the development of the administration and interpretation of the law, and failure to evolve a system of case law which adjudication by commission should be expected to produce. All of these criticisms have varying degrees of validity for the different commissions. However, Congress and the executive branch of the government must share much of the blame for the difficulties which have become apparent, and much of the criticism should be aimed at them. Commissions cannot be expected to function as independent and objectively oriented agencies when Congress continuously assigns to them such conflicting legislation that obedience to one part brings conflict and contradiction with another. Nor can commissions command respect when the executive branch of the government persists in using the power of appointment as a means of providing rewards for political support or as a means of furthering programs that Congress will not sanction directly. Such reform as may be necessary needs to begin with Congress, which should recognize the fact that it cannot evade ultimately its responsibility by constantly shifting it to the shoulders of a commission. Similar remarks apply to the executive branch, which must understand and acknowledge the meaning of an independent regulatory body and the responsibilities connected with appointments necessary to make it so.

In the field of transportation the Interstate Commerce Commission has come under severe scrutiny, first of all because of the serious problems connected with national transportation policy that have emerged recently, and second because of the sharply conflicting interests of the different modes of transport that come under its jurisdiction. An appraisal of what seems to be the appropriate role of the Commission in light of modern transport conditions will be given after regulation and the issues of national transport policy have been discussed.

However, it may be noted here that the criticisms seem to center on four points: (1) the procedures used by the Commission in dealing with cases coming before it; (2) the functions, adjudicative and executive, that the Commission is called upon to perform; (3) the role of the Commission in policy making and policy formulation; and (4) the present content of the law as it relates to transport regulation and public policy.[36]

The first of these items is clearly under the control of the Commission, and most of the difficulties connected therewith could be corrected by it, although all of them could not be eliminated as long as the present burden of duties imposed upon it remains. The third item is also partially under the control of the Commission. The development of policy on matters such as interagency rate making, which enforcement of the law calls for, is a responsibility of the Commission. Criticism of what has been done here must be directed at it; but it should be recognized that neither the legislative nor the executive branches of the government have taken very decisive steps to give coherent instructions to the Commission. Nor can the latter, as a regulatory body, be expected to develop and formulate public policy beyond the duties assigned to it by legislation.

The second basis of criticism is one that can be resolved by Congress. The Commission is compelled to perform the duties assigned to it, even though they may be executive in nature. What ones may be appropriate for the efficient discharge of regulatory functions is a matter for Congress to decide.

The fourth criticism does not relate to the regulatory commission at all. For example, it is not relevant to an evaluation of the Interstate Commerce Commission to state that there should be a "revision of Section 4 of Part I of the Interstate Commerce Act to modify or abolish the authority of the Commission to grant railroads relief against water carrier competition."[37] That such a proposal is in the interest of sound

---

[36] See *Report on Regulatory Agencies to the President-Elect* (Landis Report), Senate Committee on the Judiciary, 86th Congress, 2d session, December, 1960 (Washington, D.C.: U.S. Government Printing Office, 1960); *Independent Regulatory Commissions*, Report of the Special Subcommittee on Legislative Oversight of House Committee on Interstate and Foreign Commerce, House Report No. 2238, Union Calendar No. 1024, 86th Congress, 2d session (Washington, D.C.: U.S. Government Printing Office, 1961); and M. L. Fair, "Some Observations on the Theory and Performance of the Independent Regulatory Agencies in Regulating Public Utility Industries," *I.C.C. Practitioners' Journal*, Vol. XXVII, No. 9 (June, 1960), pp. 957–69. For a severe criticism of the Civil Aeronautics Board, see Louis J. Hector, *Problems of the CAB and the Independent Regulatory Commissions*, Memorandum to the President (mimeographed), September 10, 1959, pp. 1–75.

[37] *Report on Regulatory Agencies to the President-Elect* (Landis Report), *op. cit.*, p. 79.

transportation economics is debatable, to say the least, but that is beside the point. It has nothing to do with the status and achievements of the Commission because the decision on the matter of the authority of the Commission must rest with Congress. Appraisal of the role of commissions in the execution of public policy requires first of all a distinction between formulation and execution. Too much of the present debate fails to take note of this.

THE INTERSTATE COMMERCE COMMISSION

Membership and Appointment

The Interstate Commerce Commission consists of eleven members appointed by the President of the United States "by and with the advice and consent of the Senate." These members are appointed for a period of seven years and may be reappointed. They are removable during their terms of office by the President only for substantially the same reasons that hold for the removal of judges, namely, inefficiency, neglect of duty, or malfeasance in office.[38] The Chairman of the Commission is elected by its members. This position, with the exception of the years 1940–43, has been rotated annually since 1910.

Scope of Authority

The scope of the Commission's statutory authority is summarized conveniently by the Special Subcommittee on Legislative Oversight as follows:

The Commission has been vested with authority to regulate various types of surface transportation in interstate and foreign commerce. The scope of this authority is briefly as follows: (1) to issue certificates of public convenience and necessity for the construction, extension and abandonment of lines of railroads; certificates of public convenience and necessity for the establishment or extension of motor common carrier and water common carrier operations; the issuance of permits for the institution and extension of motor contract carrier operations, water contract carrier operations, and freight forwarder operations; (2) to require that rates and practices of all common carriers, including freight forwarders, subject to the act be just, reasonable, and nondiscriminatory, and that such rates be published, filed with the Commission and observed; and to require that motor contract carriers and water contract carriers establish and observe just and reasonable minimum rates; (3) to regulate railroads and motor carriers, including private carriers by motor vehicles, with respect to safety of operations, standards of equipment, and hours of service of personnel whose activities affect safety of operation; (4) to require personal injury, death, and property damage insurance of motor carriers and freight forwarders for the pro-

---

[38] See, for example, *Humphrey's Executor* v. *United States*, 295 U.S. 602 (1935).

tection of the public and cargo insurance for the protection of shippers; (5) to pass upon the unification, mergers, and common control of two or more railroads, motor carriers, water carriers, express companies or sleeping car companies, and to approve or disapprove the pooling or division of traffic, service or earnings by two or more such carriers; (6) to regulate the issuance of securities by railroads and motor carriers, the financial reorganization of railroads, and the guarantee of loans to railroads; (7) to prescribe regulations governing the packaging, marking and handling of explosives and other dangerous articles which are binding upon all carriers subject to the Interstate Commerce Act and shippers, and which regulations as to marking and packing are adopted by the Coast Guard for application to water carriers; and (8) to investigate alleged violations, prosecute in court and assist the Department of Justice in prosecuting civil and criminal proceedings arising under all parts of the act and related acts such as the Elkins Act, the Clayton Antitrust Act, and the Transportation of Explosives Act. In addition to the above, the Commission has various other duties such as the prescribing of time zones under the Standard Time Act, determining reasonableness of parcel post increased rates, prescribing charges by railroads for the transportation of mail, investigations under the Medals of Honor Act, and others.[39]

It will be noted that the authority of the Interstate Commerce Commission extends only to agencies of transportation named in the legislation, and that this does not even cover all transportation for hire in interstate commerce, one particularly notable exception being air transport, which is regulated by the Civil Aeronautics Board.

Internal Organization

The wide range of duties which the Interstate Commerce Commission is called upon to discharge has resulted in a relatively complex organization, which is depicted in Figure 11–1. As of 1966 the Commission employed approximately 2,376 employees and operated on an appropriation of $27,540,000 for the fiscal year ended June 30 1966.[40]

The Chairman is the executive head of the Commission and is responsible to it in the discharge of his executive and administrative functions. He is now assisted by a Vice Chairman, this post being established in 1961. The Managing Director is the permanent staff member in charge of the activities of the Commission; he reports to the Vice

[39] *Independent Regulatory Commissions: Comparative Operating Data, etc.,* prepared for Special Subcommittee on Legislative Oversight of Committee on Interstate and Foreign Commerce, Subcommittee Print, 86th Cong., 2d sess. (Washington, D.C.: U.S. Government Printing Office, December, 1960), pp. 114–15. Items (3) and (7) have now been assigned to the Department of Transportation, as well as time zones, transportation of explosives, and investigations under the Medals of Honor Act under item (8).

[40] Interstate Commerce Commission, *80th Annual Report, June 30, 1966* (Washington, D.C.: U.S. Government Printing Office, 1967), p. 142.

FIGURE 11–1 INTERSTATE COMMERCE COMMISSION

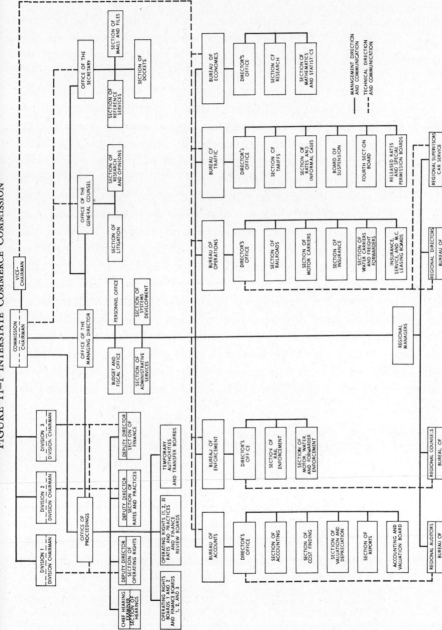

Reorganization of the Commission to account for the establishment of the Department of Transportation. Reproduced, with permission, *Traffic World*, March 18, 1967.

Chairman. The Commission conducts its work through three divisions to which the various commissioners are assigned. There are three procedural bureaus under the Office of Proceedings, in charge of a director, which processes cases for the divisions; the directors of these bureaus report to the director of proceedings who reports directly to the chairman of the Commission. The five regulatory bureaus report through the vice-chairman. All matters of general transportation importance and those involving formal hearings are acted on initially by a division whose action is final where matters of general transportation importance are not involved; otherwise, appeal may be made to the entire Commission. Hearings are normally conducted by examiners who report their findings and recommendations to the appropriate division of the Commission for formal action. Finally, employee boards may handle proceedings that do not involve issues of general transportation importance and on which no formal hearing has been held.[41]

This new administrative organization is designed to speed the handling of cases as well as to focus responsibility for writing decisions. It has been developed in response to criticisms regarding the organization of the Commission and procedures employed by it. The Commission still feels that it is handicapped by the fact that the Department of Justice is the statutory defendant when orders of the Commission are challenged. The Commission can intervene, but the fact that it has to rely upon the Department of Justice in court cases has led to considerable conflict which the Commission feels should be rectified by a change in the law which would permit the Commission to defend its own orders.[42]

✓ THE CIVIL AERONAUTICS BOARD

Membership and Appointment

The Civil Aeronautics Board is an independent regulatory commission patterned after the Interstate Commerce Commission, although it possesses much less comprehensive responsibilities, its activities being confined to air transportation. It consists of five members appointed for

[41] For a more complete description, see Interstate Commerce Commission, *79th Annual Report, June 30, 1965* (Washington, D.C., U.S. Government Printing Office, 1965), pp. 6–10. A detailed presentation of practices and procedures before the Commission will be found in Edgar Watkins, *Shippers and Carriers—Interstate Commerce,* by Burton Fuller, Vol. II (5th ed.; Atlanta, Ga.: The Harrison Co., 1962).

[42] Interstate Commerce Commission, *74th Annual Report, June 30, 1960* (Washington, D.C.: U.S. Government Printing Office, 1961), p. 160.

six years by the President, in the same manner as the members of the Interstate Commerce Commission, and holding office under the same conditions. The Chairman and Vice-Chairman are designated by the President on an annual basis.

Scope of Authority

The scope of the Board's statutory authority was summarized by the Special Subcommitte on Legislative Oversight as follows:

In general the Board performs three chief functions: (1) regulation of the economic aspects of domestic and international U.S. air carrier operations and of the common carrier operations of foreign air carriers to and from the United States; (2) investigation and analysis of civil aircraft accidents; (3) adjudication of refusals of the Administrator of the Federal Aviation Agency to issue airman certificates and of appeals from orders of the Administrator affecting air safety certificates and participation in the Administration's safety rulemaking proceedings.

Economic Regulation. The Board licenses common carriage by air by U.S. air carriers in foreign air transportation. Board orders granting or affecting certificates authorizing overseas and foreign air transportation and foreign air carrier permits are subject to Presidential approval.

The Board fixes the rates for the carriage of mail, and, in some instances, subsidy for air carriers; regulates air carriers' accounting practices; regulates mergers, acquisitions of control and interlocking relationships involving air carriers; prevents unfair competition or unfair and deceptive practices by air carriers, foreign air carriers and ticket agents; passes on contracts for cooperative working arrangements between air carriers; may fix rates in interstate air transportation and maximum and/or minimum rates in overseas air transportation, but in foreign air transportation may only remove rate discrimination. The Board may also guarantee private loans to certain classes of air carriers. The Board advises the Secretary of State in the negotiation of agreements with foreign governments for the establishment and development of international air routes and services.

Accident Investigation and Analysis. The Board investigates accidents involving civil aircraft and holds public hearings thereon where the public interest so requires; it reports the facts, circumstances, and probable causes of such accidents; it makes such recommendations to the Administrator as will tend to prevent similar accidents in the future; makes such reports public in such form and manner as it deems to be in the public interest; and conducts special studies and investigations to reduce the possibility of aircraft accidents and prevent their recurrence.

Safety Enforcement and Regulation. Upon the request of aggrieved parties, the Board reviews in quasi-judicial proceedings, conducted pursuant to the of the optimum blend of the two mechanisms. Whether the current blend is Administrative Procedure Act, denials by the Administrator of the Federal Aviation Agency of applications for airman certificates and orders of the Administrator modifying, amending, suspending, or revoking any air safety certificates

The Board may also participate as an interested party in safety rulemaking proceedings conducted by the Administrator of the Federal Aviation Agency.

Other Functions. The Board participates in the negotiation of air transport agreements with foreign governments. Also, in addition to licensing the common carrier operations of foreign air carriers, the Board authorizes the navigation of foreign civil aircraft in the United States for other purposes.

The Board exercises its powers independently. Its decisions are not subject to review by any executive department or agency, except for the approval of the President required in the Board decisions granting or affecting certificates for overseas and foreign air transportation, and foreign air carrier permits.[43]

The organization of the Board is set forth in the chart in Figure 11–2.

FIGURE 11–2

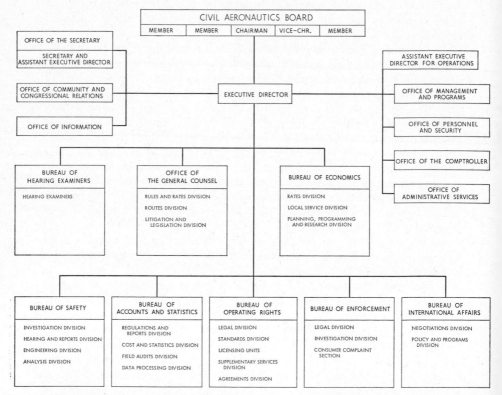

Prepared by Office of Management and Programs, Civil Aeronautics Board, July 25, 1966.

[43] *Independent Regulatory Commissions: Comparative Operating Data, etc., op. cit.,* pp. 4–5. The powers of the Civil Aeronautics Board on all matters relating to safety in aviation have now been transferred to the National Transportation Safety Board in the Department of Transportation.

THE FOUNDATIONS OF
TRANSPORT REGULATION

INTRODUCTION

The Basis of Regulation

From early times in English history, transportation had been subject to various regulations, because the supplying of transport services to the general public was what was known as a "common calling" and, under it, common carriers were required to serve all alike, at reasonable rates and without discrimination. There was also a recognition of the fact that the furnishing of transport facilities was in many respects a function of government. With the growth of private enterprise in transport the theory developed that the agencies supplying transportation were performing governmental functions under grants of authority to do so. It was on this basis that private firms were accorded the right of eminent domain. In addition, legal theory also came to hold that when the owner of private property assumed the obligation to serve all who applied, he could not renounce his responsibilities without public consent, and he became subject to the special common-law rules for enterprises affected with a public interest.

Thus the foundations for modern regulation were well established by the beginning of the nineteenth century, but it was not until the rise of the railroad to its prime position in inland transport that positive regulation began. It was the unique economic characteristics of railroads which brought this about. Had it not been for these characteristics, there is little reason to believe that regulation in transportation would have taken on anything resembling its present pattern.

Early Regulation

It was not until 1870 that any serious attempt was made to regulate transportation in a positive way in the United States. Some early restrictions had been imposed on railway charges and earnings through charters which were granted by direct legislation. These charters frequently contained schedules of maximum charges for passengers and freight, and sometimes limited earnings to a percentage of capitalization. These controls were ineffective, however, because of lack of means of supervising costs that entered into the calculation of profits available for dividends; because the maximum rates prescribed were generally higher than the most profitable ones; and because rate relationships could not be controlled by charter or by direct legislation. Even the charter limitations did not obtain when railroad charters came to be granted under general incorporation acts. In some of the New England states, commissions were created, but they were of the advisory type and had little power of control and no direct authority over rates.

Reasons for the Development of Regulation

The immediate factor in the development of the positive regulation of the railroads was the Granger movement which began in 1867 This was an agrarian manifestation of thoroughgoing discontent with economic conditions, of which antirailroad sentiment was but one phase. It was the result of the severe decline of agricultural prices following the Civil War, arising from previous inflation, overexpansion in agriculture, public land policy, and unfavorable foreign markets for grain. The railroads quickly became a focus of attention for this discontent because they had failed to provide the low freight rates that had been expected. In addition, there was a great deal of discrimination in rate making, as well as an arrogant ignoring of shippers. Finally, financial excesses and abuses, with heavy investor losses, together with much foreign ownership of stocks and bonds, aroused a great deal of local antagonism as well as resentment at "absentee" ownership.

Railroad excesses and abuses were a legitimate basis for protest and ill feeling, and would have brought legislative reaction even in the absence of other factors. If these difficulties had not been present, some form of regulation would have been inevitable because of the economic features of railroad transportation which have already been discussed. Furthermore the comprehensive type of regulation that ultimately emerged would probably have been unavoidable, abuses or no abuses. The nature of railroad economics and the inadequacy of complete reliance on competition made public intervention inescapable. Unfortunately, failure to understand the economic basis of regulation of railroads, together with the resentment which railroad practices had aroused, seriously retarded the development of a statesmanlike approach to the problems of railroad transportation. The carry-over, even to the present time, of this early lack of understanding of the nature and sources of the problem has placed severe obstacles in the way of an economical resolution of the current transport dilemma.

STATE REGULATION

The Granger Laws

The initial steps for the positive regulation of railroads came when the states of Illinois, Iowa, Minnesota, and Wisconsin enacted what became known as the "Granger laws" between 1871 and 1874. These laws had common objectives and very similar provisions, although they were not identical in their clauses. They all established maximum rate limits, Iowa prescribing rates for all distances up to 376 miles on various classes of freight and on specific commodities. Illinois and Minnesota, on the other hand, imposed the duty of prescribing a schedule of maximum rates on regulatory commissions which were set up under their statutes. The various laws endeavored to deal with place discrimination by what were known as "prorata clauses," by which rates could not be higher for shorter than for longer hauls. This applied to any distance, no matter in what direction the traffic moved, or whether it was on a branch line or on the main line. An attempt was made to preserve competition by forbidding competing railroad lines to consolidate, and personal favoritism came in for some limitation with prohibitions against free railroad passes to public officials. Finally, the Granger laws introduced the mandatory commission, which, it was noted earlier,[1] was literally an American invention and one of this country's unique contributions to the development of the regulation of private industry. It was these commissions that formed the prototype of the Interstate Commerce Commission, which was to be set up shortly thereafter.

The Granger laws enjoyed only limited direct success, and all of them except that of Illinois were repealed; for the remainder of the century, state regulation was quite ineffective. There were a number of reasons for the repeal of these laws. In the first place, both legal and administrative experience was lacking. As a consequence, in construction and application, there was insufficient adaptability. The maximum rate and distance provisions were too rigid, and the railroads frequently made the situation worse by taking full advantage of the maxima. Finally, economic conditions culminating in the panic of 1873 resulted in a rather thorough breakdown of the movement for regulation.

[1] See Chapter 11.

The results of the laws were not all negative in nature, however. A start had been made on the development of the idea of the mandatory commission, on the one hand; and on the other, the unworkability of highly inflexible laws was clearly demonstrated. More important was the fact that the testing of the legislation and its administration in the courts established the unequivocal right of the states to regulate industries affected with a public interest and demonstrated clearly that the state could, through properly worded and administered legislation, develop very broad and comprehensive powers over private business, especially that which was "affected with a public interest."

Court Interpretation of the Granger Laws

It was to be expected that legislation as highly controversial and as novel as the Granger laws would soon have to face the test of the courts. For the first time, the issue of whether the authority a legislature could exercise over business which had clearly recognized public responsibilities was different and more extensive than that which it had over purely private undertakings was squarely joined. The question came before the Supreme Court of the United States in the Granger cases, for which *Munn* v. *Illinois* (1877)[2] established the precedent. This case actually pertained only to grain elevators in the city of Chicago, but the Court held that these were part of the transportation process and that they therefore were subject to the jurisdiction of the Illinois law. Three major questions were passed upon by the Court: (1) the right to regulate, (2) the right of judicial review, and (3) the power to regulate interstate commerce. The position taken by the Court in this case on the second and third issues was not sustained in subsequent legal developments, but its decision on the first has held to the present time, even being given wider scope than was implied initially.

1. *The Right to Regulate.* The legislation of the state of Illinois was first of all challenged on the ground that the fixing of maximum rates deprived the plaintiffs of property without due process of law and therefore violated the Fourteenth Amendment of the federal Constitution. The Supreme Court held that the state had the right to regulate an industry affected with a public interest and that certain activities had fallen into that category of common law for centuries. Transportation was such an activity. This ruling of the Court has been

[2] 94 U.S. 113.

followed ever since, although the scope of the concept of an industry affected with a public interest has been broadened somewhat over the years since that time, as was explained in the previous chapter.

2. *The Right of Judicial Review.* Even if one conceded that the state did have the right to regulate, the plaintiffs contended that such a power could not be exercised without limit. They argued that the owner of property was entitled to a reasonable compensation for its use and that what constituted a reasonable compensation was for the courts and not the legislature to decide. The Supreme Court rejected this idea also, by stating that once the right to regulate had been established, the role of the courts had been exhausted. For protection against possible abuses of the exercise of legislative power, resort had to be to the polls, not to the courts. This part of the decision did not stand for long; in a short time it was reversed and the right of judicial review definitely established by the Supreme Court. The development of this in connection with fair value was discussed in the previous chapter.

3. *The Power to Regulate Interstate Commerce.* A third point which was raised in the Granger cases was the extent to which states could exercise jurisdiction over interstate commerce. At this time, there was no federal legislation whatsoever on this matter. In *Munn* v. *Illinois* the Court found that the business of the warehouses was carried on exclusively within the state of Illinois. Their regulation was therefore a matter of domestic concern; and until Congress acted with reference to the interstate relations, the state could regulate them, even though in doing so it indirectly affected interstate commerce. Some of the other Granger cases went further than this by ruling that a state could prescribe maximum rates on traffic that moved within a state even though the shipments moved to points beyond state boundaries or came from points outside them.[3] The issue that had been presented was not allowed to lie in this uncertain category for very long.

Two other matters of importance to regulation were passed upon in the Granger cases. At the time the Granger laws were enacted, most of the railroad charters gave the railroads the right to fix their own rates. Because charters were contracts,[4] the railroads argued that regulation was precluded. The Court ruled, however, that when the state had the right to regulate, the charter provisions did not carry with

---

[3] See *Chicago, Burlington and Quincy Railroad* v. *Iowa,* 94 U.S. 155 (1877); *Peik* v. *Chicago and Northwestern Railway Company,* 94 U.S. 164 (1877).

[4] *Dartmouth College* v. *Woodward,* 4 Wheat (U.S.) 518 (1819).

them the renunciation by the state of its own superior right of regulation, unless immunity from regulation was specifically and definitely conferred by the charter.

The other issue that arose had to do with the constitutionality of the mandatory commission as an instrument of regulation. It was contended that the powers conferred by the Granger laws on the commissions constituted an unconstitutional delegation of legislative powers. The Court held that these commissions could not make laws, but they could administer the ones assigned to them by the legislature.[5]

State versus Federal Authority

The indefinitely defined limits of state authority over interstate commerce under the Granger decisions were sharply delineated by the Supreme Court in *Wabash, St. Louis and Pacific Railway Company* v. *Illinois* (1886).[6] The law of the state of Illinois forbade a railroad to charge more for a shorter haul than for a longer haul for the same shipments in the same direction. The Wabash Railway charged more for shipping grain from Gilman, Illinois, to New York than from Peoria, Illinois, the former being closer to New York. The reason was severe competition at Peoria which was absent at Gilman. The state of Illinois brought suit to prevent the violation of the long-and-short-haul clause in its statute. Successful enforcement of the law would obviously have to apply to the entire rate from Gilman as well as Peoria to New York. The Supreme Court held that this was clearly and exclusively interstate traffic and therefore could be regulated only by the federal government. Even though it did nothing on the matter, the states were nevertheless powerless to act. This set the stage for and created the necessity of federal legislation to deal with problems of transportation.

The Wabash case definitely established the rule that when traffic fell exclusively within the category of what the Court ruled was interstate commerce, only the federal government could act. Two important issues, however, remained. The first was how far federal power could be extended under the concept of interstate commerce; and the second was whether, when federal authority had been established, the states could act if the federal government permitted them to do so.

The first of these issues emerged in the Minnesota rate case, which involved the validity of certain intrastate rates prescribed by the Minne-

[5] See railroad commission cases, *Stone* v. *Farmers' Loan and Trust Company*, 116 U.S. 307 (1886); 116 U.S. 347 (1886); 116 U.S. 352 (1886).
[6] 118 U.S. 557.

sota Commission.[7] The cities of Duluth, Minnesota, and Superior, Wisconsin, are adjacent to each other and compete for trade over a broad area in Minnesota. When the Commission ordered the railroads to reduce passenger fares and freight rates between points located entirely within Minnesota, these railroads were forced by competition to do the same to Superior. The impact of the reduction affected rates over a wide area, as far west as the Pacific coast. The railroads protested the orders on the ground, among others, that they involved the regulation of interstate commerce. The Supreme Court held that in the absence of Congressional action the state might pass laws affecting local interests, even though interstate commerce was indirectly or incidentally burdened. The Court did point out, however, that the states could not under any guise impose direct burdens and indicated that Congress could act even where indirect effects existed, if it so desired.

The next year, in the Shreveport case,[8] in a similar controversy, the authority of the federal government was definitely established. The Texas Commission maintained lower rates eastward from Dallas and Houston toward Shreveport, Louisiana, than the interstate rates westward from Shreveport to the same points. The Louisiana Commission complained to the Interstate Commerce Commission that the interstate railroad rates from Shreveport were unreasonable and discriminatory. The Interstate Commerce Commission agreed with Louisiana and established rates to eliminate the discrimination. The railroads contended that they could not be compelled to lower rates which were reasonable, and the state of Texas argued that Congress did not have the power to fix the intrastate charges of an interstate carrier. The Supreme Court held that the power of a state to prescribe intrastate rates could not be exercised in such a way as to defeat the legitimate exercise of federal control over interstate commerce. Congress, through the Interstate Commerce Commission, had seen fit to act and had the power to do so. The basic difference between this case and the Minnesota one arose from the fact that the Louisiana Commission had appealed to the Interstate Commerce Commission, whereas in the Minnesota case, appeal had gone directly to the courts. The Interstate Commerce Commission took action in the Shreveport case, and the Supreme Court upheld its power to do this under Section 3 of the Interstate Commerce Act, the provisions of which constituted a legitimate exercise of Congressional authority.

[7] *Simpson* v. *Shepard.* 230 U.S. 352 (1913).

[8] *Houston, East and West Texas Railway Company* v. *United States*, 234 U.S. 342 (1914).

The final step in the growth of federal power came with the Wisconsin passenger fares case.[9] The state of Wisconsin prescribed a maximum fare of 2 cents per mile for carrying passengers solely in the state. When interstate fares were increased, the Wisconsin Commission refused to follow suit. The Interstate Commerce Commission ordered the railroads to raise these intrastate fares to the interstate level, on the ground that the intrastate fares constituted an undue burden on interstate commerce. The Supreme Court held that effective operation of the Interstate Commerce Act, as amended by the Transportation Act of 1920, required that state traffic pay a proportionate share of the cost of maintaining an adequate railroad system.

It seems to be clear from the decisions of the Supreme Court that federal authority over transportation can be extended almost without limit if it is necessary to do so in order to regulate interstate transportation. The obverse of this is the extent to which Congress can permit states to exercise control, even though the effect of this on interstate commerce is substantial. The implications of the foregoing decisions are that so long as the Congressional power is not exclusive, the states can act. In the regulation of motor transport in particular, Congress has taken specific steps to limit the authority of the Interstate Commerce Commission, thereby reserving much motor carrier regulation to the states. The Shreveport rule, for example, is applicable only to railroads and common carriers by air at the present time, and the Interstate Commerce Commission is specifically prevented from applying it to motor transport by the Motor Carrier Act of 1935.[10]

Developments in state versus federal authority since the Wisconsin passenger fares case have turned largely on the interpretation of federal legislation rather than on constitutional issues.[11] The states, nevertheless, exercise extensive control over transportation, to a considerable degree because of Congressional acquiescence, particularly in the case of railroads. All of the states regulate transportation to a greater or lesser degree as a result of the revival of regulation by state commissions commencing in 1907. Authority over railroads is confined largely to local matters, although controversy has arisen in connection with abandonments and discontinuance of train service. Many of the states impose thoroughgoing control over motor transport, and even

[9] *Railroad Commission of Wisconsin* v. *Chicago, Burlington and Quincy Railway Company,* 257 U.S. 563 (1922).

[10] Interstate Commerce Act, Section 216 (e).

[11] See R. E. Westmeyer, *Economics of Transportation* (Englewood Cliffs, N.J.: Prentice-Hall, Inc., 1952), pp. 188–94, for a discussion of some minor jurisdictional conflicts.

carriers engaged in interstate operations must receive state authorization if they wish to carry intrastate traffic.[12] Intrastate common carriers by motor are now permitted to engage in interstate commerce within a given state if they register their operating authority with the Interstate Commerce Commission. This greater leeway for motor carriers is a recognition by Congress of the close relationship between motor transport and relatively local areas.

THE ACT TO REGULATE COMMERCE, 1887

The Supreme Court decision in the Wabash case eliminated all state control over transportation that fell strictly into the category of interstate commerce. If there was to be any regulation of this whatsoever, it had to be undertaken by the federal government. This could be accomplished only by statutory enactment because there is no federal common law and there was therefore no basis upon which agencies of the federal government could act in the absence of legislation. The development of state regulation and the delimitation of its scope by the Supreme Court forced Congress to act.

There was some incidental regulation by Congress relating to interstate commerce in transportation prior to 1887, such as the law of 1866, which was designed to facilitate through interstate shipments by authorizing necessary arrangements, and an act passed in 1873 relating to the conditions of carriage of livestock. In addition, there was a great deal of agitation for federal regulation, prior to 1887, as a result of the conditions which had led to action at the state level. In 1873, President Grant recommended that Congress undertake an investigation of certain phases of transportation. The Senate appointed a committee, which became known as the Windom Committee. In 1874, it made its report, the burden of which was that reliance should be placed on competition as the means of securing lower freight rates. No legislation emerged, however; meanwhile, severe railroad competition led to a deterioration of railroad rate structures and the rise of discrimination as a major issue. This was emphasized by the Cullom Committee in its report to the Senate in 1886. This Committee also found many other

---

[12] For a discussion of state regulation of motor carriers, see D. V. Harper, *Economic Regulation of the Motor Trucking Industry by the States* (Urbana, Ill.: University of Illinois Press, 1959). State regulation of air carriers is dealt with by Stuart Daggett, *Principles of Inland Transportation* (4th ed.; New York: Harper & Bros., 1955), pp. 602–9. The Pacific Southwest Airways operates a commuter service in California between San Diego, Los Angeles and San Francisco. Its services are strictly intrastate and it is not subject to the jurisdiction of the Civil Aeronautics Board.

abuses in railroad practices, and concluded that competition and self-interest could not be relied upon to give adequate protection to shippers. It decided that federal regulation was necessary to remedy the situation. The Wabash decision provided the final impetus, especially in view of the fact that about three fourths of the railway traffic in 1886 was interstate.

The Act of 1887 was but the first of a long series of legislative enactments relating to transportation that were to be passed over the ensuing years down to the present time. The most significant features of these will be dealt with in chronological succession because each added something more to the federal program. Thus the present Interstate Commerce Act, as this legislation came to be known, comprises an accumulation of legislation over a period of 80 years. Furthermore, most of the provisions of the various laws have been retained, although some of them have been modified to meet changing conditions or court decisions.

Provisions of the Act of 1887

1. *Coverage.* The Act of 1887 was made applicable to all common carriers by railroad engaged in interstate or foreign commerce. It did not apply to common carriers wholly by water, but it did include common carriers partly by water and partly by rail, where they were under common control or arrangement for continuous carriage or shipment.

2. *Reasonable Rates.* Section 1 required that all rates be just and reasonable, and provided that every unjust and unreasonable charge was unlawful. This was simply a statutory enactment of the long-standing common-law rule, although prior to this enactment there was no adequate basis at the federal level for enforcing this rule.

3. *Personal Discrimination.* Section 2 prohibited personal discrimination by making it unlawful, directly or indirectly, for a carrier, by any device, to charge one person more than another for a like and contemporaneous service under substantially similar circumstances and conditions. Certain special and quite limited exceptions were set forth in later sections.

4. *Undue Preference or Prejudice.* Section 3 was really a blanket prohibition of undue or unreasonable preference or advantage of any form to any person, place, or kind of traffic. Thus, this was not a prohibition of preferential or differential treatment, but only a limitation to what might be considered just and reasonable.

5. *The Long-and-Short-Haul Clause.* This is the well-known

Scale
Economies
?

Section 4 of the Act, which prohibited a common carrier subject to the Act from charging or receiving any greater compensation in the aggregate for transportation of passengers or of like kind of property, "under substantially similar circumstances and conditions," for a shorter than for a longer distance over the same line, in the same direction, the shorter being included within the longer distance. The Commission could grant exceptions in special cases.

6. *Pooling.* Section 5 made it unlawful for common carriers to enter into any contract, agreement, or combination for the pooling of freight, or for the division of the aggregate or net proceeds of their earnings.

7. *Publication of Rates.* Section 6 of the Act stated that schedules of rates and fares were to be printed, made available for public inspection, and filed with the Commission. There was to be strict adherence to the published schedules, and ten days' public notice was required before rates could be advanced.

8. *The Interstate Commerce Commission.* To administer the law, the Act established an Interstate Commerce Commission, which was to consist of five members appointed by the President, with the advice and consent of the Senate, for a term of six years. Later on, this was changed to eleven members appointed for a term of seven years. The Commission was to be bipartisan in composition, and no commissioner could engage in any other business, vocation, or employment while holding office. Any commissioner could be removed for inefficiency, neglect of duty, or malfeasance in office by the President. There was no limitation on reappointment. By an amendment in 1889 the Commission was ordered to report directly to Congress, thereby assuming an independent status.

In order to enable it to carry out its responsibilities, the Act gave the Commission the authority to inquire into the management of the business of common carriers. It could require the testimony of witnesses and the production of records on matters under investigation. It was empowered to order the preparation of annual reports and to prescribe a uniform system of accounts. Finally, it could undertake investigations upon complaint or on its own motion, and the findings were to be prima-facie evidence in all judicial proceedings as to every fact found.

The Act contained penalties for violation of its provisions, but these could be imposed only by the courts. The Commission could order those subject to the law to "cease and desist" from further violation, but if the respondent failed to obey the Commission's orders, it was necessary for the latter to appeal to the courts for enforcement. There was no penalty for failure to obey the Commission's orders; penalties were imposed only for violation of the law.

Judicial Interpretation

On the surface the powers of the Interstate Commerce Commission under the new law were very comprehensive and adequate for the task of effective regulation. The law still had to pass the scrutiny of the courts, however, for its meaning to be discovered. The result was that many difficulties appeared which had not been expected. Much of the wording was anything but unambiguous; and in addition, the respective positions of the courts and the Commission in regulation remained to be worked out.

First of all, definite obstacles to enforcement appeared. Opposition arose over the power of the government to compel witnesses to testify.[13] This was resolved by the passage of the Compulsory Testimony Act of 1893, which provided that no person should be prosecuted on account of any matter concerning which he might testify or produce evidence in a proceeding which alleged violation of the Act of 1887.[14] The Commission also was handicapped by the fact that when it appealed to the courts to enforce its orders, the courts insisted on rehearing all the evidence and also permitted the carriers to introduce evidence not previously presented to the Commission. The Supreme Court, in 1896,[15] expressed disapproval of this practice, but further legislation was necessary to provide adequate remedies for the difficulty.

A second difficulty appeared in connection with the prescription of reasonable rates. The Commission assumed that it had the authority to determine whether particular rates were unreasonable and that, if it so found, it could prescribe reasonable maximum rates for the future. The issue came before the Supreme Court in the maximum freight rate case of 1897.[16] The Court held that the power to designate rates for the future could not be implied from the provisions of the Act of 1887, and that this power was not among those granted to the Commission by Congress. All the Commission could do was to pronounce a particular rate to be unreasonable, and then the dispute could start all over again on any lower rate established by the railroad.

[13] *Counselman* v. *Hitchcock,* 142 U.S. 547 (1892).

[14] This was upheld in *Brown* v. *Walker,* 161 U.S. 591 (1896); see also *Interstate Commerce Commission* v. *Brimson,* 154 U.S. 447 (1894).

[15] *Cincinnati, New Orleans and Texas Pacific Railway Company* v. *Interstate Commerce Commission,* 162 U.S. 184.

[16] *Interstate Commerce Commission* v. *Cincinnati, New Orleans and Texas Pacific Railway Company,* 167 U.S. 479.

The final blow to the Commission's rate-making powers came with the decision of the Supreme Court in the Alabama Midland case in 1897.[17] This dealt with the long-and-short-haul problem. The Commission ruled that competition between interstate railways at a distant point and the absence of like competition at a nearer point did not generally create such dissimilarity as to justify higher rates for the short haul. In other words, the Commission refused to recognize the competition between interstate railways as creating a dissimilarity of circumstances, except in "rare and peculiar" cases. The Court held that competition at the more distant point constituted a dissimilarity of conditions sufficient to make section 4 inapplicable. The Commission thus found itself virtually without authority over place discrimination.

Results of the Act

As a consequence of court interpretation of the Act of 1887 the Interstate Commerce Commission was stripped of all authority necessary to deal effectively with the rate grievances that had led to the passage of the law. The legislation was not entirely ineffective, however. Publicity of rates had been secured, many of the grosser forms of discrimination had been eliminated, valuable statistical data had been accumulated, and experience in the pitfalls of the law had been acquired. Finally, and most important, the Interstate Commerce Commission had become firmly established so that Congress was ready to undertake steps to make it an effective enforcement agency. This resulted in a series of acts that were passed during the first decade of the twentieth century. Much of this legislation was to receive railroad support before long because management came to realize that railroads could not operate satisfactorily under the rules of the Sherman Antitrust Act. Competition faced definite limitations in railroad transport, yet if this was to be given recognition, a substitute for Sherman Act restrictions had to be found. At the same time, and for similar reasons, the antitrust law was inadequate to protect the shipping public.

THE ELKINS ACT, 1903

The need for strengthening the law relating to personal discrimination and rebating had become apparent even to the railroads themselves. The Elkins Act made the published tariff the only lawful one, and any departure from it was a punishable offense. Any departure

---

[17] *Interstate Commerce Commission* v. *Alabama Midland Railway Company*, 168 U.S. 144.

from the published tariffs was made a conclusive test of discrimination. The railroads, their agents, and their officers were liable in the event of violation of the law; and the recipients of rebates were liable, as well as the carriers which gave them. Finally, the courts were given jurisdiction to enjoin violations of the law.

THE HEPBURN ACT, 1906

Provisions of the Act

1. *Extension of the Commission's Jurisdiction.* This legislation was the first positive step designed to give the Interstate Commerce Commission real authority over the railroads. It extended the Commission's jurisdiction to cover express and sleeping-car companies, switches, spur tracks, terminal facilities of every kind even to the extent of authority over the charge for switching services performed by industrial railways, and for privately owned railroad cars. Pipe lines for the transportation of any commodity (other than water or gas) were also made subject to the provisions of the law when they were in fact common carriers in interstate commerce.

2. *Regulation of Accounting.* Recognizing that control over accounting was a fundamental basis for effective regulation, the Hepburn Act provided that detailed annual reports were to be rendered by all common carriers, under oath, three months after the close of each year. The Commission could require other reports and was to have access at all times to the accounts. The Commission was given the power, at its discretion, to prescribe the forms of all the accounts and records. It promptly proceeded to set up a uniform accounting system in accordance with these provisions.

3. *Control over Maximum Rates.* The Hepburn Act provided that after full hearing and upon complaint the Commission could prescribe maximum rates and the regulations and practices thereafter to be observed. The Commission, however, could not prescribe the maximum rates in the first instance; it could act only after existing rates had been found to be unreasonable or otherwise unlawful. It was also given the authority to establish through routes, the maximum rates to apply on such through routes, and the division of the joint rates among the carriers participating in them. Finally, it was empowered to fix the maximum amount to be paid by a carrier for any service rendered or any instrumentality furnished by the owner of property transported by the carrier.

4. *The Commodities Clause.* Many railroads owned coal mines and engaged in the production of other commodities, and this had led

to a good deal of discrimination. By charging high rates on the commodities they produced, they could enjoy a distinct advantage over competitors who had to ship over the rail lines. To deal with this problem, Congress enacted the "commodities clause." This provided that no railroad should transport in interstate commerce any commodity, other than timber and its manufactured products, produced by it, except such commodities as were necessary for its use in the conduct of its business as a common carrier. This is the clause which some people think should also be applied to petroleum pipe lines.

5. *Procedure for Enforcement.* The Hepburn Act strengthened greatly the Commission's powers of enforcement. The orders of the Commission were to take effect within not less than thirty days from the time of issuance, and if a carrier failed to comply, the Commission or any injured party might apply to the courts for an enforcement order. The courts were directed to enforce the orders, provided they were "regularly made and duly served." The penalty for disobeying an order of the Commission was $5,000 for each offense, and each day's violation constituted a separate offense. Moreover, the orders of the Commission were binding unless suspended or set on one side by a court. However, if they were disobeyed, the Commission had to appeal to the courts to enforce them; this was rarely necessary.

Judicial Interpretation

One of the most significant results of the Hepburn Act was that it established the Interstate Commerce Commission on the firm legal footing that it enjoys today as an independent regulatory agency. Whatever may be the evaluation of the Commission and its policies, its shortcomings can scarcely be ascribed to the limitations on its authority that may be imposed by the courts. The decisions in cases under the Hepburn Act settled this; for in these cases the Supreme Court gave clear-cut expression of the fact that it recognized that the Interstate Commerce Commission had become a full-fledged administrative tribunal and that it intended to support that position.

The attitude of the Court was first set forth in *Interstate Commerce Commission* v. *Illinois Central Railroad Company* (1910).[18] Here, the Court stated that:

Plain as it is that the powers just stated are the essence of judicial authority . . . it is equally plain that such perennial powers lend no support whatever to the proposition that we may, under the guise of exerting judicial power, usurp

---

[18] 215 U.S. 452. See also *Baltimore and Ohio Railroad Company* v. *United States,* 215 U.S. 481 (1910), and *Interstate Commerce Commission* v. *Chicago, Rock Island and Pacific Railway Company,* 218 U.S. 89 (1910).

merely administrative functions by setting aside a lawful administrative order upon our conception as to whether the administrative power has been wisely exercised. Power to make the order and not the mere expediency or wisdom of having made it is the question.[19]

The most explicit and detailed summary of the position of the Supreme Court was set forth in *Interstate Commerce Commission* v. *Union Pacific Railroad Company* (1912),[20] which was discussed in the previous chapter. From this time forward, the most significant litigation pertaining to regulation in transportation involved either the constitutionality of legislative provisions or the interpretation of the statutes and the scope of the authority conferred by them.

The commodities clause gave rise to some problems of interpretation because of the meaning of the term *any interest direct or indirect.* The Supreme Court had taken the position in other cases that ownership of stock in a corporation did not constitute ownership of the property. In accordance with this it held that the Delaware and Hudson Railroad, through ownership of stock of a coal company, had no interest in the coal that was shipped that would make it subject to the commodities clause.[21] This ruling was modified, however, in *United States* v. *Reading Company* (1920).[22] In this instance the Reading Company was a holding company which owned the Philadelphia and Reading Railway Company and the Reading Iron and Coal Company. The Court took the position that the relationships were so close that the coal company was in effect a mere agency or department of the railroad. It therefore ordered the Reading Company to give up either its coal or its railroad properties. On the other hand, at a later date, in *United States* v. *Elgin, Joliet and Eastern Railway Company* (1936),[23] the Court held that there was no violation of the commodities clause resulting from the transportation of products of several subsidiaries of the United States Steel Corporation, even though the railroad was controlled by United States Steel.

Despite this halting interpretation of the law by the Supreme Court, the main difficulties which gave rise to the legislation do not

[19] 215 U.S. 452, 470 (1910).

[20] 222 U.S. 541. See Chapter 11, p. 278.

[21] *United States* v. *Delaware and Hudson Railroad Company,* 213 U.S. 366 (1909). It should be noted that an attempt to prohibit specifically the control of subsidiary industrial companies through stock ownership was defeated in the Senate. See W. Z. Ripley, *Railroads: Rates and Regulation* (New York: Longmans, Green & Co., 1913), p. 515.

[22] 253 U.S. 26.

[23] 298 U.S. 492. See also *United States* v. *South Buffalo Railway Company,* 333 U.S. 771 (1948). For a detailed description of the interpretation of the commodities clause, see J. Guandolo, *Transportation Law* (Dubuque, Ia.: William C. Brown Co., Publishers, 1965), chap. 34.

seem to be of significance today. The railroads at present are urging the repeal of the clause because it applies to them alone and there is no effective way of preventing carriage of products by motor carriers owned by the producers of the products, especially if it is private carriage. The same remarks apply to water carriers, and many industrial firms own these. In other words, the divorcement of carriers from manufacturing under the commodities clause applies only to railroads. However, this of itself is not an argument for the repeal of the commodities clause. It could still be made effectively to apply to all common carriers. Whether this is in the interest of efficient transportation needs to be examined on broader grounds than the mere fact that it is applicable to the railroads alone.

THE MANN-ELKINS ACT, 1910

Extension of the authority and jurisdiction of the Interstate Commerce Commission was carried a step further by the passage of the Mann-Elkins Act. This legislation served to remedy the limitations imposed by the Supreme Court before the Hepburn Act, and it gave the Commission more positive control over rate making than it had previously enjoyed. It also extended the Commission's jurisdiction to telephone, telegraph, and cable companies, whether wire or wireless, which were engaged in transmitting messages in interstate or foreign commerce.

Provisions of the Law

1. *Control over Rates.* Prior to the Mann-Elkins Act the Interstate Commerce Commission had been able to establish maximum rates where the existing ones had been found to be unreasonable. However, it could take action only after the rates had gone into effect and only, therefore, after the damage had been done, if the rates proved to be unreasonably high. Furthermore the railroads were still able to act in concert in raising their rates despite the Supreme Court decisions in the Traffic Association cases.[24] To provide a means of dealing with the issues arising from these developments, the Mann-Elkins Act empowered the Commission to suspend the proposed changes in railroad rates by providing that when any new rate, fare, or classification was filed with the Commission, the latter should have the authority, either upon complaint or on its own initiative, to suspend the proposed changes for a period not exceeding 120 days, during which time it was to determine the lawfulness of the proposed changes. An additional

[24] See Chapter 10, p. 251.

suspension period of six months was permitted if the first period was insufficient to arrive at a conclusion. (At the present time, the total suspension period is seven months.) The proposed changes became effective unless suspended by the Commission, and also if determination of the issues at stake had not been made when the period of suspension permitted by law had expired. When increases were requested, the burden of proof to justify the new rate as increased was placed upon the railroad. Any interested party might register objections to the increase or the increased rate.

Further to strengthen the authority over rates, the Commission was given the power to fix maximum rates after a hearing taken on its own motion. It was given control over the classification of freight, and shippers were given the right to designate the through routes over which their freight was to be carried, subject to such regulations as the Commission might prescribe.

2. *Long and Short Haul.* Commission authority over the long and short haul was restored by the elimination of the phrase *under substantially similar circumstances and conditions.* Henceforth the long-and-short-haul prohibition was to apply under all conditions, unless the Commission specifically granted exceptions. No common carrier was to charge any greater compensation for a through rate than the aggregate of the intermediate rates; and furthermore, whenever a railroad reduced its freight rates to compete with a water route, it might not subsequently increase these rates unless the Commission found that the proposed increase rested on changed conditions other than the elimination of water competition. Congress evidently intended to compel a much greater conformity to the distance principle than had obtained theretofore.

3. *The Commerce Court.* It was felt that a specialized transportation court should be established to expedite cases arising under the Interstate Commerce Act and to secure greater uniformity of decisions. This part of the legislation was largely due to the insistence of President Taft, who was particularly interested in the problems of enforcement by regulatory agencies. The Commerce Court was to consist of five judges assigned to the Court by the Chief Justice of the United States for a period of five years. All cases were to go directly to it, with appeal only to the Supreme Court.

Application of the Law

In the years immediately following the enactment of the Mann-Elkins Act, the railroads made a number of requests for rate increases.

The Commission exercised its powers of suspension and, after investigation, denied the applications[25] until after World War I broke out in Europe.

In a new series of cases the Commission granted some rate increases, but in the main the petitions of the railroads were denied.[26] Recognition of the fact that responsible price regulation necessitates something more than a negative attitude had not yet taken hold. The idea that the Commission should occupy the positive role of regulating rates so that the carriers could receive adequate revenues was to come later. Even with that development the suspension powers have been a serious handicap to effective and sufficiently expeditious rate adjustments, especially in times of rapidly or relatively rapidly rising prices, with the result that railroad revenues have seriously lagged behind railroad needs. Suspension proceedings (labeled Investigation and Suspension) have resulted in inordinate delay, expensive litigation, and obstruction by literally all parties opposed to rate increases, which has included nearly everybody but the railroads. In recent years these proceedings have applied not only to rate increases but also to reductions, a development which has made adjustment to competition by the railroads a tedious matter.

The Commission took immediate steps to deal with the long-and-short-haul situation. This was a particularly troublesome issue in transcontinental traffic and in Southern territory, where the basing-point system of pricing had obtained for many years. At first the Commission sanctioned a graduated zone system of rates to the Pacific coast,[27] but by 1918 the transcontinental rate structure had been brought into conformity with the long-and-short-haul principle,[28] although the blanketing of rates in both directions on many commodities still remains, as was pointed out earlier.[29] The rate structure of the South was also gradually modified over a period of time so as to end long-and-short-haul violations.

The Commerce Court proved to be a conspicuous failure. First of all, it interferred unduly with the orders of the Interstate Commerce Commission, contrary to the ruling in the Illinois Central case, and as a result was frequently reversed by the Supreme Court. Second, one of

[25] *Advances in Rates—Eastern Case,* 20 I.C.C. 243 (1911); and *Advances in Rates— Western Case,* 20 I.C.C. 307 (1911).

[26] 31 I.C.C. 351 (1914); 32 I.C.C. 325 (1914); 35 I.C.C. 497 (1915); 45 I.C.C. 303 (1917).

[27] 21 I.C.C. 329 (1911); 21 I.C.C. 400 (1911).

[28] 48 I.C.C. 79 (1918).

[29] Chapter 10, p. 241.

the members of the Commerce Court was found guilty of corruption. As a consequence, the Court was abolished by Congress in 1913. Jurisdiction that had been assigned to the Commerce Court was transferred by the District Court Jurisdiction Act[30] to the district courts of the United States. The statute provided that no restraining order or injunction against an order of the Commission could be issued unless the case had been heard before three judges, at least one of whom had to be a circuit judge. Appeals from these special courts were to be carried to the Supreme Court of the United States.

THE PANAMA CANAL ACT, 1912

The strategic position of the railroads with regard to inland transport meant that they could exercise effective control over water competition through ownership of carriers on competing water routes, ownership of water terminal facilities, and refusal to co-operate on through shipments requiring some rail haulage. That the rivalry between rail and water carriers led to many practices by railroads to limit that competition is evident. This was the reason for the restrictions imposed upon railroads in their competition with water carriers by the Mann-Elkins Act. There was widespread feeling that railroad control of water competition should be removed, a feeling that was enhanced by the prospective opening of the Panama Canal.

To meet the possible threat to water competition through the Canal by transcontinental rail traffic, and to break up railroad control of water traffic on the Great Lakes and in coastwise trade, Congress passed the Panama Canal Act in 1912. This legislation made it unlawful for any railroad to have any interest of any kind in a common carrier by water with which it competed or might compete, or in any vessel carrying freight or passengers on the same routes. In the case of the Panama Canal the prohibition was absolute. For other traffic by water the Commission was authorized to permit existing interrelations to continue, if it was of the opinion that they were being conducted in the interests of the public, and if water competition was not reduced or prevented thereby. The law further provided that the Commission should have the authority to establish physical connection between the line of a rail carrier and the dock of a water carrier, to establish through routes and maximum joint rates over such rail and water lines, and to require rail carriers that had entered into arrangements with a water carrier for handling through business between interior points in

[30] 38 Stat. 219 (1913).

the U.S. and a foreign country to extend such arrangements to other steamship lines operating from that point to the same foreign country.

Upon the passage of the Act the Interstate Commerce Commission undertook an immediate investigation of rail-water carrier relationships in accordance with the instructions of the law. The Commission held that where the competition was real and substantial, it had no choice but to bring about the separation of ownership of rail and water carriers. As a result, there was a considerable unscrambling of relationships, particularly on the Great Lakes.[31]

Little controversy over the problem emerged after 1915 until recently. The issue came squarely to the fore again with the application of the Southern Pacific Company and the Illinois Central Railway, in 1959, for permission to acquire joint ownership of the John I. Hay Company barge line on the Mississippi River.[32] The Commission denied the application on the grounds that the applicants had failed to establish that the considered transaction (1) would be consistent with the public interest, (2) would not prevent the applicant common carrier by water from being operated in the interest of the public and with advantage to the convenience of commerce and the people, (3) would not exclude, prevent, or reduce competition on the routes by water under consideration, and (4) would carry out the precepts of the national transportation policy. Four commissioners dissented from the decision. That the issues involved are by no means dormant is evident from application of other railroads to operate barge lines. The Commission, on the other hand, has given its approval to American Commercial Lines, Inc., to acquire Terminal Transport Co., a motor carrier with extensive operating rights extending from Florida through the midcontinent area. The Commission held that the provisions of the Interstate Commerce Act is not applicable to water carriers, and that it was not required that the motor service be limited or restricted to that which is auxiliary or supplementary to the water service.[33]

THE VALUATION ACT, 1913

Probably the main idea behind the Valuation Act was to furnish the Interstate Commerce Commission with some standard by which to

[31] According to A. G. Ingersoll, President, Federal Barge Lines, St. Louis, Missouri, of the thirty Commission-authorized, rail-controlled water operations, only one was still in operation in 1961.

[32] *Illinois Central Railroad Co. et al.—Control etc.—John I. Hay Co.,* 317 I.C.C. 39 (1962).

[33] *American Commercial Lines, Inc.,* 97 M.C.C. 380 (1965). Sustained in 265 F. Supp. 549 (1966).

test the reasonableness of railway rates and the reasonableness of proposed increases. The passage of the Hepburn Act of 1906 and the Mann-Elkins Act of 1910 indicated the need for some such legislation. The Valuation Act was based essentially on the yardstick set forth in *Smyth* v. *Ames*. Under the law the Commission was directed to ascertain and report in detail on each piece of property used for common carrier purposes, the original cost to date, the cost of reproduction new, the cost of reproduction less depreciation, and to indicate the methods by which these costs were obtained. Likewise, it was directed to report separately all other values and elements of value, and the methods of valuation employed. In addition, it was to ascertain the property held for other purposes than those of a common carrier, together with the original cost and present value of it. Finally, the Commission was to show the value of the property of every carrier as a whole and, separately, the value of its property in every state and territory. The final valuations ascertained by the Commission were to be published and were to be prima-facie evidence of the value of the property in all proceedings under the Interstate Commerce Act, and in all judicial proceedings brought to enjoin or set aside an order of the Commission.

The use that has been made of valuation in determining the general level of rates was discussed in Chapter 9. There, it was pointed out that the concept of fair return on fair value has not played a significant role in the fixing of railroad rates. Moreover, there has been no judicial determination of what constitutes fair value for the setting of railroad rates, in the light of the legislation which set forth the considerations to which the Commission must give due weight. The Commission has, however, used what amounts to prudent investment in passing upon the issuance of new securities; it uses the same base for measuring and reporting upon the fair return earned annually by the railroads, and in its cost-fixing investigations.[34]

APPRAISAL OF REGULATION TO 1920

The development of state and federal legislation on transportation down to 1920 laid the foundation of regulation by providing the legislative and administrative experience, by establishing firmly the constitutional basis of regulation, and by resolving the problems relating to the position of the independent commission in the scheme of regula-

[34] For a discussion of the uses made of valuation of railroad properties, see Daggett, *op. cit.,* pp. 625–29; see also M. L. Fair and E. W. Williams, Jr., *Economics of Transportation* (rev. ed.; New York: Harper & Bros., 1959), pp. 566–73.

tion. This was accomplished principally at the federal level, because of the withdrawal of the states after their experience with the Granger laws. On the other hand, it was under state regulation that the full implications of the control of monopoly were unraveled. The development of public policy on the issues of fair return on fair value took place only at the state level, and it was the commissions in a few states, such as California, Massachusetts, and Wisconsin, that pointed the way to comprehensive regulation of monopoly in industries affected with a public interest. The foundation for this had been laid at the federal level, but there does not seem to have been any appreciable grasp of the fact, until the end of World War I, that successful regulation of the railroads had to be cast in the public utility mold.

The right of the government to regulate industries affected with a public interest was established as a result of state legislation, but the role of the independent commission in regulation and its relation to the judiciary was settled largely as a result of litigation centering around the Interstate Commerce Commission. Almost all of the legal controversy involving actions of the Commission since 1920 has been on the interpretation of statutes. The authority granted to the Interstate Commerce Commission has led many to feel that it has enjoyed less interference than the state commissions. However, it should be recognized that when state laws were comprehensive and clear, state commissions received essentially the same judicial support as the federal Commission. The clash between the judiciary and the state authorities occurred largely over the matter of fair return on fair value, and this issue was never squarely joined by the Interstate Commerce Commission with the courts.

The period down to 1920 also established clearly the constitutional boundaries of state versus federal authority over transportation. The result of litigation from the Wabash case to the end of the period was to resolve doubts in favor of the federal government. What this meant was that the Interstate Commerce Commission could be given jurisdiction over intrastate transportation, particularly rates, whenever it was necessary to protect and make effective some regulation of interstate commerce.[35] Within this limitation the division of authority between state and federal governments became a political rather than a legal consideration, and therefore rested in the hands of Congress.

The regulatory program of the federal government down to 1920 was essentially restrictive and negative in nature. The Interstate Commerce Commission was given the authority to limit and suspend rates,

[35] *Illinois Commerce Commission* v. *Thomson*, 318 U.S. 675 (1943).

and to impose limitations on rate-making practices, but it did not possess nor did it exercise any positive responsibilities with regard to the welfare of the railroads. The theory was that regulation was solely for the purpose of protecting the shipper and that the Commission's only responsibility was to him. The assumption seemed to be that competition would protect the railroads, whereas in fact the conditions which gave rise to the need for regulation were of the very kind that made it impossible for competition to afford the necessary protection. In other words, the conditions necessary for effective competition were absent, and regulation was powerless to impose or introduce them. The failure to grasp the nature of railroad economics resulted in a failure to develop a coherent theory of regulation, which the states had already been able to do for public utilities.[36]

What the next step in the development of federal regulation might have been had World War I not intervened, it is impossible to say, although it is quite likely that the move would have been in the direction of positive regulation.[37] The extreme and unbalanced traffic burden, together with the rapid rise in prices, led the federal government to take over the operation of the railroads in December, 1917. Mr. W. G. McAdoo was appointed Director General of the Railroads, and all employees and officers became employees of the federal government. Each railroad was guaranteed a profit on its railroad operations during the period of federal control, equal to the average annual profit for the preceding three years. During the period of federal operations the government resisted rate increases, while it was compelled to meet increases in wages and other costs. The result was a deficit, estimated at around $1.5 billion, by the time the railroads were returned to private hands. More important than this, however, was the distorted

[36] Gabriel Kolko in *Railroads and Regulation 1877–1916* (Princeton, N.J.: Princeton University Press, 1965), takes the position that the Act of 1887 was to lend stability to railroad cartels which the expansion of the industry had prevented. The inadequacy of the Commission's power to achieve this purpose brought about the passage of the Acts of 1903, 1906, and 1910. It is true that one of the objections of the legislation was to impose limitations on competition, but the alternatives to this are not clear. Kolko constantly refers to the railroad problem but nowhere does he give an indication of what it was, nor why it arose. There are good grounds for argument on the economic desirability of many of the provisions of the legislation, but a long line of distinguished scholars has approved much that was done, and many even wanted further extension of control. Professor H. J. Davenport once astutely observed: "One should altogether despair of what the future may achieve who is compelled to condemn all that the past has done. That our predecessors saw imperfectly was unavoidable; but that they did not see at all is incredible."

[37] See F. H. Dixon, *Railroads and Government* (New York: Charles Scribner's Sons, 1922), pp. 15–21, for conflicting views on the responsibility of the Interstate Commerce Commision.

relationship of costs and income that had developed, and which raised the problem of what to do with the railroads when the war was over.

There was a sharp division of opinion on what the postwar policy should be. Former Director General McAdoo proposed to continue government operation for an experimental period of five years. The final decision was to turn the railroads back to private ownership under strict regulation of the public utility type. This was what the Transportation Act of 1920 was designed to achieve.

RAILROAD REGULATION
SINCE WORLD WAR I

INTRODUCTION

The Transportation Act of 1920, which was enacted shortly after the signing of the peace treaty that ended World War I, constitutes a landmark for transport in general in the United States, and for railroads in particular. First of all, it should be recognized that at this time railroad transport constituted for all practical purposes the inland transport system of the country. The national transport problem and the railroad problem appeared literally to be one and the same thing, and the legislation was designed to establish national policy for the years to come.

Second, this legislation was the culmination of the growth of federal regulation over the preceding 30 years, the development of which was traced in the previous chapter. It rounded out the Interstate Commerce Act by providing control over all those areas of rail transport not yet under Commission jurisdiction which seemed to be essential for thoroughly comprehensive regulation. In doing so, it put the regulation of transportation squarely in the public utility pattern of regulated monopoly. This established the basis for the policy and procedure for transport regulation which has remained literally unimpaired as far as legislation and administration are concerned over the succeeding 47 years to the present day.

Third, while it marked the culmination of the development of regulation of the years preceding World War I, it was really outmoded almost as soon as it was passed because the new technology in transport, lurking in the background, burst into the open with full vigor almost before the ink of the President's signature was dry. The underlying assumptions were invalid literally before the debates were finished; railroads alone were no longer to be *the* inland transportation system of the country. The alternative sources of supply disclosed themselves immediately, although the impact and implications of them were not completely felt for some time. In addition, the alternative sources, especially motor transport, possessed totally different economic structures from that which characterized the railroads.

Thus the legislation of 1920 marks the division between the old and the new periods of transport in the twentieth century. However, it was based entirely on the assumptions of the old period and the theory of public policy and transport economics that accompanied them. These remarks are not designed to cast blame on those who passed the legislation. Indeed, in light of the circumstances at that time, they did a rather creditable job. The significant thing is that, for good or for ill, they established the framework and almost the detail of regulation that have held to the present time. What is needed today is a clear recognition of the fact that the underlying assumptions were soon to be proven incorrect by the course of events, and that this has necessitated an approach to public policy, as completely new as the Act of 1920 constituted, in keeping with assumptions which are in accordance with the facts of the present time.

THE BASIS OF THE NEW POLICY

Regulation of transportation down to World War I had developed on the theory that competition was an inadequate means of protecting the interests of the consuming public, although its effects on the different railroads was not understood. The two principal shortcomings of competition seemed to be that it was unable to limit discrimination and unreasonable advances in rates. Although the monopoly position of the railroads was emphasized, there was little grasp of the fact that limitations imposed upon maximum rates necessitated the adoption of some measure of reasonableness that would protect the legitimate interests of the railroads. Moreover, it was apparently assumed that discrimination and maximum reasonable rates constituted two distinct issues, presumably on the ground that the only significant aspects of discrimination were personal and distance. The implicit assumption was that competition would provide the necessary incentive for the railroads to protect their interests and that protection against exploitation of the shipper was all that was necessary to ensure an adequate system of railroad transport. It was not understood that the monopoly features of railroads made competition, acting alone, an inadequate device to protect the interests of either side. Recognition of this began to emerge during World War I, but even the members of the Interstate Commerce Commission were sharply divided on the issue, some taking the position that the government had no direct responsibilities to the railroads, others holding that revenue requirements were a necessary concern of the regulatory authorities.[1]

Nevertheless, there was a growing awareness of the fact that the regulation of both specific rates and the general level of rates had to be more than merely restrictive in nature if it was to be successful. This awareness emerged from both legal and economic considerations. On the legal side the decision in *Smyth* v. *Ames* pointed up the fact that there were limitations on the powers of public authorities to restrict the earnings of private enterprise, particularly in those situations where private concerns were denied the privilege of withdrawing from offering their services at their own discretion. This had not been given explicit recognition by the courts in the case of railroad transportation under the control of the Interstate Commerce Commission, but the issue was bound to be joined if Congress took direct steps to limit the earnings of the railroads. On the economic side it was becoming apparent that if the railroads were to be able to appeal to investors for new funds, earnings had to be adequate to attract these, and public authority would have to accept the responsibility of permitting rate increases that would meet these requirements, even though shippers might protest. Successful regulation could not shirk the task of reconciling shipper and carrier interests.

Railroad finance, with its accompanying problems of overcapitalization and bankruptcies, had been a matter of public concern for some time. Under the authorization of the Mann-Elkins Act of 1910, President Taft appointed the Railroad Securities Commission to investigate the question of whether the Interstate Commerce Commission should be given control over the issuance of railroad securities. This Commission in its report of 1911 took the position that there was no relation between capitalization and the rates which were charged, and that financing the enterprises was a matter of private concern. What was not recognized, among other things, was that an adequate return was necessary to attract new investment, but that the investment would not be forthcoming if the capital structure was unsound. Furthermore the courts had already taken the position that financial structure and financial requirements had to be taken into consideration in the determination of a fair return. The public was hardly likely to assent to establishing rates high enough to ensure solvency and profitability of enterprises suffering

[1] See F. H. Dixon, *Railroads and Government* (New York: Charles Scribner's Sons, 1922), pp. 15–25.

from an excessive issuance of securities and financial irresponsibility. The states which had embarked upon the most comprehensive regulation of public utilities had already made the control of public utility security issues one of the main features of their legislation.

Public policy in the era of railroad development encouraged the building of competitive lines. This resulted in overbuilding, excessive competition, weak roads competing with strong roads, and perennial bankruptcies. If the railroads had constituted a competitive industry, the market presumably would have provided the necessary corrective measures. This was not possible, however, because of the limitations on withdrawal from service of investment dedicated to the public service, as well as the physical and economic immobility of a good deal of the capital of railroads. Combination and consolidation, which might have resolved much of the problem in the early days, was ruled out by a vigorous application of the antitrust laws. The measures that might have been adopted by the railroads were precluded by various statutes, while at the same time nothing was done to provide a substitute. Rate regulation designed to protect the public was based on the theory of monopoly because it was recognized that monopoly could not be eliminated, yet railroad organization was required to follow the path of competition. Because rates on competitive traffic had to be the same for all the railroads, regulation could not escape the difficulties inherent in such a situation. If these rates were permitted to be high enough for the weak lines, they would be too high for the others; and if they were limited to reasonable levels for the strong ones, they would be disastrous to the weak. Some attempt to resolve this dilemma was inescapable.

If comprehensive regulation of rates and earnings was to be achieved, it was necessary to exercise extensive control over service. What constitutes reasonable prices must be evaluated in conjunction with quality and adequacy of service. Otherwise, restrictions on earnings can be countered by various kinds of reductions in service. In addition, public requirements on interchange, car service, and schedules of service cannot be left to private discretion where competition is an inadequate means of protecting public interest in an industry that is recognized as being essential to the public at large.[2]

All of the foregoing problems of regulation were dealt with in the

[2] The special problems of labor in railroad transportation resulted in the inclusion of legislation regarding it in the Transportation Act of 1920. The provisions, however, were not under the jurisdiction of the Interstate Commerce Commission and are not part of the Interstate Commerce Act. They will not be dealt with here but will be discussed in Chapter 20 in connection with the special problems of labor in transportation.

Transportation Act of 1920. This legislation did not supersede previous enactments; it merely built upon them. The Interstate Commerce Act therefore came to consist of the previous legislation with the additions made in 1920 and with only slight modification of some provisions of the previous laws.

THE TRANSPORTATION ACT OF 1920

Transitional Provisions

The Transportation Act of 1920 first of all provided for the termination of federal control over the railroads on March 1, 1920. To facilitate the adjustment to private operation, the Act extended the federal guarantee of earnings for a period of six months, that is, down to September 1, 1920. In addition, arrangements were made whereby reimbursement of the government for improvements made during the period of federal control could be carried out over a period of 10 years, and where necessary because of financial embarrassment, railroads could borrow from a loan fund, for periods up to 15 years, to buy new equipment or meet maturing obligations.

Control over Rates

Regulation of railroad rates by the Interstate Commerce Commission was extended to give the latter more complete authority than it had possessed previously but, more important, also to provide the Commission with a standard of reasonableness by which it could gauge the appropriate general level of rates, together with the responsibility of adjusting rates to meet that standard. This was the famous rule of rate making.

Rule of Rate Making. In exercising its power to establish just and reasonable rates, the Commission was directed to initiate and establish rates under which the carriers as a whole, under honest, efficient, and economical management, could earn a fair return on the fair value of railroad property held for and used in the service of transportation. The Commission was required to determine from time to time, and make public, the percentage of such aggregate property value that constituted the fair return; the percentage had to be uniform for all the rate groups designated by the Commission.[3] For the first two years the fair return was to be 5.5 per cent, but the Commission could increase this at its discretion for certain purposes up to an amount not to exceed

---

[3] The three rate groups established by the Commission corresponded to the Official, Southern, and Western classification territories.

6 per cent in total during that time. At the end of the two-year period the Commission was to set the fair return; it established it at 5.75 per cent.

It should be noted that the law provided no guarantee to the railroads, nor did it ensure that any particular railroad would earn the stipulated amount. It established a standard for the railroads as a whole, that is, an average, which obviously could not be achieved by every line as long as earning power was unequal. Furthermore the standard was in effect a maximum which, presumably, the Commission was to aim at, year in and year out, regardless of traffic and economic conditions. The law did not prescribe an ultimate rate of fair return, but the implication was clear that Congress regarded 6 per cent as the ceiling.

Recapture of Earnings.   The law recognized that a fair return for the railroads as a whole would result in the stronger roads receiving more than what was regarded as fair, while the weaker ones would earn less. To deal with this situation, a provision was included whereby a particular road was permitted to earn up to 6 per cent. One half of any amount above this was to be retained by the carrier and placed in a reserve fund by it, to be used for specified purposes. The other half was to be turned over to the Interstate Commerce Commission to be used to establish and maintain a contingent fund. The Commission was authorized to make loans from this fund to railroads, provided that they could give reasonable assurance of their ability to pay the interest charges. The interest rate on these loans was to be 6 per cent. The primary purpose of this arrangement was to provide the weak roads with credit and facilities.[4]

Minimum Rates.   The Act of 1920 gave the Commission the power to prescribe the minimum rates which railroads could charge on all shipments. This was a recognition of the fact that as long as the railroads were free to set their own minimum rates, they could discriminate in favor of certain commodities or places, even though the Commission possessed the power to set maximum rates. Moreover, as far as the law was concerned, lack of public control over minimum rates invited rate wars unless the railroads entered into agreements or arrangements with each other to prevent them. Such arrangements were not expressly sanctioned by the law. It was presumed that giving the Commission control over minimum rates settled the issue. In addition, the Commission was

---

[4] The constitutionality of the recapture clause was upheld by the Supreme Court in *Dayton–Goose Creek Railway Company* v. *United States,* 263 U.S. 456 (1924), but was never implemented because of the dispute over valuation. See *St. Louis and O'Fallon Railway Company* v. *United States.* 279 U.S. 461 (1929).

given the power, after a hearing, to prescribe the proper rate, regulation, or practice. In other words, it now could fix minimum, maximum, or precise rates. No standard was contained in the legislation to guide the Commission on what constituted an appropriate minimum rate, although the amendment to the long-and-short-haul clause stipulated that when the Commission granted exceptions to it, the rate to the more distant point had to be reasonably compensatory. Again, however, the meaning of this term was left for the Commission to define.

Regulation of Intrastate Rates. The conflict between the state and federal governments over state-made rates that affected interstate commerce was discussed in the previous chapter. The sanction of the Supreme Court for the exercise of broad federal powers over these rates resulted in a more explicit designation of the authority of the Interstate Commerce Commission by Congress. The Act of 1920 provided that the Commission should prescribe the rate, fare, and classification for railroad services in such manner as to remove preference or discrimination in interstate or foreign commerce arising from state-made rates. This simply embodied the Shreveport rule in the Interstate Commerce Act. The duty of the Commission to initiate rates that would yield a fair return made this provision necessary if interstate commerce alone was not to be compelled to carry the burden of providing adequate revenues for the railroads. The Commission could now require intrastate rates to be raised if it considered them to be too low.

Intercorporate Relations

The Act of 1920 constituted somewhat of a departure, in theory at least, from previous policy based on competition between railroads, by including provisions that sanctioned the consolidation of competing railroads, the acquisition of control of one railroad by another through either lease or stock ownership, and the pooling of traffic or earnings. In every case, however, approval by the Interstate Commerce Commission was required. These provisions were adopted to afford relief from the application of the antitrust laws to the railroads and, in the case of consolidation, to encourage the formation of a limited number of railroad systems of approximately equal earning power.

The Act instructed the Commission, as soon as practicable, to prepare and adopt a plan for the consolidation of the railroads in the country into a limited number of systems. Competition, however, was to be preserved as fully as possible, and existing routes and channels of trade were to be maintained whenever practicable. The capitalization of each new system was not to exceed the value of the properties as determined by the Commission. After the adoption of the plan, which was to be preceded by hearings in which all interested parties could participate, the railroads desiring to consolidate would make application to the Commission. After hearings, of which the governor of every state in which the properties of the applying railroads were located had to be notified, the Commission could grant final approval if it deemed the consolidation in the public interest. The consolidations were permissive, not compulsory; no railroad could be compelled to enter into the consolidation.

The Act also provided that the Commission could authorize one carrier to control another by lease, by purchase, or in any other manner not involving consolidation if the arrangement was in the public interest. The Commission could act in this situation, as in consolidation proceedings, only after application by the carrier. It could not take the initiative, but its sanction was to grant immunity from the antitrust laws.

Carriers were also to be permitted to pool their freight or earnings if given specific approval to do so by the Commission. However, limitations were imposed upon the dealings that carriers might have with each other, by making it unlawful for any person to be an officer or director of more than one carrier without the authorization of the Commission. In other words, the railroads were expected to act independently except where specific exemption to the contrary was provided.

Regulation of Securities

The Act provided that no railroad could issue any securities or assume any obligation or liability in respect of the securities of any other person without the consent of the Interstate Commerce Commission. In order that railroads might meet short-term situations, however, the law was not to apply to notes maturing not more than two years after the date of issue, and aggregating not more than 5 per cent of the par value of the securities of the railroad. The jurisdiction of the Commission over the regulation of security issues was exclusive; it was not necessary for the railroad to secure the assent of any other agency, although the governors of the appropriate states were to be notified, so that presentation could be made when hearings were held, if that was desired. The law also explicitly stated that approval by the Commission was not to be construed as implying any guarantee or obligation on the part of the United States. It should also be noted that the Commission had no control over securities already issued. Its powers to bring about reasonable capitalization where it did not exist were therefore some-what limited.[5]

Control of Service

Effective control designed to impose limitations on competition among firms of a particular industry necessitates some regulation of the conditions of entry. Many state public utility laws had resolved this question by requiring new applicants under their supervision to secure certificates of public convenience and necessity. This meant that a new enterprise, or one serving a new area, had to secure permission from the state authority by proving that the service it proposed to provide was in the public interest and not being adequately rendered by an exist-ing firm. The Interstate Commerce Commission did not possess such control over railroads, and they could undertake construction to tap new markets at their own discretion. The Act of 1920 remedied this de-ficiency by giving the Commission control over new construction. Henceforth, no railroad could undertake extensions without first receiv-ing from the Commission a certificate that public convenience and neces-sity required such extensions. The Commission was also given the power to require extensions if it deemed this to be in the public interest.[6]

In keeping with its authority over extensions the Commission was also given control over railroad abandonments. After the effective date of the Act, no railroad could abandon all or any portion of a line of railroad, or the operation thereof, without securing permission from the Interstate Commerce Commission. This was designed to protect com-munities dependent upon particular railroads, and also to enable rail-roads to discontinue the operation of unprofitable branch lines, which local interests might resist strenuously.

The Act of 1920 made it the duty of every railroad to furnish adequate and safe car service. This term was defined to include the use, control, and supply of cars as well as their movement and distribution. It even included locomotives and other vehicles, and the supply of trains. Under emergency conditions, which cover a wide variety of cir-cumstances, the Commission may suspend the operation of carrier rules

---

[5] The Railroad Modification Act of 1948 (62 Stat. 162), incorporated as section 20 (*b*) of the Interstate Commerce Act, provides that the terms of railroad securities may be altered or modified if approved by the Commission and if 75 per cent of the principal amount or shares of the securities affected is approved by the holders thereof. This may make it possible for carriers facing financial difficulties to avoid the prolonged and costly procedures of receivership and reorganization.

[6] The restrictive interpretation by the Supreme Court on compulsory extensions ren-dered this power virtually inoperative. See *Interstate Commerce Commission* v. *Oregon-Washington Railroad and Navigation Company*, 288 U.S. 14 (1933).

and orders and issue its own, governing the distribution and use of equipment and the priority to be accorded traffic of various sorts.

Prior to 1920 the Interstate Commerce Act imposed upon the railroads the obligation to afford all reasonable and proper facilities for the interchange of traffic between their respective lines. The interpretation and application of the law had led to difficulties which were resolved by the Act of 1920. This gave the Commission an explicit grant of authority to require the joint use of terminals, by making it possible to compel a carrier to share its facilities with other carriers. This could be done, however, only on the conditions (1) that the grant was in the public interest, (2) that reasonable compensation be paid to the owning carrier, and (3) that the requirement should not impair the ability of the grantee to handle its own business.

REASONS FOR LEGISLATION AFTER 1920

For a period of thirteen years following the passage of the Transportation Act, no new legislation of any significance was passed to alter or extend the Interstate Commerce Act.[7] Yet during this period, events were taking place which were to alter the very foundations upon which the policy of regulation had been erected and which were in time to require a complete overhauling of the entire program.

The rule of rate making, so carefully constructed in the Act of 1920, broke down under administration and the pressure of events. In the first place, the Commission responded slowly and with considerable resistance to requests by the railroads for rate increases. Whatever the reasons for this may have been, the railroads during the period of the 1920's failed to achieve an average return equal to the fair return prescribed by law. This was inevitable, of course, if the legal fair return was to be the maximum at any time. In 1931, when the impact of the depression of 1929 was felt, the Commission even authorized an increase in rates. This is an example of "inverse" rate making which

[7] In 1925, Congress passed the Hoch-Smith Resolution, which required the Interstate Commerce Commission, in adjusting freight rates, to take into consideration the conditions which at any time prevailed in the several industries insofar as it was legally possible to do so, to the end that commodities could move freely. The Commission was directed to make an investigation of the rate structures, and then to make such changes as might be necessary to correct any defects found to exist. This Resolution was passed specifically to express Congressional desire to afford relief to agriculture. It did not amend the Interstate Commerce Act, nor in effect did it legally alter it. This at least seems to be the interpretation placed on it by the Supreme Court (*Ann Arbor Railroad Company* v. *United States*, 281 U.S. 658 [1930]). In other words, it did not give the Commission any power it did not already possess, whatever else it may have done.

adherence to a rigid concept of a fixed rate of return, year in and year out, necessitated. This is in keeping with the logic of the concept, no matter how bad the economic reasoning may be.[8] Then, too, the reverse which the Commission suffered at the hands of the Supreme Court in the St. Louis and O'Fallon case ended the possibility of arriving at a workable and acceptable fair value, and the implementation of the recapture provisions.[9]

The consolidation provisions of the law suffered a somewhat similar fate. The Commission published a tentative plan in 1921 which called for 19 or 21 major railroad systems in the country. After extensive hearings, it adopted a "final" plan for 19 systems in 1929. The railroads were not compelled to act, however, and practically nothing was accomplished because they did not feel that the proposals were in their interest and the strong roads showed no desire to absorb the weak ones. The depression, with its severe impact on investment and financial markets, put an end to any developments that might have taken place.

The development of new technology in transportation, especially that which led to the rapid growth of motor, pipe-line, and air transport, completely altered, in the course of a few years, the position of the railroads in the national transport structure. They were now compelled to face the intense rivalry of these agencies for traffic. In the ten-year period down to 1930 the motor vehicle made its greatest impact on passenger traffic and by the end of the period was the most important provider of intercity service. Much of this was in private cars, and the overwhelming portion of it was for comparatively short distances, but the diversion of traffic and the limitations which it imposed on passenger fares introduced a factor of severe competition which soon seriously impaired railroad revenues from the passenger business. Somewhat similar remarks are applicable to the development of motor trucking. Its impact was delayed until the decade of the 1930's, but by 1940 it was a major force to be reckoned with. The competition from this source was particularly severe on relatively short-haul movements, especially in the high-grade, high-revenue traffic. The effect of this competition was even more severe, therefore, in revenue than in tonnage terms. The airplane may be said to have come of age by the beginning of World War II; in a short time after that conflict, it was to equal the

<hr>

[8] See Interstate Commerce Commission, *46th Annual Report, June 30, 1932* (Washington, D.C.: U.S. Government Printing Office, 1933), pp. 16–17.

[9] Whether the railroads could have earned an average fair return during this period equal to the prescribed standard is a matter of debate, but they were not given the opportunity to attempt to do so.

railroads in intercity first-class travel, and today it exceeds the railroads in passenger mileage in all categories. Finally, pipe lines not only deprived the railroads of most of the petroleum traffic they had enjoyed but, of much more significance, introduced a new source of fuel in oil and natural gas that was rapidly substituted for coal for both domestic fuel and power.

These rapid and drastic technological changes in transportation made it apparent that the concept of a regulatory policy based on the idea of a railroad monopoly of the supply of transport of the country was outmoded. Whatever might be the appropriate economic solution to the problems that had emerged, one thing was quite clear: A new orientation of policy which would recognize the newer agencies and adapt the program of regulation to it was inescapable. A new and more difficult railroad problem had been created. World War II delayed the full import of what this meant, but it did not alter the course of events. A national transportation policy was called for in a much broader sense than had been the case at any previous time.

Even if economic conditions had remained relatively stable, a solution to the complex transportation problems that the new transport structure created would have been difficult. The Great Depression, which commenced in 1929, of itself brought about a crisis in rail transport. The railroads had been forced to borrow heavily for new capital, especially in the 1920's, with the result that railroad indebtedness amounted to some 60 per cent of rail capitalization for the country as a whole. The drastic reduction in traffic and revenues as a result of the depression, aggravated by growing competition, made it impossible for the railroads as a whole to earn their bond interest charges in 1931. The fear was widespread that every railroad in the country would go into receivership unless the government took some action to prevent this from happening.[10] The situation called for emergency legislation as well as the development of long-run policy. For good or for ill, the latter was strongly conditioned by the general economic philosophy of the country at that time, which was that competition had to be curtailed.

Legislation for the regulation of transport since 1920 has therefore had three main purposes or objectives. The first was to remedy the deficiencies of the Act of 1920 with regard to the rule of rate making, and to consolidation. The second was to extend regulation to the other agencies of transportation, in the belief that the regulation of railroads

---

[10] The Reconstruction Finance Corporation, with the approval of the Interstate Commerce Commission, made loans to many of the railroads to tide them over their immediate difficulties.

alone had, in the light of new developments, led to a situation that made it impossible for the railroads to compete equitably and successfully, and that unregulated competition among the carriers of each of the newer agencies was ruinous. This was the result of the generally accepted premise that competition in transport was everywhere of a different nature from that which prevailed in industry in general, and that if it was not restricted by special rules, it would be unworkable. As a consequence, the extension of regulation to the other agencies adopted the same basic framework that had already been developed for the railroads.[11] The third purpose was to announce a national transportation policy that would guide the Interstate Commerce Commission in its administration of the regulatory program.

THE EMERGENCY TRANSPORTATION ACT, 1933

The immediate purpose of this legislation was to deal with the crisis with which the railroads were faced. The provisions of the part of the law that dealt with this were only temporary in nature. The others were permanent amendments to the Interstate Commerce Act.

Emergency Provisions

The Act created the Office of Federal Coordinator of Transportation. The Coordinator was to be appointed by the President from the membership of the Interstate Commerce Commission. The carriers were to establish three regional co-ordinating committees, one each in the East, South, and West. The railroad employees were also to select three regional committees. All of these were to work with the Coordinator in bringing about economies of operation through co-operation among the railroads and with the employees.

The objective of this provision to bring about a reduction in costs of operation and promote efficiencies through the elimination of unnecessary duplication of facilities and to permit the pooling of equipment, joint use of tracks and terminals, and other co-operative efforts. However, the number of employees could not be reduced (except for death, retirement, or resignation); no employee was to be placed in a worse position regarding compensation as a result of the operation of the Act; and the carriers were to compensate their employees for losses and expenses incurred by them by transfer from one locality to another. The limitations imposed by this section of the legislation prevented any-

[11] The legislation and regulation applicable to the other carriers will be dealt with in the two following chapters.

thing of significance from being accomplished by the time the emergency legislation terminated in 1936.

The second function of the Coordinator had more lasting results. He was to investigate and consider other means for improving transportation conditions in the country. Two major reports were issued by his office. The first related to the regulation of transportation and transportation conditions in general.[12] The second was an exhaustive study on public aid.[13] The first of these, among other things, recommended the regulation of motor and water transportation.

Amendments to the Interstate Commerce Act

Rule of Rate Making. This legislation repealed the rule of rate making of the Act of 1920 and substituted the following:

> In the exercise of its power to prescribe just and reasonable rates the Commission shall give due consideration, among other factors, to the effect of rates on the movement of traffic; to the need in the public interest, of adequate and efficient railway transportation service at the lowest cost consistent with the furnishing of such service; and to the need of revenues sufficient to enable the carriers, under honest, economical and efficient management, to provide such service.

At the same time, the recapture clause was repealed retroactively, and the Commission was instructed to return to the various railroads all of the excess earnings that had been paid to it under its provisions.

The best that can be said for the new rule of rate making is that it still left the Commission with some responsibility for the adequacy of carrier earnings which had been part of the philosophy of the Act of 1920. In other words, the Commission's role in regulation, in theory at least, was still a positive one, and not purely negative as it had been before 1920. On the other hand, the phraseology was almost devoid of meaning unless spelled out, and this was not done. It set up no standards of any content to guide the Commission, and it left the railroads without any objective gauge by which they could support their requests

---

[12] *Regulation of Railroads,* Senate Document No. 119, 73d Congress, 2d session (Washington, D.C.: U.S. Government Printing Office, 1934); *Regulation of Transportation Agencies,* Report of the Federal Coordinator of Transportation, Senate Document No. 152, 73d Congress, 2d session (Washington, D.C.: U.S. Government Printing Office, 1934); *Report of the Federal Coordinator of Transportation,* House Document No. 89, 74th Congress, 1st session (Washington, D.C.: U.S. Government Printing Office, 1935); *Fourth Report of the Federal Coordinator of Transportation on Transportation Regulation,* House Document No. 394, 74th Congress, 2d session (Washington, D.C.: U.S. Government Printing Office, 1936).

[13] Federal Coordinator of Transportation, *Public Aids to Transportation,* Vols. I–IV (Washington, D.C.: U.S. Government Printing Office, 1938–40).

for general rate increases. The Commission still had to control the general level of rates and maximum rates, but without a meaningful mandate from Congress. Whatever criticisms may be leveled at the Commission for its administration of the new "rule" over the ensuing years, Congress must be accorded the primary blame for its failure to face squarely the issues which maximum rate control presented in the new situation that had developed in transportation.

Consolidation. The use of the holding company in the period after 1920 had found an inviting outlet in the railroad field, and some notorious and disastrous attempts to build new railroad empires had attracted public attention. The Act of 1933 dealt with this problem by providing that all combinations, irrespective of the way in which they were achieved, required the consent of the Interstate Commerce Commission. Holding companies were specifically mentioned, and those used to effect railroad combination were thus brought within the scope of the law.

THE TRANSPORTATION ACT OF 1940

Motor carriers had been placed under the control of the Interstate Commerce Commission by the Motor Carrier Act of 1935, and water carriers were included in the Act of 1940. Thus, when the latter legislation was passed, the Commission was responsible for the regulation of carriers by rail, motor, water, and pipe lines. Air transportation was consigned to the independent Civil Aeronautics Board. With the extension of the power of the Interstate Commerce Commission, Congress felt that it was necessary to make a declaration of national policy to set forth the general considerations which should govern the Commission's regulation of the different agencies subject to its jurisdiction, with regard to their relations with each other.

The Declaration of National Policy

The declaration, which was a preamble to the Act of 1940, was made part of the Interstate Commerce Act. It is thus an expression by Congress of the general policy which it expected the Commission to follow, but it precedes Part I of the Act and does not, therefore, embody any specific rule of law as to the various sections. So far, Congress has not amplified it by any specific legislation. The declaration of policy reads as follows:

It is hereby declared to be the national transportation policy of the Congress to provide for fair and impartial regulation of all modes of transportation subject to the provisions of this Act, so administered as to recognize and preserve the inherent advantages of each; to promote safe, adequate, economical and efficient service and foster sound economic conditions in transportation and among the several carriers; to encourage the establishment and maintenance of reasonable charges for transportation services, without unjust discriminations, undue preferences or advantages, or unfair or destructive competitive practices; to cooperate with the several States and the duly authorized officials thereof; and to encourage fair wages and equitable working conditions;—all to the end of developing, coordinating and preserving a national transportation system by water, highway, and rail, as well as other means, adequate to meet the commerce of the United States, of the Postal Service, and of the national defense. All of the provisions of this Act shall be administered and enforced with a view of carrying out the above declaration of policy.

This declaration of policy was a recognition on the part of Congress that successful regulation henceforth had to give consideration to the problems of competition, or allocation of traffic among the agencies, as well as to the problems confronting the separate modes. In other words, Congress formally acknowledged that interagency competition was a matter of public concern that had to be dealt with by the Commission. The particularly vital points in the declaration were impartial regulation of all modes of transportation subject to the jurisdiction of the Commission, preservation of the inherent advantages of each type of transportation, promotion of sound conditions in the transportation industry, and condemnation of destructive competitive practices. None of these instructions were defined or implemented by further legislation, and there is little evidence to show that they had any effect on the Commission in its resolution of the issues that came before it. In fact, it could well contend that its policies to date had conformed to the instructions it was now told to follow. The outbreak of World War II postponed the inevitable controversy over the application of the declaration for over a decade, after which the issues with which we are faced today led to further legislation. These issues will be discussed in connection with the Transportation Act of 1958.

Rate Making

The Commission was given the power to remove rate discrimination against any region, and to bring this about, it was instructed to institute an investigation of the interterritorial and intraterritorial rates in general. This investigation led to the prescribing of the *Uniform Freight Classification* and the uniform class rate structure discussed in Chapter 10. The Interstate Commerce Act was also amended so as to confine consideration of the effect of rates on the movement of traffic "by the carrier or carriers for which the rates are prescribed." This was to prevent the Commission from prescribing railroad rates which were designed to protect the traffic of another mode. The application of this provision has also been a matter of uncertainty and acute controversy.

In addition, the Act provided that the burden of proof was on the carrier to justify any proposed changes in rates, classification, or rules, and any carrier was expected to prove that rate reductions as well as increases were just and reasonable. This provision was prophetic of the competitive situation that was to develop in the postwar period, when applications by railroads to reduce rates to meet competition and endeavor to recover lost traffic became a major point of controversy in interagency rivalry and public policy. The earlier resistance to rate increases was to be replaced by intense opposition by rival modes to railroad rate reductions, and the Interstate Commerce Commission was to prove to be as hard to convince on this score as it was in previous years in the opposite direction.

Land-Grant Rates

The Act of 1940 released the land-grant railroads from the obligation of transporting mail or civil traffic, both persons and property, for the United States at reduced rates. This was extended in 1945 to require the federal government to pay full rates on military as well as civil traffic.[14]

Consolidation

Railroad consolidation according to a fixed plan, but undertaken voluntarily, as envisaged in the Transportation Act of 1920, had yielded practically no results. The Act of 1940 ended the requirement that consolidations should conform to a plan laid down by the Interstate Commerce Commission and substituted in its place the provision that consolidations henceforth could be initiated by the railroads without the necessity of fitting into any plan developed by the Commission. Combination could now take place by consolidation or other means of unification, provided that the Commission found such combination consistent with the public interest, that other railroads in the area upon request might be included, and that any increase in the fixed charges resulting from the combination had to be consistent with the public interest. In addition, the Commission was required to include in its sanction the provision that for four years, at least, the employees af-

---

[14] Section 22 of the Interstate Commerce Act permits carriers to transport property at free or reduced rates for the U.S. government, but the tenders for such transportation must be submitted to the Commission and must be open for public inspection.

fected by the consolidation could not be placed in a worse position with respect to their employment as a result of the combination. Recently, there has been a vigorous reawakening of interest in consolidations, some of which have aroused a great deal of public interest; but so far, the Interstate Commerce Commission has given little indication of its position on public policy on this matter.[15]

Board of Investigation and Research

Congress, recognizing that the Act of 1940 did not resolve the transportation problem, and acting on the recommendation of the Interstate Commerce Commission, set up a Board of Investigation and Research. It was to consist of three members, appointed by the President with the consent of the Senate. The appointment was to be for two years, but the President was authorized to extend the life of the Board for two years. Its existence was terminated in 1944. It was directed to study and report upon the relative economy and fitness of rail, motor, and water carriers, the extent to which public funds had been provided for the use of these carriers without adequate compensation from them for the use of the facilities that had been provided, and the extent to which taxes had been imposed upon these carriers by the various agencies of government. The Board was also empowered to investigate other matters it might consider to be important for the improvement of transportation and for the development of a national transportation policy. The Board did not make a report on national policy, but it did prepare a number of informative studies.[16]

THE TRANSPORTATION ACT OF 1958

Reasons for the Legislation

With the end of World War II and the restoration, more or less, of the conditions of a peacetime economy, competition in transportation among the various modes quickly assumed new vigor. As a consequence, the issue of the appropriate basis for competition in rates for traffic which might be moved by any of the agencies became an acute one. A number of governmental agencies issued reports on the national transportation problem, but none of them came up with programs that could form the

[15] The Interstate Commerce Commission also has the responsibility of enforcing section 7 of the Clayton Act when applicable to common carriers. The conflict between this and the powers of the Commission under the Interstate Commerce Act is now a matter of litigation. For further discussion, see Chapter 18.

[16] For a list of these, see D. P. Locklin, *Economics of Transportation* (6th ed.; Homewood, Ill.: Richard D. Irwin, Inc., 1966), p. 253.

basis of a comprehensive revision of policy.[17] In 1954, President Eisenhower set up an Advisory Committee on Transport Policy and Organization. This Committee issued its report in April, 1955,[18] the burden of which was that federal policies should be amended to permit greater reliance on competitive forces in transportation and to assure the maintenance of a modernized and financially strong system of common carrier transportation. Legislation was presented to Congress on the basis of this report but foundered on the controversy of what came to be known as the three "shall nots." The railroads argued that the regulatory authorities should exercise their rate-making power over the various agencies (1) without regard to the effect of such rates on the traffic of a rival agency, (2) without regard to the relation of such rates to the rates of any other agency, and (3) without regard to the question of whether the rates were lower than those necessary to meet the competition of the carrier of another agency. Extensive Congressional hearings, together with a report by the Senate committee under Senator George Smathers,[19] resulted in the Transportation Act of 1958.[20] This legislation was passed by Congress in response to what seemed to be a rapidly mounting railroad crisis arising from a decline in railroad traffic resulting from the business recession, financial losses arising from unprofitable passenger operations, and the difficulties faced by many railroads in raising new capital that was urgently needed. This law was therefore primarily of an emergency nature that could serve only as a stopgap pending a thorough revision of national policy.

Provisions of the Law

Guaranteed Loans. The Interstate Commerce Commission was authorized to guarantee loans to railroads up to a total of $500 million outstanding at any time, to enable the railroads to finance capital investment in road and equipment and for maintenance work. These

---

[17] See *Issues Involved in a Unified and Coordinated Federal Program for Transportation,* Report to the President from the Secretary of Commerce (Washington, D.C.: U.S. Government Printing Office, December 1, 1949); and *Domestic Land and Water Transportation,* Progress Report of the Senate Committee on Interstate and Foreign Commerce, Senate Report No. 1039, 82d Congress, 1st session, October, 1951 (Washington, D.C.: U.S. Government Printing Office, 1951).

[18] *Revision of Federal Transportation Policy* (Washington, D.C.: U.S. Government Printing Office, 1955). This was known as the Weeks Report.

[19] *Problems of the Railroads* (Smathers Report), Report of Subcommittee on Surface Transportation, Committee on Interstate and Foreign Commerce, U.S. Senate, 85th Cong., 2d sess. (Washington, D.C.: U.S. Government Printing Office, April, 1958).

[20] Public Law 85–625 (1958).

loans were to be guaranteed only if the Commission found that without the guaranty the borrowing railroad would be unable to obtain the necessary funds on reasonable terms, that the term of the loan was not more than fifteen years, and that there was reasonable assurance that the loan would be repaid within the time fixed for repayment. If the loan was for financing or refinancing expenditures for maintenance of property, the borrowing railroad could not declare any dividends so long as any principal or interest remained unpaid. This provision for guaranteeing loans was of a temporary nature and was to expire at the end of March, 1961. In April, 1961, however, it was extended to June 30, 1963.

Intrastate Rates. Upon petition of a carrier questioning the lawfulness of any intrastate rate, fare, or charge, the Commission was instructed forthwith to institute its own investigation and to give special expedition to the hearing and decision thereon, even though a state agency had not acted. In addition, the finding might be made without a separation of interstate and intrastate property, revenues, and expenditures, and without considering in totality the operations of any carrier or group or groups of carriers wholly within any state. This appears to be primarily Congressional affirmation of the authority it was assumed that the Interstate Commerce Commission possessed, but which was placed in doubt as the result of two Supreme Court decisions in 1958.[21]

Discontinuance of Train Service. The Interstate Commerce Commission was given jurisdiction over the discontinuance or change of the operation or service of passenger trains and railroad ferries. Where operations across state lines were subject to any state law or regulatory authority, the carrier might invoke the jurisdiction of the Commission by giving thirty days' notice of discontinuance of service. The service could then be abandoned unless the Commission decided otherwise. If the operation was entirely within the boundaries of a state, a petition to discontinue might be filed with the Commission. After holding hearings in the state where the operations occurred, the Commission might sanction discontinuance if it found that public convenience and necessity would permit it, and if it found that continuance would constitute an unjust or undue burden on the interstate operations of the carrier.

---

[21] *Chicago, Milwaukee, St. Paul and Pacific Railroad Company* v. *Illinois*, 356 U.S. 906 (1958); and *Public Service Commission of Utah* v. *United States*, 356 U.S. 421 (1958).

Amendment to the Rule of Rate Making. The rule of rate making embodied in Section 15 (*a*) of the Interstate Commerce Act was amended by the following:

> In a proceeding involving competition between carriers of different modes of transportation subject to this Act, the Commission, in determining whether a rate is lower than a reasonable minimum rate, shall consider the facts and circumstances attending the movement of the traffic by the carrier or carriers to which the rate is applicable. Rates of a carrier shall not be held up to a particular level to protect the traffic of any other mode of transportation, giving due consideration to the objectives of the national transportation policy declared in this Act.

The purpose of this amendment, presumably, was to instruct the Commission to adhere to its position in the new automobiles case,[22] in which it said that it would not hold the rates of one mode of transport up to a particular level in order to preserve the rate structure of another mode, nor use restraints on rate competition as a means of allocating traffic among the modes.[23] In other words, it appeared to be a declaration against "umbrella" rate making.

However, there seem to be two major obstacles to an unambiguous interpretation of the new rule. The Commission is required to give due consideration to the objectives set forth in the declaration of the national transportation policy. This apparently has been interpreted by some members to mean that this policy may require the continuance of "umbrella" rate making, at least in some areas of intermode competition.[24]

The second obstacle arises in connection with the appropriate cost basis for calculating minimum rates for interagency competition. On this issue the members of the Commission seem to be as sharply divided as the contestants. There is apparent agreement that fully distributed costs are not always the proper basis for minimum rates, and that out-of-pocket costs may be used on occasion. However, in the *California-Oregon Lumber case,*[25] the majority held that out-of-pocket costs

---

[22] *New Automobiles in Interstate Commerce,* 259 I.C.C. 475 (1945).

[23] There does not seem to have been any consistent adherence to this policy, however. See E. W. Williams, Jr., *The Regulation of Rail-Motor Rate Competition* (New York: Harper & Bros., 1958), chap. viii.

[24] *Commodities—Pan-Atlantic Steamship Corporation,* 313 I.C.C. 23 (1960); see also 309 I.C.C. 587 (1960); *Interstate Commerce Commission* v. *New York, New Haven and Hartford Rr. Co.,* 372 U.S. 744 (1963).

[25] 308 I.C.C. 345 (1959). See also *Limestone in Trainloads—Prairie du Rocher, Illinois, to Baton Rouge, Louisiana,* 313 I.C.C. 71 (1961). The issue now seems to be squarely joined in *Ingot Molds, Pa. to Steelton, Ky.,* 323 I.C.C. 758 (1965); 326 I.C.C. 77 (1965), which is now on appeal to the Supreme Court.

should include "the variable portion of a reasonable return after Federal income taxes, and make a contribution to the transportation burden. Out-of-pocket costs include those operating expenses, rent, taxes, and return which vary with changes in traffic volume and can be assigned directly to specific traffic movements." Three members dissented from this concept of out-of-pocket costs.

The problem within the Commission itself is not merely one of differences of opinion on the accounting and statistical computations of the various kinds of costs. It is rather a lack of agreement on the cost principles that should be adopted in rate making. Furthermore the various carriers are dissatisfied with the law, although the railroads seem to have gained some ground in that they have been given authority to reduce rates to meet competition which probably would not have been accorded prior to the legislation.[26] Vigorous action by the motor and water carriers to secure the repeal of the amendment lends support to this. There is little evidence to indicate that the Commission is more likely to develop a consistent or coherent rate policy under the new amendment than under previous legislation.[27] This problem is dealt with at greater length in Chapter 17.

[26] See *East Central Motor Carriers Association* v. *Baltimore and Ohio Railroad Company, et al.,* 314 I.C.C. 5 (1961); *Commodities—Pan-Atlantic Steamship Corporation,* 313 I.C.C. 23 (1960); see also 309 I.C.C. 587 (1959).

[27] See Williams, *op. cit.,* pp. 215 f., and *National Transportation Policy* (Doyle Report), Preliminary Draft of a Report to the Senate Committee on Interstate and Foreign Commerce, 87th Cong., 1st sess. (Washington, D.C.: U.S. Government Printing Office, 1961), pp. 390–407. See D. F. Pegrum, "Do We Have a New Rule of Rate Making?" *Traffic World,* February 7, 1959, pp. 50–54, for an analysis of why the new rule was unlikely to bring about any significant change in policy, and R. W. Harbeson, "The Regulation of Interagency Rate Competition under the Transportation Act of 1958," 30 *I.C.C. Practitioners' Journal* (1962), p. 287, for an analysis of the application of the law in which he reached the same conclusion.

THE REGULATION OF
MOTOR TRANSPORT

INTRODUCTION

The general approach to the regulation of motor transport in the United States has been similar to that which has been applied to rail transport. In its economic aspects, it has developed out of railroad regulation, and on the same assumptions that led to the elaborate framework that characterizes the latter. The application of this regulation to motor transportation, however, is faced by many more complexities because of the varied sources of supply of motor carrier services, the impossibility of bringing all suppliers (or producers) under the same types of control that have been applied to the railroads, and the predominantly localized nature of the services which are performed. The latter has resulted in a division of authority among governments, especially the state and federal agencies, that was neither necessary nor tolerable for rail transport. In addition to these factors, the totally different economic structure of the motor carrier industry from that of the railroads has introduced the problem of forcing prices and competition into the framework of monopoly regulation where the essential ingredients for such an approach do not exist. An appraisal of the effectiveness and consequences of this to the control of motor transportation will be deferred until a description of the coverage of the regulation and the procedures involved has been given.

STATE REGULATION

The regulation of motor carriers did not begin anywhere until railroad regulation had become thoroughly mature. The control of motor carriers was undertaken first of all at the state level. The reasons for the development of state regulation were many and confused. At the beginning, it emerged in the form of control of jitneys or individual automobiles carrying passengers for hire in local urban transportation. This type of transportation introduced a threat to the street and urban railways; it also posed a problem of safety of operations and liability to passengers. The immediate pressure for regulation came from the established agencies that wanted protection against the competition. A similar situation soon emerged in intercity transportation as the highway systems were extended, particularly in states like California. There was need for control over the use of highways with regard to the weights of vehicles and loads, safety, and speed. Many of the reasons for legislation to control the use of the highways were applicable to all operators. The prevalent idea was, however, that all carriers for hire should be regulated as common carriers, and the railroads understandably fostered this notion. As a consequence, motor carrier regulation became a mixture of measures to govern the use of the highways, extract charges for their use, protect shippers and passengers against irresponsibility of carriers, and protect existing transport agencies.

The legislation that resulted from this mixture of motives was not based, therefore, on any clear-cut understanding of the problems of motor carrier regulation, nor of the fact that many if not all of the objectives, except the protection of existing carriers, could have been achieved without resort to the type of control imposed upon the railroads. Indeed, if there had been no railroads or railroad regulation, it is doubtful that the pattern of motor carrier regulation would have borne any resemblance to that which exists today. The latter is the result of demands to extend control to all carriers alike, and of the widespread feeling that all transportation for hire is supplied under conditions that differ markedly from those applying to industry in general, therefore requiring detailed control beyond that which is applicable to the latter.

Limitation on Powers of Regulation

Apart from safety measures and similar controls, the first attempts at state regulation were designed to treat all carriers for hire as common carriers. This met with rebuff at the hands of the Supreme Court. The right to regulate common carriers was not challenged, but the question of whether all carriers for hire could be compelled to be common carriers and regulated accordingly was another matter. In 1923 the state of Michigan enacted legislation which sought to regulate contract carriage by providing that any person transporting goods for hire on the public highways was a common carrier. In 1925 the Supreme Court declared this to be unconstitutional on the ground that a state could not make a common carrier out of a contract carrier by legislative fiat.[1] The next year the Court declared unconstitutional a California law which attempted the same thing, on the ground that a state could not require an individual to assume the responsibilities of a common carrier as the price of the privilege of doing business upon the highway.[2] The state of Texas met the issue by a new approach. In 1931, it enacted legislation which required contract carriers to obtain permits before they could operate. The state Commission was given broad powers of control, including the authority to set minimum rates. The Supreme Court upheld both provisions of the Texas law,[3] thereby approving public regulation of carriers for hire, whether common or contract. Although contract carriers cannot be required to assume common carrier obligations, they can be compelled to secure state authorization before they can undertake operations, and furthermore the state can regulate the prices they charge. This regulation has taken the form of minimum rate controls, although maximum rates may also be imposed, as is permitted in California. In practice, however, the regulation has been confined to minimum rates.

State versus Federal Authority

The state has no more power to regulate interstate commerce, as such, by motor carrier than by rail. However, the fact that the motor carrier must use state-owned highways over which the state exercises control has made it possible for the states to require carriers to secure certificates or permits from the state authorities, but the state cannot refuse to grant permission to operate solely on the condition that the route is adequately served. It may, nevertheless, refuse to allow an interstate carrier to carry on an intrastate business because on this traffic the carrier becomes an intrastate operator. Furthermore the state authority can exercise control over the rates of the intrastate traffic even though in doing so, it may affect interstate commerce, because the federal law regulating motor carriers specifically excludes them from the Shreveport rule. This is a matter of legislation, however, and not court ruling.

Although the states may impose regulations on interstate carriers for the purpose of promoting safety on the highways or conserving their

---

[1] *Michigan Public Utilities Commission* v. *Duke*, 266 U.S. 570 (1925).

[2] *Frost and Frost Trucking Company* v. *Railroad Commission of California*, 271 U.S. 583 (1926). See also *Smith* v. *Cahoon*, 283 U.S. 533 (1931).

[3] *Stephenson* v. *Binford*, 287 U.S. 251 (1932).

use, it cannot do so when the intent is to limit competition. This was decided in *Buck* v. *Kuykendall* (1925).[4] Buck wanted to operate a bus line over the highway from Seattle, Washington, to Portland, Oregon, to transport passengers between those two cities. He secured a license from Oregon, but the state of Washington refused to grant him a certificate of public convenience and necessity on the ground that Seattle and Portland were already adequately served by railroads and bus lines. The Supreme Court held that the intent of the refusal was to limit competition rather than to promote safety and protect the highways. The refusal was therefore held to be unconstitutional. In other words, the states could not regulate, directly, interstate commerce by motor vehicle. This was in keeping with the Wabash decision of 1886.

Nature of State Regulation

Economic regulation by the states varies widely as to scope and coverage. Most of the laws, however, distinguish between regular common carriers and other carriers for hire. The regular common carriers are required to secure certificates of public convenience and necessity. To qualify for one of these, the applicant must prove that public convenience and necessity will be served and that the carrier is fit, willing, and able to provide the service. This requirement of proof, and the fact that the burden of proof is on the applicant, means that if in the opinion of the requesting authorities the public is already adequately supplied with transport facilities, the certificate will not be granted. This serves to impose severe restrictions on competition in the regular common carrier business. Those who receive permission are generally subject to the same kind of regulation that is imposed upon the railroads as common carriers. Other carriers for hire are variously classified in the different states but are usually required to secure permits. These are ordinarily granted if the applicant can prove that it is fit, willing, and able to render the service it proposes to offer, and can meet the responsibilities imposed by the law. The restrictions on competition here are less severe than those applicable to regular common carriers, and the regulation is much less comprehensive.[5] Usually, only the minimum

---

[4] 267 U.S. 307.

[5] In some states, irregular-route common carriers are recognized. These can operate under permits, but they are subject to general common carrier obligations. For a detailed discussion of state regulation, see D. V. Harper, *Economic Regulation of the Motor Trucking Industry by the States* (Urbana: University of Illinois Press, 1959); also H. W. Nicholson, "Motor Carrier Cost and Minimum Rate Regulation," *Quarterly Journal of Economics,* Vol. LXXII (February, 1958), pp. 139–52.

rates of these carriers are subject to regulation, and as a rule they can abandon all or part of their service at will.

The states also exercise extensive control over motor transport through taxation, size and weight limitations, safety regulations, and operating authority for carriers engaged in interstate commerce. These vary so widely from state to state as to impose severe impediments on interstate commerce.

Nearly all the states require some form of "operating authority" from interstate carriers, but the requirements, procedures, and fees vary among the states. A few states require appearance by the carrier at hearings in order to obtain an operating authority to traverse the state, and compel the carrier to show his financial responsibility to conduct a motor carrier business, and to report the commodities he expects to carry, the territory or points between which he proposes to operate, and the equipment he intends to use. Even the carrier which is exempt from federal regulations must file for an operating authority from the state it wishes to traverse. All interstate carriers must comply with the size and weight limitations imposed by the state jurisdictions, and these vary quite widely. In addition to this, all carriers are required to pay a wide assortment of taxes for the privilege of using the state highways. The effect of these state regulations is to impose considerable limitation on the operation of motor carriers in interstate commerce.

Regular-route carriers must comply with all the requirements of the different states through which the route passes between origin and destination. Irregular-route carriers may be able to avoid some of the more onerous restrictions by avoiding a particular state. This leads to circuitous hauling, but it may be more economical than a more direct route.[6] It is possible that more uniformity may be achieved through federal action; at the present time, however, this applies only to maximum weights.[7]

[6] For a detailed discussion of state regulations affecting interstate commerce, see Agricultural Marketing Service, U.S. Department of Agriculture, *Effects of State and Local Regulations on Interstate Movement of Agricultural Products by Highway*, Marketing Research Report No. 396 (Washington, D.C.: U.S. Government Printing Office, 1961). See also *Interstate Trade Barriers Affecting Motor-Vehicle Transportation*, Board of Investigation and Research, Senate Document No. 81, 79th Congress, 1st session, September, 1944 (Washington, D.C.: U.S. Government Printing Office, 1944).

[7] The Federal Highway Act of 1956 provides that appropriations for the interstate system are to be withheld from any state that permits the portion of that system within its borders to be used by vehicles carrying a weight in excess of 18,000 pounds per axle, or an overall gross weight of 73,280 pounds, or such maximum weights as were permitted on July 1, 1956, whichever is the greater. See also American Trucking Associations Inc., *Summary of Size and Weight Limits* (Washington, D.C., August 8, 1966).

FEDERAL REGULATION

Reasons for Federal Regulation

Federal regulation of motor transport was the result of a long period of argument and controversy. This centered on the desirability of regulation as well as on the form it should take. There was little disagreement over federal regulation of interstate bus transportation, but trucking was another matter. The trucking business did not emerge with any significance in interstate commerce until the 1930's, and at that time its role in the transport system was not clear. The loss of traffic which the railroads suffered as a result of the depression which began in 1929 was aggravated by the rising competition from motor carriers. The railroads sought, therefore, to preserve their position by demanding regulation to curb this competition. In addition, rapid development of competition among the motor carriers led the principal companies to organize to secure means of curbing the competition among themselves. The prevalent idea, expressed in the National Industrial Recovery Act, was that limitations had to be imposed on competition everywhere in industry.

The objectives of regulation of motor carriers were set forth in the report of the Coordinator of Transportation in the following terms:

The public interest in transportation may, then, be summarized as requiring at least the following: (1) A minimum of outright duplication of facilities or services; (2) a transportation system which is well organized and functions in an orderly, dependable way, rather than one which is unstable, uncertain, and a breeder of discriminations; (3) responsibility in both the narrow and the broad sense indicated above [this relates to the maintenance of truck or bus service on which the shipper or traveler has come, perhaps entirely, to depend]; (4) financial stability and good credit.

There are some who think that the thing to do is to let down the bars and allow the competitors to fight it out to the finish. This would, of course, require practical abandonment of railroad regulation, leaving redress of grievances to the courts. The eventual result might be a kind of coordinated system of transportation, achieved through survival of the fittest but the greater competitive strength of the railroads would be likely to distort the results. The fact is that this plan of free-for-all competition has never worked successfully, either here or elsewhere. It has been tried and found wanting.

On the other hand, a partial and incomplete system of regulation, such as we have had, will not work.[8]

[8] Regulation of Transportation Agencies, Report of the Federal Coordinator of Transportation, Senate Document No. 152, 73d Cong., 2d sess. (Washington, D.C.: U.S. Government Printing Office, 1934), p. 23. See also D. P. Locklin, Economics of Transportation (6th ed.; Homewood, Ill.: Richard D. Irwin, Inc., 1966), pp. 666–68, for a detailing of the objectives of motor carrier regulation.

The alternatives, as seen by the Coordinator at this time, were to abandon the regulation of transportation to the antitrust laws, or to subject all of the agencies to the same type that had been developed for the railroads. No analysis was made of the fundamentally different economic characteristics of the various agencies, nor was any consideration given to a program of regulation that might be in accordance with these differences. Instead, legislation was recommended that would regulate common carriers by motor essentially in the same way that railroads were controlled, and force the other motor carriers as much as possible into the same mold. This became the basis of the Motor Carrier Act of 1935, which has survived with minor modifications to the present time.

The Motor Carrier Act of 1935

General Provisions. The Act began with a declaration of policy which set forth the main objectives of the legislation. This declaration was similar to that which was later included in the Transportation Act of 1940, except that the latter applied to all agencies under the control of the Interstate Commerce Commission, whereas the one in the Act of 1935 applied to motor carriers only. The legislation made it clear that Congress did not intend to extend its jurisdiction into the field of intrastate commerce by going so far as to state that common carriers operating wholly within a single state could transport passengers and goods moving in interstate commerce between points within the state without obtaining the permission of the Interstate Commerce Commission, provided that the carrier was operating lawfully under the jurisdiction of a state regulatory agency.[9]

If an application or complaint filed with the Commission does not involve more than three states, it must be referred to a joint board consisting of a representative of the commission of each of the states. Joint boards may be used at the discretion of the Interstate Commerce Commission in proceedings which involve more than three states. The decision of such a board becomes final if exceptions to its report are not filed within twenty days after the original report is filed, or if the Commission does not review the case.

Classification of Carriers. The Act classified carriers into five distinct groups: (1) common carriers, which are those enterprises that

---

[9] The Commission, under Public Law 89–170 (1965) is now in the process of working out procedures with state authorities to effect uniformity among the states in registration of I.C.C. operating authorities, registration and identification of vehicles, filing of evidence of insurance, and improvement of economic regulation. There is fear on the part of private carriers that this may serve as a basis for some form of regulation of private carriers.

hold themselves as being ready to serve the general public; (2) contract carriers, which are those that operate for hire under special arrangement or, in other words, specific contract; (3) private carriers, or those who transport goods of which the carrier is the owner; (4) brokers, or persons who sell transportation but do not actually perform transportation services; and (5) exempt carriers, which are not subject to the control of the Commission except for those provisions in the law which gave the Commission the authority to prescribe qualifications and maximum hours of service of employees, and to make rules relating to safety of operation and standards of equipment.

Common Carriers. The authority of the Commission over common carriers by motor vehicle parallels that of its control over railroads, although there are some minor exceptions.

1. *Certificates of Convenience and Necessity.* Every common carrier must secure a certificate of public convenience and necessity before undertaking to supply transportation service or before extending operations to additional points or over other routes.[10] To secure a certificate, an applicant must prove to the satisfaction of the Commission that it is fit, willing, and able to perform the service it proposes to offer, and that such service is required by present and future public convenience and necessity. The certificate must indicate the service to be rendered, and the route or area to be covered. It may be suspended, changed, or revoked for willful failure to comply with the law. Finally, it may be transferred, subject to rules prescribed by the Commission.

2. *Rates and Fares.* The law provides that all rates and fares must be just and reasonable. They must be published, and strict observance to published tariffs is required. Thirty days' notice must be given for all changes in rates and fares, and all proposed changes may be suspended by the Commission, pending investigation, for a period not exceeding seven months. The Commission also has the power to prescribe the maximum, minimum, or actual rate to be charged, in lieu of the one found to be unreasonable or unlawful.

The Act prohibits every unjust and unreasonable charge, as well as any undue or unreasonable preference or advantage in rates to per-

---

[10] The "grandfather" clause entitled carriers to a certificate as a matter of right if they were bona fide operators on June 1, 1935, and had operated continuously since then. Certificates remained in effect indefinitely as long as the carrier complied with the law and the orders of the Commission. The clause applied to common and contract carriers alike. In applying this to contract carriers, the Commission usually limited them to the same class of customers they had been serving. This type of restriction came to be known as the "Keystone" restriction (*Keystone Transportation Company, Contract Carrier Application,* 19 M.C.C. 475 [1939]).

sons, places, or commodities. However, motor carriers are not subject to the long-and-short-haul clause, the reason being that the competitive structure of motor transport makes long-and-short-haul discrimination very unlikely and of no importance. Although the Commission has adequate powers to deal with such discrimination if it should arise, it is nevertheless important to note that Congress has steadily refused to repeal the prohibition with regard to railroads, despite the fact that the Commission's control over rates is more complete in other respects than it is over motor carriers. The conclusion seems to be inescapable that the strict regulation of common carriage by motor vehicle is more for the protection of the carriers than of the shipping public. In this connection, it may be noted that the Act does not require motor carriers of property to establish through routes and joint rates with other motor carriers, although these may be established on a voluntary basis. They may be required for motor carriers of persons.

3. *Consolidation, Mergers, and Acquisition of Control.* The general provisions of the Interstate Commerce Act relating to railroad combinations are also applicable to common carriers by motor. If combination is to be authorized by the Commission, it must be "consistent with public interest," except that approval was not required if the number of vehicles involved is not more than twenty if a motor carrier is an applicant. This provision of the law was modified in 1965 by exempting consolidations if operating revenues did not exceed $300,000. However, the Commission still has the power in all consolidations to prescribe rules governing the transfer of certificates and permits and must give its approval for the transfer of any operating rights. If a railroad is seeking control, then the proposal may be granted only if it will enable the railroad to use motor vehicles to public advantage in its operations, and will not unduly restrain competition, regardless of the number of vehicles involved in the application. Commission approval of a combination carries with it exemption from the antitrust laws insofar as may be necessary to enable the combining carriers to do anything authorized or required by the order.

4. *Issuance of Securities.* The issuance of securities by motor carriers is subject to the same provisions as those which apply to the railroads, apart from exceptions in favor of the large number of small firms operating in the industry. At the present time, the approval of the Commission is required only if the total par value of the securities of the carrier, outstanding and to be issued, exceeds $1 million. Notes with a maturity of two years or less may be issued up to an amount not in excess of $200,000 without Commission consent.

5. *Protection of the Public.* The Commission may require the carriers to purchase surety bonds and insurance to protect the shipping and general public, or require adequate evidence that obligations arising from transport operations can be met. It is authorized to prescribe regulations governing qualifications and maximum hours of service of employees, safety of operations, and standards of equipment. These provisions apply to all common, contract, and exempt carriers in interstate commerce, and to private carriers of property.[11]

6. *Accounts.* The Act empowers the Interstate Commerce Commission to prescribe the form of accounts and reports, require special reports, and have access to the books and records of all common carriers, contract carriers, and brokers. In addition, it may require information on any contract or agreement involving any of these or any person in relation to traffic regulated by the law. These provisions may also be applied to private carriers of property at the discretion of the Commission.

7. *Dual Operation.* The Act forbids any common or contract carrier from acting in both capacities over the same route or within the same territory unless the Commission finds it to be in the public interest to permit such an operation. The theory behind this restriction was that where a carrier could offer both types of service, it would be tempted to discriminate in favor of the large shipper by granting him contract rates. It is difficult to see how this could be of any particular danger in view of the fact that the large shipper would have the advantage of being able to secure the services of a competing contract carrier in any case. This provision emphasizes the persistent attempt of public policy to separate common carriage from other carriage for hire on the basis of the supplier of the service rather than on the basis of the service supplied. This may have been reasonable when transportation service was rendered under monopoly conditions, but it does not appear to offer any advantages under competitive ones.

Contract Carriers

Most of the provisions of the Motor Carrier Act apply with equal force to contract carriers. A contract carrier by motor vehicle is any carrier which, under special and individual contracts or agreements, transports passengers or property in interstate or foreign commerce by motor vehicle for compensation. Such carriers are subject to the Act in the same way as common carriers with regard to safety, accounts and reports, consolidations, security issues, qualifications and maximum hours of

---

[11] All of these have now been transferred to the Department of Transportation.

service of employees, and safety of operations and standards of equipment. However, the Act recognizes that contract carriers offer a more individualized and specialized type of service than common carriers. It therefore provides for control of competition only insofar as it may be deemed necessary to prevent the contract carrier from interfering unduly with the business of the common carrier. It is assumed that the shipper is able to protect himself through his own arrangements or the contract with the carrier. Therefore the contract carrier does not have to provide bonds or insurance to cover loss or damage to goods carried, since it is not liable, as is the common carrier, for the safe transportation of the goods committed to its care. The contract carrier, however, must be able to assure the Commission that it can meet its public liability obligations.

Permits. Every contract carrier in interstate commerce must secure a permit, and before such permit may be issued, the applicant must prove that it is fit, willing, and able to perform the service of a contract carrier, and that the proposed operation is consistent with the public interest and the national transportation policy. The permit must specify the business which the carrier may undertake, and such reasonable conditions as the Commission may specify. The "grandfather" clause was also applicable to contract carriers.

Rates. The original provisions required contract carriers to file their minimum rates with the Commission. This was changed in 1957 to the actual rates charged, to which the carrier was compelled to adhere. This was to supply the common carriers with the information on the actual rates being granted by their competitors. Thirty days' notice is required for reductions in rates, and the Commission, after hearing, may prescribe the minimum below which the actual rates cannot go. The suspension provisions with regard to common carrier rates are also applicable to contract carriers.

Private Carriers and Brokers

Private carriers under the Act are those which transport goods in interstate commerce for themselves; that is, the services performed by these carriers are not for hire. The Commission has interpreted the term *private carriers* quite strictly by requiring that such a carrier be organically part of the business which owns it and be specialized to meet the peculiar operating needs of that business. This is to prevent subterfuge by an enterprise engaged primarily in transportation which may acquire title to the goods which are being transported solely or primarily for the purpose of transporting them. As a consequence, when a subsidiary corporation is used to perform the transportation, the primary business of that concern is transportation, and it is not, therefore, a private carrier.[12] Furthermore the Commission is generally opposed to granting permission to private carriers to engage in contract or common carriage.[13] The desire of the carriers to undertake such transportation arises from the possibility of obtaining back hauls which will result in more economical and balanced traffic loads. This, of course, would increase competition with the common and contract carriers. The dividing line between private carriage not subject to regulation and that which may be regulated is a matter of much controversy. The principal difficulty arises in connection with the endeavors of carriers who haul their own products in one direction to secure a backhaul for the empty vehicles. In the Cahaba case[14] the company hauled its own steel in one direction and backhauled salt. The Commission found that Cahaba was legitimately engaged in the business of selling and distributing salt and that the backhaul was therefore private carriage. This is to be distinguished from "buy and sell" operations where the carrier merely buys the product, to be sold at destination, in order to obtain a backhaul. This is illegal.

A broker is a person who is not a carrier or a carrier's agent, but who sells or arranges for transportation by motor vehicle. He must secure a license from the Commission to engage in such business and is required to conform to the same rules regarding accounts and reports as the motor carriers. He must furnish bond or other security to ensure financial responsibility for the service he undertakes to perform.

Exempt Carriers

The Act also excludes eleven classes of vehicles operated for hire from all of its provisions and therefore from control by the Interstate Commerce Commission, except for the qualifications and maximum hours of service of employees, and safety of operation or standards of equipment. These exemptions fall into three main categories. First of all, there are those that are essentially local in nature, for which the exemption is absolute, except as to safety regulations. Carriers in this

[12] See *Schenley Distillers Motor Division Inc., Contract Carrier Application,* 44 M.C.C. 171 (1944); affirmed in 326 U.S. 432 (1946); and *Schenley Distillers Corp., Contract Carrier Application,* 51 M.C.C. 65 (1949), affirmed in 340 U.S. 925 (1952).

[13] For an analysis of exceptions to this policy, see F. M. Porter, "Federal Regulation of Private Carriers," *Harvard Law Review,* Vol. LXIV (1951), p. 896. See *Geraci, Contract Carrier Application,* 7 M.C.C. 369 (1938); and *Bales, Common Carrier Application,* 9 M.C.C. 709 (1938).

[14] *Cahaba Steel Co., Common Carrier Application,* M.C.–125165 (1966); see also *Red Ball Motor Freight* v. *Shannon,* 337 U.S. 311 (1964).

category include school buses, taxicabs, hotel vehicles, trolley buses, motor vehicles used incidentally in transportation by air, and motor vehicles operating under the authority of the Secretary of the Interior, principally for the purpose of transporting persons in and about the national parks and national monuments. Second, motor vehicles controlled and operated by farmers in transporting agricultural commodities and products from the farm, or agricultural supplies to the farm; motor vehicles controlled and operated by co-operative associations as defined in the Agricultural Marketing Act of 1929; motor vehicles used exclusively in carrying livestock, fish (including shellfish), or agricultural commodities (not including manufactured products thereof); and motor vehicles used exclusively in distributing newspapers are all exempt. The exclusion of transportation of agricultural commodities in interstate commerce from regulation is the one that is the most significant of all, and the one which has given rise to the most controversy. Third, the Act also provides for the exemption from regulation by the Commission of carriers transporting passengers or property wholly within a municipality, between contiguous municipalities, or within a zone adjacent to and commercially a part of a municipality, if those carriers are lawfully engaged in intrastate transportation, even though the traffic may actually cross state boundaries. This exemption, however, can be modified if the Commission, in the discharge of its duty, finds it necessary to do so. The same provisions are applicable to casual, occasional, or reciprocal transportation of passengers or property in interstate commerce for compensation, by persons not engaged in transportation by motor vehicle as a regular occupation or business.

These exemptions, especially those applying to agricultural commodities, are another indication of the difference between motor and rail transport, and constitute a recognition of the fact that Congress has not found it necessary to impose common carrier obligations on the suppliers of transport service for an important segment of the economy, to ensure adequacy of transport facilities, or to protect the shipper, nor even to subject these carriers to the regulations to which contract carriers, as defined in the Act, must conform.

ADMINISTRATION OF THE MOTOR CARRIER ACT

The administration of the Motor Carrier Act has required a great deal of attention by the Interstate Commerce Commission, which has published some 100 volumes of decisions to date dealing with them alone, under Part II of the Interstate Commerce Act, together with special reports and decisions contained in the reports dealing with

Part I of the Act. The following discussion deals only with details of what seem to be the outstanding issues of motor carrier regulation that have come before the Commission.

Control of Entry

The administration of the Motor Carrier Act by the Commission indicates clearly the intention to impose severe limitations on competition among motor carriers coming within the jurisdiction of the Act, and even on the competition of these carriers with the railroads. The conclusion seems to be warranted that the Commission is more concerned with protecting the competitors than it is with protecting competition. Indeed, it is doubtful that the Commission has ever recognized the distinction between the two.

The Grandfather Clause. When the Commission first undertook the administration of the Act, it was faced with over 89,000 applications by common and contract carriers for certificates or permits which would legalize their existing businesses. The objective of the grandfather clause was to protect carriers who were genuinely in operation before the Act took effect. The applicants, on the other hand, sought as broad and extensive operating rights as they could obtain. For regular-route common carriers the practice followed was to restrict the operating rights to the routes and points already being served by the applicant. In the case of irregular-route and anywhere-for-hire common carriers, authority was generally restricted to areas or points already served, although broader authorizations were sometimes granted where this seemed to be required. Irregular-route common carriers were also subject to certain commodity restrictions, the Commission in the first instance confining the operations to commodities previously handled. The Supreme Court, however, ruled that if a carrier had held itself out to transport general freight and had hauled a wide variety of general commodities, the Commission could not prevent the carriage of others in the same general class merely because they had not been transported before.[15] In granting permits under the grandfather clause, the Commission did not limit the authorization to the particular shippers that had been served, but it usually confined the carriers to the same general class of shippers with whom they had previously had contracts. This came to be known as the "Keystone" restriction.[16]

Certificates and Permits for New Operations. When applica-

---

[15] *United States* v. *Carolina Freight Carriers Corporation*, 315 U.S. 475 (1942).

[16] *Keystone Transportation Company, Contract Carrier Application*, 19 M.C.C. 475 (1939). But the Supreme Court has held that a contract carrier rendering specialized service does not become a common carrier because it reaches for new business within the limits of its license (*United States* v. *Contract Steel Carriers*, 350 U.S. 409 [1956]).

tion is made by a common carrier to expand the authority of its certificate or to establish new operations, it must contend with a public policy that is designed to restrict the expansion of existing firms and the entry of new firms. The applicant must prove that public convenience and necessity require the granting of the certificate. This is usually an onerous and expensive burden.[17] The Commission has held that existing carriers will normally be given the privilege of handling all the traffic in the territory served by them if they can do so efficiently and economically. Only positive proof to the contrary will result in permitting a new firm to enter. Even the showing that rates would be reduced as a result of the introduction of competition is not a determinative factor in demonstrating public convenience and necessity, since this might result in rates that are too low for the occupant—a contention that is invariably advanced by the existing certificate holder. Where rail service only is available, the Commission generally follows the principle that shippers are entitled to access to service both by rail and by motor carrier.

Presumably, permits for contract carriers are less difficult to secure than certificates for common carriers; at least this would seem to be the intent of the law. However, the restrictions imposed upon operating rights granted under the grandfather clause indicated that the Commission would be no more lenient than a strict interpretation of the law required. An applicant for a permit for contract carrier operations must prove that the granting of a permit to it will be consistent with public interest, and in evaluating this consideration, the Commission has always paid attention to the possible effect of approval upon shippers and upon other carriers. Furthermore the Commission has endeavored to restrict contract carriers to a limited number of contracts; and in this, its hand has been strengthened by Congress, which amended the Motor Carrier Act in 1957 to provide that a contract carrier must be one that is engaged in transportation under continuing contracts with one person or a limited number of persons. When it denied a permit to a contract carrier on the ground that adequate common carrier service was available it met reversal in the courts. In *I.C.C.* v. *J.–T. Transport Co.,*[18] the Commission held, that the shippers did not

---

[17] See D. F. Pegrum, "Effects of Regulation on Small Business in Motor Transport," *I.C.C. Administration of the Motor Carrier Act,* Hearings before Select Committee on Small Business, U.S. Senate, 84th Congress, 1st session, November, 1955 (Washington, D.C.: U.S. Government Printing Office, 1956), pp. 465–70; also *Competition, Regulation and the Public Interest in the Motor Carrier Industry,* Report of the Select Committee on Small Business, 84th Congress, 2d session, Senate Report No. 1693 (Washington, D.C.: U.S. Government Printing Office, 1956).

[18] *Interstate Commerce Commission* v. *J.–T. Transport Co. Inc., et al.* 368 U.S. 81 (1961); 74 M.C.C. 324 (1958); 79 M.C.C. 695 (1959); see also *U.S.* v. *Contract Steel Carriers,* 350 U.S. 409 (1956).

require a different type of service that could not be supplied by the existing common carrier and that there was a presumption that services by existing carriers would be adversely affected. The Supreme Court ruled that the 1957 amendments to the legislation were made to establish a regime under which new contract carriage could be established if the "distinct need" of the shippers indicated that it was desirable. It therefore upheld the application. Mr. Justice Frankfurter wrote a vigorous and lengthy dissent the gist of which was that shipper preference is not a sufficient ground for granting an application and that it was congressional policy to limit entrance to contract carriage as a means of preserving the capacity of available common carriers to meet the nation's transportation needs. The Commission has adhered as closely to the latter position as the courts and the law will allow.

The Commission has also refused to permit a contract carrier to participate in piggyback (T.O.F.C.) arrangements.[19] In 1964 it ruled that Plan III should also be available to for-hire motor and water carriers, and was upheld by the Supreme Court on this ruling.

Trip Leasing. This is an arrangement whereby motor carriers obtain the use of equipment and personnel from other carriers, especially from for-hire carriers that are exempt from regulation. This enables a regulated carrier to supplement its own vehicle supply; it also provides a means for other carriers to find a load for the return trip of their own trucks. This is particularly true for haulers of agricultural products whose traffic is principally in one direction. The Commission has objected to this practice on the ground that it leads to great difficulty in enforcing the safety provisions of the Act,[20] and also that it gives the carriers who lease the equipment a cost advantage over those who supply their own. In addition, it aids the exempt carriers by giving them the opportunity to secure revenue for the return trip. Congress amended the Act in 1956 so as to deprive the Commission of the power to regulate the duration of equipment leases or the compensation for leased vehicles with respect to most of those used for hauling agricultural commodities and certain related products. For most other classes of vehicles the rule of the Commission provides that the lease must not be for less than 30 days. To maintain the status of private carriage the shipper

[19] *Iron and Steel Articles—Eastern Common Carriers,* 305 I.C.C. 369 (1959); *Movement of Highway Trailers by Rail,* 293 I.C.C. 93 (1954); see also footnote 19, Chapter 5, above.

[20] This objection seems to have little force in view of the fact that the law provides that the provisions with regard to qualifications and maximum hours of service, and safety of operation or standards of equipment, apply to all carriers in interstate commerce. Transference of safety control to the Department of Transportation will remove this argument, but the Commission will probably continue to endeavor to protect regulated carriers.

(lessee) must assume the risks normally involved in private transportation. In order to avoid the authority requirements of the law, a vehicle lease arrangement must result in the lessee exercising management over the operations and assuming the responsibilities, the duties, the risks, and the burdens of transportation. Legitimate leasing arrangements are bound to be the subject of continuous litigation.[21]

Railroad Control of Motor Carriers. In recent years, many of the railroads have sought vigorously to enter the motor freight business and have taken the position that they should be permitted to receive certificates on the same grounds as other applicants. The grandfather clause applied to railroad operation of motor transport in the same way as it did to other persons. The Commission, however, has interpreted the law even more strictly with regard to railroad applications for new certifications than it has to other applicants. The principle which has been applied to date is that railroad operation of motor carriers must be auxiliary or supplementary to railroad service. A certificate will not be granted if it will result in duplicating service, thereby leading to competition with the railroad itself, if it will compete with another established motor carrier, or if it will invade to a substantial degree territory adequately served by another rail carrier.[22]

This principle was given more explicit meaning by the imposition of what are known as "key-point" restrictions. Under this arrangement the motor carrier affiliate of a railroad may provide co-ordinated service to and from points on its lines, but such service cannot be between the larger cities, known as "key points," which are concentration and distribution centers. The motor affiliate may transport freight between local points, from local points to key points, or vice versa, but it cannot move the traffic through the key points. The movements to and from the key points must be part of a rail haul.[23] However, the Commission has permitted a railroad subsidiary to conduct unrestricted common carrier operations within a limited territory on the ground that authorized motor carriers within the area were not rendering the type of service required by the public.[24] Despite this, there has been little relaxation of the strict limitations imposed upon the rail operation of motor carriers.

[21] See *United States* v. *Drum,* 368 U.S. 370 (1962).

[22] See *Pennsylvania Truck Lines—Control—Barker Motor Freight,* 1 M.C.C. 101 (1936), 5 M.C.C. 9 (1937), 5 M.C.C. 49 (1937).

[23] *Kansas City Southern Transport Company, Inc., Common Carrier Application,* 10 M.C.C. 221 (1938), 28 M.C.C. 5 (1941). The restrictions imposed on railroad operations of bus lines have not been as severe as those on freight lines.

[24] *Rock Island Motor Transit Company—Purchase—White Line Motor Freight Company,* 40 M.C.C. 457 (1946), 62 M.C.C. 880 (1953).

Consolidation and Mergers

In view of the Commission's policy of restricting entry, it is not surprising that it does not accord great weight to the possibility that consolidations will lead to an undesirable restriction of competition.[25] On the other hand, it has been concerned with the effect of consolidation of connecting carriers on other carriers with whom the acquiring carrier had interchanged traffic. Thus the Commission refused to permit the acquisition of the Keeshin Freight Lines by the Pacific Intermountain Express, which would have established a single transcontinental line. Pacific Intermountain Express interchanged traffic with a number of eastern lines at St. Louis and Chicago. The acquisition of Keeshin would have adversely affected the other lines with whom Pacific Intermountain Express had interchange arrangements.[26]

The Commission must approve the conditions of consolidation, but it generally gives considerable latitude to the judgment of the operators if the price does not seem to be excessive and if the buyer is able to demonstrate that he can meet the obligations incurred. However, the amount paid for operating rights, and the amount paid for the property in excess of its physical value, must be charged to surplus and cannot, therefore, be used in any proceeding to determine the reasonableness of rates. The theory of motor carrier regulation is clearly the same as that of public utilities.

In 1966, applications before the Commission for unification amounted to 306 as compared with 359 in 1965. Most of these involved relatively small carriers but some were large mergers. Pacific Intermountain Express merged with All States Freight Inc., to form a coast to coast carrier, with total operating revenues of $100,243,000. Of the authorizations in 1965 involving the 100 largest motor carriers of property, two others had operating revenues of over $100 million—Consolidated Freightways with $155,539,000 and Roadway Express Inc., with $123,082,000. There are now seven companies offering complete coast to coast service.

Rate Regulation

Although motor carriers for hire have been subject to a large amount of competition, much of which is outside the bounds of public control, the Commission has nevertheless been concerned with the gen-

25 See *Associated Transport, Inc.—Control and Consolidation,* 38 M.C.C. 137 (1942); and *McLean Trucking Company* v. *United States,* 321 U.S. 67 (1944).
26 *Pacific Intermountain Express—Control and Purchase,* 57 M.C.C. 341 (1950), 57

eral level of rates, and has imposed restrictions on it by refusing from time to time to grant carrier requests for rate increases. In imposing these restrictions on the level of rates for motor carriers, the Commission has not endeavored to adopt the rule of fair return on fair value. Instead, it has gauged the adequacy of the rate level by the operating ratio. This has been adopted as the standard because the Commission has found that the investment is so small relative to the volume of business done that the margin of revenue over expenses required to pay a normal rate of return on capital invested would be so small that a slight miscalculation of probable revenues or expenses might leave the carrier with operating revenues insufficient to pay operating expenses.[27] Just how one goes about deciding what constitutes a reasonable margin of revenues over expenses for such purposes has never been clearly explained. Nor, for that matter, has any clear reason been expounded as to why it is necessary to prescribe a general level of rates under such circumstances. The difficulties of setting an appropriate general level for motor carriers is the same as that of prescribing workable maximum prices for any other competitive industry. It is considerably more complicated than for railroads, which have presented difficulties that have not yet been resolved. The Commission pointed out in one case that rates could not be raised sufficiently to give all the carriers adequate revenues. It said that if that were possible in the light of competitive reasons, most of the carriers would make excessive profits.[28] The best that one can say for this type of reasoning is that it is economic nonsense. If there are too many carriers for all of them to be profitable, the solution is to let competition set the level of rates and let those carriers who cannot survive get out. Protection of public interest in such a situation has a peculiarly hollow ring, especially when accompanied by restriction of entry.

Similar remarks may be made concerning the Commission's administration of the minimum rate provisions. Although much has been made of destructive rate cutting and ruinous competition among motor carriers, economic analysis fails to show how it can emerge. How it can develop in motor transport any more than among competitors in industries outside of transport has not been explained, and in its deci-

---

M.C.C. 467 (1951). The Commission also refused to permit International Transports to establish a transcontinental single-line, heavy-haul trucking operation on the objection of competing truckers that they were supplying such service through leases.

[27] See *Middle West General Increases,* 48 M.C.C. 541, 552–53 (1948).

[28] *Increased Common Carrier Rates in the East,* 42 M.C.C. 633 (1943). The issue is before the courts again, see footnote 24, Chapter 9.

sions the Commission has thrown no light on the matter. It is not sufficient to justify the fixing of minimum rates by stating that "the important considerations here are that there is a rate war, that carriers have
lost and are losing traffic because of rates which as a whole are substantially lower than necessary to yield adequate revenues, and that to
regain and retain traffic they are engaging in destructive competitive
practices. *We know of no other way of correcting this situation than by
placing a floor below which rates may not go without our prior approval.*"[29] This is clearly a case of protecting competitors rather than protecting competition; it is also likely to prove to be a successful device
for eroding the common carrier unless more effective means are discovered for limiting supply than are now available. Common carrier
obligations can be maintained and adequate notification of rate changes
can be required without resort to minimum price fixing.

Back-haul rates have been another source of endeavors to adhere
to a policy of fully allocated costs and to limit competition. In this
connection the Commission has stated:

An unbalanced condition of truck traffic, because of the greater number of
operators, is apt to be somewhat of an individual matter. That is to say, the
traffic of one truck operator may preponderate in one direction, whereas that of
a competing operator may preponderate in another. As between operators, therefore, the application of the "out-of-pocket" cost method of making rates might
well result in a breakdown of the rate structure in both directions.[30]

This, however, seems to be a clear case of joint supply in which an
operator will have to count his costs and revenues in both directions,
seeing to it merely that he secures sufficient revenue from the total of the
movements. Neither direction needs to pay for the fully allocated
costs (including those that are joint), and competitive pricing will make
the necessary adjustments between the two. If two carriers operate in
opposite directions, they must operate in the same direction, and each
can participate in the traffic both ways if permitted to do so. Joint costs
are not the cause of ruinous competition. The problem that has arisen
is not from joint supply and backhaul but from unbalanced traffic and
excess capacity resulting from restrictive conditions attached to the
certificates of public convenience and necessity granted by the Com-

[29] *Class and Commodity Rates, New York to Philadelphia*, 51 M.C.C. 289, 298–99
(1950), (italics supplied). See Locklin, *op. cit.*, pp. 699–700. For a study that concludes
that the fixing of minimum rates for motor carriers leads to higher than necessary costs
to shippers and results in an oversupply of carriers, see Nicholson, *op. cit.*, p. 139.

[30] *Refrigerator Material, Memphis, Tennessee, to Dayton, Ohio*, 4 M.C.C. 187, 189
(1938).

mission. Alleged ruinous competition can all too easily become a guise for protecting competitors as opposed to protecting competition.

Agricultural Exemptions

Administration of the exemption of for-hire movements of agricultural products under the Motor Carrier Act raised two very controversial issues. On both, the Interstate Commerce Commission endeavored to follow a narrow and restrictive interpretation, and on both it was forced to give ground under court decisions and public pressure. As a result of these, the Commission, first of all, now exempts from control, motor vehicles while being used in transporting agricultural commodities if the vehicles are not used at the same time in transporting commodities which are not exempt. A substantial part of trucking of the exempt commodities is back haul by regulated carriers, and when they are engaged in such haulage, the rates they charge for it are completely free of control by the Commission.[31] The second issue related to the scope of commodities which were exempt. At first, the Commission interpreted these to include all products raised or produced on farms by tillage and cultivation of the soil; forest products; live poultry and bees; and commodities produced by ordinary livestock, live poultry, and bees. It also limited its interpretation so as to exclude products which had undergone very simple packaging or processing. However, successive court decisions compelled a broadening of the exemptions, until the Supreme Court finally adopted what came to be known as the "substantial identity test," which meant that where "the commodity retains a continuing substantial identity through the processing stage we cannot say that it has been 'manufactured.' "[32] The Commission had already recommended to Congress that the exemptions be limited to the movement of commodities from farm to market, or to the first processing point. Congress, however, merely responded in the Act of 1958 by limiting them to those which already obtained, together with returning a few items, such as frozen fruits and vegetables, cocoa beans, coffee beans, tea, bananas, imported wool, and some others to the nonexempt category.

[31] For an extensive discussion of agricultural exemptions, see C. C. Linnenberg, Jr., "The Agricultural Exemptions in Interstate Trucking: Mend Them or End Them?" *Law and Contemporary Problems*, "Transportation," Part V, Vol. XXV (Winter, 1960), pp. 139–83; also *National Transportation Policy* (Doyle Report), Preliminary Draft of a Report to the Senate Committee on Interstate and Foreign Commerce, 87th Congress, 1st session (Washington, D.C.: U.S. Government Printing Office, 1961), pp. 516–29.

[32] *East Texas Motor Freight Lines, Inc.* v. *Frozen Fruit Express*, 351 U.S. 49 (1960).

Opposition to the exemption of agricultural commodities from regulation arises on two main grounds. The first is that of safety, and the responsibility of the carrier to its client. Both of these objections may be dismissed as not relevant to the problem of regulation. Safety regulations and enforcement are not a part of economic regulation; they could be developed and applied much more effectively in the hands of some executive agency. Responsibility to the general public and shippers is a matter of law—court decision and legislation. Commissions do not develop this nor prescribe the rules. The objections on this score are not greatly different for exempt carriers from those which apply to contract carriers, and there is little possibility of bringing the exempt commodities extensively under common carriage.

The second ground of opposition lies in the effect of the exemptions on regulated carriers, particularly common carriers by motor and rail. The endeavor of these to eliminate the exemptions is understandable because they desire protection against competition from others, to say nothing of protection from each other. The contention that it is desirable in order to stabilize rates and protect shippers does not carry much force when the shippers themselves are overwhelmingly in favor of the exemptions and seem to have little concern with rate instability. The argument that exemptions should be ended in order to protect the common carrier assumes that common carriage in this area of transportation is necessary in the public interest, or that it is necessary to put this traffic in the hands of common carriers in order to give them enough business to be able to continue their other common carrier obligations, or both. The first objection is answered by the lack of shipper demand for regulation. The second constitutes a contention that common carriers should be supported by those who do not need them. If this has any validity, then it must mean that the agricultural shippers would be "subsidizing" others. In fact, the Doyle Report says as much: "We should all expect to pay our share of the public service costs of regulated transportation as reflected in commodity prices."[33] The principal evil from exemption, if there is one, seems to arise from excluding certain

---

[33] *National Transportation Policy* (Doyle Report), *op. cit.*, p. 525. The implication of the discussion, in the report, on agricultural exemptions is that other transport subsidizes the farmer. "If transportation is not to be required to subsidize farmers and fishermen, the agricultural exemption problem takes a different direction than heretofore" (p. 526). If this means that agricultural traffic is being supported by other transportation, it is patently wrong. If it means that agricultural commodity movements do not pay enough for the use of the highways, this would apply equally well to all other carriers. If it means that all carriage for hire should be subject to entry control and price regulation, then it indicates that the authors must favor the equivalent of unfair practices acts and resale price maintenance for everybody.

carriers from the privilege of participating in the traffic. The remedy to this, particularly in light of the characteristics of motor transport and pervasive competition, lies not in imposing further restrictions, but rather in removing many that now place limitations on competition. For example, reductions in restrictions on trip leasing would lead to a greater utilization of existing equipment and in less unused capacity. Similarly, much greater flexibility in rate making for all common carriers would serve to reduce the incentives to private trucking. It may be hard to justify these exemptions in the light of traditional transportation policy, with its strict control over pricing, but under contemporary conditions it is more difficult to justify restrictions which stifle the capacity of regular carriers, especially common carriers, to compete on equal terms.

Motor vehicles controlled and operated by a cooperative association as defined in the Agricultural Marketing Act of 1929, as amended, or by a federation of such associations, if the federation possesses no greater powers or purposes than the cooperative associations, are exempt from economic regulation. In a case involving the Northwest Agricultural Cooperative Assn. Inc., the cooperative transported farm supplies back to its members and also used empty space for backhauling nonfarm-related commodities for nonmembers of the association. The Commission ruled that this was illegal and it was upheld by the district court. The Court of Appeals however, reversed the district court.[34] It found that the transportation on the backhauls was small in relation to the overall transportation operations, but also that a cooperative association would lose its character if its nonfarm-related business exceeded that which was necessary and incidental to its farm-related business (presumably something in excess of 50 per cent of the total). This decision has aroused much opposition from the regulated carriers, especially since the Department of Defense has stated that it will not refuse to route freight on exempt trucks if lower rates can be obtained thereby and has already approved four cooperatives as qualified to haul its traffic. Again protection of competition versus protection of competitors rears its head.

The Gray Area

Another area of motor carrier transport that has recently attracted considerable attention is one which has been labeled the

[34] *I.C.C.* v. *Northwest Agricultural Cooperative Assn. Inc.*, 234 Fed. Supp. 496 (1964); 350 F. 2d 252 (1965); certiorari denied by U.S. Supreme Court, 382 U.S. 1011 (1966). See 96 M.C.C. 616 (1964).

"gray" area. In most of its aspects it is an extension of private carriage and agricultural exemptions. Although it is supposed to be of considerable public concern because of public danger with regard to safety of operations and because of the need for protection of shippers from "illegal" operations, the basic issue seems to arise in connection with unauthorized transportation, that is, transportation that is not sanctioned unless under certification or permit from the Interstate Commerce Commission. In other words, this is transportation that escapes control in that it does not fall into the exempt category and does not proceed under authorization. This apparently is its worst offense. The principal offenders seem to be those engaged in "buy and sell" operations and trip leasing, although the following is also given as an example: "Transportation of house trailers, or mobile homes, is performed in many areas by unauthorized carriers, no doubt in part because few carriers in these areas possess authority from the Commission for such transportation."[35]

As already mentioned, the major objection to this type of operation seems to be that it results in loss of traffic to regulated carriers. Curiously enough, another objection is that it diverts equipment from trip leasing. "Gray area operations have absorbed part of the equipment ordinarily leased by authorized carriers. Vehicles formerly available to the authorized motor carriers under trip lease during peak seasonal periods or other times may now be unobtainable to the extent that they have been unlawfully leased to shippers."[36] In short the so-called problem of unauthorized transportation" in interstate commerce seems to be that of diversion of traffic from regulated carriers. The fact that it is able to compete and provide a more acceptable alternative to shippers appears to be of little consequence. Demonstration of harm to the economy, the public in general, and economical regulated transport is lacking. The opposition illustrates an attitude of long standing—that if something is illegal, it is economically undesirable. Even the Commission's own staff has doubts as to the undesirability of gray area operations.

Although gray area operations are by definition unauthorized, their development suggests that in some respects they fill a need of a part of the shipping public. . . . Nonetheless, assuming a public need for certain types of services now handled in the gray area, an important question for consideration by legislative, administrative and regulatory agencies dealing with transportation is how

---

[35] Bureau of Transport Economics and Statistics, Interstate Commerce Commission, *Gray Area of Transportation Operations,* Statement No. 6010 (Washington, D.C., June, 1960), p. 69.

[36] *Ibid.,* p. 76.

to provide for these needed services within the scope of presently authorized transport services or authorizations to be granted in the future.[37]

CONCLUSION

Public policy for motor transport has been based on the same general theory that developed in connection with the railroads. It has been predicated on the idea that transportation is basically monopolistic in nature and that this is true of all the agencies of transport. At no time in the regulation of motor transportation has the idea emerged that it possessed all of the characteristics of a competitive industry and that whatever regulation of it is necessary in the public interest must be within the framework of competition. Motor transport has none of the economic characteristics of the railroads, and endeavors to force it into this mold have failed in their objective. Restriction of entry can restrict competition among common carriers, among contract carriers, and between both groups, but it is powerless to deal with exempt carriage and with private carriers. Furthermore the restrictions serve to maintain higher rates than are necessary for both types, at least insofar as these are not affected by nonregulated competition, and it thereby stimulates exempt and private carriage, with the consequent possibility of encouraging a continuous oversupply of facilities.

The establishing of minimum rates by public authority encounters all the difficulties of minimum price fixing where firms are directly competitive. The only successful way to make this work is by restricting entry so as to create monopoly—a policy that can scarcely be defended on economic grounds even if one grants the dubious assumption that it can be made effective. Similarly, the regulation of the general level of rates and maximum rates is not necessary in the public interest, to say nothing of the fact that a reasonable gauge of what they should be has not been developed and, by the very nature of the economics of motor transport, cannot be.

The reasons for the difficulties and shortcomings of regulation are the small scale of operations, the multiplicity of operators, and the various categories into which they fall. Even if the law did not provide for the distinction between common, contract, and private carriers, the facts of motor carriage would compel it, at least as long as private enterprise in business and the right of a person to supply his own transportation remain. As has already been stated, if there had been no railroads, and

---

[37] *Ibid.*, p. 105. The Doyle Report is equivocal on this matter. See *National Transportation Policy*, pp. 507–14. Gray area operations also exist in water and air transport.

if motor transport had developed without them, the pattern of regulation would have been totally different. The historical precedent of railroad regulation does not warrant the carrying-over of its procedures to something for which it was never devised and does not fit, nor does the presence of the railroads today necessitate it or support it.

At the present time, much is made of the need to protect the common carrier, and the assumption is also prevalent that common carriage calls for rate regulation. What this means for interagency competition will be discussed in a subsequent chapter, but as far as common carriage by motor vehicle is concerned, the elaborate scheme of control of entry, rate regulation, and the accompaniments to these are unnecessary, at least for the protection of public interest. If there is a place for common carriers in motor transport, the competitive price mechanism will indicate it, if it is given a chance to operate, and the necessary services will be forthcoming. To say that the failure to restrict competition in this area prejudices the small shipper ignores the fact that the large shipper has other alternatives at his disposal.[38] Nor does enforcement of common carrier obligations require control of entry and rate fixing. Certification could still be retained to ensure that the supplier was fit, willing, and able, and common carriage could still be required to assume the usual obligations. Similarly, if desired, the obligations of contract carriers could be increased to afford more protection to the shippers with whom the contracts are made, and exemptions could be diminished—or for that matter, eliminated—if it were felt that such was in the public interest. All this could be done without the present restrictive controls; that is, it could be accomplished fully within a competitive framework.

The authority of the Interstate Commerce Commission over hours of work of employees, standards of equipment, and safety is not an integral part of economic regulation. This is more properly a matter for executive and policing control, rather than for quasi-judicial and quasi-legislative administration. It is rather absurd to give a body like

---

[38] Regulated carriers have failed miserably to meet the needs of the small shippers. "Complaints from shippers indicate a continued trend in which some motor carriers subject to our jurisdiction refuse to handle what they consider undesirable freight. With the high-level economy affording near-capacity operations for many motor carriers, a preference at times is given to higher paying freight, while low-rated commodities are ignored." Interstate Commerce Commission, *80th Annual Report, 1966* (Washington, D.C.: U.S. Government Printing Office, 1967), p. 20. It is also reported that the growth in total volume of small shipment traffic moving by regulated carriers has been insignificant since 1946. The Regular Common Carrier Conference of the American Trucking Associations now shows signs of taking this matter seriously.

the Interstate Commerce Commission such a task when applied to the enormous number of private vehicles on the highway.[39]

Finally, the problems of the gray area, whatever they may be, are largely legal in nature. The rapid growth of this form of motor transport is indicative of the breakdown of regulation. The restrictions imposed upon common and contract carriers impede their flexibility and adaptability to such an extent that they are unable to meet the public demands for service. The argument that the gray area needs to be curbed for reasons of public safety can scarcely be taken seriously. The contention that it must be controlled to protect the shipper falls into the same category. The responsibility of the state is adequately discharged if shippers are able to ascertain the kind of carrier they are employing and the responsibilities that fall on it. If shippers are willing to take the risk of transporting by other than common or contract carriers, it is difficult to see why the state should prevent them from doing so. It may be that the state may wish to impose liability responsibilities on all carriers for hire, but this does not necessitate restrictions on the types of commodities that can be transported, nor on the number of carriers engaged in transporting them. The pressure to curb gray area activities arises not from concern for the shipper but from the desire to reserve, by restrictive means, as much traffic as possible for common carriers. The more severe the limitations that are imposed, the greater will be the pressures to evade them, because something more than a few recalcitrants is involved.[40]

[39] This responsibility has now been transferred to the Department of Transportation.

[40] For an analysis of the theory of motor carrier regulation, see D. F. Pegrum, "The Economic Basis of Public Policy for Motor Transport," *Land Economics,* Vol. XXVIII, No. 3 (August, 1952), pp. 244–63. See also J. R. Meyer *et al., The Economics of Competition in the Transportation Industries* (Cambridge: Harvard University Press, 1959), chaps. iv, vii, and viii. For a detailed and critical analysis of entry control, see J. C. Nelson, "The Effects of Entry Control in Surface Transport," National Bureau of Economic Research, *Transportation Economics* (New York: Columbia University Press, 1965), pp. 381–422.

REGULATION OF AIR, WATER, AND PIPE-LINE TRANSPORTATION

REGULATION OF AIR TRANSPORTATION

INTRODUCTION

The regulation of air transportation falls into a somewhat different category from that of rail, motor, and water transport in that policy regarding air transportation has involved both regulation and promotion. The same agency has had to deal with each of these, as a result of which it has been engaged in economic regulation and the administration of subsidy and public aid at the same time. The Interstate Commerce Commission has never been faced with the problem of administering subsidies and public aid. The fact that the Civil Aeronautics Board has been required to be both a regulatory and a promotional agency has had a significant influence on the policies it has adopted.

The regulation of air transportation has also been closely associated with public responsibility on technical developments in the industry, particularly as they have related to safety of passenger operations. As a consequence, there has been a considerable amount of mingling of control designed to promote safety in aviation with economic regulation. This has been accompanied by public participation in the development of technical aids for navigation and airports. Legislation over the years has brought about a changing allocation of responsibilities for the carrying-out of the various programs, although economic regulation has remained in the hands of the Civil Aeronautics Board. Nevertheless the latter, in developing its policies, has been compelled to pay attention to technical problems, and this may have had, and still may have, some bearing on its decisions regarding competition or the limitations on it.

THE AGENCIES OF CONTROL

Early Legislation

At the outset, federal policy on aviation was concerned with matters of navigation, safety, and promotion. The first federal interest in air transportation came through the activities of the Post Office Department, which began to experiment with air mail as early as 1911. In 1916, Congress made some appropriations to the Post Office for experimental air-mail service. In 1918, air-mail service between Washington and New York was begun with airplanes provided by the War Department. In the same year the Post Office took over the operation with its own equipment and in the course of the next two years extended service to Chicago, San Francisco, Minneapolis, and St. Louis. Until 1924, air-mail route operation was limited to daylight flying; but in that year, night service was begun west of Chicago, and by 1925 a night airway system from coast to coast had been established.

By 1925 the initial experimentation stage was over, and the development of government service had reached the point where private operation of both mail and passengers seemed feasible. Congress responded to the changed situation by passing the Air Mail (Kelly) Act of 1925 and the Air Commerce Act of 1926. The first of these authorized the Postmaster General to award contracts for the carriage of mail to private companies on the basis of competitive bidding. This gave the carriers an assured source of income upon which they could undertake to build a passenger and express business. The Air Commerce Act provided for the construction and maintenance of civil airways and aids to navigation, and the regulation of private and commercial operators with regard to matters of safety by the Department of Commerce. During this period and down to 1934, air transportation was largely under the control of large manufacturing enterprises interested in promoting air transport through air-mail payments as an outlet for airplanes which they were undertaking to produce.

The unsatisfactory nature of air-mail contract arrangements led to a revision of the legislation by Congress in the Air Mail acts of 1934 and 1935. Under this legislation the Postmaster General was to award air-mail contracts and enforce air-mail regulations. The Interstate Commerce Commission was to set fair and reasonable rates of mail pay, and the payments were to be kept within the limits of anticipated postage revenues. Finally, the Bureau of Air Commerce in the Department of

Commerce was to regulate safety in air transport, and was made responsible for airway maintenance and development.

The Air Mail Act had serious deficiencies. By 1938 the air transport industry faced critical financial difficulties; many of the major lines faced the threat of bankruptcy, and much of the original investment in air lines had been dissipated. Financial difficulties were also aggravated by a series of accidents in the winter of 1936–37 which served to undermine public confidence. Meanwhile the aviation industry had been separated into two definite parts, namely, transport and manufacturing. This led to the passage of the Civil Aeronautics Act of 1938, which established comprehensive federal control over all phases of interstate air transportation.

Early airport development was financed approximately equally by municipalities and private investors. The Air Commerce Act of 1926 prevented the federal government from participating in the direct operation and construction of airports. However, funds were advanced through the Civil Works Administration and the Federal Emergency Relief Administration during the depression of the thirties, and after 1933 federal contributions became the principal source of funds. The Civil Aeronautics Act of 1938 removed the limitations on federal participation in airport development and provided specific powers for the planning of airport development and improvement. As a result of the recommendations of the Civil Aeronautics Authority the federal government in 1940 embarked upon a comprehensive program of airport development.

The Civil Aeronautics Act of 1938

The Civil Aeronautics Act provided for comprehensive control of civil aviation in the United States and for regulation of for-hire air transport engaged in interstate commerce, similar to that which was exercised over other carriers by the Interstate Commerce Commission. To carry out the provisions of the law, Congress established a Civil Aeronautics Authority, to which were transferred the functions previously assigned to the Department of Commerce and the Interstate Commerce Commission. The Authority was to consist of five members appointed by the President with the advice and consent of the Senate, the term of office being six years. It was the intention of Congress that the Authority should be an independent regulatory commission comparable to the Interstate Commerce Commission. The Act also established, within the Authority, an Administrator and an Air Safety Board. The

Administrator was to be appointed by the President with the advice and consent of the Senate, but he could be removed from office at the will of the President. It was his duty to foster the development of civil aeronautics and air commerce, and to encourage the establishment of civil airways, landing areas, and other air navigation facilities. In addition, he might be assigned other duties by the Civil Aeronautics Authority. The Air Safety Board was to consist of three members appointed by the President with the consent of the Senate, to hold office for a period of six years, but the law contained no provisions for removal from office during the period of appointment. The Air Safety Board was a fact-finding body set up to investigate aircraft accidents and to make recommendations to the Civil Aeronautics Authority for measures to prevent them. Although the Board was to make its reports to the Authority, it was nevertheless required to exercise and perform its powers and duties independently of the latter.

The organizational structure of the Civil Aeronautics Authority was modified by Reorganization Plan No. 4, promulgated by President F. D. Roosevelt in 1940. The name of the five-man regulatory body was changed from the Civil Aeronautics Authority to the Civil Aeronautics Board; the Administrator became the Administrator of Civil Aeronautics, and the Air Safety Board was abolished. The functions of the Air Safety Board were transferred to the Administrator, whose organization became known as the Civil Aeronautics Administration (C.A.A.). The Administrator was made responsible to the Department of Commerce, and the Civil Aeronautics Board was also placed in the Department of Commerce. The Board, however, retained its complete independence as a regulatory agency, but the Secretary of Commerce was given control over its budgeting and accounting.

THE FEDERAL AVIATION ACT OF 1958[1]

The complex problems relating to the use of air space and conflict among the various agencies concerned with air navigation were climaxed by two serious accidents in 1958. Congress took immediate action to deal with the situation by passing the Federal Aviation Act of 1958. This law continued the functions of the Civil Aeronautics Board as set forth in the Act of 1938 as modified by the reorganization plan. It also incorporated the separation of mail pay from subsidy, as provided by Reorganization Plan No. 10 of 1953. In addition, it created the Federal

[1] Public Law 85–726, 85th Cong., 2d sess. (1958); 72 Stat. 731; 49 U.S.C. par. 1301 *et seq.*

Aviation Agency to take over the functions of the Civil Aeronautics Administration. The new law now embraces all legislation relating to the regulation of aviation, continuing the powers of the Civil Aeronautics Board, just as though the law had not been passed. Regulation of air transport can therefore be discussed as though the present law had been passed in 1938.

The Civil Aeronautics Board

Declaration of Policy. The Federal Aviation Act contains a declaration of policy to guide the Board in its economic regulation of air transport. This declaration is similar to the one embodied in the Interstate Commerce Act, although it contains no statement with regard to wages and working conditions, nor does it make any reference to other forms of transportation. It is evident that Congress intends that the Board shall regulate air transportation independently of, and without regard to, the effects of its actions and policies on the other agencies. There is also a provision in the law which declares that every citizen of the United States has a public right of freedom of transit through the navigable air space of the United States.

Certificates of Public Convenience and Necessity. The Act provides that no air carrier shall engage in air transportation unless it has a certificate of public convenience and necessity from the Board. However, the Board may, if it sees fit, grant exemption from this provision to any air carrier not engaged in scheduled air transportation, and to any scheduled air carrier if its operations are conducted during daylight hours. The original Act contained a "grandfather" clause, but this was deleted in the new law. When a certificate authorizes the transportation of mail, the carrier must provide necessary and adequate facilities and service, and must transport mail whenever required to do so by the Postmaster General. No certified carrier is permitted to abandon any route or any part thereof without the sanction of the Board. No foreign air carrier may engage in air transportation between the United States and another country unless it receives a permit from the Board. All certificates authorizing United States nationals to engage in overseas or foreign air transportation and all permits to foreign companies must receive the approval of the President of the United States.

Rates and Fares. The rates and fares of all air carriers must be published, and the tariffs containing these must be open to public inspection. All tariffs must be strictly observed, and rebates are prohibited. Thirty days' notice is required for all changes in rates, and the Board may suspend proposals for such changes for a period up to 180 days. No domestic or foreign air carrier may give any undue preference or unreasonable advantage to any person, locality, or description of traffic. Certified air carriers are required to establish just and reasonable rates, reasonable through service with other air carriers, and safe and adequate service, equipment, and facilities. The Board, after hearing, may prescribe the lawful rate to be charged or the maximum and/or minimum rate. On the overseas traffic of American lines the Board can prescribe the maximum and/or minimum rates, but not the exact one. The Board, however, does not have authority over rates to or between foreign countries served by American lines.

The Act also contains a rule of rate making somewhat similar to that of the Interstate Commerce Act, except that there are no instructions to consider the effects of the rates of air carriers on other modes. The rule requires that the Board shall consider, among other factors:

(1) The effect of such rates upon the movement of traffic; (2) the need in the public interest of adequate and efficient transportation of persons and property by air carriers at the lowest cost consistent with the furnishing of such service; (3) such standards respecting the quality of service to be rendered by air carriers as may be prescribed by or pursuant to law; (4) the inherent advantages of transportation by aircraft; and (5) the need of each air carrier for revenue sufficient to enable such air carrier under honest, economical, and efficient management, to provide adequate and efficient air carrier service.

Air carriers may establish through service and joint rates and fares with other common carriers. When the common carriers are subject to the jurisdiction of the Interstate Commerce Commission, matters concerning joint arrangements may be referred to a joint board consisting of an equal number of representatives designated by the chairmen of the Board and the Interstate Commerce Commission. The joint boards enjoy the same powers as the Civil Aeronautics Board possesses with regard to through service and joint rates between air carriers.[2]

Transportation of Mail. The Postmaster General is authorized to make rules and regulations necessary to ensure the safe and expeditious carriage of mail by aircraft, provided that these are not inconsistent with orders or regulations of the Board, but anyone aggrieved by the schedules established by the Post Office may apply to the Board for review. The Board is directed to fix and determine the fair and

[2] On February 1, 1967, the Civil Aeronautics Board announced that it and the Interstate Commerce Commission had established informal procedures for the cooperative assembling of information and the joint gathering of data on the coordination of intermodal air-surface transportation. See Civil Aeronautics Board, Docket No. 16946 (Feb. 1, 1967) and I.C.C. Docket, *Ex Parte No. 251* (Feb. 1, 1967). See also: *Air-Truck Coordination and Competition,* I.C.C. Bureau of Economics, Statement No. 67–1 (Feb. 1967).

reasonable rates of compensation for the transportation of mail by aircraft, and may fix different rates for different carriers and different classes of carriers. The rates thus established must be such as to give the carrier adequate revenue from mail and other sources to maintain and continue the development of air transportation to the extent and quality required for the commerce of the United States, the Postal Service, and the national defense. However, the Postmaster General is required to pay only the amount to which the carriers are reasonably entitled for the service performed in transporting the mail, the Board being required to make up the difference between this and the total payment needed by the carrier out of appropriations made for that purpose. Thus the Post Office is supposed to be relieved of the airmail subsidy, but the Board still has the responsibility of deciding what the service pay shall be.

Intercorporate Relations. The law prohibits all mergers, consolidations, or acquisition of control involving two or more air carriers unless permission is granted by the Civil Aeronautics Board. Similar provisions apply to such arrangements between an air carrier and any person engaged in any other branch of aeronautics, a foreign air carrier, or any other common carrier. All consolidations, mergers, or acquisitions of control may be sanctioned by the Board only after hearings have been held on the application. Furthermore, if the applicant is a carrier other than an air carrier, such an applicant is, for the purpose of these proceedings, considered to be an air carrier. In other words, the Interstate Commerce Commission does not have the power to sanction the extension into air transportation of carriers under its jurisdiction.

Aircraft Accident Investigations. It was the duty of the Board to investigate accidents and report the facts, and to make recommendations to the Administrator of the Federal Aviation Agency to prevent such accidents in the future. The Board had to provide for appropriate participation of the Administrator, but he could not participate in the determination of the probable cause of an accident. If military aircraft were involved, appropriate arrangements for the participation of the military authorities had to be made. When substantial questions of public safety arose, the Board could establish a Special Board of Inquiry, consisting of one of its members acting as Chairman and two public representatives appointed by the President.[3]

Methods of Competition. The Act gives to the Board powers, similar to those possessed by the Federal Trade Commission, to deal

---

[3] These functions have now been transferred to the National Transportation Safety Board in the Department of Transportation. See Chapter 21.

with unfair or deceptive practices, or unfair methods of competition in air transportation or the sale thereof. It may issue cease and desist orders if it finds that these conditions exist.

Accounts and Reports. All air carriers may be required to make such annual and other reports as are ordered by the Board. The latter is instructed to prescribe the forms of all accounts and records.

The Federal Aviation Agency

The Federal Aviation Act of 1958 provided for a separate agency to exercise federal control over the physical facilities of civil aviation. The military was required to co-operate with the agency so as to assure conformity to plans and policies for the use of navigable air space.

The Administrator of the Federal Aviation Agency is appointed by the President with the advice and consent of the Senate. He is responsible for the exercise of all powers and the discharge of all duties of the Agency. In carrying out these responsibilities, he is answerable only to the President. He is, however, expected to co-operate with state, territorial, municipal, and other local agencies in the discharge of his duties.

It is the duty of the Administrator to give full consideration to the requirements of national defense, and of commercial and general aviation, and of the public right of freedom of transit through the navigable air space. To this end he is authorized and directed to make plans, policies, and rules for the use of navigable air space, and to acquire, improve, and operate air navigation facilities. In other words, he has charge of the national airways system. All federal funds to be expended in connection with any landing area can be disbursed only on his recommendation, and he must be informed even on all military installations. The same remarks apply to all other airports and landing space, even though the expenditure of federal funds is not involved. The Administrator is instructed to develop long-range plans for air navigation and landing facilities. Included in this is the administration of the Federal Airport Act of 1946, and the allocation of federal aid made available under this legislation to airport projects which conform to the National Airport Plan. This plan, which was originally developed, and revised annually, by the Civil Aeronautics Agency, is now under the direction of the Administrator. He also took over all of the functions previously exercised by the Secretary of Commerce under the Federal Airport Act. All certifications and registrations of aircraft are under the Federal Aviation Agency, as well as the prescription of safety rules and regulations. It should be remembered. however, that investigation of aircraft accidents is the responsibility of the Civil Aeronautics Board, although it has no powers to prescribe any rules or regulations to promote safety. In addition, if the Administrator denies the application of an airman for a certificate for flying, appeal may be had to the Board. Similarly, any action on the part of the Administrator amending, suspending, or revoking the certificates which he has granted may be appealed to the Board, whose decision on the matter is binding on the Administrator.[4]

STATE REGULATION

The role of the states in the regulation of air transportation is of relatively minor significance, particularly in light of the extensive powers of the Federal Aviation Agency, the fact that the bulk of air transportation is interstate commerce, and the sole responsibility and authority of the federal government over air-mail transportation. In addition, the Federal Aviation Act does not preclude the exercise of regulatory authority under the Shreveport rule, as does the Motor Carrier Act. Nevertheless, state and local authorities can, and some do, exercise considerable authority over safety and navigation, as well as over economic matters such as fares and security issues. Where the service performed by the carrier is solely intrastate and its business does not go outside that category, state authority can act without federal interference. Where interstate activities are also involved, the issue is not so clear, unless there is a substantial federal question, in which case federal power is supreme. For example, in *Western Air Lines* v. *Public Utilities Commission of California* (1954)[5] the Supreme Court declined to interfere. Western Air Lines had raised its air coach fares between Los Angeles and San Francisco with the approval of the Civil Aeronautics Board. The California Commission ordered an investigation of the fares. It approved the increase in fares as of the date of the order (May 7, 1951) but required Western Air Lines to refund the excess of fares collected between March 1, 1951, and May 7, 1951. With the responsibility for adequate revenues for interstate air carriers and those carrying mail in the hands of the federal government, it would appear to be desirable that the issue should be clarified so as to leave control in the hands of the Civil Aeronautics Board. However, developing technology indicates that much strictly local service by air may develop in the near future. This may well be an area for the desirable exercise of state authority. The more

[4] All of the functions of the Federal Aviation Agency have now been transferred to the Department of Transportation.

[5] 342 U.S. 908.

precise delineation of state and federal jurisdiction than exists today will have to await developments, but it is by no means certain that almost exclusive control will or should be placed in the hands of the federal government.[6] If competition develops extensively and air transport becomes thoroughly self-sustaining, there will be even less reason for it.

REGULATION BY THE CIVIL AERONAUTICS BOARD

One of the most difficult tasks, perhaps the most difficult, of the Civil Aeronautics Board pertains to the policies to be adopted in granting permission to carriers to offer service for hire. At the present time, this covers certificates of public convenience and necessity to common carriers offering trunk service, feeder and local services, all-cargo freight carriers, and supplemental or irregular carriers. The Board does not possess the authority for economic regulation of contract carriers, although it has asked Congress to pass regulation giving it this power.[7]

Certification of Carriers

Trunk-Line Certification. Regulatory policy, which requires that common carriers be certified to offer service, makes it incumbent on the applicant to prove public convenience and necessity. This usually carries the implication that the existing occupant of a route will be afforded protection against competition if it is rendering adequate service and if competition by another carrier will impair its operations. At the same time that it provided for certification, however, the Civil Aeronautics Act instructed the Board to consider competition to the extent necessary to assure the development of a sound transportation system, and it also prohibited the Board from approving consolidations which would lead to monopoly. There was no clear understanding of the role that competition might be expected to play, nor the extent to which effective competition might be possible in air transportation. Moreover, the requirement that the Board fix air-mail rates in accordance with the needs of individual air lines, which, at the outset at least, meant that the mail was to subsidize air transport, was bound to result in some limitations on certification. In other words, the Board was faced at the very beginning with the necessity of trying to reconcile a number of contradictory instructions.

[6] In California, Pacific Southwest Airways serves as a commuter line between the major cities, without airmail contracts and without federal regulation. It is one of the most successful airlines in the country and offers severe competition to the major trunk lines.

[7] Civil Aeronautics Board, *Annual Report, 1961* (Washington, D.C.: U.S. Government Printing Office, 1962), p. 10.

When the Act became effective in 1938, it was necessary to give existing air lines "grandfather" rights under the law for the routes then in bona fide operation by them. Eighteen trunk-line carriers received certificates at that time, although only eleven are in operation today. No new air carrier has been certified for trunk-line service since the original act was passed. Certification in this area, therefore, has been confined to the granting of new routes to existing carriers.

At the beginning of its administration the Board followed a cautious policy of certification of new services, seeking to protect existing carriers and, in extension applications, to favor the carriers already serving the same general area. In 1943, however, the Board stated what came to be known as the "presumption" doctrine.[8] This meant that there was a presumption in favor of permitting direct competition in air carrier services where traffic appeared to be sufficient to support them. As a result of this policy a considerable amount of additional direct competition developed rapidly, and even more indirect competition. The Board soon came to the conclusion that it had proceeded too far, too fast, in the sanctioning of competition, especially when the government had to guarantee the success of operations through air subsidies. A more restrained policy was therefore put into effect under which greater attention was given to the preservation of air-line earnings and the promotion of stability in the industry. In other words, the theory underlying public convenience and necessity came to the fore again. However, the rapid growth of air passenger transport in the country led the Board by 1955 to alter its policy again by authorizing the development of competitive services on a large scale. Most of the increased competition has taken place on the more heavily traveled routes. The granting of certificates for new operations has indicated a tendency to favor the weaker lines in order to strengthen them and to lessen the disparity between them and the Big Four. No plan that seems to have been clearly thought through has been evident in the implementation of the policy.

The lack of a clear-cut recognition and comprehension of policy was evidenced in the Los Angeles/San Francisco—Vancouver, B.C. case involving the application for a certificate of public convenience and necessity for a through route to Vancouver, British Columbia, by Western Air Lines and United Air Lines.[9] This case was complicated by the fact that the Board could issue only one certificate because it was to a foreign country. Nevertheless, the principles underlying the

[8] *Transcontinental and Western Air, North-South California Service,* 4 C.A.B. 373 (1943).

[9] *Los Angeles/San Francisco—Vancouver, B.C. Case,* Civil Aeronautics Board, Docket No. 16984 *et al.,* January 25, 1967.

decision were in line with domestic policy. The Examiner awarded the certificate to United Air Lines on the ground that it was already serving Vancouver with a stopover in Seattle, and on the basis of the various criteria the Board had traditionally applied. He pointed out that no case had been cited in which the carrier established in the market had been supplanted by a competitive newcomer as the dominant carrier. The Board reversed the Examiner and awarded the certificate to Western Air Lines because the certification of Western would make available to the traveling public the benefits of competitive service. If the Examiner was unable to ascertain the criteria used by the Board it is difficult to see how anyone else can.

The Board seems to be guided by the idea that regulation is necessary to preserve competition because without such regulation competition would result in the elimination of so many companies that competition would be destroyed. How this could happen when it seems to be recognized that economies of scale have definite limitations in air transport is somewhat of a mystery. What this amounts to is that the Board favors a policy denoted by that euphemistic term "regulated competition"[10] which means dividing traffic by administrative fiat among competitors who are restricted to the numbers necessary to preserve all of the competitors.

These strictures must be tempered somewhat by the fact that the subsidy provisions of the law are still applicable if any of the carriers should fail to earn a fair return. In addition, the trunk lines are still required to continue service to points which may not be profitable, thereby giving rise to internal subsidy. What the policy of the Board would be if these two limitations were removed is impossible to say and the Board has failed to indicate its reaction to them.

Local and Feeder Service. The local service carriers—or as they are frequently called, "feeder" air lines—operate over routes between smaller cities, and between these cities and the larger centers. The Board decided in 1944 to authorize and support this type of service which was independent of the trunk-line systems. At the outset it was

---

[10] Many motor carrier applicants for certificates have espoused "regulated competition" rather vigorously. They have argued for competition when seeking admission and have then opposed additional entrants once they have obtained their routes.

In authorizing Pacific Airlines to offer nonstop service between Burbank, California, and Las Vegas, Nevada, "The CAB noted the Pacific Air Lines is still faced with a greater amount of competition from other federally regulated carriers in its major markets than any other local service carrier, and also with competition from unregulated Pacific Southwest Airways to a unique extent. The Board said its action is designed to allow Pacific to compete on a more equal footing—not necessarily in the same market PSA serves—without significantly altering the competitive balance among regulated carriers." (Civil Aeronautics Board, *Release,* June 13, 1967.)

decided to establish such transportation on an experimental basis where there appeared to be a justifiable expectation of success at reasonable cost to the government. Applications of this type were assigned on an "area" basis. Initially, the certificates were granted only for a three-year period, but when the question of renewal came up for consideration, the issue that emerged was whether the Board intended to establish two separate air-line systems in the country, namely, the domestic trunk-line carriers, which would serve only the larger communities without subsidy, and the local service lines, which would have to be more or less permanently subsidized by the federal government. The Board espoused this policy. At the present time, certificates for local service carriers are virtually in the same permanent category as those for trunk lines.

The Civil Aeronautics Board adopted the general policy of imposing restrictions on feeder air lines so as to prevent direct competition by them with the trunk lines. Usually, they are required to serve all points on their routes on all flights, although there are modifications of this. In addition, when a feeder line offers services to local points between major terminals, it may be able to sell tickets for travel between those terminals, but it cannot operate nonstop flights; as a consequence, it offers only incidental competition to the trunk lines.

Survival of feeder service is almost completely dependent on subsidy. Recently, the Board has made some attempts to reduce the costs from this by the adoption of a "use it or lose it" policy. Under this, service will be withdrawn from points from which, over a test period, the carrier did not enplane a minimum of five passengers a day. Nevertheless, it expected an increase in subsidy payments in the future because of the expansion of local services, although it hoped that this trend might be reversed at some future date to some reasonable possible cost.[11] Virtually all of the subsidy of $68 million in 1960 was for local services of one form or another.[12]

The Civil Aeronautics Board has now adopted a new policy to permit the local service airlines to compete directly on a nonstop basis with trunk-line carriers in 101 major markets less than 300 miles apart, but without subsidy on this service. It hopes to cut subsidy payments without any serious impact on the trunk lines. On March 31, 1967 the Board took under consideration a revised class subsidy rate formula for the 13 local service carriers. Subsidy payments under the revised formula would be related to services between each pair of points

[11] Civil Aeronautics Board, *Annual Report, 1960*, p. 23.
[12] *Loc. cit.*

for each of the carriers, and would be made for up to two round-trips per day in subsidy eligible operations. Under this formula and on the assumption that local service passenger revenue continues to grow by at least 20 percent, per year, the Board estimates that the net subsidy for 1967 will be $54 million.[13]

All-Cargo Carriers. In the period immediately following World War II, literally hundreds of new air transport ventures were undertaken under the nonscheduled exemptions granted by the Civil Aeronautics Board. Many of these developed business on an exclusive-cargo basis in what were really scheduled operations. In 1949 the Board certified four of the new companies for a temporary period of five years. These temporary certificates were granted on what was characterized as a "promotional" basis, although it was recognized that they were in competition with the air-freight service of the scheduled air lines. It was felt that these freight lines, operating without benefit of air-mail subsidies, would develop an efficient service that would serve as a yardstick for measuring the efficiency of other carriers of cargo. As a further step in enforcing self-sufficiency, the Board refused to authorize these all-cargo carriers to carry express for the Railway Express Agency or to transport mail. However, by 1956 all four of the all-cargo carriers were authorized to transport express, and in 1956 they were granted permission to carry mail for one year on a nonsubsidy basis. In 1958 the Board denied the request to put the all-cargo carriers on a mail subsidy basis but left the basic question open for future consideration.[14]

In August, 1964 the CAB adopted a policy designed to make the all-cargo carriers specialists for large volume airfreight in all-cargo aircraft. It was intended that the combination carriers would concentrate on small volume shipments. The Board established blocked-space service as the exclusive domain of the all-cargo carriers, the blocked-space service affording special rates in exchange for a contracted volume of traffic during a given period of time. Slick Airways and Flying Tiger were certified for the service, while American, TWA and United were denied the privilege of filing similar tariffs.[15] American Airlines challenged the ruling in the courts but the decision of the Board was upheld.[16]

[13] For a discussion of local service subsidies, see H. R. Swaine, "A Proposal for Control of Local Service Subsidies," *Journal of Air Law and Commerce,* Vol. XXXI, No. 3 (1965), pp. 181–97. All subsidy to helicopter services was discontinued as of the end of 1965.

[14] *Ibid.,* p. 8.

[15] Civil Aeronautics Board, *Annual Report, 1965,* p. 40.

[16] *American Airlines Inc.* v. *Civil Aeronautics Board,* 359 F. 2d 624 (1966); certiorari denied by the U.S. Supreme Court, 385 U.S. 843 (1966).

The Board's policy obviously is that of encouraging the development of freight service. The reason for confining blocked-space to the all-cargo carriers is another illustration of encouraging competition by dividing traffic and restricting entry. The combination carriers could have been accorded the same rights, without any special advantage accruing to them, if they had been required to restrict blocked-space to all-cargo planes, with minimum rates covering the full cost of the service of such planes, or, in other words, by a complete separation of the services of the combination planes from the all-cargo ones.[17]

At the same time, however, routes of the all-cargo carriers are limited as to the cities which may be served, Flying Tiger at present being confined to 14 cities. It is now applying to add 12 cities to its present transcontinental system, "at a time when there are indications that the climate of the Civil Aeronautics Board may be receptive to such requests."[18] Why all-cargo lines should be limited in the cities they serve when they are not subsidized nor supported by airmail contracts is curious indeed. One must assume that the purpose is to protect the freight business of the trunk lines, even though the latter are not allowed to compete for "blocked-space" traffic.

Supplemental or Irregular Carriers.   Soon after the Civil Aeronautics Board took office in 1938, it acted to exempt from regulation air carriers engaged solely in nonscheduled operations. Following World War II, these grew rapidly in number, as a result of which the Board required all "irregular air carriers" to obtain letters of registration in order to be able to continue operations after June 10, 1947. Further restrictions were applied to the large irregular carriers, which aroused bitter opposition. The Board undertook an investigation in 1951 leading to a report in 1955 which enlarged somewhat the scope of operations of these carriers.[19] The Board recognized the value of the charter operations and the various specialized services performed by these carriers. It accordingly authorized unlimited charter operations in the carriage of passengers and property, and individualized ticketed operations by each carrier not to exceed 10 trips per month in the same direction between any single pair of points. This gave the irregular carriers a sort of roving authority to go where they pleased as long as they stayed within the 10-trip limit. The regularly certified carriers protested this

---

[17] It should be remembered that the all-cargo lines carry freight for the military under government contracts for which the CAB establishes minimum rates "consistent with sound economic conditions," that is, to afford protection for the carriers against too much competition. Flying Tiger was the only carrier as of March, 1967 offering domestic blocked-space service.

[18] *Aviation Week and Space Technology,* May 1, 1967, p. 27.

[19] *Large Irregular Air Carrier Investigation,* Civil Aeronautics Board, Docket No. 5132 (decided January 28, 1959).

ruling, and the Circuit Court of Appeals held that the Board lacked the authority to issue certificates which restricted the number of flights to be provided and which were not for linear-type routes.[20] The Board felt that this was a severe blow to its efforts to promote supplemental air service. It therefore asked Congress for amendatory legislation. Congress responded by enacting temporary legislation on July 14, 1960, which essentially continued the law as applied by the Board for 20 months pending further Congressional action.[21]

In 1961 Congress amended the Federal Aviation Act so as to provide a basis for certifying supplemented air carriers on a restricted basis. In 1965 the CAB held public hearings on the domestic applications of supplemental carriers. In March, 1966 the Board awarded certificates to 10 carriers permitting charter operations and also the right to charter aircraft to tour operators who would in turn sell package tours to individual members of the general public. The Board held that the charters would economically strengthen the supplemental carriers without having a materially adverse effect on the certified route carriers. The inclusive tour charters were authorized for a five-year period, but the other certificates were for an indefinite period.

The Board has also authorized air taxi carriers to provide scheduled and demand services for the transportation of passengers, property, and mail under limited conditions in aircraft not exceeding 12,500 pounds gross take-off weight. These carriers are not eligible for subsidy, but they operate with a high degree of flexibility and with virtually no restrictions. The CAB now proposes to grant authority to air taxi carriers to utilize aircraft having a maximum certified take-off weight of over 12,500 pounds, when the maximum passenger-carrying capacity does not exceed 12 persons.[22] These carriers operate under a blanket exemption without certification.

Rates and Fares

Passenger Fares. Despite the fact that passenger transportation has been the most significant area of air transport development since the

---

[20] *United Air Lines* v. *Civil Aeronautics Board*, 278 F. (2d) 446 (1960). This order was vacated by *All-American Airways, Inc.* v. *United Air Lines, Inc.*, 364 U.S. 297 (1960), pending further Congressional action.

[21] Civil Aeronautics Board, *Annual Report, 1960*, pp. 35 and 45. As a result of action by the President under a letter dated January 9, 1961, the Board undertook reconsideration of the certificates granting the 10-trip limit and unlimited charter operations to 22 supplemental carriers, but continued the permission pending a final decision (*Large Irregular Air Carrier Investigation*, Civil Aeronautics Board, Supplemental Order and Opinion, January 17, 1961).

[22] Civil Aeronautics Board, *Annual Report, 1966*, pp. 9–10.

Civil Aeronautics Board assumed its regulatory authority, and despite the fact that the regulation of air transportation has been predicated on the general theory of control that has governed public policy for transportation in this country, the Board has never developed or announced any general principles for the determination of passenger fares for air travel. So far, the air lines have been given more latitude in setting passenger fares than in making freight rates, but the Board has on a number of occasions taken action to restrict the rate-making discretion of the carriers. From time to time, fares have been adjusted on an *ad hoc* basis. Immediately after World War II, it intervened to reduce passenger fares; then in 1949, it permitted a rise in fares. In 1953, it sanctioned the coach-type fares, with the stipulation that there was to be a 25 per cent differential between coach and first-class charges, this being necessary, in the opinion of the Board, to reflect the cost differentials and to reflect an adequate distinction between the two. No development of policy took place, however; no attempt was made to encourage passenger fares that would eliminate reliance on air mail; and no attempt was made to permit a free pricing policy that would reflect any sort of an economic equilibrium in air passenger transport.

An investigation into the lawfulness of passenger fares was instituted in 1943, but was not pushed to its conclusion. Similarly, another one, undertaken in 1952, was dropped in 1953, but the Board did state that it would not sanction increases unless earnings fell below a level necessary to provide a fair return over a reasonably extended period which included the good years as well as the bad. Finally, a general passenger fare investigation was undertaken in May, 1956.[23] In the decision rendered in November, 1960, the Board concluded "that the record before us is inadequate to the fixing of the fare level. However, the record does permit us to formulate significant standards which will contribute to the regulation of fares."[24]

Probably the real difficulty of the Board, which led to its indecision, lay in its inability to resolve the problem of fixing the appropriate

[23] *General Passenger Fare Investigation*, Civil Aeronautics Board, Docket No. 8008 *et al.*, May, 1960 (decided November 25, 1960) (mimeographed).

[24] *Ibid.*, p. 5. This conclusion was reached despite the long-drawn-out nature of the proceedings, and the comprehensive report of Examiner Ralph L. Wiser. Moreover, the Board could have requested the additional information necessary to reach a definitive conclusion, which it claimed was lacking. Eastern Air Lines (*Eastern Air Lines* v. *Civil Aeronautics Board*, 294 F. [2d] 235 [1961]) filed suit challenging the right of the Civil Aeronautics Board to terminate the investigation without deciding the lawfulness of existing fares. The Supreme Court denied *certiorari*, 368 U.S. 927 (1961). For an extended discussion of the passenger fare problem, see Nelson Lee Smith, "Regulation of Returns to Transportation Agencies," *Law and Contemporary Problems*, "Transportation," Part I, Vol. XXIV, No. 4 (Autumn. 1959), pp. 702–32.

level of prices for competitive firms, coupled, in this case, with the additional fact that it was able to fall back on subsidy to sustain the "weak lines." The Board rejected the operating ratio as the appropriate standard for measuring the general level of rates, and concluded that "only the rate of return on investment indicates the appropriate end result."[25] It concluded that the industry required an over-all return of 10.25 per cent over an extended period of time for the Big Four, and 11.125 per cent for the Intermediate Eight, the weighted average for the domestic trunk-line system being 10.5 per cent. The dilemma which the Board faced, to which it can scarcely be given any credit for indicating a resolution, is best revealed by a quotation from a conclusion in the opinion:

The problem of accommodating the requirements of the weak and strong carriers is, of course, one of the most difficult to be found in regulation. Clearly general fare increases cannot be regarded as the panacea capable of solving the problem. There are other tools which are more appropriate for use in dealing with the less profitable carriers. First, an over-all examination of the general passenger fare structure, an issue excluded from this proceeding, might well result in bringing the costs and revenues of the individual carriers into closer alignment. Second, as the Examiner pointed out, carriers whose needs are not met by general fare level adjustments can seek higher fares, although competitive aspects would preclude them from charging such fares except on some few noncompetitive segments (assuming, of course, that such fares are otherwise lawful). A third tool is that of route realignments designed to produce a more balanced competitive structure. Finally, we are authorized by Section 406 of the Act to grant subsidy payments where we find that such compensation is required in the interests of commerce, the Postal service, and national defense. Whether, and to what extent, any of these approaches should be used will, of course, depend on all surrounding circumstances. Suffice it to say, however, that the Board has available to it a number of techniques for dealing with problems not amenable to solution by regulation of the general level of fares.[26]

Thus stands the situation with regard to air-line passenger fares at the present time, although an informal study of the passenger fare structure is programmed for completion in 1967.

Freight Rates. The policies of the Civil Aeronautics Board have been even less definitive with regard to freight rates than with passenger fares. This is partly the result of the experimental nature of freight movements by air, partly the result of competition between all-cargo lines and the domestic trunk lines, and partly the result of the role of subsidy payments in the development of air transport. Prior to 1944, no

[25] *General Passenger Fare Investigation,* Civil Aeronautics Board, Docket No. 8008 *et al.,* p. 10.

[26] *Ibid.,* pp. 76–77.

air-freight rates had been published by the air lines. In that year, American Airlines introduced an air-freight service with rates that averaged approximately 44 cents a ton-mile, including pickup and delivery. Shortly thereafter, other lines undertook to transport freight under tariffs developed on a ton-mile basis. At the same time, a number of nonscheduled carriers began to offer freight service throughout the country. In 1947 the Board permitted noncertified cargo carriers to operate on a scheduled basis. American, Capital, and United air lines met the challenge by proposing rates of approximately 12 cents a ton-mile on many commodities—a sharp contrast to the mail rates of 45 cents to 60 cents a ton-mile which they were receiving. The Board instituted an investigation into air-freight rates which resulted in the establishment of minimum freight rates.[27] These were (1) a minimum rate of 16 cents per ton-mile for the first 1,000 ton-miles of any shipment and (2) a minimum of 13 cents per ton-mile for anything above 1,000 ton-miles for any shipment. In 1953 the Board granted the request of the cargo lines to increase the minimum 25 per cent. This applied to all carriers of air freight. Lower rates were permitted for back hauls. The all-cargo carriers have also sought to be given the privilege of carrying mail, but so far they have not been put on a mail subsidy basis.

Airmail Compensation

Under the Civil Aeronautics Act of 1938 the Civil Aeronautics Board was required to fix air-mail rates so as to give the carriers whatever revenue was necessary, over and above other sources, to ensure the development of air transportation. In 1951 the payment was divided into two parts, separating mail pay from subsidy. The requirement to do this was incorporated into the Federal Aviation Act of 1958.

Initially, air-mail rates were set so as to build the revenues of the carriers up to the required level. The rapid growth of other sources of air-line income led the Board to appraise the need for air-mail revenues by an allocation of costs on a pound-mile basis between mail and commercial services, although this was not the only factor which was used in fixing mail rates. Two kinds of mail rates were developed: the "service" rate, based on fully distributed costs for carriers which had achieved commercial self-sufficiency, and the "need" rate for those which had not reached this status. In 1951 the service rate for the Big Four was set at 45 cents per ton-mile. This was adjusted in 1954 to a line-haul charge of 30.17 cents per ton-mile, to which were added terminal

[27] *Air Freight Rate Investigation,* 9 C.A.B. 340 (1948).

charges ranging from 3.32 cents per pound to 33.21 cents, depending upon the nature of the airports. These rates apply also to feeder lines. The additional revenue to which the carrier may be entitled under the law is provided by subsidy.

In 1965 domestic airmail rates, by informal conference with the carriers and the Post Office, were reduced by about 8 per cent. The rate through 1966 consisted of a line-haul charge of 27.33 cents per ton-mile plus a sliding scale for terminal charges. This rate expired as of December 31, 1966 and a new scale was proposed by the Examiner which would reduce the line-haul charge to 26.33 cents per ton-mile, commencing January 1, 1967. This recommendation is under review by the Board.

The critical issue with regard to airmail compensation turns on the matter of costs. Express, freight, and half-fare family-plan passenger revenues are treated as by-products and not assigned fully distributed costs.[28] The allocation of those costs, which cannot be traced directly, between passengers and mail, entails arbitrary apportionment and probably overstates the air-mail costs. This surmise seems to be supported by the rates the carriers are willing to offer for air freight. In any case the position of the air lines would be precarious without the air mail. The extent to which air mail involves a hidden subsidy is therefore a debatable question.

Regulation of Service

The Civil Aeronautics Board under both the original and the present law is given control over the standards of service of the carriers under its supervision. Until recently, there has been no direct interference with carrier operations on this score. However, since 1958 the Board has been giving more attention to the problem of adequacy of service.[29] Rulings in a number of cases since 1958 seem to indicate that the Board regards its obligations for regulation of the air lines to be in the same category as that of public utility commissions in such areas as electricity and natural gas. In other words, there seems to be a definite move to replace reliance on competition, as the means of compelling adequacy of service, by orders from the Board, even where competition is direct and could be relied upon as a sufficient disciplinary force on those carriers that wished to stay in business.[30]

[28] Passengers and their luggage are assigned an arbitrary weight of 200 pounds.
[29] See *National Transportation Policy* (Doyle Report), Preliminary Draft of a Report to the Senate Committee on Interstate and Foreign Commerce, 87th Congress, 1st session (Washington, D.C.: U.S. Government Printing Office, 1961), Part VII, chap. 12.
[30] *Ibid.*, pp. 708–20.

The raw root of the adequacy of service question is whether the air transportation needs of the public will be satisfied by dependence on profit incentive in a competitive market, unrestricted by government control, or whether the regulatory structure within which this competition is to operate to satisfy transportation needs is so designed that the profit incentive will not do the job, requiring, therefore, further Government control, resulting ultimately in Government assumption of managerial reins as well as regulation.[31]

Carried to its logical conclusion, the Board's policy leads to the necessity of equal rates for competing carriers between the same places. This serves to deprive the consumer from choosing between different types of service at different prices, which is one of the characteristics of a competitive market. Denial of this privilege by control over service is difficult to reconcile with the Board's sanctioning of irregular or supplemental carriers.

Consolidations and Mergers

Consolidations and mergers of all kinds involving air lines must be approved by the Civil Aeronautics Board. However, after hearings the Board must approve an application for merger, consolidation, or acquisition unless it finds that it is not consistent with public interest. No such acquisition may be approved if it would result in creating a monopoly, thereby restraining competition or jeopardizing another air carrier not a party to the transaction.

In implementing the policy of the Act, the Board has dealt with four types of situations: (1) mergers involving only local service carriers, (2) mergers of local and trunk lines, (3) mergers of trunk lines, and (4) acquisitions by other than air carriers.

Policy on the merging of local service carriers generally seems to favor such consolidations if a stronger enterprise will emerge. The Board requires a showing that the service areas of the merging carriers are similar, that they can readily be integrated from an operational standpoint, and that some through traffic between the areas is available. Only one merger involving a trunk line and a local carrier has been approved, and this entailed the subsidy question.[32] The basic policy, however, has been to keep trunk lines and feeder lines in separate categories. On smaller trunk lines the Board has approved mergers on similar find-

---

[31] *Ibid.,* p. 720. It should be noted that regulation of adequacy of service is quite distinct from safety regulation. Recent widespread complaints regarding service and the treatment of customers have led to inquiries by the Board that may well make the surmise in the above quotation come true.

[32] *Continental-Pioneer Acquisition Case,* Civil Aeronautics Board, Docket No. 6547 (Order No. E–8803), December 7, 1954.

ings, namely, that little diversion from other carriers would result, services would be improved, subsidies would be reduced, and no monopoly or restraint of trade would result from the mergers.

Three important trunk-line merger applications involving the Big Four and smaller trunk lines have been considered. The first was an application of American Airlines to acquire control of Mid-Continent Airlines.[33] This was refused on the ground that American Airlines was already the largest carrier and that approval would have impaired competition unduly. The second application, the request of Eastern Air Lines to acquire Colonial Airlines,[34] was approved because the Board felt that no monopoly consideration was involved; in addition, the fact that Colonial in an independent position would require subsidy was also a consideration.

The third application was that of United Air Lines to acquire Capital Airlines.[35] The latter, unable to meet its equipment obligations, was threatened with bankruptcy. The Board felt that it was faced with the choice of approving the merger, permitting bankruptcy and reorganization, or supporting the firm with subsidy. It was felt that neither of the latter possibilities was feasible. It therefore approved the merger, despite the fact that this made United the largest route system in the country, on the basis of the "failing business" doctrine.[36] It was felt that the inability to rehabilitate Capital Airlines overrode the restrictions of the law with regard to restraint of competition. Other air lines argued that the merger should be conditioned on a redistribution of some of Capital's routes, but the Board disagreed, except for two restrictions designed to protect Allegheny Airlines and Mohawk Airlines (these are local service carriers). Minority opinions agreed with the basic merger plan, but criticized the majority position which had led to such delay that merger seemed to be the only escape available at that late date.

The Board's position on the acquisition of air carriers by other transportation agencies is consistent with its stand on domestic mergers. Its application of the law has virtually excluded surface carriers from

[33] *American Airlines—Acquisition of Control of Mid-Continent Airlines,* 7 C.A.B. 365 (1946).

[34] *Colonial–Eastern Air Lines Case,* Civil Aeronautics Board, Docket No. 6998 (Orders No. E–9945 and No. E–9946), January 11, 1956.

[35] *United-Capital Merger Case,* Civil Aeronautics Board, Docket No. 11699 (Order No. E–16605), decided April 3, 1961.

[36] *Ibid.,* pp. 4 f. The Board supported its stand by citing approval of mergers by the Supreme Court under the Clayton Act where one of the parties to the merger would have to go out of business if permission to consolidate was denied. The above discussion does not deal with consolidation on overseas routes. The question of the relation of the Board's authority over consolidation and other antitrust issues is dealt with, in part by the Supreme Court in *Pan-American World Airways* v. *United States,* 371 U.S. 296 (1963).

air transportation. This policy is clearly expressed in the following quotation:

It would be expecting too much to assume that a transportation company engaged in both air and sea transportation would be in a position to provide vigorous competition between its air transportation and its surface transportation on this route. . . . Any assumption that an automatic competition between two forms of transportation, conducted by the same management and operating over the same route, could develop would be an assumption at war with the realities of business experience and of human nature. In such circumstances the transportation activities offering the larger investment interest may be expected to dominate in any competitive conflict between the two. We believe, therefore, that the maximum development of air transportation on the proposed route cannot be assured under a plan which carries the inherent danger, in the event of a conflict of interest, that the air transportation may find itself a captive of the surface transportation interest.[37]

The general tenor of the Board's decisions in merger cases seems to fit the philosophy of the antitrust laws. This is at variance with its approach to regulation of fares and service, which is predicated on the public utility analogy. Which of these two directions should be followed may be a matter of debate, but both cannot be pursued with success at the same time. If, as some contend, the Board should develop a plan of consolidation,[38] application of the public utility approach to the regulation of air transport is called for. If, on the other hand, a competitive structure is to be envisaged, then the other policies should be shaped accordingly.

Appraisal of Civil Aeronautics Board Policy

Evaluation of economic regulation by the Civil Aeronautics Board must recognize the contradictions contained in the governing legislation. The law seems to presuppose the application of the type of control which was developed for rail and motor carriers, yet the emphasis on competition and the prevention of monopoly can be implemented only through the encouragement of a competitive structure. At the same time, provision for the payment of subsidy should preclude freedom of entry, unless the public purse is assumed to be unlimited. The Board cannot be blamed for these inconsistencies.

On the other hand, the Board's actions have been characterized by continuous vacillation, delay, and inconclusiveness. It is literally impossible to go through the record and discover any development of pol-

[37] *Additional Service to Latin America,* 6 C.A.B. 857, 903–4 (1946). For an extended argument for a contrary policy, see T. W. van Metre, *American Transportation Policy* (Washington, D.C.: National Federation of American Shipping, 1944).

[38] See H. D. Koontz, "Domestic Air Line Self-Sufficiency: A Problem of Route Structure," *American Economic Review,* Vol. XLII, No. 1 (March, 1952), pp. 103–25.

icy, either that air transport should be treated as a regulated monopoly or that it should be controlled in the pattern of a competitive industry. The two exceptions to this indecisiveness are the separation of local service from trunk-line carriers and the exclusion of other agencies from participation in air transportation. Certification policies have exhibited no consistent behavior, unless it can be said that they have been consistently contradictory, as evidenced by the proposal to certify the large irregular carriers to provide competition for the trunk lines. If regulation was to be in the public utility pattern, then certification clearly should have been limited. The Board, however, does not seem to have favored this, nor do the economics of air transport warrant it. Certification policy should have given recognition to this fact and should have been developed accordingly.

The rate policy of the Board has been the most inept of all, if it can be called a policy. No pattern of rates or fares has been developed, and after twenty-four years of regulation no general investigation has been completed. No principles have been established to guide the formulation of particular fares, nor have any reasons been given why rate making should not be on a strictly competitive basis. Limitations have been imposed on requests for increases in the level of rates, without a measuring rod having been developed for gauging the reasonableness of the applications, and in the face of a professed desire to make the air lines self-sustaining and independent of government support. In fact, no reasons have been advanced to support a policy which imposes restrictions on the maximum limit to fares. Furthermore, there has been no reconciliation of the rates which the carriers are permitted to charge on freight with the much higher service rates for the carriage of mail.

It seems to be quite evident that regulatory policy for air transport is in need of a complete overhauling. Whatever theory one may hold regarding the economic structure of air transportation that regulation should assume, workable public policy for the industry cannot pursue courses of action based on the theories of competition and monopoly at the same time. At the present time, it would probably be possible to force air transport into the mold of monopoly,[39] but this would not be in keeping with the economic structure of the industry; nor do there seem to be any good reasons for attempting to do so. The Board could probably develop policy in keeping with the competitive nature of the industry without any change in the law, except perhaps for the elimination of the subsidy provisions. In the absence of Congressional

---

[39] This differs from motor and water transport, where the technological aspects preclude such a possibility, at least as long as one assumes private enterprise. Future technological developments may also make it impossible in air transport.

action, however, it is unlikely that any significant changes will take place in the foreseeable future. They will probably have to wait for Congress to indicate the kind of policy it wishes to be applied to air transportation.[40]

After a comprehensive study of CAB regulation of passenger traffic, Samuel B. Richmond concludes

It is clear that both competition and direct regulation can, in appropriate circumstances, be substituted one for the other, as mechanisms for seeking to serve the public good in the economic phases of the air transport industry. The difficult problem, and that which is yet unresolved, is the determination of the optimum blend of the two mechanisms. Whether the current blend is viable is not yet clear. . . .

The optimum blend of competition and regulation is a dynamic quantity. Its movement through the transition from reciprocating engine to jet to supersonic equipment as well as to vertical take-off equipment with its repercussions on alternative modes of surface travel cannot be predicted. However, it is to be hoped that the Civil Aeronautics Board, in making its decisions about competition and the many related economic and financial problems, will as a general policy and whenever possible, act to preserve and strengthen rather than weaken competition in the air transport industry.[41]

It is to be hoped that the CAB will find it possible to move more consistently in the direction of a thoroughly competitive structure in air transport.[42] What the functions of the Board will be if this takes place remains to be seen.

[40] For severe criticisms of the Civil Aeronautics Board and current policies, see Louis J. Hector, *Problems of the CAB and the Independent Regulatory Commissions*, Memorandum to the President (mimeographed), September 10, 1959; and Horace M. Gray, "The Airlines Industry," in Walter Adams (ed.), *The Structure of American Industry* (3d ed.; New York: Macmillan Co., 1961). See also *National Transportation Policy* (Doyle Report), Part VII, chap. 12. Although this chapter of the report seems to be critical of the Board's policies, no over-all evaluation is given, nor does the report integrate the problems of air transport policy with that of the other agencies. See also Lucile S. Keyes, *Federal Control of Entry into Air Transportation* (Cambridge: Harvard University Press, 1951).

[41] Samuel B. Richmond, *Regulation and Competition in Air Transportation* (New York: Columbia University Press, 1961), pp. 256–57.

[42] Professor Richard E. Caves has suggested that this could be accomplished gradually by arranging "the network of air routes into three parts. Class 1 would be the city-pair routes large enough to sustain more than one carrier with entry unrestricted. Class 2 would be those local-service cities or routes that probably could not be served without subsidy. Class 3 would be a residual of cities or city-pair markets that would be profitable for a single carrier. The critical first step would be to open the class of large city-pair markets to all certified carriers not receiving subsidy. . . . The second step would be to eliminate restrictions on entry of new carriers to city-pair markets in Class 1. . . . A final step, once the situation had again stabilized reasonably, would be to consolidate the first and third class markets, leaving only subsidized local-service routes subject to separate regulation." Richard E. Caves, *Air Transport and Its Regulators* (Cambridge, Mass.: Harvard University Press, 1962), pp. 447–48. One might add that the final step would be to eliminate all subsidy.

REGULATION OF WATER TRANSPORTATION

REGULATION TO 1940

The regulation of domestic water transportation down to 1940 was carried out in a limited way by different agencies under a number of laws passed by Congress from time to time. One aspect of the regulation pertained to water carrier operations as they related to rail transport. In 1887 the Interstate Commerce Act gave the Commission jurisdiction over carriers engaged in transportation partly by railroad and partly by water, where both were under common control or arrangement for continuous carriage. The Hepburn Act of 1906 gave the Commission the authority to establish through routes and rates for joint rail-water services, and the power to fix maximum joint rates and to establish the divisions of such rates between rail and water carriers. The Mann-Elkins Act of 1910 limited railroad departures from the long-and-short-haul principle to meet water competition, a provision which was strengthened by the Act of 1920. Finally, the Panama Canal Act of 1912 imposed severe restrictions on railroad operation of water carriers, in addition to giving the Commission authority to require a railroad to make physical connection with the dock of a water carrier. This aspect of regulation was obviously designed to protect water carriers against competition by the railroads.

The second aspect of the regulatory program pertained to control of independent, port-to-port operations by water carriers. The Shipping Board Act of 1916 created the United States Shipping Board and gave it authority to promote and regulate deepwater shipping. In domestic commerce, this was limited to carriers operating regular routes in coastwise or intercoastal trade, and to common carriers on the Great Lakes. Maximum rates, fares, and charges had to be published and filed with the Board. They could be changed only after ten days' notice. The Board could not fix minimum or actual rates. The Intercoastal Shipping Act of 1933 required common and contract carriers operating in intercoastal service via the Panama Canal to publish their actual rates. In 1938 the law was amended to give the Federal Maritime Commission, which had replaced the Shipping Board, the authority to set minimum rates for domestic deepwater common carriers, but this did not apply to those plying the Great Lakes.

REASONS FOR THE ACT OF 1940

In the period following World War I, domestic shipping, particularly in the coastwise and intercoastal trade, was subject to very severe competition and declining earnings. It was felt that regulation was necessary to cure this evil.

> [Unregulated] competition may be quite as much of a public evil as unregulated monopoly. This is a fact which it takes time to learn, but which the country has learned well from much sad experience. The Interstate Commerce Act and the National Industrial Recovery Act were both founded upon it. The present chaotic conditions in the water-carrier industry produce results which plainly are contrary to the public interest.[43]

From this point of view the Federal Coordinator then proceeded to point out the difficulties in the domestic shipping industry which created the need for regulation in the public interest.

According to the report, unregulated competition in the shipping industry produced an instability of rates that was harmful to the conduct of commerce and industry. An inevitable consequence was unjust discrimination between shippers, with the advantage going to those with the biggest tonnage. Chaotic conditions produced financial demoralization and impaired credit, which made it impossible for the coastwise and intercoastal trades to secure private capital for the support of their fleets. Finally, the absence of effective regulation prevented the desirable coordination between all forms of transportation. The Coordinator then made a series of recommendations for legislation which became the basis for the provisions for regulating domestic water carriers in the Transportation Act of 1940, which placed them under the jurisdiction of the Interstate Commerce Commission.

THE TRANSPORTATION ACT OF 1940

The regulation of domestic water carriers under the Act of 1940 follows the same general pattern as that which applies to motor carriers. In addition to the provisions under Part III of the Interstate Commerce Act, which relate specifically to water carriers, those which are regulated are subject to the long-and-short-haul clause of the Act and to the consolidation requirements. However, there is no financial regulation and no control over abandonments, and the Shreveport rule is not applicable. Moreover, the exemptions are more extensive than for motor carriers.

Provisions of the Act

The law recognizes two types of carriers subject to regulation, namely, common carriers and contract carriers. Private carriers are

---

[43] *Regulation of Transportation Agencies,* Report of the Federal Coordinator of Transportation, Senate Document No. 152, 73d Congress, 2d session (Washington, D.C.: U.S. Government Printing Office, 1934), pp. 10–11.

exempt, as also are carriers engaged solely in transporting the property of a person owning all or substantially all of the voting stock of the carrier; there are other incidental exemptions, such as for carriers operating within a single harbor. In addition to these exemptions, there are those that apply to the type of shipment which is made. Transportation of bulk commodities is excluded where a contract carrier transports not more than three commodities in the cargo space of the vessel, but this does not apply to carriers engaged in interstate commerce through the Panama Canal. Liquid cargoes in bulk in tank vessels are exempt, as is also contract carriage by water, which by reason of the inherent nature of the commodities transported, their requirement of special equipment, or their shipment in bulk is not actually and substantially competitive with transportation by any common carrier subject to the Interstate Commerce Act.

With the exceptions already noted, common carriers by water are subject to essentially the same controls as are common carriers by motor. They must obtain certificates of public convenience and necessity, although a "grandfather" clause protects those who were in bona fide operation on January 1, 1940. A common carrier cannot receive a certificate as a contract carrier, and vice versa, although the Commission may find reason for special exceptions. Finally, certificates may not be revoked once they have been granted, but in 1965 Congress empowered the Commission to revoke certificates for failure on the part of the carrier to provide service thereunder.

Contract carriers by water are subject to regulations similar to those prescribed for common carriers except for the differences dictated by the nature of their business. They are required to secure permits and must publish their minimum rates. Thirty days' notice of change must be given. Contract carriers may not engage in common carriage without special permission, but they may transport commodities covered by the exemption provisions.[44]

The Act contains no provision prohibiting private carriers from transporting goods for hire. Moreover, the grandfather clause protects them in the contract or common carrier business which they enjoyed

---

[44] Senate hearings are now being held on S. 1314 (April, 1967) the effect of which would be (1) to repeal the custom of the trade provision which places a restriction on the movement of exempt dry-bulk commodities unless they were transported prior to June, 1939; (2) to repeal the limitation which restricts the number of dry-bulk commodities to three which may be carried in a tow of vessels at any one time; and (3) to repeal the prohibition against the carriage of both regulated and nonregulated dry-bulk commodities in the same tow of vessels. The water carriers obviously want greater freedom of action than they are willing to accord the railroads.

prior to January 1, 1940. The Commission may grant certificates or permits to private carriers if it finds it in the public interest to do so.

Conclusions on the Legislation

The present law to regulate water carriers was passed for the purpose of protecting domestic water transport from destructive competition within itself. The theory was that competition could be limited through certification and permits, and by control over rates. The Commission has found little reason to prescribe maximum rates, and not much has been done with regard to minimum rates. Similarly, activity on certificates and permits has been of slight importance.

The experience of twenty years of regulation under the Act has little to commend it. The legislation was incapable of providing a resolution of the difficulties that have beset domestic shipping. Common and contract carriage cannot be preserved by endeavors to limit competition for the carriers of these two types when so much water transport is exempt. Nor will the regulation of water carriers protect them against the other agencies of transportation. The fact is that water transportation is a highly competitive industry, and if common and contract carriers cannot stand the competition, they cannot survive unless they are subsidized directly. The significant and economical part of domestic water transportation in this country does not need regulation for its continued existence. The public utility type of regulation constitutes a useless policy for industries that totally lack the necessary characteristics; indeed, it will be positively harmful if it is anything but innocuous.

REGULATION OF PETROLEUM PIPE LINES

THE PIPE-LINE PROBLEM

The only significant type of pipe-line transportation that is for hire at the present time is that which transports crude oil and liquid petroleum products such as gasoline. Pipe lines that are used for transporting water are normally an integral part of a water system which acquires the water and transports it for resale directly to consumers or to distribution systems. Thus the transportation is an integral part of the whole process of supplying water, and the pipe lines are part of the total plant. Where the ownership is private, the water companies are regulated as public utilities, the rates covering the total costs of acquisition, transportation, processing, and distribution. Essentially the same remarks apply to natural gas pipe lines. These normally undertake to deliver the gas at the city gate or directly to consumers, one of the functions of the pipe-line company being to acquire the gas which is to be delivered from the various field sources available. In other words, the natural gas pipe-line companies are not engaged merely in transportation; they also undertake the responsibility of acquiring the gas for the buyers.

Petroleum and products lines occupy a dual capacity. The large oil-refining companies in particular undertake to explore for oil and pump much of it in the fields. They also refine it in a relatively limited number of large centers. The pipe lines are used to connect their extraction and refining facilities. However, there are also independent refiners and independent producers in the fields, the former requiring oil and the latter requiring market outlets for their crude products. They are largely dependent on the pipe-line facilities which are mostly in the hands of the large integrated companies. This ownership integration in the oil industry, from extraction to refining, has given rise to sharp differences of opinion on the desirability of separating pipe-line ownership from extraction and refining.[45] Whatever the ultimate resolution of the ownership problem of petroleum pipe lines may be, it seems clear that as carriers for hire they will have to be recognized as falling into the public utility category and to be regulated accordingly.

FEDERAL REGULATION

The regulation of transportation in interstate commerce by pipe lines was included in the Hepburn Act of 1906, in which Congress declared that all interstate pipe lines transporting oil or other commodities, except water and natural or artificial gas, were subject to all the applicable provisions of the Interstate Commerce Act.[46] This law was amended in 1920 apparently so as to place all petroleum pipe lines in interstate commerce in the category of common carriers.

[45] See, for example, G. S. Wolbert, Jr., *American Pipe Lines* (Norman University of Oklahoma Press, 1952); and E. V. Rostow, *A National Policy for the Oil Industry* (New Haven: Yale University Press, 1948). See also Leslie Cookenboo, Jr., *Crude Oil Pipe Lines and Competition in the Oil Industry* (Cambridge: Harvard University Press, 1955), for a careful review of the entire controversy. Cookenboo favors joint ventures among majors, independents, and anyone else interested therein (p. 130), although he recognizes a good many difficulties in this as a resolution of the problem. A comprehensive analysis of the organization and structure of the petroleum industry will be found in M. D. de Chazeau and A. E. Kahn, *Integration and Competition in the Petroleum Industry* (New Haven: Yale University Press, 1959). It is interesting to note that the Doyle Report does not discuss the problem at all. The Southern Pacific Co. operates two pipe-line systems which are completely independent of oil companies.

[46] The commodities clause did not apply to pipelines.

The status of petroleum pipe lines in interstate commerce has been a matter of lengthy controversy which has not yet been clearly settled. If they were all in fact common carriers under the law, they could be compelled to transport oil for independent refiners or producers at just and reasonable rates. In the pipe-line cases[47] the Supreme Court upheld the Commission's order requiring the pipe-line companies to file tariffs and accept the Commission's jurisdiction, because they carried everybody's oil to market even though they compelled outsiders to sell it to them before doing so. However, in a sharply divided opinion the Court in 1951[48] refused to regard as a common carrier a pipe line used solely to carry its owner's products to market. This still leaves unsettled the question of whether a pipe line in interstate commerce can be compelled to accept common carrier status if its services are sought after and needed by independent producers or refiners.

In regulating those carriers which are under its jurisdiction, the Commission has dealt with two main problems. The first is that of establishing reasonable minimum tender requirements; these apply particularly to trunk lines. Minimum tender requirements vary from 100,-000 barrels to 10,000 barrels, the Commission finding in the *Reduced Pipe Line Rates Case*[49] that tender requirements above the latter were unreasonable. The second problem facing the Commission is that of standards for the reasonableness of the level of pipe-line rates. High rates are obviously no burden on the owning lines, but may severely restrict the independents. The Commission has applied the fair return principle, under which it has allowed 8 per cent on the fair value as determined by it, although it seems to consider 10 per cent reasonable for products lines.[50]

Pipe lines are also subject to the Elkins Act of 1903, which prohibits rebating and other forms of personal discrimination by common carriers. Under a consent decree which the Department of Justice obtained in 1941, the pipe lines agreed not to pay dividends to any shipper-owner which were in excess of 7 per cent of the stockholder's share of the value of the pipe-line property as determined by the Interstate Commerce Commission.[51] Earnings in excess of 7 per cent on the valua-

[47] 234 U.S. 548 (1914).

[48] *United States* v. *Champlin Refining Company,* 341 U.S. 290 (1951). See also *United States* v. *Uncle Sam Oil Company,* 234 U.S. 548 (1914); and *Valvoline Oil Company* v. *United States,* 308 U.S. 141 (1939).

[49] 243 I.C.C. 115 (1940).

[50] *Ibid.,* p. 142; and *Minnelusa Oil Corporation* v. *Continental Pipe Line Company,* 258 I.C.C. 41, 53 (1944).

[51] See Wolbert, *op. cit.,* pp. 165–69, for a copy of the decree.

tion of the pipe line had to be placed in a special surplus account to be used principally for new construction or the retirement of debt.

Regulation appears to have reduced the earnings on pipe-line properties,[52] although competition in the oil industry may also have been a factor. Whether this has had any appreciable effect on the relative position of the independents, and therefore on competition in the industry, is a matter of dispute. The question of competition is also related to problems of domestic production of oil, as well as importations from foreign sources. It will be difficult to divorce transportation from the other aspects of the oil industry and to break up vertical integration. Competition from overseas sources of supply, brought in by company-owned tankers, cannot be ignored in evaluating the appropriate basis for pipe-line ownership.

[52] See D. P. Locklin, *Economics of Transportation* (6th ed.; Homewood, Ill.: Richard D. Irwin, Inc., 1966), p. 606, for computations of rate of return on pipe-line investment from 1921 to 1963.

PART IV

National Transportation Policy

TRANSPORTATION AS A NATIONAL PROBLEM

INTRODUCTION

The preceding sections of this book have dealt with the functions of transportation, its development, economic structure, and the processes of public regulation. There remains the task of examining some of the major problems from the standpoint of the transport structure of the country as a whole, and the formulation of national policy. This will entail some repetition of material already covered, although frequently in a somewhat different context. The purpose of this is to delineate the issues that are involved in developing an economical transport system for the United States, particularly under the objectives and assumptions of a private enterprise economy. In a strictly logical sense an economical system of transportation will be based on the same economic considerations for any country, provided that the basic assumptions are the same. In fact, however, they cannot be the same for transport policy developed for various countries; they will differ with the different institutional arrangements, with the variations in individual choice conditioned by these arrangements, and with the different governmental structures and procedures that give rise to peculiar jurisdictional problems, and recognition of local needs.

The presentation in this chapter will also involve duplication, in abbreviated form, of a good deal that will be elaborated in the chapters that follow. Even though this means repetition of a sort, it seems desirable to survey the issues of national policy as a whole so as to provide a perspective of the over-all issues in advance of examining them in detail. It should be recognized that this examination of transportation as a national problem is as significant to management and the practitioners in transportation as it is to the students of public policy, because it is only within the setting of public policy, or the established rules of the game, that they can carry on their activities. The success of the latter turns, in part, on what is permitted by public policy. In addition, the difficulties which are encountered as a result of public action can be discovered only by the operations for which management is ultimately responsible. The role of national policy is as significant, therefore, to it as are the internal operations of the enterprises.

TRANSPORTATION—A PERENNIAL PROBLEM

Uniqueness of the Transport Problem

Transportation presents a unique problem for national policy because of its intimate relation to community life. In fact, the idea of a unified community or body politic is impossible in the absence of adequate means of transportation and communication. Throughout history the body politic has found it necessary to participate directly in the supplying of transport facilities. Even in a country where the utmost possible development of private enterprise prevailed, public participation would be necessary, especially under modern conditions. It has never been feasible to divorce transportation from community concern or interest, because it literally forms the physical framework of a community, and it constitutes the spatial arteries that keep community life going. Transportation routes are decisive factors in the location of economic activity, thereby evoking public interest in the development and maintenance of them.[1]

Transportation agencies are obliged to use public facilities. Water transport must utilize the inland waterways, coastal waters, and harbors of the country, and these cannot be left solely to private exploitation or development. Navigational aids cannot satisfactorily be provided by private enterprise alone, nor left to complete reliance on competitive forces. Similar remarks apply to air transport. Railroads must be permitted to exercise the power of eminent domain, a procedure which, directly or indirectly, requires the use of governmental powers. Motor transport must be able to use the highways, the provision of which also entails resort to the powers of eminent domain. In other words, transportation, unlike most other economic activity, needs the aid of the government in securing the necessary route facilities, whether the services be sup-

[1] Somewhat similar remarks apply to what we call public utilities, but the latter are commonly much more local in nature and do not involve as much interchange of goods and services between peoples and communities. Furthermore, today, public utilities form a homogeneous group of industries as far as their economic structure is concerned, and each firm can be treated pretty much in isolation. Transportation consists of a heterogeneous group in economic structure, and firms cannot be treated in isolation. Pervasive competition characterizes transportation; easily delineated monopoly characterizes public utilities.

plied by public or private enterprise. But the participation by government does not stop at this point. Public investment is unavoidable. No feasible means for supplying streets and highways, to say nothing of water and air navigational aids, by which complete reliance can be placed on private enterprise, has yet been developed. Public investment in the routes over which much of our transport takes place is inescapable. Thus, transportation, even in a private enterprise economy, constitutes a mixed system of ownership and investment. It is the unavoidability of this mixed system that is one of the reasons why economical allocation and utilization of resources in transport constitutes such a complex problem.

Transportation presents a unique problem for public policy in that the suppliers constitute a group of industries, some of whose services are readily substitutable for each other, while some are not readily substitutable or are even specific to the particular agency. This would not present any particular difficulties if the agencies had similar economic characteristics and therefore were amenable to the same type of regulation or control. This, however, is not the case. Railroads and pipe lines are natural monopolies, while motor, air, and water carriers are competitive in nature. Furthermore a large amount of transport service is not for hire; it is supplied by the owners of the facilities for themselves. Much of this is readily substitutable for services which are sold for hire, and much of the for-hire traffic can move into the private category if for any reason the for-hire service is unsatisfactory. The regulation of railroads developed in the same pattern as the regulation of public utilities. Water, air, and motor transport lack the economic characteristics of public utilities. Even when the enterprises in these agencies operate as carriers for hire, they do not fit the category, and when they serve only their owners, they cannot be brought under public regulation. Public policy must give recognition to this diversity and cannot proceed successfully on the theory that a single type of regulation is applicable to all of them.

Another unique problem in transportation arises in connection with the role of the common carrier. Although this concept did not start with the railroads, nor was it confined to them even in their early days, present law relating to common carriers and the responsibilities they must discharge is largely the product of railroad regulation. The railroads became complete common carriers, probably because of their monopolistic position and the public functions they were discharging. As a consequence, the idea has developed that transport for hire is presumed to fall into the common carrier category, unless there are compelling reasons to the contrary, and that those engaging in the business of a common carrier should be restricted to this type of undertaking. So far, there has been no basic departure from this theory, despite the impact of the new technology.

The need for common carriage, and public imposition of the obligations incident thereto, arise from the nature of much of the transportation for hire. Shippers transfer physical possession of the goods they ship to the enterprise that transports them, with the expectation that they will be delivered at destination in the condition in which they were received. Shipper and receiver may be different people, and in addition, more than one transport firm may be involved. The practical impossibility of every shipper entering into a specific contract for every shipment he makes, and then being forced to undertake individual suit for redress if the conditions of the contract are not fulfilled, makes a general law for common carriage with the stipulated obligations and, over a wide range, almost automatic enforcement a necessity for an effective transport system. At the federal level, at least, the law must be a matter of legislation, and even at the state level the common law itself is inadequate.

Despite the public need for the common carrier, it does not follow that there is any presumption in favor of the idea that the common carrier alone is essential to the transport structure, nor does it follow that the common carrier needs to be protected. Other carriers for hire are equally essential to the transport system of the country, especially in motor and water transport, to say nothing of those which are not for hire. Concern over the decline of the relative position of the common carrier fails to take account of the changing structure of transport, with the inevitable decline of the common carrier. Present feeling that the latter needs to be protected also neglects to take into consideration the fact that common carriage relates to the obligations assumed and therefore does not necessarily require that the firm assuming them must not be allowed to do anything else. If permission to engage in the business of transportation beyond the common carrier role is not prejudicial to shippers, it is difficult to see why restrictions which may have been quite valid in the past should be maintained under present circumstances. Furthermore the idea that the common carrier must be protected against competition from others assumes, first of all, that this can be accomplished and, second, that the services that are being offered cannot support themselves. The extent to which these assumptions may be valid will depend upon the effectiveness of competition in present-day transportation. Analysis of the considerations which should be weighed in the development of public policy on this issue necessitates evaluation of the role of competition in transport under modern conditions. Suffice it to say at this point that protection of the common carrier and restriction of its activities solely to common carriage do not seem to be necessary in the interests of an economical, efficient, and adequate transport system.

The Changing Nature of the Problem

Transportation policy has been developed within the framework of monopoly theory. As a result, restrictions have been placed on freedom of decision by management, prices have been regulated in a comprehensive manner, and competition has been limited by severe control over conditions of entry. Limitations on competition have been imposed on the premise that competition in transportation can be ruinous, with harmful results to the carriers as well as to the consumers. Moreover, the common carriers have supported restricted entry, once they have obtained permission to operate, although all of them seek authorization to compete effectively against rival agencies at the very time that they endeavor to limit the rival's privilege of doing the same thing.

The complexities surrounding the competition among the various agencies arise primarily from the totally different economic structures among them. Purely competitive or purely monopoly theory is inadequate for transport as a whole, and so is oligopoly. The monopoly theory under which regulation developed to its present stage is no longer applicable to the entire field even of common carriers, nor has competition replaced it entirely over the whole range of services. Public policy, as well as the behavior of carriers, must accommodate themselves to both, because neither can be eliminated.

The problem is further complicated by the inescapability of public ownership. Whereas, in the period of railroad supremacy, regulation was a definite alternative to public ownership, today the latter is inescapable for a large part of the investment in transport. This poses the new issue of criteria for public investment and criteria for user charges. This is distinct from the problem of regulation and independent of it. Furthermore, public ownership can no longer comprehend the entire inland transport system, and would not resolve the basic problem of economical allocation and utilization of resources. Nationalization of rail transport cannot resolve the problem of economical allocation and utilization of resources to railroads in this country unless all the costs relevant to such calculations are ascertained for them and assigned to them. If this were to be the case, then competition would have to be given as full scope as the structure of the industry permits—an arrangement that is more readily operational under private ownership. If this were not done, then the idea of an economical transport system would be categorically abandoned.

The Formulation of Public Policy

Problems of transportation have occupied the attention of the legislative and executive branches of the federal government from the very beginning of this country as a nation. They have been concerned with the promotion and development of the different elements of the transport system from time to time, and with regulation of the various agencies. Down to 1920 the focal point of the latter was the railroads; since then the other agencies and the relation of them to the railroads has come under increasing scrutiny. Over the years the center of attention of national policy has been on regulation and public control. At the same time, there has been a great deal of activity in the promotion of transport, other than railroad, but until recently little consideration has been given to the co-ordination of promotional activities with national policy; and to date, scant recognition of the need for this and the implications of it has been afforded by governmental authorities.[2]

The full import of the impact of technological change on the transport structure was not grasped until after World War II. Recognition of the growing need for a thoroughgoing examination of the transportation problem in its postwar setting led President Eisenhower to appoint a Presidential Advisory Committee on Transport Policy and Organization on July 12, 1954, with instructions to make a comprehensive review of over-all federal transportation policies and problems, and to transmit recommendations regarding them for the President's consideration. The resulting report (known as the Weeks Report) marked a departure from previous ones by its emphasis on "pervasive" competition in modern transportation, although it did not spell out the meaning and implications of the term.[3] Since then a number of other reports

[2] See C. L. Dearing and W. Owen, *National Transportation Policy* (Washington, D.C.: Brookings Institution, 1949). This volume contains a summary of reports on proposals for reorganizing national transportation activities over the years 1933 to 1947. See also *Unified and Coordinated Federal Program for Transportation,* Report to the President from the Secretary of Commerce, December 1, 1949 (Washington, D.C.: U.S. Government Printing Office, 1949) (Sawyer Report); and *Domestic Land and Water Transportation,* Progress Report of the Senate Committee on Interstate and Foreign Commerce, Senate Report No. 1039, 82d Congress, 1st session, October, 1951 (Washington, D.C.: U.S. Government Printing Office, 1951).

[3] *Revision of Federal Transportation Policy,* Report of Presidential Advisory Committee on Transport Policy and Organization (Washington, D.C.: U.S. Government Printing Office, 1955).

have been issued,[4] the Doyle Report being the latest and in many respects the most comprehensive; at least it is the largest.

All of the reports since 1954 have placed considerable emphasis on the desirability of reducing governmental restraint on transport and of affording greater opportunity for the play of competitive forces. However, none of them has developed the economic premises upon which such an approach must be founded, nor has any of them explored the implications in terms of the limitations on and the functions of regulation under such circumstances. Curiously enough, all of them imply more positive regulation in many directions than now exists, by the suggestion that carriers be compelled to comply with rate regulation based upon an ill-defined standard of cost orientation. Restrictions on competition are also proposed for the purpose of protecting the common carrier. There seems to be little understanding of the fact that competitively compelled rates will resolve the problem of cost-price relationships, and that all that is necessary, at most, is to prevent predatory practices and unreasonably high monopoly profits, if there is any possibility of obtaining them. None of the reports seems to grasp the fact that much of the field of transportation is not even amenable to regulation based on the theory of monopoly.

In short, despite the plethora of reports and studies to date, Congress will find little that will assist it in a positive way to arrive at the legislative changes necessary to adapt national policy to the radically altered status of transport today, and to recognize the pervasiveness of competition which all acknowledge. As far as the reports are concerned, literally everything recommended can be accomplished within the framework of existing statutory enactments. All that would be necessary would be to change the outlook of the regulatory authorities. Unfortunately, this is unlikely to come about with anything less than drastic legislative modifications and, in addition, the adoption of

[4] *Problems of the Railroads* (Smathers Report), Report of Subcommittee on Surface Transportation, Committee on Interstate and Foreign Commerce, U.S. Senate, 85th Congress, 2d session (Washington, D.C.: U.S. Government Printing Office, April, 1958). One of the immediate results of this was the setting-up of the study group that issued the Doyle Report. *Adequacy of Transportation Systems in Support of the National Defense Effort in the Event of Mobilization* (Kilday Report), Hearings of Subcommittee on Armed Services, House of Representatives, 86th Congress, 1st session (Washington, D.C.: U.S. Government Printing Office, 1959), pp. v–xx. U.S. Department of Commerce, *Federal Transportation Policy and Program* (Mueller Report) (Washington, D.C.: U.S. Government Printing Office, March, 1960). This was accompanied by an Appendix by E. W. Williams, Jr., and D. W. Bluestone, *Rationals of Federal Transportation Policy* (April, 1960). *National Transportation Policy* (Doyle Report), Preliminary Draft of a Report to the Senate Committee on Interstate and Foreign Commerce, 87th Congress, 1st session (Washington, D.C.: U.S. Government Printing Office, 1961).

new criteria for the economic allocation and utilization of public investment. Finally, the labor problem in transportation has been almost completely ignored.

Thus the formulation of public policy for transport to date has lacked the necessary comprehensiveness in scope as well as in the economic analysis of modern transport as a whole. Part of this deficiency may be ascribed to the fact that the institutional framework within which transport services are supplied at the present time is the result of a long process of accumulation based on assumptions that may have been valid at various times in the past, but which have not been adapted to the radically new situation. This is complicated by the fact that many of the assumptions still hold, albeit in a different setting. Moreover, a complete modernization of national policy would entail drastic adjustments that might well produce severe dislocations in the transport structure for some time to come. This may well explain the apparent inability at the federal level of policy making to enunciate a comprehensive and progressive program for Congressional action. In any case, authoritative formulation is lacking at the present time, despite the acknowledged crisis, particularly with regard to railroads. To this must be added the dilemma of urban transportation, where little progress has been made in diagnosing the real nature of the problem, let alone in perceiving a resolution of it.[5]

General Objectives of Public Policy

The enormous investment, both public and private, in transportation today and the prospective requirements for the immediately ensuing decades call for an enunciation of the general objectives of public policy. In strictly economic terms this can be set forth rather simply by saying that public policy requires the economical allocation and utilization of economic resources for the transport system as a whole, and among the agencies which make up that system. What this means is that the transport that is considered necessary for the country should be obtained at the lowest economic cost and utilized in the most efficient manner. If transportation were thoroughly competitive in its entirety,

[5] For a summary discussion of this, see E. W. Williams, Jr., "An Evaluation of Our Recent Transportation Plans," *Proceedings of the Syracuse Transportation Conference* (Syracuse, N.Y.: Business Research Center, Syracuse University, April 10, 1961), pp. 22–27. President Kennedy sent a message to Congress in April, 1962, with proposals for revising regulation and aid to urban transport. President Johnson succeeded in establishing a Department of Transportation in 1966. Both of these developments will be discussed in later chapters. For a discussion of conflicts in national transportation policy, see D. F. Pegrum, "Conflicts in Transport Policy," *Transportation Journal,* Vol. VI, No. 1 (Fall, 1966), pp. 5–16.

and if investment in it could be made in completely competitive fashion, the solution would be simple, because the market could be relied upon to resolve the problem. Unfortunately, the situation is not that simple.

The pervasiveness of competition today affords the opportunity to place heavy reliance on competition as the means of efficiently allocating traffic among the various agencies and carriers on a price basis. It is in this area that modification of the present program of regulation is called for. Regulation alone, however, can resolve the questions of competition only within the cost conditions imposed upon the competitors by legislation or by public aid. Thus, for competition to be effective in the public interest, equality of conditions must be established. To meet the economic objective of an efficient system, public policy must see to it that tax burdens, user charges, public aid, and labor legislation are administered so as to eliminate as far as possible handicaps on any of the agencies. Public investment in transport should be scrutinized in the light of public needs as measured by the best economic gauges possible.

Even though an economical transport system were obtained by applying the foregoing criteria, there would remain the problem of national defense. The transport problems of national defense loom large in any country. These cannot be gauged in the market place, and what is necessary to develop an adequate inland system for this purpose must be the result of the appraisal of the military as well as other authorities. Nevertheless, it is still incumbent on these to obtain in the most economical way what is deemed necessary for defense and explicitly to acknowledge the additional costs which this entails. In short, national defense considerations do not alter the objective of an economical transport system, even though the direct criteria of the market place for measuring the need are inapplicable.

PUBLIC INVESTMENT AND PUBLIC AID

Public Aid and Subsidy

Public aid and subsidy in transportation constitute three different items in the governmental participation in financing transportation. Public investment encompasses the expenditures by government in highway, water, and air transport route and terminal properties.[6] Public aid consists primarily of the provision of transport facilities for users who are not required to pay the full cost of them, the deficiencies being made up from general tax revenues. Subsidy may most conveniently be

[6] This should also include investment in urban transport, in which the federal government is now participating, in addition to its present aid to highways in urban areas.

thought of as direct payments made to assist a particular agency. At the present moment, this is confined in domestic transport to feeder air lines, although there may be some disguised subsidies in the air-mail payments to the trunk-line carriers. As far as subsidies are concerned, the justification may be that of fostering an "infant industry," even though the public need for this in transport is by no means self-evident and the criteria for the amount that is necessary are totally lacking.

Public investment and public aid are another matter, exhibiting less readily ascertainable costs, more difficulties in arriving at the appropriate amount of public expenditures, and greater complexities in meeting the costs if any or all of them are to be recovered by users. If it is assumed that the primary burden of the transport system of the country is to be borne by the users of the services, it is necessary to ascertain the total economic costs for each kind of transport, to require the users of each of the agencies to meet those costs through adequate charges, and to develop means of assessing the costs equitably on the various users. If economical transport is an objective of public policy, then gauges must be devised for measuring the appropriate amount of public investment that should be made. The most difficult agency for which it is necessary to develop adequate criteria for this at the present time is motor transport because of the mixture of commercial and non-commercial uses, the large element of common costs in highway investment, and the technical inability at the present time to relate use to the quality of highway service that is provided.

Criteria for Public Investment

To date, there has been little development of economic criteria for ascertaining the total amount of public investment that should be made in transport or of the total economic costs involved in the proposals for such investment.[7] Gauges for economical public investment will probably have to start with some workable agreement on the components of the economic costs that should be included in the facilities that are to be provided.[8] Although this presents some theo-

---

[7] Many engineering studies have been made by state highway departments and by the Bureau of Public Roads, the Department of Agriculture, and other agencies of the federal government. These, however, have been based on the principle assumption of need, estimated without the restraining influence of some form of rationing which the utilization of economic goods requires. See Williams and Bluestone, *op. cit.*, p. 42.

[8] For a discussion of this as it relates to the use of water resources, see J. Hirshleifer, C. de Haven, and J. Milliman, *Water Supply: Economic Technology and Policy* (Chicago: University of Chicago Press, 1960); J. Krutilla and O. Eckstein, *Multiple Purpose River Development* (Baltimore: Johns Hopkins Press, 1958); and O. Eckstein, *Water Resource Development* (Cambridge: Harvard University Press, 1958).

retical difficulties, a workable approach seems feasible if all the explicit costs are included, together with the implicit costs of tax equivalents on public property used by transport.

Measurement of the benefits of public aid afforded by the explicit costs assumed by government has been attempted, particularly through the use of the benefit cost ratio. This approach endeavors to measure the allocation of costs between users and nonusers by apportioning them on the basis of estimated benefits.[9] Apart from the difficulties encountered in ascertaining such benefits outside the market place, the allocation of part of the costs of highways, for example, to property owners benefited by the undertakings would call for the same treatment for railroads. If this were done for transport, it would seem to be logical to extend it to all industry; this would result in moving resource allocation farther than ever from the price mechanism. This is explicitly recognized in the Highway Cost Allocation Study prepared by the Federal Highway Administrator for the Department of Commerce.[10] Recognition of this fact led to the conclusion that "[in] the allocation of tax responsibility for the support of the Federal Aid Highway Program, care should be taken that the allocation is as nearly as possible neutral with respect to the competitive position of other modes of transportation."[11]

User Charges and Resource Allocation

Even though the foregoing questions are resolved, there still remains the problem of recovering from the various users the total amount they are called upon to bear. This issue arises in its most complex form also in motor transport. If costs could be traced with any degree of accuracy among the various classes of users, the total to be recovered could be distributed among them on that basis. A good deal of study has been given this matter, and there is evidence that considerable progress has been made in tracing responsibility. However, joint and common costs form an important part of the costs of public investment, and the allocation or recovery of these on an economical basis presents particularly difficult issues, especially in the light of conflicting interests and keen competition among the agencies. Nevertheless, growing

[9] For this method of measuring public aid to transport, see Federal Coordinator of Transportation, *Public Aids to Transportation,* Vol. IV (Washington, D.C.: U.S. Government Printing Office, 1940), pp. 12–154.

[10] *Final Report of the Highway Cost Allocation Study,* House Document No. 54, 87th Congress, 1st session (Washington, D. C.: U.S. Government Printing Office, 1961), p. 74.

[11] *Ibid.,* p. 277. Railroads and pipe lines at present are the only other modes to which this stricture can apply today.

recognition of the nature of the problem together with the development of techniques for identifying the separable costs will result in reducing the amounts that are not traceable, thereby narrowing the limits of judgment as to the appropriate means of recovering the balance.

COMPETITION, CO-ORDINATION, AND INTEGRATION

The role of regulation in the process of supplying transport services has been that of filling in the deficiencies, actual or alleged, of competition and the market place as adequate safeguards of public interest. If competition had been able to operate as effectively as it has for industry in general, it is reasonable to assume that no special policy of transport regulation would have developed but that transport enterprises would have been subject to the same general rules applicable to other competitive undertakings. The development of public policy and the economic structure of transportation has precluded this possibility. Instead, regulation reached its present status on the theory that railroads were essentially monopolistic in character and that the controls applied to them should be extended at least to the common carriers of the other agencies. The rise of the new transport structure has modified radically the conditions upon which the theory was developed. Competition has now become a pervasive influence to which public policy must be adapted.

Competition in Transport

Competition in transportation at the present time manifests itself in two ways. First of all, there is the competition among the enterprises of a particular mode or agency, and second, there is the competition among the enterprises of the different modes. If competitive forces were the same within each of the agencies, these two would constitute one and the same problem. This, however, is not the case.

The role of competition among the firms of the different modes of transport varies because of the differences in the economic structure of them. As has already been pointed out, railroads and pipe lines fall into the category of natural monopolies, while water, air, and motor carriers exhibit the characteristics of competitive industries. This is the basis for the two distinct problems of intra-agency and interagency competition. The fact that the government provides the route facilities for motor, water, and air transport is an important basis for this distinction in a private enterprise economy, but interagency competition will be present under any system. The competitive abilities of each mode will be affected by the burden of costs which may be imposed upon it by public policy. Thus the competitive relationships among the agencies will be influenced by user charges, but the competitive structure of transport will not be.[12]

Intra-agency Competition. Competition among the firms of each of the modes of transport, that is, intra-agency competition, presents a distinct problem for regulation because of the different economic structures of each. If railroads and pipe lines were the only two modes serving the public in inland transportation, they would have to be regulated as natural monopolies. This presents severe complications under the present geographical pattern of railroads because of the excessive duplication of facilities. This has been a persistent problem for railroad regulation because of the failure to develop a program of consolidation in keeping with the natural monopoly features. The growth of competition from the newer modes, especially motor carriers, has not changed this structural problem. What it has done is to give the shipper a wider range of alternatives which has greatly reduced the monopoly powers of the railroads. Public policy for the latter today, therefore, must give careful consideration to two crucial questions, namely, (1) the development of a geographical pattern of ownership based on the natural monopoly characteristics and (2) the adaptation of rate regulation to the severe competition offered by the other modes.

The situation within motor, air, and water carriers is in a totally different category. If competition among the firms is not deliberately restrained by public action, or by private agreements, exploitation of the shipper will not occur. In other words, rate regulation is economically unnecessary. Even where entry is restricted, rate regulation is of little benefit to the shipper because of the alternatives of nonregulated carriage available to him. Its chief purpose to date in water and motor transport has been to protect the carrier, not he shipper. As has already been pointed out, the situation in air transport is not quite so obvious, but it is significant to note that the Civil Aeronautics Board's achievements in this direction have been singularly unimpressive. It seems evident that current regulation of motor, water, and air transport is out of tune with the economics of these industries. Regulation of competition in competitive industries is a contradiction of terms.

Interagency Competition. The regulation of competition among

12 If all transportation were publicly owned and operated, motor transport would fall into a category very similar to that of railroads because of the costs entailed in providing the surface routes. Water and air transport would remain essentially as they are today as far as the economic characteristics are concerned.

the different agencies applies first of all to rates. The basic question here is whether such regulation is necessary in the interests of the shipper. This rests on the question of the appropriate relationship of rail rates to those of the other carriers. There is little support for the idea that railroads should or can be protected against the competition of the other carriers. Instead, it is the issue of how much leeway should be accorded to the railroads to meet this competition and therefore of the minimum to which railroad rates should be permitted to go. Analysis in previous chapters led to the conclusion that the economical basis for minimum pricing was the relevant economic costs. Rate making for interagency competition rests on the same basis as pricing for competitive undertakings.

Competition and the Common Carrier. In the period since World War I the proportion of total traffic carried by common carriers has declined drastically because of the rise of the alternative means of moving traffic, and the inability of government to bring many of these into the common carrier category or even within the scope of regulation. The fact that common carriers supply a necessary service and must assume special obligations in doing so has given rise to the idea that they must be protected against competition if they are to survive.[13] That some form of protection of the shipper is necessary seems to be obvious. He needs to be assured that the obligations assumed by the common carrier will be performed properly. However, he is under no obligation to use this means of transportation.

The argument that the common carrier needs protection against competition among common carriers must rest for support on the economic considerations involved in the issues of interagency and intra-agency competition. The need for protection against noncommon carrier competition rests on the answer to two questions: (1) the extent to which such protection can be made effective and (2) the *raison d'être* of the protection. Despite the persistent attempts of regulation, commencing with the Motor Carrier Act of 1935, to extend protection, little success has been achieved, and endeavors to restrict noncommon carriage competition are likely to yield the opposite results. The idea that

[13] This idea has been fostered also by the holders of certificates of public convenience and necessity, particularly in air and motor transport, who regard these certificates as powerful safeguards against competition from firms of their own mode. The railroads typically interpose their opposition when motor carriers apply for certification of service that will compete with them; motor carriers respond in kind when the railroads seek to introduce new service. The Interstate Commerce Commission now regards the loss of traffic by regulated carriers as the principal problem for public transportation. See Interstate Commerce Commission, *75th Annual Report, June 30, 1961* (Washington, D.C.: U.S. Government Printing Office, 1962).

limitation is necessary because of the special obligations of the common carrier assumes that these benefits to the shipper are not worth the additional price he is willing to pay for them; that is, the differential benefits of common carriage over noncommon carriage are so slight as to yield no adequate price to support the former. The one form of control that does seem to be essential relates to the obligations undertaken for the services that are offered. If a carrier holds itself out to transport certain types of traffic as common carriage, then it should be held fully responsible for the discharge of the obligations pertaining thereto. If this is done, the shippers will be able to make a free choice through the medium of the market. The development of policy along these lines raises the question of whether the concept of the common carrier should apply to the firm or merely to some of the services performed by it. This will be dealt with in a later chapter.

Co-ordination of Transport

Shippers quite frequently find it necessary to employ the services of more than one carrier, either of the same mode or of a different one, to move their goods from origin to destination. This requires some form of co-ordination of transport facilities. It may be provided by the shipper himself, as, for example, when he delivers freight to a railroad in his own trucks or in those hired from someone else; or it may be undertaken entirely by the carriers. In the latter case the service is rendered just as though the shipper were dealing with only one carrier.

Co-ordination first began in a significant way with the railroads on a voluntary basis. With the passage of the Interstate Commerce Act in 1887 the Commission was given authority which was extended by subsequent legislation to the comprehensive powers it now exercises over railroads.[14] The Hepburn Act of 1906 gave it the power to establish through routes and rates on traffic by rail and water. Thus, co-ordination among railroads may be compelled, as well as between railroads and water carriers. Voluntary co-ordination of this character may be carried out by motor carriers among themselves and with rail and water carriers, but the Commission cannot compel it. The same remarks apply to water carriers. The Civil Aeronautics Board has no compulsory authority over air lines, but with its consent they may enter into voluntary arrangements among themselves or with other modes.

---

[14] For a detailed history of this development, see Bureau of Transport Economics and Statistics, Interstate Commerce Commission, *Historical Development of Transport Coordination and Integration in the United States,* Statement No. 5015 (Washington, D.C., April, 1950).

Co-ordination among carriers, then, may be achieved by compulsory or voluntary means. There is little argument concerning the use of compulsion for interchange of traffic between railroads, although the details of administration have created considerable controversy. The compulsory features when applied to rail-water routes and rates have been the basis of bitter disputes. Most of the Interstate Commerce Commission's efforts in this direction have been to protect and strengthen the water carriers which have sought to participate in traffic that would otherwise move by rail.[15] Moreover, the railroads have been restricted severely in quoting through rail rates that would compete with the through rail-water rates between the same points.

The absence of compulsory co-ordination for the other carriers may be explained by their competitive structures, Congress apparently adhering to the belief that competition will result in whatever co-ordination is necessary. So far, this policy seems to have worked satisfactorily; to the extent that competition is effective, voluntary arrangements by carriers seeking traffic will be worked out, and discriminatory treatment is unlikely to present any significant problem. The railroads are in a somewhat different category, but present rules which require interchange to protect existing carriers serve to deprive the railroads of traffic which would benefit them, but for which, under the circumstances, they cannot compete.

Consolidation and Integration

Co-ordination of transportation services may also be developed through consolidation of carriers of the same mode or integration of carriers of different modes under common ownership. The first method is a matter of particular attention at the present time with regard to railroads. The second is principally concerned with railroad ownership of other modes.

Consolidation. Early attempts to consolidate railroads encountered resistance under the antitrust laws. The Transportation Act of 1920 provided for a plan to which consolidations were required to conform, but implementation of it was to be on a voluntary basis. The idea of an over-all plan was dropped in the Act of 1940, the law being changed so that the consent of the Interstate Commerce Commission is now required and consolidations that take place must be in the public interest.

[15] For a contrary evaluation of the policy of the ICC, see J. L. Frye, "An Analysis of Rail-Water Coordinate Service," *Transportation Journal,* Vol. VI, No. 3 (Spring, 1967).

The need for extensive consolidation among railroads is now generally conceded, but the pattern which this should follow is subject to much difference of opinion. Some favor consolidations which would preserve extensive competition among the resulting systems; others argue for a limited number of regional groupings. At the present time, the Commission is faced with a large number of applications for merger. So far, it has given no indication of the consolidation pattern it favors. Before approval of the requests is granted, it would seem that the desirable pattern in the light of railroad and transport economics should be settled at the policy level of government.

Consolidation policy for the other modes presents a different problem. Motor and water transport are so competitive as to warrant the conclusion that the antitrust laws alone would be adequate to safeguard public interest. This would be especially true if restrictions on entry were modified. The air carrier problem is complicated by current policies on mail payments, subsidy, and certification. If these were developed to conform to the competitive characteristics of the industry, and if the apparent limitations on economies of scale were recognized, then it is likely that antitrust would be adequate for it also.

Integration.   Integration or interagency ownership has been advocated principally on the grounds that it would provide for more economical transport and would be more convenient for the shipper—first of all, because he could get any of the services from one company and, second, because co-ordination among the agencies would be easier to develop. These assumptions require careful examination in light of policy.

It is very doubtful that any economies of scale can be realized by interagency ownership. The limitations on economies of scale that apply to all the modes, although not with equal force, make it difficult to see how more efficient transport can be supplied by transport companies than by independence of ownership of the modes. The railroads as such would not be helped unless the effect were to reduce intermodal competition because the competitive rates received by the other modes which they owned would not be able to shoulder any of the railroad burden. In other words, it would not help to resolve the railroad problem.

Co-ordination would offer as much of a problem at present unless huge transport monopolies were established, an unlikely possibility. It is difficult to see how dealing with a single firm would offer any real advantages to the shipper in light of present competitive opportunities. Moreover, if it had any effect on interagency competition, the result would be to diminish it rather than to enhance it. In addition, it would be unlikely to promote more thoroughgoing co-ordination because the transport companies would be loath to co-operate with the competitive carriers of the other modes.

Railroad ownership of motor carriers for the performance of ancillary services is a somewhat different question. The general policy of the Interstate Commerce Commission has been to oppose ownership of motor carriers by railroads, but it has permitted it when the services to be offered are purely ancillary in nature. Thus, it permits the railroads to operate motor carriers to perform terminal services, to replace abandoned branch-line services, and to substitute for local traffic between key points where the freight has had a prior rail haul or will have a subsequent one. These arrangements seem to be designed to afford co-ordination of local and through traffic without impairing competition. When railroads enter into piggyback operations with their own motor vehicles, they compete with the line traffic of motor carriers by use of the rails rather than the highways. Integration by railroads with other carriers, particularly motor, for the purpose of supplying ancillary services may enable the railroads to compete more effectively to attract traffic to their lines without restricting the processes of competition.

TERMINAL PROBLEMS

Terminals in many respects constitute the most complex problem in the field of transportation today. Before the rise of the modern transport structure, it centered largely on the railroads. Where cities were served by more than one rail line, each had its own passenger and freight facilities. The problems connected with these related to terminating and originating traffic and the interchange of through traffic. In the cities served by a number of rail lines,[16] delays, congestion, inconvenience, and wasteful duplication were the result, to a considerable extent, of railroad competition. Steps both voluntary and compulsory have been taken to deal with the difficulties by interchange arrangements and even unification, but the basic problem has remained and has even become aggravated with the growth of traffic. To this must be added the requirement of adequate rail-water connections at those points where water traffic is of significance. Harbor development and control have been largely matters for local and state authorities to deal with, but the federal government, through the Corps of Army Engineers, has also participated in planning and financing.

[16] Chicago is served by 23, St. Louis by 16, and New York by 12.

The growth of air transportation has created another terminal problem somewhat similar to that of rail and water. The airport constitutes the terminus of the traffic movement by the airplane. At the present time, most of the airports are owned and managed by municipal authorities, federal participation being confined to those airports receiving aid in accordance with the National Airport Act of 1946. The location of these termini, particularly with the development of the "jets," has become a matter of great importance because of the technical problems of operation and the relation of the location to the terminal movement of the traffic they generate. The need of more than one airport for the large centers complicates the problem. If air freight should develop to significant proportions, new considerations would arise.

The most difficult issues, in some respects, connected with terminals are presented by the motor vehicle. For the most part, its terminal consists of the roadways and the plants and the buildings of the customers. The motor carrier supplies terminal services to the other carriers; it is the most important transport agency within the city and metropolitan areas; and it moves a large volume of intercity traffic that may pass through the centers, originate in them, or may be destined to them. Thus the terminal aspects of motor transport are an inextricable part of the present urban transport complex.

In some respects the terminal problems of each of the modes may be dealt with independently of each other, and to a certain extent this is necessary because they cannot be divorced from the functioning of each carrier as a whole. Railroad terminals, for example, cannot be separated from the other aspects of railroad operations. Because, however, of the relationship of the terminal facilities and services connected with the different modes to urban transport and the position occupied by the motor vehicle in it, policies with regard to terminal problems must be developed as part of an over-all approach to metropolitan transportation before a satisfactory program can emerge.

THE LABOR PROBLEM

Labor Legislation

The problem of labor in national transport policy falls into a somewhat different category than the other topics of this chapter. Yet in some ways, it is so closely related with it both historically and in its special relation to some of the modes that it warrants separate treatment. Public policy with regard to labor in transportation has never been integrated, at least in any unified way, with the regulation of transport itself. Thus the Interstate Commerce Commission and the Civil Aeronautics Board have no authority over labor and labor relations except that the Motor Carrier Act gave the Interstate Commerce Commission authority over qualifications and maximum hours of service of employees of motor carriers, whether for hire or private, in connection with its responsibilities for safety of operation; and it was responsible for the safety of operations of rail carriers.[17] Even this modicum of authority has been transferred to the Department of Transportation.

Nevertheless, there has been a long history, beginning with the Erdman Act of 1898, of federal legislation with labor problems that have arisen in connection with rail transport, culminating in the Railway Labor Act of 1926 and its subsequent amendments. This legislation was made applicable to air lines in 1936. There is also separate legislation relating to railroad retirements and unemployment benefits. The law governing labor disputes may be administered through a number of agencies established under it, while that relating to retirements and unemployment is under the Railroad Retirement Board. These laws and their administration will be dealt with in a subsequent chapter.

The Uniqueness of the Labor Problem

The labor problem in transportation is unique in a number of different ways. Special attention has been accorded it, particularly in railroad transportation and more recently in air transport, because of the responsibilities of operating employees for the safety of the traveling public. The detailed rules incident to the operation of railroad trains, and the relatively long period of training necessary, have contributed to the preferred position of these uniquely skilled employees in the field of transportation. The requirements of health, skill, and special training for air-line pilots have also resulted in strict standards of public control and a strategic position for the pilots.

The key positions occupied by these members of the transport personnel, because the traffic cannot move without them and there are no ready substitutes for them, have made it possible for them to secure special benefits and special privileges not generally accorded even to the other employees of the same modes. Historically, this preferred position developed in connection with the railroads. Even today the

---

[17] The Transportation Act of 1940 provides that when a consolidation takes place, the employees shall be protected for a period of four years from the effective date of the consolidation, so that employees affected by the transaction will not be "in a worse position with respect to their employment" (Interstate Commerce Act, Part I, Section 5 [2] [f]). Protection may also be afforded employees in the case of abandonment.

operating staff enjoys special protection not received by other railroad employees under such legislation as the full-crew laws, for example, although the legislation regarding consolidation and abandonment has extended these benefits somewhat.

The unique position of part of the labor force at least in railroads arises from dependence of the public on the railroads and on a particular railroad. A shutdown of the entire railroad system of the United States would paralyze the commerce of the country literally overnight, and even for one strategic railroad the same results would obtain for a whole area. A concerted refusal to work by engineers, firemen, brakemen, and conductors can bring the transport system to a halt at once. In none of the other modes have such devastating possibilities been present until recently. Probably the key point in the explanation of this lies in the monopoly position so long occupied by the railroads and the fact that even today they are the core of the transport system of the country. This has made it possible for the key personnel to organize more effectively than in any other industry and at the same time has stimulated the public attempts to develop ways and means of resolving disputes without resort to strikes and shutdowns.

Transport Technology and the Labor Problem

The monopoly position of railroad transportation led to the growth of comprehensive control over rates and the rate level that today characterizes our regulatory policy. An effective program for limiting profits to those which are fair also requires control of the costs which enter into the calculation of those profits. The costs which are competitively determined can be accepted as reasonable or fair. What is a fair wage for strategically organized labor, however, is another matter; and so far, we have lacked adequate criteria by which to measure this.[18] The Interstate Commerce Commission has been compelled to accept wages as costs and adjust rate levels accordingly. As long as the railroads can meet the demands and earn the necessary profits, their position is not prejudiced, even though they might resist the demands. The only victims of this situation are the shipper and the ultimate consumer. If the railroads were to come under public ownership, the taxpayer would also enter the picture unless some better means of dealing with the situation were developed than is available today.

The impact of changing technology on labor relations remains to be seen. Technology has revolutionized transportation in the last forty

---

[18] For a discussion of this problem, see F. H. Dixon, *Railroads and Government* (New York: Charles Scribner's Sons, 1922), chaps. vii, xiii, and xxiv.

years; competition has now become the order of the day, and even though labor organizations should be able to maintain monopolistic positions in some segments, they no longer deal with management that enjoys the same powers to any significant degree. Consequently, if transportation remains in private hands, and if it cannot depend upon the government for subsidy, labor costs in transport will have to conform to general competitive conditions. This may make it possible for labor problems to be settled through the medium of collective bargaining, and it may also make it possible to develop means of adjusting labor disputes other than by strikes, because even with pervasive competition, strikes, especially against the railroads, carry too great a threat of immediate paralysis of the operation of the economy.

AGENCIES OF PUBLIC POLICY

Public policy in transportation involves government in economic regulation as well as in the administration of public funds for the provision of transport services. Thus, it differs from that which is applied to industry in general in that the government specifically displaces a considerable part of the forces of the market place, on the one hand, and participates in managerial and investment functions, on the other. As was pointed out in a previous section of this chapter, these two aspects of public policy are distinct from each other. Yet they are immediately related, particularly through the impact of public investment on the total allocation of economic resources to transportation and among the different agencies.

Regulation of Transport

Regulation in transportation is primarily concerned with the control of rates and competition. This has been extended to cover such other aspects of operations as service, finance, and accounting. This comprehensive control is necessary where the sources of supply of transport services fall strictly into the public utility pattern. The Interstate Commerce Commission was given additional responsibilities over safety and conditions of operation. Thus, its functions were extended far beyond those which are essential to comprehensive public utility control.

The appropriate scope of the functions of the independent regulatory commission in transport has turned on three questions. The first is the nature and extent of economic regulation that is necessary under contemporary conditions. The second is the feasibility of giving to these commissions functions that are essentially of an executive nature. The third is that of developing national transportation policy and of coordinating the various aspects of it. The establishment of the Department of Transportation in April, 1967, has now placed the last two of these functions in the executive branch of the government. Although the respective roles of the Department, the Congress and the commissions remain to be worked out, it appears that the primary responsibility of the commissions will be that of regulation as directed by the laws of Congress.

The desirable scope of the regulatory powers must be evaluated in light of what seem to be the reasonable minimum requirements and possibilities of regulation at the present time. If one assumes that transport regulation must continue in the public utility pattern that has characerized it to date, then the elimination of much of the minutia that occupies the attention of the Commission today is well-nigh unavoidable. On the other hand, if full play is accorded competitive forces, then the need of rate regulation and restriction of entry in the competitive modes will disappear; even rate regulation for railroads would call only for minimum controls to prevent predatory practices and perhaps some power over maximum rates. This pattern of control is unlikely to emerge rapidly, but developments in this direction can reduce the enormous amount of detail now engrossing the attention of the regulatory authorities.

Reform of commission procedures either by legislation or by internal reorganization to reduce delays, expense, and obstacles to competitive adaptation must be based on a theory of the function of regulation in transportation if it is to be effective. Present criticisms[19] would largely be overcome if regulation were reduced to conform to the requirements of current competitive conditions. The reduction of the detailed duties of commission regulation made necessary by present legislation would make it possible for the Interstate Commerce Commission to devote more attention to the development of policy, or at least proposals for policy, on matters such as consolidation and interagency ownership, which can be formulated only within the framework of a theory of transport organization based on the economics of transport.

Similar considerations apply to the question of whether there should be a single federal commission for the regulation of transportation, two separate ones as is presently the case, or commissions for each

[19] See, for example, *Report on Regulatory Agencies to the President-Elect* (Landis Report), Senate Committee on the Judiciary, 82d Congress, 2d session, December, 1960 (Washington, D.C.: U.S. Government Printing Office, 1960).

of the agencies. A single commission under present laws would not serve to reduce existing cumbersomeness and delay in the administration of the regulatory program. It would also entail mixing promotion and regulation, which the Interstate Commerce Commission now escapes. On the other hand, extensive reduction of regulatory functions, together with separation of them from those that are executive in nature, might make a single commission more feasible than is currently the case.

Administration and Promotion

The discharge of executive functions such as the prescription and supervision of safety measures is really foreign to the idea of an independent regulatory commission. Nevertheless, it was a rather logical extension, under the circumstances, of the need for control of service by the Interstate Commerce Commission if rate regulation was to be effective. The proliferation of duties in this respect, especially with the development of motor transport, made this a particularly onerous burden on regulation. In motor transport the effective discharge of safety regulations must rest upon police and highway authorities, not the regulatory agencies. These functions belong in the executive branch of government. The distinction between safety regulations and service requirements will become less difficult to make if the force of competition is given more recognition in public policy.

Administration of public aid, subsidy, and public investment do not fall within the scope of regulation. The difficulties faced by the Civil Aeronautics Board in reconciling its responsibilities on air-mail payment and subsidy with those of regulation illustrate this. Furthermore, public aid, subsidy, and public investment are not really related to the process of regulation. They are, however, an integral part of transport policy. Until recently there was no single agency or department in the federal government for co-ordinating the programs of public investment in inland transport and for developing policy with regard to financing and the recovery of the costs of them. These duties have been scattered among a number of different agencies, often with conflicting responsibilities.[20] Of at least equal significance is the fact that no co-ordination exists today between public investment and the over-all need for transport facilities. Nothing resembling an economical system of transportation can be obtained as long as the present contradictions

---

[20] See Dearing and Owen, *op. cit.,* chap. vi and pp. 351–71; and *National Transport Policy* (Doyle Report) Part III. The extent to which this has been remedied by the establishing of the Department of Transportation remains to be seen.

persist and transport services are supplied by undertakings that are wholly privately owned, on the one hand, and by those receiving large amounts of public support, on the other. The deficiencies of this approach can be remedied only by administrative unification that will view investment needs in transportation as a whole, and the imposition of a substantial equality of burdens on the users of each mode.

Federal, State, and Local Responsibilities

The complex interrelationships of local, state, and interstate transportation call for close co-operation between these three levels of government, with reasonably clear-cut recognition of the responsibilities of each. Because of the predominantly interstate character of rail, pipe-line, and air transport, and federal jurisdiction over the waterways, primary authority over these modes rests in the hands of the federal government and will undoubtedly remain there. Some conflicts and contradictions still exist, however, particularly with regard to water and air terminals. These are mostly under the control of local authorities, although some state participation exists in the case of water. The principal problem that emerges here is connected with financing and assessing the appropriate costs on the users of the facilities. User charges for these are a matter of local jurisdiction and exhibit little uniformity in policy. As far as the taxpayer is concerned, this may be regarded as a matter for local decision, but the impact of it on the competitive relationships among the different agencies of transport is another question. Federal investment policy in harbors and airports will require re-examination if a program of user charges for the recovery of federal funds is to be developed.

The major problem of reconciling federal, state, and local policies arises in connection with motor transport. Here, public investment is made by all three levels of government, but jurisdiction over use rests in the hands of state and local authorities. The imposition of user charges by the federal government will encounter some severe limitations unless the co-operation of state authorities in particular is obtained, because of the large amount of intrastate vehicular traffic. However, if the federal government is able to assess effective user charges to recover the federal stake in the highway system, a significant step will have been taken toward equalizing competitive conditions. To this problem of the motor carrier should be added that of developing acceptable arrangements on weights, sizes, and safety standards of vehicles moving in interstate traffic.

Another problem concerning the locus of governmental responsibility in transport has recently emerged at the urban or metropolitan level. To date, this has been primarily a matter of local concern and may well remain so. However, the federal government is already involved through its provision of funds for highway construction, particularly the national interstate system, which embraces many of the major routes through metropolitan centers and even forms part of the freeway systems of cities such as Los Angeles. In addition, the problem of mass movement of people in the large metropolitan centers has attracted the attention of authorities in the federal government. The plea so far has been for federal aid for local development. If this is accorded, the pressures are hardly likely to stop at that point.

CONCLUSION

The foregoing discussion should make it clear that there are many facets to the national transport problem. The impact of modern technology has resulted in the emergence of a group of industries with independent functions in many respects and with close interrelationships in others. The differing economic characteristics of the various modes are such as to make it doubtful that a single approach embracing all of them would prove to be workable. While the objective of national policy should be to meet the nation's transport requirements in the most economical way, this is not easy to accomplish with the mixture of private and public investment, national and local transport needs, and the demands of national defense. Moreover, the present situation is the result of a long historical accumulation of legislation, court and commissions decisions, and administrative actions. These create an inertia that is not easy to overcome, while agreement on what should be overcome and how it is to be done can scarcely be said to have reached the stage of decisiveness. Finally, it must be recognized that the underlying assumptions of national policy must be that of a private enterprise system in transportation.

The basic *modus operandi* must be those of the pricing system, the market place, and competition. In peacetime we rely primarily on the market mechanism operating within rules established on the assumption that competition, private interest, and private initiative can and will perform the functions of central management.[21] The market mechanism has some limitations but not as many as has frequently been supposed. More reliance on them than present policy employs will

[21] See M. A. Copeland, "Institutionalism, and Welfare Economics," *American Economic Review,* Vol. XLVIII, No. 1 (March, 1958), pp. 1–17.

simplify both regulation and administration. It is difficult, therefore, to subscribe to a policy designed to copy the military approach.

   . . . We could learn from the study of military techniques which, despite all we hear to the contrary, work in the largest, most complex undertaking known to man—general war.

   The military starts with a definition of what it wants to do—generally and specifically. It estimates the situation, the resources, and as best we can define them, the enemy capabilities. It lays a plan of action under which each task will contribute to the final goal, keeping each action within its variable resources. It tries to provide alternatives against the unexpected. When it moves, it moves in coordinated fashion, with determination, and it doesn't quit if obstacles appear. If the systems approach has been well worked out, it wins.[22]

Apart from colliding head-on with the fundamental presuppositions of private enterprise, implementation of this point of view would pose a major threat to a free society. National policy today calls for an analysis of the various problems of transport and for steps to resolve them through the medium of the private enterprise system, not through centralized governmental direction and management. The following chapters undertake to deal with these matters in greater detail.

[22] Speech of Major General Doyle, *Traffic World,* April 22, 1967, p. 110.

COMPETITION
AND REGULATION
IN TRANSPORTATION

INTRODUCTION

Competition in economic activity is a matter of alternatives. If resources can be put to different uses, there will be competition among these uses for the resources that can be applied to them, and there will be competition among the resources to serve the various purposes to which they may be put. The effectiveness of the competition will depend upon the extent to which the resources and uses may be substituted for each other: The greater the possibilities of substitution, the greater will be the competition; and the lesser the possibilities of substitution, the lesser will be the competition. For example, there is no direct competition between automobiles and steel, but automobile manufacturers compete with each other for the sale of their products and for the purchase of steel; similar remarks apply to the producers of steel. The production of automobiles and steel is undertaken by two different industries, and there is no direct rivalry between them. On the other hand, although the production of steel and aluminum is carried on by two different industries, there is a good deal of substitutability of the products and hence competition between them, and this would exist even though each were operating as a monopoly, or if one were a monopoly and the other was not.

As has already been pointed out, transportation consists of a group of industries. Competition in the supplying of transport services is similar to that in the rest of the industrial structure, namely, intra-industry or intra-agency, and interindustry or interagency. Public policy for industry in general does not distinguish between these two classifications of competition, and the principal center of public attention is confined to intra-industry competition and the behavior of particular firms. Transport policy, on the other hand, must recognize both types of competition because of the differences in the economic characteristics

422

of the various agencies of transport, and because there is a wide range of substitutability of services among them. Each of the modes has features which call for separate treatment, and there is the special problem of the standards for competition among them. The pervasiveness of competition in this field refers to the over-all competitive situation which has developed with the new technology, but it must not be interpreted to mean that each mode is thoroughly competitive within itself.

INTRA-AGENCY COMPETITION

Competition in Rail Transport

Types of Competition. Competition among railroads takes on a number of different forms. The most obvious is where they compete directly with each other as parallel lines for traffic between given points. It is this type which gave rise to intense rivalry, rate wars, and ruinous practices. A somewhat similar situation is found when important trade centers are connected by rival roads having markedly different distances and operating conditions. For example, traffic may move from Portland, Oregon, to Ogden, Utah, by the Union Pacific over a distance of 945 miles, or it may go by way of the Southern Pacific for 1,487 miles. This is known as indirect or circuitous routing. Even though railroads were organized into regional monopolies, strong competition among them would still exist because of market conditions. Florida, Texas, and California compete with each other for the market for citrus fruits in the manufacturing region of the Great Lakes and the Atlantic coast. Similarly, seaports may compete for export trade that may pass through any of them. Thus, competition among railroads may take on a number of different forms. The one that gives rise to the most difficult problems is that involving parallel and rival routes between the same centers.[1]

Control of Competition. Railroad competition in the period immediately following the Civil War resulted in severe rate wars. It has been reported that cattle were hauled from Chicago to New York for $1.00 per carload in 1873.[2] The chaotic competitive situation that developed before the inauguration of federal regulation led the railroads

---

[1] For a discussion of the different forms of railroad competition, see Stuart Daggett, *Principles of Inland Transportation* (4th ed.; Harper & Bros., 1955), chap. xix.

[2] See D. P. Locklin, *Economics of Transportation* (6th ed.; Homewood, Ill.: Richard D. Irwin, Inc., 1966), chap. 15, for illustrations; also Eliot Jones, *Principles of Railway Transportation* (New York: The Macmillan Co., 1925), chap. v.

to resort to a number of different devices to curb competition among themselves. They worked out agreements to divide territory, to maintain specific rates, and to pool traffic or revenues. All of these arrangements had a precarious standing at common law, and of course there was no way of compelling adherence to them as a matter of contract at the federal level. Pooling agreements were ended with the Act to Regulate Commerce in 1887, and rate agreements ran afoul of the Sherman Act of 1890.[3] In the cases involving rate agreements, the law was on the side of the majority of the Supreme Court, which held them to violate the Sherman Act, but economics was on the side of the minority, which took the contrary point of view.

The failure to control competition by rate agreements and pooling led to the development of three other means, namely, rate bureaus, combination and consolidation, and limitations on competition by regulation. The latter has already been described in connection with the legislation that has given the Interstate Commerce Commission its present comprehensive control over railroads; combination and consolidation will be discussed in the next chapter. Rate bureaus were set up on a regional basis as organizations through which proposals for changing rates were channeled. Adherence to the recommendations of the committees representing the participating railroads was a voluntary matter, but this was nevertheless a means of collective action on rate making. This, too, encountered the obstacle of the Sherman Act, despite the control over rates exercised by the Interstate Commerce Commission. Finally, Congress passed the Reed-Bulwinkle Act in 1948, by which rate bureaus and their operations are now lawful for railroads, provided that the Commission sanctions their procedures and that each individual carrier has the right to take independent action if it does not want to accept the recommendations of the committee of which it is a member.

One of the complicating features of railroad competition arises from the problem of the weak and strong roads.[4] This is the result of the unequal earning capacity of railroads that are directly competitive with each other for much of the traffic on which each of them depends. If two or more railroads are competing for the same traffic, they will have to charge the same rates on it. One of them, however, may be in a decidedly advantageous position, and therefore be able to offer rates which may be lower than the other one can afford to charge, thereby de-

[3] *United States* v. *Trans-Missouri Freight Association,* 166 U.S. 290 (1897); *United States* v. *Joint Traffic Association,* 171 U.S. 505 (1898).

[4] See J. C. Nelson, *Railroad Transportation and Public Policy* (Washington, D.C.: The Brookings Institution, 1959), pp. 214–18.

priving the latter of the traffic; or the rates may be such that the road in the disadvantageous position may have to accept traffic at rates which, although above relevant costs, may be inadequate because the rest of its traffic is unable to make up the necessary difference. When such a situation persists, the weaker road may be in a chronically unsound financial condition. Uncontrolled competition under such circumstances may lead to disastrous results to all of the competitors. Controlled competition may preserve the stronger roads, leaving the weaker roads in a continuously unsatisfactory position; or it might conceivably result in the strong roads being compelled to maintain such high rates as to yield unreasonable profits, deprive them of traffic which they could move more economically, and at the same time burden shippers dependent on them alone with charges that they otherwise would not have to bear. In any case, such a situation results in uneconomical rail transport. This is because competition between natural monopolies is ruinous if it extends to a significant portion of their business. This will be so even if the roads are of comparatively equal competitive strength.

The Role of Competition.   Competition of some kind or another among railroads is unavoidable unless a single system is established for the entire country. Such competition, however, may not be uneconomical if, through appropriate organization, duplication of facilities and services and excess capacity are eliminated. To date, public policy on railroad organization has been designed to preserve direct competition, on the one hand, and to regulate it, on the other. This is a contradiction in terms which can scarcely result in a resolution of the problems which such competition presents.

If railroad transportation in the United States is to realize its full potential of efficiency, competition among the systems will have to be much more limited than it is at the present time. However, it seems to be clear that there will be a good deal of competition if private ownership remains, no matter what solution is adopted. How much regulation or control this will call for will depend upon the amount of direct rivalry that continues to exist and the effectiveness of competition from the other modes. If, as far as circumstances will permit, railroads are recognized as natural monopolies and organized on that basis, the need for control of competition among them will be greatly reduced. The extent to which rate control will then be necessary to protect the shipper will depend upon the effectiveness of competition from the other agencies. It may well be that intermodal competition will prove to be a more effective safeguard of public interest than any comprehensive form of rate regulation we have as yet devised.

Even if a program of consolidation for railroads were developed on a predominately regional basis, competitive freedom on rates among them, including, as it would have to, abolition of rate making by agreement, is likely to develop but slowly. The rate structure of the country has grown up over a long period of time with many restrictions on competition that have had significant effects on traffic routes and the location of firms and industries. Then too, the railroads themselves have shown considerable reluctance to accept the full consequences of a freely competitive pricing structure. These issues are illustrated by the difficulties that have arisen as the result of court action overruling the Interstate Commerce Commission's authority to maintain differentials on export traffic to the Atlantic ports north of Baltimore.[5] The problem is likely to become more acute if present proposals for consolidation in Eastern territory are carried out. The controversy that has developed over the absolute "rate-break" rule on grain rates in Western territory is another illustration of a similar nature.[6] The western railroads evidently want protection against the eastern ones to prevent a shift in industry from their territory. The railroads also registered opposition to placing them solely under antitrust laws, including the Robinson-Patman Act, as a condition for removing bulk commodities and agricultural products from rate regulation. The rail carriers do not seem to be ready to go the whole way in accepting competition as the regulator of rates in intra-agency competition. Competition among the modes still leaves many of the railroad problems unsolved.

Competition in Motor Transport

Competition in motor transport is of a much simpler type than that which characterizes railroads. As has already been pointed out, the economic structure is such as to make it possible for competition to function as a fully effective force for establishing economical prices. Limitations on competition among carriers are not necessary to protect them against ruinous competition and the consequences arising from it. In fact, it is literally impossible to protect them from extensive competition within the industry because of the amount of motor transport that lies outside the scope of regulation. Moreover, the policy of restriction that has been tried to date has come perilously close to breaking down, as evidenced by growth of the "gray" area and "illegal" transportation for hire. The concern which this development has created arises from the

[5] *Boston and Maine Railroad* v. *United States,* 202 Fed. Supp. 830 (1962).
[6] *Western Rail Grain Rates,* 358 I.C.C. 358 (1966).

restrictions that have been placed upon the regulated carriers with regard to their freedom to compete. Endeavors to resolve the dilemma are likely to meet with little success under the current theory of regulation because it requires comprehensive control of the entire industry, both carriage for hire and that which is not for hire. The possibility of this is so remote that it does not merit serious consideration. In addition, the extension of regulatory authority would result in an increase of motor transport facilities rather than the reverse, thereby aggravating instead of alleviating the problem of excess capacity. In theory, regulation should result in prices that would approximate those which competition will yield. Where competition is inescapable, it is scarcely sound policy to impede it and then endeavor to secure the fruits of it by public regulation.

If competition in an industry is to be effective, it is necessary that resources be both legally and economically mobile. Resources are economically mobile in motor transport; both investment and facilities are easily transferred to other uses. Plant or equipment may be shifted to new market demands and new market areas. Ready transferability may also be achieved by new investment or disinvestment with a consequent shift of capital to or from motor transport. Because most of the investment in it is in facilities that have a relatively short life and in equipment that can be moved easily from one use to another, or to new market areas, the utilization of resources can respond readily to the demand for them.

If resources are to be legally mobile, it must be possible for them, as far as the law is concerned, to be free to move from one use to another, and from one market to another. There must be freedom to transfer the physical equipment according to the wishes of the producers, or to convert it or divert it to other uses. In other words, there must be both freedom of entry and freedom of exit. If freedom of entry is denied by law, special privilege is accorded to an entrant to an industry or market, or to an existing producer, and this affords protection against the pressures of competition. The protected carrier is no longer faced with the threat of an alternative supplier of similar services who may be willing to risk his resources in the belief that his venture will be successful.

The limitations on competition in motor transport in the United States today are the result of legal restrictions, not of the economic characteristics of the industry. These restrictions serve primarily as a protective device for the common carrier, although they also do the same thing for the contract carrier in a somewhat more limited way. How effective they are in fact is an uncertain question, as evidenced by widespread demands of the protected carriers for more rigid controls, and concern over the growth of the "gray" area. The focal point of the issue is really the common carrier, and whether it in the public interest needs protection. There is the additional question whether, in fact, it can be afforded effective protection against competition. However, public need for common carriage is not a valid ground for protecting common carriers by restriction of entry.[7]

Competition in Other Modes

Competition within the other modes of transport partakes of the nature of either of the previous two and therefore requires no elaboration. Pipe lines are natural monopolies, and over-all competition would be unworkable. This has been recognized in natural gas. No problems have yet arisen on this issue for petroleum pipe lines because of their direct association for the most part with the oil industry.[8] The same remarks apply to water transport as were made for motor, except that regulation has been much less restrictive and has been aimed at protecting the water carriers against the railroads rather than against themselves. Restriction of competition within the industry has had little effect on its behavior, and even if vigorous attempts were made to broaden and enforce the law, they would be very unlikely to solve any of the problems that exist.[9]

As has already been pointed out, air transportation is an industry which is competitive in its structure. The Civil Aeronautics Board has acknowledged this but has done little so far to develop a consistent policy of any sort.[10] It is evident, however, that intra-agency policy will

---

[7] See D. F. Pegrum, "Effects of Regulation on Small Business in Motor Transport," *I.C.C. Administration of the Motor Carrier Act,* Hearings before Select Committee on Small Business, U.S. Senate, 84th Cong., 1st sess., November, 1955 (Washington, D.C.: U.S. Government Printing Office, 1956), pp. 465 f.; J. C. Nelson, "The Effects of Entry Control in Surface Transport," in National Bureau of Economic Research, *Transportation Economics* (New York, 1965), pp. 381–422.

[8] It is interesting to note that barge lines in California protested rates on the competing Southern Pacific Pipe Lines Inc., on the ground that the California Public Utilities Act required that water carriers be protected against competing land carriers. The Commission, in a divided opinion, ruled against the barge lines on purely technical grounds, and refused therefore to deal with the rate issue of incremental versus fully distributed costs. *The River Lines* v. *Southern Pacific Pipe Lines Inc.,* case 7238, Decision No. 66695, January, 1964.

[9] Restriction of common carrier competition between the mainland and Hawaii has been a source of almost continuous controversy. It certainly has done nothing to improve the lot of the shipping and traveling public.

[10] In 1961, the CAB asked Congress to enact legislation that would give it economic regulatory control over contract carriers by air. It took this step on the grounds that it had been necessary for the Interstate Commerce Commission to exercise control over contract motor carriers in order to safeguard the public good. Civil Aeronautics Board, *Annual Report, 1961* (Washington, D.C.: U.S. Government Printing Office, 1962), p. 10.

have to be developed independently of that for the other modes. It also seems to be clear that the competitive nature of the industry will have to occupy the center of the stage of any program that is economically sound and based on the assumption of self-sufficient private enterprise. In addition, the Board will have to resolve the problem of the respective positions of freight and passenger traffic in airline competition and organization.

INTERAGENCY COMPETITION

The Problem of Interagency Competition

Interagency competition has been a controversial issue in American transport policy since the beginning of the century. Until the emergence of the motor carrier, it was confined to the rivalry of rail and water carriers. Public policy on this question has continuously been directed to the protection of the water carrier, this being based on the grounds, alleged or real, that the railroads were able to use their monopoly position to control or eliminate water transport. With the rise of the new agencies in transport since World War II, competition between rail and motor carriers has become very intense. For the most part, pipe-line transportation is so much cheaper than rail that the latter makes very little effort to compete for traffic in crude oil, but competition for the movement of liquid products is quite active.[11] Some competition between pipe lines and water carriers is also evident. The air lines compete for passenger traffic and are trying to make some inroads on freight, but the relationship of their rates to those of other carriers so far has not raised issues on the principles of pricing to be used for the interagency rivalry. These have been confined to the competition between the railroads, on the one hand, and the water and motor carriers, on the other.

The problem of interagency competition has arisen from the need for developing policy with regard to price competition where the rival modes possess strikingly different economic characteristics. If the railroads had the competitive features of the other two agencies, the issue would probably not have emerged, despite the fact that the governing principles would still have been the same. In other words, differential pricing or discrimination would not produce any difficult problems. It is because the relevant costs for railroads for minimum price decisions on particular items of traffic fall well below average costs that the controversy arises. The extent to which such pricing should be permitted as a means of securing traffic which may also be moved by other modes is the special problem of interagency competition.

[11] See Locklin, *op. cit.,* p. 605.

Inherent Advantages

Congress gave explicit recognition to interagency competition in the declaration of national policy in the Transportation Act of 1940 when it directed the Interstate Commerce Commission to administer regulation so as to recognize and preserve the inherent advantages of each mode. It presumably strengthened its instructions in the Transportation Act of 1958 when it said that the rates of a carrier were not to be held up to a particular level to protect the traffic of any other mode of transportation. Unfortunately, this gave no criteria for measuring what constituted a reasonable minimum rate, nor did it clearly relieve the Commission of the responsibility of protecting water carriers.

It may be assumed that Congress intended that transport services should be supplied by the carriers most economically able to do so. If this is the case, then it must rest on the meaning of inherent advantages in economics. Economical decisions are those that result in allocating resources to uses that satisfy those wants that are deemed most important at the time the decisions are made. When the pricing process is most completely effective, the resources are being used to their best possible advantage and are being put to the uses they are most capable of fulfilling. That is to say, they are being used according to their inherent advantages. Inherent advantages, therefore, may be defined as those advantages which a producer possesses as a result of greater efficiency of operation, which make it possible for him to attract customers to his business at lower relative prices than those that a rival producer or supplier of alternatives can offer.[12]

The idea of inherent advantages is implicit in an economical allocation of resources and therefore is implicit in all competitive concepts. So much is this the case that the term is not even used in the field of industry in general. It appeared in transport legislation apparently because of the diverse economic characteristics of the industries and because of the fact that monopoly and competitive situations were inextricably mixed in a way not found elsewhere in our industrial structure. The desire of Congress to preserve the inherent advantages of the different modes arose out of its concern over the effects of competition among them on each of them, especially the effects of railroad competition on the other agencies. Congress, however, did not recognize the differences in the economic characteristics of the various agencies. It

---

[12] See D. F. Pegrum, "Why Inherent Advantages Are Important," in *Essays on Inherent Advantages of Railway Service* (New York: Simmons-Boardman Publishing Corp., 1954), pp. 9–12.

probably assumed that they all needed to be treated alike. This led to the further assumption that there was no distinction between intra-agency and interagency competition. The need for and basis of this distinction has already been pointed out.

If inherent advantages are to be realized, then traffic should be permitted to move by the low-cost carrier. This seems to be recognized by the Interstate Commerce Commission, except where it is following the legislative mandate to protect the water carriers, but the gauge for the low-cost carrier is the issue which is in dispute.[13] The criterion which the Commission appears to be following is that which approximates average cost. However, as has already been pointed out, this is not the appropriate measuring rod for the economical minimum price which competition may compel. This economical minimum is the relevant costs of moving the traffic in question, and these costs are the specific and variable.

From the standpoint of economics, attempts to limit or eliminate differential pricing which increases the use of economic resources is against public interest. Given the investment or the technical necessities of a plant, prices for particular products or services that are below average costs are economically sound as long as they cover the costs that would not be incurred if the production did not take place. This assumes, of course, that the firm is better off at these prices than at any others that it could get for these services or for the use of the resources that produce them. That is, it assumes that the prices are market-oriented and not quoted for predatory purposes. Rates that attract traffic which increases the net revenue of the carrier that can get it are in the public interest and are a necessary part of public policy that relies on competition. The fact that the rates may be based on costs which are "below average" is not a relevant consideration.

Rate making on these principles may be hard on some competitors. That, however, is the essence of competition. The purpose of public policy in an area where pervasive competition prevails is to preserve competition, not to sustain competitors. The competition must be fair, but fair competition has meaning only as it enables enterprises to succeed by the sale of their product to consumers who have alternative choices. This does not recognize survival by preying upon or devouring rivals, but it does make survival dependent upon the ability to attract

---

[13] See *New Automobiles in Interstate Commerce*, 259 I.C.C. 475 (1949); *Lumber— California and Oregon to California and Arizona*, 308 I.C.C. 345 (1959); and Howard Freas, *Aspects of Transportation Based on Regulatory Experience in the United States*, a paper delivered to the High Authority Coal and Steel Community, Luxembourg, October 10, 1958 (mimeographed).

customers by superior services or lower prices, or both, in open markets with rivals.

The protection of competition demands the prevention of predatory pricing. When a seller is worse off by selling a product or service than he would be if he did not sell it, and knowingly does this to get business from a competitor, then he is engaged in predatory pricing. It is this sort of behavior in transport that the regulation of interagency competition should seek to prevent, and no other. It should be noted that differential pricing should not be limited by public authority merely to that which is necessary to meet the competition of a carrier of a rival agency. It will be to the interest of the carrier and the public to go lower than this if, as a result, the net revenue is increased by the generation of traffic which makes for a fuller utilization of the carrier's plant.[14]

Commission Policy on Interagency Competition

The Transportation Act of 1958 was, among other things, supposed to establish criteria for rate competition among the modes. Unfortunately, it did nothing to resolve the issue of the minimum below which the rates on traffic for which the different modes competed. This matter has been one of continuous controversy within the Commission and before the courts. It remains completely unsettled at the present time. A brief review of some of the leading cases will illustrate this.

In *Interstate Commerce Commission* v. *New York, New Haven and Hartford Railroad Co.,*[15] the Supreme Court overruled the Interstate Commerce Commission which had denied the appellee railroads the right to reduce rates for trailer-on-flatcar service between certain points served by coastal water carriers. The Commission took the position, that although the proposed rates equaled or exceeded fully distributed costs, the reduced T.O.F.C. rates were an initial step in a program of rate reductions that could fairly be said to threaten the continued operation, and thus the continued existence, of the coastwise water carrier industry generally. It also held that the coastwise shipping was important for the national defense, the shipping public, and the economy of the coastwise ports and coastal areas. The objectives of the National Transportation Policy required a differential between rail rates and those of Sea-Land and Seatrain. It therefore

[14] See for example, *Petroleum from Los Angeles and El Paso to Arizona and New Mexico*, 287 I.C.C. 731 (1953); see also D. F. Pegrum, "Is Minimum Rate Regulation Necessary in the Public Interest?" *Transportation Research Forum* (Boston, 1963), pp. 41–45.

[15] 372 U.S. 744 (1963).

prescribed a differential of 6 per cent over Sea-Land for T.O.F.C. service. The Supreme Court reversed the Commission on the ground that something more than even hard competition must be shown before a particular rate can be deemed unfair or destructive. Then it added "The principal purpose of reference to the National Transportation Policy, as we have seen, was to prevent a carrier from setting a rate which would impair or destroy the inherent advantages of a competing carrier, for example, by setting a rate below its own fully distributed costs, which would force a competitor with a cost advantage on particular transportation to establish an unprofitable rate in order to attract traffic."[16] This can hardly be said to throw much light on the basic problem.

In *Grain from Idaho, Oregon and Washington to Ports in Oregon and Washington,*[17] the respondent railroads proposed to establish reduced rates on grain and grain products. The railroads faced competition from motor truck operators at rates lower than those of the railroads. There was also competition from barge operators on the Columbia River system. The Commission found that "the data of record leaves no doubt that on a fully distributed cost basis, the motor-barge mode is the low cost mode of transportation. . . . Fully distributed cost is utilized here as the criteria determinative of the low-cost carrier because the primary competition which respondents seek to meet is regulated barge or motor-barge and not private or other carriage not subject to Commission regulation. This is the general rule. As an exception to that rule, an out-of-pocket basis has been approved, for example, where the dominant competitive force was unregulated trucking."[18]

At the same time the above case was being heard, the Commission was also dealing with one of its most controversial cases *Grain in Multiple-Car Shipments—River Crossings to the South,*[19] the so-called Big John case. In the summer of 1961 the Southern Railway filed schedules on all grain rates from certain Ohio and Mississippi river crossings to specified points in southern territory. Southern proposed schedules subject to aggregate minima of 450 tons (in 5 cars), 900 tons (in 10 cars) and 1,800 tons (in 20 cars). Southern had acquired

---

16 *Ibid.,* p. 759.

17 319 I.C.C. 534 (1963).

18 *Ibid.,* p. 560. For a full discussion of this case and its implications, see J. C. Nelson, "Competitive Issues in Grain Transport in the Pacific Northwest," *Transportation Research Forum* (1964), pp. 10–20.

19 321 I.C.C. 582 (1963); 325 I.C.C. 752 (1965).

over 500 of the "jumbo" cars (100 tons capacity). Division 2 of the Commission, in dealing with the question of what constituted the low-cost mode in this case, held that "it is manifest that in competitive rate making where one mode does assert the inherent advantage of low cost in performing a service, sound economics plainly require that all costs, including 'public costs' which go to make up the asserted inherent advantage must be considered," that the public costs were those incurred by government on the waterways for the benefit of the barges, and that fully distributed cost comparisons were the basis of determining the low-cost mode. It also found that without the public costs the barges would be the low-cost mode, that Southern's rate proposals were compensatory in that they were significantly above out-of-pocket costs, and that Southern was subject to substantial unregulated truck competition. The Division therefore approved Southern's schedules.

In July, 1963, the full Commission took the case under consideration. It held that the public costs were irrelevant to any proceeding determining inherent cost advantages, that fully distributed costs constituted the basis for gauging the low-cost mode, and that where the majority of the traffic is moving by an unregulated mode the inherent advantages should be measured by a cost standard that will encourage increased movement by a regulated mode. The full Commission modified the rates approved by Division 2 by requiring an increase of approximately 16 per cent in the multiple-car rates to protect the low-cost barge lines. The case was appealed to the courts and the federal court set aside the Commission's order on the ground that the Commission had exceeded its statutory authority and that the decision was not supported by substantial evidence in the record.[20] In January, 1965, the Supreme Court vacated the order of the district court, remanding the case to the Interstate Commerce Commission to give the latter the opportunity to justify its original order by adequate findings.[21] On reconsideration the Commission found that the Southern rates from Ohio and Mississippi river crossings were designed to meet competition from unregulated truck movements,[22] and were therefore legal.

[20] *Cincinnati, New Orleans and Texas-Pacific Ry. Co.,* v. *United States,* 229 F. Supp. 572 (1964).

[21] 372 U.S. 642 (1965), *per curiam.*

[22] *Grain in Multiple-Car Shipments—River Crossings to South,* 325 I.C.C. 752 (1965).

The final case to be considered in this connection is *Ingot Molds Va. to Steelton, Ky.*[23] In this case the respondent railroads proposed reduced rates on ingot molds and ingot mold stools of $5.11 when moved in single shipments of not less than 600 gross tons, minimum of 112,000 pounds per car (12 or fewer cars) on one bill of lading. This proposed rate was equal to the overall charges to the receiver for the barge movement. The existing rail rate was $11.86 subject to a carload minimum of 100,000 pounds. The reduction was to enable the railroads to compete for the traffic. Division 2 of the Commission found that the proposed rate exceeded the railroads' out-of-pocket costs but was below the fully distributed costs. While adhering to the principle of fully distributed costs the Division found that the barge lines had been moving the traffic at rates, voluntarily established, which did not cover their fully distributed costs. Therefore, the barge lines were not entitled to protection against rates which were presumably profitable to them. Upon reconsideration the full Commission reversed the decision of Division 2. It held that the rail carriers would get all the traffic at equal rates. "In circumstances such as here presented where both the proponent carrier and the competing carrier are regulated the Commission consistently has utilized the fully distributed cost standard to determine which mode of carriage possesses an inherent cost advantage."[24] On a fully distributed basis, the low-cost mode of transport is barge-truck and not to recognize this would impair the ability of a carrier not only to compete but to exist. This case is now on appeal to the Supreme Court.

The foregoing cases indicate the complete confusion and division of the Commission on the appropriate basis for minimum rate making in interagency competition. The opinion of Examiner J. S. Kaplan, already discussed, on *Rules to Govern the Assembling and Presenting of Cost Evidence* provides a thorough resumé of the chaotic thinking within the Commission. It is quite clear, however, that the basic position of the Commission is that of protecting competitors, not protecting competition. Regulated carriers are to be protected against competition from other regulated carriers, but unregulated carriers deserve no such charitable consideration. So far, the courts have done little to clarify the situation. Perhaps the Supreme Court will find an answer, but one should not be too optimistic. The Court may well fail to decide

---

[23] 323 I.C.C. 758 (1965), and 326 I.C.C. 77 (1965).
[24] 326 I.C.C. 77 (1965), 83. See also *Carbon Blacks, Southwest to Ind., Ohio and Mo.,* 325 I.C.C. 138 (1965).

the question of whether the railroads may merely *meet* competition, or whether they may also be entitled to *make* it.

THE COMMON CARRIER PROBLEM

From the development of the railroad as the principal means of inland transportation down to comparatively recent times, transportation for hire was provided primarily by the common carrier. The growth of the other agencies, especially the motor vehicle, has marked the decline, in relative terms at least, of the importance of common carriage in the movement of traffic. This has led to the contention that special steps need to be taken to protect the common carrier from the inroads of other means of transport, because of the unique obligations it is compelled to assume, and because of the necessity for a strong system of common carriage to meet the transportation requirements of the country.[25]

An examination of this question must recognize at the outset that enterprises in all of the modes fall into the category of common carriers and that, therefore, it is distinct from the issue of intra-agency and interagency competition; it is, instead, that of common carriers versus noncommon carriers. Although the railroads constitute the only mode which is exclusively devoted to common carriage, the question of whether the common carrier needs special protection is one that centers upon a particular type of obligation rather than upon a particular agency of transportation.

The need for common carrier service arises from the dependence of the shipping public upon carriers for hire that can supply transportation services on a regular and dependable basis without it being necessary for the shipper to seek out the supplier and make special contractual arrangements with him for each particular shipment. Common carrier obligations are assumed voluntarily by the carrier, but they become a matter of public responsibility for it once this status is acquired. Furthermore, when an enterprise assumes the status, it may be prevented from engaging in noncommon transport if public authority so decrees. Railroads have thus become exclusively common carriers,

[25] *Revision of Federal Transportation Policy,* Report of Presidential Advisory Committee on Transport Policy and Organization (Weeks Report) (Washington, D.C.; U.S. Government Printing Office, 1955); U.S. Department of Commerce, *Federal Transportation Policy and Program* (Mueller Report) (Washington, D.C.: U.S. Government Printing Office, March, 1960), and appendix thereto, *Rationale of Federal Transportation Policy* (April, 1960); and *National Transportation Policy* (Doyle Report), Preliminary Draft of a Report to the Senate Committee on Interstate and Foreign Commerce, 87th Cong., 1st sess. (Washington, D.C.: U.S. Printing Office, 1961).

whereas enterprises in motor, water, and air transport have been able to escape the category if they refuse to undertake the accompanying obligations.

Common carriers acquire their position by standing ready to offer their services on a regular basis to all who seek them, at reasonable prices and without discrimination. This is usually the result of a special grant of privilege from public authority, although it may ensue from action of the carrier which puts it into that category. Over the years, particularly since the Interstate Commerce Act was passed, common carriers have been compelled to afford protection to shippers which has not been imposed upon other carriers for hire. In addition, common carriers are not permitted to discontinue services once they have been proffered, without the consent of public authority. Thus a firm which wishes to operate as a common carrier is compelled to assume obligations that are not imposed upon other carriers for hire. Nor under present conditions are the common carriers able to compete for a considerable portion of present-day traffic under the same conditions as their less restricted rivals.

Prevailing policy requires a common carrier to confine its activities to that kind of business. This policy is based on the theory that if a firm is permitted to engage in both common and noncommon carrier transport, there will be discrimination against those who are forced to rely on the common carrier services. This theory has not been followed consistently, however, for motor and water transport. Any motor carrier may haul exempt commodities in interstate commerce so long as it does not violate the "tainted vehicle" doctrine, and water carriers may transport bulk commodities without restriction if they are not included in the same tow with common carrier haulage. Railroads are denied both of these privileges, and common carriers by motor cannot, as a general rule, engage in contract carriage. When the railroad industry enjoyed a virtual monopoly over inland transport, restrictions of this sort may have been reasonable, but with the totally changed conditions of today, it is difficult to see how they can afford protection to the shipper against discrimination in rates or service.[26] To argue that to permit carriers to engage in both common and noncommon carrier services would lead to discrimination must mean that the shipper who is able to take advantage of contract or exempt carriage, or to supply his

[26] This has been recognized in both Canada and Great Britain. In the latter country, where the railroads are under government ownership, management is permitted to engage in pricing in the same manner as any private enterprise. The same thing would probably happen in this country if the railroads came under public ownership.

own, is the beneficiary of discrimination against the one who relies on common carriage. This clearly seems to be the position taken in the Doyle Report.[27] The logic of this is that all transportation for hire should be forced into the common carrier mold, and probably all private carriage as well. This can scarcely be regarded as a practical solution to present-day problems. The alternatives that are available to shippers as the result of technological developments in transportation call for a relaxation of restrictions on common carriers, not the opposite extreme. If common carriage is necessary, it will pay for itself, provided that noncommon carriage is not given aid and privileges denied to those who may offer common carrier services. If protection of the common carrier is effective only because shippers, who would use other sources of supply if they were given the opportunity, are denied the privilege in order to assist in carrying the burden created by those unwilling to pay for the common carriage, the policy is uneconomical. It should be remembered in this connection that while concern has been expressed over the fate of the common carrier, the I.C.C. has spent much of its recent energies in limiting competition among common carriers on the alleged ground of preventing them from destroying each other.[28]

EQUALIZING COMPETITION

If competition is to be effective in bringing about an allocation of traffic among the suppliers of transport services in accordance with their relative efficiencies, conditions must be established under which that competition is permitted to take place so that the carriers which can haul the traffic most economically are allowed to do so. At the present time, the restrictions of regulation rest very unevenly on the different modes with regard to the traffic which can be taken by more than one of them if rates are used as the arbiter of allocation. This is also true for carriers within the modes, particularly motor and water. In addition to this, there are inequalities in the cost burdens which are imposed on the different agencies.

These inequalities are primarily among the modes rather than be-

---

[27] *National Transportation Policy,* Part VII, chap. iv. This report recommends severe restriction on noncommon carriage in order to protect common carriers and to compel those who do not patronize the common carrier at present to do so in order to support those who do. Surely this is discriminatory and uneconomical at one and the same time.

[28] See D. F. Pegrum, "Effects of Regulation on Small Business in Motor Transport," *I.C.C. Administration of the Motor Carrier Act,* Hearings before Select Committee on Small Business, U.S. Senate, 84th Cong., 1st sess., November, 1955 (Washington, D.C.: U.S. Government Printing Office, 1956), pp. 465 ff.

tween common carrier and noncommon carrier firms. They arise principally from public provision of facilities used by motor, water, and air transport. Railroads and pipe lines are required to carry all of the costs of supplying their services, including the costs of acquiring and maintaining the capital in the roadways they use, together with property taxes on them. Similar costs are not imposed on water carriers and air lines, and are only partially assessed on highway users. The equalization of competitive conditions therefore involves two distinct issues; one is in the area of regulation, and the other is in the administration of the program of public investment.

The inequality in competitive rules has two aspects. One of these arises in connection with restrictions placed on those enterprises which operate as common carriers that compete for traffic that may be hauled by other firms. The effect of this is felt most heavily by the railroads because they are unable to escape common carrier restrictions in any way, but it also constitutes a competitive handicap to common carriers in motor transport which are restrained in a somewhat similar fashion. Contract carriers, apart from possible limitations on the minimum rates they may quote, are able to negotiate freely with shippers, who are thereby given a wider choice of alternatives. At the same time, the carriers themselves are not bound to offer unprofitable services or to continue to serve if they do not wish to do so. They are also freed from ordinary common carrier liability. Consequently, they are able to transport freight not available to common carriers because the latter cannot compete on equal terms. The restrictions serve to protect the contract operators.

However, it is recognized that contract carriage is an important transport service. Public policy distinguishes between the firms that perform different functions rather than between the functions themselves. If the differentiation were based on functions and on the services offered, carriers could operate in both a contract and a common carrier capacity without any more prejudice to shippers than exists under present circumstances. In addition, this would aid in preserving the common carrier enterprise by giving it a wider base on which to seek traffic. The exemptions granted to motor carriers on agricultural products and to water carriers on bulk commodities are afforded on the theory that competition is an adequate safeguard to the shipper. To date, there has been no serious attempt to change these regulations, except by common carriers who cannot participate in the haulage. Under present competitive conditions, permission for common carrier enterprises to move this traffic on equal terms with those who are now able to do so would increase rather than lessen competition and at the same time would make it possible for the common carrier to secure a greater diversity of traffic.[29]

The second aspect of inequality of competitive rules arises from the restrictions on freedom of pricing that are imposed on common carriers. They are required to publish their rate schedules, adhere to them, secure permission to make any adjustments of them, and avoid personal discrimination and undue preference or prejudice. In addition, proposed rate changes may be suspended while the reasonableness of the new rates is being investigated. The result of these regulations has been to introduce a rigidity into pricing procedures and structures that constitutes a severe handicap to attempts to adjust to a highly competitive situation. The possibility of extending regulation sufficiently to remedy the inequities is quite remote. The alternative, therefore, is to relax these restrictions so as to equalize the competitive opportunities of the common carriers.

The regulation of minimum rates was not instituted to protect shippers, but instead to control possible rate wars among railroads[30] and, more specifically, to protect water transport against railroad competition. If, however, traffic is to be allocated economically among the various agencies and carriers, they should be allowed to compete for business on the basis of its profitability to them. This means that they should be permitted to charge anything above the relevant specific costs of a particular service if they are better off by doing so. Minimum-rate regulation is not an economic necessity except as a means for preventing predatory or deliberately destructive competition. There is no need to retain maximum rate controls over motor and water common carriers if entry restrictions are relaxed. The same remarks apply to air transport. It may be that maximum controls should be retained for railroads because of lack of reasonable alternatives to shippers on certain types of traffic, but even if this is so, application of the authority should give recognition to the over-all needs of the carrier for an adequate return. Finally, the opportunity to compete equally on a price basis calls for an end to the power of the regulatory authorities to suspend proposed rate changes. This follows logically from the foregoing

[29] The Doyle Report recommends that the mixing rule which prohibits hauling bulk and common carrier traffic in the same barge, tow, or vessel be repealed. Curiously, it does not propose parallel changes for common carriers by motor, and advances no suggestion whatsoever that concessions should be made to railroads on bulk commodities and agricultural commodities. The reasons for the differences in proposed treatment are nowhere set forth. See *National Transportation Policy*, pp. 516–33.

[30] There had not been any of these for over twenty years prior to the enactment of the legislation in 1920.

proposals, but common carriers might still be required to give advance notice, say thirty days, of intention to change rates.

Equalizing conditions of competition by shaping regulatory policy to that end would go far toward bringing about a more efficient utilization of economic resources devoted to transportation, but it is unable to do anything about reducing the handicaps to effective competition imposed by the unequal cost burdens resulting from present policies connected with public investment in transport facilities. This is a matter which is outside the scope of regulation. Removal of these inequalities requires, first of all, ascertaining the total economic costs of supplying the public facilities and, second, assessing those costs on the users of the facilities as nearly as possible in accordance with the responsibility for incurring them. If this is impracticable for political or other reasons, then relief, sufficient to restore the balance, should be granted to the modes, railroads and pipe lines, which are compelled to carry the full costs without the benefit of public aid or support. This point is discussed in the chapter on financing transportation, and it is unnecessary to deveolop it further here.[31]

THE PRESIDENT'S MESSAGE

Recognition of the pressing problems that are burdening our transportation system today led President Kennedy to submit to Congress on April 5, 1962, a message relative to the transportation system of the nation.[32] After the preamble and a statement on basic national transportation policy, the message was divided into four parts. Part I dealt with intercity transportation, Part II with urban transportation, Part III with international transportation, and Part IV with labor relations and research. Only the preamble and Part I will be discussed in this chapter. The part of the message dealing with labor relations contained no concrete proposals relating to transportation nor any recommendations for legislation. After stating the need for a co-ordinated program of research, the President stated that he expected the Secretary of Commerce to develop a comprehensive research program for the government for later consideration by the Congress.[33]

[31] See Chapter 19.

[32] *The Transportation System of Our Nation,* Message from the President of the United States, April 5, 1962, House of Representatives, Document No. 384, 87th Congress, 2d session (Washington, D.C.: U.S. Government Printing Office, 1962). The full text of this message is reproduced in Appendix I at the end of this book.

[33] Problems of international transportation are not discussed in this book. Part II, relating to urban transportation, will be dealt with in Chapter 24.

A Basic National Transportation Policy

In reviewing the problems besetting transportation, the President stated that a chaotic patchwork of inconsistent and often obsolete legislation has evolved from piecemeal development, with the result that it has failed to keep pace with the changing structure. The regulatory commissions have been required to make thousands of detailed decisions based on out-of-date standards, while, at the same time, management has been shackled in exercising its initiative. Rate-making and other controls require some carriers to provide some services at a loss and some to charge rates high in relation to cost so as to shelter competitors; some carriers are subject to rate regulation, while others are not; and finally, some enjoy the use of public facilities without bearing all the costs of them. Less federal regulation and subsidization is necessary for a healthy intercity framework, and current federal policies must be reshaped in the most fundamental and far-reaching fashion.

The basic objective of national transportation policy must be to assure the availability of economical transportation services without waste or discrimination at the lowest economic cost. Chronic excess capacity should be avoided, and the efficient use of those resources devoted to transportation requires that users be provided with the incentive to select the service they desire at the lowest total public and private cost. "This basic objective can and must be achieved primarily on unsubsidized privately owned facilities, operating under the incentives of private profit and the checks of competition to the maximum extent practicable. The role of public policy should be to provide a consistent and comprehensive framework of equal competitive opportunity that will achieve this objective at the lowest economic and social cost to the Nation."[34] To achieve this, there must be equal opportunity for all forms of transport and the users through greater reliance on the forces of competition and an equalization of competitive conditions resulting from imposing the full cost of service upon the users. Common carriers should be aided in their endeavors to maintain their status by being given relief from the burdens of regulation that handicap them against unregulated competition.

The message recognized that the regulatory pattern that has grown up around transportation would have to be modified on a gradual basis if serious disruption was to be avoided. To assist in the process, the President requested the chairmen of the Civil Aeronautics

[34] *The Transportation System of Our Nation, op. cit.,* p. 3.

Board, the Interstate Commerce Commission, and the Federal Maritime Commission to meet at frequent intervals to discuss the regulatory problems affecting the various modes of transportation, and to seek coordinated solutions through legislation and administrative action to improve the regulatory process. A number of specific recommendations were made to initiate the carrying-out of the program.

Equal Competitive Opportunity under Diminished Regulation

The first of the recommendations related to control over rates and the creation of equal competitive opportunity under diminished regulation. The message stated that extending to all other carriers exemption from approval or prescription of minimum rates on bulk commodities, as applied to water carriers, would permit the forces of competition and equal opportunity to replace present cumbersome regulation. The public interest, however, would be protected by leaving intact the Interstate Commerce Commission's control over maximum railroad rates, and other safeguards, such as the prohibition against discrimination and requirements on car service and common carrier responsibility. In a similar way, exemptions on agricultural and fishery products would be extended to all carriers. How these proposals would be incorporated into legislation was not spelled out; presumably, the message intended that only minimum rate regulation would be removed on bulk and agricultural commodities as far as common carriers are concerned.

It was also recommended that Congress enact legislation that would eventually limit control of intercity passenger rates to maximum fares only. To prevent rate wars, Congress was asked to make certain that carriers freed from rate regulation would be covered by existing laws against monopoly and predatory practices.

Consistent Policies of Taxation and User Charges

The President recommended the repeal of the 10 per cent transportation tax on intercity railroad and bus transportation, but the imposition of a 5 per cent tax on air-line tickets and air-freight bills. He also suggested a continuation of the 2-cents-per-gallon net tax on gasoline for commercial air lines and extension of it to jet fuels. The same charges were to be extended to all fuels used on inland waterways; but vessels employed in the fisheries, foreign trade, or in trade between the Atlantic and Pacific ports of the United States, or between the United States and any of its possessions, would be exempt. Similarly, vessels in coastal trade which are too large to use the intercoastal waterways would be excluded. The objective of these recommendations was to recover through user charges the expenditures of the federal government on waterway facilities.

Evenhanded Government Promotion of Intercity Transportation

To achieve this, the President recommended legislation that would make the domestic trunk air carriers ineligible for operating subsidies in the future. In addition, he requested the Civil Aeronautics Board to prepare a schedule for the termination of subsidies to the three certified helicopter services, and to develop a plan for a sharp reduction of subsidies to the local service or feeder air lines.

Protection of the Public Interest

The President directed the formation of a group of agency representatives designated by the Attorney General, the Secretary of Commerce, the Secretary of Labor, the Chairman of the Council of Economic Advisers, and the heads of other agencies involved in a particular merger case to undertake two tasks: (1) to formulate general administration policies on mergers in each segment of the transportation industry and (2) to assist the Department of Justice in developing a government position on each merger application. The criteria for mergers should be (1) maintenance of effective competition among the alternative forms of transportation; (2) preservation of economical, efficient, and adequate service to the public; and (3) assistance to affected workers to make necessary adjustments. Possibly, all of this meant that control over mergers was to be taken out of the hands of the Interstate Commerce Commission and the Civil Aeronautics Board, although this was not clear. Nor was any position indicated on intermodal integration.

Congress was requested to declare, as a matter of public policy, that through routes and joint rates should be vigorously encouraged, and to authorize all transportation agencies to participate in joint boards. In addition, legislation should be enacted to encourage experimental rates and services, and to explore every possible simplification of rate structures.

Conclusion

When President Kennedy's message is viewed in the light of existing legislation and its application, it is clear that some drastic changes were envisaged. The most significant of these related to the extension of rate-making freedom to a large portion of the tonnage now moving in interstate commerce. Congress, particularly under the leadership of Mr. Oren Harris of the House of Representatives, under-took to implement the rate-making proposals of the President.[35] The essence of the proposed legislation was to remove bulk commodities from rate control and to extend the agricultural exemptions to all carriers. The antitrust laws were to be applicable to this traffic, but section 3 of the Interstate Commerce Act relating to undue or un-reasonable preferences was to be retained. It was inevitable that the proposals would generate violent opposition. Even the railroads were quite unhappy with the possibility of being subject to section 2 of the Clayton Act (Robinson-Patman) and section 3 of the Interstate Commerce Act. Had the legislation passed it would have resulted in interminable legal battles over conflicting statutory provisions, issues of primary jurisdiction, and rivalry among regulatory agencies. The legislation failed to reach the floor of Congress despite efforts to achieve a last minute compromise,[36] and there seems to be no prospect for legislative changes at least before a new Congress convenes in 1969. Neither the legislative nor the regulatory branches of the gov-ernment have been able to develop policy, in a period of well nigh 50 years, to meet the problems of pervasive competition arising from the changing structure of transport.

[35] See *Transportation Act—1963,* Hearings, Committee on Interstate and Foreign Commerce, House of Representatives, 88th Cong., 1st sess., Parts 1, 2, 3 (Washington, D.C.: U.S. Government Printing Office, 1963).

[36] In a belated effort, those supporting the legislation proposed that the transporta-tion of the commodities to be excluded from rate regulation "shall not be performed at a rate below the costs to the particular carrier or carriers that would not be incurred if the service to which the rate applies had not been rendered." The proposal would have pro-hibited the Interstate Commerce Commission or any court from suspending or enjoining the rates prior to a final determination by the Commission that the rate was below the level of the avoidable or incremental cost floor. This approach should have been adopted when the legislation was first drafted.

CONSOLIDATION AND INTEGRATION

MEANING AND PROBLEM

Consolidation and merger, as discussed in this section, refer to any form of combination of properties of a carrier of a particular mode which results in the management and operation of them as a unit. This unification may be achieved in different ways such as merger, outright consolidation, or long-term lease, but it does not include the combination of carriers of different modes. The latter is usually referred to as integration or diversification. It will be discussed in the following sections.

The problems of consolidation, particularly with regard to public policy, are quite different for the various modes. This intermodal difference, like many others that have already been discussed is the result of the contrasting economic characteristics of the modes. In the case of railroads, it emerges in connection with an industry in which competition is of limited applicability and therefore poses the question whether policy shall be predicated on an attempt to preserve competition among the systems as much as possible, or whether recognition of the monopoly features shall predominate through the creation of regional or nationwide systems. Motor and water carriers do not raise the issue of the desirability of monopoly, but rather the reverse, as a consequence of which consolidation can be viewed entirely in a competitive setting. Much the same remarks apply to air transport, except that subsidy, especially for feeder lines, imposes limits on the competition that should be permitted. One further item of difference among the modes is also significant. Railroads can serve only the areas which their lines contact. This means that there is no satisfactory way of organizing them separately as local lines and through lines; they have to be both, or at least through lines also have to be local. Motor carriers, on the other hand, may be primarily local in nature, or they may be established to haul

446

interstate traffic on a long-distance basis, or they may do both. That is, the territorial scope of consolidation for them poses no special problems, whereas it is crucial for the railroads.

Considerations of economies of scale also play a different role among the modes. The limitations of these on the efficiency of operations of motor, water, and air carriers are matters of direct concern to the operators because, given freedom of entry, competition will impose effective restraint on overexpansion. As long as they operate in a strictly private enterprise category, monopoly is unlikely to present a problem, and if it were to do so, antitrust would provide an effective remedy. Railroad consolidation, on the other hand, from the very nature of the industry, cannot be successfully dealt with by antitrust, and cannot be limited to economical size by the restraints of the market. This is why there is so much controversy over the scope of consolidations and what constitutes the appropriate number of enterprises for an economical railroad system for the country. It is a problem very similar to that which arises in connection with electrical utilities where, unfortunately, there is no very adequate gauge for the optimum size of the market area which such a utility should serve.

Consolidation as an issue in transport policy is therefore primarily concerned with the railroads. It is with this mode only that plans have been developed as a matter of public policy and Congress has endeavored to prescribe standards or specific measures.

RAILROAD CONSOLIDATION

The Problem of Consolidation

Railroad consolidation presents a unique problem because if there is to be unified operation, the roadway must be a continuously connected one. In this respect the situation is like that which confronts public utilities. For the latter industries, however, each enterprise can be isolated and be given a complete monopoly of the area it serves. This is possible only within limits for railroads, unless a single system is established for the entire country, because of the direct competition between them at important centers they serve. On the other hand, consolidation cannot follow the pattern which permits them to tap whatever markets they desire, because of the problem of ruinous competition. In other words, if consolidation is to be predicated on monopoly, or at least the reduction of competition among the railroads, the problem of the geographic scope of each system must be resolved. If it proceeds on the theory of competition, it cannot be successful whether the methods employed be voluntary or compulsory. It is the failure to recognize this fact that has led to the current impasse. If the monopoly basis had been recognized very early in railroad history, the difficulties of the proper geographical scope of each system could have been largely avoided. The competitive approach, however, became the basis of policy. This resulted in public insistence on competition, particularly at large centers, duplication of facilities, entrenched property positions, and vested labor interests, all of which resist a rational approach to resolution of today's problem.[1]

History of Consolidation

From the standpoint of public policy the history of railroad consolidation may be divided into three periods. The first was from the beginning of the railroads down to 1904, during which time the industry enjoyed a free hand. The second was from 1904 to 1920, when the antitrust laws were vigorously applied, practically bringing an end to consolidation. The third was from 1920 to the present time, during which period various attempts by government have been made to promote consolidation, with limited success so far, however.[2]

Railroad consolidation first began as a combination of end-to-end lines to form through routes, the first of these of consequence being that of the New York Central Railroad, which was established in 1853 to form a single railroad undertaking from Buffalo to New York. In the ensuing twenty years, this was followed by the organization of a number of other similar enterprises. The next step in the consolidation movement was the formation of railroad systems by which the various roads sought to gain entry to new markets and the markets of competitors by extensions and acquisition of transverse lines. The resulting systems, together with the construction into the West, established the railroad framework essentially as it exists today. The ownership

---

[1] For a discussion of some of the obstacles, see R. J. Sampson, *Obstacles to Railroad Unification* (Eugene: Bureau of Business Research, University of Oregon, 1960); see also Michael Conant, *Railroad Mergers and Abandonments* (Berkeley, Calif.: University of California Press, 1964).

[2] This has been expressed somewhat differently as follows: "We have had three periods of consolidation; one is the entire period to 1904 when we didn't want it but when we had a tremendous amount of it; two, that between 1904 and 1920 when we forbade it by law and when it was practically slowed down to almost zero; and three, the period since 1920 when we wanted it, but have had so little" (*National Transportation Policy* (Doyle Report), Preliminary Draft of a Report to the Senate Committee on Interstate and Foreign Commerce, 87th Congress, 1st session (Washington, D.C.: U.S. Government Printing Office, 1961), p. 230. Chapter iv of Part V of this report presents a good discussion of the consolidation problem.

pattern was confined almost entirely to each of the three major railroad territories of the country. However, a third step followed, in which the objective became that of restraining competition through the building of huge corporate empires.

The effect of the third step was to bring the railroads of each of the different regions under the dominance of one or two combinations. Commencing in the 1890's, the New York, New Haven and Hartford proceeded to acquire the railroads in the New England territory. By 1911, it had obtained control of almost all of the lines in that area, together with numerous electric railways, steamship lines operating along the coast, access to the coal fields of Pennsylvania, and an outlet to the Great Lakes. Thus, it had a practical monopoly of transport for the region. In the trunk-line territory, the New York Central and the Pennsylvania had emerged as the two dominant systems by 1900. As a result of a series of transactions, these two companies acquired large stockholdings in the other railroads of the territory such that by 1902, between them they controlled the Eastern territory. In addition, they had joint interests in a number of the most important railroads in the region. Similar developments took place in the Southern region, where the Morgan financial interests, through acquisition of stock, literally eliminated competition among the railroads of the South. The most spectacular development in railroad combination took place in the Western region with the attempt of E. H. Harriman to monopolize the transcontinental routes. Through control of the Union Pacific, Mr. Harriman obtained a large stock interest in the Southern Pacific and a half interest in the San Pedro, Los Angeles and Salt Lake, and 13 per cent of the stock of the Santa Fe, which enabled him to elect two directors to its board. He obtained large stock holdings in the Northern Securities Company, which controlled the Great Northern and Northern Pacific, which two railroads jointly owned the Chicago, Burlington and Quincy. As a result of these developments the Union Pacific secured control of every line of railroad reaching the Pacific coast between Portland and the Mexican border, except the Santa Fe, as already noted. In addition, stock interest was acquired in the Illinois Central (29.59 per cent), the Baltimore and Ohio, the New York Central, the Chicago, Milwaukee, and St. Paul, the Chicago and North Western, and others. Finally, in 1907, it added the Central of Georgia, which provided a through line from the West to a port on the southern Atlantic coast.

Had these combinations succeeded, the railroads of the country would have come under the control of a very few corporate giants—wide in scope and with whole regions under single control.[3] It was this final stage of the first period in the development of railroad consolidation that ran afoul of the Sherman Act, with the result that little of significance has been accomplished since then.

The first evidence that the railroads were clearly vulnerable to the Sherman Act was afforded by the Traffic Association cases of 1897 and 1898, but the decisive blow came in the Northern Securities case.[4] The dissolution of this holding company under the order of the Supreme Court marked the beginning of the breakup of the Harriman empire;[5] it also resulted in the elimination of some of the other combinations. In addition, the Clayton Act of 1914 gave the Interstate Commerce Commission the authority to enforce Section 7 as it applied to railroads. This forbade one corporation from owning the stock of another where the effect of such ownership was to substantially lessen competition or tend to create a monopoly. Application of this law by the Commission made it necessary for the railroads to dispose of their stock interests in competing lines. Thus the effects of the "grand" phase of railroad consolidation were almost completely obliterated.

The third period in the history of railroad consolidation, from 1920 to the present, which has been characterized by various attempts on the part of the government to promote consolidation, has resulted in few mergers of significance to the present time. Not a single consolidated system proposed by the Interstate Commerce Commission under the plan which was developed in accordance with the Transportation Act of 1920 has emerged. There have been some mergers, and some attempts were made to evade the legislation by the use of the holding company device, but this means was terminated by the Transportation Act of 1933. Recently, a number of proposals for the formation of large systems by merger have been put forward, but only one of these has received final approval as yet.[6] Moreover, the pattern of the proposals indicates clearly that railroad management has evolved no definite theory of the basis on which consolidation should take place, nor has the Interstate

[3] For an exhaustive treatment of these developments, see W. Z. Ripley, *Railroads: Finance and Organization* (New York: Longmans, Green & Co., 1915); and Eliot Jones, *Principles of Railway Transportation* (New York: The Macmillan Co., 1925), chap. xvii.

[4] *Northern Securities Company* v. *United States,* 193 U.S. 197 (1904).

[5] See also *United States* v. *Union Pacific Railroad Company,* 226 U.S. 61 (1912); *United States* v. *Southern Pacific Co.,* 259 U.S. 214 (1922).

[6] See *National Transportation Policy* (Doyle Report), pp. 247, 252–57; J. W. Barriger, Jr., *Why Consolidation?* Paper, Transportation Management Institute, Stanford University, Stanford, California, July 17, 1959; see also Bureau of Transport Economics and Statistics, Interstate Commerce Commission, *Railroad Consolidations and the Public Interest—A Preliminary Examination,* Mimeograph Statement No. 6201 (Washington, D.C., March, 1962).

Commerce Commission given any indication of its position on the matter.

Public Policy on Consolidation

The Transportation Act of 1920 signaled a new departure on the part of Congress toward railroad consolidation, in that it sought to encourage the formation of a limited number of systems. It accordingly instructed the Interstate Commerce Commission to draw up a tentative plan and, after hearings were held on it, to prepare a final one to which all subsequent consolidations were to conform. However, the instructions required that competition was to be preserved as fully as possible, and existing routes and channels of trade and commerce were to be maintained wherever it was practicable to do so. In addition, the systems were to be of substantially equal earning capacity. Nevertheless, the railroads were not compelled to undertake the consolidations, but all mergers that were made had to conform to the plan.[7] The "final" plan of the Commission was issued in 1929 and provided for either 19 or 21 systems.[8]

The lack of accomplishments under the Act of 1920 and the growing recognition of the need for consolidation led Congress to replace the earlier provisions by those of the Act of 1940. The idea of an over-all plan was abandoned, and instead the Commission was directed, in applying the "public interest guide," to give consideration, among other things, (1) to the effect of the proposed transaction on adequate transportation service to the public; (2) to the effect upon the public interest of the inclusion, or failure to include, other railroads in the territory involved in the proposed transaction; (3) to the total fixed charges resulting from the proposed transaction; and (4) to the interests of the employees affected by the consolidation arrangements. Thus the matter was really tossed into the hands of the Commission by Congress to guide consolidation without any mandate as to the theory of organization. How much discretion the Commission actually possesses under this legislation, is still a matter of extreme controversy.

During the period between 1930 and 1940 a number of proposals for consolidation were formulated. One of these was advanced by the National Transportation Committee under the chairmanship of ex-

[7] Professor W. Z. Ripley of Harvard University was retained by the Commission to draw up the plan. He submitted his report in 1920, and the next year the Commission issued its tentative plan. Professor Ripley's report was published as an appendix to it, 63 I.C.C. 455 (1921).

[8] 159 I.C.C. 522 (1929). For a discussion of the history of this, see *National Transportation Policy* (Doyle Report), *op. cit.,* pp. 234–40.

President Calvin D. Coolidge. This committee recommended regional consolidation, under which the regional operating companies would be unified by a top holding company for the entire country.[9] In the same year, 1933, Mr. Frederick H. Prince of Boston drew up what became known as the Prince Plan. This proposed that the Class I railroads of the country be consolidated into seven large systems, two in the East, two in the South, and three in the West. Then, in 1938, President F. D. Roosevelt appointed a "Committee of Three" from the Interstate Commerce Commission to study the problem; it recommended that the Commission be given authority to require unification. In the same year, however, the President appointed a committee that became known as the "Committee of Six," which opposed compulsory consolidation. The report of this committee formed the basis of the provisions in the Transportation Act of 1940, which is the last word on the subject by Congress to date. Recently, J. W. Barriger, Jr., now President of the Missouri-Kansas and Texas Railroad, has proposed that the railroads be consolidated into two nationwide systems, operating from coast to coast. One of these would encompass the entire West and the Official territory; the other would occupy the Mississippi Valley and the Southern territory.[10]

The Recent Merger Movement

In the years since 1957 the Interstate Commerce Commission has received some 50 applications for acquisitions, mergers, and consolidations. About one half of this number have been approved by the Commission. Five have been denied. The only approval of a major merger that has been tested finally in the Supreme Court is that of the Atlantic Coast Line and the Seaboard Airline. At the present time the situation can only be described as chaotic with the prospects of a long drawn out legal and political battle.

The first merger in the development of the present situation was that of the Norfolk and Western Railway with the Virginian Railway.[11] The Commission sanctioned the merger of these two "strong" roads in which it took the position that public interest would not be adversely affected by such lessening of competition as might result. This was followed by the authorization of three consolidations of major east-

---

[9] The research staff of the committee was organized by Dr. Harold G. Moulton, President of the Brookings Institution. The report was published as *The American Transportation Problem* (Washington, D.C.: Brookings Institution, 1933). This report took the position that voluntary consolidation was not likely to be a success (p. 858).

[10] Barriger, *op. cit.,* p. 24. The Prince Plan was also drawn up by Mr. Barriger.

[11] *Virginian—Norfolk and Western Merger,* 307 I.C.C. 401 (1959).

ern railroads, namely: control by the Chesapeake and Ohio of the Baltimore and Ohio; merger of the Norfolk and Western with the Chicago, New York and St. Louis (the Nickel Plate); and merger of the Pennsylvania and New York Central railroads. At the same time the Commission denied the application for merger of the Great Northern, the Northern Pacific, and the Chicago, Burlington and Quincy railroads.

Acquisition by the Chesapeake and Ohio Railway of the controlling stock interest in the Baltimore and Ohio Railway was the result of extensive behind-the-scenes financial maneuverings with Swiss bankers from which the Chesapeake and Ohio emerged victorious. Application was made to the Interstate Commerce Commission for approval of control.[12] This was granted principally on the ground that the Baltimore and Ohio was on the verge of financial collapse and could be saved only by immediate assumption of control by the Chespeake and Ohio. In his dissent from the decision Commissioner Tucker contended that the approval sealed the pattern of consolidation of the eastern railroads without any coordinated appraisal of the merger proposals for that territory. The case-by-case approach, he said, prevented a realistic and effective role by the Commission in the decisional process required by section 5(2) of the Interstate Commerce Act.

The second major merger development in the Eastern territory was that of the Norfolk and Western Railway with the New York, Chicago, and St. Louis Railroad (The Nickel Plate).[13] After extensive hearings, Examiner Lester Conley ruled in favor of the merger, with the inclusion of some smaller lines and conditions designed to protect the public interest. He held that the new system would be enabled to provide more effective competition on certain traffic and that in no instance would the public be deprived of an adequate competitive rail service as a result of the unification. The recommended order of the Examiner became the order of the Commission in June, 1964.

Application for the merger of the Pennsylvania Railroad and the New York Central Railroad was filed with the Commission in March, 1962.[14] This proposal encountered vigorous opposition from the very beginning. Initially, it was supported by the applicants on the ground that the two railroads were in severe financial straits, and that they could

---

[12] *Chesapeake and Ohio Railroad—Control—Baltimore and Ohio Railroad,* 317 I.C.C. 261 (1962). For a description of this, see *Railway Age,* January 2, 1967, pp. 17 ff.

[13] *Norfolk and Western Railway Co. and the New York, Chicago, and St. Louis Railroad Co. Merger,* 324 I.C.C. 1 (1964).

[14] *Pennsylvania Railroad Company—Merger—New York Central Railroad Company,* 237 I.C.C. 475 (1966).

protect themselves from competition from the other merged railroads and from other modes of transport only by consolidation. The proposal, if approved would "create an hour-glass shaped system flared on the east from Montreal, Canada, through Boston, Massachusetts to Norfolk, Virginia, and on the west from Mackinaw City, Michigan, through Chicago, Illinois to St. Louis, Missouri, operating about 19,600 miles of interlaced road sprawling between the Great Lakes on the north (with some trackage in Canada) and the Ohio and Potomac rivers on the south."[15] The Commission held that public interest would be served by the merger, and noted that the Department of Justice had submitted no evidence to support its proposal for four systems in the Eastern district. The Commission disclaimed responsibility for initiating a plan for consolidation in that territory. It held that it had exclusive and plenary powers over carrier consolidation, which made it unnecessary to make specific findings under section 7 of the Clayton Act. (Curiously the Commission held that the railroads had been able to meet water competition by reduced rates, and cited the Southern Grain Rates case. The reduced rates in this instance had gone into effect only as a result of court action.) The Commission held in abeyance the disposition of the Erie-Lackawanna, the Delaware and Hudson, and the Boston and Maine railroads until it passed upon the application of the Norfolk and Western and the Chesapeake and Ohio to merge. Commissioner Tucker concurred in the approval of the consolidation, but only because he did not see how it could be avoided in light of previous merger approvals. He also noted that the proposed merger of the Norfolk and Western and the Chesapeake and Ohio presented the Commission with a hopeless dilemma.

Appeal of the Commission's order was carried to the Supreme Court in *Baltimore and Ohio Railroad Co.* v. *United States* (1967).[16] The sole question before the Court was "whether, in the light of findings as to the necessity of protection for the so-called protected railroads, the Commission erred in permitting the consummation of the merger prior to and without awaiting determination of the inclusion provisions."[17] Five justices held that the Commission was in error and remanded the case to the Commission for further consideration. Mr. Justice Brennan, in a scathing criticism of the Commission's procedures concurred in the decision, and held that the Commission did possess the authority to consolidate all the merger proceedings and to evolve some rational plan. Mr. Justice Douglas joined in the opinion

[15] *Ibid.*, p. 489.
[16] 18 L. ed. 2d., 159 (1967).
[17] *Ibid.*, p. 165.

of the majority but contended that the Commission's findings did not satisfy the standards of section 5 (2) (C) of the Transportation Act of 1940. Justices Fortas, Harlan, Stewart, and White dissented from the majority on the ground that the Commission's order was well within its powers.

The Commission now has the case under reconsideration and it is also conducting hearings on the application of the Norfolk and Western and the Chesapeake and Ohio to merge. It has ordered the Norfolk and Western to acquire the Erie-Lackawanna, the Delaware and Hudson, and the Boston and Maine. This issue has now been carried to the courts. The prospects of early settlement of the consolidation program of eastern railroads is quite dim, particularly in view of the intense rivalry that has now developed among the major protagonists.

The only recent case in which the impact of the Clayton Antitrust Act (section 7) has been adjudicated by the courts was that of the merger application of the *Seaboard Airline Railroad Company—Atlantic Coast Line Railroad Company.*[18] The Commission held that the Transportation Act of 1940 retained the provision of immunizing mergers from the operation of the antitrust laws, but that it deleted the requirement of the Act of 1920 relating to the preservation of competition. It then took the position that the exemption afforded by the Interstate Commerce Act cuts across the antitrust laws and avoids the necessity of their enforcement by the agency exercising regulatory jurisdiction. After examining the various aspects of the proposal the Commission concluded that the effects of the curtailment of competition resulting from the merger would be far outweighed by the advantages. It also noted that, because of the basic economic characteristics of railroads, it was not realistic to insist that intramodal rail competition must be preserved at all places, at all times, and under all circumstances. Commissioner Webb dissented vigorously from the decision to approve. He argued that in no prior case had the Commission destroyed so much competition with so little justification; that the tests of the Clayton Act had been totally destroyed; and that the decision was a bold grab for power in which the courts were not likely to acquiesce. The case was appealed and a three-judge district court set aside the order of the Commission on the ground that the latter had not conformed to the tests of the Clayton Act.[19] Appeal was taken to the Supreme Court which, in a *per curiam* decision, held that

---

[18] 320 I.C.C. 122 (1963).

[19] *Florida East Coast Ry. Co.* v. *United States,* 242 F. Supp. 14 (1965). For a discussion of mergers under the Clayton Act, see D. F. Pegrum, *Public Regulation of Business* (rev. ed.; Homewood, Ill., Richard D. Irwin, Inc., 1965), chap. 15.

the Commission was not bound by the Clayton Act tests if it concluded that the merger would assist in effectuating the overall transportation policy.[20] The case was remanded to the district court which upon reconsideration approved the merger. This was affirmed by a *per curiam* ruling of the Supreme Court on April 10, 1967.

A number of merger applications have been filed in recent years by railroads in the Western district but none of major importance have been approved so far.[21] The major application in this region was that of the Great Northern Railway, the Northern Pacific Railway and the Chicago, Burlington and Quincy Railroad to merge to form the Great Northern Pacific and Burlington Lines, Inc.[22] This proposed merger would have joined, formally, two of the major transcontinental lines to the ports of the Pacific Northwest and the strongest road of the Granger territory, the Chicago, Burlington and Quincy, which is jointly owned by both of them. The merger itself would have given official sanction of a unification that was largely already existent in fact. A majority of six members voted to deny the merger; five dissented, some very vigorously and caustically. The majority held that the applicants were all strong lines, in no need of financial salvation, and offering strong competition among themselves, and with the Chicago, Milwaukee, St. Paul, and Pacific. The majority was also fearful of the effects on the "weak" Milwaukee railroad and on others serving the area involved. It felt that arrangements necessary to safeguard the positions of other railroads would be difficult to work out and that they were unnecessary under the circumstances. The minority of the Commission attacked the majority position, particularly Commissioner Walrath who argued that the majority had misapplied the law, had been inconsistent and inept in its analysis, and had contradicted its verdict in the Pennsylvania–New York Central case.

It is difficult to find fault with Commissioner Walrath's evaluation of the reasoning of the majority. On the other hand, approval of the application would have resulted in the same conditions in the Western region that now obtain in the Eastern, which should be avoided if possible. It should be noted, now, that the Commission has reopened the case for further consideration.

[20] *Seaboard Airline Railroad* v. *United States,* 382 U.S. 155 (1965).

[21] In 1960, both the Southern Pacific and the Atchison, Topeka and Santa Fe applied to acquire control of the Western Pacific Railroad. Both applications were denied. Finance Docket 21314 (1965).

[22] *Great Northern Pacific and Burlington Lines, Inc.—Merger—Great Northern Railway,* Finance Docket 21478 (1966). On Nov. 30, 1967 the Commission reversed itself by approving the merger.

A Program for Consolidation

From the foregoing presentation, it is clear that there has been agreement for the past forty years that consolidation of railroads is necessary, but there has been no consensus as to the format it should take. There seems to have been no explicit recognition of the fact that the nature of railroad economics indicates clearly that the monopoly characteristics of railroads should be controlling in any feasible plan. Even if this is granted, however, the appropriate size of the various systems offers grounds for marked differences of opinion. Mr. Barriger apparently sees very little limitation in the economies of size, while Professor Kent T. Healy suggests that these are quite severe. The practical solution would seem to lie somewhere between these two extremes. Railroad transport is rapidly becoming primarily that of long-distance haulage. On the other hand, nationwide systems, in light of the physical and economic geography of the country, appear to offer dubious advantages.[23]

The controversies, conflicts of interest, financial manipulations, and maneuverings that have accompanied the present surge of railroad mergers prompted Congress to consider legislation that would have amended section 7 of the Clayton Act to effect a moratorium on the larger merger decisions so that Congress, the administration, and the Interstate Commerce Commission would have the time to investigate their overall impact, and to develop new criteria and safeguards for the acceptance of some of these mergers "in the public interest." Hearings by the U.S. Senate were held under the direction of Senator Kefauver.[24] Witnesses with widely varying points of view presented an array of testimony on the issues involved in railroad consolidation. As to be expected, some favored the moratorium, others registered strong opposition; some supported consolidation into a few large systems, others voiced total disagreement with this. Professor W. N. Leonard urged Congress to assume leadership in the matter, but he went

---

[23] The comparison with the two Canadian systems is of doubtful merit in light of the markedly different geographic and economic conditions of the two countries. In addition, the Canadian developments have not solved their problems. See *Report of the Royal Commission on Transportation* (Ottawa: King's Printer, February, 1951), especially pp. 282–93.

[24] *Railroad Merger Legislation,* Hearings, Subcommittee on Antitrust and Monopoly of the Committee on the Judiciary, U.S. Senate, 87th Cong., 2d sess., Parts 1 and 2 (Washington, D.C.: U.S. Government Printing Office, 1962). *The Railroad Merger Problem,* Report of the Subcommittee on Antitrust and Monopoly, 88th Cong., 1st sess. (Washington, D.C.: U.S. Government Printing Office, 1963). Part 1 of the Hearings are a very valuable source of information on the various points of view on the railroad merger problem.

further than the other witnesses by recommending "the creation of a new agency specifically created to plan and create consolidations along lines laid down by Congress, with power to approve merger plans of carriers, or to propose and carry through its own plans."[25] The proposed legislation, however, did not reach the floor of the Senate.

The Bureau of Transport Economics of the Interstate Commerce Commission issued a staff report on *Railroad Consolidations and the Public Interest* in 1962.[26] The study pointed out that proponents and opponents of mergers present their views adequately in most instances, but no voice speaks before the Commission for the public as a whole in most consolidation cases. After reviewing various aspects of the merger problem and analyzing a number of individual cases it suggested possible additions or changes to present methods, but concluded that the utility of additional or modified criteria could not be fully determined without further research as a sequel to the study. The sequel has not yet appeared.[27] The creation of the Department of Transportation in 1967[28] has added a new element to the situation. Presumably, the Department will be influential, and will possibly provide executive leadership for future mergers. How this will affect the present situation remains to be seen.

It is clear that a fresh start on the policy for railroad consolidation is needed at this time. Congress should give a clear mandate to the appropriate agency that competition as envisaged in the Transportation Act of 1920 is no longer a controlling factor. If the Interstate Commerce Commission is to continue to be the agency charged with the responsibility of working out the program, it should announce the principles in quite precise terms upon which consolidation may take place, and this before any further consolidations are permitted. If the Commission together with the railroads can work out an acceptable plan, so much the better; but if not, then Congress will have to assign the responsibility to someone to compel the development and the implementation of one.

OTHER AGENCIES

Consolidation of motor and water carriers at the present time presents no unique problems. In fact, there do not seem to be any good

---

[25] *Railroad Merger Legislation, op. cit.,* p. 313.

[26] *Railroad Consolidation and the Public Interest,* Staff Study, Bureau of Transport Economics and Statistics (Washington, D.C., 1962).

[27] The White House also released a Report of the *Interagency Committee on Transport Mergers* which set forth general criteria applicable to mergers in the railroad and airline industries (March 6, 1963). This report shed little light on the subject matter of the title.

[28] See Chapter 21, below.

reasons why they cannot be dealt with under the antitrust laws in the same manner as the railroads were prior to 1920. There is little likelihood of the emergence of any developments such as those which beset the railroads, because of the different economic characteristics of these two industries. If there is a reason why the responsibility for supervising mergers in water and motor transport should be left with the Interstate Commerce Commission, then the latter should be required to discharge its functions in the spirit of the antitrust laws and not according to the inept combination of competition and monopoly that has characterized the policy toward the railroads.[29]

Consolidation policy for motor carriers is complicated at the present time by restrictions on freedom of entry. The law gives the same exemption from the operation of the antitrust laws as applies to the railroads. The preservation of competition among carriers is significant chiefly as it aids in the attainment of the objectives of the National Transportation Policy.[30] Merger proposals, therefore, do not have to meet the tests of the antitrust laws. The economics of the motor carrier industry seem to make this exemption inadvisable, even though the administration of the Clayton Act might be left with the Commission. In the fiscal year ending June, 1966, the Commission authorized a number of major mergers leading to the establishment of firms operating on a nationwide basis.[31] Restriction of competition among these carriers by present certification policies raises serious questions on the effectiveness of competition among common carriers by motor vehicle, particularly in light of concerted action in rate making which is now the common practice.

The same remarks could be made with regard to air transport were it not for the fact that the Civil Aeronautics Board is still saddled with the responsibility of financial success through mail pay and subsidy. As

---

[29] See Walter Adams and J. G. Hendry, *Trucking Mergers, Concentration, and Small Business; an Analysis of Interstate Commerce Commission Policy, 1950–56,* Report for the Senate Select Committee on Small Business, 85th Congress, 1st session (Washington, D.C.: U.S. Government Printing Office, 1957). The author cannot view the growth of mergers in the trucking industry with the alarm expressed in this report, although he feels that the policy of certification pursued by the Interstate Commerce Commission is not conducive to healthy competition. On the other hand, the views of the minority of the Committee in its report, *Mergers and Concentration in the Trucking Industry,* 85th Congress, 2d session (Washington, D.C.: U.S. Government Printing Office, 1958), that free competition would end up in ruinous competition and the bankruptcy of small firms, are scarcely in keeping with the structure of competitive business, nor with the appropriate policy for competitive enterprise in this country. They evidently support the idea of restricting competition in order to preserve it.

[30] See *Interstate Commerce Commission Activities 1937–1962,* Supplement to the *75th Annual Report* (Washington, D.C.: U.S. Government Printing Office, 1962), p. 203.

[31] Interstate Commerce Commission, *80th Annual Report, 1966* (Washington, D.C.: U.S. Government Printing Office, 1967), p. 43.

long as this remains, feeder air lines should continue to operate on an exclusive basis. The trunk lines present a different problem. The first issue that has to be settled regarding them is certification and the route pattern. Until this is resolved, no sensible basis for consolidation can be established. If competition is to be the basis of policy, then the desirability of mergers should be judged in this light. If this is not to be the pattern, the Civil Aeronautics Board should develop a program of certification on the opposite hypothesis and proceed to design the areas to be served by the different carriers accordingly. The present indecisive attitude reaps the bad effects of following both theories. In the opinion of this author the approach should be based on the premise that air transport is a competitive industry, and steps should be taken to develop its organization and operation in accordance with that premise.[32]

INTEGRATION AND DIVERSIFICATION

THE NATURE OF THE ISSUE

Integration and diversification, although frequently used to mean the same thing, are in many respects two separate issues in transport policy. Integration, or common ownership of the various modes, refers to the unification of them into transportation companies prepared to offer the services of any of them to their customers. At the present time in this country the proposals are confined for the most part to enterprises providing domestic services, little interest being shown, for example, in railroad ownership of overseas shipping lines. This common ownership may encompass the supplying of only ancillary or supplemental services by the railroads using other carriers, or it may embrace competing carriers of the different modes.

Diversification is commonly used to mean the same thing as the foregoing, but it may also refer to common ownership of other modes in territories beyond the existing territories served by the railroad, thereby extending its market area into areas served by other lines, but through the medium of competing modes—not by the railroad but by the controlling corporation. Current proposals for diversification also indicate intentions of expanding beyond transportation into other areas of industrial activity. This is evident by the request for the repeal of the commodities clause of the Hepburn Act, and by the recent move of the Chicago and North Western Railway to acquire the Essex Wire Corpo-

---

[32] See Chapter 15, above, for a discussion of merger proceedings.

ration, a firm that makes wire, cable switches, and auto parts in 54 U.S. and Canadian plants. Other railroads are engaged in somewhat similar diversification.

It is clear that when integration is concerned with transportation enterprises only, it is a matter of transport policy. When it involves diversification into other industries, it becomes a question of public policy with regard to industrial organization and the corporation. This is quite distinct from public policy on transportation, raising very different issues. The problem of transport policy will be dealt with first.

INTEGRATION FOR ANCILLARY PURPOSES

Integration of transport for ancillary or supplemental purposes refers to the operation of the facilities of other modes by a carrier whose principal business undertakings are concerned with one of the agencies. The arrangement relates primarily to the railroads which wish to utilize motor transport as an immediately co-ordinated service in connection with their railroad traffic. Thus, they may wish to supply pickup and delivery service at terminals so that complete transportation from origin to destination may be rendered by them. This may also apply to local traffic movements to and from intermediate points that have a prior or subsequent movement by rail under the "key-point" rule sanctioned by the Interstate Commerce Commission. Similarly, the railroads may provide their own piggyback transportation by owning and operating the trailers to be moved on flatcars, and the motive equipment to assemble and deliver the trailers. Other examples of ancillary services of a somewhat similar nature could be detailed.

The utilization of other modes for providing ancillary services makes it possible for the railroads to co-ordinate transportation in a way that is convenient to the shipper. It may also aid the railroads in their competition with rival modes by attracting traffic that otherwise might move entirely by the other means. If shippers are given the option of providing their own ancillary services by whatever devices they see fit, and if the piggyback service is available to other carriers or shippers who wish to supply their own trailers, there is little ground for complaint that this participation by railroads constitutes unfair competition or a threat to competition in transport. In addition, it is likely to provide a stimulus to the development of piggyback movements, thereby encouraging more economical transportation.

The substitution by the railroads of motor transport for abandoned branch-line services presents issues that are somewhat more complicated. The branch lines have usually been discarded because motor carriers have taken their business. The substitution of railroad-owned motor carriage puts the railroad companies directly into the motor carrier business. This may involve motor traffic only, or it may be a means whereby the railroads can retain the branch-line traffic that was part of a through movement, which in the absence of railroad participation might go all the way to destination by the other mode. Insofar as the through traffic is concerned, the substitution by the railroads is of an ancillary nature because competing motor carriers would be given the same through-rate privileges; insofar as it is local, it puts the railroad squarely in the motor carrier business. The latter raises the issue of public policy concerned with the question of the development of transportation companies. In this case, it may be difficult to separate the two, but there may be good reasons for permitting this substitution, even though transportation companies are not approved.

TRANSPORTATION COMPANIES

Permission to create transportation companies is now being sought by the railroads, and the Association of American Railroads is being used as a spokesman for this program.[33] The proposals for the formation of transportation companies, opposed by the motor, water, and air carriers, have grown out of the loss of freight traffic by the railroads to the other modes. The argument is advanced that the shipper today is confronted with the necessity of determining the most economical and efficient means of moving his goods. This quite commonly involves the use of more than one agency, especially motor carriers. Formation of transportation companies, it is contended, would afford the shipper complete transportation service under one management, and would result in more efficient and more economical use of all transport facilities and equipment. The point is also made that integration of the different modes by common ownership would add to the financial stability and strength of the carriers by reducing the chance of failure of the entire enterprise if any one of the types of service being offered should fail, that is, if any one of the modes in the combined undertaking should turn out to be unsuccessful. Finally, it is urged that the railroads are required to pay heavy taxes to help build highways, airways, and airports, and improve waterways, for use by their competitors.

In evaluating the merits of transportation companies, it should be

[33] See Association of American Railroads, *Magna Carta for Transportation* (Washington, D.C., 1961), chap. viii.

recognized at the outset that this involves different questions than those that arise in connection with the privilege of supplying ancillary services. The latter does not result in common ownership of facilities supplying line-haul services, but the essence of transportation companies is to do just this. Furthermore the provision of ancillary service has the advantage of providing for effective co-ordination, whereas common ownership of the modes for line-haul traffic assumes independent and, theoretically at least, competitive movements.

The economies which may be realized from common ownership are dubious, to say the least, as is evident from the earlier analysis of economies of scale in the various modes of transport. The different agencies would undoubtedly be organized as separate corporations which would afford little opportunity for "spreading the overhead," in addition to the fact that the competitive nature of motor, water, and air transport would make it impossible for them to absorb any significant amount of the railroad burden. Moreover, common ownership by the railroads of competing modes would not assist the railroads as such unless it resulted in reducing the competition among the different agencies of the same company. If this were the outcome, it would be the result of the development of transport monopolies, a possibility that is denied by the proponents, and one that clearly would not be in the public interest. In other words, transportation companies will not solve the problems of the railroads per se, and will not improve their competitive capabilities.

The formation of transportation companies is also related to the problem of consolidation, and this issue should be resolved before policy questions on integration are decided. Railroad consolidation, as already noted, might take the form of competitive, regional, or national systems. The last two seem to be the only feasible possibilities. If the regional plan is adopted, then it would seem logical to confine the transport companies to the same areas unless they were to be allowed to penetrate each other's territories through the medium of other modes. How this could be of any assistance to the railroads in the resolution of their problems is difficult to understand. On the other hand, if companies were to be confined to the territory of a particular railroad, it would not necessarily be economical to confine the motor transport to the same territory, and it would certainly be undesirable to do this for air. In addition, the threat of regional transport monopoly, or at least dominance of a particular corporation, would be very real because it would be organized around the inescapable monopoly structure of the railroad. If a limited number of national systems were established, the threat to anything resembling healthy competition in transport would be too great to be tolerated. Furthermore, transport companies, with the continued existence of rate making by agreement would serve to reduce competition and would probably require more detailed regulation than we have at present.

The suggestion that if railroads, through the taxes imposed upon them, are required to contribute to the support of the other modes, they should be allowed to participate in the operation of them in order to receive some of the benefits derived from the taxes, seems to be too trivial to warrant serious attention. This is clearly not the way to resolve the problems which public aid presents. Operation of other agencies, as already pointed out, will not solve the problems of the railroads even if the former are the beneficiaries of public aid. The resolution of this problem lies in equalizing competitive conditions among the modes, something that integration is powerless to achieve. The real essence of this proposal lies in the argument that diversification will promote financial stability. Just how this would come about, or precisely what it means, has not been spelled out, but it could not be of assistance to the railroads as a means of transport unless it was the result of suppressing competition presented by the other agencies. One must assume that the financial stability which is referred to relates to the controlling corporation rather than to the railroad which would be one of the methods of transportation owned by the corporation. This is quite a different matter and needs to be dealt with in connection with the problem of diversification in general.

Ownership of pipe-line companies by railroads or the corporations controlling them possibly falls into a slightly different category. The construction of pipe lines as common carriers independent of the oil companies has much to commend it, where this is feasible. Pipe lines and railroads are not strongly competitive because of the differences in costs, which favor the pipe lines. Moreover, the pipe lines are natural monopolies, and common ownership would not result in diminution of competition with the other means of transport. The pipe lines may also use the railroad right of way, thereby making more complete utilization of a resource devoted to rail transport. Whether this will result in any material social benefit that could not be obtained from independent ownership of the pipe line may be an open question, but as far as transport organization is concerned, no serious disadvantages are apparent.

DIVERSIFICATION

Diversification arises when a corporation undertakes to supply various services or to produce various commodities that are not directly related to each other in the production process, or in fact are quite independent of each other in the operating processes. The combination of these is the result of corporate organization, commonly the holding company device, which may combine totally unrelated activities for financial reasons. This is the situation where railroads own pipe lines or overseas shipping companies. The proposals advanced at the present time go farther than this, however. In seeking to secure the repeal of the commodities clause, the railroad corporations want the privilege of acquiring industries in fields other than transportation. This raises two major questions.

The first relates to the organization of the railroads themselves. This emerges in its extreme form with the proposal for two nationwide railroad systems, or even one under an American Telephone and Telegraph type of combination. Apart from the problems which this sort of a railroad giant would present, permission to integrate other modes of transport would entail so much control over the transportation system of the country by a single enterprise as to make a mockery out of effective competition, to say nothing of the diseconomies of scale. If to this were added the privilege of diversifying into nontransport industrial activities, concentration far beyond anything now in existence would be the result. Any serious attempt to preserve an effective competitive enterprise system could not countenance such a development.

If some form of regional consolidation is contemplated, a similar situation would emerge, although it would not be so extreme. Nevertheless, transport companies formed around regional railroad consolidation would result in enterprises with decisive dominance over the transport facilities of the region. If to this were added the privilege of diversifying into other industrial activities, regional consolidation would be promoted to an extent incompatible with a competitive system.

One of the problems of industrial organization and public policy that has not yet been resolved is the scope of diversification which should be permitted to modern corporate enterprise.[34] This issue cannot be developed here. Suffice it to say, however, that there is pressing need for the development of criteria for the scope of corporate undertakings compatible with private enterprise and the competitive system on which

[34] See Pegrum, *Public Regulation of Business, op. cit.,* chap. 20. For a discussion of the diversification program of the Chicago and North Western Railway, see *Time,* June 23, 1967 p. 88. This diversification into wire manufacturing and chemicals is obviously an attempt to enhance corporate profits, not to solve railroad or transport problems. The prestige and borrowing power of the railroad is a definite advantage for the acquired firms. The agreements currently being advanced for the advantages of diversification are similar to those used on behalf of the phenomenal development of the holding company in the 1920's.

it relies. Until we have more clear-cut answers to this question, transport companies and a fortiori transport companies with industrial diversification should not be permitted. At the present time the railroads have enough problems, as railroads, to occupy their energies. One of the first of these is consolidation. Until a solution of this is worked out, permission to form transportation companies and to engage in further diversification should be withheld.

Chapter

19

FINANCING
TRANSPORTATION

INTRODUCTION

The Allocation of Economic Resources

The basic problem of public policy as it relates to the financing of transportation is concerned with three issues: (1) the total allocation of economic resources to the provision of transportation for the country, (2) the allocation of the total among the various modes of transport, and (3) the allocation of the burden of paying for these resources among the beneficiaries of the services that are rendered by the transport system. The economic resources that are devoted to the transport sector of the economy consist of the capital costs together with all of the other outlays which are necessary to maintain and operate the system. Most of these costs are explicit; but some of them may be implicit, even though certain nuisance costs are omitted in ascertaining the total. The allocation problem rests primarily on the capital investment to be made in transport as a whole, and the proportions of this in the various modes. In addition, however, it encompasses the costs that are entailed in maintaining and utilizing the facilities. These are conditioned to a very large degree by the way in which the capital funds are provided, the extent to which the users of the facilities are required to pay for the use which they make of them, and the methods by which the payments are imposed. The bulk of the transportation services of the country are supplied directly to the consumer by private operators, but the provision of the "highways" for motor, water, and air transportation is the immediate responsibility of government at the present time; essentially similar remarks apply to their terminal facilities. It is because of this that the most critical issues of resource allocation to transport, and among the various agencies, turn on investment policies in the public sector and the appropriate assessment of the costs of this public sector on the beneficiaries thereof.

467

If the economic resources of the country are to be allocated to transportation in an economical way, the amount of these that is devoted to transport must be such that any part of them would not be more valuable if assigned to some other activity, and vice versa. This means that, insofar as possible, investment needs in transportation should be measured in terms of alternatives, so that resources will flow into transportation if they will be more valuable there than in some other use, and will not flow in, or will move out, if other opportunities are better. In terms of a free price economy, this would mean that price inducements would indicate the need for services and therefore resources in the transport sector. Even if price indicators are not directly available, some economic gauge of requirements must be developed if transportation is to be supplied on a rational rather than an arbitrary basis. In economic terms the situation is no different here than it is in other areas of the economy.

The allocation problem does not end with the total that is required by transportation. The different modes have their respective claims. The same general principles apply to intermodal assignment of resources, as to allocation to transport and nontransport uses. The amount of resources to be assigned to each mode should be subject to the test that they will not be more valuable if put to any other use in transportation or elsewhere. If it were possible to utilize the market completely to supply this test, the amount required by each mode would be available for it, and the total for transport as a whole would be ascertained by summation. Under such circumstances, allocation among the modes would take the same pattern as allocation among the various industries in the economy.

The final problem in this connection pertains to the allocation of the burden of costs upon the beneficiaries of the services rendered by the agencies of transport. Where goods or services are supplied completely by private enterprise, allocation of the burden is settled by the mechanism of the market. This does not always mean that it is free from arbitrary or whimsical action, but insofar as competition is effective, this will be eliminated. The same remarks apply to transportation where competition operates. If all of the supply of transport services were subject to workably effective competition, the allocation of the transport burden among users would present no unique questions. Unfortunately, the problem is not susceptible to such a relatively simple solution, even though a much closer approximation could be obtained than is presently the case.

The Unique Problem in Transport

The unique problem in the financing of transport services today arises from the inescapable mixture of private and public investment among the agencies and within some of them. Railroad financing at the present time is forced to rely on private investment induced by the revenues which the carriers are able to obtain from the transport services they sell. This is so even where they may obtain government-guaranteed loans under the provisions of the Transportation Act of 1958, because these loans are not to be made unless there is assurance that they will be paid back in the contract period. Similarly, even though public bodies may undertake to "subsidize" commuter passenger services, the payments which are made are for specific services which are to be rendered and are for the purpose of covering the costs the commuters are unable or unwilling to bear. In these instances it is the commuter who is being subsidized by the public funds, not the railroad.

In the case of water, air, and motor transport the investment in the "highways" and the bulk of the terminal facilities is made by public authority relying for the most part on its taxing power. Except for the St. Lawrence Seaway and the Panama Canal the domestic waterways are toll-free; that is, they are supplied without cost to the water carriers. The air lines are not assessed with any direct costs for the use of the airways, and they by no means contribute fully to the costs of the airports which are publicly owned, and this includes all of the important ones. The motor carriers use highways, roads, and streets that are provided from public funds paid for out of taxation. Although taxes are assessed on the users, these taxes do not cover all of the explicit costs incurred in the provision of the highways. Even if these three modes of transport were required to pay user fees to cover all of the costs of the public investment, they would still not be saddled with the responsibility of assuming the risk of the investment; that risk belongs to the taxpayer, not the carrier. Its investment problems are confined to the equipment and facilities it owns.

Public investment in water and air transport could be gauged in the same manner as if the entire plant were privately owned. This could be done by refusal to make expenditures that would not be met by prospective revenues. In other words, theoretically, at least, government could handle this on the strictly business basis of pricing the services to make the undertaking a going concern independent of the general taxpayer. Motor transport, however, offers a more complex problem. It is pretty generally held that the construction and maintenance of highways, especially if these be interpreted to include local roads and streets, are for purposes that go beyond highway transportation. As a consequence, some reliance is placed on taxation of others than the users. How much this should be, and how to calculate the amount of the cost that should be borne by the taxpayer, is a disputed question. There is the additional complication that road facilities are used by a variety of vehicles. The appropriate burden to be placed on each, even if the burden is known, is a problem that has by no means been resolved to date.

The Equalization of Competition

If all investment in transportation were a matter of private decision based on choices that were conditioned by thoroughly competitive situations, there would be no special problem of resource allocation to transport in total, or among the agencies. This situation is not possible today; and indeed, in many respects it has never obtained in this area of economic endeavor. Public participation, directly or indirectly, has always characterized transportation. The existence at the present time of the different modes and the wide range of competition among them, however, has created the relatively new problem of developing a policy which will provide for substantial equality of competitive opportunities for the different modes to obtain the traffic which may be moved by any of them. If each were so unique in its own sphere of activity that interagency competition did not exist, each agency could be dealt with in isolation. The impossibility of this makes it imperative that the choice to shippers among the services that can be supplied by the different agencies—that is, the substitutable services—be afforded on the basis of the relative costs of the services. If these relative costs are to be the measure of the relative efficiencies of the agencies, they must be derived from the total economic costs which the supplying of transport service by each agency entails. The focal point, under modern conditions, of ascertaining these economic costs and imposing them upon the users lies in the areas of public aid and public investment.

Public aid and public investment are not the only aspects of financing transport. They loom large in public policy, however. Moreover, the historical development of transportation has very largely followed the pattern dictated by public aid. A considerable portion of the highway and terminal facilities of all the modes has resulted from either public aid or public investment; nor has this feature of transportation diminished with the emergence of the modern system. On the contrary, the opposite has been the case, and the proportion of the public sector of resources in transport has increased, despite the fact that the enterprises which supply the services directly are privately owned.

No unique question of financing the operators of air, water, or motor carriers has arisen, apart from public participation, nor does it seem likely to. Pipe-line finance has never been a matter of concern. The railroads have offered a distinct problem because of the large amount of capital required as a whole, and for each system. In addition, the dependence of the public on a particular railroad, and the close relationship in the past of railroad rates to railroad finance, has prompted public intervention. This again emerges from the monopoly features of railroads. Today the issue has taken on a different turn because of the rise of comprehensive interagency competition. Railroad financial structures are no longer a causal factor in railroad rate making.[1]

HISTORY OF PUBLIC AID

Public investment and public aid for transportation have characterized the history of the development of the United States from its very beginning as a nation. The history of this may be divided into three periods, each identified by a different policy. The first period, which extended down to the financial crisis of 1837, was one of public investment in canals and inland waterways with private operation of the vessels, and some construction of roads for land communication. The second period was the railroad era, which may conveniently be said to have come to an end in 1920, during which time inland transport was developed primarily under private ownership, with various kinds of public aid, land grants being the best known. The third period, from World War I to the present, constitutes a new phase, with vast public expenditures on highway, water, and air transport. At the same time, reliance has been placed on private operators to provide the transport services, while railroads and pipe lines have depended entirely on private ownership. This third period, therefore, is characterized by a mixed system of ownership in a sense that was not applicable to the earlier periods, and one that is likely to remain for the indefinite

---

[1] This is precisely the position that was taken by the Railroad Securities Commission established in accordance with the provisions of the Mann-Elkins Act of 1910, but the conditions at that time were quite different than they are now.

future. These three periods overlap each other somewhat, but the contrast between them is such that each stands out clearly from the other.

The Early Period

The early period, commencing with the establishment of the federal government, may be said to have extended to 1837. During this time the development of transportation facilities was largely a matter of public undertakings, with the state and local governments playing the major role. At the very outset of the growth of internal transportation, turnpikes were built by private stock companies as continuous lines for through traffic, with the costs being met by tolls imposed on the users. Some 180 turnpike companies were chartered by New England alone by 1810.[2] State aid was often given to these companies; and in 1808, Albert Gallatin, Secretary of the Treasury, proposed that the federal government undertake a program of comprehensive internal improvements. One result of this was the Cumberland Road or "National Pike."

The principal improvement in transportation during this period came with the construction of the canals. The most significant of these was the Erie Canal, which was built by the state of New York. The success of this venture led to a mania of canal building, especially in the states of the Atlantic seaboard and the Great Lakes area. Down to 1838, state debts amounting to over $60 million for canals and $6.6 for roads were incurred. The financial crisis of 1837 brought an end to this phase of transport development.[3] The failure of the state projects and the repudiation of indebtedness by many of the governments led to the inclusion of provisions in many state constitutions prohibiting the use of state funds or credit for internal improvements. Transportation facilities for the remainder of the century were to be provided by private concerns, many of which, however, received aid from states or the federal government.

The Railroad Era

The first period of transport development in this country came to an end in part because of the emergence of the railroad and the rather rapid recognition that it was the superior means of inland transportation. Some considerable public aid and public investment for railroads had been made by 1837, a total $42.8 million of debts having been

---

[2] For an account of these developments, see E. L. Bogart, *Economic History of the American People* (2d ed.; New York: Longmans, Green & Co., 1935), pp. 312 f.

[3] *Ibid.*, p. 328.

incurred by the states for this purpose down to 1838. After the financial crisis of 1837, however, railroad construction was left almost entirely in private hands, with the investment coming from private sources, particularly from Europe. Public aid entered the picture through such channels as guarantees of securities, grants of rights of way, land grants, and tax privileges, most of it being confined to the grants and special privileges.

The total amount of public aid that was accorded the railroads is a matter of considerable dispute. This is partly the result of different methods of computing the aid in monetary terms and partly the result of inadequate records. It is not necessary to undertake any serious analysis of the question here because for all practical purposes the direct aid came to an end before the outbreak of World War I and therefore does not enter the picture of public policy in a significant way in the modern period.

In the part of the country westward from the Ohio and the Mississippi, public aid consisted primarily of land grants. Indirect aid was given through charters, many of which afforded tax exemptions for a period of time, and some of which even granted banking privileges.[4] The principal public contribution to railroad construction was made by the federal government during the period from 1850 to 1871 in the form of land grants. As pointed out in Chapter 3, these land grants consisted of rights of way and alternate sections of land on each side of the rights of way, these sections being granted to the railroads for the purpose of enabling them to obtain the capital to undertake construction. The total acreage deeded under this arrangement amounted to just over 131 million acres. The total aid in monetary terms of private citizens and local, state, and federal governments was estimated by the Federal Coordinator of Transportation to have amounted to $1.4 billion.[5] A similar study made by the Board of Investigation and Research

---

[4] See C. W. Wright, *Economic History of the United States* (New York: McGraw-Hill Book Co., Inc., 1941), pp. 346–50.

[5] Federal Coordinator of Transportation, *Public Aids to Transportation,* Vol. I (Washington, D.C.: U.S. Government Printing Office, 1940), p. 19. This also included the benefits estimated to have been received from interest savings on money borrowed from the Reconstruction Finance Corporation during the 1930's. An illustration of the method by which the Coordinator arrived at the total public aid to railroads is afforded by the following quotation from Vol. II (1938), p. 66: "Many railroads have also been aided in securing funds for construction of their lines through subscriptions to their stocks by citizens of communities into or through which their lines were built. As in the case of the contributions of cash, securities, and other property by citizens in aid of the construction of railroads . . . , these subscriptions have generally been made collectively in furtherance of the common efforts of the citizenries of the communities to secure the building of railroads into or through such communities. Consequently, they were public aids." The conclusion seems to be warranted that the total estimated public aid to railroads in this study is grossly overstated.

which was set up under the Transportation Act of 1940 estimated the total to be about $624 million.[6]

In connection with public aid to railroads, it should be noted that the railroads were required to give the federal government land-grant rates which, because of competitive conditions, had to be met by other roads not receiving the grants. When these benefits are matched against the public aid, the conclusion seems to be warranted that the government was ultimately repaid the aid which the railroads received.[7] Whatever may be the final verdict on this controversy, it is clear that railroad transportation, especially as distinct from the corporate enterprises, is today not receiving any public aid, direct or indirect, for which the federal government does not expect full compensation, or for which public agencies are not receiving services that are being rendered in return for the compensation the railroads are receiving. Furthermore, most of the aid extended to the railroads was not designed to enable them to compete with other forms of transport, but rather to encourage the supplying of transportation services to a vast continent that was without practicable commercial facilities in advance of the markets that could have supported them.[8] This may have resulted in overexpansion and waste of resources, but that is a matter of past history, the lesson and legacy of which should be not to repeat the same mistake again. Excessive development of railroads in the nineteenth century can scarcely be regarded as an argument for a repetition of the policies in other areas of transportation today.

The Modern Period

This period, which may be said to have begun with the end of World War I, marked a new departure in public participation in providing for transportation facilities. Heretofore, public aid had been

[6] See Board of Investigation and Research, *Public Aids to Transportation,* House Document No. 159, 79th Cong., 1st sess. (Washington, D.C.: U.S. Government Printing Office, 1945), chap. iii. For a succinct comparison of the two studies, see R. E. Westmeyer, *Economics of Transportation* (Englewood Cliffs, N.J.: Prentice-Hall, Inc., 1952), pp. 58–66.

[7] See Stuart Daggett, *Principles of Inland Transportation* (4th ed.; New York: Harper & Bros., 1955), chap. xxxiv. This is similar to the conclusion of the Board of Investigation and Research: "Rates and tax compensation have fully counterbalanced these aids [land grants] which were extended many years ago" (*op. cit.,* p. 57).

[8] For a critical evaluation of the effects on economic growth by public aid to rail transport, see R. W. Fogel, *Railroads and American Economic Growth: Essays in Econometric History* (Baltimore, Md.: The Johns Hopkins Press, 1964). That there has been too much uncritical acceptance of the economic benefits to society arising from public aid is all too clear, but Fogel's estimates and assumptions are not without bias either. He tries to prove too much. See also John B. Lansing, *Transportation and Economic Policy* (New York: The Free Press, 1966), chap. 7.

confined largely to assisting the railroads in the construction of their lines, but in the modern period it has taken the form of large-scale public investment in highway, water, and air transport, and expenditures on the maintenance of their routes and a major portion of the terminal facilities. The operation of the equipment has been left in the hands of private firms which use the publicly supplied "highways." This arrangement, which makes government the largest single proprietary interest in transportation, is unlikely to be changed in the foreseeable future. The federal government has become the largest single owner of transportation plant in the country, but the stake of all governments has grown at an exceedingly rapid pace since 1947. As a consequence, the problem of financing the enormous outlays on motor, air, and water transportation has been assumed by government, in contrast to the predominantly private financing of the previous period. From the very nature of the routes used by these modes, this seems to be an inescapable development.

Table 19–1 sets forth the federal, state, and local expenditures on domestic transportation facilities in this country to date as estimated by the Association of American Railroads. While these estimates may be subject to some debate they clearly indicate the magnitude of government expenditures on transportation today. These estimated expenditures represent the total outlays by all levels of government since 1921, and the only element of direct subsidy is that which has been paid to the airlines, amounting to $1,120,024,000 from 1939 to 1967. It is significant to note that of the total governmental expenditures on transport of $277.7 billion, $215.2 billion have been spent since 1947, $57.3 billion by the federal government and $158.1 billion by state and local governments. Of the total federal expenditures for this period, $42.9 billion have been for highways, $9.3 billion for air transport, and $5 billion for domestic waterways. State and local expenditures amounted to $148.6 billion for highways, $4.5 billion for waterways, and $5 billion for airports. Thus the total expenditures at all levels on highways amounted to approximately $191.5 billion. During the period since 1947, private expenditures on railroads for construction and maintenance of way have amounted to $26.4 billion.

The problems connected with the financing of transportation in the country at the present time therefore fall into two categories:) (1) financing the privately owned and operated portion of the transport system—in the case of railroads and pipe lines, this covers the total financing, that which is to provide for the roadway facilities as well as that which supplies the operating equipment; and (2) fi-

TABLE 19–1

SUMMARY OF GOVERNMENT EXPENDITURES FOR DOMESTIC TRANS-
PORTATION: AIRWAYS, AIRPORTS, AIRLINE CASH SUBSIDIES,
HIGHWAYS, AND WATERWAYS*

Expenditures for Years	Federal	State and Local†	Total†
Prior to 1947......$13 732 604 489		$48 742 721 615	$62 475 326 104
1947..........	534 102 370	2 994 000 000	3 528 102 370
1948..........	678 790 053	3 497 000 000	4 175 790 053
1949..........	861 384 324	3 873 000 000	4 734 384 324
1950..........	896 368 978	4 208 000 000	5 104 368 978
1951..........	896 308 768	4 644 000 000	5 540 308 768
1952..........	963 935 839	5 046 000 000	6 009 935 839
1953..........	1 080 333 685	5 591 000 000	6 671 333 685
1954..........	942 875 734	6 593 000 000	7 535 875 734
1955..........	1 055 817 154	6 839 000 000	7 894 817 154
1956..........	1 221 572 828	7 821 000 000	9 042 572 828
1957..........	1 944 045 184	8 332 000 000	10 276 045 184
1958..........	3 109 201 771	8 355 000 000	11 464 201 771
1959..........	4 014 005 304	8 197 000 000	12 211 005 304
1960..........	3 653 121 876	8 588 000 000	12 241 121 876
1961..........	3 952 733 676	9 263 000 000	13 215 733 676
1962..........	4 192 748 321	9 782 000 000	13 974 748 321
1963..........	4 875 639 438	9 967 000 000	14 842 639 438
1964..........	5 446 984 000	10 109 000 000	15 555 984 000
1965..........	5 329 295 000	10 789 000 000	16 118 295 000
1966..........	5 751 205 000	11 480 000 000	17 231 205 000
1967 (est.)....	5 846 641 000	12 055 000 000	17 901 641 000
Total........$70 979 714 792		$206 765 721 615	$277 745 436 407

* This table summarizes expenditures for all types of facilities. Data are for fiscla
years, except highway expenditures which are on a calendar year basis. Not included are Merchant Marine and Coast Guard expenditures. The totals for these are: $21,130,000,000 and
$7,519,000,000 respectively.

† Does not include state and local expenditures for waterways prior to 1947.

SOURCE: Association of American Railroads. These figures have been compiled from
official government publications. See also *National Transportation Policy* (Doyle Report),
Preliminary Draft of a Report to the Senate Committee on Interstate and Foreign Commerce,
87th Cong., 1st sess. (Washington, D.C.: U.S. Government Printing Office, 1961), pp. 166–84.

nancing the publicly supplied highways, waterways, and airways, and
financing the privately owned equipment and facilities—in this instance, it is in the sector involving public investment that the most
acute and difficult problems arise.

FINANCING THE RAILROADS

Nature of the Problem

Providing for the financial requirements of railroad transportation
differs from that of motor, water, and air, first of all, because at the

present time, it is achieved through the medium of private enterprise and, second, because each system or enterprise must be operated as a unit; that is, the roadway and motive equipment are technically so constructed that they must be treated as a unit for operating
purposes.[9] In the other three modes, on the other hand, the roadway is
separate from the enterprises supplying the services, with the result
that a multiplicity of carriers can use it. If the federal government were
to take over the railroads, and it were assumed that the undertaking was
still to be self-liquidating, the same basic problems would remain as
are now present, although the responsibility for meeting them would
be shifted to different hands. If the government were to acquire the
roadway,[10] leaving the operations in private hands, user charges would
have to be imposed on each operating company. Just how these would
be levied offers some interesting grounds for theoretical speculation.

The problem of financing the railroads today centers on the ability
of the private corporations to secure adequate revenues to maintain and
operate their enterprises, together with the acquisition of new capital
from outside investors. The sources of capital funds for the railroads
are internal and external. The external sources are the capital markets
for stocks, bonds, and other securities. The principal internal sources
are depreciation and retirement charges, and undistributed earnings
from transportation and non-transportation income. Professor J. C. Nelson estimated that 43.6 per cent of gross capital expenditures from
1946 to 1955, inclusive, came from external sources and 56.44 from
internal. Almost all the funds from external financing were obtained
from equipment obligations; these amounted to 40.33 per cent of the
gross capital expenditures. They are the most marketable of railroad
securities. "More than half of all postwar gross capital expenditures
was financed by funds which became available from various depreciation charges to operating expenses, from drawing down accumulated
reserves of cash and temporary cash investments, and from net income
from transportation and non-transportation operations not paid out to
stockholders in the form of dividends."[11] From 1947 to 1962, gross
capital expenditures by railroads averaged just over $1 billion a year,
with only $833 million in 1962. Since then, however, the total has
been over $1 billion a year, reaching $1.95 billion in 1966.

[9] The same is true of pipe lines. The financing of these is not discussed in this
chapter because they are, for the most part, directly related to the petroleum industry and
offer no special problems at present that differ from corporation finance in general.

[10] This proposal has even been advanced by the president of Western Maryland
Railroad as a means of counteracting public investment in the other "ways."

[11] J. C. Nelson, *Railroad Transportation and Public Policy* (Washington, D.C.: The
Brookings Institution, 1959), p. 219.

Capital Requirements

Investment in the railroads of this country at the end of World War I amounted to approximately $24 billion, and it is generally conceded that this was not excessive. Today, some 50 years later, it is about $27.5 billion, an increase of only $3.5 billion, despite the modernization program, the effects of inflation, and the enormous economic growth of the country. In spite of gross capital expenditures averaging $1.15 billion a year since 1947, almost no new net investment has been made. Railroads cannot, therefore, be characterized as a growth industry at the present time. Whether they should be or can be depends upon the role one assumes they should occupy in the modern transport structure. Although they transport about 75 per cent more ton-miles of freight than they did at the end of World War I, this is being done with only a small increase in capital investment. This indicates a substantial improvement in railroad efficiency, at least as far as capital expenditures are concerned.

On the other hand, the absolute decline in passenger-mile transport and the deficit on the passenger business that has been incurred emphasize the decreasing importance of capital expenditures on this once lucrative phase of railroad transportation. Whether all of this adds up to a need for net new capital investment depends upon the place the railroads are expected to occupy in the transport system of the future. Whatever may be the verdict on this question, it is clear that the ability of the railroads to secure capital funds, either to maintain the present investment or to expand, depends on their ability to earn sufficient revenues to supply their capital needs from internal and external sources. Ultimately, earning capacity will have to be the test of the need for capital in railroad transportation.

The estimated capital requirements of the railroads in the years ahead were the subject of extensive study by the Brookings Institution, which arrived at four estimates.[12] Two of these were the result of a questionnaire sent to forty-one Class I railroads requesting projections for the period 1956–65, with the assumptions (1) that the railroads would continue to carry about 50 per cent of the intercity traffic or (2) that they would increase their share to 55 per cent. It was also assumed that national transportation policy would remain much as it was

---

[12] *Ibid.*, chap. xi. See also *National Transportation Policy* (Doyle Report), Preliminary Draft of a Report to the Senate Committee on Interstate and Foreign Commerce, 87th Cong., 1st sess. (Washington, D.C.: U.S. Government Printing Office, 1961), Part II, chaps. iii and iv, and J. W. Barriger, Jr., *Super-Railroads for a Dynamic American Economy* (New York: Simmons-Boardman Publishing Corp., 1956).

in 1956, that the figures were in 1955 dollars, and that present technology would continue to prevail. The third estimate was obtained
from the study by John Barriger, Jr., and the fourth from the Interstate
Commerce Commission, *Ex Parte 206.*[13] Table 19–2 sets forth these

TABLE 19–2

ESTIMATES OF RAILROAD CAPITAL REQUIREMENTS
(In Millions of Dollars)

	Brookings Assumption[1]	*Brookings Assumption*[2]	*Barriger*	*Ex Parte 206*
For equipment	$ 938	$1,045	$ 750	$1,000
Roadway and structures	486	518	1,250	500
Total Annual	$1,424	$1,563	$2,000	$1,500

SOURCE: *National Transportation Policy* (Doyle Report), Preliminary Draft of a Report to the Senate
Committee on Interstate and Foreign Commerce, 87th Congress, 1st session (Washington, D.C.: U.S. Government
Printing Office, 1961), p. 53 (corrected for arithmetic errors).

estimates. Three of these are nearly the same in amount, but Mr.
Barriger's is considerably higher. He projected a complete modernization program, commencing in 1956 and ending in 1963, at a cost of
$20 billion, with normal peacetime traffic requirements of 750 billion
to 800 billion ton-miles of freight, nearly 50 per cent more than the
actual revenue ton-miles of 1960. The estimates made by Mr. Barriger,
for an annual basis were approximately the same as actual results for
1966 when capital expenditures were about $1.95 billion and
freight ton-miles were 738.3 billion. The total capital expenditures,
however, for the years 1953 to 1966 inclusive have amounted to only
$14.5 billion. The actual results have fallen considerably short of the
estimated needs, especially if inflation is taken into account.

The ability of the railroads to meet capital requirements depends
upon whether they can attract the projected volume of traffic at rates
that are sufficiently remunerative to provide the funds. Unfortunately,
the record on this score since 1946 is not encouraging. The highest
rate of return since 1946 was 4.31 per cent in 1948; it has been below 4 per cent in 15 out of the 20 years since 1946, and in every year
since 1955, falling to 1.97 per cent in 1961. Since then it has risen
steadily to approximately 3.9 per cent for 1966. This is the best showing since 1955. The rise in both rate of return and capital expenditures has been stimulated by the 7 per cent investment tax credit by

[13] *Increased Freight Rates,* 299 I.C.C. 429 (1956), 300 I.C.C. 633 (1957); also
Ex Parte 212, 302 I.C.C. 665 (1958), 304 I.C.C. 289 (1958). This estimate was for the
years 1956–60.

the federal government. The return must also cover interest charges. The railroads reduced their total funded debt of approximately $11.6 billion in 1932 to $8.3 billion in 1947. It was $8.5 billion in 1959 and $7.94 billion in 1963 (figures since then are not available). One must conclude that the long-run financial outlook for the railroads as a whole is quite uncertain with serious difficulties ahead unless some rather drastic steps are taken to assure continuation of the improvement in this position that has appeared during this period of a high level of national prosperity.

It is important to observe that the foregoing is a depiction of the railroad situation in the aggregate. The differences among the individual railroads are very marked. For example, the Pocahontas lines are strong, and so are most of the western transcontinentals. Much of the difficulty centers around the weak roads, but the financial plight of the New York Central and the Pennsylvania indicates that the problem is more deep-seated than this. Railroad capital will be hard to obtain as long as the industry as a whole continues in its present condition, and little short of a drastic overhauling of national transportation policy is likely to alter this.[14]

The Passenger Deficit Problem

Long-Run Trends. Railroad passenger traffic, amounting to approximately 40 billion passenger-miles in 1926, declined to a low of 17.3 billion in 1933 as a result of diversion of passenger travel to the private automobile, which grew so rapidly after 1920, and the impact of the depression following 1929. By 1940, travel by railroad had recovered to 24.8 billion passenger-miles, and in 1944 it achieved an all-time peak of 97.3 billion passenger-miles. It has declined rapidly since then and by 1966 had dropped to 17.1 billion, of which 4.2 billion was commutation traffic. In the period since 1936, operating revenues from passenger service have exceeded the operating expenses, as calculated by the Interstate Commerce Commission, only in the years 1942 to 1945.[15] The prospect is that the decline in passenger traffic will continue. Examiner Hosmer, who conducted the hearings for the Commission, stated: "At the present time the inescapable fact . . . seems to be that in a decade or so this time-honored vehicle

---

[14] for a general discussion of this, see D. F. Pegrum, "Investment in the Railroad and Other Transportation Industries under Regulation," *American Economic Review,* Vol. XLVII, No. 2 (May, 1957), pp. 416–29. See also Eastern Railroad Presidents Conference, *Eastern Railroad Problems: The Serious Situation and Its Causes* (Jersey City, N.J., October, 1961).

[15] *Railroad Passenger Train Deficit,* 306 I.C.C. 417 (1959).

[the passenger coach] may take its place in the transportation museums along with the stagecoach and the steam locomotive." The Doyle Report reached the conclusion that railroad intercity passenger service meets no important needs that cannot be provided for by other carriers, and possesses no uniquely necessary services. The committee felt that eventually there will be an important demand for rail passenger service within the large urban regions developing in the United States, but that this requirement is 10 to 20 years in the future.[16] Whatever the prospects for intercity rail passenger service may be, the fact is that the current burden for most railroads of supplying passenger service is too great to carry in view of the over-all revenue problems.

Nature of the Passenger Deficit. The precise amount of the passenger deficit, and therefore the burden it places on the freight traffic, is a matter of dispute. The Interstate Commerce Commission requires the railroads to separate their expenses into those solely related to passenger service, those solely related to freight service, and those which are common to both. The latter are then divided between freight and passenger traffic essentially on a fully distributed basis. Calculated by this formula, the deficit has ranged from $426.5 million in 1947 to $723.7 million in 1957, in the former year amounting to 35.4 per cent of the net railway operating income derived from freight, and 44 per cent in the latter. The deficit for 1966 was $420 million. However, this does not indicate how much better off the railroads would be if they were to discontinue passenger service than they are at present, because the reduction in the common costs that might take place has not been ascertained. If the deficit is measured on an avoidable cost basis, it is probably only about 20 or 30 per cent of that which is estimated on the basis of fully distributed costs. This would place it in the order of $125 million for 1966.[17] Whatever the actual situation may be, it is clear that the railroads as a whole are suffering from a passenger burden on freight revenues that constitutes a serious threat to their financial health.

Unfortunately, the aggregate situation does not provide a particularly useful portrayal of the impact of the deficit. Some railroads regard their passenger traffic as definitely worth retaining. Nevertheless, each of the major regional groupings shows aggregate deficits. This leads to the conclusion that the railroads which find passenger traffic unprofitable to them should be permitted to abandon it. Such a procedure would be of benefit to both the shippers of freight and the

[16] *National Transportation Policy* (Doyle Report), p. 322.
[17] See Nelson, *op. cit.*, chap. ix.

railroads. This solution, however, presents serious difficulties because of the importance of the latter in urban commuter service for many of the large cities.

The areas in which the commuter traffic by railroad between the suburban areas and the central business district is of prime importance in the movement of metropolitan passengers are New York, Chicago, Philadelphia, Boston, and San Francisco. The total rail commutation traffic declined from 345 million passengers in 1947 to an all-time low of 192.6 million in 1965, but the peak-hour traffic into the center of the cities has remained relatively stable. The concentration in the peak hours, however, has resulted in maximum capacity operation for only twenty hours per week. There is no specific cost information that makes it possible to ascertain the amount of the passenger deficit that is attributable to this traffic. Moreover, the deficits on commuter travel fall on particular railroads that offer this service to the large metropolitan centers. Hence the commuter problem needs to be viewed separately from the intercity passenger question.[18]

The rail passenger traffic problem has become acute in recent years because of the burden of it on railroad finance and because of the role of some railroads in urban transportation. If intercity traffic were the only consideration, sound reasons could be advanced for permitting the railroads to discontinue it where it was to their advantage to do so. If national defense requirements demand a continuance of a certain minimum of passenger service that otherwise would not be forthcoming, the federal government should pay for it directly. There does not seem to be any good reason why the shipper of freight and the railroads should be made to carry the load. A considerable portion of the commuter rail service cannot be abandoned, certainly not in the near future. The metropolitan area should be required to make up the difference between the revenues from commuter fares and the expenses incurred in rendering the amount of service that is deemed necessary. A financially sound and economical national railroad system cannot be expected to carry this load.

Conclusion

The foregoing presentation indicates that the problem of financing the railroads as a whole is a critical one at the present time. Under existing public policy of regulation and government promotion of other modes, the railroads, judged by normal private business stand-

[18] See *National Transportation Policy* (Doyle Report), Part VII, chap. vii. The problem of urban transportation is dealt with at greater length in Part V, below.

ards, are suffering from overinvestment. Nevertheless a considerable number of individual roads does not fall into this category. Whether a thoroughgoing revision of national policy would alter the situation so as to bring about a need for more new capital in the railroads cannot be assumed with certainty. Nor is it clear what the situation would be if the passenger deficit problem were resolved. However, the evidence warrants the conclusion that if the latter issue were met head on in an economical fashion, if the railroads were given the opportunity to compete fairly and on equal terms with the other modes, and if a consolidation program based on the underlying structure of natural monopoly were worked out, rail transport would have no problem of survival under private ownership. Admittedly, this is a large order, but sooner or later it will have to be filled whether the railroads remain in private hands or are taken over by the government, if economical transport is to be achieved.

FINANCING MOTOR TRANSPORT

Introduction

The Distinct Problem of Motor Transport. The problems connected with the financing of the motor transport system of the country are quite different from those of financing the railroads; indeed, they are more complex than those of any of the other modes. In the first place, the responsibility for providing the highways, local roads, and streets rests in the hands of public authorities and is a separate consideration from that of supplying the motive equipment. Even a large portion of the terminal accommodations as such is supplied by others than the operators of the vehicles. Second, the financing of the motive equipment and part of the terminal facilities relies on private finance and for the most part makes an appeal to the general investor for funds.[19] Third, the price mechanism as a gauge for resource allocation to motor transport is faced with severe limitations. This is especially true of investment in the roadway facilities. It should be noted that the greater part of the economic resources devoted to highway transportation is in the rolling stock and is directly subject to the measuring rod of the market, but the burden placed on the operators of the vehicles for the use of the roadways has a critical bearing on the effectiveness of this gauge as a determinant of economical transport.

---

[19] See C. A. Taff, *Commercial Motor Transportation* (3rd ed.; Homewood, Ill.: Richard D. Irwin, Inc., 1961), chap. 10; also W. J. Hudson and J. A. Constantin, *Motor Transportation* (New York: The Ronald Press Co., 1958), chap. xii.

The Problem of Measuring Resource Needs. The basic issue of finance for the motor transport system arises in connection with the determination of the amount of investment required to supply the necessary roadway facilities. The roadways of the country are, for the most part, constructed from funds appropriated by governmental agencies through taxes of various kinds. They are available to all who wish to use them, and up to the present time, no means has been developed whereby the quality of the service afforded by the roads and the cost of the particular service utilized by the motor vehicle can be correlated. In other words, the market or economic demand for the different types of highways and streets is unavailable as a means of measuring how much of each should be built. Moreover, current policy divides public investment costs between users and nonusers, as a consequence of which motor transport does not cover the total costs of the routes which it utilizes. Thus, at the present time, an objective test of whether there is too much or too little public investment in roads and streets is lacking. This has an additional implication with regard to the total supply of motor transport, in that the supplier and user are not forced to equate the total costs which the services entail with the demand for them.

The second problem of financing, namely, that which involves the provision of the motive equipment, is a matter of private decision. This presents no particularly unique problems, whether the vehicles be for hire or for private purposes. The decisions can be made directly through the price mechanism; and given the defective conditions of supply of highway facilities, it is reasonable to assert that this area of motor transport does not entail an uneconomical allocation of resources.

Allocation of Costs between Users and Nonusers. Another significant issue connected with investment in the motor transport industry centers on the question of the allocation of costs between users and nonusers. It is assumed that road facilities are for general public benefit as well as for users. Policy based on this assumption calls for an allocation of costs between users and nonusers. The division of costs in this manner means that property owners and the general taxpayer are required to carry part of the burden, the remainder falling directly on the users of the roadways. Recently, the federal government has undertaken an elaborate study of this problem.[20] This study comes to the

---

[20] *Final Report of the Highway Cost Allocation Study,* prepared by the Federal Highway Administrator for the U.S. Department of Commerce, House Document No. 54, 87th Cong., 1st sess. (Washington, D.C.: U.S. Government Printing Office, 1961); and Part

conclusion that the burden of costs, at least of the major highways, should be borne by the users, but even if this is done, the problem of supplying funds for streets and local roads still remains.[21]

Allocation of Costs among Users.   Even when the total costs that are to be borne by the users are ascertained, there is still the difficult task of developing means of determining the costs incurred for the various users and assessing these costs upon them. In essence, this is really no different from the pricing problem faced by any multiproduct firm. It is complicated, however, by a number of factors. First of all, there is a multiplicity of public agencies participating in the undertakings, and there is no assurance that they will arrive at a uniformity of procedures. However, the adoption of a firm policy by the federal government with regard to its investment plans would go a long way to remedy this difficulty. Second, means for ascertaining the responsibility for highway costs are not easy to obtain. Joint costs loom large, and the cost components of speed, grades, curves, loads, and so forth are such as to make the determination of even the specific costs a very complex task. Finally, there would be the problem of devising appropriate means for assessing and collecting the charges even though an appropriate schedule were worked out. A truck or a car may use a superhighway, a street, or a local road. These represent different services and different qualities of service, but no feasible device has been developed as yet for differentiating among them. This means that the superior facilities will be sought out because such choice as does exist leads to the selection of the superior road, with the result that others are underutilized. This is particularly the case with freeways and city streets. In other words, no economical device for rationing the use of particular roadways is available at present.

Equalizing Competition

The foregoing problems are inherent in the technical structure of motor transport and would present the same problem of economical allocation and utilization of resources even if it were the only means of land transportation. The matter is further complicated, however, by the fact that it is only part of the transport system and that it is in

---

VI, House Document No. 72, 87th Cong., 1st sess. (Washington, D.C.: U.S. Government Printing Office, 1961). Part VI deals extensively with the economic and social effects of highway improvements. See below for further discussion of this study.

[21] The problem of allocating highway funds to the various highways and roads is dealt with by R. W. Harbeson, "Some Allocational Problems in Highway Finance," in National Bureau of *Transportation Economics* (New York: National Bureau of Economic Research, 1965), pp. 138–160.

competition with other agencies, especially the railroads. If resources are to be allocated economically to transportation and among the agencies, it is necessary that choices in the use of transport facilities be dictated by the relative total economic costs of supplying them. In other words, public policy must seek every possible means of equalizing competitive conditions among the various agencies. One of the most critical phases of this problem today is in the field of public investment in transport, especially in roadway facilities for motor, water, and air transportation. Without a reasonable equalization of cost burdens among the different carriers in the transport system of the country, regulation is powerless to equalize competitive conditions, even though it places the maximum reliance possible on competition among carriers.

DEVELOPMENT OF THE HIGHWAY PROGRAM

With the rapid settlement of the continental United States in the fourth quarter of the nineteenth century and the spread of the railroad network, the need for the development of local roads became apparent. At first, highway construction was undertaken almost entirely by local governments. Then, in 1891, New Jersey passed legislation designed to encourage the connection and extension of local highways into a state system. Other states soon followed suit, and one by one, state highway departments or agencies were established. Impetus was given to this development by the growth of automobile ownership, which increased from four motor vehicle registrations in 1895 to 2,490,932 in 1915, and to 10,493,666 by 1921. The federal government established the Office of Public Roads Inquiries in the Department of Agriculture in 1893; the name of this was changed to the Office of Public Roads in 1901. This finally became the Bureau of Public Roads in the Department of Commerce in 1949. In 1966, this was transferred to the Department of Transportation under the Federal Highway Administration.

Federal Highway Legislation

With the rapid rise of the automobile the need for federal participation to provide for interstate traffic became apparent. The first provision for federal aid came with an appropriation of $500,000 under the Post Office Appropriation Act of 1912, to be allotted to the states for the improvement of post roads.

The Federal Aid Road Act of 1916. This legislation was the first step in the development of a permanent plan for co-operation between the states and the federal government. It also marked the beginning of federal aid to the states in the construction of an integrated system of highways. Congress appropriated $75 million to be used during the succeeding five years to aid the states in improving rural post roads. Federal support was to be limited to $10,000 per mile, exclusive of the cost of bridges over 20 feet in length, and was to be matched dollar for dollar by the states receiving the aid. To be eligible, a state also was required to create a highway department to co-operate with the federal government.

Federal Highway Act of 1921. A more systematic development of federal policy came with the Act of 1921, which limited federal aid to a designated system of interstate highways. The amount of construction in any year for which a state could obtain federal aid was limited to 7 per cent of the existing system of improved highways in the state. The state had to match the federal aid it received. This became known as the federal-aid primary system.

In subsequent years, further aid was extended under relief and public works legislation. Relief funds were granted to state and local governments without the requirement of matching funds and were afforded for construction outside the federal-aid primary system. Finally, the Highway Act of 1944 provided for the designation of a national system of interstate highways, not to exceed 40,000 miles, which would connect all major centers in the country and join with continental routes at the nation's borders. Aid was to be extended for streets in urban centers over 5,000 population and to secondary roads without regard to mileage limitations.

Federal Aid Highway Act of 1956. As early as 1934 the idea was expressed in Congressional debates that the amounts being authorized by the federal government for highway expenditures would be returned to the Treasury from taxes levied directly on the road user, and indirectly through sales taxes. In 1954, recognition was given to the need for more rigorous participation by the federal government in highway building. The Federal Highway Act of 1954 set up a committee which was headed by General Lucius Clay to develop and recommend a plan to this end. This report outlined a ten-year program from 1955 to 1964 for highway development,[22] although no immediate action was taken. The Federal Aid Highway Act of 1956, however,

[22] *Needs of the National Highway Systems, 1955–84,* House Document No. 120, 84th Congress, 1st session (Washington, D.C.: U.S. Government Printing Office, 1955); *National Highway Program,* House Document No. 93, 84th Congress, 1st session (Washington, D.C.: Government Printing Office, 1955).

was the outcome of these developments. It marked a new departure in federal policy. First of all, it provided for a highway trust fund from which all federal-aid highway expenditures were to be made. It was to be built up from motor vehicle fuel taxes, taxes on vehicles and tires, and a tax on trucks and buses with a gross weight exceeding 26,000 pounds. No disbursements were to be made except from the trust fund. The law authorized total expenditures by the federal government of $46.2 billion over a period of thirteen years, amounting to an annual rate of $3.1 billion from 1960 through 1967. The law designated a national system of interstate and defense highways of 41,000 miles to be financed on a 90 per cent federal and 10 per cent state basis. The remainder of the federal program concerned the primary, secondary, and urban highways—often known as the ABC program—which were to be financed on the basis of 50 per cent federal aid and 50 per cent state. The objective, as far as the federal government is concerned, was to provide for highways on a "pay as you go" basis,[23] and although revenues for the trust fund have been inadequate to maintain the projected rate of construction, advances to the fund by the Treasury Department have been made on the assumption that tax collections for the fund will provide for reimbursement.

FINANCING THE HIGHWAY SYSTEM

Extent of Public Investment

The bulk of the expenditures on the road system of this country have been made since 1921. The total amount, actual and estimated, for all governments from 1921 to 1966 is $231.9 billion, to which the federal government has contributed $47.5 billion, the state and local governments $184.4 billion. Since 1947, total governmental expenditures on roadway facilities have amounted to $175.8 billion, the federal contribution being $38.6 billion, of which $32.7 billion have been spent since 1956. The state and local disbursements since 1947 total $137.3 billion, of which $69.7 billion have been spent since 1956. An indication of the current magnitude of public resource allocation to motor transport is afforded by the outlays for 1966, which consisted of $4.5 billion by the federal government and $10.8 billion by state and local authorities for a total of $15.3 billion. It is evident that pub-

---

[23] The financial requirements of the federal-aid primary, secondary, and urban highway programs (the ABC program) take precedence over the requirements of the interstate system.

lic expenditures have grown at a rapidly increasing rate in the postwar years, and particularly since 1956.[24]

Sources of Highway Funds

The revenue for financing the nation's highway program is derived primarily from various kinds of taxes, although in some states tolls are collected on the turnpikes or toll roads to repay the bonds issued to finance them.[25] The taxes which provide the sources of revenue for financing the highways are of various kinds and are used to refund general bond issues of state and local authorities floated to provide the outlays initially, or to carry out a "pay as you go" program. As already noted, federal policy is now committed to "pay as you go," the revenues being derived from taxes on motor fuel; a manufacturer's tax on trucks, buses, and trailers; taxes on tires, inner tubes, and tread rubber; and a vehicle use tax of $3 per 1,000 pounds on all vehicles over 26,000 pounds.[26]

State and local revenues are obtained from fuel taxes, registration fees, weight-distance taxes, and property taxes. At the present time, some 85 per cent of state expenditures are derived from user taxes, either directly imposed or through federal aid. Local county and city sources still rely heavily on general property taxes as well as on appropriations from general funds, these providing some 66 per cent of the expenditures for highway and street purposes. County, township and municipal governments raised $2,657 million for highway purposes in 1964, of which $1,029 million were from property taxes and assessments. At the present time "approximately 18 per cent of the revenues for all highways and streets are derived from non-motor-vehicle tax payments, chiefly at the local level in the form of benefit assessments, local property taxes, and appropriations from general funds."[27]

The rapidly rising costs of highway construction and mainte-

[24] For an extensive presentation of the federal program since 1956, see U.S. Department of Commerce, *Highway Progress, 1965,* Annual Report of the Bureau of Public Roads (Washington, D.C.: U.S. Government Printing Office, 1965).

[25] Over two thirds of the mileage of the toll roads has been incorporated into the interstate system. The tolls will continue to be charged on these roads until the bonds are retired. There is little likelihood of any significant development of such highways in the future. At present, there are about 3,262 miles of toll roads.

[26] See American Trucking Association Inc., *Highway Financing,* Current Report, September, 1966; *National Transportation Policy* (Doyle Report), *op. cit.,* pp. 188–89.

[27] *Supplementary Report of the Highway Cost Allocation Study,* House Document No. 124, 89th Cong. 1st sess. (Washington, D.C.: U.S. Government Printing Office, 1965), p. 29.

nance are the source of serious concern to the trucking industry,[28] as well as to the governments who have to raise the funds. It seems unlikely that the Interstate Highway program will be completed by 1972; as a consequence, the highway trust fund taxes will have to be extended beyond that date. Additional taxes will also probably have to be levied.

Highway Cost Allocation

Ascertaining the appropriate basis for allocating the costs of providing highways involves three major considerations: (1) calculating the total costs that are incurred, (2) determining the responsibility of users and nonusers for them, and (3) tracing the costs to be met by the various motor vehicles on the basis of the costs incurred for them. The total expenditures on roadways can be obtained from the records, but these do not make up the total economic costs. At least two implicit items are of considerable significance. These are the tax equivalents comparable to those imposed on railroad rights of way on resources allocated to the highways, and the interest cost on the government's equity in highway investment. The second consideration arises from the fact that benefits from highway construction are derived by nonusers as well as users. The third involves the devising of appropriate means of assessing the costs allocated to highway users on the different kinds of vehicles that travel over them. The second problem only will be dealt with in this section.

In the Act of 1956, Congress directed the Secretary of Commerce to study highway cost allocation with regard to the effects on design, construction, and maintenance of federal-aid highways of the various vehicles; the proportionate share of the resulting costs to be borne by each class of users; and any direct or indirect benefits, in addition to those derived from direct use of the highways, attributable to public expenditures on them. The Secretary of Commerce, in co-operation with other federal and state agencies, completed the study in 1961.[29]

Highways serve a number of different purposes, which leads to a rather widespread acceptance of the conclusion that not all of the costs of providing them ought to be imposed upon the immediate users. Highways afford access to land in both urban and rural areas without

[28] See Motor Transport Economics, *Highways—The Years beyond 1972*, Current Report, February, 1965; National Highway Users Conference Inc., *Highway Maintenance* (Washington, D.C., 1964).

[29] *Final Report of the Highway Cost Allocation Study*, House Document No. 54 and House Document No. 72, 87th Cong., 1st sess. (Washington, D.C.: U.S. Government Printing Office, 1961).

which the land would be practically useless and worthless. They also perform a "community service function" that makes community life and activity possible. In addition, they provide one of the principal avenues of intercommunity and long-distance transportation for commercial, recreational, and national defense purposes.

The study of the Secretary recognized these considerations and examined at considerable length a number of different methods that have been advanced for a division of costs between users and non-users.[30] It concluded that definitive answers to questions of cost allocation between users and nonusers could not be reached solely through analysis. It did not arrive at a quantitative evaluation of the total benefits to be derived from the federal-aid program by others than the direct users of the highways. It recognized that there was a vast array of non-user benefits that emerge from highway improvements, but pointed out that similar results obtained from every justifiable investment, whether from public or private funds. It stated that "The existence of a dividend to the economy over and above the user benefits provided by highway investment does not of itself prove that there should be a proportional tax contribution from non-user or general revenue sources." [31] The study recognized that some nonuser sources of revenue were necessary, particularly for local roads and streets, but concluded that for all federal-aid systems, 92 per cent of the needed revenues should be derived from users and only 8 per cent from nonusers.[32] This recommendation for the allocation of total costs was based on the premise that "In the allocation of tax responsibility for the support of the Federal-aid highway program, care should be taken that the allocation is, as nearly as possible, neutral with respect to the competitive position of other modes of transportation."[33]

The Allocation of User Costs

After the total costs to be borne by highway users have been determined, there still remains the question of allocating these costs to the various users. As has already been mentioned, this problem, in theory at least, is similar to that which is faced by any multiproduct firm. It is more difficult, however, to identify the specific and the joint costs. In addition to this, no adequate means of pricing the specific services rendered by the specific highways and streets has been developed. This

---

[30] *Ibid.,* House Document No. 54, especially Part II.

[31] *Ibid.,* p. 73 and p. 122.

[32] *Ibid.,* p. 147.

[33] *Ibid.,* p. 277; see also pp. 245 ff.

complicated the problem of the study for the Department of Commerce because the means available for collecting the revenues are inadequate for distinguishing between the uses which vehicles make of federal-aid highways and roads, and the uses they make of other roadways. Similar remarks apply to user charge programs developed by the states.

The study examined four different methods for allocating costs among users. One of these was the incremental theory of cost responsibility, which assumes that highway costs are variable with the weight and size of the vehicle and that, starting from a basic road design cost, there are successive design costs to be added to meet requirements of progressively heavier vehicles. Another method, assuming that road facilities have been built for use by mixed traffic and that the costs occasioned in construction are essentially joint, endeavored to apportion the costs according to the amount of relative use or benefits derived by the various classes of motor vehicles from the highways. A third method, called the cost-function method, divides the costs into three categories: (1) costs that are affected by vehicle size or weight, (2) costs that vary with the use of the highways, and (3) costs that are independent of both vehicle size or weight and traffic volume. The fourth method employs gross ton-miles as the measure of cost responsibilities. This method has the advantage of relative simplicity and availability of data. Although the study seemed to favor this as the most feasible approach at the time, it pointed out that it was defective as a measure of the value of service received by the various vehicles, and that it was not recommended as a single solution to the problem of allocating cost responsibility.

Further exploration of the allocation problem was carried out by the Secretary of Commerce and submitted to the Congress in 1965.[34] This study made use of highway tests on cost responsibility, and evaluated the allocation of costs on the basis of the previous criteria. It allocated total costs, however, to users in accordance with the revenue provisions of the Federal Highway Act of 1961.[35] It also expressed a clear preference for the incremental theory of cost allocation[36] because it is thoroughly grounded in highway engineering research, while the differential benefit method is untried and involves assumptions of doubtful merit. The study found that the ratio of cost alloca-

---

[34] *Supplementary Report of the Highway Cost Allocation Study,* House Document No. 124, 89th Cong., 1st sess. (Washington, D.C.: U.S. Government Printing Office, 1965).

[35] *Ibid.,* p. 29.

[36] This method is under attack by the trucking industry because it lends to the imposition of a greater share of the costs on the heavy trucks.

tions to payments made for 1964 was 1.00 for automobiles and 7.34 for 5-axle tractor semitrailer combinations.[37] It seems clear that the larger combinations on the highways will have to assume a larger share of the total burden. The total tax contributions to the trust fund for 1964 were estimated to be:[38]

	Million Dollars	Percent
Private and for-hire vehicles		
Automobiles............................	$2,041.7	60.87
Buses..............................	38.8	1.15
Single-unit trucks..................	668.5	19.93
Combinations.....................	593.3	17.69
Publicly owned vehicles..............	12.0	0.36
Total........................	$3,354.3	100.00

FINANCING AIR TRANSPORT

Introduction

Financing air transportation is similar to that of motor transport, in that it is characterized by public and private participation and is likely to remain in that category for the indefinite future. It presents a simpler problem, in principle at least, than does motor transport because the use of the publicly supplied facilities is confined to a more limited group of users and the use can be channeled more readily through specific facilities. As far as commercial civil aviation is concerned, the users can be confined to particular routes, and the terminal facilities can be specifically controlled. As a consequence, user costs can be more directly traced and user charges more specifically applied if full recovery becomes the practice for national policy.

To date, only limited steps have been taken to apply user costs for the facilities supplied by the federal government or through federal aid. In addition, private operation of air transport in this country enjoys the benefit of direct public subsidy. At the present time, this is expended on the domestic feeder lines (except for Northeast Airlines which in a somewhat anomalous category); although the law still provides for subsidy to trunk lines if it is necessary. The record indicates that none of the important airports are on an economically self-sustaining basis, despite the fact that a considerable portion of their revenue is

[37] *Ibid.*, p. 4. These ratios apply to construction costs only.

[38] *Ibid.*, p. 322. This was the total going into the highway trust fund except for $70 million from nonuser sources.

obtained from nonairline sources. The federal Aviation Agency reports that the combined net operating loss for the two Washington, D.C., metropolitan airports was $6,263,962 for fiscal 1965.

Airway Investment

The national airways system is provided entirely by the federal government. The Association of American Railroads reports that the total federal expenditures on the federal airways system from 1925 to 1967, inclusive (the latter year being estimated), amounts to $7.6 billion for establishment, administration, maintenance, and operation, including flight and medical standards programs. The total expenditure on this account was $557.7 million for 1961 and $722 million for 1966.[39] These outlays have shown a rapid and persistent rate of increase since 1949, being almost seven times as large in 1966 as in the former year.[40]

The FAA reports that the system making up the U.S. air control and navigation system represents a national investment of some $1.25 billion, and costs about a $0.5 billion annually to operate and maintain.[41] Moreover, there have been no explicit user charges for the use of these facilities by private and commercial planes. Although there has been an excise tax on aviation gasoline, it has been credited to the highway trust fund, and no tax has been imposed on jet fuel. The 5 per cent tax on air passenger fares was continued when other passenger fare taxes were removed in 1961. This was credited to the general fund but was considered as a user tax. It was made permanent in 1965.

Airport Investment

Most airports in the United States are owned and operated by local government units. Beginning in 1933, the federal government made large grants under work relief programs. More than 71 per cent of all civil airport outlays in the 1933–40 period were from federal work relief funds. Through 1944, the federal government contributed 72.1 per cent of all estimated capital expenditures for U.S. civil airports.[42]

[39] See also *National Transportation Policy* (Doyle Report), *op. cit.*, p. 182; Federal Aviation Agency, *Second Annual Report* (Washington, D.C.: U.S. Government Printing Office, 1960), p. 37.

[40] For a projection of these expenditures, see *National Transportation Policy* (Doyle Report), *op. cit.*, p. 196.

[41] Federal Aviation Agency, *Seventh Annual Report* (Washington, D.C.: U.S. Government Printing Office, 1966), p. 35.

[42] See Nelson, *op. cit.*, p. 101; and J. H. Frederick, *Commercial Air Transportation* (4th ed.; Homewood. Ill.: Richard D. Irwin, Inc., 1955), p. 41.

In 1946, Congress enacted the Federal Airport Act. Under this legislation the federal government's share of the cost of a project is limited to 50 per cent of the investment in the case of Class 3 or smaller airports and no more than 50 per cent for the larger ones. To be eligible for federal aid, an airport must be included in the "national airport plan," which is revised annually by the Federal Aviation Agency. According to the latter, approximately $1.3 billion will be necessary for the major components for new acquisition and construction for the fiscal years 1966–70.[43]

The Association of American Railroads reports that $2.6 billion were expected as grants-in-aid down to 1966; state and local governments expended $6 billion, before deduction of revenues received by them, during the same period. Total federal, state, and local expenditures on airports down to 1966 amounted to $8.8 billion.

Subsidy to Air Transport

In addition to public aid from federal, state, and local governments, air transport has been directly subsidized from its very beginning by airmail payments by the federal government. Down to 1955, airmail payments had been set by the Civil Aeronautics Board so that, together with other revenues, they provided an adequate net profit to the air carriers. There was no separation of the calculation of service mail pay from subsidy until 1951. On the basis of applying the subsidy ratio (59 percent) as determined by the Civil Aeronautics Board for the years prior to 1951, and adding to the figures thus obtained the direct subsidy payments as reported by the Board since then, the Association of American Railroads calculated the total domestic subsidy from airmail and direct payments since 1939 as $1.1 billion, $1 billion of that being paid since 1947. The Civil Aeronautics Board reports that no subsidies have been paid to domestic trunk lines since 1956, except to Northeast Airlines for local service in the New England area. Airlines rendering international service have received no subsidy since 1958. On the other hand, local service airlines, three helicopter services, and airlines in Alaska and the Hawaiian Islands received a total subsidy of $83.1 million in 1964. Efforts to reduce this have resulted in eliminating the subsidy to helicopter service for 1967, with total payments amounting to $68.1 million for 1967 for the others, of which $60.7 million is for local service in the continental United States. This was $64.7 million in 1966.[44]

---

[43] See Federal Aviation Agency, *Seventh Annual Report, op. cit.,* p. 67.

[44] Civil Aeronautics Board, *Subsidy for United States Certified Air Carriers* (Washington, D.C., October, 1966).

Financing the Air Lines

Although air transportation has been supported continuously by public subsidy, with the recent exception of the trunk lines noted above, it has presumably been the assumption that it would in time achieve financial independence. At the present time, this is the situa-situation for domestic trunk-line passenger service. However, the current outlook is none too clear. The introduction of the jets produced a serious financial challenge in 1960 and the following three years.[45] Since then earnings have increased rapidly with a reported rate of return on investment of 9.6 per cent for 1964, 11.2 per cent for 1965, and 9.7 per cent for 1966. At the same time, total indebtedness for the domestic trunk lines has grown from 28 per cent of total invested capital in 1955 to over 60 per cent in 1966, indicating a serious burden of debt for an industry of this type.[46] The introduction of the jumbo jets and other rising costs may well threaten another crisis. There is obviously no prospect of eliminating subsidy for the local feeder services for the indefinite future, if these are to continue to be offered.

From the foregoing, it is obvious that air transport is far from being an economical and self-sustaining industry. At present the trunk lines face serious problems, even with the public support of airway and airport facilities. The feeder air lines cannot survive without subsidy. It is clear, therefore, that user charges adequate to support public expenditures on civil airways and airports attributable to civil aviation cannot be borne by the industry, and this is likely to be the situation for the indefinite future. At the present time, the industry does not seem to be in the position to bear any user charges of consequence unless there is a substantial contraction of service, and probably considerable liquidation.

FINANCING DOMESTIC WATER TRANSPORT

Total and annual governmental expenditures for the support of the domestic waterway system are not available. The Doyle Report states, however, that for the period from 1917 to 1960, "No less than $7.1 billion in federal funds have been expended in aid of navigation.

---

[45] The net loss for 1961 was $34.6 million after interest and taxes, according to the Air Transport Association of America.

[46] Federal Aviation Agency, *National Aviation Goals*, pp. 153–75.

This sum includes about $5.7 billion for navigation improvements by the Corps of Engineers; $219 million for similar work by the Tennessee Valley Authority; some $1.7 billion for United States Coast Guard work relating to navigation; and $158 million for charts and other aids by the Coast and Geodetic Survey."[47] The Association of American Railroads estimates that the federal government expended $5.1 billion on inland waterways from 1947 to 1967 and that state governments spent $4.5 billion in the same period. No charges whatsoever are made for the recovery of federal funds except for the Panama Canal and the St. Lawrence Seaway, both of which are international waterways, although they also serve domestic commerce. All vessels of whatever nationality using the Panama Canal pay tolls. The same remarks apply to the St. Lawrence Seaway. The St. Lawrence Seaway Development Corporation is required to prescribe tolls which will make this project self-liquidating. The costs which are to be covered, however, relate only to navigation; all joint costs were charged to the hydroelectric phase of the project. The Corporation is not required to pay taxes equivalent to corporate income and excess profits taxes; nor is it responsible for the additional outlays on the Great Lakes and the harbors which are necessary to make the project feasible. The cumulative deficit from operations of the Seaway down to 1965 was $19 million.[48]

It is not necessary here to discuss the arguments pro and con on tolls for waterways.[49] Suffice it to say that if public policy is to achieve an economical transport system and an economical allocation of resources, users of the domestic waterways should be required to pay tolls that will cover all future economic costs attributable to them. If

[47] *National Transportation Policy* (Doyle Report) *op. cit.*, p. 167.

[48] St. Lawrence Seaway Development Corporation, *Annual Report*, 1965, p. 13. The Minister of Transport, Canada, in "Report as to the Self-Sufficiency of Seaway Tolls and Proposed Charges Related to the Financial Requirements of the St. Lawrence Seaway" stated:
"The fact that the opposition to the proposed tolls was expressed during the public hearings should not be allowed to obscure the realities of the situation. It is thoroughly understandable that those interests that will have their costs most directly affected by a tolls increase—the users of the Seaway—would express opposition. At the same time it should also be recognized that since the opening of the deep waterway in 1959 the Montreal-Lake Ontario section has sustained a loss of approximately $47 million. In addition, all of the operating cost of the Welland section, amounting to $35.2 million, has been a charge to the Canadian taxpayer. Therefore, of the total operating losses for both sections of $82.2 million, Canada's share has been $71.5 million, which is 87 percent, under the circumstances where about only one-half of the trade benefits accrue to Canada. Unless there are adequate user charges, the losses will continue to accumulate and will amount to hundreds of millions of dollars." Quoted from *Traffic World*, January 14, 1967, p. 8.

[49] See *National Transportation Policy*, *op. cit.*, pp. 197–210, for a treatment of this.

they are unable to meet these costs, Congress should take steps to eliminate further expenditures.[50]

TAXATION OF WAY AND IMPUTED INTEREST

The provision of highway, airway, and waterway facilities by government entails both explicit and implicit costs. The latter are not included in the public budgets, in the estimates of public expenditures in aid of transport, or in the costs to be covered by user charges. The two major items of implicit costs are imputed interest on the public investment equity in highway, air, and waterway transport and the property tax equivalent on the publicly owned facilities of these agencies. Both of these items are recognized in the highway cost allocation study,[51] although what they amount to is not developed in monetary terms. The Doyle Report discusses the property tax burden on railroads and oil pipe lines at length.[52]

The highway cost allocation study takes the position that a property tax equivalent should be charged on the entire highway investment (1) to preserve neutrality in the comparison of alternative investment opportunities or (2) to balance comparable costs among competing forms of transportation. The Doyle Report estimates that railroads pay almost $200 million in taxes on roadway or right-of-way properties, and pipe lines approximately $1.5 million. It states that "the property tax on right-of-way of railroads and pipelines still stands as a unique and burdensome tax on these carriers which keeps them in a relatively tax discriminated status."[53] As a remedy for this situation the committee recommends a federal law that would exempt railroads and pipe-line right-of-way property from ad valorem property taxation by the states, a federal tax law that would remove tax discrimination against railroads and pipe lines, or both.

Solution of the problem of unequal tax burdens on the different

[50] What the effect of such tolls would be on inland waterway transportation cannot be forecast, but American Waterways Operators, Inc., contends that it would practically eliminate domestic water transport. See *To Rob Our Youth*, published by the National Waterways Conference, Inc. (Washington, D.C., 1962). The effect on domestic Great Lakes traffic would probably be slight; but if this were done for improvements on the Great Lakes, it would add to the cost of shipping that uses the St. Lawrence Seaway, thereby increasing the problems of the latter.

[51] *Final Report of the Highway Cost Allocation Study*, House Document No. 54, pp. 37–38.

[52] *National Transportation Policy* (Doyle Report), Part VII, chap. i.

[53] *Ibid.*, p. 449.

modes of transport presents severe complexities.[54] It is difficult to see, however, why transportation should enjoy any unique position with regard to taxes if an economical allocation of resources between transport and nontransport users is to obtain. Therefore, it would seem to be appropriate to assess comparable tax burdens on the "roadways" provided by investment for all modes of transport, whether privately or publicly owned, just as on other industries.

The other major element of imputed costs connected with the supplying of transport facilities by public investment is imputed interest. "The highway taxpayer, whether user or other, may be said to forego investment opportunities in the amount of taxes paid. Interest on this amount is a measure of his sacrifice. The highway improvements to which he contributes should, in the benefits he derives compensate him, or more than compensate him, for this sacrifice."[55] This is a recognition of the fact that capital is not a free good and that costs are entailed in supplying it, whether they be expressed or implied. Railroads have to earn a return on the equity in their property if they are to continue in business, and neutrality and equity in competition require the same for publicly supplied investment, whether supplied by taxation or by borrowing. So far, little attention has been given to the calculation of this interest for transportation; but recently, studies dealing with the same problem have been undertaken in the field of publicly owned utilities.[56]

CONCLUSION

The foregoing lengthy, but nevertheless condensed, discussion of financing the transport system warrants the conclusion that motor, air, and water transport are not required to bear all the costs of public investment attributable to them. This makes for inequities in competition among the modes and, from the public point of view, leads to a

[54] For a discussion of some of the issues, see C. Lowell Harriss, "Taxation of Public Utilities: Considerations for the Long Run," *The Tax Magazine,* October, 1965, pp. 660–66; H. Benishay and G. R. Walker, Jr., "Tax Burden Ratios in Transportation," *Land Economics,* February, 1967, pp. 44–55.

[55] *Final Report of the Highway Cost Allocation Study,* House Document No. 54, p. 37.

[56] See O. Eckstein, *Water Resource Development* (Cambridge, Mass.: Harvard University Press, 1958); J. Krutilla and O. Eckstein, *Multiple Purpose River Development* (Baltimore, Md.: The Johns Hopkins Press, 1958); and J. Hirschleifer, C. de Haven, and J. Milliman, *Water Supply: Economic Technology and Policy* (Chicago: The University of Chicago Press, 1960).

relative overuse of the agencies relying on public investment and underuse of the others. In addition, "there is a definite indication . . . that the heavier trucks and combinations (particularly the latter) should be paying considerably more in relation to the payment by the lighter vehicle groups, than they do now."[57] If this is so, competition with carriers relying completely on their own resources is even more inequitable.

Under existing conditions, there is evidently overinvestment in transportation. The railroads as a whole are unable to secure adequate revenues for their operations, while motor, air, and water transport do not cover the full economic costs attributable to their activities. If public policy were to require each of the modes to cover its full costs, there would undoubtedly be a considerable reduction in air and water transport, and probably in motor trucking. If, in addition, the competitive rules among the modes were equalized, a further shift would occur. Whether this would require more investment in railroads, or whether it would result in a more effective utilization of existing resources, is a matter of conjecture. The conclusion is warranted, however, that present policy has resulted in an excess allocation of economic resources to transportation and a misallocation among the modes.[58]

[57] *Final Report of the Highway Cost Allocation Study,* House Document No. 54, *op. cit.,* p. 27; see also *Supplementary Report of the Highway Cost Allocation Study, op. cit.*

[58] See E. W. Williams, Jr., and D. W. Bluestone, *Rationale of Federal Transportation Policy,* U.S. Department of Commerce, April, 1960; D. F. Pegrum, "Investment in the Railroad and Other Transportation Industries under Regulation, *American Economic Review,* Vol. XLVII, No. 2 (May, 1957), pp. 416–29.

Chapter 20

THE SPECIAL
PROBLEM OF LABOR

INTRODUCTION

The problems relating to labor in the field of transportation have loomed large in public policy in this country for over three quarters of a century. Down to 1934, in domestic transportation, the unique issues and developments were centered on railroads. In 1936 the Railway Labor Act was extended to cover air transportation. At the present time, these are the only two modes with which special federal legislation is concerned. Labor in the other three modes is subject to federal enactments that apply to other industries.

Federal and state commissions regulating transportation do not have any authority over labor and labor relations except that the Interstate Commerce Commission, in exercising its authority over safety of operations of motor transport in interstate commerce, has control over hours of work and the qualifications of employees. The development, therefore, of labor policy has followed a course independent of that of regulation. Because of the responsibility of commissions for the control of the costs of the enterprises whose prices they regulate, some students of transportation have taken the position that this division of authority is anomalous and that the Interstate Commerce Commission should have been given control over wages.[1] The need for this, or even the feasibility of it today, apart from the fact that it would be unacceptable to labor, in the light of the changed conditions in transport, will be discussed later.

Uniqueness of the Labor Problem

Labor costs loom large in the supplying of transport services. In railroad, air, and motor transport, wages make up over 60 per cent of

[1] See F. H. Dixon, *Railroads and Government* (New York: Charles Scribner's Sons, 1922), chap. xxii.

the operating expenses. This points up the need for economy and efficiency in the utilization of manpower. It is not this of itself, however, which gives rise to the unique problems of labor in transport or to the powerful and special position occupied by some of the labor organizations throughout the world, especially in the railroad industry.

One of the most obvious differences between labor in transport and in most other areas lies in the responsibility for public safety, especially on the part of the employees engaged in the control and movement of the vehicles. This calls for a relatively high degree of skill and training, in some cases extremely high, and a strong sense of public responsibility. This is particularly true of those who operate the motive equipment, for they are literally on their own from point of departure to destination, despite the extensive development of automatic control devices. Many of these employees cannot readily be replaced except from a continuous pool of trained personnel and, because of the time spent in the occupation, cannot easily transfer to other employment after years of service. Job security and the problem of unemployment have therefore become critical issues.

Closely connected with the foregoing is the fact that transportation requires continuous performance. Overtime pay, night work, Sundays, and legal holidays fall into a different category than they do for industry in general. In addition, intercity transportation at least, commonly entails time away from home, with the necessary provisions for accommodations to take care of this. As a consequence, a pattern of working rules and conditions, and pay scales, especially in railroad transportation, has developed over many years that is the most complex in existence.

Transport requires a continuity of operations that is more vital to public welfare than almost any other industrial activity except public utilities. Apart from the need for prompt and efficient service, there is the inescapable requirement for continuous performance. Even where alternative means of transport are readily available, a work stoppage may interrupt the movement of goods, people, or livestock before the journey is completed. A nationwide strike of any of the key operating personnel of the railroads would paralyze the economy of the country, even today, in about forty-eight hours. Work stoppage on a major railroad in a particular area would have the same effect on a large region, and possibly on the commuting services of important centers.

Prior to the growth of competitive means of transport, this situation was probably more obvious than it is today because of the nearly complete dependence of the country on rail transport alone. The division of traffic, however, among the agencies has not materially altered the key positions of certain carriers and certain groups of operating personnel, at least for the short run and for any particular crisis. Transportation is still an activity in which many of the suppliers are clearly affected with a public interest, which means that the public using the services is vitally affected by the actions of a particular carrier or group of carriers or carrier employees acting in concert.

The labor problem in domestic transportation arose with the railroads as they grew into the prime transport agency of the country. Present methods for dealing with critical issues involving railroad labor were established in the legislation of 1926 as modified by the amendments in 1934. The same procedures have been extended to air transportation, but so far no steps have been taken in this direction for the other modes. Meanwhile the technological structure of transport has literally been revolutionized by the growth of intense competition among different agencies as well as by rapid change within each. Railroad employment, which amounted to 2,000,000 employees in 1920, had dropped to 1,220,784 in 1950 and 630,895 in 1966. The payroll in 1950 was $4.6 billion, and in 1966 it was $4.9 billion. In the airlines, on the other hand, employment has risen from 13,300 in 1939 to 244,038 in 1966, while the payroll has gone up from $24 million in 1939 to $2.1 billion in 1966. Despite this increase in employment the introduction of jet-powered airplanes injected a crisis into labor relations in this industry because of the threat to employment of operating personnel and the failure to resolve the issues of the appropriate type of crew. It is in railroad and air transport that the most critical labor controversies have arisen so far; and unfortunately, no satisfactory means of dealing with them has yet been devised.

THE RAILROAD LABOR PROBLEM TO 1926

Railroad Labor Organizations

No effective organization of railroad employees occurred until the Civil War. The first to organize in a significant way were those engaged in train service operation. In 1863 the engineers founded the Brotherhood of Locomotive Engineers; in 1868 the Order of Railway Conductors was established. This was followed in 1873 by the Brotherhood of Locomotive Firemen and Enginemen, in 1883 by the Brotherhood of Railroad Trainmen, and in 1894 by the Switchmen's Union of North America. These five unions, known as the "Big Five" of railroad labor, have remained independent of the American Federation of Labor. Most of the other craft unions in the railroad industry were organized near the end of the nineteenth century.[2] The majority of these "nonservice" unions are affiliated with the American Federation of Labor. There is also a third group of unions with membership among railroad employees, such as the International Brotherhood of Electrical Workers, but these have been of minor importance in shaping railway labor policy.

Except for the Brotherhood of Railroad Trainmen and the Brotherhood of Locomotive Engineers, the first two groups of unions formed an association in 1929 of executives known as the Railway Labor Executives' Association, which speaks for all the railway unions in negotiations with the carriers on general wage scales. It also represents the employees on matters coming before Congress.

It is evident that while railroad labor is highly organized and to a certain extent unified, it is also very diversified. A large number of unions, some independent, others more or less affiliated with each other, together with a craft union type of organization that has promoted a considerable conflict of interest among railroad employees, has created a congeries of railroad labor relations that may break down at any point and threaten continuity of operations of the entire railroad system. There is the additional fact that bargaining for many of the unions must, in effect, be on a nationwide basis because interruption of service on a particular railroad as a result of independent action could halt movement of traffic throughout the national network. This would make effective rail transport almost impossible. Public policy has endeavored to grapple with problems of this nature for the past 80 years.

Railroad Labor Legislation to 1926

The Arbitration Act of 1888. Labor unrest in the railroad industry during the 1870's and the 1880's led to the passage of the Arbitration Act of 1888. This was the first of five laws enacted down to 1920 to deal with railroad labor disputes and the first of seven to the present time. This Act provided for voluntary arbitration of disputes between carriers and their employees, but no special machinery was created to implement the provision. The legislation proved to be completely ineffective as a means of dealing with the Pullman strike of

---

[2] However, only a minority of railroad employees were members of railroad unions prior to World War I. The government during this conflict encouraged all classes of railroad employees to organize. Now over 80 per cent are unionized.

1894. A temporary commission appointed by President Cleveland indicated the need for further legislation.

The Erdman Act, 1898.   This legislation was limited to the settlement of disputes involving employees connected with the operation of trains, but it did inaugurate procedures for mediation and arbitration. The administration of the law was the responsibility of the Chairman of the Interstate Commerce Commission and the Commissioner of Labor. If interested parties could not settle a dispute by negotiation, either party could invite the government officials to settle the issue by mediation or conciliation. If this failed, it was the duty of the officials to try to get the disputants to arbitrate. If they agreed, each side was to select an arbitrator, and these two were to select a third member who would be the neutral chairman. The award of the board was final and binding, and was to remain in effect for a minimum period of one year.

The Erdman Act proved incapable of dealing with issues that were really vital to either side, especially since so much rested on the judgment of one neutral arbitrator. The severe disputes over wages in 1912 led to repeal and replacement of the legislation in the next year.

The Newlands Act, 1913.   This legislation recognized the need for continuity of personnel and machinery to deal with railroad labor disputes. It established a Commissioner of Mediation and Conciliation who was to serve full time and for a period of seven years. He was to be assisted by two other government officials appointed by the President, the three forming a Board of Mediation and Conciliation. This Board could act upon its own without waiting for an invitation. If the disputants agreed to arbitration, the Board of Arbitration could consist of three members or six. It was required to reach a verdict in thirty days, but its decisions were not binding on the parties. If a dispute was settled by mediation or arbitration, either party could call upon the Board of Mediation to interpret the meaning or define the application of the terms of settlement.

The Newlands Act functioned successfully until the concerted movement of the four service brotherhoods in 1916 for the eight-hour day. Attempts to settle this controversy were unsuccessful; and on August 28, 1916, the unions called for a strike which was to commence on Labor Day, September 4. President Wilson immediately asked Congress for legislation to resolve the issue.

The Adamson Act, 1916.   This law provided for a basic eight-hour day for train service employees operating trains in interstate commerce. The President was instructed to appoint a commission of three men to report on the operation of the eight-hour day. Pending the completion of the investigation, and for thirty days thereafter, wages for the eight-hour day could not be reduced below the standard daily wages being paid when the Adamson Act was passed. The railroads challenged the constitutionality of the legislation in the courts. While the case was pending, the brotherhoods called for a strike to take effect on March 17, 1917. President Wilson requested that the controversy be submitted to a committee of the Council of National Defense. This was agreed to by both sides. The date of the strike was postponed to March 19, and on that day the railroads agreed to put the Adamson Act into effect without waiting for the decision of the Supreme Court. On the same day the Court, by a vote of five to four, upheld the law[3] on the ground that Congress had the power to meet a national emergency that could not be handled in any other way. During the period that the government operated the railroads while the war was on, the eight-hour day became standard for all railroad employees.

The Transportation Act of 1920. During the period from December, 1917, to March, 1920, the railway carriers were under the control of the United States Railroad Administration. The Director General, Mr. William Gibbs McAdoo, created a Division of Labor coordinate with the other divisions of the Railroad Administration to advise and assist him on labor relations. A Board of Railroad Wages and Working Conditions, advisory to the Director General and composed of three representatives of management and three of the employees, was set up to make recommendations for changes in wages and working conditions. Three railway boards of adjustment, bipartisan in nature, were also established to deal with controversies arising out of the application or interpretation of existing wage schedules. Under these arrangements, railroad labor made impressive gains in its power of collective bargaining, in the standardization and nationalization of practices and policies, and in the development of union organization. With the difficulties presented by the return of the railroads to private hands, it was clear that a fresh start for dealing with the problems of railroad labor was in order. Unfortunately, the compromise legislation which was incorporated in the Transportation Act of 1920 established machinery and procedures inadequate to deal with the difficult problems which were presented by the return to private ownership and the impact of the immediate postwar deflation. The law providing the machinery for settling labor disputes was contained in Title III of the

[3] *Wilson* v. *New,* 243 U.S. 332 (1917).

Act of 1920, but the Interstate Commerce Commission had no jurisdiction over it, nor was there any connection between the regulatory
provisions of the Act and those relating to labor.

The Act created two principal means for dealing with labor disputes. The first of these was railroad boards of labor adjustment that
could be established by agreement between the railroads and the employees. They could be local, regional, or national in nature and could
intervene in cases involving grievances, rules, or working conditions
on their own motion, on the application of either side to the dispute,
on the petition of one hundred interested workers, or on the request of
the newly created Railroad Labor Board. If an adjustment board
failed to achieve settlement, the case was to be turned over to the Railroad Labor Board.

The Railroad Labor Board, which was the second means for dealing with disputes, was to consist of nine members appointed by the
President and selected equally from management, unions, and the public. This Board was given exclusive jurisdiction over wage controversies, in addition to deciding disputes not settled by the adjustment
boards. It was also required to establish rates of wages and standards of
working conditions which, in the opinion of the Board, were just and
reasonable. Decisions of the Board required the concurrence of a majority which had to include at least one public member where wages
were at issue. The law contained no antistrike provisions nor any means
of enforcing the decisions of the Board.

The legislation failed to achieve its principal objectives. It was unable to resolve any of the major controversies that arose. The adjustment boards were not established, with the result that the Labor Board
became overburdened with disputes they were intended to settle. In
addition, it failed to arrive at any practicable standards of just and
reasonable wages, and instead became engaged in wage determintion
without the authority commensurate with the responsibilities it was
supposed to assume.

The Railway Labor Act of 1926

The Railway Labor Act, which replaced all previous legislation
designed to deal with labor disputes, incorporated all of the measures
that had been included in previous laws, except for the noncompulsory
wage determination of the Act of 1920. Its coverage was also extended
to all railroad employees. In thus relying on collective bargaining,
with conferences and conciliation or mediation as the primary methods
of settling disputes, it represented the accumulated experience of the

previous forty years. Amendments made in 1934 to overcome difficulties that arose in connection with establishing adjustment boards and problems arising from company-dominated unions completed, with minor changes, the machinery for settling railroad labor disputes that we have today.

All disputes between a carrier and its employees are to be considered and, if possible, settled by conference between representatives of labor and management. The representatives are to be chosen by each of the disputants respectively without interference from the other side.

The National Railroad Adjustment Board

The Act of 1926 provided that bipartisan adjustment boards were to be set up by agreement between the carriers and the unions to handle disputes arising out of grievances. Difficulties were encountered in establishing these, however. This led to the creation of the National Railroad Adjustment Board by the legislation of 1934. This agency was given exclusive jurisdiction over disputes arising out of grievances, or out of the interpretation of agreements concerning rates of pay, rules, or working conditions.[4] The Board is composed of 36 members, 18 selected by the carriers and 18 by the unions. For operational purposes the Board is organized into four divisions, each of which has jurisdiction over a particular class of employees. If a division fails to reach a decision in a case, a neutral referee is to be selected to break the deadlock. The decisions of the adjustment boards are final and binding on both parties. If a carrier fails to comply, labor can file civil suit against it, but no corresponding remedy is afforded the carrier.

National Board of Mediation

The Act of 1926 provided machinery for dealing with disputes that could not be settled by collective bargaining. The government could step in to try to resolve the issues through mediation, arbitration, and emergency boards. A National Board of Mediation, consisting of three members appointed by the President with the advice and consent of the Senate, was created by the Act of 1934. The term of office of the members is three years. This Board has jurisdiction over disputes involving rates of pay or changes in rules and working conditions where the parties to the dispute have been unable to effect a set-

[4] Public Law 89–456 (1965) provided for special adjustment boards to resolve labor disputes otherwise referrable to the National Railroad Adjustment Board. The special boards are to be established 30 days after request by either carriers or employees.

tlement. Either party may invoke the services of the Board, or the latter may act on its own motion in the case of an emergency. The function of the Board is to endeavor to bring about settlement through mediation. It does not decide the issues. It also has the duty, in the event that there is disagreement among the employees on who is to represent them, to investigate and, if necessary, to conduct an election by secret ballot to obtain the representatives.

Arbitration

If the National Mediation Board is unable to achieve the settlement of a controversy, it must endeavor to bring about arbitration. Both sides must agree if there is to be arbitration, and if this is done, the award is binding. A board of arbitration may consist of three or of six members, one or two being appointed by each side. The remainder are to be selected by the party artibrators, but if they cannot agree, the National Mediation Board is required to act.

Emergency Boards

If arbitration is refused and the dispute remains unsettled, and if the National Mediation Board has reason to believe that interstate commerce is seriously threatened, the Board must notify the President. He may at his discretion create an emergency board to investigate the dispute and report its findings to him. After the appointment of the emergency board and for thirty days subsequent to its report, no change, except by agreement, may be made in the conditions out of which the dispute arose.

Results of the Railway Labor Act

It was the intent of Congress, in adopting the Railway Labor Act as amended in 1934, to provide an agency for the authoritative adjustment of grievances and disputes over the meaning and application of agreements concerning rates of pay and working rules. It also intended that the Mediation Board should be a means of stabilizing the relations of the railways and their employees. Undoubtedly, a good deal has been accomplished on both counts. However, under the stress of problems arising in connection with World War II and subsequent inflation, the President of the United States found it necessary to seize the railroads and place them under government control four times following 1941 after all other measures to avoid strikes had been exhausted. As matters now stand, existing machinery is unable to resolve issues that are vital, especially to the unions. Seizure of the railroads by the government has impaired the role of collective bargaining; but more than that, it has encouraged militant action by the unions, which have nothing to lose as a consequence of seizure. Some means of restoring the balance is urgently needed.

THE COORDINATOR'S REPORT

The combined impact of competition from the newer modes of transport and technological developments, such as dieselization of motive power, central traffic controls for line operations, and automation in the freight assembly yards, on railroad employment and labor practices has developed into a crisis that has once more threatened a complete breakdown in labor relations. The emerging difficulties were clearly seen by Coordinator Eastman in 1934. The depression of the 1930's had a particularly severe impact on the railroads because of the precipitous decline of traffic, the rise of the new competition, and the heavy debt structure of a large proportion of the railroads. One of the major tasks imposed on the Coordinator under the Emergency Transportation Act of 1933 was to investigate the railroad situation and to make recommendations designed to introduce measures to improve railroad efficiency and to reduce costs of operation. Probably the most critical aspect of the whole problem related to employment and railroad labor relations, because almost all the measures available to increase efficiency and reduce costs aggravated the already serious unemployment situation. In addition, the restrictions imposed upon the displacement of labor by railroad consolidations practically eliminated these as a means of cutting costs. The comprehensive discussion by the Coordinator of the labor problem[5] has a startlingly contemporary ring because of the close parallel of the problems of thirty years ago with those of today, and the unfortunate lack of any substantial progress in dealing with them up to the present moment.

THE PRESIDENTIAL RAILROAD COMMISSION

On November 1, 1960, the President established a Presidential Railroad Commission to consider, in accordance with an agreement between carriers and the labor organizations of the "Big Five" brotherhoods, a controversy over wages, rules, working conditions, and social

[5] See *Report of the Federal Coordinator of Transportation,* House Document No. 89, 74th Congress, 1st session (Washington, D.C.: U.S. Government Printing Office, 1935), pp. 62–98.

security of the members of these unions. The Commission consisted of five carrier, five employee, and five public representatives under the chairmanship of one of the representatives of the public, Simon H. Rifkind. The Commission submitted its final report to the President on February 26, 1962.[6] It was written and agreed to unanimously by the public members. The railroad representatives accepted it but in a separate statement said they were disappointed with many of the recommendations. However, they felt that the public interest required that they agree. The labor representatives disagreed with virtually every phase of the report, refused to sign, and filed separate statements. One member, Mr. A. F. Zimmerman, submitted a letter only, in which he stated that his views would be reported directly to the President.

The report covered the subjects of wages, rules and working conditions, and social security for the operating employees of the railroads of the entire country. The traditional procedures for emergency boards were not followed because it was felt the issues were unusually broad and complex. Consequently, every appropriate method to understand the practices of the industry and the issues involved was employed. Separate recommendations for action were made for each of the topics dealt with. The report concluded (1) that the rules governing the manning of engines and trains need to be revised to permit the elimination of unnecessary jobs and at the same time to safeguard the interests of the individual employees adversely affected, (2) that the entire complex and intricate system of compensation needs to be overhauled, and (3) that the procedures for the administration of rules and the disposition of grievances need to be revised.[7] The Commission felt that the solution to the issues has to be found within the framework of collective bargaining, but that a period of transition, probably of considerable length, is essential because it is not prudent to make a sharp and precipitate break with the past.

In short, the report concludes that the entire structure of the relations of railroad management and labor needs to be overhauled drastically and that existing means for doing so constitute an unsatisfactory way of performing the task.

There is no reason for the public to continue to support from public funds neutrals used in deciding cases involving operating employees under the First Division of the National Railroad Adjustment Board. The parties should here bear the same responsibilities they do in industry in general. Yet it is imperative

[6] *Report of the Presidential Railroad Commission* (Washington, D.C., February, 1962) (mimeographed).

[7] *Ibid.*, p. 11.

that there be procedures for settling disputes over the application and administration of collective bargaining agreements. The parties together with responsible government agencies and officials need to review systematically this area.[8]

The vigorous opposition of the labor representatives indicated that resolving the issues that have been so thoroughly exposed would be a very painful task.

Labor relations in the railroad industry since the report of the Presidential Commission have been little short of chaotic. Disagreement immediately arose over the implementation of recommendations of the Commission, particularly those relating to work rules and the employment of firemen, the so-called featherbedding issue. When all means to settle the dispute failed, Congress took action by passing legislation[9] which established a seven-man tripartite board to dispose of the issues relating to the use of firemen on other than steam power, and to consist of road and yard crews. The award of the Arbitration Board was to continue for a maximum of two years from the date it took effect, unless the parties agreed otherwise. The award was finally implemented after extended legal proceedings on April 2, 1964. Conflict over the award continued, and on March 31, 1966, the firemen struck eight major railroads. They were ordered back to work by the U.S. District Court for the District of Columbia and were fined for contempt for failing to do so for four days.

Disputes between the railroads and employee groups resulted in Presidential intervention involving telegraphers in 1962, and operating employees (work rules) in the spring of 1964.[10] In 1967, the dispute with the International Association of Machinists led Congress to consider action to prevent a strike. The Senate and the House of Representatives were unable to agree on legislation and a nationwide strike resulted. Congress reacted promptly by passing a law which reinstated government authority to prohibit the strike, and required labor and management to accept a government dictated settlement of the wage dispute if the issue remained unresolved at the end of 90 days. President Johnson appointed a five-man board charged with the duty of devising a mandatory settlement if agreement could not be reached within the 90-day period. If there is no voluntary agreement the board's recommendations will be binding until January 1, 1969.

[8] *Ibid.*, p. 340. For a careful summary of the railroad labor problem, see John T. Dunlop, "Manpower in Operating Classifications on the Railroads," in National Bureau of Economic Research, *Transportation Economics* (New York, 1965), pp. 423–36.

[9] Public Law 88–108 (1963).

[10] For a summary of the labor controversies, see Association of American Railroads, *A Review of Railroad Operations* (Washington, D.C., annually 1962 to 1966).

RAILWAY SOCIAL SECURITY

The depression of the 1930's resulted in legislation that established a separate social security system for railway employees. Retirement benefits prior to this had been regarded as a management problem. Many railroads had established their own pension plans, but down to 1928 the regulations of the Interstate Commerce Commission permitted pensions to be charged to operating expenses only as they were paid out.

Railroad Retirement Act, 1936

This law makes all railroad employees eligible for retirement at 65 years of age, although they may continue to work beyond that age if they wish to do so. Workers who have completed 30 years of service can retire at 60; if they are permanently disabled, they can retire at that age regardless of length of service. An employee may shift from one railroad to another without losing pension rights. The annuities are computed on the basis of a formula which is based on length of service and average monthly income. The law also provides for a minimum annuity.

The Retirement Act is administered by a Railroad Retirement Board of three members, who are appointed by the President with the advice and consent of the Senate for a term of office of five years. This Board certifies the individuals who are to receive pensions to the Secretary of the Treasury, who authorizes payment from the railroad retirement account, which is under his jurisdiction. The funds for the railroad retirement account are derived from a tax on the income of the employee and an excise tax on the payroll of the carrier. Carriers and employees contribute equal amounts to the account. The rates are higher than those of the Social Security Act.

The Railroad Labor Unemployment Insurance Act, 1938

This Act removed railroad employees from coverage by the unemployment insurance acts of the states and Title IX of the United States Social Security Act. In place of this, all employees are made eligible for unemployment insurance payable to them from funds derived from a tax on the payrolls of the carriers. This created one federal system of railroad unemployment insurance.

Extension of Benefits

Benefits under railway social security were expanded rapidly after the original laws were passed, the most important changes being made in 1946. The legislation of that year assured that railway workers were to be covered by the most comprehensive protection in the United States against the five major hazards of economic security—old age, disability, death, unemployment, and sickness.[11] Moreover, these benefits were provided through legislation developed on the principle of a separate railway social security system. Recent enactments have again increased and extended benefits obtainable under the railroad retirement system.[12] In 1965, the federal program of health insurance (medicare) was established and included those under the railroad retirement system. In 1966,[13] a five-year temporary program of employer-financed annuities supplemental to regular retirement benefits under the railroad retirement system was set up. This law also provided for increases for retirement-survivor beneficiaries.

One further item relating to the security of railroad workers should be mentioned. The Transportation Act of 1940 provided that the Interstate Commerce Commission, in dealing with consolidations, was to require a fair and equitable arrangement to protect employees. No consolidation was to be approved if it worsened a worker's employment status in the four years following the effective date of the Commission's order. Employees with less than four years' service were to be protected for a period equal to the time they had been on the carrier's payroll before the consolidation order. In addition, the Commission generally has written labor protection clauses into abandonment orders that have been issued since 1942.[14]

THE LABOR PROBLEM IN AIR TRANSPORTATION

The Railway Labor Act

The role of the federal government in dealing with labor problems in air transportation differs from that in connection with railroad labor in that it is confined to the settlement of labor disputes. This is carried out under the provisions of the Railway Labor Act, which was

[11] *Annual Report of the Railroad Retirement Board for the Year Ending June 30, 1947* (Washington, D.C.: U.S. Government Printing Office, 1948), p. 11.

[12] See Public Law 89–97 (1965).

[13] Public Law 89–699.

[14] See L. A. Lecht, *Experience under Railway Labor Legislation* (New York: Columbia University Press, 1955), for a comprehensive treatment of the railroad labor problem since the beginning of World War I. For careful summary treatments, see Dixon, *op. cit.,* chaps. vii, viii, xiii, xxii, and xxiv; K. Healy, *The Economics of Transportation* (New York: Ronald Press Co., 1940), chaps. xvi and xvii; E. R. Johnson, *Government Regulation of Transportation* (New York: D. Appleton-Century Co., Inc., 1938), chap. xi; Eliot Jones, *Principles of Railway Transportation* (New York: Macmillan Co., 1925), chaps. xx and xxvi; and H. G. Moulton, *The American Transportation Problem* (Washington, D.C.: Brookings Institution, 1933), chap. ix.

extended in 1936 to cover the employees of air carriers engaged in interstate commerce.

The coverage and procedures of the Labor Act as applied to the air lines are the same as for the railroads. The Act authorizes a National Air Transport Adjustment Board similar to the National Railroad Adjustment Board, but one has never been established. However, system boards of adjustment have been created by agreements between the carriers and the unions. These seemed to have functioned reasonably well in dealing with employee grievances and interpretation of agreements on rates of pay, rules, and working conditions.

The National Board of Mediation performs the same duties for the air-line industry that it does for the railroads. If collective bargaining breaks down, it offers its services for mediation, and if this fails, it endeavors to secure arbitration of the controversy. If this also fails, the Board may notify the President and recommend the creation of an emergency board. A number of such boards have been set up but the results of their activities cannot be counted as successful in bringing about a satisfactory resolution of the issues at stake.

Labor Organizations

As of March 1, 1959, thirty-one labor unions represented the employees of the nation's certified air lines. Ten of these are so-called "independent locals," and the other twenty-one are national in scope. The three largest unions in terms of air-line employee membership are the International Association of Machinists, the Transport Workers Union, and the Air Line Pilots Association. There is also the Flight Engineers International Association, which represents the mechanic-qualified engineers, except for Northwest Airlines, where the International Association of Machinists has jurisdiction. Something over 55 per cent of air-line employees are organized.

Labor Problems

The most difficult labor problems in the air-line industry are of recent origin and have arisen out of the introduction of jet aircraft. This has created fears concerning job security, particularly with the flight personnel, as well as the jurisdictional dispute between the Air Line Pilots Association (ALPA) and the Flight Engineers International Association (FEIA). This dispute has turned on the question of whether the occupant of the third seat in the cockpit should be a member of ALPA or FEIA. The problem of job security centers on hours of work and rates of pay, especially for the flight personnel. The financial problems of the air lines, the powerful position of the flight personnel, and the inferior bargaining position of the other employees point up the chaotic conditions in air-line labor relations at the present time.

Mutual-Aid Pact

On October 28, 1958, six of the major air lines, including the "Big Four," entered into what has been called the "mutual-aid pact." This agreement, which any other certified air carrier may join by singing and filing a copy with the Civil Aeronautics Board, obligates each party to pay the one suffering a strike an amount equal to its increased revenues attributable to the strike while it lasts, minus applicable direct expense. The obligation arises only if the strike is called before the employees exhaust the procedures of the Railway Labor Act, or if the employees strike to enforce demands in excess of or opposed to the recommendations of an emergency board. The CAB approved the agreement because it found that it did not constitute an impediment to bona fide collective bargaining, and did not violate the Railway Labor Act. The objective of the agreement was to prevent the individual carriers being "whipsawed" by powerful unions by successive strikes against the different airlines. This agreement has been put to use on a number of occasions, the last being in 1966.

Results of the Legislation

The Railway Labor Act as amended was the outcome of long years of experience in dealing with railroad labor disputes and was designed for that purpose. Whatever its merits and defects in this respect, it is ill-suited to grapple with the problems of a young and totally different industry. The Mediation Board has been unable to deal with the major controversies, and this is not surprising; its duties to the railroads alone constitute a big enough task. The emergency boards are *ad hoc* and therefore unable to provide any continuity or development of policy. If it is assumed that labor problems in air transportation need to be dealt with by legislation other than that which governs labor relations for industry in general, then a new law geared to the special problems of the air lines is called for. Current controversies offer little prospect of being resolved by present arrangements, and the prospects of a successful application of only those procedures afforded industry in general are not very bright.[15]

[15] For a current discussion of labor problems in air transportation, see the following in *Law and Contemporary Problems,* Vol. XXV, No. 1 (Winter, 1960), pp. 3–56: E. L. Oliver, "Labor Problems of the Transportation Industry"; A. M. Wisehart, "The Airlines' Recent Experience under the Railway Labor Act"; and W. V. Henzey, "Labor Problems in the Airline Industry."

OTHER TRANSPORT INDUSTRIES

There is no special legislation for dealing with the labor problems of other carriers in domestic commerce. This is not because of the absence of labor disputes but rather because Congress has felt that the issues can be dealt with most satisfactorily by employees acting through collective bargaining or other means.

The rise of motor transport to its present significance in intercity and interstate transport has recently brought the national aspect of this industry to the fore, particularly with the activities of the International Brotherhood of Teamsters under Mr. James Hoffa. Truck drivers constitute the largest single group of employees in the Teamsters' Union, some 90 per cent of over-the-road drivers being members. The membership is organized into local unions, each of which is a member of a joint council for the geographical area in which the union is located. Each of the organizations within the Teamsters' Union is chartered by and responsible to the International Brotherhood, which is independent of the American Federation of Labor-Congress of Industrial Organizations.

The multiemployer areawide type of agreement was the predominant type of labor agreement covering intercity trucking until recently. Negotiations between employers and employees were generally carried on by five employer groups, each of which covered a particular region of the country. The Teamsters Union, however, under the leadership of Mr. Hoffa set a nationwide master contract as its goal. This move was met by the truck operators who formed The Trucking Employers Inc. as the national bargaining unit for about 10,000 motor freight carriers. The first master contract was signed in March, 1967, after severe controversy which posed the threat of a nationwide strike.[16] Present bargaining procedures and organization of employers and employees pose the possibility for the future of strikes that could bring the nation's trucking industry to a standstill. The importance of trucking in the national transport system is such that a nationwide strike of key personnel could paralyze the economy almost as much as a similar event on the railroads. Existing means for settling railroad disputes are not satisfactory for the highly competitive and diversified trucking industry any more than they are for the airlines. Various procedures might be adopted to anticipate developments, but

[16] Local strikes in various areas of the country occurred because of refusal of area unions to ratify the agreement. The Teamsters Union, however, finally was able to overrule the locals after meetings in Washington under the Secretary of Labor.

current arrangements are quite inadequate. Congress will have to take some positive steps before long.

CONCLUSION

Areas of Conflict

The most acute areas of conflict over labor relations in transportation to date have been in railroad and air transport. The railroad problem is long-standing; and at the present time, it can scarcely be said that much genuine progress has been made toward resolving the basic issues, particularly as they have emerged under the impact of technological change. The problem in the air lines has developed primarily since the end of World War II, but has become particularly acute with the introduction of jet-powered aircraft. To date, motor transport has not presented issues that have been sufficiently acute to warrant special action comparable to that which has been applied to railroads and air lines. However, practices within the Teamsters' Union and chaotic conditions in labor in motor transport have attracted public attention and created considerable concern. The same remarks apply to labor in the domestic shipping industry.

The attention which has been given to the railroad labor problem may be attributed first of all to the position of the railroads in the transport structure. The exclusive position occupied by them, together with the dependence of so many areas on the particular railroad serving them, meant that stoppage of transportation on any of them could have a disastrous effect in a very short time. The immediate dependence on the operating employees for the movement of trains gave these employees a uniquely strategic position. With the interconnection of rail systems throughout the country the formation of craft unions within this group facilitated unified action and strengthened their hands in collective bargaining, even if it was with only one railroad. The public had a large stake in labor-management relations, apart from the effects of strikes, because of the concerted action of railroads with regard to rates. When regulation of these was undertaken, the logic of the situation called for public control of labor costs, as for all others, by the regulating agency. However, this was not done. The Interstate Commerce Commission has never had any say over railroad labor matters.

Somewhat similar remarks apply to the air-line industry because of the key position occupied by the pilots and flight engineers in particular. The potential for "whipsaw" tactics or even a nationwide strike, now that the industry has come to occupy such an important place in the movement of passengers, makes essential the development of means at the federal level for peaceful and equitable adjustments. Route certification which limits competition, and public subsidy, actual or lurking in the background, add further emphasis to the need for safeguarding the public interest in agreements that are made. Under these circumstances, it hardly seems reasonable to rely on the largesse of either labor or management.

Until recently, at least, the motor trucking industry has offered no such difficulties because of the widespread competitive situation. The possible effective development of nationwide bargaining may have altered the situation because of the growth of transcontinental trucking systems and because of the increasing dependence on intercity and interstate traffic on the trucking industry. Union organization that could bring a halt to all commercial or all for-hire trucking in a particular area or for the nation as a whole would create a situation almost as perilous as that which would result from similar action in the railroad industry. However, the major problem in the trucking industry at present seems to rest not in the need for special machinery for dealing with labor disputes, but in the need for examination of the issues posed by the unionization under a single authority of all motor trucking in a given area or in the nation as a whole.

Effects of Changing Technology

Technological developments that have brought about the rise of the new transport structure have affected the problems connected with adjusting labor disputes in two ways. First of all, the more effective competition becomes among the various modes, the greater are the limitations upon the discretionary powers which labor leaders can exercise, as long as the organizations for collective bargaining for the various modes are independent of each other. In other words, competition imposes restrictions on the powers which labor unions are able to exercise, just as it does on management. In a private, competitive enterprise system, limitations on the monopoly powers of labor are as essential to its success as are those on management. Second, competition within the modes has the same effect in the absence of area-wide or nationwide collective bargaining for the particular mode or the key personnel of it. Limitations on the effectiveness of this competition, such as exist in the railroad industry or which are the result of restrictions on entry imposed by public regulation, may to some extent offset the competitive effects. However, in motor transport, for example, the presence of private carriage and unregulated carriage for hire assures extensive competition among the suppliers of transport services.

The possible difficulties in labor relations that might emerge, if transport companies embracing the different modes on a wide scale were formed, should be given careful consideration when evaluations of the merits of intermodal integration are being made. The inducements to create company-wide unions would be very great and the problems of collective bargaining would become more difficult than they are today even in the railroad field. Moreover, a national organization for all the workers, especially operating personnel, in these transport companies, would be a tempting objective, quite possibly not too difficult of accomplishment. If a more competitive structure is to be the goal of national policy in transportation, it will be necessary for the federal government to recognize the implications of this in all its phases and not confine attention merely to pricing policies and ownership organization.

National Transportation Study

Despite the importance of labor problems in transportation in general, and in the railroad industry in particular, the Doyle study group did not examine this question, on the grounds that the Interstate and Foreign Commerce Committee does not have jurisdiction on labor matters, and that limitations on time and budget precluded the exhaustive study that should be given this conflict that has retarded development for the past generation.[17] However, it did make a general assessment of the centers of responsibility for perpetuation of long-term labor differences in transportation.

The report concluded that responsibility must be divided four ways between the public, government, management, and labor leadership. The general public was given the first blame for its failure to acquaint itself with the facts and for the apathy it displays. This gives pressure groups the opportunity to exert whatever influence they can muster to further their own interests. The principal blame, however, was laid at the door of government. The executive and legislative branches have avoided preventive action and have entered the arena only after the crises have arrived. This is an avoidance of the duties and responsibilities of public leadership which government is supposed to provide. The remaining responsibility was divided equally between

[17] *National Transportation Policy* (Doyle Report), Preliminary Draft of a Report to the Senate Committee on Interstate and Foreign Commerce, 87th Cong., 1st sess. (Washington, D.C.: U.S. Government Printing Office, 1961), Part VII, chap. x.

management and labor. Both sides have shown an intransigence which has led them to positions from which they are unwilling to retreat, despite the pressures of changing technology and the need for adjustments to meet the new situations which these have created.

The study group also felt that the coexistence of separate social security systems under the Railway Labor Act is wasteful at the administrative level of government and difficult to justify. It contended that railway labor does not differ from any other labor, requires no special treatment in view of labor legislation of the past generation, and in no way justifies added cost in government to handle a specialized program apart from labor as a whole.

On the other hand, the report stated that the vital nature of transportation justifies continued special attention to labor problems. Accordingly, it made six recommendations that are essentially hortatory in nature except for one item which is included as a footnote. This was that a Transportation Labor Board should be established in the Department of Transportation (the creation of which was recommended in another connection). It would provide a forum for continuing labor-management discussion, a research agency specializing in transportation labor, and a means for impartial analysis of the over-all public interest in relation to transportation labor questions. It should be composed of representatives of government, labor, management, and the using public, and be supplied with adequate resources to perform its functions. However, its function would not include mediation, which should remain in the Department of Labor. How this sort of an arrangement could possibly aid in resolving the present critical problems of labor in the field of transportation is not spelled out.[18]

[18] Legislation establishing the Department of Transportation (1966) contained no provisions regarding labor disputes.

Chapter 21

REGULATION AND ADMINISTRATION IN TRANSPORT POLICY

INTRODUCTION

Effective realization of public policy in transportation requires a distinction between regulation and administration of the legislative enactments of Congress. Regulation, as has already been pointed out, takes on a judicial character in the task of interpreting and applying the laws which Congress has passed; it is also legislative in nature, in that it entails the responsibility of filling out the details of the statutes to meet the continuously changing situations which arise in connection with the supplying of transportation services. On the other hand, the formulation of over-all transportation policy is a function of the executive branch of government. The administration of programs of public aid and public investment is also an executive matter. Between these two broad areas the control of transportation by government encompasses the supervision of many activities of the private operators which may fall within either the executive or the regulatory function. The appropriate allocation of these may be somewhat difficult to determine, but in general the line may be drawn between those which are intimately related to the regulatory process and those which are not. Thus, service standards, freight car supply, and common carrier obligations may be regarded as the responsibility of the regulatory commission, while safety standards for motor vehicles and operating personnel can be supervised by an executive department.

In the development of public policy to date the tendency has been to give the regulatory commission authority over all matters relating to the transport agency under its control, although responsibility for safety measures in aviation was transferred to the Federal Aviation Authority, and labor problems have always been kept out of the hands of the commissions. It has also been assumed that the latter were responsible for developing policy, within the broad mandates laid down by Congress, for the modes of transport under their control. There has, however, never been a unified approach to transport problems because of inconsistencies in the laws and in the administration of them.[1]

The declaration of national policy in the Transportation Act of 1940 contained the implicit assumption that the Interstate Commerce Commission could develop a coherent transport policy within the framework of the existing law. What was not understood was that the rise of the newer agencies, with the vast amount of public investment that was involved, necessitated a distinction between regulation and promotion that had not been particularly significant theretofore. In addition, the volume of detail that the new regulatory program entailed, together with the highly conflicting interests of the various modes, has burdened the Commission with so much work that the regulatory procedure has broken down. A new approach which recognizes the totally different structures that have emerged in transportation is now an urgent necessity.

THE ROLE OF REGULATION

THE INDEPENDENT REGULATORY COMMISSION

The Role of Regulation in Transport

For over three quarters of a century and particularly for the last 50 years, transportation in the United States has been subject to detailed and comprehensive regulation, especially as applied to common carriers. This policy has been developed on the assumption that the competitive forces of the market were, under the rules applicable to industry in general, inadequate to afford the safeguards considered necessary in the public interest. As a consequence, a vast accumulation of regulatory prescriptions has become embodied in the law, and these form the institutional framework within which the rendering of the bulk of transportation service for hire takes place. The impact of changing technology on the means of supplying transportation during the last 30 years, however, has altered radically the fundamental assumptions upon which the regulation was erected; indeed, some would say that it has swept these assumptions away completely. Nevertheless, this does not warrant the eradication of the whole corpus of trans-

[1] See *National Transportation Policy* (Doyle Report), Preliminary Draft of a Report to the senate Committee on Interstate and Foreign Commerce, 87th Congress, 1st session (Washington, D.C.: U.S. Government Printing Office, 1961), Part IV, chap. ii.

portation law that has been developed, because nothing would be left to take its place if this were done. What is needed is a careful revision of legislation and of regulatory policy that will give full recognition to the changed conditions.

The revisions that are called for depend on the evaluation that one makes of the nature of the contemporary transport structure and the way in which it can function efficiently. There seems to be little disagreement with the view that transportation today is subject to highly competitive conditions over a wide range of activities, but there is lacking a convincing consensus on what should be done to deal with the situation. If regulatory controls are to be extended and existing detailed supervision over pricing and other activities retained, as advocated by the Doyle Report, then regulation must become more comprehensive than at present, and the processes of administration altered radically to cope with the mounting volume of work the regulatory authorities will have to face. On the other hand, if greater reliance is to be placed on competitive forces and pricing is to be accorded the freedom which the present situation seems to warrant, the task of regulation assumes a different character, and the commissions will be burdened with much less adjudicatory responsibility than is presently the case.

Even if the rate-making powers of the Interstate Commerce Commission were reduced to that of control over minimum rates solely for the purpose of preventing predatory competition, and regulation of maximum rates were limited to undue preference, unreasonable discrimination, and unreasonable profits, responsibility for administering the other parts of the Interstate Commerce Act that are not directly connected with rate regulation would still remain. Enforcement of common carrier obligations would still be necessary, as would certification of common carriers to assure the shipper that he was dealing with a firm authorized to perform these services. Co-operative arrangements such as car pooling, traffic interchange, joint use of terminal facilities, and operation of rate bureaus under the Reed-Bulwinkle Act would require scrutiny by regulatory authorities. In addition, co-ordination of services by through routes and joint rates calls for continuous supervision, especially for railroads. In other words, even though extensive relaxation over rate making, control of entry, and abandonment of unprofitable lines and services were to take place, continuous regulation of a more comprehensive nature than is required for industry in general is still needed in transportation. The fact that so much attention has been focused on control of rates, entry, and abandonments has obscured the other distinctive functions of regulation in transportation that are not readily amenable to court or executive supervision. Finally, it should be noted that whatever steps in the direction of deregulation may be undertaken, reorganization of regulation will have to come about gradually because of the complex interrelationships and procedures that have evolved under policies that have been developing since 1887.

Inadequacy of Antitrust

Apart from the fact that deregulation, if it is to be undertaken, must emerge gradually, the antitrust laws are an inadequate device for dealing with the peculiar problems of transportation. More important, the means at present available for enforcing them are not adapted to the requirements of transport. To burden the Federal Trade Commission with the task of applying to transport the laws it is called upon to enforce would place it in a more awkward position than it now seems to occupy, to say nothing about the complete absence of rules or experience applicable to transportation. The Sherman Act, as it has been interpreted with regard to restraint of trade and monopoly, is not the appropriate means for dealing with the problems of railroad consolidation or transport integration.[2] In addition, co-operative arrangements for interchange of traffic, car pooling, joint use of terminals, and rate bureaus would require exemption and therefore special administration under other legislation. Finally, common carrier responsibilities in interstate commerce that have developed under the jurisdiction of the Interstate Commerce Commission would have to be retained or incorporated in new legislation that would need to be adjudicated without continuous resort to the courts.

Despite the effectiveness of pervasive competition, transportation still possesses characteristics of both public utilities and competitive industries. The Sherman and Clayton acts are still applicable insofar as they are not waived by special exemptions. The unique features of transportation are such, however, that a great many practices, unnecessary and undesirable for other industries, must still be sanctioned. These need to be administered in conjunction with, and in light of, over-all national policy for transportation.

Criticism of Commission Regulation

Criticisms of the performance of the independent regulatory commission range all the way from opposition to the exercise of control

---

[2] None of the present important railroad mergers would ever pass muster under the Clayton Act and probably would not survive the Sherman Act if they were carried out.

over private enterprise by an agency that is directly independent of the legislative, executive, and judicial branches of the government, to thoroughgoing disagreement with the laws which it has to administer and with the interpretation of them. As a consequence, the proposals which have been advanced may insist that this sort of governmental agency be abolished altogether, or that there be reconstruction of both the legislative mandates and the procedures which commissions employ. That regulation in transportation needs to be overhauled is not very debatable, but this is just about as far as agreement goes. Before any practicable approach to workable reconstitution of the regulatory process can be undertaken successfully, it is necessary to reach some accord on the functions which regulation must perform.[3] A blanket indictment of all commissions at the federal level is not in order because they perform such diverse functions that they have few problems in common. Furthermore, in transportation, abolition of the Interstate Commerce Commission and assignment of its quasi-judicial duties to the courts would impose an intolerable burden on the latter if present legislative enactments were retained. So far, those critics who would eliminate the Interstate Commerce Commission and the Civil Aeronautics Board have not stated their case in terms of the scope and details of regulation which would obtain if present procedures were done away with. The first step in this approach must be that of spelling out the task that has to be performed before the means of executing it has been set up.

Those who criticize regulation in transport on the ground that it has become cumbersome, contradictory, and susceptible to unwarranted delays have recommended that the executive functions now performed by the commissions be assigned to the executive branch of

[3] For different points of view on the controversy, see M. M. Carrow, "Administrative Adjudication: Should Its Role Be Changed?" *George Washington Law Review,* Vol. XXVII, No. 3 (January, 1959), reprinted in *Major Administrative Process Problems,* Hearings of the Subcommittee on Interstate and Foreign Commerce, House of Representatives, 86th Congress, 1st session (Washington, D.C.: U.S. Government Printing Office, 1960), pp. 768–90; L. J. Hector, *Problems of the CAB and the Independent Regulatory Commissions,* Memorandum to the President (mimeographed) (September 10, 1959); *Report on Regulatory Agencies to the President-Elect* (Landis Report), Senate Committee on the Judiciary, 86th Congress, 2d session, December, 1960 (Washington, D.C.: U.S. Government Printing Office, 1960); and E. S. Redford, *National Regulatory Commissions —Need for a New Look* (College Park, Md.: Bureau of Governmental Research, College of Business and Public Administration, University of Maryland, 1959). For a brief summary of some of the recent reports, see M. P. Arth, "Federal Transport Regulatory Policy," *American Economic Review,* Vol. LII, No. 2 (May, 1962), pp. 416–25. See also M. H. Bernstein, *Regulating Business by Independent Commission* (Princeton: Princeton University Press, 1955); *National Transportation Policy* (Doyle Report), Part IV; and M. L. Fair, "Some Observations on the Theory and Performance of the Independent Regulatory Agencies in Regulating Public Utilities," *I.C.C. Practitioners' Journal,* Vol. XXVII, No. 9 (June, 1960), pp. 957–69.

the government, and that internal organization and procedures be thoroughly revised so as to make for more efficient administration. Reform of this type would retain the quasi-judicial and quasi-legislative duties. However, much of the criticism that applies to the Interstate Commerce Commission is inescapable under present legislation because of the ever-present threat of appeal of decisions to the courts. This necessitates strict compliance with the law and the accumulation of voluminous records in each case of importance. This is evidenced in the recent cases involving the highly controversial issues surrounding minimum rates for interagency competition and the applications for consolidation by railroads and by airlines.

One significant factor that has made the task of the Interstate Commerce Commission particularly difficult has been the contradictory and often indefinite nature of the legislation that it has been charged with enforcing.

When terms requiring exercise of judgment are used in administrative law much uncertainty and confusion resulting in excessive litigation could be avoided if the lawmakers expressed their intent and understanding of the term [*sic*]. In transportation law, it has proven difficult to interpret the intent of Congress regarding such phrases as "*undue* preference;" "compensatory;" "*destructive* competition;" and the like. Such terms lack precision in a modern world of rapid development. More precise explanation of the intent of Congress, modified from time to time as changing circumstances might require, would greatly simplify the regulatory problem for all concerned in the process.[4]

Congress has failed to provide the Commission with a workable standard for ascertaining the reasonableness of the general level of rates at the same time that it has imposed upon the Commission the task of dealing with the issue. No steps have been undertaken to clarify the ambiguities of the declaration of policy in the Transportation Act of 1940, and the revision of the rule of rate making in the Act of 1958 was sufficiently vague to satisfy all parties. Similarly, the attitude of Congress has been vacillating and uncertain on policy for railroad consolidation and intermodal integration. Nor has there been a sufficient consensus among economists or other students of transportation on guidelines for these matters that would indicate to the Commission that it was following any generally accepted point of view.[5]

---

[4] *National Transportation Policy* (Doyle Report), p. 120.

[5] One would find it exceedingly difficult to extract a unified economic policy from the Sawyer, Weeks, Mueller, and Doyle reports, yet these have been the principal government documents in the last 17 years setting forth proposals for policy in the regulation of transportation. The message of President Kennedy (discussed below) is a radical departure from previous recommendations.

Reorganization of Transport Regulation

Reorganization of the Interstate Commerce Commission to meet the changed problems in transport pertains to three main categories, namely, (1) restriction of activities to quasi-judicial and quasi-legislative matters, thereby eliminating those that are of an executive nature; (2) modification of procedures so as to provide for more expeditious handling of the more or less routine matters of regulation, thereby freeing the Commissioners to devote their time to major issues and policies; and (3) consideration of whether there should be a single commission for transportation or multiple administration of regulation.

Restriction of Activities. Much of the detailed work of the Commission has pertained to supervision of technical operating matters that do not fall into the category of regulation, but rather are of a police and executive nature. Supervision of standards of equipment, of safety operations and of operating employees of all motor carriers of property in interstate commerce, and of weights and measures for vehicles are duties that are much more within the competence of executive agencies. This has been recognized in air and water transport. When railroads were the sole concern of the Interstate Commerce Commission, there were possibly adequate reasons for assigning these tasks to one agency, although labor and personnel matters were never within its jurisdiction. However, motor transport has introduced an entirely new problem that calls for separation of policing responsibilities from regulating economic activities, especially when the executive duties extend to all motor carriers of property in interstate commerce. The line of demarcation in many instances is not too easy to draw, but the basis for excluding the duties imposed on the Commission that are of a purely technical operating nature is not difficult to obtain. The recent creation of the Department of Transportation, discussed below, relieves the Commission of these responsibilities, and may, therefore, return it to the basic concept of regulatory agency. This alone, however, will not accomplish the whole task. The Commission still has to extricate itself from the vulnerable position of protecting carriers against competition from each other while treating nonregulated transport as unwanted and illegitimate offspring.

Reorganization of Internal Operations. Reorganization of the internal operations of the Commission must consider the regulatory functions it may have to perform in the future. If the regulatory duties remain essentially as they are at present, means must be adopted whereby the details of regulation can be performed by a staff working within clearly defined rules and policies laid down by the Commission, thereby giving the latter the opportunity to develop broad lines of policy on the most significant issues. At the same time, there is need for an executive officer who can manage and direct the internal affairs. If rate making were placed on a competitive basis with standards clearly defined by the Commission, a large part of the current volume of work would disappear. Similarly, elimination of control of entry of motor carriers by confining certification merely to assurance of ability to discharge common carrier responsibilities, that is, that they are "fit, willing and able," would free examiners and staff from the unwieldly volume of work now imposed upon them. Recommendations for internal reorganization to date have assumed the continuation of the present regulatory duties. It is not surprising that little accord has been reached on what should be done.

Single or Multiple Commissions. The third area of discussion on reconstruction relates to the question of whether there should be a single commission to regulate transportation or more than one. The Doyle Report recommended a single Federal Transportation Commission that would have jurisdiction over operating rights of all regulated carriers (air, highway, merchant marine, rail, and domestic water, including brokers and freight forwarders), with consideration of extension of economic regulation to pipe lines; (2) rates and services covering all aspects of intramodal and intermodal services and rate making, including shipping conference agreements; and (3) approval and promulgation of safety regulations for air, highway, and rail carriers, as well as investigation of accidents involving such carriers. All other functions of the Civil Aeronautics Board, the Federal Maritime Commission, and the Interstate Commerce Commission would be transferred to a Department of Transportation in the executive branch of the government.[6] The Commission would consist of fifteen members who would serve for a term of office of ten years.

If the present scope of regulation of transportation is to be retained, or even expanded, as suggested by the Doyle Report, it is difficult to see how any reorganization entailing the concentration of control in the hands of a single agency can be worked out in a way that will deal with the present difficulties; in fact, it is hard to see how matters would not get much worse. If this is to be the direction of public policy, then separate commissions for each of the modes would be much more

---

[6] *National Transportation Policy* (Doyle Report), pp. 107–8. The Weeks and Mueller reports did not mention the subject of organization procedure and regulation, nor did the message of April, 1962, by President Kennedy to the Congress.

workable. Separate commissions could focus their attention on each agency independently of each other. Each could deal with the problems of its own mode without the distracting and conflicting claims of the rivals and would be compelled to recognize the competitive claims of its own charge. The competitive pressure of independent and separate responsibility would serve as a stimulus to imagination and initiative that is lacking at the present time. Competition is an excellent antidote to bureaucracy and vested interests. Problems relating to questions of interagency co-ordination could be handled through joint boards.

If, on the other hand, national transportation policy is reconstructed so as to make a clear-cut separation of regulation and administration, and if regulation is reduced so as to place prime reliance on competition, then there is a strong case for a single commission.[7] The task of regulating the economic aspects of motor and water transport would be drastically reduced, and even railroad regulation would be a much less burdensome undertaking than it is today. The necessity would still remain of distinguishing between the regulatory requirements of each mode. Whether internal organization would be more effective on an agency basis or on a functional basis would depend upon the duties of such a commission as spelled out in the legislation, although the larger problems of the railroads would seem to call for some modal specialization. In any case the commission would be able to supervise and co-ordinate transport regulation as a whole, as well as assist in developing transport policy within the quasi-judicial, quasi-legislative framework. The place of air transportation in this organization would depend upon the type of revision accorded the Civil Aeronautics Act. If the promotional functions were removed from the jurisdiction of the Civil Aeronautics Board, regulation of air transport could be combined with the others in a single agency. If present duties were to be retained, a separate agency could probably function more satisfactorily.

Reorganization of regulation and the functions of the regulatory commission in the execution of the transport policy of this country turn on a number of factors. A workable program must separate regulatory and executive responsibilities. Decisions must be reached on the role that competition is to be permitted to exercise within the various modes and among them. Finally, the part to be played by competitive pricing, and the scope of managerial discretion in pricing policies, are

---

[7] This is the proposal set forth in C. L. Dearing and W. Owen, *National Transportation Policy* (Washington, D.C.: Brookings Institution, 1949). This study was made at the request of the Hoover Commission on government reorganization.

the crux of the whole matter. Until Congress resolves these questions, little progress is likely to be made in bringing about a solution to the current critical issues, despite the fact that the commissions could go a long way, if they made up their minds to do it, toward dealing with them even under present legislation.

THE ROLE OF ADMINISTRATION

EXECUTIVE RESPONSIBILITIES

The federal government is engaged in a wide range of strictly administrative, operating, and policing functions in the transport activity of the country. It is also the largest single investor in transportation property, the provider of a large part of the funds for highways, most of the funds for waterways, and all of them for airways and air navigational facilities, as well as subsidies to air transport and aid to airports. In addition, it undertakes the programming of much of the transport development of the country and participates in the formulation of national transportation policy. Thus, there are three distinct categories of an executive nature in the federal government's role in transportation. These categories are (1) the administration of operating and policing functions such as supervision of safety of operations of the various modes; (2) the programming of federal investment, supervision of the expenditure of federal funds, and determination and collection of charges for the use of federal facilities; and (3) the formulation and development of national transportation policy, including the provision and administration of transportation for national defense purposes. Prior to the creation of the Department of Transportation, the task of administering the functions under the first category were divided between the regulatory agencies and the executive branch. Those in the other two categories, except for the administration of subsidies by the Civil Aeronautics Board and the Federal Maritime Commission, and the program for guaranteed loans to railroads by the Interstate Commerce Commission, were under executive control, with, however, practically no co-ordination of any kind.

ADMINISTRATIVE ORGANIZATION

The administrative tasks relating to federal participation in providing transportation services, other than those discharged by the Interstate Commerce Commission and the Civil Aeronautics Board, have been dispersed among a number of federal agencies. The National Security Resources Board, the Office of Defense Transportation, the National Advisory Committee for Aeronautics, the Department of the Treasury, the Department of the Army, and the Department of Commerce all participated without any co-ordinating machinery to unify their activities. The two major defects of this division of authority were in programming and the development of a coherent and unified national transportation policy.

Transport promotional programs lack central direction. Although the Federal-aid highway program, administered by the Bureau of Public Roads, and the merchant marine program administered by the Maritime Administration, are conducted under policy direction of the Undersecretary of Commerce for Transportation, no central leadership exists in the promotion of other transportation programs, or in relating each program with the others. To illustrate, air mail subsidies are administered by the CAB, while the FAA is responsible in other promotional areas for air transportation. The Corps of Engineers, Department of the Army, is responsible generally for rivers and harbors work, while the Coast Guard, Department of the Treasury is responsible for various aids to navigation. Both the Corps of Engineers and the Coast Guard have responsibility for safety in navigation. The shining example of uncoordinated promotion is, of course, the unplanned impact of the Federal-aid highway program on transit and traffic problems of some of our larger metropolitan areas. There is some degree of executive control of program funds through the Bureau of the Budget, but there is no central organization responsible for directing policy planning and coordination of these programs in the public interest.[8]

The second major defect in administrative organization was that there was no single authority in the executive branch of the government that could be held responsible for the formulation and execution of national transportation policy. The Undersecretary for Transportation in the Department of Commerce could not perform this task because he lacked control over many of the different agencies that administer transportation matters that are vital to national policy. Drastic reorganization of the executive branch of the government was as essential to the resolution of the critical transportation problems of this country as is reform in regulation.

PROPOSALS FOR REORGANIZATION

That reorganization of the executive branch of the government with regard to transportation is beset by serious difficulties is evidenced by the proposals of the many special commissions, committees, and

---

[8] *National Transportation Policy* (Doyle Report), p. 95.

study groups that have been created to examine the problems over the last 40 years.[9] Dearing and Owen list nine such groups that were set up in the 15 years down to 1949.[10] To these must be added the Sawyer, Hoover Commission, Doyle, and Landis reports.

The common theme running through the parts dealing with the organizational problems in the executive branch of the government was that some means of effecting co-ordination of the various activities, especially in programming and public investment, was necessary; but beyond this, agreement came to an end. The Sawyer Report[11] suggested that a central research group be established to evaluate and appraise all of the various promotional activities, but did not indicate to whom it would be responsible. The Hoover Commission recommended that all major nonregulatory transportation activities of the federal government be transferred to the Department of Commerce.[12] It proposed that the Office of Undersecretary of Transportation in the Department of Commerce be established[13] to deal with transportation matters assigned to the Department. The Commission rejected the idea of a Department of Transportation under a Secretary of Transportation who would be a member of the Cabinet. The Task Force of the Commission accepted the proposal advanced by Dearing and Owen for this type of organization. The organizational structure that was devised would have been according to modes of transportation, each division being under an assistant secretary.[14] The Doyle Report advanced essentially the same type of arrangement, except that it recommended organization along functional rather than modal lines.[15] The Landis Report rejected the idea of a Department of Transportation[16] on the ground that none of

[9] See D. I. Mackie, "The Necessity for a Federal Department of Transportation," *Journal of Law* (Emory University Law School, Atlanta, Georgia), Vol. VIII, No. 1 (1959), p. 46, for a detailed survey of these. See also *National Transportation Policy* (Doyle Report), pp. 97–98.

[10] Dearing and Owen, *op. cit.,* p. 382.

[11] *Unified and Coordinated Federal Program for Transportation* (Sawyer Report), Report to the President from the Secretary of Commerce, December 1, 1949 (Washington, D.C.: U.S. Government Printing Office, 1949), p. 20.

[12] Commission on the Organization of the Executive Branch of the Government, *Task Force Report on Regulatory Commissions* (Washington, D.C.: U.S. Government Printing Office, 1949), Appendix N, chap. iv.

[13] This was created in 1953, without, however, any substantial modifications of existing arrangements in the executive departments.

[14] Dearing and Owen, *op. cit.,* p. 391.

[15] *National Transportation Policy* (Doyle Report), pp. 111–15. It also recommended a Transportation Labor Board in the Department, only, however, to provide a forum for impartial discussion and analysis (*ibid.,* p. 681, n. 46).

[16] *Report on Regulatory Agencies to the President-Elect* (Landis Report), pp. 75–77.

the proposals so far had been based on sufficient experience to merit adoption. The report also took the position that the office of Undersecretary of Transportation is not sufficient for the task because, by virtue of the vast and important responsibilities of the executive branch in transport, these responsibilities cannot be subordinated to the Secretary of Commerce. The report therefore recommended that the development of the co-ordinating function be placed in the Executive Office of the President "in an office already constituted to perform staff and not personal functions for the President."[17] President Kennedy's message of April, 1962, omitted discussion of the problems of administrative reorganization.

THE DEPARTMENT OF TRANSPORTATION

President Johnson's Message, March 2, 1966[18]

In his message to Congress, President Johnson stated that "America today lacks a coordinated transportation system that permits travellers and goods to move conveniently and efficiently from one means of transportation to another, using the best characteristics of each." In order to coordinate the executive functions of the transportation agencies in a single coherent instrument of government which would give policy guidance and support for each means of transportation, he recommended that Congress establish a Cabinet-level Department of Transportation. He stated that the role of the Department would be to: coordinate the principal existing programs that promote transportation in America; bring new technology to a total transportation system by promoting research and development in cooperation with private industry; improve safety in every means of transportation; encourage private enterprise to take full and prompt advantage of new technological opportunities; encourage high-quality, low-cost service to the public; conduct systems analyses and planning to strengthen the weakest parts of today's system; and develop investment criteria and standards, and analytical techniques to assist all levels of government and industry in their transportation investments.

Coordination of the executive functions of various agencies of the government was to be achieved by consolidating in the Depart-

---

[17] *Ibid.*, p. 77.

[18] The message is printed in full in *Creating a Department of Transportation*, Hearings, Subcommittee on Government Operations, House of Representatives, 89th Cong., 2nd sess. (Washington, D.C.: U.S. Government Printing Office, 1966), pp. 36–49.

ment of Transportation, the Office of Undersecretary of Commerce for Transportation, the Bureau of Public Roads, and the federal-aid highway program, the Coast Guard, the Maritime Administration, the safety functions of the Civil Aeronautics Board, the safety and car service functions of the Interstate Commerce Commission, the Great Lakes Pilotage Administration, the St. Lawrence Seaway Development Cooperation, the Alaska Railroad, and certain minor transportation-related activities of other agencies. This list represented the consolidation into one department of the duties of those agencies whose primary functions are transportation promotion and safety. The economic regulatory functions of the Interstate Commerce Commission, the Civil Aeronautics Board, and the Federal Maritime Commission were to remain unchanged.

The President recommended that the airline subsidy program remain with the Civil Aeronautics Board because of its relation to air carrier service, but the Secretary of Transportation should participate in Civil Aeronautics Board proceedings that involve international aviation policy. The navigation program of the Corps of Engineers was to be left with that body, but the Secretary should be involved in the planning of water transportation projects. In addition, the Secretary, with the approval of the President was to issue standards and criteria for the economic evaluation of federal transportation investments generally. The secretaries of the Department of Transportation, and Housing and Urban Development were to recommend to the President, within one year after the new Department was established, the most effective means and procedures for a unified federal approach to urban transport problems.

One of the principal parts of the message related to safety in transportation. The President therefore recommended that there be created under the Secretary of Transportation a National Safety Transportation Board independent of the operating units of the Department. The Board was to consist of five members appointed by the President. He also recommended a new highway safety program that would be administered by the Secretary.

Other recommendations in the message related to: safety at sea; air accident compensation in international aviation; research and development; supersonic transport aircraft; aircraft noise; improved marine technology; high-speed ground transportation research and development; and systems research on transportation. Responsibilities for these matters were to be divided among different agencies for the present time.

Congressional Action

The Senate and the House promptly held extensive hearing on bills incorporating most of the President's recommendations to secure the viewpoints of all interested parties. There was general, although not unanimous agreement in support of the creation of a Department of Transportation, but wide divergence of opinion on the details of the bills introduced into both Houses of Congress. All of the witnesses, expressing views of the different modes, proposed amendments designed to protect their interests. Fears were expressed that the new Department would impinge severely on the regulatory functions of the Interstate Commerce Commission, the Civil Aeronautics Board and the Maritime Commission. Members of the committees insisted that every step would be taken to safeguard against this. Representatives of the different modes were also anxious to have specific representation in the new organization. This was because it was obvious from the proposed legislation that the new Secretary would be inflential in developing policy for the modes, and in critical regulatory issues involving them.

The most crucial issues in the proposed legislation related to safety regulation, investment criteria and standards for federal funds in transportation, and the respective roles of Congress and the Secretary on the latter, as well as the responsibility of the Secretary to Congress on the development of national transportation policy. The legislation as finally approved by the Senate and the House of Representatives placed safety regulation and investment criteria, with reservations, in the new Department, with the proviso that the criteria has to be approved by Congress.[19] The legislation was approved on October 15, 1966 and the Department placed in operation on April 1, 1967 with Alan S. Boyd, former Undersecretary of Transportation as the first Secretary of the Department of Transportation.[20]

The Department of Transportation Act, 1966

Section 2 of the act set forth the general objectives of the legislation. Among these objectives was the provision "to develop and rec-

[19] See *Creating a Department of Transportation, op. cit.,* and *Establish a Department of Transportation,* Hearings, Committee on Government Operations, U.S. Senate, 89th Cong., 2nd sess., (Washington, D.C., U.S. Government Printing Office, 1966); also *Department of Transportation Act,* House of Representatives, 89th Cong., 2nd sess., Report No. 1701, *Department of Transportation Act,* Report No. 2236, and *Establishing a Department of Transportation and for Other Purposes,* U.S. Senate, 89th Cong., 2nd sess., Calendar No. 1627, Report No. 1659 (Washington, D.C.: U.S. Government Printing Office, 1966).

[20] Public Law 89–670 (October 15, 1966).

ommend to the President and to the Congress for approval national transportation policies and programs to accomplish these objectives with full and appropriate consideration of the needs of the public, users, carriers, industry, labor and the national defense."

Section 3 established an executive department, known as the Department of Transportation under a Secretary who was to be appointed by the President by and with the advice and consent of the Senate. There was to be an Undersecretary similarly appointed who could act in the absence of the Secretary and who would perform such functions, powers, and duties as the Secretary prescribed. The law provided for four Assistant Secretaries appointed by the President to perform such duties as prescribed by the Secretary. There was also to be an Assistant Secretary for Administration. The section established within the Department, a Federal Highway Administration, a Federal Railroad Administration, a Federal Aviation Administration, and Transferred the Commandant of the Coast Guard to the Department. The office of Federal Highway Administrator was transferred under the title of Director of Public Roads as the operating head of the Bureau of Public Roads.

Section 4 contained provisions requiring consultation with other agencies of government to maintain a coordinated transportation system, and specifically provided that:

Nothing in this Act shall be construed to authorize, without appropriate action by Congress, the adoption, revision, or implementation of (A) any transportation policy, or (B) any investment standards or criteria. All orders and actions in the exercise of functions transferred were to be subject to judicial review in the same manner as before the transfer. The Secretary and the Secretary of Housing and Urban Development were to cooperate on their respective transportation policies and were to report within one year, and annually thereafter on studies and legislative recommendations. In addition, they were to report, within one year after the effective date of the Act, to the President and the Congress "on the logical and efficient organization and location of urban mass transportation functions in the Executive Branch."

Section 5 established within the Department a National Transportation Safety Board. It was to exercise the functions, duties, and powers transferred to the Secretary with regard to, (1) determining the cause or probable cause of transportation accidents and reporting the facts, and (2) reviewing on appeal the suspension, amendment, modification, revocation, or denial of any certificate or license issued by the Secretary or an administrator. The Board was to make public, among other things, (1) every recommendation made to the Secretary or an administrator, (2) every special study conducted, and (3) every action of the Board requesting the Secretary or an administrator to take action. The section specifically provided that "the Board shall be independent of the Secretary and the other offices and officers of the Department" in the exercise of its functions. Finally, the Board was to consist of five members appointed by the President with the consent of the Senate, to hold office for five years. Not more than three were to be from the same political party.

Section 6 transferred, in detail, provisions of numerous laws to the Secretary but specifically left to the various administrators the enforcement of the safety laws. This section also placed the administration of the Alaska Railroad in the hands of the Secretary.

Section 7 dealt with transportation investment standards. Subject to the requirement to cooperate with other federal agencies, the Secretary was:

to develop and revise standards and criteria consistent with national transportation policies, for the formulation and economic evaluation of all proposals for the investment of Federal funds in transportation equipment or facilities, except such proposals as are concerned with (1) the acquisition of transportation facilities or equipment by Federal agencies in providing transportation services for their own use; (2) an interoceanic canal located outside the contiguous United States; (3) defense features included at the direction of the Department of Defense in the design and construction of civil air, sea, and land transportation; (4) programs of foreign assistance; (5) water resource projects; or (6) grant-in-aid programs authorized by law. The standards and criteria developed or revised pursuant to this section shall be promulgated by the Secretary upon their approval by Congress.

The standards and criteria for economic evaluation of water resource projects are to be developed by the Water Resources Council.

For the purpose of such standards and criteria the primary direct navigation benefits of a water resource project are defined as the product of the savings to shippers using the waterway and the estimated traffic that would use the waterway; where the savings to shippers shall be construed to mean the difference between (a) the freight rates or charges prevailing at the time of the study for the movement by the alternative means and (b) those which would be charged on the proposed waterway; and where the estimate of traffic that would use the waterway will be based on such freight rates, taking into account projections of the economic growth of the area.

The Water Resources Council was expanded to include the Secretary of Transportation on matters pertaining to navigation features of water resource projects. Every survey, plan, or report formulated by a federal agency which includes a proposal as to which the Secretary has promulgated standards and criteria must be prepared in accordance with the information supplied by the Secretary for that purpose. Every proposal has to be coordinated with the Secretary and all other units of government, after which it will be transmitted to the President for his action.

Section 8 amended many laws to bring them into conformity with the new legislation, including the transfer of the St. Lawrence Seaway Development Corporation which was to report directly to the Secretary.

Section 14 directed the Secretary "to submit to the Congress within two years from the effective date of this Act, a proposed codification of all laws that contain the powers, duties, and functions transferred to or vested in the secretary or the Department by this Act."

CONCLUSION

The creation of the Department of Transportation marks a new turn in the federal approach to development and administration in national transport policy. It will bring together, under one head, about 100,000 employees and 31 agencies and bureaus dealing with transportation. It will administer about $6 billion of federal funds now devoted to transportation. The recommended budget for the fiscal year 1967–68 is $31.4 million. Thus, for the first time, a large part of the executive responsibilities of the federal government in transportation will be combined under one head with Cabinet status. In addition, the legislation contemplates that the Secretary will be the executive spokesman for national transport policy and will be responsible for developing and initiating measures for transport as a whole,—regulated and nonregulated. How all of this will be carried out, and how the multifarious duties and responsibilities assigned to the Secretary will be coordinated into a coherent program remains to be seen. The legislation gives little clue as to how this will be accomplished, and probably could not have done so. The sheer task of internal organization will take some time and it is unlikely that any very definitive stance will be observable before the election of 1968, at which time a new Secretary might take over, with very different ideas from those of his predecessor. Effective implementation of the legislation will obviously take some time, and working relationships between the Secretary, the Congress, and the regulatory agencies are likely to emerge but slowly and quite possibly with considerable friction.

Although the legislation clearly indicates that a sharp line is to be drawn between regulation and administration, the basis of a satis-

FIGURE 21–1

DEPARTMENT OF TRANSPORTATION—ORGANIZATION AND RESPONSIBILITIES

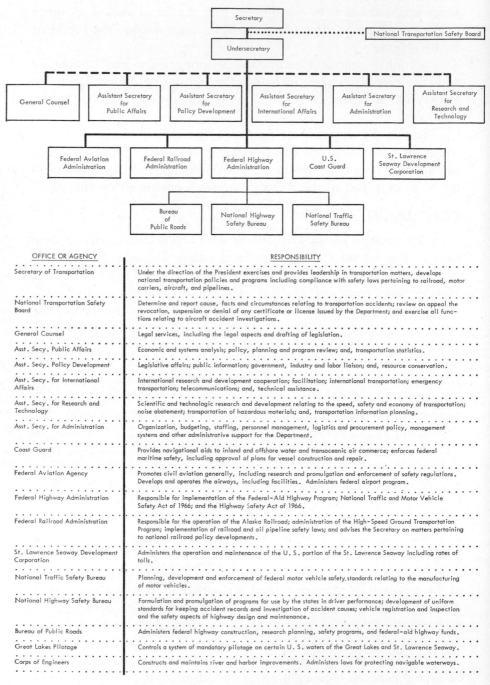

OFFICE OR AGENCY	RESPONSIBILITY
Secretary of Transportation	Under the direction of the President exercises and provides leadership in transportation matters, develops national transportation policies and programs including compliance with safety laws pertaining to railroad, motor carriers, aircraft, and pipelines.
National Transportation Safety Board	Determine and report cause, facts and circumstances relating to transportation accidents; review on appeal the revocation, suspension or denial of any certificate or license issued by the Department; and exercise all functions relating to aircraft accident investigations.
General Counsel	Legal services, including the legal aspects and drafting of legislation.
Asst. Secy. Public Affairs	Economic and systems analysis; policy, planning and program review; and, transportation statistics.
Asst. Secy. Policy Development	Legislative affairs; public information; government, industry and labor liaison; and, resource conservation.
Asst. Secy. for International Affairs	International research and development cooperation; facilitation; international transportation; emergency transportation; telecommunications; and, technical assistance.
Asst. Secy. for Research and Technology	Scientific and technologic research and development relating to the speed, safety and economy of transportation; noise abatement; transportation of hazardous materials; and, transportation information planning.
Asst. Secy. for Administration	Organization, budgeting, staffing, personnel management, logistics and procurement policy, management systems and other administrative support for the Department.
Coast Guard	Provides navigational aids to inland and offshore water and transoceanic air commerce; enforces federal maritime safety, including approval of plans for vessel construction and repair.
Federal Aviation Agency	Promotes civil aviation generally, including research and promulgation and enforcement of safety regulations. Develops and operates the airways, including facilities. Administers federal airport program.
Federal Highway Administration	Responsible for implementation of the Federal-Aid Highway Program; National Traffic and Motor Vehicle Safety Act of 1966; and the Highway Safety Act of 1966.
Federal Railroad Administration	Responsible for the operation of the Alaska Railroad; administration of the High-Speed Ground Transportation Program; implementation of railroad and oil pipeline safety laws; and advises the Secretary on matters pertaining to national railroad policy developments.
St. Lawrence Seaway Development Corporation	Administers the operation and maintenance of the U. S. portion of the St. Lawrence Seaway including rates of tolls.
National Traffic Safety Bureau	Planning, development and enforcement of federal motor vehicle safety standards relating to the manufacturing of motor vehicles.
National Highway Safety Bureau	Formulation and promulgation of programs for use by the states in driver performance; development of uniform standards for keeping accident records and investigation of accident causes; vehicle registration and inspection and the safety aspects of highway design and maintenance.
Bureau of Public Roads	Administers federal highway construction, research planning, safety programs, and federal-aid highway funds.
Great Lakes Pilotage	Controls a system of mandatory pilotage on certain U. S. waters of the Great Lakes and St. Lawrence Seaway.
Corps of Engineers	Constructs and maintains river and harbor improvements. Administers laws for protecting navigable waterways.

Prepared by the Transportation Association of America.

factory working relationship between the Department and the Commissions will have to be established. For example, the controversial question of railroad consolidation may give rise to some fundamental conflicts of policy. The Interstate Commerce Commission is proceeding, or endeavoring to proceed, with railroad consolidation on a decidedly *ad hoc* basis. The Secretary may not agree with this, yet some major moves may be made without his cooperation, a step that would most likely prevent any successful attempt to secure an overall approach to the problem. Moreover, agreement between the Secretary and the Commission may not even be possible, in which case the issue may be tossed into the lap of Congress. Similarly, controversies seem to be in the offing over strictly regulatory issues. The Secretary appears to be much more in favor of hard competition than is the Commission. Mr. Mackey, Assistant Secretary for Transportation Policy Development is reported to have said,

> Had the department been in existence over the past few years—the cases we probably would have taken part in would have included every major rail merger at the Interstate Commerce Commission, every major route case—such as the pending Trans-Pacific case—at the Civil Aeronautics Board and, perhaps, even the 'Big John' and the 'Ingot Molds' cases at the I.C.C. . . . Someone has already solved transportation's easy problems for only hard ones are left. Our approach to regulation is that it is good only when it enhances the benefits flowing naturally from a market economy. Regulation for the sake of regulation is, we feel, undesirable.[21]

The Department has already sharply criticised an examiner's report on recommended procedures to widen the use of the Interstate Highway System by motor freight common carriers. The Department contended that the proposed regulations would place an unwarranted procedural burden on any regular route carrier wishing to include any part of the Interstate System as a regular operating route.[22] The impact of intervention of this sort on the regulatory independence of the Interstate Commerce Commission will bear watching.

One of the main purposes of the legislation, and the most controversial, related to standards and criteria for the investment of federal funds in transportation. The law establishes no criteria for highways and air transport but leaves these for the Secretary to develop for the approval of Congress. How he will go about this matter remains to be seen but it is safe to say that the administration of this section of the law will promote more controversy than its enactment. The determination of the appropriate investment in these modes vis-à-vis the

---

[21] The American Waterways Operators, Inc., *Weekly Letter,* May 6, 1967, pp. 3–4.
[22] *Ex Parte* MC-65 (1967).

railroads presents a problem that will require much more "equalization of competitive opportunities" by other means than exists at the present time, if a meaningful resolution is to ensue. The law itself establishes the standards for investment in waterways. The provisions represented a distinct victory for the waterway interests by rejecting the order of the Bureau of the Budget of November, 1964, to the Army Engineers requiring the latter to make their economic evaluations on the basis of cost of service in the area affected by the construction of the navigation project, using as the basis for such calculations water-compelled rates by other modes which might be expected to be in effect after the waterway project was completed. Instead, the comparison is to be that of those rates which would be charged on the proposed waterway with those being charged by other modes before the waterway comes into existence. In other words, the results that would ensue from competition are ignored. The effects on policy for federal expenditure are bound to be slow in forthcoming, if, indeed, they emerge at all. One would have to be very optimistic to assume that marked changes in public investment in transport are to be obtained through the operation of the present section 7.[23]

The provisions of the law regarding safety in transportation provoked almost as much controversy as those relating to investment. Although the National Safety Board is supposed to be autonomous, fears were voiced that the investigation of accidents, the determination of their causes, and the steps to be taken to prevent their recurrence were ultimately under the same control. Many felt that investigation and safety regulation should be regarded as separate tasks and should be placed in independent hands. This had been done for air transport when these functions were separated in 1958 between the Civil Aeronautics Board which was given the responsibility for investigation, and the Federal Aeronautics Administration which handled safety regulation. Opponents of the new legislation felt that it returned to the unsatisfactory conditions that prevailed prior to 1958. The future record under the National Safety Board will have to supply the answer to this question, although there seem to be good reasons to suppose that it is better equipped to carry out these assignments for rail, water, and motor carriers than the agencies previously charged with them.

The problems of urban transport were avoided in the legislation

---

[23] The law does not seem to give the Department of Transportation a particularly potent weapon with which to combat "Mike Kirwan's Big Ditch" (*Reader's Digest,* June 1967, pp. 59–64), if it is disposed to do so.

except that the Secretary of Transportation and the Secretary of Housing and Urban Development were to study the problem and report to Congress within one year after the effective date of the act on the organization and location of urban mass transportation functions in the executive branch. Thus, one of the most critical and pressing of the transportation problems requiring coordination and unification at the federal level has been postponed to the future without any indication of the possible outcome. This will certainly handicap the Secretary in developing criteria and recommending federal investments, particularly in highways.

The passage of the Department of Transportation Act marks a clear-cut turning point in the respective roles of regulation and administration in national transportation policy. It seems quite safe to say that regulation will occupy a relatively less, and perhaps absolutely less, important role in transport than it has done in the last 80 years. Policy development is now to be focussed in the executive branch of the government. Whether this will result in severe inroads on regulation remains to be seen, but the Department is bound to have strong influence on regulatory theory. If the Department follows an aggressive approach to the implementation of "pervasive competition" much present regulatory detail will vanish. The pressures of changing technology are working inexorably in that direction. These two factors are bound to modify the scope of activities of the Interstate Commerce Commission and the Civil Aeronautics Board. What will be the role of regulation in transportation as we have known it remains to be seen. The policy of Commissions of protecting regulated carriers from competition among themselves seems destined to suffer severe curtailment, and the Interstate Commerce Commission's "double standard" for competition among regulated carriers and between them and nonregulated ones has probably gone by the boards. A new day has dawned for the development and application of national transport policy but the weather which will accompany it has yet to be ascertained.

PART V

Urban Transport

THE URBAN
TRANSPORTATION
PROBLEM

INTRODUCTION

The basic problems of intercity and interstate transportation have had the benefit of thorough examination over the years. Even with the relatively recent impact of new technologies and the emergence of the modern transport structure, these have come to be reasonably well understood. This does not mean that solutions to all the difficulties have been worked out at either the management level or that of public policy. There is anything but unanimity of opinion on what ought to be done to meet the radically altered circumstances of the last quarter of a century. But the exhaustive factual exploration and analysis at all levels of investigation have provided the information upon which action can be based. The outlines of the problems themselves and the lines upon which the attack on them must take place are established with sufficient clarity that concerted action is now possible. The principle obstacles to prompt and constructive reform at the present time arise from conflicting interests, the readjustments among agencies and carriers that are inescapable, and the sheer inertia that the accumulation of past policies has induced.

In contrast to this, urban transportation, with all the complexities that it involves, is almost unexplored territory. Even the scope of the problem has not been outlined. Thus the Doyle Report states: "The basic function of urban transportation systems is to move people, the basic function of cities is to provide people with a place to live and work with comfort and convenience. We have tended to lose sight of these fundamentals in the auto age and have concentrated on moving and storing vehicles to the exclusion of analysing the functional transportation problem, and taking appropriate action."[1] This completely

[1] *National Transportation Policy* (Doyle Report), Preliminary Draft of a Report to the Senate Committee on Interstate and Foreign Commerce, 87th Congress 1st session (Washington, D.C.: U.S. Government Printing Office, 1961), p. 596.

ignores the fact that the movement of people is only one phase of the urban transportation problem, and that the enormous amount of freight traffic has its origin and destination, or both, in the urban centers. In addition, these centers are the points through which people move to and from other places. After a brief examination of the metropolitan transportation dilemma, the factors affecting it, and alternative solutions that have been advanced, Wilfred Owen says:

We have the assurance, therefore, that the problem of congestion in urban areas has been precipitated by the automobile; that the automobile, on the contrary, has been our escape from congestion; that the automobile and mass transportation are both guilty of promoting congestion; and finally that neither is the primary culprit, but rather a host of other factors that have resulted, thanks to modern technology, in the successful attempt to crowd too many people and too much economic activity into too little space. And of the city itself we are told that preservation of the vast investment in urban America will assure both economic salvation and atomic annihilation.[2]

It is clear that the present difficulties connected with urban transportation are the result of the impact of technological developments in transport. The most immediate and probably the most important of these is the result of the development of the automobile. However, it should be noted that transportation has always presented serious problems in the large cities of the world, and it is not self-evident that this is worse today than in the past. Rising standards of living and increased mobility of people have introduced new questions of how to service their traffic needs economically. These have brought severe repercussions on land utilization and location of activity, together with individualized passenger movements heretofore unknown. New arrangements are called for, and to date the focus of attention has been on passenger traffic.

The same forces, however, have also affected the means of moving freight and the distribution of goods. The impact here has been as pronounced as on the movement of people. Yet almost no attention has been given to this problem, and practically no systematic analysis of it has been undertaken to date. We are almost totally uninformed as to the way that transportation has shaped the structure of our cities, or conversely, how transport has responded to meet changes induced by other forces. Transportation in cities is as important for moving goods as it is for moving people. The relationship of intercity to intracity movements has always had an important influence on urban transport

problems. Before the automobile a reasonable line of demarcation between the two existed because of the nature of transport technology.
Some of this still persists, but the automobile has introduced a radical
change because much of both intercity and intracity traffic mingles on
the streets and highways in the metropolitan area in an indiscriminate
way. To date, no means of separating these two kinds of automobile
traffic has been devised, although a certain amount of by-passing of
through traffic has been developed for the smaller areas. In other words,
the terminal problem has taken on a fundamentally different aspect,
and so far we have taken no steps to analyze it as a whole.

Public investment in transport for intercity traffic has introduced
severe complications to the problems of total resource allocation to
transportation as well as economical allocation and utilization among
the modes and carriers. In metropolitan transportation these problems
focus on the impact of motor vehicle transport although air transportation, particularly recent developments, has introduced a new dimen-
sion. The participation of local, state, and federal governments in the
provision of highways within the urban areas means that each has a
significant role in supplying the facilities, the most important for the
main routes falling into the hands of the state and federal governments. The federal government provides 90 per cent of the funds for
the national defense interstate system, which constitutes key arteries
in the metropolitan motor routes, as well as 50 per cent for the ABC
system.[3] The participation by the three levels of government means,
first, that all of them are directly involved in planning the principal
highway and street systems; second, that financing of the routes entails the development of devices by each for raising the necessary
revenues; third, that intercity and metropolitan transport movements
become inextricably intertwined as soon as they enter the urban
area, at least under present programs of development; and fourth,
that a very large proportion of the local traffic movement is removed
from the direct controls of the price mechanism, which complicates
the problem of congestion and makes it particularly difficult to ascertain the appropriate role for mass passenger traffic systems. Thus,
public investment in transportation presents its most serious complications in the urban areas.

In addition, therefore, to the economic problems of urban transportation, there is that of the appropriate type of governmental organi-

---

[3] According to the Doyle Report, 38.6 per cent of all federal highway funds were
spent in urban areas between July 1, 1956, and December 31, 1959. See *National Transportation Policy*, p. 594.

zation to deal with the issues. Every metropolitan area has its own unique situation, yet each is affected by the policies of government at the different levels of participation. The challenge to public administration is as serious and complex as it is to economics. Moreover, transportation is only one of the many aspects of metropolitan governmental questions today, and cannot very well be dealt with in isolation because of the interaction of policies connected with all of them, particularly those arising from public expenditures and taxation.

EMERGENCE OF THE PROBLEM

The modern problem of transportation in the urban and metropolitan centers of this country stems from the impact of the new technologies on the means of moving people and goods. In this respect, it is primarily the product of the automotive vehicle. This has induced a change in the structure of urban centers and may be a strongly contributing factor to the increasing urbanization of the United States. It may be doubted, however, that transportation is the primary force in the latter development. Mechanization of all phases of production is probably the most decisive factor, but transportation is one, and a very important, aspect of the change. What the characteristics of urbanization would have been if the individualization of transportation had not been part of the movement is impossible to say; but the effect of the changes in the means of transport has been to challenge the typical structure of the metropolitan center, and to engender shifts in the location of activities in it in a way that is most baffling to those who are trying to resolve the problems that have been created. Plans and programs based on the assumption that the structures which grew up around the earlier means of transport are developed on the premise that the basic framework has been created, and that the problem of public authority is to adapt current means of transportation to this situation. On the other hand, the part that transportation has played in creating these structures, and the way it may compel modification of them, does not seem to have occupied a very prominent role so far in the formulation of public policy.

The Rise of the City

In their economic functions, at least, the important cities of the world arose as trade and commercial centers. They were the focal points of surrounding regions, and gateways between them and the outside world. Because of this, and the limitations imposed by land transport, they were typically located on waterways, frequently with access to the sea. Their geographic structure was strongly water-oriented and their size severely limited by horse and foot transportation. They were the meeting place of land and water routes, and until the development of the railroad, all of the cities of this country were located on water facilities. The rise of the railroad as the principal means of land transportation removed many of the limitations on location, at the same time that it made possible the concentration of industrial production at the key transport points of the country.

Industrialization and Transport

The application of mechanical power to production made modern industrialism possible in the manufacturing processes, and its utilization for transportation made it economical to assemble raw materials, bring in the food and other needs of the urban population, and provide market accessibility for the products of the factories. Rail terminal facilities and rail-water connections thus became the focal points of the industrial activities of the cities. Until additional means were provided for the movement of goods and people within the centers, transport was a severely restraining factor on the spread of the urban area. All industrial and commercial activity was closely dependent upon rail connections. Residence was strictly confined by location of employment because of the lack of commercial passenger facilities.

The first major break-through in this pattern came with the application of electricity to transportation. The development of the street and interurban as well as the subway and elevated railways, at the close of the nineteenth and the beginning of the twentieth centuries made possible the growth of residential areas independent of the railroads as such. They still, however, imposed upon the city dweller the necessity of residing in close proximity to these new passenger agencies as well as providing ready access to his place of work. In other words, this means of urban passenger transportation required concentration of population at both ends of the travel route; a high density of traffic was indispensable. The street railway provided no significant change for the movement of goods, but it did introduce important modifications in the urban residence patterns, as well as facilitating the rapid growth of cities. It was this transport innovation that conditioned the geographic structure of American cities until after World War I. By that time the street and interurban railways clearly faced an uncertain future, although one eminent student of transportation stated in 1927: "There is yet no satisfying evidence that the space-occupying automobile will dominate the city streets, nor that the highway will provide as good a bearing surface as the rail where mass movements of passengers are concerned."[4] On the other hand, there were those who felt that this means of transport had a future of no more than twenty years.[5]

Revolution by the Automobile

The extremely rapid decline of mass passenger transportation by rail and the crisis facing rapid transit, even in those cities where it remains, are the result of the revolution in urban transport brought about by the use of the automobile. From a situation in which literally all urban passenger traffic for any distance was provided by rail at the end of World War I, the movement of people has changed to that whereby over half of all persons entering and leaving metropolitan areas with populations over 250,000 are traveling by automobile. The percentage in the large cities ranges all the way from 17 per cent in New York to 30 per cent in Chicago, 64.8 per cent in San Francisco, and 95 per cent in Los Angeles. The role of rapid transit assumes slightly more important proportions for weekday movement of people entering the central districts, except for New York, the percentages being 83 for New York, 66.8 for Chicago, 32.1 for San Francisco, and 31 for Los Angeles. The shift, however, especially in terms of the impact on urban transport facilities, is not quite so simple as these figures might indicate because of peak-hour movements in the mornings and evenings, five days a week, for a total of twenty hours per week. Thus, 90 per cent of this peak traffic for the central business district of New York moved by public carriers, and 71.5 per cent of it in Philadelphia.[6] In Los Angeles, 86.7 per cent of all home-to-work movements on an average weekday in 1958 was by automobile, but 54.4 per cent of the revenue passengers of the Los Angeles Metropolitan Transit Authority were workers, and 85 per cent of these rode during the peak hours. Only 7.5 per cent of all persons traveling to work used transit, however, which means that a mere 6.4 per cent of the working population used rapid transit and 85 per cent of this was in the peak hours. On the other hand, 52.5 per cent of the persons in the central business district at

[4] Stuart Daggett, *Principles of Inland Transportation* (1st ed.; New York: Harper & Bros., 1928), p. 98.

[5] *Ibid.*, p. 97. For the meteoric career of interurban railways, see G. W. Hilton and J. F. Due, *The Electric Interurban Railways in America* (Stanford: Stanford University Press, 1960).

[6] Owen, *op. cit.*, chaps. ii and iii. The above figures were taken from the 1956 edition of Owen, but they have changed only slightly since then. A different classification used by Owen in the revised edition makes comparison difficult. See Table 8 in appendix of each edition.

the time of peak accumulation were brought in by public transit vehicles, according to a 1957 count.[7] Among other things, this is a clear indication that the central business district is of much less significance as a place of employment in Los Angeles than it is in the other large cities.

Urban passenger transportation is not merely a matter of moving people to and from work. It also involves traffic for shopping, arrivals and departures at the terminals of intercity agencies, airports, docks and railroad depots, and to a limited extent bus terminals. It also includes travel to and from the metropolitan areas for business, recreational, and other reasons. It is in the intercity traffic rather than within the centers themselves that the automobile has assumed the overwhelming role, 90 per cent of intercity travel at the present time being by private car. Yet a large part of this enters into the urban complex because all of the traffic destined to or originating in the city is part of the metropolitan traffic pattern. Moreover, the statistics for the leading counties in this country indicate that there is one passenger car for every three persons, or one per family. This ranges from 5.3 persons per car or 1.8 families per car in New York to 2.3 persons per car or 0.8 families per passenger car in Los Angeles. These two counties rank the highest in population and in car registrations; Los Angeles is first in truck registrations and New York third in the United States, and they mark almost the extreme limits of persons per passenger car and families per car. No counties have fewer persons per car than Los Angeles—Wayne County, Michigan, Nassau County, New York, and Dallas County, Texas, have 0.7 households per car, Los Angeles has 0.8. New York has the highest number of persons per car and the highest number of families. Philadelphia and Cook County, Illinois, rank second and third. Cook County and Los Angeles have the largest number of truck registrations, with Los Angeles ranking first in both cars and trucks.[8]

The radical change brought about by the automobile in the movement of people in the urban centers has been accompanied by parallel shifts in the transportation of goods. Unfortunately, quantitative information on this aspect of the urban transport revolution is almost completely unavailable. The volume of traffic within the metropolitan

[7] Coverdale and Colpitts, Consulting Engineers, *A Study of Public Transportation Needs in the Area Served by the Los Angeles Metropolitan Transit Authority* (New York, May, 1959). No comparable figures are available since 1957.

[8] Automobile Manufacturers Association, *Automobile Facts and Figures* (Detroit, Mich., 1966), p. 22. The average for the 15 leading counties in the United States in terms of car registration is 2.8 persons per car and 0.8 households per car.

areas that is moved by the various agencies is an unknown quantity. For the greater part, it is divided between rail and truck facilities, although water plays its part in a number of the more important centers. Pipe lines for water, gas, and petroleum would have to be included if a complete picture were to be obtained. The critical movements, however, rest with the rails and the trucks because they perform the bulk of the distributive functions within the urban centers, and the trucks also use the city streets in connection with their intercity haulage. Some idea of the role of the truck is afforded by the estimate that "80 per cent of the freight transported in Southern California is distributed in vehicles that collect goods at only one origin and deliver in relatively small amounts to many scattered destinations. Another 10 per cent is distributed to scattered destinations by pipelines; and the remaining 10 per cent is moved in relatively large quantities from origin to a single destination (from mine to factory for example)."[9] The Chicago study estimated that trucks accounted for 21.9 per cent of all weighted vehicle trips made on the average weekday in 1956 in the study area.[10]

The terminal facilities for rail and air transport are relatively fixed, possibly for a long time. Water terminals are permanent from the standpoint of urban traffic planning. Truck terminals are, for the most part, dependent on the other modes, and the location of the customers. The movement of goods by this means is therefore dependent on the structure of the urban center which is served. For the immediate present it must be assumed that the intracity traffic which relies upon the terminals of rail, water, and air transport will focus on those points. Industrial activity that must be served directly by rail or water transport will have to locate accordingly or at least be accommodated by the extension of rail spur lines. The remainder will be able to respond to the influence of other forces. This does not warrant the assumption that manufacturing that is dependent on rails will continue to be concentrated in central city areas, because the greater flexibility in the movement of products by the automotive vehicle makes it possible to locate in outlying districts that are served by the railroads.

The Inertia of the Past

One final point should be mentioned in connection with the emergence of the present urban transport problem. The enormous con-

[9] Southern California Research Council, *An Approach to an Orderly and Efficient Transportation System for the Southern California Metropolis* (Los Angeles: Occidental College, 1961), p. 37.

[10] Department of Public Works and Buildings, State of Illinois, *Chicago Area Transportation Study*, Vol. II (Springfield, Ill., 1960), p. 48.

centration of economic activity in the central areas of the large cities of this country has resulted in a huge capital investment in land, buildings, and other facilities. This creates inertia and vested interest against decentralization, with its consequent obsolescence and decline in property values. This in itself is a serious obstacle to adaptation to new conditions, especially when the latter take place rapidly. Efforts of downtown businessmen's associations and other organizations to halt the feared blight of the central city areas by counteracting the centrifugal influence of the automobile is evidence of this, as is also the well-nigh universal assumption that other and more effective means of surface transport must be developed if strangulation is to be avoided. The historic pattern of the modern city based upon the earlier means of transportation dies a hard death.

TRANSPORT AND THE URBAN STRUCTURE

Transport and Urban Development

It has already been pointed out that the rise of the modern metropolitan center with its high degree of concentration of population and industry came with the development of land transport by rail. The ensuing concentration was most marked where the railroads joined water facilities that gave easy access to heavy raw materials, and markets to other countries. At the same time, mass rapid transit by rail, and freight movement by the same means, meant that industry had to be concentrated where immediate rail transport was available. In addition, residential location was conditioned by the proximity of rail transport, which in turn depended upon a high density of traffic movement if the service was to be profitable at a reasonable price. Thus the large metropolitan center developed within relatively confined geographic limits. This was the typical structure at the end of World War I.

The growth and importance of electricity and electrical transmission reduced, or even eliminated, many of the advantages of concentration as far as the source of mechanical power was concerned, and the increasing efficiency of telecommunications operated in the same direction. Pipe-line transportation of petroleum and natural gas had a similar effect. The decisive factor as far as transportation developments were concerned, however, came with the utilization of the automotive vehicle in its various forms. Much of the transport was still dependent on water and rail, but industrial production was no longer bound by a working population dependent upon rails for their means of transport. Shopping and other centers were freed from similar restrictions. It is important to recognize the fact that if modern industrial life had grown up around present-day means of communication and the automobile, current concentration in central cities would not have emerged, or at any rate it would have been vastly different from the present pattern. The powerful forces which these new developments have generated raise the pertinent question of whether the central city area as we know it today can be saved, especially by intensified attempts to retain or revive the means by which it was created. In other words, the study of metropolitan transportation today must recognize three issues: First, there is the present problem of intense concentration of traffic and the pressing need to do something about it; second, there are the powerful forces making for decentralization that must be reckoned with at the same time that the problem of concentration is being handled; and third, there are the pattern and character of the metropolitan center of the future as it is being conditioned by the newer technologies, as it may be compelled by defense requirements, and as we may wish to shape it by sociological considerations. For those who would mold the future of the cities according to neatly devised plans that can be detailed on drawing boards, it is well to offer the reminder that, given the conditions that were in existence prior to the new transport technologies, it is unlikely that they would have been able to plan urban areas materially different from those that are now the source of our difficulties.[11]

The Changing Economic Function of the Central City

Probably the most notable feature of urban change since World War I has been the rapid growth of fringes and the loss of population in the central core areas of the cities. This has been accompanied by a pronounced shift in the employment patterns in the central city areas, denoting a corresponding change in their economic functions. As population has shifted to the suburbs, the neighborhood retail trade has accompanied it. This has been more rapid in some metropolitan areas than in others; but in the thirteen largest metropolitan centers in the

---

[11] "It would seem best to define the public transit problem in urban areas as that of finding ways to meet these transit riders' different needs and requirements with reasonable economy and to reject those approaches to the public transit problem that place the emphasis upon reshaping the city and its growth pattern to suit certain aesthetic tastes of particular groups. The latter approach not only raises issues of political philosophy and morality in a democratic society but also is likely to be self-defeating, for the technological forces at work reshaping our cities are numerous and not observably very sensitive to manipulation or modification by the presence, or lack of presence, of public transit." John R. Meyer, John F. Kain and Martin Wohl, *Technology and Urban Transportation* (Santa Monica, Calif.: Rand Corp., June, 1962), p. 40.

country the central cities have all registered a decline in their retail trade employment, and the central business districts have registered an even sharper decline. A similar shift, although not as severe, has occurred in employment in the wholesale trades. Manufacturing employment has also declined, but the pattern is somewhat more complex. The central cities have been experiencing this transition since the beginning of the century, but it has not affected all types of manufacturing in the same way. "More and more the central city has come to specialize in the 'communications oriented' segment of manufacturing, the uncertain and the exotic type of manufacturing specialization. And there is every reason to expect that to the extent that manufacturing remains in the central city these forms of specialization will grow more pronounced still." [12] Employment in office jobs exhibit less recognizable changes. Financial institutions of various kinds have always found the central cities to be the most satisfactory focus of their activities. According to Vernon, in eight metropolitan areas in 1947, every major branch of the financial community—banking, insurance, and security dealers —had more than four fifths of its employment in the central cities. These also attracted advertising agencies, employment agencies, management advisory services, and addressing and mailing services, so that in 1948 the thirteen central cities (covered in the Vernon study) accounted for 94 per cent of the employment in their metropolitan areas' business services.[13] Yet despite this, there was an outward distribution of employment in these activities. Vernon summarizes this by stating that office activities in the nation are expanding and will continue to expand, but apart from this he sees only a growing obsolescence in the rest of the central city beyond its central business district. The outward movement of people will be matched by an outward movement of jobs. Beyond the central business district, but within the confines of the central city, there is likely to be a long-run decline in the intense use of space for sites and homes; and he sees little prospect of anything that will halt this trend.[14] Whether this evaluation is too extreme may give rise to differences of opinion, but it certainly seems to be in keeping with the influences of transportation that have been so power-

[12] Vernon, *The Changing Economic Function of the Central City* (New York: Committee for Economic Development, 1959), p. 54.

[13] *Ibid.,* pp. 56–57.

[14] It may be noted that the *Chicago Area Transportation Study* does not seem to support this view. It expects stability for 1980 in the completely built-up parts of that urban region. It does not discuss shifts in the types of activities. For a summary presentation of this study, see J. B. Lansing, *Transportation and Economic Policy* (New York: The Free Press, 1966), chap. 15.

ful in the past, the greater availability of less expensive sites for homes and plants, and the rising standards of living of the population.

The Los Angeles Industrial Structure

Resolution of the transportation problems that have arisen in the development of the modern metropolitan centers must take into consideration the influence of transportation on the changes that have occurred, and vice versa. One of the vital questions is the effect that transportation has on the pattern of the structure, on the one hand, and the extent to which transportation may be utilized to mold the structure, on the other. Little investigation on this score has been carried out to date. The present author undertook a research project the purpose of which was to throw some light, if possible, on the influence of the modes of transport on the location of industrial activity within the Los Angeles area. This influence will probably vary from one metropolitan center to another, but Los Angeles, because of its rise to eminence with the growth of the automobile, is a particularly interesting laboratory. Here, it may be assumed that the influence of the automotive vehicle has been of greater significance than anywhere else. The author therefore endeavored to ascertain the pattern of locational development since 1920, this date being the starting point because of the area's phenomenal growth since then, and also because it ushered in the automobile era.

The center of the city of Los Angeles is located on the Los Angeles River just after it passes from the north through the gap between the Santa Monica and San Gabriel mountains. This point is where the routes from the east, after entering Southern California through the only two mountain passes available, cut through the Puente Hills to converge on the main entrance from the north. It was through these two avenues of approach that the railroads met at the original center which, in 1890, was a small city of 50,000 people without any significant access to the sea. The railroad pattern of the area fanned out west to Santa Monica Bay and south to San Pedro. The advantages of port facilities finally cast the lot to the region to the south; and in 1909, Wilmington and San Pedro were consolidated to become the port of Los Angeles, twenty-two miles from the central city. By this time the railroad structure of the metropolitan area was established almost precisely as it is today. (See Figure 22–1.)

In 1924, which was the approximate beginning of the phenomenal growth of the Los Angeles metropolitan area, industrial activity was confined to the central city served by railroads and street railways,

FIGURE 22-1

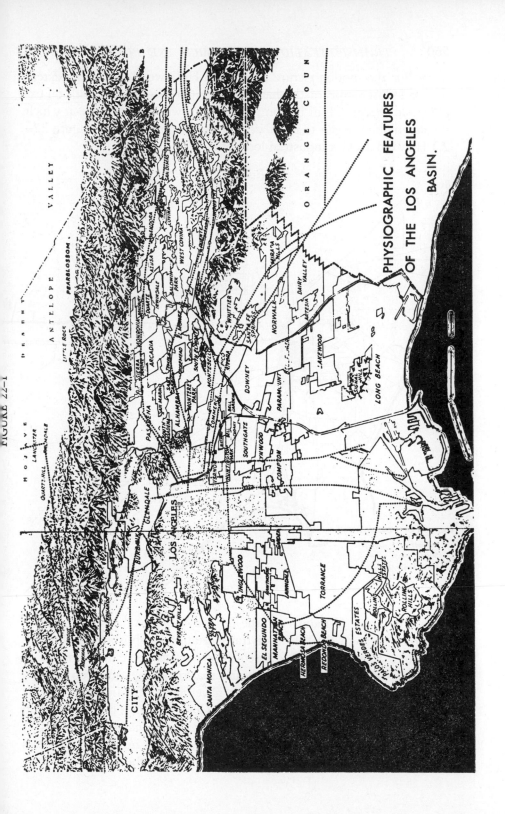

PHYSIOGRAPHIC FEATURES
OF THE LOS ANGELES
BASIN.

except for the motion-picture industry in Hollywood, and some extension of industry toward the harbor, particularly connected with oil exploitation at Signal Hill in Long Beach. This was also the time at which the automobile began to exert its powerful influence. (See Figure 22–2.) How did it affect industrial location?

FIGURE 22–2

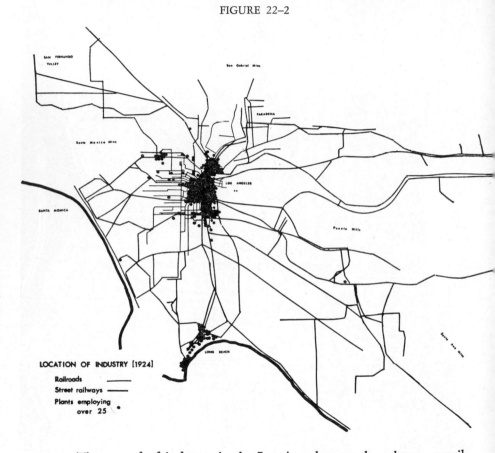

LOCATION OF INDUSTRY [1924]

Railroads ———
Street railways ———
Plants employing ·
    over 25

The spread of industry in the Los Angeles area has shown a striking conformity to the fabric of transportation established by the railroad lines forty years ago. Moreover, there has been little change in these lines since then, which indicates that they have not been built to accommodate the new locations that have developed. Industrial plants (identified by the Standard Industrial Classification) have located in all directions from the center of the city, the dispersion in terms of distance being as pronounced for those with five hundred employees or more as for those with less, and as marked for those not located on spur lines as for those that are. Furthermore the dispersion of plants not located on spur lines shows a similar pattern, with more clusters, however, characterizing the spread. It is also instructive to note that the pattern follows the rail fabric, with a relatively minor exception in the Hollywood area.

The service industries (Standard Industrial Classification) show a similar type of dispersion over the metropolitan area, although somewhat less oriented to railroads and rail spur lines. The major departure here is in the so-called "Wilshire corridor" from the center of the city west for a distance of twelve miles, and in the adjacent Hollywood area. It is in this region, and especially in those activities employing from 50 to 250 employees, that complete independence of rail transport is evident.[15]

The first feature of the development in Los Angeles that seems clear is that the plants in the metropolitan area employing fifty or more people are located along routes marked out by rail transportation before the automotive vehicle played any part. The only exception to this is the Wilshire corridor and the Hollywood area, where the industries are almost all of the service type. The second feature is that there is a remarkably uniform dispersion of all industries, particularly over the areas to the north, south, and west. There is a greater concentration of all activities in the central city area, but a greater total of all plant locations in the larger metropolitan area. Finally, the service activities are heavily oriented to the west side of the central city, to the Wilshire corridor, and to the Hollywood area. (See Figures 22–3 and 22–4.)

The influence of the automobile on industrial location in Los Angeles would thus appear to be twofold. First of all, it has engendered the dispersion of industry in all directions along the transport routes carved out by the rail lines over the wide expanse of 2,200 square miles of the metropolitan area. Second, it has spread the center of the service activities of the region from the west side of the central city along the Wilshire corridor and up into Hollywood. The centrifugal force of the automobile precludes Los Angeles from becoming the type of metropolitan center that one associates with very large cities, and this despite physiographic features that would have dictated otherwise in the absence of automotive transport. It may well be that this

---

[15] A detailed presentation and analysis of this whole development in the Los Angeles metropolitan area is given in D. F. Pegrum, *Urban Transport and the Location of Industry in Metropolitan Los Angeles,* Occasional Paper, No. 2 (Los Angeles, Calif.: Bureau of Business and Economic Research, University of California, 1963).

FIGURE 22-3

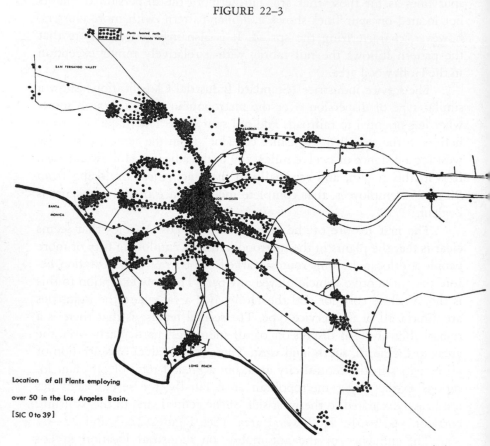

Location of all Plants employing
over 50 in the Los Angeles Basin.
[SIC 0 to 39]

powerful influence will prevent the older centers from maintaining their present structures, as Vernon suggests.

The Los Angeles Residential Structure

The growth of the metropolitan area of Los Angeles from a total population in 1900 of 108,920 inhabitants to 6,646,248 in 1960 has been the most phenomenal of any city in the world. The major portion of this growth has been since 1920 when the total was 951,615. This has been coincident with the development of the automobile as a vehicle of urban transport.

Down to 1920, the central area (which is larger than the central business district) registered the largest growth in population, but from 1920 to 1960 it lost that position in both relative and absolute terms, and from 1950 to 1960 suffered an absolute decline of 5.9 percent. (Figure 22-5.) The greatest growth has been registered

FIGURE 22–4

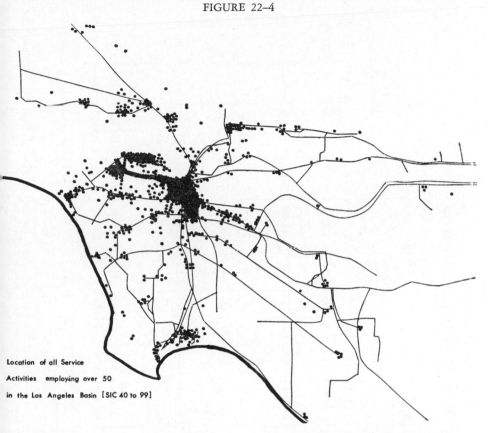

Location of all Service
Activities employing over 50
in the Los Angeles Basin [SIC 40 to 99]

in the southwest, the west, and the San Fernando Valley. At the
present time all of the regions surrounding the central area have a
population of more than 1 million each. Furthermore, the trend in
the surrounding regions has been continuous since 1920, and all of
them surpass the central area in total population. (Figures 22–6 and
22–7.) The growth pattern down to the Census of 1960 warrants
the prediction that by 1970 the southeast will have the largest residential population, the valley will be second, the west and east will
be very close for third and fourth places, respectively, and the central
area will remain at the bottom of the list and possibly continue to
decline.

Approximately 68 percent of employment in industries with
more than 50 employees was in the combined valley, central and
western areas. There was, however, a widespread scattering of industrial activity over the entire metropolitan region, with clustering
around numerous points throughout the area. In contrast with the

FIGURE 22-5

LOS ANGELES METROPOLITAN AREA* POPULATION, 1900–1960
(By major area)

Sub-areas**	Major Area	1900	Per cent Change 1900–1910	1910	Per cent Change 1910–1920	1920	Per cent Change 1920–1930	1930	Per cent Change 1930–1940	1940	Per cent Change 1940–1950	1950	Per cent Change 1950–1960	1960
1) 2)	Valley (2)	5,846	201.3	17,616	86.6	32,869	525.7	205,769	54.1	317,050	91.7	607,700	75.4	1,065,969
3) 4) 5)	East (3)	31,598	153.3	80,042	66.0	132,901	100.7	266,752	31.1	349,488	65.3	577,828	72.2	996,408
6) 7) 8) 9) 10)	Central (1)	102,479	205.5	313,104	81.7	568,886	25.6	714,559	13.6	811,584	5.9	859,219	−5.9	808,991
11) 12) 13)	West (4)	8,536	187.2	24,517	168.8	65,904	612.2	469,362	32.2	620,691	52.1	944,232	34.4	1,269,209
14) 15) 16) (Orange County)	South-east (5)	32,461	121.9	72,020	109.7	151,055	335.3	657,614	21.3	797,516	68.4	1,342,901	86.6	2,505,671
	TOTAL	180,920	180.4	507,299	87.6	951,615	143.2	2,314,056	25.2	2,896,329	49.6	4,331,880	53.4	6,646,248

*The Los Angeles Metropolitan Area comprises Los Angeles and Orange counties.

**The subareas are:

1. San Fernando Valley
2. Glendale
3. Pasadena
4. Pomona-Foothill
5. Alhambra
6. Northeast
7. East
8. Central (including downtown Los Angeles)
9. Wilshire
10. Hollywood
11. Beverly Hills-Westwood
12. Santa Monica Bay
13. Adams-Inglewood
14. Southeast
15. Whittier-Norwalk
16. South Coast

SOURCES: 1900–1920: U.S. Bureau of the Census, *Fourteenth Census of the United States, Vol. I, Population* (Washington, D.C.: Government Printing Office, 1921), p. 354. Table 55 gives population by "minor civil divisions." These were aggregated to equal approximately the five major areas used by the Security-First National Bank.
1920–1960: Security-First National Bank, *Monthly Summary of Business Conditions in Southern California*.

distribution of industry, the three residential districts—valley, central, and west—contain only 49 percent of the population of metropolitan Los Angeles. It seems, therefore, that a substantial movement of workers takes place from the east and southwest into the west and central areas, and into the southwest corner of the valley area. The source of the workers in the various areas is unknown, but it is clear that the daily movement of people to and from work in Los Angeles involves a decidedly complex regional interchange and

FIGURE 22–6

Los Angeles Metropolitan Area Population Growth, 1920–1960

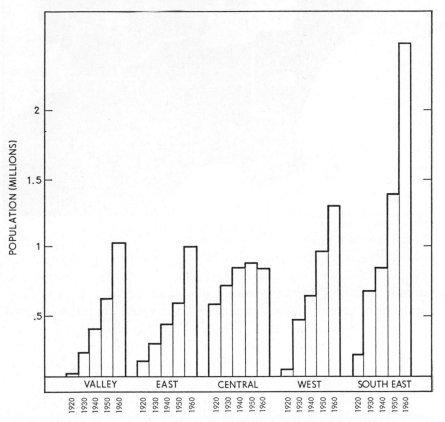

dispersion which, unlike such movement in most metropolitan centers, does not focus on the downtown central city area, nor even on the central area of residential population.

Rail passenger transport facilities for metropolitan Los Angeles in 1920 consisted of electric interurban lines and street railways.

FIGURE 22-7

LOS ANGELES POPULATION
Percentage Distribution by Area, 1960

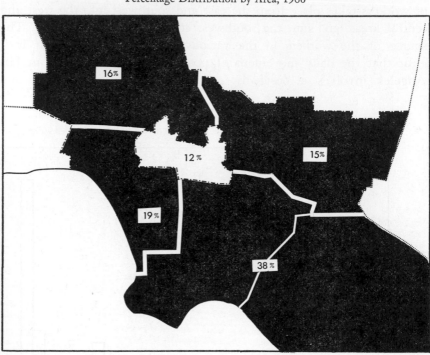

The interurban lines formed part of the railroad routes while street railways were confined almost entirely to the central residential area. (Figure 22-8.) In the years after 1920, the interurban lines shrank steadily from the periphery toward the center, and the street railways experienced continuous contraction. All street and interurban railway service for passengers ended on March 31, 1963.

The development of freeways, which commenced with the 8.2 mile Arroyo Seco in 1940, amounted to only 45 miles in 1953 but grew to 260 miles in 1963. A system of 550 miles is planned for 1970 and 800 miles by 1980. The freeway pattern seems to have been determined by residential growth and location rather than vice versa.[16] Despite the enormous and explosive growth of the metro-

[16] For a detailed presentation, see D. F. Pegrum, *Residential Population and Urban Transport Facilities in the Los Angeles Metropolitan Area,* Occasional Paper, No. 3 (Los Angeles, Calif.: Bureau of Business and Economic Research, University of California, 1964).

FIGURE 22-8

RAIL PASSENGER SERVICE IN THE LOS ANGELES AREA: 1920

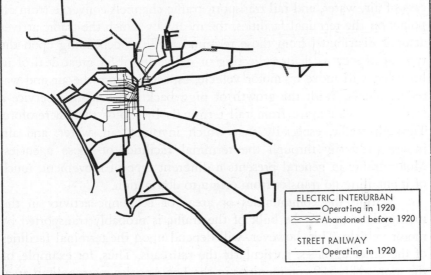

ELECTRIC INTERURBAN
——Operating in 1920
~~~~~Abandoned before 1920

STREET RAILWAY
——Operating in 1920

politan area, Los Angeles probably has more transport mobility than any other center of comparable size.[17]

The Pattern of Traffic Movements

The pattern of the movement of traffic, both passenger and freight, in a metropolitan area will depend upon the relative importance of rail, motor, and water facilities in the region, the location of industry and economic activity, and the location of the residential population. These factors, together with the significance of the metropolitan center as the focus of regional activity, give rise to three basic patterns of traffic movement.

The three basic patterns of traffic within a metropolitan area are essentially the same for the transport of people as for goods, although the movement of people is much more segmentized and individualized, on the whole, than is that of freight. These three basic movements are (1) the movements of traffic into the area, out of it, and through it;

[17] See Meyer, Kain, and Wohl, *op. cit.;* also Karl Moskowitz, "Living and Travel Patterns in Automobile-Oriented Cities," Automobile Manufacturers Association, *The Dynamics of Urban Transportation,* Symposium (Detroit, Mich., 1962), pp. 3.1–3.13.

(2) the movement within the communities themselves; and (3) the traffic movement among the communities.[18]

Freight traffic into and out of the area involves the collection or distribution of the goods through the various terminal points. In the case of air, water, and rail transport, traffic channels converge from all points on the terminal facilities, the means by which the traffic arrives at or is distributed from those terminal facilities depending upon the type of agency used for collecting or delivering it. A great deal of it, however, will move by motor vehicle, especially from the air and water terminals. With the growth of piggyback and container service a larger part will move from rail terminals by motor than heretofore. Through traffic, especially that which involves rail, water, and air, moves primarily through the terminal facilities of those agencies. Motor traffic in general presents a different type of movement, much of it entailing no transfer from origin to destination.

Within the communities or areas of economic activity in the metropolitan center the bulk of the traffic is probably transported by motor vehicle. This, however, will depend upon the terminal facilities of the other agencies, particularly the railroads. Thus, for example, of the more than 519 communities in the Los Angeles metropolitan area, 321 have no rail facilities and are served exclusively by trucks and private automobile. As rail terminals are consolidated and moved to the periphery of metropolitan areas, truck traffic will increase relatively, unless rail spur lines are developed to counteract this—an unlikely development. Similarly, as airfreight increases in significance, the internal movement by motor vehicle will also increase. Plans for resolving urban traffic problems will have to face the fact that the bulk of the freight traffic in the area will move by motor vehicle. All of the latter which enters into intercity traffic will obviously be handled this way as well as that which is moved by air. How much rail freight will also entail a supplementary movement by motor vehicle will depend upon the way the rail terminal arrangements are developed; but the prospects, regardless of the role railroads will play in the transport structure of the country in the future, are for an increased volume of motor freight relative to the total freight movements in the metropolitan centers. Plans for street and highway programs must take this into account, even to the point of considering specialization so as to separate freight and passenger routes in many cases.

---

[18] For a careful analysis of the various phases of traffic movement in urban areas, see R. B. Mitchell and C. Rapkin, *Urban Traffic* (New York: Columbia University Press, 1954).

THE COMMUTER PROBLEM

The commuter problem in its broadest sense is concerned with the movement of people from their various residences to their places of work. This is concentrated in the morning hours from 7:00 A.M. to 9:00 A.M. and in the evening from 4:30 P.M. to 6:30 P.M. for five days a week. In a narrower sense the problem involves the movement of people from the suburbs to the central business areas by mass transit. This problem has become extremely acute in certain cities, particularly with regard to the role of railroads in providing the necessary service. The Doyle Report contains an extensive discussion of this problem.

The Rail Commutation Problem

The Doyle Report states that the most pressing aspect of the commuter problem is the deterioration of railroad service and the discontinuance of trains caused by the steady loss of revenue in furnishing the service.[19] The most important areas where rail commutation is significant in the movement of people between the suburbs and the central business district are New York, Chicago, Philadelphia, Boston, and San Francisco, with a fringe business operated in and out of Pittsburgh, Washington, and Baltimore. The difficulties in maintaining this commuter service by the railroads arise from three basic causes: (1) fundamental changes in public habits and desires, (2) competition that has severely reduced rail freight revenues, and (3) a worsening of the long-time unfavorable cost-price relationships in rail suburban services.

The fundamental change in public habits and desires has been occasioned by the widespread use of the automobile, the general reduction in the work week from six to five days, the change in the pattern of use of leisure time, and the general rise in living standards. The Doyle Report found that the total rail commutation traffic declined from 345 million passengers in 1947 to 221 million in 1957, but that the peak-hour traffic on the major routes into the center of the cities was stable or increasing. However, the increases were confined to the Long Island Railroad in New York City, between 1953 and 1958, and the Burlington, the Chicago and North Western, and the Milwaukee lines in the Chicago area.[20] The other railroads in the Chicago area suf-

---

[19] *National Transportation Policy* (Doyle Report), p. 554. The report from page 552 to page 582 deals with various phases of the problem. See also Owen, *op. cit.,* chap. iii.

[20] The Interstate Commerce Commission reported that commuter revenue passengers declined to a 10-year low in 1965 with 192.6 million passengers. There were increases in

fered declines, apparently the result of the greater development of multilane and expressway facilities on the south side of Chicago. All of the other railroads in the different areas suffered declines.

Revenue and Expense Squeeze

For many years the revenue from rail freight traffic has made up for the passenger service deficit and thus has been literally responsible for continuing suburban railroad passenger service. The major portion of commuter service is rendered by railroads in the Eastern District, and it is the railroads in this area that have the highest proportion of passenger revenues—and therefore expenses—in relation to freight revenues. This has brought about a revenue-expense squeeze particularly because suburban fares have historically been very low and probably have never covered the costs where suburban traffic has been great enough to require separate trains to serve commuters. The early fares were priced on the theory that commutation was a by-product of the regular intercity services. The Doyle Report states that the most destructive practice, economically, has been the granting of discounts to peak-hour users, an economically unsound and irrational pricing practice.

Action to Keep Commuter Trains Running

Action to keep the commuter trains running has been taken by the railroads, by the cities and states where the problem is acute, and by the federal government. The railroads have endeavored to overcome the losses by reduction of operating expenses, but without significant success. Material costs have been largely outside the control of management, as well as labor costs and taxes. Some reductions have been possible through discontinuance of train service where this has been permitted by public authority.

Action by Cities and States. Pressure on rail commutation services has led local and state governments to take steps to alleviate railroad financial burdens. The action has varied from one metropolitan area to another but has included tax relief, direct cash payments to rail carriers, loans to re-equip, efforts to organize public corporations or authorities competent to deal with the situation, and over-all mass transportation planning activity.[21] An important element of tax relief was granted to the Long Island Railroad in 1954 by the state of New York. Massachusetts made direct payments to the New Haven for the

---

the Chicago area on both the Chicago and North Western and the Illinois Central railroads. *Eightieth Annual Report*, 1966, p. 85.

[21] *Ibid.*, p. 566; see also Owen, *op. cit.*, pp. 113–18.

continuation of commuter services commencing on July 1, 1958. The city of Philadelphia in 1958 entered into contracts with the Reading and Pennsylvania railroads which first of all involved direct payments. This resulted in the establishment in January, 1960, of a nonprofit public corporation which sets all schedules, collects all revenues, and pays the Reading and Pennsylvania railroads for the complete service rendered at a contractual rate. The city has also invested in property improvements and new coaches which it leases to the railroads.

Action by the Federal Government. The principal action by the federal government has come through the Transportation Act of 1958, which was designed to make it easier to discontinue unprofitable passenger services. In addition, the Interstate Commerce Commission may guarantee loans for new equipment. The discontinuance provisions of the Act of 1958 have been beneficial to the railroads mostly in intercity service. The loan guarantee provisions have not been applied directly to commutation equipment.

Conclusion. In summarizing its survey of the commutation problem, the Doyle Report concludes:

1. Rail commutation revenues have seldom recovered the cost of the service; the deficits have been made up from freight profits.
2. The continuing losses from suburban services have forced the railroads to discontinue many trains.
3. Enough alternative commuter transportation exists to reduce the proceeds from fare increases due to the number of riders lost with each increase.[22]

THE PRICING PROBLEM

Rationing of Service

Perhaps the most difficult aspect of the urban transportation problem arises from the fact that the use of the automotive vehicle has not been matched by the development of means for rationing the use of road facilities in terms of the types of services received or the time at which they are utilized. The streets and main arteries are economic goods which are therefore scarce, and unless they are to be constructed and used wastefully, some means of rationing needs to be devised. The rationing device that is most generally effective is the price mechanism. This is particularly difficult to apply to motor transport, as was pointed out in connection with highways, but it is much more complex in the urban areas because of the technical difficulties. The main problem cen-

---

[22] *Ibid.,* p. 582. The recommendations for dealing with this difficult problem will be discussed in Chapter 24.

ters on the freeways and other principal arteries that are burdened with the peak loads. At the present time, the selection of particular routes at particular times by the driver is based on convenience to him, except for limited restrictions that may be placed on trucks or buses on occasion. In other words, the driver makes his choice among the roads and streets as though they were a free good that does not need to be economized.[23] What is needed is specific rationing of specific use of the highways on specific occasions if we are to achieve an efficient utilization of them. The consequences of failure to do so are expressed by Professor W. S. Vickrey in the following terms:

> In the absence of any pricing of highway usage we seem to be faced with the following dilemma. Either we construct a highway system of extravagant proportions, which, while no greater than needed to carry its volume of traffic without congestion, is nevertheless much larger than the users would be willing to pay for if they had their choice between paying their share or doing without the facility or with one less ample, and being relieved of the corresponding share of the cost. Alternatively, we construct a highway system that is severely congested during the rush hours, sufficiently so that resort to rail transit is the better alternative, if that is available, or possibly to bus transit if the busses can be sufficiently insulated from the impact of congestion, itself an expensive arrangement to provide. Nor is there any particularly attractive middle ground. Specific pricing of highway usage is needed and needed badly.[24]

Possible Devices

It should be noted that user taxes do not resolve the problem just discussed, because they cannot be related to the specific use in question. Out-of-town and urban usage cannot be distinguished in these tax devices, nor the use of specific routes. If taxes could be based on permits or licenses for specific use and policing utilized to secure adequate compliance, direct pricing could be employed and would be much more effective. It must be emphasized that the inadequacy of tax devices in this connection is not part of the question of whether motorists as a whole contribute their full share to the provision of the facilities, but rather the inability of this means to achieve an efficient allocation of the total services that are provided. The result is either congestion or oversupply.

Considerable emphasis has been placed upon the parking problem

[23] See D. F. Pegrum, *The Los Angeles Metropolitan Transportation Problem—A Preliminary Analysis* (mimeographed) (Los Angeles: University of California, March, 1957), for a more extensive discussion of this.

[24] *Transportation Plan for the National Capital Region,* Hearings before the Joint Committee on Washington Metropolitan Problems, November, 1959, 86th Congress, 1st session (Washington, D.C.: U.S. Government Printing Office, 1960), p. 469. See also W. Vickrey, "Pricing as a Tool in Coordination of Local Transportation," National Bureau of Economic Research, *Transportation Economics* (New York, 1965), pp. 275–91.

as related to motor traffic congestion. This does not seem to offer any particular problem, especially if street parking is eliminated where it seriously impedes traffic or leads to congestion. Parking facilities can be provided and made to pay for themselves.[25] This is one way that the uneconomical use of motor vehicles can be checked, but this is not likely to offer much relief from the flow of traffic, or the relative use of the various routes.

Truck traffic presents somewhat different problems than the passenger car. It has been suggested that heavy trucks may be eliminated from main arteries during peak hours; also, that steps be taken to promote the movement of freight traffic by truck at other times of the day than during the peak hours. Devices such as these, if accepted by the business community, would afford some relief. The truck parking problem can be eased considerably by the requirement that all commercial firms provide adequate off-street loading and unloading facilities, with means for entrance and exit that do not create serious impediments to the flow of the street traffic. These proposals do not do much more than scratch the surface of the basic problem.

It has been suggested that free mass transportation to commuters is the answer to the difficulties. The Doyle Report states that the best means of reducing urban transportation costs is "by giving commuters free mass transportation which would cost less than providing the additional highway and parking facilities needed for their autos."[26] This point of view seems to be based on the idea that the city user of automobiles is heavily subsidized through taxes. This may be challenged. Parking does not need to be subsidized; it can be provided on an economical basis, and pricing can be applied directly to ration its use. The issue rests, therefore, on the public support given to the motor vehicle through its use of the highways.

A study by the Transportation Center at Northwestern University examined the question of aid to private automobiles in the Chicago urban area and the effect which this might have on the demand pattern for automobile and transit service. It came to the conclusion that the true situation lies somewhere between a subsidy of $17.56 per vehicle per year to an overpayment of $4.85 by the vehicle.[27] The general con-

---

[25] See Wilbur Smith and Associates, *Transportation and Parking* (New Haven, Conn.: 1966).

[26] *National Transportation Policy* (Doyle Report), pp. 553 and 608.

[27] *Basic Issues in Chicago Metropolitan Transportation* (Evanston, Ill.: Transportation Center, Northwestern University, June, 1958), pp. 54–55. A careful summary of the studies undertaken at the Center is given by M. Reinsberg, *Metropolitan Transportation* (Evanston, Ill.: Northwestern University, 1961). This will be discussed in Chapter 24 below.

clusion to be drawn is that, nationally, urban traffic contributes more highway user tax revenue than is spent for city streets from all sources.[28] In any case, if indirect aid is given, it is not of sufficient importance to influence the choice of the travelers. It may also be added that if free mass transit were provided, it would have to be established that it was cheaper than provision of automobile facilities—something that the proponents have not done. In addition, free transit, instead of reducing waste, would merely promote it in another direction, scarcely an economical way of dealing with the problem; nor would it make for much reduction in street and highway expenditures even if it did divert some traffic because it would affect only the peak loads and not, therefore, the basic highway investment costs. There are few proponents of mass transit who contend that it can be placed on a fully self-supporting basis.

Recent technological developments have introduced the possibility that electronic devices for metering urban motor traffic on the main arteries may be available in the not distant future at reasonable cost. A model of this was introduced at the hearings on the transport problems of the city of Washington by the Link Aviation Corporation.[29] If transit plans are being developed for the year 1980, it is reasonable to assume that the technical difficulties of metering or pricing can be solved by that date. How an application of pricing to the urban highway problem would affect the use of rapid transit may be an open question, but plans for developing the latter should take this into careful consideration before huge public expenditures are made on a means of transport that even in a more favorable technological and economic setting proved to be a failure.

THE PROBLEM OF ORGANIZATION

The Nature of the Problem

One of the most complex aspects of metropolitan transportation today centers on the appropriate type of governmental organization. This is because virtually all levels of government from the immediately local to the federal participate in providing or controlling various phases of urban transport. At the same time, the services are supplied by private enterprises, by federal, state, and local governments, and by special bodies such as the New York Port Authority, the Southern California Rapid Transit District, and the Chicago Transit Authority. Some of the transport enterprises are regulated by the Interstate Com-

[28] For a similar conclusion, see Owen, *op. cit.*, p. 155.
[29] *Transportation Plan for the National Capital Region*, pp. 458–63 and 472–507.

merce Commission, whose control over the railroads is of particular importance, some by state commissions, some by local authorities, with a large part of the urban traffic subject to no control at all. For all of the complex web of routes and carriers that form the "system" of transport for a particular metropolitan area, there is at the present time no co-ordinated authority for the planning or administration of public policy, and no central authority for financing the public aspects of the undertakings—in fact, no co-ordinating device either by the market or by public agency for any transport purpose. To characterize the present situation as haphazard is charitable, to say the least.

Multiplicity of Jurisdictions

The development of policy for transportation in a large metropolitan area is complicated, first of all, by the number of different means of transport, both for freight and for passenger purposes, that are available in the area. The primary function of the railroads is in intercity transportation, but in some centers it is crucial for mass commuter service. In addition, the terminal facilities are the centers for the gathering and distributing of the traffic which originates in or is destined to the area. The relation of these terminal points to the urban traffic problem is therefore critical and must be part of the over-all plans for urban movement. In a similar although less complex way, airports which are the termini for intercity passenger traffic, and are largely under local jurisdiction, are a significant factor in the local picture. Water terminals are mainly under local control and, located by geography, exert their most important influence on freight traffic. Automobile transport presents the most difficult questions because of the intermingling in a more or less indiscriminate fashion throughout the entire range of freight and passenger traffic, both metropolitan and intercity.

Because of this complexity of the metropolitan transport structure, no single public authority can exercise any exclusive jurisdiction over all the agencies or the services rendered by them. All levels of government are involved in some way or another, yet the issues are more or less unique to each metropolitan center. Furthermore, each of the areas is composed of a large number of governmental units operating with a considerable degree of independence of each other, yet dealing with transportation, much of which moves as though no jurisdictional boundaries were in existence. Thus, for example, in the Los Angeles area there are some 519 different communities with over 100 significant suburban shopping areas. There are about 2,000 local government units, more than 300 of which are concerned with transportation, and the 125 towns and cities have planning commissions, each acting largely independently of each other.[30] If to this is added the unavoidable participation of the state and federal governments, the difficulties of co-ordinated action become apparent. So far, no steps have been taken anywhere to bring about unification of action and policy, although proposals have been advanced to deal with the issues, at least at the stage of policy formation. Some of these will be discussed in Chapter 24.

PROBLEMS OF FINANCE

Financial problems, as they relate to the urban transport structure per se, are concerned with rapid transit and with highways and streets. Although there seems to be general agreement that urban rapid transit must be handled as a local—that is, metropolitan—problem, there are differences of opinion on how it should be provided. Some feel that it should be developed on an economical basis so as to be self-sustaining, others feel that tax support is necessary, while still others hold to the position that it should be supplied free of charge to users with all the revenues coming from the taxpayer. As matters stand at present, mass rapid transit seems to offer little prospect of standing on its own feet, at least on the scope envisaged by the major areas that are trying to develop or revive it. If these programs are to be carried through, public aid is unavoidable. This means that some single authority for the metropolitan area must be established to conduct the operations because of the numerous political jurisdictions that are involved. Some of these proposals will be examined later, but it should be noted that they do not deal with the urban transport problem as a whole, nor with the financial issues it raises.

The processes of financing mass rapid transit are relatively simple if it has been agreed that there is to be a single agency and if the decision has been made between self-support and public aid. Financing the facilities for motor transport offers no such simple prospect at the present time. Federal, state, and the multiplicity of local governments all participate through a variety of tax measures which, on the whole, are developed independently of each other. Freeways and many of the

---

[30] For a fuller discussion of this, see D. F. Pegrum, *The Los Angeles Metropolitan Transportation Problem; Transportation in the Los Angeles Area;* Final Report of the Citizens Traffic and Transportation Committee for the Extended Los Angeles Area (Los Angeles, August 1, 1957); Southern California Research Council, *op. cit.* See also Owen, *op. cit.,* chap. vi, for a more general discussion.

through arteries are part of state-wide programs integrating the state-wide system, rather than being tailored to local needs, yet they are an integral part of the urban transport structure and are utilized by motorists in that way. The national system of interstate and defense highways has also become part of the metropolitan highway system. The federal government bears 90 per cent of the cost of these roads and at the same time levies special taxes to cover the construction expenditures which are disbursed through the highway trust fund. Finally, streets and other roads are provided by the various local authorities out of special taxes levied by them, property taxes, and revenues allocated by state authorities out of gasoline taxes, motor vehicle taxes, and other levies for highway purposes.

Thus, there is literally no co-ordination of financial policy for streets and highways in the metropolitan areas, either in the planning of the networks and their utilization, or in the means of financing them. Without some resolution of this chaotic situation, providing for urban transportation is bound to be inefficient and wasteful.

Chapter 23

TRANSPORT TERMINALS

INTRODUCTION

Terminals are an integral and vital part of both intercity and urban transportation. Generally speaking, they are regarded as the points of concentration at which traffic on the intercity carrier ends its journey, or is interchanged for further movement when transferred for continuance to ultimate destination in another center. Thus, airports are the places at which air traffic between cities is originated or terminated, or where interchange between the planes of the same or other carriers is effected. Water ports, with their docks, wharves, and roadsteads, are the exchange areas of land and water transport. Rail terminals are more complicated, on the whole, than the foregoing two. They are the points at which all intercity traffic by rail, both passenger and freight, makes or breaks bulk, the assembling or distribution being carried out by various means. In addition, they are the points of interchange for the same or different carriers moving through the main centers to other destinations. Motor terminals may be somewhat similar to those of railroads in the sense that they may be concentration points for incoming and outgoing traffic, but they are much less extensive in scope because of the lack of need for large switching yards, equipment servicing facilities, and extensive passenger accommodations. There is also the fact that a large amount of motor traffic moves from the initial point of departure to ultimate destination without the necessity of reshipment of any kind. Finally, the motor vehicle can use the roads and streets with little restriction and is thus not limited in its movement as is the motive equipment of the railroads.

The problem of transport terminals, therefore, has three major aspects: (1) the relation to the movement of traffic between centers involving assembly, distribution, and interchange; (2) the relation to the urban transport pattern in which the issues center on the assembly and distribution of traffic, thereby affecting urban traffic flow, land utilization, and the location of industry; and (3) the technical questions of operation, co-ordination, and location. Terminals are thus a part of the national transportation system at the same time that they are an integral phase of the urban transport structure. To date the most critical issues regarding terminals have centered on the railroads, with their problems of access to the principal metropolitan centers, traffic interchange among the different lines, and connections with water carriers. This is partly because the location of railroad terminals and the land which they utilize has been very largely at the option of the carriers. In those cities where a number of lines meet, competition for sites has created a multiplicity of facilities where, by the nature of the services performed, monopoly, or at least unified operation, is more in keeping with the situation. Water terminals are severely circumscribed by geographic conditions, but unification and more efficient operation have been an important issue at all of the major ports. The rapid development of air transport and the demands of space for the safe operation of the large intercity planes, particularly jets, has given rise to new and complex problems of location and the movement of traffic to and from the airports. So far, this has focused primarily on passenger traffic, but as airfreight develops to significant proportions, new complications for urban traffic will arise. Motor terminals present the simplest problems because of the highly individualized features of the traffic movements and the opportunities, over a wide range, to avoid rehandling of traffic, especially freight.

THE GENERAL NATURE OF THE TERMINAL PROBLEM

The terminal problems connected with transportation have been recognized as of major importance for the last fifty years. Until recently, however, they have not been viewed as possessing two distinct yet intimately related features, the first being that of incoming, outgoing, and through traffic, and the second being the effect of these on traffic patterns and requirements within the metropolitan centers.

When the terminal problem first attracted attention, just after the turn of the century, it centered on the railroads, with their multiplicity of freight and passenger facilities in the large cities which resulted from the competition of numerous lines for favorable sites and convenient access to the concentrated traffic of the major centers. Congestion, delays, high cost of terminal operations, and the strategic positions occupied by some of the railroads in key centers pointed up the need for developing ways and means of co-ordinating terminal operations, speeding up traffic service, and reducing expense. The problem was principally related to rail transport because of the necessity of direct rail connections for shippers, except for traffic that could be moved conveniently for short distances by horse-drawn vehicles, and because of the reliance of passengers on the railroads for intercity travel.

The large seaports also presented the problem of co-ordination of water terminal facilities within the harbor areas, and the linking of these with the railroad lines serving the centers. Some form of unified connection with the docks was needed because cargo, both incoming and outgoing, moved over railroads to and from land destinations within the metropolitan areas as well as to outside points.

These same terminal problems still remain, but they have been modified, quite drastically in some ways, by the development of air and automotive transport. The airplane has introduced the necessity of large land requirements which has made location because of land costs, as well as considerations of safety and noise, a critical problem in airport sites. In addition, traffic to and from the terminals, especially that of passengers, has become a significant consideration to the air lines, as well as to authorities concerned with the flow of vehicles within the urban area. Motor terminals may be dispersed throughout the metropolitan region because of the small amount of space required for loading and unloading passengers, but busses utilize the streets for all of their journeys and thus merge intercity and metropolitan traffic in a way that is quite different from the other carriers. The same remarks apply to trucks, except that a much greater proportion of the traffic is independent of the depots because of direct connections with the shippers' facilities.

Rail traffic, as such, ends its movement with the rail lines, whether at passenger stations, freight depots, or spur lines to plants. The railroads enter directly into the urban traffic movement only as their lines cross streets and occupy land space. However, it is necessary to distribute freight and passengers from the main terminal points, and it is in this way that they become a vital part of the urban transportation complex. In addition, the large assembly yards required for modern freight trains, and the extensive facilities needed for the long intercity passenger trains, utilize large amounts of surface space in the metropolitan areas. The technical developments in rail transport with the emphasis on long-distance intercity traffic, together with the increasing use of the automotive vehicle for gathering and distributing purposes in the urban areas, has given impetus to considerations of relocation, consolidation, and unification of railroad terminals so as to reduce costs, improve efficiency, and relieve urban congestion.

Each of the different modes of transport has its own peculiar terminal problems as they relate to its special function in the national transport system. These may be examined from the standpoint of the different modes and the various carriers both as competing means of transportation and as a part of a system which, in many of the services that are offered, requires direct co-operation. There is the additional point, however, that terminal facilities, as narrowly defined, are an integral part of the metropolitan transportation complex. Effective planning for the development of means for dealing with the movement of traffic within the metropolitan areas must consider the traffic which focuses on these terminals and its relation to the movements within the area itself. So far, little has been done to co-ordinate these two phases of the metropolitan transportation problem. Resolution of modern urban transport questions must be based on a recognition of the fact that the terminal phases of intercity transportation are an integral and vitally important segment of traffic movements within the metropolitan area.

RAILROAD TERMINALS

Most railroads provide both passenger and freight services. These require separate facilities, but the intercity traffic moving over the main lines of the carriers converges on the metropolitan areas over single routes from which the passenger and freight trains must be separated as they move into the terminal points. Passenger trains begin and end their journeys at single depots located in the central part of the city, but those hauling freight begin or end their line haul at classification yards where the cars are assembled for departure or separated for dispatch to the designated unloading points. In addition to these terminal facilities, railroads must also have roundhouses for locomotives, together with maintenance and service shops and yards for other rolling stock in the immediate vicinity of their main terminals. The major repair and service centers may be concentrated at other points. The principal feature of railroad terminals and railroad terminal operations, therefore, relates to arrangements for the receipt or delivery of traffic originating in or destined to the urban center, and the transference of traffic that moves through it to other destinations. It is in the major metropolitan areas that the railroad terminal problem presents its most serious complications for the carriers, the patrons, and urban transportation.[1]

Passenger Terminals

Despite the enormous investment in rail passenger terminals—much of which is now obsolete—these form the simplest type of rail terminal service because the trains can operate into and out of them as units, the passengers load and unload themselves, and a relatively small amount of goods passes through them. In addition, they are a single point of origin or destination as far as the railroads are concerned, since the passengers must provide their own means of moving to and from the depots. Most of the terminal districts of the country are served by three or more line-haul railroads, Chicago having 23, St. Louis 16, and New York 12, but Los Angeles and San Francisco have only three each, with San Francisco proper having only one. The passenger terminal problem, therefore, varies widely and is more complicated where the number of entering lines is large.

The city of Chicago has six major passenger terminals located in the central area. Because it is the hub of lines converging from all directions, the transfer of passengers going through the city to other destinations presents a problem, except where it is between trains which use the same terminal. Transfer between depots is effected by the use of taxicabs, the fare for which is covered by the rail ticket. The transfer traffic enters into the metropolitan flow, however. To date, no ready solution to the complexities has been found because of the large number of separate lines that enter the city, and the volume of passenger traffic handled by them.

The railroads in Los Angeles have resolved the problem by the construction of a Union Depot owned and operated by the Southern Pacific, Union Pacific, and Santa Fe railroads jointly. This is located in the center of the city. Construction of it in 1939 was a comparatively simple task because of the availability of land for the rail operations and adequate parking facilities. In addition, the previous depots were in close proximity to each other. The prospects for a solution of this type in the areas where it is most needed are dim indeed.

---

[1] For a good presentation of the situation in Chicago, see H. M. Mayer, "Localization of Railway Facilities in Metropolitan Centers as Typified by Chicago," *Journal of Land and Public Utility Economics,* Vol. XX, No. 4 (November, 1944), pp. 299–315. See S. Daggett, *Principles of Inland Transportation* (4th ed.; New York: Harper Bros., 1955), chap. 24 for a discussion of air and rail terminals.

Freight Terminals

Terminal Freight Traffic.   The freight traffic which moves through the major terminal centers may be through traffic, carload local traffic, or less-than-carload (l.c.l.) shipments. Each of these requires a different type of handling and facilities.

Through traffic is that which moves through the terminal area without rehandling. It does, however, require the breakup of the incoming trains and the regrouping of cars for outgoing haulage either over the same or over another road. Most of the classification yards for sorting this traffic are well within the metropolitan areas and, not infrequently, close to the center. This is because of developments preceding the recent rapid growth of the metropolitan areas, and because of the fact that through traffic is only part of the consist of the freight trains. This makes it impracticable to regroup through traffic at different points from those where the local traffic is handled. In addition, the need for interchanging a considerable portion of it with other lines makes it necessary to have adequate connections with them. Increasing length of freight trains, together with the use of the hump or gravity operation for switching, and electronic classification devices, has resulted in modernization and increasing lengths of yards. This is leading to reorganization and relocation that may move many of the major primary yards to outlying areas, thus eliminating some of the congestion in the more concentrated central parts of the city. Illustrations of this are found in the Southern Pacific yards at Roseville, California; Los Angeles, California; and Houston, Texas; and in the Proviso yard of the Chicago and North Western in Chicago.

Carload local traffic originates in or is destined to a particular urban area. If the entire movement is over the road of a single carrier, it must be delivered to the designated destination point from the main terminal yard or returned to the latter from the loading points. These may be warehouses, plants, factories with their own industrial lines and interior switching facilities, special terminals such as "produce," or public tracks where loading and unloading is undertaken by the consignee with final delivery by trucks. Much of the traffic by piggyback is typically of the latter type. All of this carload traffic requires an extensive network of trackage facilities into the industrial areas and to the major plants and warehouses.

Less-than-carload traffic calls for arrangements for collecting relatively small shipments at a multiplicity of points and then reassembling them into freight cars for a single destination or in "pedlar" cars that unload at way stations. The assembling or unloading may take place at freight depots located in various parts of the metropolitan area, on sidings set up for the purpose, or by "trap" or "ferry" cars that pick up or deliver less-than-carload freight at warehouses. This procedure was developed as a competitive device by railroads to secure traffic located at some distance from their depots, but nearer those of rival carriers. The development of truck transport has changed this considerably, first by the introduction of pickup and delivery service, by which the railroads undertake, either with their own motor vehicles or by contract with an independent motor carrier, to provide services to the door of the shipper or consignee. The piggyback and container techniques are an extension of this practice, but are much more expeditious and efficient when the size of the shipments is sufficiently large to warrant their use.

Traffic Interchange

The multiplicity of terminals in the large metropolitan centers, resulting from the number of independent railroads serving them, means that facilities must be provided for the exchange of all types of freight among them. This applies equally well to freight originating in or destined to places within the area as it does to through traffic, because all of the railroads cannot contact all of the firms that use their facilities. Even as it is, there is probably considerable waste from excessive duplication of accommodations. Various types of interchange arrangements among the carriers, however, serve to alleviate the problem somewhat and to provide shippers with reasonably expeditious service and access to the different railroads.

Line-haul carriers undertake to handle all carload traffic at any point within a terminal area connected to their tracks. When another carrier is involved, this service may be performed for an extra charge imposed upon the shipper for the switching. Frequently, where there is competition for the traffic, the line-haul railroad will absorb the switching charge so as to make its rate to destination the same as that of its competitor. This is commonly known as "reciprocal" switching, in that there is no separate terminal cost for the shipper, but the railroads pay each other for the services that are performed.

Belt-line railroads are used in many centers to handle traffic interchange. These are lines which perform terminal services only by providing connections in the terminal area between the line-haul carriers. Chicago is served by a number of these. The "outer" belt line (the Elgin, Joliet and Eastern Railway) extends from Porter, Indiana, to

Waukegan, Illinois, for a distance of 130 miles. This line is outside the main classification yards, but it has direct physical connections with all the main lines entering Chicago, and constitutes the means of interchange of through carload traffic. Chicago is also served by three other belt-line routes, the peripheral, the intermediate, and the inner, all of which are within the area encompassed by the outer belt line and more or less concentric to the heart of the city. No switching charges are imposed on shippers located on any of these three lines. Chicago also has the Chicago Tunnel System for delivering less-than-carload freight within the central business district. It is a common carrier that issues through bills of lading for the traffic which moves over the line-haul carriers. In many of the port cities of the country, belt lines are used in the port areas to unify the connections between the various railroads and the multiplicity of wharves to and from which freight may move. Ownership of belt lines may be private, public, or joint. The Chicago outer belt line (Elgin, Joliet and Eastern Railway) is owned by the United States Steel Corporation, and a large proportion of its traffic is for that enterprise. The other belt-line routes in Chicago are not under unified ownership. The belt line which serves the port of San Francisco is owned and operated by the state authority which administers the port. The port of Los Angeles is served by the Harbor Belt Line Railroad under which all railroad facilities in the area were consolidated into a single-terminal railroad in 1929. It is owned and operated jointly by the Board of Harbor Commissioners, the Southern Pacific Company, the Union Pacific, and the Santa Fe. The operations are under a general manager who reports to the Board of Operations, which consists of one member from each of the three railroads and one from the City of Los Angeles Harbor Department. "Universal" freight stations may be operated in connection with belt-line railroads, thereby achieving some unification in the movement of less-than-carload traffic in the metropolitan area. These are depots at which both inbound and outbound freight is handled for all railroads. There are five such stations in Chicago.

Complete unification of rail terminal facilities may be accomplished through joint action by the railroads whereby operation of the terminal properties is placed in the hands of a single organization. The leading illustration of this is the Terminal Railroad Association of St. Louis, which was formed in 1889. This organization resulted from the difficulties of the nine eastern railroads reaching East St. Louis and the seven western lines entering St. Louis proper to provide terminal facilities on opposite sides of the Mississippi River and to have separate bridge operations over it. The Association was formed to resolve this problem. It is owned and operated by fifteen trunk-line railroads. It has a union passenger depot which is used by all the trunk lines, as well as two bridges across the Mississippi, with access to a third which is owned by the city of St. Louis. The bulk of the classification and interchange of traffic, both carload and less than carload, is handled by the Association, which also provides extensive loading and unloading facilities throughout the area. These arrangements do not preclude the railroads from delivery on their own rails or to other railroads with which they have connections. In other words, the Association does not handle all the traffic within the area, but it does resolve the problems of interchange, and it gives all the railroads access to the entire area without excessive duplication of facilities.

Produce Terminals

The rapid development of shipments of perishable commodities in the period after World War I and the need for providing specialized facilities and expeditious distribution resulted in the establishment of produce terminals in the larger cities. These are usually jointly owned or operated, and in any case commonly used, by many carriers. Such a terminal provides storage and consignment tracks, refrigerator and cooler space, auction rooms, inspection platforms, and icing platforms. One feature of the produce terminal is that it helps the shipper to sell his goods through a central auction. The commodities usually arrive early in the morning so that they can be dispatched to the buyers at the beginning of the business day, especially if they are highly perishable. With a few exceptions a single produce terminal is characteristic of the larger terminals. The produce terminal in Los Angeles handles a large amount of perishable agricultural products brought in by trucks in overnight hauls from considerable distances.

Authority over Terminals

Railroad terminals are private property, and a railroad cannot be expected to disadvantage itself seriously by affording the accommodation of its facilities to other lines. Prior to 1920 the Interstate Commerce Act imposed upon the railroads the obligation to afford all reasonable, proper, and equal facilities for the interchange of traffic between their respective lines. However, a common carrier was not required to give the use of its tracks or terminal facilities to another engaged in like business; but if a carrier voluntarily opened its terminal to the use of others, it was obliged to avoid discrimination among the various railroads. The Act of 1920 gave the Interstate Commerce Commission the power to require a carrier to give the use of its terminal facilities to another carrier, provided that (1) the grant should be in the public interest, (2) reasonable compensation should be paid, and (3) the requirement should not impair the business of the carrier making the concession. As a result of this, the Commission has been able to promote a good deal more co-ordination in interchange than existed theretofore, but little other progress has been made in terminal unification.

Conclusion

The railroad terminal problem has developed as a result of the tremendous growth in intercity traffic over the years, the number of competing railroads at important centers, and the rapid growth of metropolitan areas. Considering these factors, it is doubtful that any advance planning at the time the molding forces were exerting their influence could have achieved any more satisfactory results. Even if one were able to wipe the slate clean at the present time and start afresh, it is difficult to envisage the organizational and locational pattern that would be relevant for the future. Consolidation of railroads into a limited number of systems would introduce some modifications. Changing technological developments are also having their impact, but as long as the railroads are the medium for mass intercity freight traffic, large terminal facilities will have to be provided within the metropolitan areas to handle it. Although inertia, because of private property interests, competing railroads, and the existence of the terminal facilities that have grown up over time, presents impediments, the real problem lies deeper. As Mayer says: "No comprehensive plan has been evolved that considers in detail the relationships between the railway pattern and the other elements of the urban agglomeration in order to insure that the railway facilities will function more effectively as integral parts of the metropolitan area as a whole."[2] Until a better comprehension of the emerging metropolitan complex is obtained, and until there is a better understanding of the role of the different agencies in the transport structure, resolution of the major problems will have to be by improvisation, largely by the carriers themselves, as adaptations to the exigencies of business requirements.

[2] Mayer, *op. cit.*, p. 315.

AIRPORTS

The Air Terminal Network

The major problem of air terminals, like that of railroads, centers on the large metropolitan areas which are the focal points of the principal intercity traffic. For general planning purposes the Federal Aviation Agency classifies air terminal areas into three groups: (1) the large hub, which handles 1 per cent or more of continental United States passengers; (2) the medium hub, with 0.25 per cent to 0.99 per cent; and (3) the small hub, with 0.05 per cent to 0.24 per cent. In 1959, there were 23 large hubs, made up of the largest metropolitan centers; 38 medium ones, exemplified by cities such as Reno, Nevada; Salt Lake City, Utah; and Columbus, Ohio; and 93 small hubs, such as Tucson, Arizona; Wichita, Kansas; and Little Rock, Arkansas. Of the 549 communities in the continental United States that had scheduled air-line service, traffic was concentrated in the 154 hub communities. The 23 large ones accounted for over two thirds of all the passenger originations and an even greater proportion of the mail and cargo.

For planning purposes within the hubs the airports are classified into three groups: (1) airports capable of accommodating the turbo-jets, (2) airports able to serve all other scheduled air carriers, and (3) airports for general aviation which serve civil aircraft other than scheduled air carriers. Those that are capable of handling the jets also accommodate a large percentage of all other segments of civil aviation. This is also true for the second group of airports. The growing complexity of the air terminal situation in the hub area is illustrated by the fact that the national airport plan for the fiscal years 1962–66 recommended a total of 22 airports for the Los Angeles metropolitan area by 1966, two of these to accommodate the largest turbo-jets, 17 for other scheduled air carriers, and three for general aviation.[3]

Ownership and Management

Airports may be publicly or privately owned, but the large ones capable of handling the turbo-jet planes are all owned and administered by some public agency, commonly municipal or the equivalent. The tremendous demands for land space for airports, the desire of cities to

---

[3] The information for this section was compiled from Federal Aviation Agency *National Airport Plan, Fiscal Years 1962–1966* (Washington, D.C.: U.S. Government Printing Office, 1961). Los Angeles has recently (1967) acquired the Ontario airport as part of its municipal complex, although it is outside the city limits.

promote aviation in their areas, together with federal aid for construction, have promoted public ownership. In addition, individual air lines would be quite incapable of financing their own airports under present technical conditions because of the large terminal facilities required by the long-distance aircraft. Air terminals, therefore, have to be utilized on a joint basis. This might be done through joint ownership and operation by the air lines, but they could scarcely carry the burden of the costs under current conditions. Even with federal aid, public borrowing at low interest rates, and exemption from property taxes, most airports find it difficult to meet operating expenses, and none of the largest, at least, would be likely to survive on a private enterprise basis.[4]

Airport administration and management vary widely throughout the country. Administration may be under an existing department of the city government; under a separate airport department; under an airport commission, the members of which are selected by the city government; or under an airport authority. The Port of New York Authority is the responsible agent for the airports in the area under its jurisdiction. The Los Angeles International Airport is under an Airport Commission of five members appointed by the Mayor. It operates through a general manager with a professional staff, but is responsible to the city government for all of its actions. Financing, concessions, and so forth are matters over which the city government exercises ultimate, and much direct, authority.[5]

The landing areas of airports are under the direct control of the airport management, and revenues from these are obtained through landing fees. The method of handling the building area varies from one airport to another. At the new International Airport for Los Angeles, each trunk-line carrier has its own "satellite" terminal building owned by the airport but leased to the carrier, which must supply all the interior furnishings. Revenues are also received from hangars and ground facilities of the air lines, parking areas, and restaurants. Some airports—for example, San Francisco—have hotels on the airport grounds. These nonlanding area sources of revenue are an important item of budgeting in airport finance. They should not, however, as a matter of principle be used as a means of disguising the costs that belong to the supplying of facilities to the carriers. These should be as-

---

[4] The Federal Aviation Agency estimated that the development costs of its four-year plan would amount to $751.4 million for the air carrier airports and $331 million for general aviation airports, for a total of $1,082,420. *Ibid.,* p. 212.

[5] See Sheldon W. Stahl, "The Los Angeles International Airport—An Economic Analysis" (Ph.D. thesis, University of California, Los Angeles, 1964).

certained as accurately as possible and stated separately. If this is not done, the appropriate basis for carrier charges cannot be developed.[6]

Airport Location

One of the most difficult problems connected with airports is that of determining the appropriate location. It illustrates forcefully the complexities of advance planning with rapidly changing technologies. A great many existing airports are encountering serious locational disadvantages, and if plans could be remade, many of them would be placed elsewhere than as at present. A large number will find their functions severely modified for the future, but the appropriate location of the new ones to be constructed is very difficult to determine. If in the course of a relatively few years hence, freight transported by jet planes should constitute a significant proportion of air traffic, present airports would be totally inadequate and present locations a major source of difficulty. Probably an entirely new air terminal complex would have to be developed to deal with this situation.

Those responsible for deciding on the location of airports, especially the main ones in the hub area, have to evaluate a large number of factors, many of which commonly conflict with each other. Climatic and surrounding physical geographic considerations are important because of the problems of navigational safety. Large areas are required to provide for the long landing strips which are necessary for the most modern planes. Noise, the potential damage to surrounding properties, particularly from take-offs, and the need for adequate clearance and approach even outside the port area are matters that have to be weighed. These will be even more important if supersonic jets are brought into commercial use. The relation of the airport to the metropolitan area it serves is a major consideration. Facilities must be provided for moving traffic to and from the terminals. Most of the business they afford enters into the surface movements of the areas. The distance of the location from the focal points of the traffic which the airports generate is another factor. The new airports which are being constructed are being located farther and farther away from the centers of the cities they serve. For example, two possible sites are being examined for the second large airport for Los Angeles; one is some 35 miles east of the heart of the city, the other is some 75 miles to the north in the Antelope Valley, which is separated from the Los Angeles area by mountain

[6] The Federal Aviation Agency opposes the levying of any charges by airport management for the recovery of federal funds, which it believes should be borne by the nation as a whole (Federal Aviation Agency, *National Aviation Goals,* Report of the Task Force (Washington, D.C.: U.S. Government Printing Office, September, 1961), p. 93.

ranges with peaks rising to over 10,000 feet. The air terminal problem in its relation to metropolitan areas may soon become more difficult to resolve than that of the railroads.

The planning of airports and their location must be considered at both the federal and the local levels. If an airport is to be eligible for federal aid, it must be part of the national airport plan developed by the Federal Aviation Agency. Not only must the physical structure of the airport meet its approval, but the location also has to be satisfactory.

A closely related matter is accessibility, which is so basic to airport value that the road and highway plan of the Federal Government must embrace the closest liaison between the FAA, the Bureau of Public Roads, the appropriate state and local agencies, to assure adequate access to air terminal areas from the communities served. Any Federal program for assistance to communities in providing mass transit facilities should take into account the potential of such facilities in improving the ties between the central city and its airports.[7]

The problem of noise from jet transports and the effect of this on surrounding property owners and residential population has already created serious problems including the threat of lawsuits from property owners. The introduction of "jumbo" jets, and perhaps supersonic aircraft will intensify the difficulties. The Los Angeles City Council has taken notice of this fact (July 27, 1967) by voting to impose a $1 tax on all departing or arriving passengers, and on each ton of air cargo or airfreight loaded or unloaded at the terminals. This was one of the conditions for approval of a $75 million airport revenue bond issue intended as the first phase of a $500 million master plan development of the Los Angeles municipal airports. The tax revenues to be paid into "a noise abatement fund" to be used by the Airports Department for soundproofing of homes, schools, and churches in the affected areas. Secretary Boyd has advanced a somewhat similar suggestion. Whether this will get at the root of the problem is debatable to say the least. It would seem to be more realistic to place the burden more directly on the industry thereby bringing it to a clear-cut recognition of the economic responsibilities of changing technology. It is clear that the development of air transportation has not simplified the matter of resolving the problems of the metropolitan transport complex, or the administrative procedures and devices for dealing with the issues.

MOTOR TERMINALS

While the problem of terminals is a matter of major concern for railroads and air transport, it is a relatively minor matter for the motor

[7] *Ibid.,* p. 95.

transport industry as a whole. This does not mean that terminal expenses are unimportant. In fact, they constitute a significant portion of the total expenses for over-the-road truck haulage between large centers, and they have shown signs of a rather serious increase. On this, one study points out that:

Terminal costs . . . are for the most part chargeable only to L.T.L. (less than truck load) shipments. L.T.L. traffic ordinarily must be picked up and delivered by local trucks and in most instances must pass through the terminal dock and be loaded into and unloaded from the over-the-road vehicle. The truck load traffic need not be handled through the terminal—it is loaded directly at the point of origin into the over-the-road vehicle and delivered directly in the same vehicle to the consignee at the point of destination. In part, then, the fact that terminal costs per ton have risen so much more sharply than average revenue per ton may be attributable to the fact that L.T.L. business has been expanding in relation to total tonnage carried by motor carriers.[8]

Passenger Terminals

Bus passenger terminals are for suburban and intercity travelers, and in most cities are of very modest proportions because of the lack of need for large loading facilities. Each bus can move in quickly, load, and enter upon its journey with a minimum of time. In addition, small depots in the suburban areas can be established to load and unload passengers on the routes served, thereby avoiding much of the concentration in the downtown area. Traffic congestion in midtown Manhattan led the Port of New York Authority to establish a Union Bus Terminal for intercity and suburban buses, and some other cities have bus terminals which are also centers of transportation to airports. In most, however, airport delivery is to hotels or other designated points.

Freight Terminals

As already pointed out, freight terminals for trucks are for the purpose of handling less-than-truckload traffic, the truckload freight being moved directly between point of origin and final destination. Intercity trucking companies find it necessary to have terminal facilities for assembling and distributing the small shipments, but these usually can be located outside the congested areas.

The old idea seemed to be to get into the center of things even at the expense of efficient and economic handling of freight. The new and enlightened idea is

[8] Shields and Company, *The Motor Carrier Industry* (New York, 1956), p. 35. Consolidated Freightways reported the construction of a $2,850,000 truck terminal in Chicago (the most expensive ever built by a trucking company). It was to be opened by the end of 1962 (*Traffic World,* June 30, 1962, Part I, p. 29).

to find a location with plenty of space, build a platform that will permit the handling of freight at the least possible cost, and have plenty of space for parking the vehicles off the street. It has been proved that the careful routing of trucks to generally avoid congested traffic areas is economically sound in the pickup and delivery operation even though more miles may be travelled.[9]

New York City again is a notable exception to this because of the congested conditions in downtown Manhattan. The Port Authority of New York has constructed two union motor truck terminals within its area to handle the huge volume of l.t.l. traffic that moves in and out, as well as a truck terminal for rail freight. In Los Angeles, United Parcel Service has constructed a highly mechanized depot near the center of the downtown retail area for sorting its shipments for delivery within the metropolitan area and to outside points. The Chicago Union Truck Terminal is the largest in that city and serves twenty noncompeting carriers. In general, motor carriers prefer to have their own terminals; and considering the nature of the intercity trucking industry, this is likely to remain the pattern in most cities for the foreseeable future. With so much truck traffic moving directly from origin to destination, the advantages of terminal unification seem to be rather small.

WATER TERMINALS

Water terminals differ from those of other carriers in that the location, as it relates to the particular area served, is rather precisely determined by geographic conditions. Harbors develop at the economical and strategic meeting places of land and water routes. Locational possibilities are therefore quite limited, and location for the most part is taken as a fixed factor in port location and development.

The major transport problem in the metropolitan areas that are ports, especially seaports, is that of providing adequate interchange facilities between the land and sea agencies without aggravating congestion on the waterfront, which seems to be inescapable, at the same time that ready access to the docks and wharves serving the general public is afforded to all shippers. This is the problem of rail-water connections, and it is commonly dealt with by some kind of rail coordination, as previously described.

The problems of port administration vary widely, but they present their greatest complexities in seaport areas where harbor facilities are such that a number of different cities may each have ports that serve

---

[9] *Financing the Motor Carrier Industry*, Regular Common Carrier Conference of the American Trucking Associations, Inc. (Washington, D.C., 1952), p. 43.

the entire region. New York is the outstanding illustration of this; the harbor area of San Francisco is somewhat similar; and metropolitan Los Angeles has two immediately adjacent ports, namely, Long Beach and Los Angeles. Only New York has achieved a degree of unified administration of the port area which is a single geographic region but is divided on a city and also on a state basis.

The functions of port administration may be grouped into four categories: (1) navigation administration, (2) trade and traffic promotion, (3) waterfront facility administration, and (4) metropolitan transportation development. The last of these is a minor function except for the establishment of terminal rail connections undertaken by some administrations and the metropolitan transport responsibilities of the Port of New York Authority.

Administration of the important seaports is usually under a central agency established for that purpose. The primary responsibilities are generally in the hands of local agencies. The federal government, however, may have an important role through the Department of Defense, the Coast Guard and the Customs Bureau under the Treasury Department, the Immigration Bureau under the Department of Justice, and the Department of Agriculture in connection with imports of agricultural products. Thus, port administration entails the co-ordination of a great many activities and agencies at both local and federal levels. This cannot be isolated from the metropolitan transportation problem, even though many of the duties, especially that of management of port facilities, can be handled quite separately.[10]

THE PORT OF NEW YORK AUTHORITY

The Port of New York Authority is the most comprehensive undertaking in this country to date to deal with the complex problems of co-ordination and unification of transportation in a metropolitan area. It is a self-supporting, nonpolitical agency of the states of New York and New Jersey, created as a means for resolving the transportation difficulties of the largest and most important metropolitan area of the country, which spreads into two states and constitutes the greatest focal point of domestic and foreign commerce in the world.[11]

[10] For a detailed discussion of port administration, see M. L. Fair, *Port Administration in the United States* (Cambridge, Md.: Cornell Maritime Press, 1954).

[11] According to Owen, the Bi-State Development Agency created by the compact between Missouri and Illinois in 1949 for the city of St. Louis is the most comprehensive regional planning agency that has been set up so far. It is modeled on the Port of New York Authority. See Owen, *op. cit.,* p. 177.

The Interstate Compact

The harbor area of the New York metropolitan region centers on the Hudson River as it meets the Atlantic Ocean. The lower reaches of the river, which constitute the harbor area, also serve as a boundary line between the states of New York and New Jersey. The bulk of the maritime commerce developed on the New York side of the harbor, but most of the trunk railroads entered the area and located their terminals on the New Jersey side. Communications across the river were maintained by car-float, lighterage, and ferry services. In fact, there were no vehicular crossings over or under the waterways between New York and New Jersey when the Port Authority was created in 1921. Congestion, conflicts over rate differentials, and rivalries between interests on both sides of the harbor led to the organization of the New York–New Jersey Port and Harbor Development Commission, which was set up by the two states to develop a comprehensive plan to resolve the difficulties. Because of the problems of dual sovereignty, it was decided to utilize the clause in the Constitution of the United States which permits states to enter into compacts with each other to solve common problems. In 1921, both states adopted legislation providing for a compact which supplemented the agreement of 1834 that dealt with boundary lines. This compact creating the Port of New York Authority was signed on April 30, 1921, and assented to by Congress.[12]

Powers and Jurisdiction

The compact of 1921 created a Port of New York District with specific boundaries that included roughly the metropolitan region within a radius of twenty-five miles of the southern tip of Manhattan, and placed it under the jurisdiction of the Port of New York Authority. This agency constituted a body "both corporate and politic, with full power and authority to purchase, construct, lease and/or operate any terminal or transportation facility" within the Port District. It was empowered to make charges for the use of the facilities, to acquire real estate, and to borrow money, but it was given no power to levy taxes. It was authorized to make recommendations to the two state legislatures and to Congress to facilitate the carrying-out of its purposes, and was instructed to prepare a comprehensive plan for the development of the

[12] For a detailed history of the Authority, see E. W. Bard, *The Port of New York Authority* (New York: Columbia University Press, 1942). The material in this section is drawn largely from F. L. Bird, *A Study of the Port of New York Authority* (New York: Dun & Bradstreet, Inc., 1949). See also, *The Port of New York Authority, Annual Report, 1966,* for a summary of activities and operations.

port region for the two legislatures. This plan was presented in 1922 and was based largely on the report of the Port and Harbor Development Commission that had previously been established to recommend a solution to the difficulties besetting the area. It provided for the complete reorganization of the railroad terminal system and contained extensive proposals concerning trucking, ferries, vehicular tunnels, markets and food distribution, and the handling of grain and fuel.

The Port Authority is composed of twelve commissioners, six appointed by the governor of each state. Each serves for a term of six years and without financial compensation. The commissioners determine policies, approve plans and financial appropriations, and appoint the executive director and general counsel. The Authority is an instrumentality of the two state governments, but it enjoys a very high degree of autonomy. It is given complete tax immunity, paying no taxes to the municipalities or the states on its property, its income, its gasoline and other purchases, and its motor vehicle registrations. It pays no federal taxes, and interest on its bonds is immune from federal income taxes. However, because of the difficulties that arose over relief from local property taxes when the Authority undertook to acquire property for terminals, the legislatures of the two states granted it permission to enter into voluntary agreements with municipalities to make payments in lieu of taxes equal to those previously levied on the property which was acquired.

Terminal Unification

The primary purpose of the Authority when it was originally formed was to bring about a reorganization of the railroad terminal system, which was the most pressing problem at the time. Relatively little has been accomplished on this score, partly because the Authority lacks the regulatory and coercive powers to compel the railroads to accept the provisions of the comprehensive plan, and partly because of the enormous technical and operational problems connected with the carload traffic of the trunk-line railroads. In addition, urban rail passenger traffic has presented issues for which no ready financial solution is available. Apart from some co-ordination of railroad operations on the New Jersey waterfront, the principal achievement in rail transport was the construction of the union freight terminal for less-than-carload traffic in midtown Manhattan in 1932.

Vehicular Traffic. Prior to 1927, ferryboats provided the only means for vehicles to cross the Hudson River between the New Jersey and the New York sections of the metropolitan area. This impeded travel because of the crossing time that was required, and the increasing congestion at the ferry terminals with the rapid growth of automobile traffic. The Holland Tunnel was constructed under the river in 1927 by separate commissions of the two states. The operation of this was turned over to the Port Authority in 1930. The George Washington Bridge was put into operation in 1931 and the Lincoln Tunnel in 1937. In addition, three other bridges were constructed to connect New Jersey with Staten Island. Thus, there are six vehicular crossings of the Hudson between New Jersey and New York City, all under the control of the Authority. Ferries continued to compete with the fixed river crossings but have steadily declined in importance. By 1947, they handled only about 12 per cent of the total vehicular traffic crossing the river. The ferry service across the Hudson River from Jersey City will soon be abandoned with the introduction of the Aldene Plan adopted by the state of New Jersey.

Bus and Truck Terminals.   Immediately after the end of World War II the Port Authority undertook to construct motor terminals which were to be co-ordinated with access to the Hudson River tunnels. One union motor truck terminal is located in downtown Manhattan and one in Newark, New Jersey. The function of the union truck terminals is to provide centralized points of interchange between the large over-the-road trucks handling less-than-truckload freight and the smaller vehicles which collect and deliver the shipments in the central areas. The Railway Express Agency occupies 192 truck berths on the first floor and basement of the Port Authority building. The union bus terminal is located in midtown Manhattan. It is for intercity and suburban buses. It is used by a large majority of the bus companies entering the area. No new bus terminals may be constructed by private companies in the central area, nor may there be any permanent enlargement of any existing terminals, except those under the control of the Port Authority.

Marine Terminals.   Waterfront development of New York harbor on both sides of the river is a conglomerate of docks, wharves, and other terminal facilities, some privately owned and some under municipal control. They are scattered among the three cities of Newark, Hoboken, and New York, with only a minimum of co-operation and co-ordination to date. A large part of the facilities is antiquated in terms of modern transportation, and much of the waterfront lacks modern and efficient handling equipment. The Authority acquired the Grain Terminal from the state of New York in 1944 and completely rehabilitated it. In 1947 the Authority entered into an agreement with the city of Newark whereby it acquired a long-term lease of the properties of the port of Newark and undertook to develop that water front. The Authority has prepared a comprehensive program for unification, co-ordination, and modernization of the waterfront facilities and their connections with the land transport of the area. So far, only a minimum of success has been achieved, and much remains to be done by way of overcoming political, financial, and other obstacles before the basic problems besetting the New York harbor area can be resolved. At the present time the Authority operates six marine terminals in the New York-New Jersey harbor area.

Air Terminals. The Port Authority operates four airports and two heliports. The John F. Kennedy International Airport is used for long-distance and overseas flights. La Guardia Airport serves the requirements of short-haul traffic for the east side of Manhattan and other areas east of the Hudson, while Newark airport serves the west side and the New Jersey section of the Port District. The Authority acquired Teterboro Airport in New Jersey as a supplementary airport for general aviation. Studies are now being undertaken for the location and construction of a fourth major airport. The two heliports are located in Manhattan.

Rail Transportation

The Port Authority acquired the Hudson and Manhattan Railroad in 1962. This constitutes its only excursion into rapid transit so far. The financial problems of the railroad were such that the legislatures of New York and New Jersey entered into convenants with bondholders of the Authority to protect them against dilution of already pledged revenues by any additional commuter rail deficits. The Authority cannot use funds for any additional commuter railroad purposes unless it determines that the new facilities will be self-supporting. This limitation can be overcome by state subsidies.

World Trade Center

In 1962 construction of a World Trade Center was authorized. Construction was commenced in 1967 after the legality of the project was upheld in the courts. The Center is to be completed over a five-year period. The estimated cost is over $270 million.[13]

Investment

The cumulative investment in the Port Authority amounted to $1,584,037,000 at the end of 1966. The funded debt was $832,849,-

[13] See *Via Port of New York Authority*, April, 1962, and *Annual Report, op. cit.*

000. Debt retired through income and reserve funds over the life of the Authority to 1966 totaled $944,960,000.

Conclusion

The Port Authority of New York was designed primarily to effectuate unification, in terms of operation, of the terminal facilities in the New York harbor area of the two states of New York and New Jersey. Originally, this was mostly a matter of co-ordination and unification of rail and water terminals and connections between them. Attention was also directed to the problems of river crossings of the Hudson. Subsequent developments of motor and air transport have added some terminal aspects of these to its activities. With the exception of the Hudson River crossings, its efforts have been confined to attempts to resolve the terminal problems of rail, water, motor, and air carriers. Its achievements on this score have undoubtedly been outstanding, although they have fallen considerably short of the original objective, particularly in rail and water co-ordination and unification. Resolution of the problems of motor traffic has been limited to the Hudson River crossings and less-than-carload freight. How much more can be accomplished by a single agency remains to be seen. It has been unable to do much about motor vehicle traffic in general and so far has not dealt with urban passenger traffic in general, mass transit, or commuter travel. Whether it can serve as a satisfactory medium for dealing with these questions is still to be answered. If it is burdened with this task, it will find that this phase of the transportation problem of the New York area will be much more difficult to deal with than anything it has yet faced.

As mentioned earlier, the Authority is financially self-sustaining, without taxing power, and independent of direct public aid for its operations. It could not maintain this position if it were required to assume the burden of the metropolitan mass transit and commuter problem.[14] The fact that it is financially self-sustaining, however, must not be interpreted to mean that all of the economic costs entailed in its operations are covered by its revenues. The tax exemptions on the property it administers and on the bonds it sells, as well as the federal airport aid it receives, are important sources of financial assistance. How it would fare without this is an open question. It is not intended here to imply that this procedure is inadvisable, but it does need to be evaluated in terms of the over-all financial problems of the metropolitan area, and the economic costs of supplying the transportation services.

---

[14] See Bird, *op. cit.*, for a detailed analysis of the financing and financial operations of the Authority.

Burdens transferred from one segment of the economy may be too great for the others to bear.

The greater are a city's economic and governmental functions, the larger is the proportion of its potential taxable resources that escapes taxation. Note, for example, the relatively high percentages of tax exempt property in New York and in the state capitals listed [Boston and Providence]. At the same time more expenditures are required, much of which must come from the city's budget. Little wonder, then, that a large metropolis, partly deserted by its residents, badly needs financial help from the outside.[15]

[15] J. Gottmann, *Megalopolis* (New York: Twentieth Century Fund, 1961), p. 752. Owen characterizes New York City as existing in a chronic state of bankruptcy, Owen, *op. cit.*, p. 150.

Chapter 24

PROPOSED SOLUTIONS TO THE URBAN TRANSPORT PROBLEM

INTRODUCTION

Urban transportation problems have been the subject of very extensive investigations in most of the large centers for many years. Under the impact of the automobile, the "crisis" in mass rapid transit, and the huge demands for funds for roadway construction in urban areas, the issues have risen to the level of attracting the serious attention of the federal government. In many ways the transportation question is but one phase of the problems that the rapid urbanization of this country has created for metropolitan areas.[1] In some respects, at least, it is the most significant economic problem and can be viewed independently of the others. However, in its economic aspects it is the most complex question facing the metropolitan areas, at the same time that it defies solution by any single unit of government because in every area it embraces the responsibilities and activities of many of them. Any feasible resolution, therefore, of the problems of metropolitan transportation must be based upon the development of means for coordinating and unifying the actions of the responsible public authorities of the various regions.

The following survey of some approaches to the current problems of urban transportation is designed to highlight some of the contrasting situations in different areas of the country, suggestions that have been advanced for dealing with them, and the proposed program of the federal government.[2]

[1] See R. C. Wood, *Metropolis against Itself* (New York: Committee for Economic Development, March, 1959).

[2] The state of New York is working on a master plan for the City of New York which is not discussed here because it is still in the formative stage. Under the proposal, $1 billion for rapid transit would be provided from a statewide bond issue. The plan calls for the Metropolitan Commuter Transportation Authority to become a "holding" agency of the Long Island Railroad, the New York City Transit Authority, the Triborough Bridge and Tunnel Authority, and for whatever agency is set up to handle the commuter service

THE DOYLE REPORT

The Urban Transport Problem

The Doyle Report examined the problem of commuter services provided by the railroads, particularly in New York, Chicago, Philadelphia, and Boston, at some considerable length.[3] It concluded that (1) rail commutation services have seldom recovered the cost of the service, and the deficits have been made up from freight profits, a situation which cannot long continue; (2) the continuing losses from suburban service have forced the railroads to discontinue many trains, in conflict with the needs of commuters for efficient transportation; (3) enough alternative commuter transportation exists to reduce the proceeds from fare increases because of the number of riders lost with each increase; and (4) suburban rail service is primarily a local metropolitan area problem, and the major efforts to continue the service must be local efforts. However, federal involvement through credit, rate and services regulation, taxes, and the federal-aid highway program is so important that the federal government must join in helping to resolve the difficulties. The report stated that the most important forces affecting the services were external to the railroads and largely beyond the control of the managements.

As an immediate step to deal with this issue, the report recommended that (1) the Act of 1958 should be amended to provide for direct loan of federal funds by the Interstate Commerce Commission for suburban capital improvements; (2) the federal discontinuance statute should be extended to three months, the time within which the Interstate Commerce Commission must act on notice to discontinue, and the burden of proof should affirmatively be placed on the railroad seeking discontinuance; and (3) The federal income tax statutes should be so adjusted that state and local financial support for necessary passenger service made available by either tax relief or direct payments to carriers will not be absorbed by taxation of corporate profits.[4]

---

of the New Haven Railroad. Presumably this would still leave the Hudson and Manhattan Railroad under the Port of New York Authority. See *Railway Age,* April 3, 1967. See also *Rapid Transit Systems in Six Metropolitan Areas,* Staff Report to the Joint Committee on Washington Metropolitan Problems, 86th Congress, 1st session (Washington, D.C.: U.S. Government Printing Office, November, 1959).

[3] *National Transportation Policy* (Doyle Report), Preliminary Draft of a Report to the Senate Committee on Interstate and Foreign Commerce, 87th Congress, 1st session (Washington, D.C.: U.S. Government Printing Office, 1961), Part VII, chap. vii. The details of this were set forth briefly in Chapter 22 above.

[4] *Ibid.,* pp. 581–82.

The report then proceeded to examine the twentieth-century urban revolution in terms of the effects of the automobile on the residential patterns of the metropolitan area, and their impact on mass rapid transit. Unfortunately, it confined its attention almost exclusively to this phase of metropolitan transportation. It appraised the rapid growth of passenger traffic by automobile with rather serious misgivings, and expressed the opinion that the capacity which needs to be added to the urban transport systems to raise standards of service and to reduce transportation costs could best be provided "by giving commuters free mass transportation which would cost less than providing the additional highway and parking facilities needed for their autos."[5] The report also emphasized the fact that no over-all planning or co-ordination for metropolitan transportation exists in any urban center of the country. Yet local, state, and federal authorities all participate on an extensive scale in the provision of the facilities. Because of the complexities of the problem and the conflict of jurisdictions, it concluded that the major trends in the development of urban transport establish the federal interest in sound metropolitan transportation. It therefore made the following recommendations: (1) Co-ordination of federal facility and redevelopment programs by the Executive Office of the President must be more effective than at present—at the top policy level in Washington and also at the field level. (2) Comprehensive transportation and land use planning must have greatly increased emphasis and financial support from the federal establishment. (3) The federal government should undertake a substantial program of basic research in urban transportation and development problems. (4) Following initiation of the above recommendations, a detailed study of further federal financial aid to metropolitan transportation will be in order.[6]

Suggested Plan for Federal Legislative Aid

The report also contained a suggested plan for use of federal legislative aid in forming metropolitan authorities.[7] This was drawn up on the basis of extensive investigation, although it stated that it was primarily for the purpose of stimulating thought and further research rather than presenting a finished legislative proposal. The plan was advanced because the study committee concluded that present-day metro-

[5] *Ibid.*, p. 553. At the same time, the report stated that "Planners and administrators are going to have to rationalize the financing of urban transportation and move in the direction of making the entire operation self-sustaining" (p. 607). No attempt is made to reconcile these contradictory positions.

[6] *Ibid.*, pp. 619–20.

[7] *Ibid.*, Appendix K, pp. 632–46.

politan areas, some of which have hundreds of governments, including districts or authorities, within their defined boundaries, are not able to produce results in solving problems which afflict the entire metropolitan area.

A detailed table of contents of the draft statute was presented. This was then analyzed under two main headings, the first involving federal participation and aids, and the second the powers and standards to be used in the administration of metropolitan districts established to deal with the entire supply of passenger transportation for each.

Legal Organization and Framework. The scope of the authority established under the legislation encompasses any mode for transporting people in large numbers, and would include all private, common, and contract carriers by rail, bus, taxicab, automobile, or any other power-driven means engaged in this activity within the metropolitan district. Federal power would be utilized to facilitate the formation of districts, but the effectuation of the arrangements would be voluntary, becoming operative in a state only upon ratification by that state. "The metropolitan transportation authority (hereafter the MTA), the fundamental administrative body created, is a single-function authority empowered to plan, regulate, and, if desired, operate, mass transportation within its respective metropolitan district."[8] One aspect of the proposal, especially emphasized by the report, was its voluntary nature. There was to be no federal compulsion to join the plan. Each state would do so of its own choice by legislative enactment. There were also to be provisions whereby a state could withdraw at any time. Financing was to be based on general obligation bonds based on the credit of the constituent jurisdictions, but federal aid would be available to all who met the required legislative standards. Finally, the judicial acts of the MTA would be subject to review initially by the state commission, possibly by the Interstate Commerce Commission, and ultimately by the courts.

When a state agreed to participate in the program, the President of the United States would appoint five commissioners, who must legally reside in the state, to the state mass transportation commission. The state, in conjunction with local authorities, would form the metropolitan district. The President would then appoint the three members of the MTA, two of whom should be residents of the district, both state and district appointees being subject to the approval of the Senate of the United States. The statute should provide for interstate metropoli-

[8] *Ibid.*, p. 635.

tan districts, and also should give the MTA original jurisdiction on all matters other than the designation of a metropolitan district.[9]

Substantive Powers of the Metropolitan Transportation Authority. The report stated that five basic powers would be required for the accomplishment of the objectives envisaged. First, the MTA would be required to develop a long-range master transportation plan. (Presumably, however, this would be limited to movement of people since this was the purpose for which the MTA was to be created.) Second, the MTA would be given the authority to control, regulate, and to the extent necessary, operate, all mass transportation and mass transportation facilities and equipment within the metropolitan district in order to achieve a balanced and maximum utilization of all facilities and modes.[10] Third, the control over entry should be broad enough to produce the most desirable route structures and the best balance of modes. This would also include authority over route extensions and revisions as well as consolidations and mergers. Fourth, the MTA would have the power to tax the movement of and license all mass transportation modes so as to obtain operating revenues. The most suitable source of revenue for most of the metropolitan agencies would be a tax on the use or movement of mass transportation vehicles, including automobiles. This tax would be levied on use, not ownership, and therefore might include tolls. Licenses for use during designated hours or within designated areas also might be employed.[11] Fifth, the MTA should have the power to raise capital funds through the issuance of obligations and the flotation of private, state, or federal financial indebtedness. One of the stated advantages of the proposal is that, as a federal agency, it would not be subject to state constitutional debt limitations.

Conclusion

In conclusion, the report stated that:

Such an authority could be administered by the people from the area under strict requirements to plan for the best interests of the metro. Since the members of the State Commission and the Metropolitan Transportation Authority would be clothed in Federal vestments they would, on the one hand, be subject to the public scrutiny and financial checks that go with this investiture, and, on the

---

[9] For organizational charts of this statutory proposal, see *ibid.,* pp. 639–41.

[10] Presumably this would apply also to private automobiles, since they were included in the definition of mass transportation, although how the controls would be implemented is not indicated.

[11] *Ibid.,* p. 645.

other hand, have a freedom of financial and operating action across jurisdictional lines which local governments collectively have not been able to bestow.

Students and close observers of metropolitan problems, particularly transportation, are unanimous in the belief that if action of the scope and freedom comprehended in this proposal is not taken that transportation congestion will become a destroyer of the centers of American production and wealth.[12]

Three crucial questions stand out in this proposal, none of which has been given careful attention in the report. The first is that of financial independence, which is supposed to be one of the objectives. The MTA will be financially independent in only one sense: It will secure its revenues from taxes and from state and federal aid. This certainly would involve no equation of expenses and revenues from use. Second, it represents very extensive exercise of public authority, especially at the federal level. How ultimate federal dominance could be escaped is difficult to imagine. Third, there is no analysis whatsoever of the over-all transportation problem of metropolitan areas; and, as pointed out previously, the movement of goods and terminal problems are as vital a part of metropolitan transportation as travel by people.

THE WASHINGTON PROGRAM

The Mass Transportation Survey Report, 1959

In 1959, President Eisenhower transmitted to Congress the report of the National Capital Planning Commission and the National Capital Regional Planning Council on the mass transportation survey of the Washington region. This report, entitled *Transportation Plan—National Capital Region,* was undertaken in accordance with the National Capital Planning Act of 1952 (66 Stat. 781) and was under the authorization of the Second Supplemental Appropriation Act of 1955 (69 Stat. 33) under the joint direction of the Commission and the Council, in co-operation with representatives of the public utility commissions of the states of Maryland and Virginia and the District of Columbia.[13]

The study confined its attention to the problems of mass passenger transportation in the national capital region and was concerned primarily with accommodating weekday traffic, because this accounted

[12] *Ibid.,* p. 646. Surely the last paragraph is purely gratuitous, to say the least.

[13] National Capital Planning Commission–National Capital Regional Planning Council, *Transportation Plan—National Capital Region* (The White House, 1959), Letter of Transmittal. See also *Metropolitan Transportation,* Staff Report for Joint Committee on Washington Metropolitan Problems, 85th Congress, 2d session (Washington, D.C.: U.S. Government Printing Office, 1958).

for most of the congestion on the transportation system, and because the region's economic well-being depends on this traffic.[14] It examined population growth and employment in the area, projecting the trends to 1980. It stated that the most important determinant of the shape of the future region was the existing pattern of land use. Therefore, even with the estimated population increase of one million, the metropolitan pattern would be much the same as it is today—a central city built up at high densities, with downtown Washington being the focus of the region. The transportation plan that was developed assumed that

. . . the future transit system would be similar to that of today offering relatively slow service by transit vehicles which would share the local streets and highways with other traffic. The projections thus produced an estimate of the minimum number of trips likely to be made by public transit and the maximum likely to be made by private automobile, since it is reasonable to expect that transit service of at least the present quality will continue to be provided.[15]

The report also stated that joint action of the District of Columbia and the two states and their political subdivisions was necessary because "Each part of the region of course has an important stake in the creation of new transportation facilities: to protect present property values in the District of Columbia; to safeguard the Federal Government's current and planned investment in the Nation's Capital; to enable suburban residents to travel from home to work in a satisfactory manner."[16]

The plan recommended a regional transportation system consisting of (1) a network of freeways on which people could travel quickly between any two parts of the region, even at hours when traffic is heaviest; (2) a new kind of fast, comfortable public transit service between the suburbs and downtown Washington, consisting of modern buses traveling on eight freeway routes, and modern rail transit service on four routes; (3) arterial streets and highways in addition to the freeways; and (4) expanded and improved local transit service. The cost of building and equipping these facilities was estimated at approximately $2.5 billion, express bus and rail facilities accounting for about $565 million of the total, and parking facilities $119 million. An annual deficit of $16 million was estimated when the region's population reaches three million people (1980). The deficit was after the amorti-

---

[14] *Ibid.*, p. 9.
[15] *Ibid.*, p. 35.
[16] *Ibid.*, p. 77.

zation of capital costs, but without any provision for taxes on the properties.

To bring this system into being, the report recommended (1) approval of the present interstate compact between Virginia and Maryland establishing an interstate agency to regulate transit in the Washington metropolitan area; (2) a temporary public corporation to complement the efforts of the regulatory agency, and empowered to acquire rights of way and construct express transit facilities and to operate them or provide for their operation by private firms, and to assist in the financing; and (3) a second interstate compact creating a new interstate agency to succeed the preceding two organizations with the power to construct and own transit facilities, and to operate them or provide for their operation by private firms. This agency should be authorized to obtain funds by borrowing and by exercising limited taxing powers, and from transit fares.[17]

Joint Committee on Washington Metropolitan Problems

The Joint Committee on Washington Metropolitan Problems was set up in accordance with House Concurrent Resolution No. 172 of the 85th Congress (1957), which provided for a complete study of all matters pertaining to the problems created by the growth and expansion of the District of Columbia and its metropolitan area. It conducted extensive hearings on a number of phases of the problems of the region, including metropolitan transportation, publishing the results in a final report[18] which was made, however, before the mass transportation survey was completed. In summarizing the conclusions from the hearings on transportation, the Committee said that there could be little argument on the facts concerning decentralization which was taking place in the area, but that there was little agreement on what they meant. Decentralization, it stated, was a response to the advance of transportation and communications technology which would not be halted or reversed by improvements in the central city.[19] Hence, consideration should be given to the probability that the forces now changing our large cities are in fact creating a wholly new kind of metropolis. The metropolitan expansion, coupled with fundamental changes in travel habits and transportation technology, has disorgan-

[17] *Ibid.,* p. 1.

[18] *Meeting the Problems of Metropolitan Growth in the National Capital Region,* Final Report of the Joint Committee on Washington Metropolitan Problems; House Concurrent Resolution No. 172, 85th Congress; Senate Report No. 38, 86th Congress, 1st session (Washington, D.C.: U.S. Government Printing Office, 1959). This report also contains a list of the special studies made for the Joint Committee (pp. 4–5).

[19] *Ibid.,* pp. 10–11.

ized the older systems of mass transportation, and defined an all but impossible problem for those who would rehabilitate mass transportation.[20] The report did not present a metropolitan development plan, but it did describe the institutions and organizations that needed to be created for such a plan to be formulated and carried out.[21] For transportation, it recommended a regional organization, the ultimate form of which was to be determined after the report on the mass transportation survey had been received and examined.

The mass transportation survey was transmitted to Congress by the President on July 11, 1959. In November of the same year the Joint Committee held extensive hearings on the report and its recommendations.[22] As was to be expected, the witnesses presented a wide range of views and suggestions. Many, such as Elmer B. Staats, Deputy Director of the Bureau of the Budget, agreed with the recommendations and urged that proposed rail transit facilities be given highest priority. Others were highly critical of the program on the grounds that it was based on a statistical projection of existing tendencies which would merely perpetuate and aggravate current problems.[23] The District of Columbia Trucking Association criticized the plan because it ignored totally the problem of transportation of property in the region.[24]

Proposals for Action

The Institute of Public Administration made a preliminary financial and organizational report of the survey. It noted that "one of the most remarkable findings of the study is that the mass transportation

[20] *Ibid.,* p. 14.

[21] *Ibid.,* pp. 21–53.

[22] *Transportation Plan for the National Capital Region,* Hearings before the Joint Committee on Washington Metropolitan Problems, November, 1959, 86th Congress, 1st session (Washington, D.C.: U.S. Government Printing Office, 1960).

[23] For a summary of the various views, see *Organization for Transportation in the National Capital Region,* Selected Documents Prepared for the Joint Committee on Washington Metropolitan Problems, 86th Congress, 2d session (Washington, D.C.: U.S. Government Printing Office, 1960), pp. 18–111. One person has criticized the study in the following terms: "I like to hope that the recent Washington, D.C., transportation study will be the last *pre-Darwinian* study in the metropolitan field. In Washington, the region-shaping leverage of the particular transportation system built appears to have been ignored completely. The laws of metropolitan evolution were suspended. The transportation engineers were presented with a single future pattern of land development, as of twenty years hence, and asked to design three totally different transportation systems to serve it. This is as if nature could produce identical triplets, each with a fundamentally different skeletal structure" (Henry Fagin, Executive Director, Penn-Jersey Transportation Study, "Comprehensive Urban Planning," address at Conference on Transportation, National Academy of Sciences, Woods Hole, Massachusetts, August 10, 1960 [mimeographed], p. 16).

[24] *Organization for Transportation in the National Capital Region,* p. 97.

system contemplated, including the rail rapid transit component, will not eliminate the need for any highways whose construction is at all practicable from an engineering standpoint. Consequently, the region cannot, as a practical matter, save much money on highways by building the recommended rail system."[25] The need for the recommended rail service would be created principally by the estimated growth of travel into and beyond the central business district. In the absence of these travel facilities, there would be a tendency for individuals to shorten the distances between their homes and places of employment. These various elements indicated the need for a focal point in policy making "which exists nowhere today."

Nevertheless, after studying the various aspects of the mass survey, the Institute recommended (1) that the federal government contribute funds for the needed acceleration of highway construction pending the time when an interstate compact agency with taxing powers can be organized; (2) that negotiations be undertaken to create an interstate compact organization with taxing power for financing the region's share of the cost of the recommended highway network, and financing the construction and operation of a rail transit system; and (3) that machinery be set up to carry forward an immediate program of transportation improvement, entailing mass transportation improvement and a system of regional traffic and parking controls.

The Institute also issued another report for the Joint Committee in which it set forth the details of a proposed Act of Congress entitled "National Capital Transportation Act of 1960." This was to establish a national capital transportation authority which would be authorized to develop a system of transportation for the national capital region and, along with other agencies, to negotiate a compact with Maryland and Virginia for the purpose of establishing an interstate agency designed to implement generally the objectives of the Act.[26]

The Bureau of the Budget, on behalf of the administration, then transmitted to the Congress proposed legislation entitled "National Capital Transportation Act of 1960." This proposed legislation provided for (1) the creation of a Temporary National Capital Transportation Agency, (2) authorized negotiation of a compact setting up an interstate proprietary agency, and, (3) if necessary, the later crea-

---

[25] *Preliminary Financial and Organizational Report regarding Metropolitan Transportation,* Joint Committee on Washington Metropolitan Problems, 86th Congress, 1st session, August, 1959 (Washington, D.C.: U.S. Government Printing Office, 1959).

[26] *National Capital Transportation Authority,* Staff Report for Joint Committee on Washington Metropolitan Problems, 86th Congress, 1st session, October, 1959 (Washington, D.C.: U.S. Government Printing Office, 1959).

tion of a federal transportation corporation. The National Capital Transportation Agency was to be headed by an administrator and an advisory board, of which the majority were to be residents of the national capital region. It was to prepare a comprehensive, up-to-date transit development program, consisting of plans, proposed routes, and locations for the transportation of persons in the region, together with a timetable for the provision of facilities and financial estimates of costs and revenues. Before carrying out any of the aspects of the transit development program, the Agency was to submit it for review and comment to the local governing bodies and other appropriate groups of the region, as well as to the governors of Maryland and Virginia.[27]

The proposed legislation also authorized the President to abolish the Agency on or after July 1, 1963, and create a National Capital Transportation Corporation, which was to be given the powers of the Agency and also was to have full acquisition and operating powers, as a federal business enterprise, to improve transit services in the region. To finance its activities, the Corporation would be authorized to obtain funds both from appropriations and by borrowing from the Treasury Department amounts authorized in appropriation acts. Provisions were also included to authorize negotiation of a compact to create an interstate proprietary agency to carry out the objectives of the legislation.

The National Capital Transportation Agency was set up by Congress. It is headed by an administrator appointed by the President and was charged with the preparation of a transit development program in detail to be submitted to him not later than November 1, 1962.[28] Thus, after over twelve years of extensive study for an area possessing the most comprehensive facilities in the country for such an investigation, and at the expenditure of large sums of money (the survey alone cost $500,000), no plan had been developed and put into operation.

In 1965, Congress took further action by passing the National Capital Transportation Act.[29] The purpose of this legislation was to facilitate the development of a coordinated system of rapid transit, bus transportation, and highways essential to the national capital region. The National Capital Transportation Agency (1960) was authorized to design and construct a system of rail rapid transit lines and other facilities at a cost not to exceed $731 million. The scope of the project was limited to the District of Columbia.

[27] *Organization for Transportation in the National Capital Region*, pp. 3–15.
[28] The report was not submitted as of October, 1962.
[29] Public Law 89–173 (1965).

Limitations of finance and recognition of the fact that a transportation program for the region of the nation's capital had to extend beyond the boundaries of the District of Columbia led to an interstate compact to which Congress assented in the Washington Metropolitan Area Transit Authority Compact (1966).[30] This law provides for the Washington Metropolitan Area Transit Zone which includes the District of Columbia, together with parts of Maryland and Virginia. The activities are to be administered by the Washington Metropolitan Area Transit Authority governed by a board of six directors. The Board is instructed to develop and adopt a mass transit plan for the immediate and long-range needs of the Zone. Before the mass transit plan is adopted it must be submitted to some 11 agencies named in the law (section 15). After public hearings, the Board may decide upon the final plan. The Board is required to adopt capital and expense budgets and transmit them to members of the compact. It is also empowered to issue bonds on its own authorization which shall be payable out of the revenues and properties of the Authority, except that signatory parties may agree to underwrite, in whole or in part, both principal and interest.

The Authority is a governing and planning agency, not an operating body for transit facilities. The operations are to be undertaken by private transit companies, private railroads, or other persons under contract or lease with the Authority. The latter, however, retains sole jurisdiction over rates and service. The Authority is to take over all the functions and duties of the National Capital Transportation Agency on September 30, 1967.

THE CHICAGO AREA TRANSPORTATION STUDY

One of the most elaborate studies on urban transportation was initiated in Chicago in 1955 under the joint sponsorship of the state of Illinois, Cook County, the city of Chicago, and the U.S. Department of Commerce.[31] The purpose of the study was to develop a long-range transportation plan for the metropolitan region, including both highway and mass transportation facilities. The year 1980 was selected as the target year for which the plans were made. The report developed an elaborate methodology for forecasting urban growth, land use, and transport requirements. The investigators assumed that Chicago would

[30] Public Law 89–744 (1966).
[31] *Chicago Area Transportation Study,* Final Report, 3 vols., 1959–62.

follow the same pattern of development that had obtained down to 1955, and that future development would be changed little by the transportation network that would be built. (This was certainly a gratuitous assumption lacking in historical foundation, and apparently given the lie by the changing scene in Chicago over the past 15 years.) The investigators found little prospect of any significant increase in mass transportation between 1956 and 1980.

The single objective of the study was "to provide that transportation system for the region which would cost the least to build and use over a period of thirty years."[32] On this basis, estimates were made for an expressway plan of 520 miles which would require an additional 232 miles over those in existence, at a cost of $2 billion for the 20-year period. The plan for rapid transit called for effective use of existing rail facilities with improvements for movement in the Central Business District. The prime objective of this part of the plan was to conserve values in central properties. The report stated that the railroads and rapid transit were to be geared "to do the bulk job of delivering people to man the offices and purchase the goods in [this] large Central Area."[33] Plans for the two types of urban transportation, rapid transit, and automobile were developed separately and the emphasis of the study was on highway planning. Rail, water, and air terminal developments were not included in the plan. The total cost of the entire program was estimated at $2.2 billion, which meant that only $200 million was for rail transit. What course of action Chicago will follow remains to be seen.[34]

THE LOS ANGELES METROPOLITAN TRANSIT PROGRAM

Background of the Problem

The urban transport problem of the Los Angeles area is the product of the automobile age. What the region would have been like and where it would rank today among the metropolitan centers of the nation without the rise of automotive transport is difficult to envisage. The phenomenal rate of growth, however, antedated the automobile; "the Los Angeles area has grown faster during each decade since 1900 than the Standard Metropolitan areas of its size and class in the Na-

[32] *Ibid.*, vol. 3, p. 15.

[33] *Ibid.*, p. 116.

[34] According to current estimates more than 65 per cent of all cars passing through downtown Chicago on the expressways do not have downtown as their destination.

tion."[35] Even before the emergence of the automobile the population of the area was rather widely dispersed, but was served by what has been described as the most extensive streetcar and interurban railway system in the world.[36] Despite this rail framework of urban transport, the role of this means for the mass movement of passengers and the distribution of freight declined rapidly after 1920 and came to occupy a relatively minor role by the end of World War II. Today, urban passenger traffic by rail (or streetcar) has disappeared, and almost 90 per cent of the cargo in the area is moved by automobile. Finally, Los Angeles is now the second largest metropolitan area in terms of population in the country, yet the density is only about 5,638 persons per square mile for the central city, as compared with over 23,321 for New York and 12,959 for Chicago.[37] It is against this background that Los Angeles is endeavoring to resolve its urban transport problems.

The Los Angeles Metropolitan Transit Authority

The problem of moving people in the Los Angeles area was the subject of investigation of some fifty transit and traffic studies in the years between 1920 and 1949. Finally, in July, 1949, the County Board of Supervisors set up the University Presidents' Advisory Committee on Los Angeles Transportation Problems. This Committee examined all the reports that had been made to date and concluded that the factual data upon which a program could be developed were out of date and that a new study needed to be made which would "start from the beginning" and not be based on previous reports.[38] Despite the recommendations of this report for a comprehensive study of the

---

[35] Donald J. Bogue, *Population Growth in Standard Metropolitan Areas, 1900–1950* (Washington, D.C.: Housing and Home Finance Agency, December, 1953), p. 56.

For a tabulation of the growth by decades from 1850, see Coverdale and Colpitts, Consulting Engineers, *A Study of Public Transportation Needs in the Area Served by the Los Angeles Metropolitan Transit Authority* (New York, 1959), p. 16. The population of the city in 1850 was 1,610 persons and the metropolitan area 3,530. See also Chapter 22, above.

[36] See A. L. Grey, Jr., "Los Angeles: Urban Prototype," *Land Economics,* Vol. XXXV, No. 3 (August, 1959), p. 233; also G. S. Dumke, "Early Interurban Transportation in the Los Angeles Area," *Southern California Historical Quarterly,* September, 1940; G. S. Dumke, *The Boom of the Eighties in Southern California* (San Marino, Calif.: Huntington Library, 1944); G. W. Hilton and J. F. Due, *The Electric Interurban Railways in America* (Stanford: Stanford University Press, 1960), pp. 406–13.

[37] See Coverdale and Colpitts, *op. cit.,* p. 17; and W. Owen, *The Metropolitan Transportation Problem* (rev. ed.; Washington, D.C.: The Brookings Institution, 1966), Table 3, p. 232.

[38] For a more detailed presentation of these developments, see D. F. Pegrum, *The Los Angeles Metropolitan Transportation Problem—A Preliminary Analysis* (mimeographed) (Los Angeles: University of California, March, 1957).

rapid transit problem in Los Angeles, no such action was taken. Instead, the state legislature passed a bill entitled "Los Angeles Metropolitan Transit Authority Act" in 1951.[39]

Act of 1951. This piece of legislation established the Los Angeles Metropolitan Transit Authority as a public corporation of the state of California. Its jurisdiction was confined to the development of some form of monorail rapid transit for a long but relatively narrow corridor through the heart of the city of Los Angeles on routes sanctioned by the Public Utilities Commission of the state. The undertakings were to be financed by the sale of revenue bonds which were obligations of the corporation, which, however, had no taxing power and was to operate without public aid.[40] The engineering firm of Coverdale and Colpitts was engaged to study the feasibility of monorail rapid transit for Los Angeles. It concluded that monorail would not be feasible unless the Authority were relieved of many of the limitations imposed upon it, including regulation by the state Public Utilities Commission, and absence of tax relief. Recognition of the fact that the Authority was totally incapable of taking any steps to deal with rapid transit for the area, and public demands for some sort of action, attracted legislative attention once more, which led to the passage of the second Los Angeles Metropolitan Authority Act in 1957.

The Act of 1957.[41] This legislation was passed to create a special authority to establish a mass rapid transit system within Los Angeles County which was designated in the law as the "metropolitan area."[42] It also repealed the Act of 1951. The Authority was set up as a public corporation of the state of California, but the statute specifically stated that it was not a "state agency." The territorial limits of the Authority were not to be diminished or decreased as long as any bonds issued under the Act were outstanding and unpaid.

The Authority consisted of seven members appointed by the Governor of the state, each member to serve for the term of his appoint-

---

[39] Assembly Bill No. 3112, Chap. 1668, Statutes of California, 1951.

[40] For a more detailed analysis, see D. F. Pegrum, *The Los Angeles Transportation Problem—An Analysis of the Los Angeles Metropolitan Transit Authority* (mimeographed) (Los Angeles: University of California, June, 1960).

[41] The Los Angeles Metropolitan Transit Authority Act of 1957, Assembly Bill No. 1104, California Statutes, Chap. 547, 1957. For a detailed analysis of this legislation and its results, see D. F. Pegrum, "The Los Angeles Metropolitan Transit Authority," *Land Economics,* Vol. XXXVII, No. 3 (August, 1961), pp. 247–55.

[42] This does not correspond to the Standard Metropolitan Area of the Bureau of the Census. It excludes Orange County, which is the most rapidly growing section of the metropolitan area, and includes the sparsely populated mountain and Antelope Valley area to the north.

ment, the full term being four years. Members had to be residents and registered voters of Los Angeles County. They could receive compensation of $50 for each meeting but no more than $200 for any calendar month. The executive director and the secretary appointed by the Authority were full-time employees who might also be members in addition to the seven designated by the governor. The Authority might adopt whatever rules and regulations it deemed advisable with regard to its own affairs. It was not subject to the jurisdiction of the Public Utilities Commission of California, except that it was required to adopt and comply with safety regulations prescribed by the Commission;[43] nor was it required to report to any public body or officer.

In order to carry out its responsibilities to establish a mass rapid transit system, the Authority was authorized to acquire all the necessary properties of various kinds and could enter into agreements with any public utility operating any transportation facilities, either within or without the metropolitan area, for joint use, or the establishment of through routes, joint fares, and transfer of passengers. In addition, it could acquire any publicly or privately owned bus lines within or without the metropolitan area which might be integrated as feeder services within the system of the Authority. It could exercise the power of eminent domain within the metropolitan area, but no publicly owned property could be taken without the consent of the public agency nor could any privately owned public utility be taken or condemned without the consent of the utility. The law contained special provisions designed to protect both publicly and privately owned passenger transportation undertakings against arbitrary appropriation by the Authority. In addition, no new construction of "subways, elevated railways, overhead suspended transit, or any other structures constituting a method of mass rapid transit in, upon, over, under or across public streets, highways, freeways, and other public places [may be undertaken] without the consent of the city, county, or state having jurisdiction over such street, highway, freeway or other public place."

The law gave the Authority the power to issue revenue bonds to provide the capital necessary to finance the rapid transit system. These had to contain the recital that neither the principal nor the interest constituted an obligation of any county, city, or the state. All bonds and the interest thereon were exempt from all taxation in California, other than gift, inheritance, or estate taxes. The properties of the corporation and its revenues were also exempt from taxation, but the Authority en-

---

[43] How these regulations were to be enforced was not indicated.

joyed no taxing powers. Any indenture might contain a clause limiting the power of the Authority to issue additional bonds for the purpose of acquiring, constructing, or completing the system or any part thereof. The Authority was given the power to fix all charges for the use of the system subject only to "such contractual obligations as may be entered into by the Authority and the holders of the revenue bonds issued under this act."

The Los Angeles Metropolitan Transit Authority became an effective operating company on March 3, 1958, when its issue of $40 million of revenue bonds was sold. With these funds the corporation acquired the properties of the Los Angeles Transit Lines for $21,604,-000, and the Metropolitan Coach Lines and its subsidiary, the Asbury Rapid Transit system, for $13,596,374, a total of $35,200,374.[44] Since then, no changes, apart from some minor operating details and an increase of fares, have taken place with regard to rapid transit in Los Angeles.[45]

The Act of 1964. The inability of the Transit Authority established under the Act of 1957 to achieve any positive results coupled with the feeling that there were too few political controls over it, led to the State legislature to take further action by creating the Southern California Rapid Transit District in 1964.[46] This new agency took over all the functions of its predecessor.

As in the previous legislation, the district was confined to a portion of Los Angeles County, although other areas might be annexed, but by means not specified in the law. The Board of Directors consists of 11 members, 5 appointed by the Board of Supervisors of the county, 2 by the mayor of the city of Los Angeles, and 4 by a city selection committee. Members of the Board of Directors who are not members of the Board of Supervisors, the council of the city of Los Angeles, or the city selection committee serve for four years. The Board is the legislative body of the Authority and is empowered to supervise and regulate every transit facility owned and operated by the Authority. The Board is required to submit to the chief administrative officers and

[44] This total may be compared with the rate base (value for rate making) of $26,730,000 submitted by the Los Angeles Transit Lines and the Metropolitan Coach Lines in their application to the California Public Utilities Commission for an increase in fares in July, 1957.

[45] Meanwhile, various governmental agencies have lost tax revenues previously derived from the private lines. Total taxes paid by them (exclusive of social security taxes) for the calendar year 1957 were reported to the Public Utilities Commission as amounting to $3,694,423.

[46] Senate Bill, No. 41, Chap. 62, Sect. 1, Part 3, Division 10, Public Utilities Code, sections 30,000–31,520.

legislative bodies within the district, a financial report on the operations of the previous year. The chief operating officer is the general manager who is directly responsible to the Board.

The Authority is empowered to levy taxes and fix the rate of taxes if revenue requirements dictate, except that the tax revenues cannot be used to meet operating expenses. The Board may, by a two-thirds vote, incur indebtedness by general obligation bonds. These, however, must also be approved by 60 per cent of the qualified voting electors at an election held for that purpose. Revenue bonds may be issued without an election, under restricted conditions. The law also provides that the district shall not incur an indebtedness that exceeds 15 percent of the assessed value of all real and personal property in the district.

To date, the new rapid transit district has accomplished little. It has been engaged in "preliminary" studies for a backbone rapid transit route for which it has received $3.9 million in state aid from oil royalties. The purpose of the studies is to prepare a master plan as the basis for submitting a $1.6 billion bond issue to the electorate in November, 1968. Meanwhile it is seeking public subsidy for its bus system.[47]

THE SAN FRANCISCO BAY AREA RAPID TRANSIT DISTRICT (BART)

Geographical Setting

The city of San Francisco and its environs present a unique problem for rapid transit because of the geography of the area. The city itself is located on the tip of a peninsula between San Francisco Bay and the Pacific Ocean. (See Figure 24–1.) Its only land connection with the surrounding regions of the metropolitan area is down the peninsula to the lower end of the bay. Until the construction of the transbay bridge in the mid-thirties, commuter traffic was by the Southern Pacific Railway down the peninsula, and by ferries to other areas surrounding the Bay. Rail commuter service to the ferries was supplied

[47] For other studies on Los Angeles transportation, see *Transportation in the Los Angeles Area,* Final Report of the Citizens Traffic and Transportation Committee for the Extended Los Angeles Area (1957); Southern California Research Council, *An Approach to an Orderly and Efficient Transportation System for the Southern California Metropolis* (Los Angeles, Calif.: Occidental College, 1961); State of California, Division of Highways, *Los Angeles Regional Transportation Study (LARTS),* Base Year Report (1960), Vol. 1; Citizens Advisory Council on Public Transportation, *Improving Public Transportation in Los Angeles* (Los Angeles, Calif., 1967).

by two street railway and interurban lines on the east side. These and the ferries disappeared with the construction of the transbay bridge. Today the only rail commuter system is down the peninsula.

The population of the three counties that now constitute the rapid transit district was 904,702 persons in 1920 and 2,057,555 in 1960,

FIGURE 24–1

SAN FRANCISCO BAY AREA RAPID TRANSIT SYSTEM

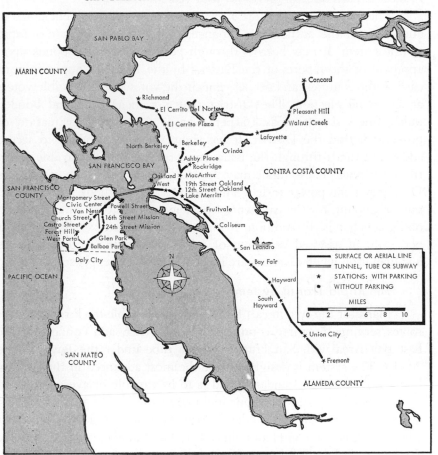

of which 740,316 were in the city and county of San Francisco. The total population of the San Francisco–Oakland standard metropolitan statistical area amounted to 2,648,762 in 1960. Rapidly growing reliance on the automobile and increasing traffic congestion of movement into San Francisco led to efforts to develop a rapid transit system in the 1950's.

Formation of the Rapid Transit District

The San Francisco Bay Area Rapid Transit District was established by the state legislature in 1957.[48] Its members are the three counties of Alameda, Contra Costa and San Francisco.[49] The District is governed by a board of 12 directors, 4 from Alameda County, 4 from Contra Costa, and 4 representing the city and county of San Francisco. Each director serves for four years.

The District may acquire necessary property by eminent domain, and is given the authority to finance, construct and operate a rapid transit system. It may borrow through general obligation bonds upon approval of the reports of the District by the Board of Supervisors of each of the counties, and 60 per cent of the votes cast by eligible voters at any bond election. The District may not incur a general bonded indebtedness that exceeds 15 per cent of the assessed valuation of property within the District. It has, however, the authority to secure additional funds through the issuance of revenue bonds payable solely from revenues. These funds may be used to acquire rolling stock. The District has the power to levy and collect taxes, without limitation on rate or amount, for the payment of principal and interest on all general obligation bonds. In addition, it may levy taxes not exceeding 5 cents per $100 of assessed valuation of taxable property, for maintenance and operation when revenues are inadequate to meet expenses.

The Rapid Transit System

Plans for the system call for 75 miles of double-track rapid transit routes serving the three counties of the District, and connecting the East Bay Area with San Francisco by a tube under the Bay (Figure 24–1). The system is designed to be the most advanced in the country by present technical standards, and is to be capable of average operating speeds of 45 miles per hour including stops. As of June, 1967, 43 miles of the system were under construction or contract. The present schedule calls for completion in 1971, but financial problems make this date rather doubtful.

Financing the System

On November 2, 1962, a proposition for the issuance by the District of $792 million general obligation bonds for the purpose of

---

[48] Chap. 1056, Statutes of California. This legislation was the prototype for the Southern California Rapid Transit District that was set up in 1964.

[49] Marin and San Matee counties were also original members but they withdrew before any financial obligations were incurred.

financing the construction of the system was submitted to the electorate. It was approved by 61.2 per cent of those who voted, the necessary majority coming from the overwhelming approval by San Francisco County.[50] To date, $370 million of the bonds have been sold.

Separate provisions and responsibilities were assigned for financing the transbay tube. The law directed the California Toll Bridge Authority to undertake the financing of the tube by using net toll revenues from the bridges across San Francisco Bay which it operates, namely the San Francisco-Oakland Bridge, the San Mateo-Hayward Bridge and the Dumbarton Bridge. Tolls are to be maintained on the latter two bridges equal to or in excess of those on the San Francisco-Oakland Bridge. The net revenues from the bridges are available for pledge by the Bridge Authority for security for bonds issued to finance the construction of the tube. The Authority is also required to finance the construction of the approaches to the tube. The District is obligated to reimburse the Authority for the costs of the approaches at the rate of $2.5 million per year, commencing on December 31, 1971 until the total cost is repaid. The total funds authorized for the construction of the tube was $180 million. In December, 1965, the Authority made $96.5 million available to the District through the sale of revenue bonds.

Cost Estimates

Initial cost estimates in 1962 for the rapid transit system were $790,493,000 for the basic system, $132,720,000 for the transbay tube, giving a total of $923,213,000. In addition, there was the estimate for rolling stock amounting to $72,875,000 to be financed by revenue bonds. New estimates in 1966, however, were $941,717,000 for the basic system and $179,878,000 for the tube, for a total $1,121,595,000, an increase of $198,382,000 over the original calculations. The estimated property tax requirements based on the original $792 million of general obligation bonds was 35.2 cents for each $100 of assessed valuation in 1966–67 rising to 69.4 cents in 1971–72.

The obvious financial difficulties facing the District led it to suggest that it might be necessary to appeal to the state legislature to raise the bonding limit and to modify the voting requirement. Failure to receive assistance from the legislature at its 1967 session has forced

[50] On November 8, 1966, the electorate of the county and city of San Francisco rejected a bond issue of $96.5 million to finance indebtedness and improvement of the San Francisco street railway and municipal system which was to provide local distribution service for the district.

the District to reconsider its program. One possibility is that the system might reduce construction to be completed in 1971 to 57 miles along with the elimination of some stations. Another possibility is to seek permission to submit a new bond issue of $87 million to the voters in June, 1968. The District is obviously facing severe financial problems long before a single train goes into operation and the resolution of the impasse is anything but clear—except that the taxpayers will have a heavier tax burden than that already forecast.[51]

PRESIDENT KENNEDY'S MESSAGE

The second part of President Kennedy's message to Congress on transportation contained his recommendations for action on the transportation problems resulting from burgeoning urban growth and the changing urban scene.[52] It was totally different in tone from Part I, which dealt with intercity transportation, in that it placed heavy reliance on long-run as well as emergency public aid.

In response to a presidential request the Department of Commerce and the Housing and Home Finance Agency undertook a study of urban transportation problems of the country. The resulting report,[53] which was submitted to President Kennedy, became the basis of his recommendations to Congress. The President's message so closely parallels the joint report that it is unnecessary to present the details of the latter. It may be noted, however, that the joint report viewed the proposed program for urban transportation as an integral part of the urban planning assistance program of the Housing Act of 1954 and the Housing Act of 1961. It also relied heavily on federal leverage and assistance, and confined its attention to the movement of people. "Mass transportation will not receive proper attention in planning and action programs, however, unless local officials see the realistic possibility of installing and effectively operating the systems which would be called for in good planning. Such a possibility is doubtful if the urban areas

[51] For a summary of the organization of the District and progress to date, see *Official Statement Relating to $70,000,000 San Francisco Bay Area Rapid Transit District, General Obligation Bonds Series G,* June 8, 1967.

[52] *The Transportation System of Our Nation,* Message from the President of the United States, House of Representatives, Document No. 384, 87th Congress, 2d session (Washington, D.C.: U.S. Government Printing Office, 1962), Part II, pp. 9–13.

[53] *Urban Transportation,* Joint Report to the President by the Housing and Home Finance Administrator and the Secretary of Commerce (mimeographed) (The White House, March 28, 1962).

must look forward to covering the total public cost from their own limited tax resources. This is the basic reason for recommending a federal program to cover two-thirds of such cost."[54]

On the basis of the joint report the President recommended that "long-range Federal financial aid and technical assistance be provided to help plan and develop the comprehensive and balanced urban transportation that is so vitally needed, not only to benefit local communities, but to assure more effective use of Federal funds available for other urban development and renewal programs."[55] Such federal assistance for mass transportation would be limited to those applications (1) where an organization or officially co-ordinated organizations are carrying on a continuing program of comprehensive planning on an area-wide basis and (2) where the assisted project will be administered through a public agency as part of a unified or officially co-ordinated area-wide transportation system.

Long-Range Program

The first instalment of a long-range program of federal aid was to be a capital grant of $500 million to be made available over a three-year period, with $100 million to be made available in the fiscal year 1963. It was to be administered by the Housing and Home Finance Agency. The assistance was to be accorded to qualified public agencies in the form of direct grants to be matched by local contributions. For rights of way, fixed facilities, including maintenance and terminal facilities, and rolling stock required for urban mass transportation systems, the grants were to provide up to two thirds of the project cost which could not reasonably be financed from expected revenue. The remaining one third was to be met by the locality or state from other sources. Federal funds were not to be used to pay operating expenses or parking facilities, except those directly supporting public mass transportation. The grant program was expected to be the major federal support, but the President recommended that the time limit on the $50 million loan authorization of the Housing Act of 1961 be removed. A community would be eligible for a grant or a loan only after the Housing Administrator determined that the facilities and equipment for which assistance was sought were necessary for the carrying-out of a program for a unified or officially co-ordinated urban transportation system as a part of the comprehensively planned development of the urban area.

[54] *Ibid.*, p. 14.
[55] *The Transportation System of Our Nation*, p. 10.

Emergency Aid

Because of the time required for organizing major planning efforts, emergency aid was proposed by a request to Congress that for a period of three years it authorize the Housing Administrator to make emergency grants (1) where there was an urgent need for immediate aid to an existing mass transportation facility or service, (2) where an official long-range program was being prepared, and (3) where equipment and facilities acquired under the emergency grant can reasonably be expected to be required for the long-range program. The emergency aid was not to exceed one half of the net project cost. It was assumed that acceptable area-wide programs would be completed in three years and that the projects would qualify for the balance of the regular federal assistance available under the long-range program.

Role of the Highways

The President recommended that the federal-aid highway law be amended to provide that the Secretary of Commerce, not later than July 1, 1965, but before approving a program for highway projects in any metropolitan area, should see that such projects are consistent with comprehensive development plans for the metropolitan area and that the federal system forms an integral part of the system of the area.[56] Provision for transit and highway facilities on the same roadway should be encouraged, and the Secretary of Commerce was requested to give favorable consideration to the reservation of special highway lanes for buses during peak-hour traffic. Finally, the Secretary of Commerce and the Housing and Home Finance Administrator were instructed to coordinate their programs through regular consultations.

Relocation Assistance

Under the federally assisted urban renewal program, moving expenses for families and businesses needing assistance is paid by the federal government, the average payment to families being about $65 and to businesses about $1,150.[57] The President recommended that similar aid be extended to persons so affected by the federal-aid highway and urban mass transportation program. The amount of payment was not

[56] The joint report stated that over 5,000 miles, or 13 per cent of the interstate highway system, are in urban areas, and they will account for 45 per cent of the total expenditure. Under federal legislation, also, 25 per cent of the ABC federal aid is specifically for the urban portions of the work on the primary and secondary highway systems (*Urban Transportation*, p. 10).

[57] *Ibid.*, p. 15.

to exceed $200 for individuals and families, and $3,000 (or if greater, the total certified actual moving expenses) for business.

Mass Transit Research and Demonstrations

As part of a comprehensive federal research program in transportation the President recommended that the Housing Administration, through a variety of procedures, should develop extensive research activities. To facilitate this, the message proposed that the $25 million authorized in 1961 for demonstration grants be made available for broad research and development undertakings as well as demonstration projects. To this amount should be added an additional $10 million from the proposed capital grant funds for 1963, 1964, and 1965.

Interstate Compacts

The final recommendation was that legislation be enacted to give Congressional approval in advance for interstate compacts for the establishment of agencies to carry out transportation and other regional functions in urban areas extending across state lines.

URBAN MASS TRANSPORTATION ACT, 1964

The proposals of President Kennedy for assistance to urban mass transportation became reality in 1964 when President Johnson signed the Urban Mass Transportation Act.[58] This legislation provided for federal grants not to exceed $75 million for fiscal 1965, $150 million for 1966, and $150 million for 1967. The Housing and Home Finance Administration was authorized to grant assistance "for carrying out a program, meeting the criteria established by him, for a unified or officially coordinated urban transportation system as part of a comprehensively planned development of the urban area, and are necessary for the sound economic and desirable development of such area." Up to two thirds of the "net project cost" could be granted, provided it could not be reasonably financed from revenues. The Administrator was also authorized to undertake research development, and demonstration projects in all phases of mass urban transportation.

The functions and duties of the Housing and Home Finance Agency were transferred to the Department of Housing and Urban Development which was established in 1965.[59] The Department of Transportation Act (1966) requires that the Secretary of Transporta-

[58] Public Law 88–365.
[59] Public Law 89–174.

tion and the Secretary of Housing and Urban Development report within one year (i.e., by April 1968) to the President and the Congress on the logical and efficient organization and location of urban mass transportation functions in the Executive Branch.

THE PROBLEM OF PLANNING

The foregoing brief survey of some selected proposals and programs for dealing with urban transport problems points up a lack of a basis for a planned approach to metropolitan transportation at the same time that it emphasizes the difficulties which face these areas. At present, there is a separate approach to the provision of facilities by the various agencies that supply the different modes. This parallels the developments of the past, which have been described as planless—although each of the agencies (especially the various forms of rail transport) had its own plans. These were largely in response to economic inducements, the construction and operation of the facilities being primarily circumscribed by the direct influences of the price mechanism and the market. Moreover, city traffic and intercity traffic were rather effectively separated technically, with transfer of movement between the two taking place at a limited number of terminal points. The terminal problem was that of co-ordinating rail interchange of traffic in certain centers, as well as rail and water facilities. The movement of people within the metropolitan area was undertaken by mass rail facilities supplied in response to revenue inducements. Land use was conditioned by the availability of these facilities as the supply of them responded to the prospects of revenue from the users. The planning that took place was in response to these factors. Still further, the structure of the cities, with the intense concentration in the central areas, was the result of the dependence on rail transport and its dependence, in turn, on the mass movement of goods and people.

The situation in today's metropolis is fundamentally different as a result of the operation of forces that have modified radically, or even eliminated, many of the conditions that molded the structure of metropolitan areas as we know them and envisage them today. The dependence of a large part of the metropolitan traffic of goods and people on rail transport has disappeared. Urban traffic movements by motor vehicle are not directly responsive to the price mechanism. Roadway facilities have to be supplied by public authority without an adequate economic gauge of precise need. Rising standards of living have created the willingness to use more expensive means of transport for convenience and for the selection of more desirable residential locations. Increased productivity in the economy has released more of the nation's population for urban activities and has accelerated urban growth.

The current need for urban transport planning and the conditions under which it has to be developed are quite different from those of the earlier setting. Whereas, prior to the automobile, they had to revolve around rail facilities, this bond has now been broken, and a large portion of the traffic is literally free to move on an independent basis. Whatever the future pattern of the large metropolitan area may be, it seems destined to be shaped, as far as transportation is concerned, by the automobile, and whatever newer devices may be developed. Unfortunately, we have as yet "no generally accepted theory of how metropolitan regions grow and change,"[60] particularly under recent transportation innovations, but most bases being employed for projecting needs are predicated on the trends to the present. This is the dilemma of transport planning. To date, it has concentrated its attention almost entirely on the movement of people. The proposals for solution place emphasis on the need for mass rapid transit to reduce congestion created by the automobile and on the need to halt the decline of the central city area in order to preserve the property values concentrated therein. Even Los Angeles is burdened with this approach.

Public participation in the supplying of transportation facilities is a necessity for every metropolitan area. The problem lies in the form that this should take and who should pay for it. The situation differs from one large center to another, and generalizations are difficult to make. If mass transportation is necessary to preserve the central city areas and the property values therein, and if the riders cannot or will not bear the burden of the costs, it would seem to be reasonable to assert that the owner-beneficiaries of the properties should shoulder the burden rather than the general taxpayer. If this failed to solve the issue, the presumption would be that the costs of the facilities were greater than the returns from them; that is, they would be uneconomical. The Doyle Report takes the position that "Planners and administrators are going to have to rationalize the financing of urban transportation and move in the direction of making the entire operation self-sustaining."[61] If this is done, mass urban transport planning will have to undergo a

---

[60] Department of Public Works and Buildings, State of Illinois, *Chicago Area Transportation Study*, Vol. II, p. 2. It may be noted that communication and public utility services for the urban areas seem to offer no peculiar problems of planning. They are built in response to demand for service as reflected through price. Sewage could be put on the same basis, if desired.

[61] *National Transportation Policy* (Doyle Report), p. 617.

complete reorientation. The present assumption seems to be that self-sustenance is not possible, nor is it a necessary condition for mass transit programs.

The automobile presents another problem. To date, we have developed no effective means of rationalizing the use of streets and highways in the metropolitan areas through a workable rationing device. This problem, as previously emphasized, has two aspects: (1) providing the total necessary revenues for the publicly supplied facilities and (2) relating the sources of the revenues to the specific use of the facilities that have been constructed. Total revenue requirements to cover all costs, explicit and implicit, can be obtained through highway user charges, even though there may be some difficulties in calculating the precise division of them among the various governmental agencies that supply the roadways. In the chapter on financing transportation, it was pointed out that motor transport does not pay for all the economic costs incurred in the provision of the roadway facilities. Wilfred Owen, however, states that "on a National basis, urban traffic contributes more highway user tax revenue than is spent for city streets from all sources,"[62] although state fiscal policy does not give the cities the benefit of this. The Transportation Center at Northwestern University examined the problem carefully for the Chicago area, and after taking into account what it considered to be all the legitimate obligations of motor vehicle users, concluded that for the year 1954 the range of subsidy for Chicago motorists was from $17.56 per vehicle to an overpayment by them of $4.85 per vehicle.[63] If these estimates approximate the facts, rehabilitation of urban rapid transit is not likely to come about as a result of increasing the costs imposed on motor vehicles, since it is scarcely to be expected that user taxes on motor vehicles in metropolitan transport will be increased solely to protect rapid transit.

The relating of the sources of the revenues to the specific uses of the facilities that have been provided raises issues that are technically more complex. Over-all roadway facilities may be adequate, yet congestion develops on many of them; and at certain critical times, "It is not uncommon to find city streets almost devoid of traffic in the vicinity of a newly opened freeway. Until recently, estimates of future traffic on proposed freeways were in part predicated on traffic diverted from city streets. With more freeways being opened the traffic diversion from existing freeways will take place."[64] Thus, congestion shifts from one

[62] Owen, *op. cit.*, p. 155.

[63] *Basic Issues in Chicago Metropolitan Transportation*, pp. 54–55.

[64] *Loop Progress, California Highways and Public Works*, January–February, 1961 (Sacramento, Calif.), p. 11.

route to another, and this is likely to take place indefinitely unless, as Professor W. S. Vickrey points out, we develop a system of extravagant proportions or embark upon a program of specific pricing for highway usage.[65] Resolution of this question is faced with severe technical difficulties. It should, however, be the object of concerted action because the automotive vehicle is unlikely to lose its place as the prime transport medium of the metropolitan areas in the period for which forecasts and plans are now being made.

Emphasis for this point is supplied by a series of studies at Northwestern University designed to appraise the future roles of the various alternative modes of metropolitan transportation.[66] After pointing out the changing pattern of traffic movements in the large metropolitan area and noting the decline in urban mass transit, the report examined three propositions advanced by the proponents of the economic desirability of public investment in urban transit. It concluded that the arguments rested on sentiment rather than on fact. (1) The "harm" that automobiles inflict on the central business district: The contention that "under the influence of private transportation, the amount of downtown land devoted to such unproductive uses as streets and parking lots has increased to the detriment of commerce and industry," was adjudged to be incorrect. The study found that the proportion of the total developed land of the city of Chicago devoted to streets, alleys, and parking lots fell from 1941 to 1956. Meanwhile, highways increased greatly the total stock of land in active use over the entire city and metropolitan area. Moreover, in monetary terms, parking lots proved to be more "productive" than vacant movie houses and outmoded office buildings. (2) The superior "efficiency" of mass transit: The study recognized that in theory a bus, subway, or commuter train might carry as many passengers per day on its right of way as a ten-, twenty-, or thirty-lane boulevard. In fact, however, transit carried only about one fourth of its peak-load capacity, and then only during the rush hours on weekdays over a limited portion of the route near downtown. Moreover, "the most efficient means of transportation is, for all practical purposes, the choice individuals make of the various transportation alternatives (including walking and bike-riding) in the day-to-day circumstances of his [*sic*] own life."[67] This matter of choice by the individual is too frequently overlooked by those who advocate public aid to transit. The

[65] *Transportation Plan for the National Capital Region,* p. 469.

[66] M. Reinsberg, *Growth and Change in Metropolitan Areas and Their Relation to Metropolitan Transportation* (Evanston, Ill.: Transportation Center, Northwestern University, 1961). This is a research summary of the seven separate studies which were made. See p. 5 for a list of these studies.

[67] *Ibid.,* p. 15.

State Mass Transportation Commission for Illinois found "that when the cost by transit is one-tenth that of the cost by automobile, about 60% of the trips are by transit; when the cost by transit is one-half that of the cost by automobile 15% of the trips are by transit; and when cost by transit is equal to the cost by automobile, only about 5% of the trips are by transit."[68] Of the total trips made by mass transit in Cook County, 15 per cent were by riders who had no other means of transport. Efficiency is a matter of the relative costs of alternatives, not the absolute costs. (3) The "benefits" to motorists: Subsidy and lowered fares would reduce congestion to the convenience of the remaining motorists. The study takes the position that "if it is fair game for one interest group to encourage use of transit, it is equally fair for a second interest group to promote the use of the automobile. An original inducement of lower transit fares might be cancelled out by the counter-inducement of price reductions in gasoline, parking, or cars."[69] The conclusion is drawn that the evidence to date is not sufficiently reliable to support the claim that the mass transit component of urban transportation is either more or less deserving of subsidy than the automobile transportation component.[70]

Mass urban transportation is in serious difficulty in every large metropolitan center of the country and shows little prospect of being able to survive in its present form without massive public aid. In terms of economic criteria, it must be rated as inefficient and uneconomical because it offers little prospect of survival under equitable competition with the alternatives. Yet it cannot at present be abandoned in many of the large centers without disastrous consequences. On the other hand, perpetuation of the present patterns offers slight prospects of lasting results, while at the same time it will entail severe tax burdens. This is the dilemma posed for the governments of most of the large metropolitan areas of the country. The efforts that are made to resolve it will have to recognize the changing structures of the modern metropolis and the altered role of the central city. The automotive vehicle has become the prime mover of urban traffic, especially people. Transportation planning for the metropolitan area of the years ahead will be forced, one way or another, to recognize this fact. Mass transportation

[68] *The Mass Transportation Problem in Illinois*, Final Report of the State Mass Transportation Commission (Chicago, June, 1959), p. 53.

[69] Reinsberg, *op. cit.*, p. 16.

[70] See also T. R. Reid, "Disposing of Some Common Myths," *Highway Highlights*, (National Highway Users Conference, Washington, D.C.), January, 1962, pp. 6–10; and A. C. Butler, "Weep Not for Los Angeles," *Highway Highlights*, June–July, 1962, p. 2.

of people may continue to occupy an important place for urban traffic in some centers, but its role is declining rapidly. Plans for the provision of transport facilities for the projected growth of the future must recognize this trend; otherwise the undertakings offer the prospect of being futile and costly at one and the same time.

In general the problem is motor transportation, and increasing automobile rather than public carrier transportation. Neither economic analysis nor transportation history suggests a return to public transportation on a scale that would be decisive. . . . Cities can never solve their transportation problems if they continue to crowd too many people and too much economic activity into too little space. Congestion in the rush hours is inevitable as long as we insist on living in suburbs, working downtown and starting off at the same time to get to the same place. In these circumstances no transportation magic can make journey to work a joy ride. We will have to avoid unmanageable transportation demands through the dispersal of population and economic activity, the preservation of open spaces, and the planning of land use densities and arrangements.[71]

All urban concentration is not merely the result of economic forces or unplanned development; high-rise centers and the resulting concentration can be limited by public authority if it wishes to do so. City planning agencies authorize the construction of high-rise buildings for both business and apartments that generate large amounts of traffic without giving any consideration to the provision of transport facilities in advance of occupancy. When the inevitable congestion occurs steps may be taken to afford relief. These steps usually involve burdens on the general taxpayer rather than on those for whom the relief is afforded. Frequently, the providing of the needed transport facilities creates additional congestion, for some time at least, by the tearing up of streets and other road construction activities after the congestion has already taken place. If this represents the level of capacity of planning authorities under such relatively simple conditions, surely one would have to be an unmitigated optimist to believe that these authorities are capable of directing the development of the orderly "dream" city that is so often proclaimed as an utter necessity if we are to escape the present "unavoidable" strangulation resulting from lack of planning.

Present transport (and other) developments represent technology running wild without attention to or responsibility for the costs involved, and the impact of these costs on the public at large, and particularly on the public treasury (cf. jumbo jets and the supersonic transport). Difficulties at the local, state, and federal levels of finance,

[71] Owen, *op. cit.,* pp. 213 and 222.

and resistance to the constantly increasing tax burden may indicate a public awakening to the fact that a callous ignoring of the market as an allocative medium brings its day of reckoning. The resort to governments at large easily disguises the fact that the taxpayer must ultimately shoulder the burden, too frequently somebody else's burden. The extensive process of matching payments for federal grants comes close to political bribery that deceives the taxpayer, wastes resources, and encourages irresponsible expenditure of public funds. The more effectively economic gauges are applied to the program of urban transport development, the more will the demands for the transport services assume manageable proportions.[72]

[72] Consulting reports almost invariably seem to favor the bias that the employer usually has. This may be explained: (1) that no firm will be hired that does not come up with the desired answer; (2) that if the desired answer does not result then the report will not see the light of day; or (3) that consulting firms have a remarkable capacity to be ambivalent, or perhaps possess such extreme tolerance that they can see or sympathize with all points of view.

APPENDIXES

Appendix I

THE TRANSPORTATION SYSTEM OF OUR NATION*

To the Congress of the United States:

An efficient and dynamic transportation system is vital to our domestic economic growth, productivity, and progress. Affecting the cost of every commodity we consume or export, it is equally vital to our ability to compete abroad. It influences both the cost and the flexibility of our defense preparedness, and both the business and recreational opportunities of our citizens. This Nation has long enjoyed one of the most highly developed and diversified transportation systems in the world, and this system has helped us to achieve a highly efficient utilization of our manpower and resources.

Transportation is thus an industry which serves, and is affected with, the national interest. Federal laws and policies have expressed the national interest in transportation particularly in the last 80 years: through the promotion and development of transportation facilities, such as highways, airways, and waterways; through the regulation of rates and services; and through general governmental policies relating to taxation, procurement, labor, and competition. A comprehensive program for transportation must consider all of these elements of public policy.

During the last session of Congress, action was taken to place our Federal-aid highway program on a sounder fiscal basis. Initial steps were taken to improve the operations of our regulatory agencies through reorganization. A beginning was also made toward meeting the needs of our cities for mass transportation. By Executive order, I recently assigned to the Department of Commerce authority for emergency transportation planning.

But pressing problems are burdening our national transportation system, jeopardizing the progress and security on which we depend. A chaotic patchwork of inconsistent and often obsolete legislation and regulation has evolved from a history of specific actions addressed to specific problems of specific industries at specific times. This patchwork does not fully reflect either the dramatic changes in technology of the past half century or the parallel changes in the structure of competition.

The regulatory commissions are required to make thousands of detailed decisions based on out-of-date standards. The management of the various modes

---

* Message from the President of the United States, House of Representatives, Document No. 384 (87th Cong., 2d sess.), April 5, 1962.

of transportation is subjected to excessive, cumbersome, and time-consuming regulatory supervision that shackles and distorts managerial initiative. Some parts of the transportation industry are restrained unnecessarily; others are promoted or taxed unevenly and inconsistently.

Some carriers are required to provide, at a loss, services for which there is little demand. Some carriers are required to charge rates which are high in relation to cost in order to shelter competing carriers. Some carriers are prevented from making full use of their capacity by restrictions on freedom to solicit business or adjust rates. Restraints on cost-reducing rivalry in ratemaking often cause competition to take the form of cost-increasing rivalry—such as excessive promotion and traffic solicitation, or excessive frequency of service. Some carriers are subject to rate regulation on the transportation of particular commodities while other carriers, competing for the same traffic, are exempt. Some carriers benefit from public facilities provided for their use, while others do not; and of those enjoying the use of public facilities, some bear a large part of the cost, while others bear little or none.

No simple Federal solution can end the problems of any particular company or mode of transportation. On the contrary, I am convinced that less Federal regulation and subsidization is in the long run a prime prerequisite of a healthy intercity transportation network. The constructive efforts of State and local governments as well as the transportation industry will also be needed to revitalize our transportation services.

This administration's study of long-range transportation needs and policies convinces me that current Federal policies must be reshaped in the most fundamental and far-reaching fashion. While recognizing that a revision of the magnitude required is a task to which the Congress will wish to devote considerable time and effort, I believe the recommendations below are of sufficient urgency and importance that the Congress should begin consideration of them at the earliest practicable date. If direct and decisive action is not taken in the near future, the undesirable developments, inefficiencies, inequities, and other undesirable conditions that confront us now will cause permanent loss of essential services or require even more difficult and costly solutions in the not-too-distant future.

A BASIC NATIONAL TRANSPORTATION POLICY

The basic objective of our Nation's transportation system must be to assure the availability of the fast, safe, and economical transportation services needed in a growing and changing economy to move people and goods, without waste or discrimination, in response to private and public demands at the lowest cost consistent with health, convenience, national security, and other broad public objectives. Investment or capacity should be neither substantially above nor substantially below these requirements—for chronic excess capacity involves misuse of resources, and lack of adequate capacity jeopardizes progress. The resources devoted to provision of transportation service should be used in the most effective and efficient manner possible; and this, in turn, means that users of transport facilities should be provided with incentives to use whatever form of transportation which provides them with the service they desire at the lowest total cost, both public and private.

This basic objective can and must be achieved primarily by continued reliance on unsubsidized privately owned facilities, operating under the incentives of private profit and the checks of competition to the maximum extent practicable. The role of public policy should be to provide a consistent and comprehensive framework of equal competitive opportunity that will achieve this objective at the lowest economic and social cost to the Nation.

This means a more coordinated Federal policy and a less segmented approach. It means equality of opportunity for all forms of transportation and their users and undue preference to none. It means greater reliance on the forces of competition and less reliance on the restraints of regulation. And it means that, to the extent possible, the users of transportation services should bear the full costs of the services they use, whether those services are provided privately or publicly.

For some 75 years, common carriage was developed by the intention of Congress and the requirements of the public as the core of our transport system. This pattern of commerce is changing—the common carrier is declining in status and stature with the consequent growth of the private and exempt carrier. To a large extent this change is attributable to the failure of Federal policies and regulation to adjust to the needs of the shipping and consuming public; to a large extent it is attributable to the fact that the burdens of regulation are handicapping the certificated common carrier in his efforts to meet his unregulated competition. Whatever the cause, the common carrier with his obligation to serve all shippers—large or small—on certain routes at known tariffs and without any discrimination performs an essential function that should not be extinguished.

Considerable research and analysis, going far beyond our present findings, will be required before we know enough about the costs and other characteristics of various forms of transportation to guarantee the achievement of these objectives in full. In the meantime, it is clear that the following fundamental reforms in our transportation policy are needed now.

PART I. INTERCITY TRANSPORTATION

Our system of intercity public transportation—including railroads, trucks, buses, ships and barges, airplanes and pipelines—is seriously weakened today by artificial distortions and inefficiencies inherent in existing Federal policies. Built up over the years, they can be removed only gradually if we are to mitigate the hardships that are bound to arise in any program of far-reaching adjustment.

As an initial step, I am requesting the Chairmen of the Civil Aeronautics Board, the Interstate Commerce Commission, and the Federal Maritime Commission to meet at frequent intervals to discuss regulatory problems affecting the various modes of transportation and to seek coordinated solutions in the form of legislation or administrative action that will improve the regulatory process.

(A) Equal competitive opportunity under diminished regulation

(1) Bulk commodities: At present, the transportation of bulk commodities by water carriers is exempt from all rate regulation under the Interstate Commerce Act, including the approval of minimum rates; but this exemption is denied to all other modes of transportation. This is clearly inequitable both to

the latter and to shippers—and it is an inequity which should be removed. Extending to all other carriers the exemption from the approval or prescription of minimum rates would permit the forces of competition and equal opportunity to replace cumbersome regulation for these commodities, while protecting the public interest by leaving intact the ICC's control over maximum railroad rates and other safeguards (such as the prohibition against discrimination, and requirements on car service and common carrier responsibility). While this would be the preferable way to eliminate the existing inequality, Congress could elect to place all carriers on an equal footing by repealing the existing exemption—although this would result in more, instead of less, regulation and very likely in higher though more stable rates. Whichever alternative is adopted, these commodities are too important a part of carrier traffic to continue to be governed so unequally by Federal rate regulation.

(2) Agricultural and fishery products: An exemption similar to that described above, and now available only to motor carriers and freight forwarders, relates to agricultural and fishery products. This exemption from minimum rates should also be extended to all carriers. Here, too, the ICC should retain control of maximum railroad rates and certain other controls, to protect the public interest in those areas where there is no effective truck or water carrier competition to keep rates down.

The combined effect of extending these bulk and agricultural exemptions will be to reduce drastically and equalize fairly the regulation of freight rates in this country. Freed to exercise normal managerial initiative, carriers will be able to rationalize their operations and reduce costs; and shippers should consequently enjoy a wider choice, improved service and lower rates.

(3) Intercity passenger rates: The traveling public, like the commercial shipper, is also uninterested in paying higher rates to subsidize weak segments of the transportation industry. Chronic overcapacity and deficits can be ended in the long run only in an industry made fit, lean and progressive by vigorous competition and innovation. But this is not possible as long as Federal agencies fix uniform minimum rates for passenger travel. I recommend, therefore, that the Congress enact legislation which would eventually limit the control of intercity passenger rates to the establishment of maximum rates only. In the case of the airlines, it may be preferable to initiate this program on a gradual or temporary basis under existing authority.

To prevent the absence of minimum rate regulation under the above three proposals from resulting in predatory, discriminatory trade practices or rate wars reflecting monopolistic ambitions rather than true efficiency, the Congress should make certain that such practices by carriers freed from minimum rate regulations would be covered by existing laws against monopoly and predatory trade practices.

While the above three recommendations relate to the most critical—and controversial—problems of unnecessary or unequal regulatory curbs on transportation, other changes in the Interstate Commerce Act and the Federal Aviation Act are needed consistent with these same principles. I recommend that legislation be enacted to:

(4) Assure all carriers the right to ship vehicles or containers on the carriers of other branches of the transportation industry at the same rates avail-

able to noncarrier shippers. This change will put the various carriers in a position of equality with freight forwarders and other shippers in the use of the promising and fast-growing piggyback and related techniques.

(5) Repeal the provision of the Interstate Commerce Act which now prevents a railroad from hauling cargo it owns. The need for this provision, which goes back to the days of oppressive railroad monopoly, has largely passed; and its current effect is to handicap the railroads in competing with other modes of transportation. The antitrust laws can insure protection against the possible abuse by a railroad of its dual status as shipper and carrier.

(6) Direct the regulatory agencies to sanction experimental freight rates, modifications and variations in existing systems of classification and documentation, and new kinds or combinations of service.

(B) *Consistent policies of taxation and user charges*

The same accidents of circumstance that have molded our transportation regulatory policies and programs have largely determined specific transportation taxes. As a result, inequities have developed and in some instances have persisted for many years.

(1) *Transportation excise tax.*—I have already recommended repeal of the 10-percent passenger transportation tax. This tax, a vestige of World War II and the Korean war, has undoubtedly discriminated against public transportation in favor of the automobile. I again recommend repeal of this tax to improve the competitive position of intercity railroad and bus passenger transportation systems, which generally are not publicly supported, and to clear the way for an equitable system of user charges for aviation.

(2) *Aviation.*—For commercial airlines, I have suggested (*a*) continuation of the 2-cents-per-gallon net tax on gasoline and extension of that tax rate to all jet fuels; and (*b*) a 5-percent tax on airline tickets and on airfreight waybills. By delaying until January 1, 1963, the effective date of all proposed changes as they affect aviation—including the repeal of the passenger tax for the airlines—ample time will be allowed for review by the Civil Aeronautics Board of any tariff adjustments that may be required by the carriers to recover the cost of user charges on fuel. The ticket and waybill taxes will be passed on directly to ultimate users.

For general aviation, such as recreational flying and company planes to which ticket and waybill taxes would not be applicable, a fuel tax of 3 cents per gallon is recommended as a minimal step toward recouping the heavy Federal investment in the airways.

All of the above taxes—in effect user charges—will recover only about half of the annual cost of the Federal airways system which is properly allocable to civil aviation. Total airways costs, which are approximately $500 million annually, have risen steadily in the past decade and will continue to grow as airways facilities and services are improved to accommodate future air traffic. Repeal of the 10-percent passenger tax as it now applies to aviation should not become effective, therefore, until the recommended user charges are in force for all segments of civil aviation.

(3) *Inland waterways.*—Also in the interest of equality of treatment and opportunity, the principle of user charges should be extended to the inland waterways. A tax of 2 cents per gallon should be applied to all fuels used in

transportation on the waterways. The recommended effective date, January 1, 1963, will allow time for review by the Interstate Commerce Commission of any adjustments that may be necessary in common carrier rates. This deferral is recommended even though the bulk of inland waterways traffic is carried by unregulated rather than regulated carriers.

The new tax should include an exemption similar to the current exemption from taxation accorded to gasoline and ships supplies for vessels employed in the fisheries, foreign trade, or trade between the Atlantic and Pacific ports of the United States or between the United States and any of its possessions. Vessels in domestic trade using facilities and routes similar to those engaged in foreign trade, and vessels in coastal trade which are too large to use the intercoastal waterways, should also be exempted.

This administration recognizes the responsibility of the Government to maintain and improve our system of inland waterways. Over $2 billion of Federal funds has already been invested in capital improvements. Expenditures for operating and maintaining the waterways are about $70 million annually, even though only a small fraction of the traffic consists of common carriers which serve all shippers and the general public. The users of the waterways include some of the largest and financially strongest corporations in the United States today, and it is surely feasible and appropriate for them to pay a small share of the Federal Government's costs in providing and maintaining waterway improvements.

(4) *Income taxes.*—Another effort to improve equity in taxation is being taken by the Treasury Department, which is reviewing the administrative guidelines now governing depreciation rates in the transportation industry. The objective of this administration will be to give full recognition to current economic forces, including obsolescence, which in their impact upon the lives of depreciable assets may affect quite differently the different modes of transportation and, therefore, their competitive relationships. In addition, I recommend that the Internal Revenue Code be amended to increase from 5 to 7 years the period during which regulated public utilities, including those in transportation, can apply prior year losses to reduce current income for tax purposes.

(C) *Evenhanded Government promotion of intercity transportation*

To achieve a better balance of Federal promotional programs:

(1) I urge favorable consideration of legislation proposed by the Civil Aeronautics Board last year to make the domestic trunk air carriers ineligible for operating subsidies in the future. These carriers provide more passenger miles of transportation service than any of the other common carriers; and, while they are experiencing temporary over capacity and have recently sustained financial losses, they have bright prospects for longrun growth and prosperity which should make them permanently independent of Government support.

(2) With respect to other aviation subsidies, the Congress has limited to $6 million the funds available in fiscal 1962 for the payment of operating subsidies to the three certificated helicopter services; and the Appropriations Committees have requested the Civil Aeronautics Board to prepare a schedule for the termination of these subsidies. I endorse this position and seek the extension of this principle. I am asking the Board to develop by June 30, 1963, a step-by-step program, with specific annual targets, to assure sharp reduction of operating sub-

sidies to all other domestic airlines as well, within periods to be established by the Board for each type of service or carrier. Rigorous enforcement of the Board's use-it-or-lose-it policy and further development of the class rate subsidy plan which the Board initiated in January 1961 with the cooperation of the local service carriers would clearly facilitate this objective. The development of single airports to serve adjacent cities, or regional airports, is also clearly necessary if these subsidies are to be eliminated and if the Federal Government and local communities are to meet the Nation's needs for adequate airports and air navigation facilities without excessive and unjustifiable costs.

(3) The Federal Government is a major user of transportation services. To assure the greatest practical use of the transportation industry by Government, I am directing all agencies of the Government, in meeting their own transport needs, to use authorized commercial facilities in all modes of transportation within the limits of economical and efficient operations and the requirements of military readiness.

(4) I also recommend that the Post Office Department be given greater flexibility in arranging for the transportation of mail by motor vehicle common carrier.

(5) Last year the Congress extended until June 30, 1963, the authority by which the Interstate Commerce Commission has been guaranteeing interest and principal payments on emergency loans to the railroads for operations, maintenance, and capital improvements for which the carriers cannot otherwise obtain funds on reasonable terms. A similar law by which the Government guarantees loans for aircraft and parts being purchased by certain certificated air carriers will expire this year. Since the Department of Commerce is already a focal point for Government transportation activities and since, in the interest of program coordination and consistency of policy these activities should be further consolidated, I recommend that the railroad loan guarantee authority, and the aviation loan guarantee authority if it is extended, be transferred to the Department of Commerce. These problems are not regulatory in nature and are clearly separable from the chief functions of the Interstate Commerce Commission and the Civil Aeronautics Board, and can be acted upon more expeditiously by an executive agency.

(D) *Protection of the public interest*

(1) Mergers: A great resurgence of merger talk has occurred in the railroad and airline industries in the last several years, and major mergers have been proposed in recent months in both industries. The soundness of such mergers should be determined, not in the abstract, but by applying appropriate criteria to the circumstances and conditions of each particular case. This administration has a responsibility to recommend more specific guidelines than are now available and more specific procedures for applying them.

Accordingly, I have directed the formation of an interagency group to undertake two tasks: First, after proper consultation with interested parties, to formulate general administration policies on mergers in each segment of the transportation industry; and second, to assist the Department of Justice in developing a Government position on each merger application for presentation before the regulatory agencies. This group will consist of agency representatives designated by the Attorney General, the Secretary of Commerce, the Secretary of Labor, the Chairman of the Council of Economic Advisers, and the heads of other agencies involved in a particular case. Under the chairmanship of Commerce, this group will examine each pending merger in transportation on the basis of the following criteria and others which they may develop:

(1) Effective competition should be maintained among alternative forms of transportation, and, where traffic volume permits, between competing firms in the same mode of transportation.

(2) The goals of economical, efficient, and adequate service to the public—and reduction in any public subsidies—should be secured by the realization of genuine economies.

(3) Affected workers should be given the assistance to make any necessary adjustments caused by the merger.

(2) Through routes and joint rates: For many years some regulatory agencies have been authorized to appoint joint boards to act on proposals for intercarrier services; but they have taken virtually no initiative to foster these arrangements which could greatly increase service and convenience to the general public and open up new opportunities for all carriers. I recommend, therefore, that Congress declare as a matter of public policy that through routes and joint rates should be vigorously encouraged, and authorize all transportation agencies to participate in joint boards.

(3) I have requested the Secretary of Defense and the Administrator of General Services to make the fullest possible use of their statutory powers, and I urge the enactment of such additional legislation as may be necessary, to encourage experimental rates and services—to explore every promising simplification of rate structures—and to encourage the development of systems that will make rate ascertainment and publication less costly and more convenient. These experiments will be pilot studies for a more general simplification of rates and for the application of new kinds of service to transportation in general.

(4) I am requesting the National Conference of Commissioners on Uniform State Laws, in cooperation with the Interstate Commerce Commission, to develop and urge adoption of uniform State registration laws for motor carriers operating within States but handling interstate commerce. The Congress should, consistent with this effort, give the Interstate Commerce Commission authority to enter into cooperative enforcement agreements with the various States, covering both the economic and the safety aspects of highway transportation.

(5) I recommend that all common carriers, including freight forwarders and motor carriers, be required to pay reparations to shippers charged unlawfully high rates.

(6) Finally, I recommend that the civil penalty now imposed on motor carriers for failure to file required reports be substantially increased; that the same civil penalty be imposed for violations of safety regulations and for operating without authority; and that the safety regulations of the Interstate Commerce Commission should be made fully applicable to private, as well as to common and contract carriers, so as to clarify the ambiguous situation prevailing at present.

PART II. URBAN TRANSPORTATION

I have previously emphasized to the Congress the need for action on the transportation problems resulting from burgeoning urban growth and the changing urban scene.

Higher incomes coupled with the increasing availability of the automobile have enabled more and more American families, particularly younger ones with children, to seek their own homes in suburban areas. Simultaneously, changes and improvements in freight transportation, made possible by the development of modern highways and the trucking industry, have reduced the dependence of manufacturers on central locations near port facilities or railroad terminals. The development of improved production techniques that require spacious, one-story plant layouts have impelled many industries to move to the periphery of urban areas. At the same time the importance of the central city is increasing for trade, financial, governmental, and cultural activities.

One result of these changes in location patterns has been a change in the patterns of urban travel. Formerly people traveled mainly along high density corridors radiating to and from downtown. Today traffic patterns are increasingly diverse. Added to traditional suburb-to-city movements are large crosstown flows which existing mass transportation systems are often not geared to handle. Also, the increasing use of automobiles to meet urban transportation needs has resulted in increasing highway congestion, and this has greatly impeded mass transportation service using those highways.

This drastic revision of travel patterns in many urban areas has seriously impaired the effectiveness and economic viability of public mass transportation, which is geared to the older patterns. A steady decline in patronage and a concomitant rise of unprofitability and financial problems have occurred. This has been particularly true of rail commuter and streetcar services limited to particular routes by fixed roadbeds.

To conserve and enhance values in existing urban areas is essential. But at least as important are steps to promote economic efficiency and livability in areas of future development. In less than 20 years we can expect well over half of our expanded population to be living in 40 great urban complexes. Many smaller places will also experience phenomenal growth. The ways that people and goods can be moved in these areas will have a major influence on their structure, on the efficiency of their economy, and on the availability for social and cultural opportunities they can offer their citizens. Our national welfare therefore requires the provision of good urban transportation, with the properly balanced use of private vehicles and modern mass transport to help shape as well as serve urban growth.

At my request, the problems of urban transportation have been studied in detail by the Housing and Home Finance Administrator and the Secretary of Commerce. Their field investigations have included some 40 metropolitan and other communities, large and small. Their findings support the need for substantial expansion and important changes in the urban mass transportation program authorized in the Housing Act of 1961 as well as revisions in Federal highway legislation. They give dramatic emphasis, moreover, to the need for greater local initiative and to the responsibility of the States and municipalities to provide financial support and effective governmental auspices for strengthening and improving urban transportation.

On the basis of this report, I recommend that long-range Federal financial aid and technical assistance be provided to help plan and develop the comprehensive and balanced urban transportation that is so vitally needed, not only to benefit local communities, but to assure more effective use of Federal funds available for other urban development and renewal programs. I recommend that such Federal assistance for mass transportation be limited to those applications (1) where an organization, or officially coordinated organizations, are carrying on a continuing program of comprehensive planning on an areawide basis, and (2) where the assisted project will be administered through a public agency as part of a unified or officially coordinated areawide transportation system.

(A) Long-range program

Specifically, I recommend that the Congress authorize the first installment of a long-range program of Federal aid to our urban regions for the revitalization and needed expansion of public mass transportation, to be administered by the Housing and Home Finance Agency. I recommend a capital grant authorization of $500 million to be made available over a 3-year period, with $100 million to be made available in fiscal 1963. Only a program that offers substantial support and continuity of Federal participation can induce our urban regions to organize appropriate administrative arrangements and to meet their share of the costs of fully balanced transportation systems.

This Federal assistance should be made available to qualified public agencies in the form of direct grants to be matched by local, non-Federal contributions. For rights-of-way, fixed facilities, including maintenance and terminal facilities, and rolling stock required for urban mass transportation systems, grants should be provided for up to two-thirds of the project cost which cannot reasonably be financed from expected revenue. The remaining one-third of the net project cost would be paid by the locality or State from other sources, without Federal aid. The extension and rehabilitation of existing systems as well as the creation of new systems should be eligible. In no event should Federal funds be used to pay operating expenses. Nor should parking facilities, except those directly supporting public mass transportation, be eligible for Federal grants.

While it is expected that the new grant program will be the major Federal support for urban mass transportation, it is important to have Federal loans available where private financing cannot be obtained on reasonable terms. I therefore recommend removal of the time limit on the $50 million loan authorization provided in the Housing Act of 1961. Federal loans would not be available to finance the State or local one-third contribution to net project cost.

Although grants and loans would be available only to public agencies, those agencies could lease facilities and equipment or make other arrangements for private operation of assisted mass transportation systems. The program is not intended to foster public as distinguished from private mass transit operations. Each community should develop the method or methods of operation best suited to its particular requirements.

A community should be eligible for a mass transportation grant or loan only after the Housing Administrator determines that the facilities and equipment for which the assistance is sought are necessary for carrying out a program for a unified or officially coordinated urban transportation system as a part of the comprehensively planned development of the urban area.

The program I have proposed is aimed at the widely varying transit problems of our Nation's cities, ranging from the clogged arteries of our most populous metropolitan areas to those smaller cities which have only recently known the frustrations of congested streets. There may, however, be some highly specialized situations in which alternative programs, for example, loan guarantees under stringent conditions, would be better suited to particular needs and the Congress may, therefore, wish to consider such alternatives.

(B) *Emergency aid*

Time will be required by most metropolitan areas to organize effectively for the major planning efforts required. Even more time may be needed to create public agencies with adequate powers to develop, finance, and administer new or improved public transportation systems. Meanwhile, the crisis conditions that have already emerged in some areas threaten to become widespread. Mass transportation continues to deteriorate and even to disappear. Important segments of our population are thus deprived of transportation; highway congestion and attendant air pollution become worse; and the destructive effects upon central business districts and older residential areas are accelerated.

In recognition of this serious situation, I also recommend that the Congress, for a period of 3 years only, authorize the Housing Administrator to make emergency grants, (a) where there is an urgent need for immediate aid to an existing mass transportation facility or service that might otherwise cease to be available for transportation purposes, (b) where an official long-range program for a coordinated system is being actively prepared, and (c) where the facilities or equipment acquired under the emergency grant can reasonably be expected to be required for the new long-range system. This emergency aid should not exceed one-half of the net project cost. Upon completion of an acceptable areawide transportation program within 3 years, these emergency projects, if a part of the ultimate system, should qualify for the balance of the regular Federal assistance available under the long-range program.

(C) *Role of highways*

Highways are an instrumental part of any coordinated urban transportation program, and must be an integral part of any comprehensive community development plan. Accordingly, I have requested the Secretary of Commerce to make his approval of the use of highway planning funds in metropolitan planning studies contingent upon the establishment of a continuing and comprehensive planning process. This process should, to the maximum extent feasible, include all of the interdependent parts of the metropolitan or other urban area, all agencies and jurisdictions involved, and all forms of transportation, and should be closely coordinated with policymaking and program administration.

Progress has already been made in coordinated transportation planning for metropolitan areas through the use of funds made available under both Federal highway and housing legislation. To increase the effectiveness of this effort, I recommend that the Federal-aid highway law be amended to increase the percentage of Federal funds available to the States for research and planning. Legislation will be submitted to effectuate this change and to provide that (a) these funds should be available for planning and research purposes only; (b) the funds be matched by the States in accordance with statutory matching requirements; and (c) any funds not used for planning and research lapse.

In addition I recommend that the Federal-aid highway law be amended to provide that, effective not later than July 1, 1965, the Secretary of Commerce shall, before approving a program for highway projects in any metropolitan area, make a finding that such projects are consistent with comprehensive development plans for the metropolitan area and that the Federal-aid system so developed will be an integral part of a soundly based, balanced transportation system for the area involved.

Highway planning should be broadened to include adequate traffic control systems, parking facilities, and circulation systems on city streets commensurate with the traffic forecasts used to justify freeways and major arterial roadways. Provision for transit and highway facilities in the same roadway, permissible under present law and already tested in several cases, should be encouraged whenever more effective transportation will result. Moreover, I have requested the Secretary of Commerce to consider favorably the reservation of special highway lanes for buses during peak traffic hours whenever comprehensive transportation plans indicate that this is desirable.

To permit the State highway departments greater flexibility in the use of Federal-aid highway funds to meet urban transportation needs, I further recommend that the Federal-aid highway law be amended to permit more extensive use of Federal-aid secondary funds for extensions of the secondary system in urban areas.

I have asked the Secretary of Commerce and the Housing and Home Finance Administrator to consult regularly regarding administration of the highway and urban mass transportation programs, and to report to me annually on the progress of their respective programs, on the needs for further coordination, and on possibilities for improvement.

(D) Relocation assistance

Last year in a message to the Congress on the Federal-aid highway program, I called attention to the problems of families displaced by new highway construction and proposed that the Federal highway law be amended to require assistance to such families in finding decent housing at reasonable cost. The need for such assistance to alleviate unnecessary hardship is still urgent. The Secretary of Commerce has estimated that, under the interstate highway program alone, 15,000 families and 1,500 businesses are being displaced each year, and the proposed urban mass transportation program will further increase the number of persons affected.

To move toward equity among the various federally assisted programs causing displacement, I recommend that assistance and requirements similar to those now applicable to the urban renewal program be authorized for the Federal-aid highway program and the urban mass transportation program. Legislation is being submitted to authorize payments of not to exceed $200 in the case of individuals and families and $3,000 (or if greater, the total certified actual moving expenses) in the case of business concerns or nonprofit organizations displaced as a result of land acquisitions under these programs.

(E) Mass transit research and demonstrations

Further, I believe that progress will be most rapid and long lasting if the Federal Government contributes to economic and technological research in the field of urban mass transportation. These research activities should be an integral part of the research program described later in this message. Important parts of this program should be carried out by the Housing Administrator directly, through contract with other Federal agencies, private research organizations, universities and other competent bodies, or through the allocation of funds to local public agencies for approved programs.

To facilitate this approach, I recommend that the $25 million authorized last year for demonstration grants be made available for broad research and development undertakings, as well as demonstration projects, which have general applicability throughout the Nation. That amount, plus an additional $10 million from the proposed capital grant funds for each of the years 1963, 1964, and 1965 should suffice for these purposes. These funds, together with research funds available under the Federal-aid highway program, can contribute to substantial advances in urban transportation.

(F) *Interstate compacts*

Finally, since transportation in many urban areas is an interstate problem, I recommend that legislation be enacted to give congressional approval in advance for interstate compacts for the establishment of agencies to carry out transportation and other regional functions in urban areas extending across State lines.

PART III. INTERNATIONAL TRANSPORTATION

We should endeavor, to the maximum extent feasible, to (*a*) gear international transportation investments to the requirements of our peacetime international trade and travel, and (*b*) provide incentives to users that will channel traffic to those forms of transportation that provide desirable service at the lowest total cost. The most critical problems associated with these policies are in the national defense area. Determination must be made as to whether the number and types of ships and aircraft adequate to meet long-range peacetime needs are also adequate to meet probable military emergencies, and if they are not, how best to meet these additional requirements.

(A) *Merchant marine*

In the Merchant Marine Act of 1936, the U.S. Government made a new start on the vexing problems of the American merchant marine in the face of repeated failure to improve its condition both before and after World War I. Subsequently, other aids in the form of cargo preference legislation, varies "trade-out," "trade-in," and tax incentives devised to stimulate new construction, and a mortgage insurance program with up to $87\frac{1}{2}$-percent Federal guarantees were added to the arsenal of protection against the industry's exposure to low-cost foreign competition.

In spite of these aids, subsidies required for both construction and operations under the 1936 act have steadily increased. Operating subsidies will rise from $49 million in 1950 to over $225 million in 1963. Ship construction costs in U.S. yards are now approximately double those in Japanese and German yards. For this reason and because of an acceleration of the program beginning in 1956 to replace war-built cargo ships, Federal expenditures for new ship construction will rise to a postwar high of $112 million in 1963.

At my request, the Secretary of Commerce has undertaken a study of the current problems of the American merchant marine. This review will involve such specific issues as the state of coastal and intercoastal shipping and the costs of service to our noncontiguous territories. It will also consider more fundamental questions of long-term adjustment: Are the criteria adopted in 1936 as guides to the establishment of essential trade routes and services relevant for the future? Are there alternatives to the existing techniques for providing financial assistance which would benefit (a) the public in terms of better service and lower rates and (b) the operators in terms of higher profits, more freedom for management initiative and more incentive for privately financed research and technological advance? What research and development efforts are most likely to increase the competitiveness of our merchant marine? Can defense readiness requirements be met adequately by greater reliance on the reserve fleet and the ships of our allies under NATO agreements? Would a smaller reserve fleet be adequate? Are the international arrangements pursuant to which world shipping operations are carried on conducive to the stability of the industry, fair but effective competition and adequate service?

I have also recommended a stepped-up research program for developing merce with estimates, under a range of assumptions as to military emergencies, of what active and reserve tonnages of merchant shipping should be maintained in the interest of national security. In addition, I have established a Cabinet-level committee, chaired by the Secretary of Labor, whose study will include the flags of convenience and cargo preference issues. When the findings and conclusions of these studies become available, I shall send to the Congress appropriate specific recommendations concerning our maritime program.

In the meantime, I have directed the Secretary of Commerce to implement fully section 212(d) of the Merchant Marine Act of 1936, for securing preference to vessels of U.S. registry in the movement of commodities in our waterborne foreign commerce; and I have directed all executive branch agencies to comply fully with the purpose of our cargo preference laws.

I have also recommended a stepped-up research program for developing ways and means of increasing the competitive efficiency of our merchant marine and related industries. Of particular significance in this effort will be the application of the principles of mass production, and the standardization of ship types and ship components, for reduction in the cost of new vessel construction. Also, I am urging that sound development in technology and automation be applied to merchant shipping as rapidly as possible, fully recognizing and providing for the job equities involved, as a major program for enhancing the competitive capability of our merchant marine.

(B) International aviation

An interdepartmental committee, headed by the Administrator of the Federal Aviation Agency, and including representatives from the Department of State, the Department of Defense, the Department of Commerce, the Civil Aeronautics Board, and the Bureau of the Budget, was established at my direction last July to undertake a study of U.S. international air transportation policies and problems. This study is presently underway, and will be completed by late summer. Concurrent with this policy study, the Bureau of the Budget is conducting a study of the organizational structure within which Government agencies carry out activities concerned with international aviation. Once these studies have been completed and evaluated, an administration policy on international civil aviation will be enunciated, with responsibilities assigned to the agencies involved according to statutory requirements.

PART IV. LABOR RELATIONS AND RESEARCH

(*A*) *Labor relations*

Technological advance in transportation must be explored and developed if we are to meet growing requirements for the movement of people and goods. New equipment often requires new skills, sometimes displaces labor, and often requires retraining or relocation of manpower. An overall reduction in manpower requirements in transportation is not inevitable, however; and the new Manpower Development and Training Act will help those transportation workers in need of new jobs or new skills.

For the long-range benefit of labor, management, and the public, collective bargaining in the transportation industry must promote efficiency as well as solve problems of labor-management relations. Problems of job assignments, work rules, and other employment policies must be dealt with in a manner that will both encourage increased productivity and recognize the job equities which are affected by technological change. The Government also has an obligation to develop policies and provide assistance to labor and management consistent with the above objectives.

(*B*) *Research*

To understand the increasingly complex transportation problems of the future, to identify the relationships of social, economic, administrative, and technical factors involved, to translate scientific knowledge into transportation engineering practice, to weigh the merits of alternative systems, and to formulate new, improved, and consistent policies—we need information that can evolve only from a vigorous, continuous, and coordinated program of research. Yet, in the field of transportation where we have many unfulfilled opportunities, research has been fragmented, unsteady, inadequate in scope and balance.

Scientific and engineering research will bring to all forms of transportation the benefits of new high strength, low-cost and durable materials, compact and economical powerplants, new devices to increase safety and convenience—improvements which have characterized the development of jet-propelled aircraft. Experiments in the maritime field have resulted in the development of a nuclear-powered merchant ship, the NS *Savannah,* which has already begun test cruises, and a hydrofoil ship, the *Dennison,* which is nearing trial runs. Transportation on land, as well as in the air and on the seas, can benefit from accelerated scientific research.

Economic and policy research will improve knowledge about the functioning of our transportation system as a whole and about the interrelation of the major branches of the industry. It should consider the new demands for transportation, the changing markets and products being handled, and the need for speed and safety. For instance, such research can consider the handling of freight as a system beginning in the shipper's plant and ending with the delivery of goods to the very doors of his customers—using new packaging, containerization and cargo handling methods that will take full advantage of new economies and convenience.

Taking advantage of new techniques that would provide convenience and efficiency, we must consider the impact of different forms of transportation investment on economic development; we must combine and integrate systems to take advantage of the maximum benefits of each mode of travel; we must now consider the Nation's transportation network as an articulated and closely linked system rather than an uncoordinated set of independent entities.

Just as a transport system must be built and operated as a whole, the different areas of transportation research must be coordinated within an overall concept. With the advice and assistance of the heads of the principal Federal agencies concerned with transportation and members of my own staff, the Secretary of Commerce is undertaking a broad evaluation of research needs in transportation and of the appropriate methods to meet these needs. I look to the Secretary of Commerce to develop a comprehensive transportation research program for the Government for later consideration by the Congress. Once such a coordinated and policy-oriented research program is underway, it will produce a flow of information of the kind that we must have to implement a comprehensive public policy on transportation.

Improved statistics for private and Government use are also urgently needed. The 1963 budget repeats a request made by the previous administration for funds to prepare for a Census of Transportation. This census will make an important beginning to supplying these much-needed data. I urge early favorable action on this request.

CONCLUSION

The troubles in our transportation system are deep; and no just and comprehensive set of goals—which meets all the needs of each mode of transportation as well as shippers, consumers, taxpayers and the general public—can be quickly or easily reached. But few areas of public concern are more basic to our progress as a nation. The Congress and all citizens, as well as all Federal agencies, have an increasing interest in and an increasing responsibility to be aware of the shortcomings of existing transportation policies; and the proposals contained in this message are intended to be a constructive basis for the exercise of that responsibility.

The difficulty and the complexity of these basic troubles will not correct themselves with the mere passage of time. On the contrary, we cannot afford to delay further. Facing up to the realities of the situation, we must begin to make the painful decisions necessary to providing the transportation system required by the United States of today and tomorrow.

JOHN F. KENNEDY.

THE WHITE HOUSE, *April 5, 1962.*

Appendix II

SELECTED REFERENCES FOR
FURTHER READING

Bibliographical material on transportation, even for the United States alone, is enormous. It includes books; articles in both professional and trade publications; reports of local, state, and federal governments; legislative hearings and investigations; reports of agencies assigned to deal with transportation problems; decisions of courts and administrative bodies; and publications of associations formed by the various modes of transport. In addition, there is a large volume of literature dealing with the technical, engineering, managerial, legal, administrative, and geographical aspects of transport. The following list of references is selected primarily from economic literature on the subject. It is intended to serve principally as an initial source of information for those who wish to pursue further study of the subject matter covered in the main text, as well as an immediate reference list to other material by those who want to investigate a particular subject more intensively. The first section contains general references and sources of information for transport economics as a whole; the remaining sections contain a more limited list of publications for immediate study of the main topics. In addition, footnote references in the main text contain references to specific sources of information. No attempt has been made to assemble anything resembling an adequate bibliography on any topic; this can be gathered according to the interests of a particular reader from sources identified below.

GENERAL REFERENCES

W. M. ACWORTH, *The Elements of Railway Economics* (Oxford: Clarendon Press, 1924). A concise treatment of theory and experience in railway economics by an eminent British student of the subject. T. C. BIGHAM and M. J. ROBERTS, *Transportation* (2d ed.; New York: McGraw-Hill Book Co., Inc., 1952). A comprehensive text on transportation in the United States with very extensive bibliographies at the end of each chapter. M. R. BONAVIA, *The Economics of Transport* (New York: Pitman Publishing Corp., 1947). This is one of the Cambridge Economic series and is a concise treatment of transport economics by a British student. A. W. CURRIE, *Economics of Canadian Transportation* (Toronto, Can.: University of Toronto Press, 1954). A descriptive and historical treatment of Canadian transportation. STUART DAGGETT, *Principles of Inland Transportation* (4th ed.; New York: Harper & Bros., 1955). A comprehensive treatment of transportation in the United States. It is especially strong on transport geography and traffic movements. It contains an extensive bibliography at the end of each chapter, as well as exhaustive footnotes. The earlier editions may be consulted for topics not contained in the last one, as well as for other references. M. L. FAIR and E. W. WILLIAMS, JR., *Economics of Transportation* (rev. ed.; New York: Harper & Bros., 1959). Deals with all phases of transportation in the United States, one whole section being devoted to transportation service. J. H. FREDERICK, *Commercial Air Transportation* (5th ed.; Homewood, Ill.: Richard D. Irwin, Inc., 1961). A comprehensive treatment of air transportation in the United States, especially in its operating aspects. It contains an extensive bibliography and the principal provisions of the Civil Aeronautics Act of 1938. A. T. HADLEY, *Railroad Transportation* (New York: Putnam & Sons, 1885). This is regarded as a classic in its field. It contains an interesting exposition of rate theory at the end of the last century. K. T. HEALY, *The Economics of Transportation* (New York: Ronald Press Co., 1940). This deals with all modes of transport in the United States, with particular emphasis on the motives and reasons for economic phenomena in this field. It also contains a careful discussion of transport costs. W. J. HUDSON and J. A. CONSTANTIN, *Motor Transportation: Principles and Practices* (New York: Ronald Press Co., 1958). A detailed account of highway development, and motor carrier operation and regulation. W. T. JACKMAN, *Economic Principles of Transportation* (Toronto: University of Toronto Press, 1937). Emphasizes economic analysis, with illustrations from Canadian experience. E. R. JOHNSON, G. G. HUEBNER, and A. K. HENRY, *Transportation by Water* (New York: D. Appleton-Century Co., 1935). A comprehensive coverage of water transportation, dealing also with both domestic and foreign shipping of the United States. E. R. JOHNSON, G. G. HUEBNER, and G. L. WILSON, *Transportation: Economic Principles and Practices* (New York: D. Appleton-Century Co., 1940). A comprehensive, descriptive study of all phases of transportation in this country (except urban). Emphasis on service and practices. Good references at the end of each chapter. ELIOT JONES, *Principles of Railway Transportation* (New York: Macmillan Co., 1924). The best single treatment of railroad economics and regulation covering the period up to 1922; also extensive references on the subject. D. KNOOP, *Outlines of Railway Economics* (2d ed.; London: Macmillan & Co., Ltd., 1923). Emphasizes economics, with special reference to railways. C. E. LANDON, *Transportation* (New York: William Sloane Associates, Inc., 1951). A valuable source of information on all phases of transportation in the United States. The references at the end of each chapter are particularly exhaustive. JOHN B. LANSING, *Transportation and Economic Policy* (New York: The Free Press, 1966). Application of economic theory to transport with emphasis on economic development. D. P. LOCKLIN, *Economics of Transportation* (6th ed.:

Homewood, Ill.: Richard D. Irwin, Inc., 1966). This is the most exhaustive and up-to-date treatment of domestic intercity transportation in the United States that is available. There is especial emphasis on railroad transportation and public regulation. There is a very thorough bibliography at the end of each chapter, and an exhaustive list of commission cases and Supreme Court decisions in the footnotes throughout. S. L. MILLER, *Inland Transportation: Principles and Practices* (New York: McGraw-Hill Book Co., Inc., 1933). The emphasis is on railroad problems and practices, and the emergence of the modern railroad problem. A. M. MILNE, *The Economics of Inland Transport* (London: Sir Isaac Pitman & Sons, Ltd., 1955). This is the most careful treatment of transportation in terms of employment and use of scarce resources that is available. It is particularly pertinent from the standpoint of the economics of transport pricing, and the basis for public policy. HUGH S. NORTON, *Modern Transportation Economics* (Columbus, Ohio: Charles E. Merrill Books, Inc., 1963). A general treatment of transport economics. NATIONAL RESOURCES PLANNING BOARD, *Transportation and National Policy* (Washington, D.C.: U.S. Government Printing Office, 1942). Part I contains an anlysis of selected problems on transport policy by different experts. Part II consists of a series of studies of each of the modes of domestic transport. W. Z. RIPLEY, *Railroads: Rates and Regulation* (New York: Longmans, Green & Co., Inc., 1913); *Railroads: Finance and Organization* (New York: Longmans, Green & Co., Inc., 1915). These two volumes constitute the standard work on American railroads and the regulation of them up to the beginning of World War I. R. J. SAMPSON and M. T. FARRIS, *Domestic Transportation: Practice, Theory, and Policy* (Boston, Mass.: Houghton Mifflin Co., 1966). A general treatise with considerable emphasis on physical distribution. C. A. TAFF, *Commercial Motor Transportation* (3rd ed.; Homewood, Ill.: Richard D. Irwin, Inc., 1961). A detailed discussion of the commercial operations of motor carriers. E. TROXEL, *Economics of Transport* (New York: Rinehart & Co., Inc., 1955). A theoretical analysis of transport and the transport agencies as a whole, with emphasis on demand, cost, and marginal-limit relations. Careful attention is given to spatial considerations. Very extensive references are afforded in the footnotes at the end of the book. R. E. WESTMEYER, *Economics of Transportation* (Englewood Cliffs, N.J.: Prentice-Hall, Inc., 1952). Covers all the modes of domestic, intercity transportation, with separate treatment of each of them. G. L. WILSON and L. A. BRYAN, *Air Transportation* (Englewood Cliffs, N.J.: Prentice-Hall, Inc., 1949). A detailed presentation of air transportation, its history, commercial operations, and regulation in the United States. It also contains extensive references after each chapter. G. S. WOLBERT, JR., *American Pipe Lines* (Norman: University of Oklahoma Press, 1952). A discussion of the role of pipelines in the oil industry and in transportation. An exhaustive list of references in footnotes and a table of cases in the appendix.

Sources of statistical and periodical information are too numerous to list in detail. The *Industrial Arts Index* and *Readers' Guide to Periodical Literature* provide references for articles in trade publications and general magazines. AMERICAN ECONOMIC ASSOCIATION, *Index of Economic Journals* (Homewood, Ill.: Richard D. Irwin, Inc., 1961–66), in seven volumes, provides a complete index by subject and author of all publications in English since 1886 in the various economic journals. Each of the modes of transport has its own association with headquarters in Washington, D.C. Each provides comprehensive information on its own carriers. In addition, there are trade journals for each. *Traffic World* (Washington, D.C., weekly) gives comprehensive coverage for all agencies of transport, together with the rulings of the federal commissions and courts. It also reports on all legislation and Congressional hearings. The Transportation Association of America issues monthly bulletins on transportation facts and figures. *I.C.C. Practitioners' Journal* (monthly) publishes articles on transport regulation and a regular list of the rulings of the Interstate Commerce Commission. The various law journals also contain articles from time to time on transport problems. A complete list of all publications of the United States government is furnished by the Superintendent of Documents (monthly). The Interstate Commerce Commission publishes its decisions in the *I.C.C. Reports* and the *M.C.C. Reports* (for motor carriers). Its annual reports contain a summary of each year's activities. It also publishes *Statistics of Railways in the United States, Statistics of Motor Carriers in the United States,* and *Statistics of Oil Pipe Line Companies.* These are annual and furnish data on all agencies under the control of the Commission. The Bureau of Transport Economics and Statistics of the Interstate Commerce Commission issues *Transport Economics* monthly, as well as special studies from time to time. Information on air transportation is furnished by the Civil Aeronautics Board in its annual reports and special studies. Its decisions are contained in the CAB reports and dockets. The Federal Aviation Agency reports its activities in its annual report. It also issues special reports on plans for aviation development. It also publishes the *FAA Statistical Handbook of Aviation* annually. The Bureau of Public Roads of the Department of Commerce reports the progress of its activities in its annual report. Statistics and other information on water transportation are to be found in the annual report of the Chief of Army Engineers. This organization also publishes special studies on water transport projects. The *Transportation Journal,* published quarterly by the American Society of Traffic and Transportation contains articles in the general field of transportation. The *Transportation Research Forum,* publishes the papers of its annual meetings. These are mostly of a technical nature.

READING SUGGESTIONS

Part I. *The Transport System*

General Texts: *T. C. Bigham and M. J. Roberts,* chaps. 1–3, transportation and the economy; chap. 5, transportation service; chap 18, co-ordination of service. *Stuart Daggett,* chaps. 1–6, the transport system and its development; chaps. 7–11, transport geography and commodity movements; chap. 22, theory of locations; chaps. 12–14, duty of service and the common carrier. *M. L. Fair and E. W. Williams, Jr.,* Part I, function and development of transportation; Part II, transportation service; chap. 16, rates and the location of industry. *K. T. Healy,* chaps. 1–9, development of the transport system. *C. E. Landon,* chap. 2, transport geography; chap. 21, effects of transportation on the location of industry and commerce. *D. P. Locklin,* chaps. 3–4, transport and location of industries;

chaps. 5–7, history of railroads; chap. 26, railroad service; chap. 28, pipe lines; chap. 30, highway transportation; chap. 33, water transportation; chap. 35, air transportation. *S. L. Miller,* Part II, railway history of the United States; Part III, the railway service. *A. M. Milne,* chaps. 1–2, the function and development of transport. *E. Troxel,* chap. 13, transport costs and location of industry. *R. E. West-meyer,* chap. 31, transportation by indirect carriers.

Other References: J. W. BARRIGER, JR., *Super Railroads for a Dynamic American Economy* (New York: Simmons-Boardman Publishing Corp., 1956). A discussion of the requirements for railroad modernization by a railroad executive. ALBERT FISHLOW, *American Railroads and the Transformation of the Antebellum Economy* (Cambridge, Mass.: Harvard University Press, 1965). ROBERT W. FOGEL, *Railroads and American Economic Growth* (Baltimore, Md.: The Johns Hopkins Press, 1964). ROBERT W. FOGEL, *The Union Pacific Railroad* (Baltimore, Md.: The Johns Hopkins Press, 1960), a study in premature enterprise. C. GOODRICH, *Government Promotion of American Canals and Railroads, 1800–1890* (New York: Columbia University Press, 1960). C. GOODRICH, J. RUBIN, J. J. CRAMER, and H. H. SEGAL, *Canals and American Economic Development* (New York: Columbia University Press, 1961). *National Transportation Policy* (Doyle Report), Preliminary Draft of a Report to the Senate Committee on Interstate and Foreign Commerce, 87th Cong., 1st sess. (Washington, D.C.: U.S. Government Printing Office, 1961), Part II, transportation trends and the decline of the common carrier; Part VII, chap. 9, piggyback and containerization. E. G. PLOWMAN, *Elements of Business Logistics* (Stanford, Calif.: Graduate School of Business, Stanford University, 1964). A discussion of integration of business and transportation. R. E. SHAW, *Erie Water West: A History of the Erie Canal, 1792–1854* (Lexington, Ky.: University of Kentucky Press, 1966). E. W. SMYKAY, D. J. BOWERSOX, and F. H. MOSSMAN, *Physical Distribution Management* (New York: Macmillan Co., 1961). This deals with the logistics of the firm; chaps. 3 and 4, transportation and product flow; chap. 6, plant location theory (with a selected bibliography on location theory).

Part II. *The Economics of Transport Pricing*

General Texts: *T. C. Bigham and M. J. Roberts,* chap. 6, transportation costs; chap. 11, the general level of rates; chaps. 12–17, rates and rate making. *Stuart Daggett,* chaps. 15–16, rate theories; chaps. 15–21, rates and rate making; chap. 23, co-operation among carriers. *M. L. Fair and E. W. Williams, Jr.,* chaps. 17–19, rate making and rate structures. *K. T. Healy,* chaps. 10–11, cost features of the different modes of transport; chaps. 13–14, pricing of transportation services. *Eliot Jones,* chap. 4, the theory of railroad rates; chap. 5, ruinous competition; chap. 6, rate systems. *C. E. Landon,* chaps. 13–20, rate theories, discrimination, and rate making; chap. 20, the general rate level. *D. P. Locklin,* chap. 8, the theory of railroad rates; chap. 9, railroad rate structures; chap. 16, the railroad rate level; chap. 17, fair value and the rate of return; chaps. 19–23, rates and rate making. *S. L. Miller,* chap. 30, theories of rate making. *A. M. Milne,* chaps. 4–5, theory of the cost of transport; chap. 6, theory of pricing of transport, economies of scale in transportation. *E. Troxel,* chap. 5, transport costs; chaps. 26–29, price discrimination and its application to transportation. *R. E. West-*

meyer, chap. 10, the general level of railroad rates; chaps. 11–13, railroad rate making and rate structures.

General Theory: J. M. CLARK, *Economics of Overhead Costs* (Chicago: University of Chicago Press, 1923), for transport purposes especially chaps. 13, 14, 15, 20, and 21. JOEL DEAN, *Managerial Economics* (Englewood Cliffs, N.J.: Prentice-Hall, Inc., 1951), chap. 2, competition; chap. 5, costs and cost concepts. J. F. DUE, *Intermediate Economic Analysis* (rev. ed.; Homewood, Ill.: Richard D. Irwin, Inc., 1953), chap. 7, theory of production and economies of scale; chap. 8, behavior of cost; chap. 10, monopoly and monopolistic competition; chap. 11, average cost pricing and price discrimination. A. C. PIGOU, *Economics of Welfare* (3d ed.; London: Macmillan & Co., Ltd., 1929), chap. 18, the special problem of railway rates. JOAN ROBINSON, *Economics of Imperfect Competition* (London: Macmillan & Co., Ltd., 1934), chaps. 15 and 16 on price discrimination. G. J. STIGLER, *The Theory of Price* (New York: Macmillan Co., 1946), chap. 8, the laws of return and cost curves; chap. 16, the theory of multiple products (see also 3rd ed., 1966).

Other References: F. M. CUSHMAN, *Transportation for Management* (Englewood Cliffs, N.J.: Prentice-Hall, Inc., 1953). A detailed presentation of rate procedures and practices. S. DAGGETT and J. P. CARTER, *The Structure of Railroad Rates* (Berkeley: University of California Press, 1947). A careful analysis of railroad freight rates on transcontinental traffic. HOWARD FREAS, *Aspects of Transportation Based on Regulatory Experience in the United States,* a paper delivered to the High Authority European Coal and Steel Community, Luxembourg, October 10, 1958 (Washington, D.C., 1958). A careful statement on cost considerations of rate making by a former chairman of the Interstate Commerce Commission. BUREAU OF ACCOUNTS AND COST FINDING, INTERSTATE COMMERCE COMMISSION, *Explanation of Rail Cost Finding Procedures and Principles Relating to the Use of Costs,* Statement No. 2–48 (Washington, D.C.: October, 1948). A careful presentation of cost theory for rate making with extensive footnote references to the literature on the subject in chap. 1. K. T. HEALY, *The Effects of Scale in the Railroad Industry* (New Haven: Committee on Transportation, Yale University, 1961). A statistical analysis of economies of scale in railroad transportation that reaches the conclusion that they are very limited. "Interterritorial Freight Rates," *Law and Contemporary Problems,* Vol. XII, No. 3 (1947). A symposium on freight rates between territories. J. B. LANSING, *Transportation and Economic Policy,* Part I, Economic Theory Applied to Transportation. J. R. MEYER, M. J. PECK, J. STENASON, and C. ZWICK, *The Economics of Competition in the Transportation Industries* (Cambridge: Harvard University Press, 1959). A thorough analysis of the costs and market structures of the different modes of transport. *National Transportation Policy* (Doyle Report), Part VI, transportation pricing. *Royal Commission on Transportation* (Ottawa: Queen's Printer, February, 1961), Vol. II, chaps. 3–4 on pricing and competition in transportation. INTERNATIONAL TRANSPORT WORKERS' FEDERATION, *Transport Policy and Problems at National and International Level* (London: Frank Cassard Co., Ltd., 1959). An interesting presentation on transport costs and pricing from the union point of view. National Bureau of Economic Research, *Transportation Economics,* conference (New York: Columbia University Press, 1965), Part I on costs.

Part III. *The Regulation of Transportation*

General Texts: T. C. Bigham and M. J. Roberts, chap. 7 the, basis of regulation; chaps. 8–9, development and extension of federal regulation of transportation. *Stuart Daggett,* chaps. 27–33, regulation of the various modes. *M. L. Fair and E. W. Williams, Jr.,* chaps. 21–27, regulation and its application to the different modes. *J. H. Frederick,* chaps. 4–9, regulation of air transportation and policies of the Civil Aeronautics Board. *K. T. Healy,* chaps. 18–24, development and results of government regulation of transportation. *Eliot Jones,* chaps. 10–14, a thorough discussion of regulatory legislation for railroads and its application up to 1917; chap. 25, the Transportation Act of 1920. *D. P. Locklin,* chaps. 10–13, regulation of railroads; chap. 14, the agencies of control; chaps. 31 and 32, motor carrier regulation; chap. 34, regulation of water transportation; chap. 36, regulation of air transportation. C. F. PHILLIPS, JR., *The Economics of Regulation* (Homewood, Ill.: Richard D. Irwin, Inc., 1965), Parts I and II, Concepts and Theory of Regulation. *R. E. Westmeyer,* chaps. 5–8, regulation of railroad transportation; chap. 19, regulation of highway transportation; chap. 23, regulation of domestic water transportation; chap. 27, regulation of air transportation.

Other References: WALTER ADAMS (ed.), *The Structure of American Industry* (3d ed.; New York: Macmillan Co., 1961), "The Airlines Industry," by HORACE M. GRAY. W. BEARD, *Regulation of Pipe Lines as Common Carriers* (New York: Columbia University Press, 1941). C. CRUMBAKER, *Transportation and Politics* (Eugene: University of Oregon Press, 1940). A thorough study of long-and-short-haul policies of Congress and the Interstate Commerce Commission. Also R. DEWEY, *Long and Short Haul Principle of Rate Regulation* (Columbus: Ohio State University Press, 1935). F. H. DIXON, *Railroads and Government* (New York: Charles Scribner's Sons, 1922). A thorough study of regulatory policy from 1910 to 1921. J. GUANDOLO, *Transportation Law* (Dubuque, Ia.: William C. Brown Co., Publishers, 1960). D. V. HARPER, *Economic Regulation of the Motor Trucking Industry by the States* (Urbana: University of Illinois Press, 1959). A comprehensive study of state regulation of motor trucking. BUREAU OF TRANSPORT ECONOMICS AND STATISTICS, INTERSTATE COMMERCE COMMISSION, *Value of Service in Rate Making,* Statement No. 5912 (Washington, D.C., November, 1959). A complete study of the use of value of service in rate-making decisions by the Interstate Commerce Commission with a list of all the cases. E. R. JOHNSON, *Government Regulation of Transportation* (New York: D. Appleton-Century Co., Inc., 1938). A complete coverage of the regulation of all modes of transportation in the United States. G. KOLKO, *Railroads and Regulations 1877–1916* (Princeton, N.J., Princeton University Press, 1965). A critical evaluation of the influence of the Interstate Commerce Commission on railroad cartelization. P. W. MACAVOY, *The Economic Effects of Regulation: The Trunk-Line Railroad Cartels and the Interstate Commerce Commission before 1900* (Cambridge, Mass.: The M.I.T. Press, 1965). *National Transportation Policy* (Doyle Report), Part V, chap. 1, regulation of transportation; Part VII, chap. 4, exemptions from regulation; chap. 12, government regulation of air transport service. S. B. RICHMOND, *Regulation and Competition in Air Transportation* (New York: Columbia University Press,

1961). W. Z. RIPLEY, *Railroads: Rates and Regulation.* A thorough treatment of railroad rate regulation to World War I. Also *Railroads: Finance and Organization.* I. L. SHARFMAN, *The Interstate Commerce Commission* (4 vols.; New York: Commonwealth Fund, 1936). An exhaustive study of the activities of the Interstate Commerce Commission. *Transportation Economics,* paper by M. J. Peck and J. R. Meyer (New York: National Bureau of Economic Research, 1965), pp. 199–241. H. B. VANDERBLUE and K. F. BURGESS, *Railroads: Rates, Service, Management* (New York: Macmillan Co., 1923). An exhaustive study of the regulatory activities of the Interstate Commerce Commission to 1923. E. W. WILLIAMS, JR., *The Regulation of Rail-Motor Rate Competition* (New York: Harper & Bros., 1958). A careful study of the policies of the Interstate Commerce Commission on rate competition between rail and motor carriers.

Part IV. *National Transportation Policy*

General Texts: *T. C. Bigham and M. J. Roberts,* chap. 20, intra-agency combination; chap. 21, labor relations; chap. 22, public aids to transportation; chap. 24, national transportation policy. *Stuart Daggett,* chap. 25, consolidation of carriers; chap. 26, co-ordination of services; chap. 34, public aid to transportation; chap. 35, some suggestions for public policy. *M. L. Fair and E. W. Williams, Jr.,* chap. 28, competition and minimum rates; chap. 29, railroad consolidation; chap. 30, co-ordination of transportation; chap. 31, national transportation policy. *J. H. Frederick,* chap. 8, airmail rates and subsidy payments. *K. T. Healy,* chaps. 16 and 17, labor problems in transport. *W. J. Hudson and J. A. Constantin,* chaps. 4 and 5, federal highway program and financing; chap. 11, labor relations in the trucking industry. *Eliot Jones,* chap. 17, railroad combinations; chap. 20, labor disputes. *C. E. Landon.* chap. 26, government promotion of transportation; chap. 27, co-ordination of transport facilities; chap. 28, labor problems in transportation. *D. P. Locklin,* chap. 25, railroad finance; chap. 29, highway finance; chaps. 37–38, transport co-ordination and interagency competition. *S. L. Miller,* chap. 36, economic analysis of inland waterways. *A. M. Milne,* chap. 7, integration of transportation. *R. E. Westmeyer,* pp. 58–66, public aid to railroads; chap. 32, basic national transportation problems; chap. 33, proposed solutions to transportation problems.

Other References: ASSOCIATION OF AMERICAN RAILROADS, *Magna Carta for Transportation* (Washington, D.C., 1961). Statement of problems and goals of public policy by the Association for the railroad industry. P. H. BURCH, *Highway Revenue and Expenditure Policy in the United States* (New Brunswick, N.J.: Rutgers University Press, 1962). R. E. CAVES, *Air Transportation and Its Regulators* (Cambridge, Mass., Harvard University Press, 1962). An economic analysis of the airline industry. M. CONANT, *Railroad Consolidation and the Antitrust Laws* (Berkeley, Calif.: Institute of Business and Economic Research, University of California, 1962). M. CONANT, *Railroad Mergers and Abandonments* (Berkeley, Calif.: University of California Press, 1964). C. L. DEARING and W. OWEN, *National Transportation Policy* (Washington, D.C.: The Brookings Institution, 1949). A study of public policy in transportation for the Hoover Commission on government reorganization. G. G. EGGERT, *Railroad Labor Disputes* (Ann Arbor, Mich.: University of Michigan Press, 1967).

FEDERAL AVIATION AGENCY, *National Aviation Goals* (Washington, D.C.: U.S. Government Printing Office, September, 1961). Task force study of national aviation goals to 1970. C. H. FULDA, *Competition in the Regulated Industries: Transportation* (Boston, Mass.: Little, Brown & Co., 1961). BUREAU OF TRANSPORT ECONOMICS AND STATISTICS, INTERSTATE COMMERCE COMMISSION, *Gray Area of Transportation Operations,* Statement No. 6010 (Washington, D.C., June, 1960). A study of transport operations lying between legitimate private carriage and that which is authorized by regulatory bodies. BUREAU OF TRANSPORT ECONOMICS AND STATISTICS, INTERSTATE COMMERCE COMMISSION, *Railroad Consolidations and the Public Interest,* Statement No. 6201 (Washington, D.C., March, 1962). An analysis of criteria for consolidation proposals. R. H. HAVEMAN, *Water Analysis and the Public Interest* (Nashville, Tenn.: Vanderbilt University Press, 1966). An analysis of federal expenditures in 10 southern states. T. E. KUHN, *Public Enterprise Economics and Transport Problems* (Berkeley, Calif.: Univeristy of California Press, 1965). L. A. LECHT, *Experience under Railway Labor Legislation* (New York: Columbia University Press, 1955). A detailed study of federal legislation and its results as applied to railroad labor. W. N. LEONARD, *Railroad Consolidation under the Transportation Act of 1920* (New York: Columbia University Press, 1946). *J. R. Meyer, M. J. Peck, J. Stenason, and C. Zwick,* chap. 9, proposals for public and private policies. H. G. MOULTON, *The American Transportation Problem* (Washington, D.C.: Brookings Institution, 1933). A study prepared for the National Transportation Committee (Committee of Six); contains a wealth of factual information and the report of the Committee. *National Transportation Policy* (Doyle Report), Part III, organization of government for transportation; Part IV, organization of transportation law; Part V, chap. 2, government assistance and user charges; chap. 3, interagency ownership; chap. 4, consolidations and mergers; Part VII, chap. 11, suspension actions of the Interstate Commerce Commission. J. C. NELSON, *Railroad Transportation and Public Policy* (Washington, D.C.: Brookings Institution, 1959). A careful analysis of the American railroad problem, supported by a mass of factual data. *Report of the Presidential Railroad Commission* (Washington, D.C., February, 1962) (mimeographed). A thorough presentation of current railroad labor problems, with recommendations for action. *Report of the Royal Commission on Agreed Charges* (Ottawa: Queen's Printer, 1955). An analysis of the application and effects of agreed charges on railway freight movements. *Report of the Royal Commission on Transportation* (Ottawa: King's Printer, 1951). A thorough investigation of Canadian transportation and its problems. *Royal Commission on Transportation* (Ottawa: Queen's Printer, 1961), Vols. I and II. Investigation of railway transportation in Canada and issues of national policy. K. M. RUPPENTHAL (ed.), *Issues in Transportation Economics* (Columbus, Ohio: Charles E. Merrill Books, Inc., 1965). A collection of papers expressing various points of view on issues in transportation. "Transportation," *Law and Contemporary Problems,* Vols. I and II (Winter, 1960). A symposium on contemporary transportation problems in the United States. *Transportation Diversification,* Hearings before a Subcommittee of the Committee on Interstate and Foreign Commerce, House of Representatives, 86th Congress, 2d session (Washington, D.C.: U.S. Government Printing Office, 1960). Statements of representatives of the various modes of transport on legislation to permit railroads to engage in other means of transportation. *The Transportation System of Our Nation,* Message from the President of the United States, House of Representatives, Document No. 384, 87th Congress, 2d session (Washington, D.C.: U.S. Government Printing Office, 1962), Part I (see Appendix I). E. W. WILLIAMS, JR., and D. W. BLUESTONE, *Rationale of Federal Transportation Policy* (U.S. Department of Commerce) (Washington, D.C.: U.S. Government Printing Office, 1960). An analysis of national transportation problems on which were based the recommendations of the Secretary of Commerce in *Federal Transportation Policy and Program* (Mueller Report) (Washington, D.C.: U.S. Government Printing Office, March, 1960).

Part V. *Urban Transport*

General Texts: *Stuart Daggett,* chap. 24, a careful discussion of rail terminal problems with good references. *J. H. Frederick,* chap. 2, a description of the airport system of the country. *W. J. Hudson and J. A. Constantin,* chap. 15, motor freight terminals. *E. R. Johnson, G. G. Huebner, and G. L. Wilson,* chap. 7, railroad freight terminal services; chap. 37, a description of water terminal facilities. *C. E. Landon,* chap. 10, a description of the terminal facilities of the various modes of transport; chap. 11, urban transport facilities, with references to numerous articles. *John B. Lansing,* chap. 15, urban transportation. *C. A. Taff,* chap. 7, a description of the different types of motor terminals and their operation. *G. L. Wilson and L. A. Bryan,* chap. 5, a description of the operation and management of airports.

Other References: F. L. BIRD, *A Study of the Port of New York Authority* (New York: Dun & Bradstreet, Inc., 1949). A study of the development, organization, and financing of the Port of New York Authority. *Chicago Area Transportation Study* (Springfield: Department of Public Works and Buildings, State of Illinois, Vol. I, December, 1959; Vol. II, July, 1960; Vol. III, 1962). A study of land use and travel patterns of the Chicago metropolitan area with forecasts of developments to 1980 with recommendations for transport planning in Volume III. COMMITTEE FOR ECONOMIC DEVELOPMENT: *The Changing Economic Function of the Central City,* by RAYMOND VERNON (New York, 1959), a careful study of the shifting structure of metropolitan areas; *Guiding Metropolitan Growth* (1960), an outline of policy planning for metropolitan areas; *Metropolis against Itself,* by R. C. WOOD (1959), a study of governmental conflicts in metropolitan areas. M. L. FAIR, *Port Administration in the United States* (Cambridge, Md.: Cornell Maritime Press, 1954). A study of the organization and management of port facilities. FEDERAL AVIATION AGENCY, *National Airport Plan, Fiscal Years 1962–1966* (Washington, D.C.: U.S. Government Printing Office, 1961). A projection of airport development for the years 1962 to 1966. JEAN GOTTMANN, *Megalopolis* (New York: Twentieth Century Fund, 1961). A comprehensive study of urbanization in the northeastern seaboard area of the United States; chap. 12 deals with transportation and traffic in the region. *The Mass Transportation Problem in Illinois* (Chicago: State Mass Transportation Commission, 1959). Final report with recommendations for dealing with the problems of mass transportation in the Chicago area. *Meeting the Problems of Metropolitan Growth in the National Capital Region,* Final

Report of the Joint Committee on Washington Metropolitan Problems (House Concurrent Resolution No. 172, 85th Congress), Senate Report No. 38, 86th Congress, 1st session (Washington, D.C.: U.S. Government Printing Office 1959). *Metropolitan Transportation,* Staff Report for Joint Committee on Washington Metropolitan Problems, 85th Congress, 2d session (Washington, D.C.: U.S. Government Printing Office, 1958). J. R. MEYER, J. F. KAIN, and M. WOHL, *The Urban Transportation Problem* (Cambridge, Mass.: Harvard University Press, 1965). A study sponsored by the Rand Corporation. R. B. MITCHELL and C. RAPKIN, *Urban Traffic* (New York: Columbia University Press, 1954). A detailed outline of the basis for research into land use and traffic movements in metropolitan areas. *H. G. Moulton,* chap. 33, problems of terminal unification; chap. 34, transportation and city planning; chap. 35, means of terminal unification. *National Transportation Policy* (Doyle Report), Part VII, chap. 7, urban transportation. An extensive analysis of the commuter problem and urban transport planning. *Organization for Transportation in the National Capital Region,* Selected Documents Prepared for the Joint Committee on Washington Metropolitan Problems, 86th Congress, 2d session (Washington, D.C.: U.S. Government Printing Office, 1960). W. OWEN, *The Metropolitan Transportation Problem* (rev. ed.; Washington, D.C.: The Brookings Institution, 1966). The most comprehensive single analysis of metropolitan transport in the United States that is available. *Rapid Transit Systems in Six Metropolitan Areas,* Staff Report to the Joint Committee on Washington Metropolitan Problems, 86th Cong., 1st sess. (Washington, D.C.: U.S. Government Printing Office, 1959). M. REINSBERG, *Metropolitan Transportation* (Evanston, Ill.: Northwestern University, 1961). A research summary of seven studies on growth and change in metropolitan areas and their relation to metropolitan transportation; an excellent summary of mass transit problems. G. M. SMERK, *Urban Transportation: The Federal Role* (Bloomington, Ind.: Indiana University Press, 1965). TRANSPORTATION CENTER, NORTHWESTERN UNIVERSITY, *Basic Issues in Chicago Metropolitan Transportation* (Evanston, Ill., June, 1958). An analysis of mass transportation problems in Chicago and the role of the motor vehicle. *Transportation Plan for the National Capital Region,* Hearings before the Joint Committee on Washington Metropolitan Problems, 86th Cong., 1st sess. (Washington, D.C.: U.S. Government Printing Office, 1959). Contains proposals by individuals and various agencies for dealing with transportation in the national capital area, and evaluation of the *Mass Transportation Survey and Plan* submitted to the Committee. *The Transportation System of Our Nation,* Message from the President of the United States, 1962, Part II (see Appendix I); see also "Urban Transportation," Joint Report to the President by the Housing and Home Finance Administrator and the Secretary of Commerce (mimeographed) (The White House, March 28, 1962). *Transportation Economics,* National Bureau of Economic Research, Part III, papers on urban transportation. *Washington Metropolitan Area Transportation Problems,* Hearings of Joint Committee on Washington Metropolitan Problems, 85th Cong., 2d sess. (Washington, D.C.: U.S. Government Printing Office, 1958). J. Q. WILSON (ed.), *The Metropolitan Enigma* (Washington, D.C.: Chamber of Commerce of the United States, 1967). The paper by Wilson on "Urban Problems in Perspective" is particularly good.

Going Places. A bimonthly bulletin published by the General Electric Co., describing developments in metropolitan transportation. *Metropolitan Transportation.* A monthly publication (Wheaton, Ill., Hitchcock Publishing Co.) on mass transportation problems and plans in various cities, with emphasis on the need for mass rapid transit.

Index

INDEX

A

Act to Regulate Commerce, 1887
  Interstate Commerce Commission, 297
  judicial interpretation
    compulsory testimony, 298
    long-and-short haul, 299
    reasonable rates, 298
  provisions, 296, 297
  results of the act, 299
Adams, Walter, 459
Additional Service to Latin America, 383
*Adequacy of Transportation Systems in
  Support of the National Defense Ef-
  fort in the Event of Mobilization*
  (Kilday Report), 31–33, 401
Administration in transport; *see also* De-
  partment of Transportation
  executive responsibilities, 531
  federal agencies, 532
  formulation of policy, 532
  Kennedy message, 534
  proposals for reorganization, 533
  Undersecretary for Transportation, 533
Advances in Rates—Eastern Case, 305
Agricultural Marketing Act, 1929, 356
Air Commerce Act, 1926, 362
Air Freight Rate Investigation, 379
Air Mail Act, 1934, 362
Air Mail (Kelly) Act, 1925, 362
Air transport
  airmail, 63
  airports, 42
  airways, 42
  beginnings, 63
  capital turnover, 142
  economies of scale, 142
  facilities, 40, 41
  federal aid to airports, 64
  financing; *see* Financing air transport
  helicopters, 65
  investment, 41
  local air transport, 65
  rate making, 193
  role of, 42
Airlines, 41
Airmail compensation; *see* Regulation,
  Civil Aeronautics Board

Airports
  air terminal areas, 588
  location
    factors, 590
    national airport plan, 591
    problem of noise, 591
  ownership and management, 588
    administration, 589
    development costs, 589
    nonlanding revenue, 589
    public ownership, 589
Alaskan Railroad, 26
American Air Lines Inc. v. *Civil Aeronau-
  tics Board,* 374
American Commercial Lines, Inc., 307
American Trucking Associations, Inc. v.
  A. T. and S. F. Railway Co., 250
American Trucking Trends, 141
Ann Arbor Railroad Company v. *United
  States,* 321
*Appraisal of the Petroleum Industry of the
  United States,* 66, 97–98
Arth, M. P., 526

B

Baltimore and Ohio R.R. Co. v. *United
  States,* 454
Bard, F. W., 595
Barriger, J. W., Jr., 450, 452, 478
*Basic Issues in Chicago Metropolitan Trans-
  portation,* 573, 628
Baumol, W. J., and Associates, 183
Benishay, H., 499
Bernstein, M. H., 526
Big Load Afloat, 38
Bird, F. L., 595, 599
Bi-State Development Agency, 594
Bluefield Waterworks and Improvement Co.
  v. *Public Service Commission of West
  Virginia,* 217, 221
Bluestone, D. W., 401, 500
Board of Investigation and Research, 329
Bogart, E. L., 472
Bogue, D. J., 614
Bonavia, M. R., 188
Boston and Maine Railroad v. *U.S.,* 242,
  426
Bricker Report; *see Domestic Land and
  Water Transportation*

Bryan, L. A., 109
Bureau of Public Roads, 62

C

Cahaba Steel Co., Common Carrier Application, 345
California–Oregon Lumber Case, 332
Carrow, M. M., 526
Carter, J. P., 142, 242
Cassady, Ralph, Jr., 169
Caves, R. E., 385
Chamberlin, E. H., 134, 158
Charleston and Hamburg Railroad, 53
Chesapeake & Ohio Railroad—Control—Baltimore and Ohio Railroad, 453
Chicago Area Transportation Study, 554, 612, 627
Chicago, Burlington and Quincy Railroad v. Iowa, 291
Chicago, Milwaukee, St. Paul and Pacific Railroad Company v. Illinois, 331
Chicago, Milwaukee and St. Paul Railway Company v. Minnesota, 273
Chisholm, Michael, 141
Cincinnati Southern Railway, 26
Civil Aeronautics Administration, 364
Civil Aeronautics Board; *see also* Federal Aviation Act, 1958; Regulation, Civil Aeronautics Board
  membership, 284
  scope of authority, 285
Class and Commodity Rates, New York to Philadelphia, 353
Clemens, E. W., 173
Colton, R. E., 251
Commerce Court, 304, 305
Commodities clause, 301, 302
Commodities—Pan-Atlantic Steamship Corporation, 332, 333
Commodity flows
  air lines, 100
  railroad, 98
  water, 99
Commodity Transportation Survey Area, 25, 99
Common carrier
  duties, 107–10
  express and package service, 111
  freight forwarders, 111
  historical nature of, 113–14
  inter-city bus, 111
  nature of, 106
  role of, 112–13
Common carrier problem
  limitation of competition, 438
  need for service, 437
  "tainted" vehicle doctrine, 437
Common law; *see* Regulation

Commuter problem; *see also* Urban transport
  actions on commuter trains
    by cities and states, 570
    by federal government, 571
    Doyle report conclusions, 571
  rail commutation problem, 569
    traffic, 569
  revenue and expense squeeze, 570
Competition; *see* Markets, classification
Competition
  equalizing
    contract carriage, 439
    inequalities among modes, 438
    inequality in rules, 439
    relevant costs, 440
    restrictions on common carriers, 439
    restrictions on pricing, 440
    unequal cost burdens, 441
  versus monopoly, 143–48
    economies of scale, 148
    effects on organization, 147
    natural monopoly, 143
    railroad monopoly, 143
    ruinous competition, 146
  in transport; *see* Common carrier problem; Competition, equalizing; Interagency competition; Intra-agency competition
Competition, Regulation and the Public Interest in the Motor Carrier Industry, 348
Competitive pricing
  application to transport, 160
  standard for public policy, 159
Compulsory Testimony Act, 1893, 298
Consolidation
  and integration, 411
    interagency ownership, 411, 412
  meaning and problem, 446; *see also* Integration; Diversification; Railroad consolidation
  other agencies
    air transport, 459, 460
    motor carriers, 458
    water carriers, 459
Constantin, J. A., 483
Continental-Pioneer Acquisition Case, 381
Contract carriers, 115
Cookenboo, Leslie, Jr., 44
Co-ordination of transport, public authority, 409
Co-operation among carriers
  freight forwarders, 250
  through routes and joint rates, 248
  other carriers, 248
  railroad cooperation
    car service rules, 247
    Fruit-Growers Express, 248

Co-operation among carriers—*Cont.*
railroad cooperation—*Cont.*
interchange, 247
interline traffic, 247
Pullman Company, 247
Copeland, M. A., 420
Costs
average, 167
and decision making, 166–67
joint and common, 165
and pricing, 161–68
of production
fixed, 162
"noneconomic," 163
variable, 163
specific, 165
traceability, 165
Counselman v. *Hitchcock,* 298
Coverdale and Colpitts, 553, 614
Creating a Department of Transportation,
534, 536
Cullom Committee, 295
Cumberland Road, 49

D

Daggett, Stuart, 15, 75, 83, 100, 108, 110,
237, 242, 249, 295, 308, 423, 474, 552
Dartmouth College v. *Woodward,* 291
Davenport, H. J., 310
Dayton—Goose Creek Railway Company
v. *United States,* 317
Dearing, C. L., 400, 530, 533
de Chazeau, M. D., 390
Decline of Coastwise and Intercoastal Shipping, 37
de Haven, C., 404, 499
Department of Transportation
congressional action, 536
investment standards, 541
organization chart, 540
President Johnson's message, 535
relation with commissions, 541
safety, 542
urban transport, 542
Department of Transportation Act, 1966,
536–40
investment standards, 538
water resource projects, 538
Dicey, A. V., 257
Diversification; *see also* Integration
meaning, 464
modern corporate enterprise, 465
Chicago and North Western Railway,
465
organization of railroads, 465
Dixon, F. H., 310, 415, 501
Domestic Land and Water Transportation
(Bricker Report), 330, 400
Doyle, Major General, 421

Doyle Report, 32, 34, 36, 111, 118, 124,
196, 330, 354–55, 358, 383, 385, 436
438, 448, 450–51, 478–79, 481–82,
489, 494, 496–98, 520–21, 523, 526–
27, 529, 532–33, 547–48, 569–71,
573, 602–6, 627
Due, J. F., 158, 166, 552, 614
Dumke, G. S., 614
Dunlop, J. T., 512
Dynamics of Urban Transportation, 567

E

Eastern Air Lines v. *Civil Aeronautics
Board,* 377
East Central Motor Carriers Assn. v. *Baltimore and Ohio Railroad Company,
et al.,* 333
East Texas Motor Freight Lines, Inc. v.
Frozen Fruit Express, 354
Eckstein, O., 404, 499
Economies of scale, 130–38
large-scale production, meaning, 136
law of diminishing returns, 130–33
nature of, 133
reasons for, 133
returns to scale, 134
in transport, 138–43; *see also* Air transport; Motor transport; Rail transport
Edwards, F. K., 189
Elkins Act, 1903
liability, 300
published rates, 299
Eminent domain, 17
Erie Canal, 51
*Equalization of Rates at North Atlantic
Ports,* 242
Establish a Department of Transportation,
536
Ex Parte 206, 479
Ex Parte 212, 479
Ex Parte 230, 124
*Explanation of the Development of Motor
Carrier Costs,* 188

F

Fagin, Henry, 609
Fair, M. L., 109, 110, 308, 526, 594
Fair return
court interpretation, 220–23
reasonable rates, 219
Fair value
and the courts, 215–19
doctrine of "end result," 219
valuation for rate making, 210
cost of reproduction, 211
historical cost, 215
market value, 210
prudent investment, 213

Federal Aid Highway Act, 1944, 62
Federal Aid Highway Act, 1956, 62
Federal Aid Road Act, 1916, 62
Federal Airport Act, 1946, 368
Federal Aviation Act, 1958; *see also* Regulation, air transportation
  aircraft accident investigation, 367
  Civil Aeronautics Board
    certificates of public convenience, 365
    declaration of policy, 365
    rates and fares, 365
      rule of rate making, 366
    transportation of mail, 367
      fair and reasonable rates, 367
      service pay, 367
      subsidy, 367
  Federal Aviation Agency, 368
  intercorporate relations, 367
  methods of competition, 367
  state regulation, 369
Federal Aviation Agency, 368
  administrator, 368
  safety rules, 368
Federal Government
  Bill of Rights, 265
  Constitution and regulation, 264–65
  form of, 264
  interstate commerce, 267–69
  powers of, 265
    implied powers, 265
Federal Highway Act, 1921, 62
Federal highway legislation, 486–88
Federal Power Commission v. *Hope Natural Gas Company*, 219–21
Federal Trade Commission v. *Ruberoid Company*, 275
Federal Transportation Policy and Program (Mueller Report), 401, 436
Federal Waterways Corporation of Delaware, 61
Fetter, F. A., 135
Final Report of the Highway Cost Allocation Study, 13, 405, 484, 490–91, 498–99, 500
Financing, air transport; *see also* Air transport
  airport investment, 494
    estimated requirements, 495
    total expenditures, 495
  airways investment, 494
    operating costs, 494
    user taxes, 494
  financing the airlines, 496
    indebtedness, 496
    rate of return, 496
  subsidy to air transport, 495
Financing, domestic water carriers; *see also* Water transport, domestic
  expenditures, 497

Financing, domestic water carriers—*Cont.*
  St. Lawrence Seaway, 497
    deficit, 497
    tolls, 497
Financing, highway system
  allocation of user costs, 491
    methods, 492
  extent of public investment, 488
  highway cost allocation, 490
  sources of highway funds, 489
  total tax contributions, 493
Financing, motor transport; *see also* Motor transport
  allocation of costs
    pricing problem, 485
    among users, 485
    users versus nonusers, 485
  equalizing competition, 485
  measuring resource needs, 484
  unique problem
    price mechanism, 483
    private finance, 483
    public authority, 483
Financing, public aid
  early period, 472
  imputed interest, 499
  modern period, public expenditures, 475–76
  railroad era, 472–73
    land grants, 478
  taxation of "way," 498
    unequal tax burdens, 498
Financing, railroads; *see also* Railroads, financing
  capital requirements
    estimates, 478, 480
    funded debt, 480
  nature of the problem
    capital expenditures, 477
    sources of funds, 477
  passenger deficit problem
    commuter problem, 482
    long-run trends, 480
    nature of, 481
Financing, transportation
  allocation of resources, 467–68
  equalizing competition, 470–71
  imputing interest, 499
  taxation of "way," 498
  unique problem for transport, 469–70
Financing the Motor Carrier Industry, 593
Fogel, R. W., 58, 474
Freas, Howard, 183, 431
Frederick, J. H., 236, 494
Freight classification
  commodity rates, 238
  Consolidated Freight Classification, 237
  development of, 236

Freight classification—*Cont.*
for other carriers
airlines, 239
Co-ordinated Motor Freight Classification, 239
National Motor Freight Classification, 239–40
territories, 236
Uniform Freight Classification, 237
Freund, Ernest, 17
Frost and Frost Trucking Company v. *Railroad Commission of California,* 107, 336
Fulton, Robert, 50

G

Gallatin Report, 72
General level of rates; *see also* Fair value; Fair return
airlines, 225
appropriate return, 226
competitive setting, 226
motor carriers, 224
pipelines, 225
railroads
legal basis, 222
record of railroad earnings, 223
theory
cost-plus pricing, 207
disadvantages, 207, 208
particular rates, 208
water carriers, 224
General Passenger Fare Investigation, 225, 377, 378
Geraci, Contract Carrier Application, 345
Gibbons v. *Ogden,* 267
Glaeser, M. G., 222
Gottmann, Jean, 600
Government Expenditures on Transport Facilities, 39
Grain from Idaho, Oregon and Washington to Ports in Oregon & Washington, 433
Grain in Multiple-Car Shipments—River Crossings to the South (Big John case) 433
Gras, N. S. B., 11
Gray, H. M., 193, 385
Gray Area of Transportation Operations, 357
Great Northern Pacific and Burlington Lines, Inc.—Merger—Great Northern Railway, 456
Grether, E. T., 169
Grey, A. L., Jr., 614
Guandolo, John, 277, 302
Guide to Railroad Cost Analysis, 183

H

Harbeson, R. W., 333, 485
Hard versus soft competition, 172–73
Harper, D. V., 295, 337
Harris, Oren, 445
Harriss, C. Lowell, 499
Hay, John I., Company, 307
Healy, K. T., 140, 514
Hector, L. J., 280, 385, 526
Hendry, J. G., 459
Henry, R. S., 57
Henzey, W. V., 516
Hepburn Act, 1906; *see also* Regulation, water transportation
judicial interpretation
authority of I.C.C., 301
commodities clause, 302
procedure for enforcement, 301
provisions, 300
Highway financing; *see* Financing the highway system
Highway maintenance, 490
Highway program, development of
federal participation
ABC program, 488
Federal Aid Highway Act (1956), 487
Federal Aid Road Act (1916), 486
Federal Highway Act (1921), 487
Highway Act (1944), 487
highway trust fund, 488
Highway Progress, 1965, 33, 34
Highway trust fund, 488
Highways—The Years beyond 1972, 490
Hilton, G. W., 552, 614
Hirshleifer, J., 404, 499
Historical Development of Transport Co-ordination and Integration in the United States, 409
Hoch-Smith Resolution, 321
Hudson, W. J., 483
Humphrey's Executor v. *United States,* 281
Hunter, Alex, 157

I

Illinois Central Railroad Co. et al.,—Control etc.— John I. Hay Co., 307
Illinois Commerce Commission v. *Thomson,* 309
Improved transportation, 11–15
Improving Transportation in Los Angeles, 618
Increased Class and Commodity Rates, Transcontinental (Motor), 224
Increased Freight Rates, 479
Independent regulatory commission; *see also* Regulation, transport
courts versus commissions, 277

Independent regulatory commission—*Cont.*
  criticisms of, 278–82
  executive functions, 276
  fact-finding, 276
  procedures, 275
  quasi-judicial, 275
  quasi-legislative, 275
Ingot Molds, Pa. to Steelton, Ky., 332, 435
Inland waterway transportation; *see* Water
  transport, domestic
Inland waterways
  investment, 61
  Mississippi System, 60
  New York State Barge Canal, 60
  Panama Canal, 61
  revival, 60
  St. Lawrence Seaway, 61
Integration; *see also* Diversification
  for ancillary purposes, 461
  branch lines, 451
  key-point rule, 461
  nature of the problem, 460
  ownership of pipelines, 464
  piggyback service, 461
  transportation companies, 460–64
    economies of scale, 463
*Interagency Committee on Transport Merg-
  ers*, 458
Interagency competition; *see also* Interagency pricing, theory
  I.C.C. policy
    confused policy, 435
    fully distributed costs, 432
    protection of water carriers, 432
    public costs, 434
    unregulated carriers, 433–34
  inherent advantages
    differential pricing, 431
    low-cost carrier, 431
    meaning, 430
    protection of competition, 432
    problem of price competition, 429
Interagency pricing, theory
  differential pricing and efficiency, 195
  interagency competition, 194
  low-cost modes, 183, 197
  multiple pricing problem, 193
  relevant costs, 196
  ruinous competition, 194
Intercity traffic
  federally regulated, 71
  freight ton-miles, 68
  passenger miles, 69
Interstate Commerce Commission
  internal organization, 282
  membership, 281
  scope of authority, 281
*Interstate Commerce Commission Activities,
  1937–1962*, 459

Interstate Commerce Commission v. *Ala-
  bama Midland Railway Company*, 299
Interstate Commerce Commission v. *Brim-
  son*, 298
Interstate Commerce Commission v. *Illi-
  nois Central Railroad Company*, 301
Interstate Commerce Commission v. *J.—T.
  Transport Co., Inc., et al.*, 348
Interstate Commerce Commission v. *New
  York, New Haven, and Hartford R.R.
  Co.*, 332, 432
Interstate Commerce Commission v. *North-
  west Agricultural Cooperative Assn.
  Inc.*, 115, 356
Interstate Commerce Commission v. *Ore-
  gon-Washington Railroad and Navi-
  gation Company*, 320
Interstate Commerce Commission v. *Union
  Pacific Railroad Company*, 302
*Interstate Trade Barriers Affecting Motor-
  Vehicle Transportation*, 338
Intra-agency competition
  in motor transport, 426
    economic mobility, 427
    legal mobility, 427
  in other modes
    air transport, 428
    pipe lines, 428
    water carriers, 428
  in rail transport, 423
    control of competition, 423
    rate agreements, 424
    role of competition, 425
    types of competition, 423
    weak and strong roads, 425
*Iron and Steel Articles—Eastern Common
  Carriers*, 349

J

Johnson, E. R., 514
Joint costs; *see* Costs
Jones, Eliot, 144, 423, 450, 514

K

Kahn, A. E., 390
Kain, J. F., 556, 567
Kallenbach, J. E., 267
Kaplan, J. S., 435
Kefauver, Estes, 457
Kennedy, J. F., President, Message to Con-
  gress, 441–45
  results, 445
Keyes, Lucille S., 385
"Keystone" restriction, 341
*Keystone Transportation Co., Contract Car-
  rier Application*, 347
Kilday Report; *see* Adequacy of Transpor-
  tation Systems etc.
Knight, F. H., 131, 132

Knoxville v. *Knoxville Water Company,* 217
Kolko, Gabriel, 59, 310
Koontz, H. D., 142, 383
Krutilla, J., 404, 499

L

Labor legislation; *see also* Railway Labor Act, 1926; Railway social security
  Adamson Act, 1916, 505
  Arbitration Act, 1888, 504
  Erdman Act, 1898, 505
  Newlands Act, 1913, 505
  Transportation Act, 1920, 506
Labor problems
  air transport
    labor conflicts, 515
    labor organizations, 515
    mutual aid pact, 516
    Railway Labor Act, 1926, 514
    results of legislation, 516
  motor transport
    Brotherhood of Teamsters, 517
    master contract, 517
    Trucking Employers Inc., 517
  uniqueness of in transport, 414, 501
    areas of conflict, 518
    Coordinator's report, 510
    Doyle Report, 520–21
    effects of changing technology, 518
    employment in transport, 503
    payrolls, 503
    Presidential intervention, 512
    Presidential Railroad Commission, 510–12
    railroad labor organizations, 503
    transport technology, 415
Land grant rates, 58
Landis Report, 280, 417, 526, 533
Lansing, J. B., 13, 474, 557
Large Irregular Air Carrier Investigation, 375
Law of diminishing returns, 130
  optimum combination, 132
Law and economic life
  meaning of regulation, 257
  regulated industries, 258
  rules of behavior, 256
  supremacy of law, 257
Lecht, L. A., 514
Leonard, W. N., 457
Linnenberg, C. C., 354
Lippincott, B. E., 161
Location of industry
  factors, 5
  freight rates, 6
  metropolitan areas, 7
  regional development, 6
  transportation, 6

Locklin, D. P., 17, 37, 75, 116, 119, 181, 233, 329, 339, 392, 423, 429
Long and short haul
  applicability, 244
  meaning, 244
  "natural" advantage of location, 245
  reasons for violation, 244
Los Angeles, structure of
  industrial, 558–62
    influence of automobile, 561
    influence of railroads, 561
  residential, 562–67
    decline of central area, 563
    distribution of population, 564–66
    growth of population, 562
    rail passenger transport, 565, 567
Los Angeles Gas and Electric Corporation v. *Railroad Commission of California,* 218
Los Angeles Regional Transportation Study, 618
Los Angeles/San Francisco—Vancouver, B.C. Case, 371
Lowe, G. E., 251
Lumber—California and Oregon to California and Arizona, 431

M

Mackie, D. L., 538
Magna Carta for Transportation, 462
Major Administrative Process Problems, 526
Mann-Elkins Act, 1910; *see also* Regulation, water transportation
  application of the law
    commerce court, 305
    long and short haul, 305
    rate increases, 305
  provisions, 303
Marbury v. *Madison,* 271
Market structures, pricing, 154–60
  competitive pricing, 154, 155
  monopolistic competition, 159
  monopoly pricing, 156
  oligopoly pricing, 157, 158
Markets, classification, 150–54
  competition, types, 150–52
  monopolistic competition, 153
  monopoly, 152
  oligopoly, 153–54
Marshall, Alfred, 24
Mass Transportation Problem in Illinois, 630
Maximum freight rate case, 298
McAdoo, W. G., 310, 314
McArdle et al. v. *Indianapolis Water Co.,* 217
McLean Trucking Co. v. *United States,* 351

Meeting the Problems of Metropolitan Growth in the National Capital Region, 608

Mergers and Concentration in the Trucking Industry, 459

Metropolitan Transportation, 606

Meyer, J. R., 141, 142, 195, 196, 222, 360, 556, 567

Michigan Public Utilities Commission v. *Duke,* 107, 336

Middle West General Increases (motor), 224

Milliman, J., 404, 499

Milne, A. M., 181, 195, 196

Mitchell, R. B., 568

Moore, D. C., 108

Moskowitz, Karl, 567

Motor Carrier Act, 1935
  administration
    agricultural exemptions
      effect on regulated carriers, 354
      substantial identity test, 354
    conclusion, 358–60
    consolidation and mergers, 351
      transcontinental carriers, 351
    control of entry
      grandfather clause, 341, 347
      "key-point" restrictions, 350
      new operations, 349
      piggyback operations, 349
      railroad control of motor carriers, 350
      trip leasing, 349
    the gray area
      "buy and sell" operations, 357
      "illegal" operations, 357
    rate regulation, 351
      back-haul rates, 353
      criticism of, 352
      general level of rates, 352
      minimum rate provisions, 352
      protecting competitors, 353
      use of operating ratio, 352
  common carriers, authority over, 341–43
  contract carriers, 343
    permits, 344
    rates, 344
  declaration of policy, 340
    Public Law 89–170 (1965), 340
  dual operation, 343
  exempt carriers, 345
  private carriers and brokers, 345

Motor Carrier Act, 1957 contract carriers, 348

Motor Carrier Industry, 592

Motor Carriers, rate making theory
  absence of ruinous competition, 190–91
  competitive features, 187

Motor Carriers, rate making theory—*Cont.*
  fixed and variable costs, 188
  joint and common costs, 190
  operating ratio, 189
  turnover of capital, 189

Motor terminals
  Chicago Union Truck Terminal, 593
  freight terminals, 592–93
  passenger terminals, 592
  United Parcel Service, 593

Motor transport
  beginnings, 62
  capital turnover, 141
  economies of scale, 140, 141
  federal aid, 62, 63
  financing; *see* Financing, motor transport
  gross revenues, 141
  growth of traffic, 63
  highway system, 33
  net investment, 33
  ownership of vehicles, 34
  role of, 35
  types of carriers, 32

Moulton, H. G., 452, 514

Mueller Report; *see Federal Transportation Policy and Program*

Munn v. *Illinois,* 215, 262, 272, 290

N

National Airport Plan, 368

National Airport Plan, Fiscal Years 1962–66, 588

National Aviation Goals, 590–91

National Highway Program, 487

National Transportation Policy; see Doyle Report

National Transportation Safety Board, 537

Natural Gas Pipeline Company v. *Federal Power Commission,* 218

Nebbia v. *New York,* 263

Needs of the National Highway System, 1955–1984, 487

Nelson, J. C., 28, 34, 191, 360, 425, 428, 433, 477, 481, 494

New Automobiles in Interstate Commerce, 332, 431

Nicholson, H. W., 337

Norfolk and Western Railway Co., and the New York, Chicago and St. Louis Railroad Co. Merger, 453

Northern Securities Company, v. *United States,* 450

Northwest Agricultural Cooperative Assn. Inc., 356

O

Oliver, E. I., 516

Organization for Transportation in the National Capital Region, 609, 611

Owen, W., 400, 530, 533, 548, 552, 574, 576, 594, 600, 628, 631

P

Pacific Intermountain Express—Control and Purchase, 351
Pan-American World Airways v. *United States,* 382
Panama Canal Act, 1912; *see also* Regulation, water transportation
  administration, 307
  railroad ownership of water carriers, 306
  through routes and joint rates, 306
Particular rates
  authority over, 227
  discrimination
    problem of, 232
    types, 233
  principles of
    assumptions of I.C.C., 229, 230
    cost of service, 229
    value of service, 231
  standards of public policy, 232
Passenger fares
  air lines, 235, 236; *see also* Regulation, Civil Aeronautics Board
  motor buses, 235
  railroads, 235
Peck, M. J., 141, 142, 195, 196, 222, 360
Pegrum, D. F., 117, 191–92, 196–97, 215, 257, 333, 348, 360, 402, 428, 430, 432, 438, 455, 465, 480, 500, 561, 566, 572, 576, 614–15
Pennsylvania Railroad Company—Merger—New York Central Railroad Company, 453
Petroleum from Los Angeles and El Paso to Arizona and New Mexico, 432
Phillips, C. F., Jr., 219
Piggyback service
  growth of, 124
  open tariff provisions, 249
  plans, 123–24
Pipe-line transport
  investment, 44
  natural gas pipe lines, 44
  oil pipe lines, traffic, 43
  routes, 44
Pipe lines
  development, 65
  product lines, 66
  rate making, natural monopolies, 191
  routes, 65
  Standard Oil of New Jersey, 65
  traffic, 65
Port of New York Authority
  interstate compact, 595
  investment, 599–600
  powers and jurisdiction, 595

Port of New York Authority—*Cont.*
  rail transportation, 598
  terminal unification, 596
    air terminals, 598
    bus and truck terminals, 597
    marine terminals, 597
    vehicular traffic, 596
  world trade center, 598
Porter, F. M., 345
Portibus Maris, De, 262
Pound, Roscoe, 259
Price discrimination
  hard versus soft competition, 172
  meaning, 168–69
  peak and off-peak pricing, 171
  relation to costs, 169–70
Price regulation, principles, 199–206
  maximum prices, 204–5
    difficulties, 205
    purpose, 204
  minimum prices, 201–4
    difficulties, 204
    purpose, 201
    requirements, 202–3
  objectives, 199–200
  precise prices, 205–6
    procedure and requirements, 206
  problem of fair prices, 199
Private carriers, 115–16
Problems of the Railroads (Smathers Report), 330, 401
Public aid; *see also* Financing, public aid
  breakdown of pricing, 75
  issues of, 74
  land grants, 74
  public investment, criteria for, 404
  and subsidy, 403
  versus subsidy, 76
Public Aids to Transportation (1938–40), 325, 405, 473
Public Aids to Transportation (1940), 474
Public ownership
  mixed system, 73
  railroads, 72
Public policy in transport
  administration and promotion, 418
  federal, state, and local responsibilities, 419
  regulation, 416, 417
Pullman Company, 29

R

Rail Freight Service Costs in the Various Rate Territories of the United States, 180
Rail transport
  capital turnover, 138
  combination and consolidation, 55–56
  economies of scale, 138–40

Rail transport—*Cont.*
  emergency of railroad problem, 58–59
  factors in development, 56
    construction company, 58
    land grants, 57
    overhead costs, 56–58
    public aid, 56
  growth of railroad system, 52–54
  land grant rates, 58
  limits to size, 140
  operating ratio, 139
  standard gauge, 53
  state construction, 54
  transcontinental lines, 56
Railroad Consolidations and the Public Interest—A Preliminary Examination, 450, 458
Railroad Merger Legislation, 457
Railroad Merger Problem, 457
Railroad Modification Act, 1948, 320
Railroad Passenger Train Deficit, 480
Railroad Securities Commission, 471
Railroads
  eminent domain, 30
  equipment facilities, 29
  freight tonnage, 29
  net investment, 28
  organization of, 29
  traffic statistics, 31
Railroads, consolidation
  Committee of Six, 452
  Committee of Three, 452
  early developments, 448–50
  National Transportation Committee, 451
  Prince Plan, 452
  program for consolidation, 457–58
  recent merger movement, 452–56
  reduction of competition, 447
  Transportation Act (1920), 450, 451; *see also* Transportation Act, 1920
  unique problem, 447
Railroads, financing; *see* Financing, railroads
Railroads, legislation after 1920
  purposes, 322–24
  reasons for, 321–22
Railroads, rate-making theory
  discrimination, 184–86
    cost problems, 185
    types in railroads, 184
  railroad costs, 179–83; *see also* Transport, pricing theory
    allocation, 182–83
    fixed, 179
    joint and common, 181–82
    variable, 181
  ruinous competition, 187
Railroads, terminals
  authority over terminals, 586

Railroads, terminals—*Cont.*
  freight terminals
    local traffic, 583
    "pedlar" cars, 583
    terminal freight traffic, 583
    through traffic, 583
    "trap" cars, 584
      piggyback, 584
  passenger terminals, 582
  produce terminals, 586
  traffic interchange
    belt lines, 584
    reciprocal switching, 584
    unification of terminals, 585
    universal freight stations, 585
Railway Labor Act, 1926
  arbitration, 509
  Emergency Boards, 509
  National Board of Mediation, 508
  National Railroad Adjustment Board, 508
  results of the Act, 509
Railway social security
  extension of benefits, 514
  health insurance, 514
  Railroad Labor Unemployment Insurance Act, 1938, 513
  Railroad Retirement Act, 1936, 513
Rapid Transit Systems in Six Metropolitan Areas, 602
Rapkin, C., 568
Rate Bureaus
  function, 250
  Reed-Bulwinkle Act, 251
  Sherman Act, 250
Rate-making theory; *see* Air Transport, rate-making theory; General level of rates; Motor carriers, rate-making theory; Pipe lines, rate-making theory; Railroads, rate-making theory; Water transport, rate-making theory
Rate systems
  freight tariffs, 239
  motor carriers, 242
  other carriers, 242
  railroad rate systems
    basing-point rates, 242
    distance scale, 241
    freight rate territories, 241
    group rate systems, 241
    port differentials, 242
REA Express, 111
Red Ball Motor Freight v. *Shannon,* 345
Redford, E. S., 526
Reduced Pipe Line Rates Case, 391
Refrigerator Material, Memphis, Tennessee, to Dayton, Ohio, 353
Regulation, air transportation
  agencies of control, 362, 369

Regulation, air transportation—*Cont.*
  airports, 363
  Civil Aeronautics Act, 1938, 363; *see
    also* Federal Aviation Act, 1958
  Reorganization Plan, No. 4, 364
Regulation, Civil Aeronautics Board; *see
    also* Civil Aeronautics Board
  airmail compensation
    allocation of costs, 380
    "need" rate, 379
    "service" rate, 379
  all-cargo carriers
    blocked space, 374
    certification, 374
    Flying Tiger, 375
  appraisal of, 383, 385
  certification of carriers, 370
    "grandfather" rights, 371
    "presumption" doctrine, 371
    regulated competition, 372
    trunk-line certification, 370
  consolidation and mergers
    policy, 383
    trunk-line merger application, 382
    types, 381
  freight rates, minimum, 379
  local and feeder service
    composition with trunk lines, 373
    subsidy, 373
    "use it or lose it" policy, 373
  rates and fares
    coach fares, 377
    general passenger fare investigation,
      377
    passenger fares, 376
    return on investment, 378
  supplemental or irregular carriers, 375
    air-taxi carriers, 376
    charter operations, 375
    Federal Aviation Act, 1961, 376
Regulation, common law basis of
  emergence of control, 260
  nature of, 258
    body of rules, 258
    method of procedure, 259
  property "affected with a public interest,"
    263
  right to regulate, 262
Regulation, motor transport
  certificates of public convenience, 337
  contract carriers, 336
  federal regulation, 339, 340
    objectives, 339
  irregular route carriers, 338
  limitations on, 335
  permits, 337
  reasons for, 334
  state regulation, 334
  state versus federal authority, 336

Regulation, petroleum pipe lines
  federal regulation
    common carrier status, 391
    Elkins Act, 1903, 391
    fair return, 391
    Hepburn Act, 1906, 390; *see also*
      Hepburn Act, 1906
    minimum tender, 391
    reduced earnings, 392
  pipe-line problem, 389
Regulation, price; *see* Price regulation
Regulation, role of the courts
  functions of courts, 270–73
    delegation of powers, 272
    division of powers, 271
    enforcement of statutes, 273
    property rights, 272
    separation of powers, 272
  judicial review, 269–70
    meaning, 269
    scope, 270
Regulation, state
  court interpretation
    interstate commerce, 291
    judicial review, 291
    right to regulate, 290
    state versus federal authority, 292–94
  Granger laws, 289–92
    limited success, 289
    mandatory commission, 289, 292
Regulation, transport
  basis of, 288
  criticism of, 525–27
    congressional vacillation, 527
    internal organization and procedure,
      527
  early regulation, 288
  inadequacy of antitrust, 525
  reasons for development, 289
  reorganization
    internal operations, 528
    restriction of activities, 528
    role of competition, 530
    single versus multiple commissions,
      529
  role of, 523–24
Regulation, water transportation
  to 1940
    Act to Regulate Commerce, 1887, 386
    Hepburn Act, 1906, 386; *see also*
      Hepburn Act, 1906
    Mann-Elkins Act, 1910, 386; *see also*
      Mann-Elkins Act, 1910
    Panama Canal Act, 1912, 386; *see also*
      Panama Canal Act, 1912
    Shipping Board Act, 1916, 386
    Transportation Act, 1940; *see also* Trans-
      portation Act, 1940

Regulation, water transportation—*Cont.*
  Transportation Act, 1940—*Cont.*
    provisions, 387–88
    reasons, 387
Regulation to 1920, appraisal, 308–10
Regulation of Railroads, 325
Regulation of Transportation Agencies, 325, 339, 387
Reinsberg, M., 573, 629, 630
Report of Federal Coordinator of Transportation, 325, 510
Report of the Presidential Railroad Commission, 511
Report of the Royal Commission on Transportation (Canada), 457
Revision of Federal Transportation Policy (Week's Report), 68, 330, 400, 436
Richmond, S. B., 385
Ripley, W. Z., 58, 302, 450–51
River Lines v. Southern Pacific Pipe Lines Inc., 428
Roberts, M. J., 141
Robertson, D. H., 135
Robinson, E. A. G., 67
Robinson, Joan, 169
Rock Island Motor Transit Company—Purchase—White Line Motor Freight Company, 350
Rostow, E. V., 390
Rules to Govern the Assembling and Presenting of Cost Evidence, 183, 435

S

St. Louis and O'Fallon Railway Company v. United States, 223
Sampson, R. J., 448
San Diego Land and Town Co. v. Jasper, 217
Sargent, J. R., 196
Sawyer Report; *see Unified and Coordinated Federal Program for Transportation*
Schenley Distillers Motor Division Inc., Contract Carrier Application, 345
Seaboard Airline Railroad Company—Atlantic Coast Line Railroad Company, 455
Seaboard Airline Railroad v. United States, 456
Service, control of
  certificates for public convenience and necessity, 117
  Civil Aeronautics Board, 117
  extra services, 119
  Interstate Commerce Commission, 116
  permits, 117
  rail passenger service, 118
  sanctions for regulated carriers, 116–19

Services
  coordination of
    joint action, 122
    through routes and joint rates, 122
    T.O.F.C., 123
    traffic interchange, 123
  terminal
    "belt" lines, 121
    freight, 121
    less-than-carload freight, 121
    passengers, 120
    reciprocal switching, 121
Shreveport case, 293
Simpson v. Shepard, 215, 217, 293
Smathers Report; *see Problems of the Railroads*
Smith, N. L., 142, 225
Smith v. Cahoon, 264, 336
Smykay, E. W., 141
Smyth v. Ames, 216
Southern California Research Council, 554, 618
Southwestern Bell Telephone Company v. Public Service Commission of Missouri, 217
Stahl, S. W., 589
State of Georgia v. Pennsylvania Railroad Company, 251
Stenason, J., 141, 142, 195, 196, 360
Stephenson, George, 53
Stephenson v. Binford, 336
Stigler, G. J., 135, 157, 165
Stocking, G. W., 158
Stone v. Farmers' Loan and Trust Co., 215, 273, 292
Study of REA Express, 111
Subsidy for United States Certified Air Carriers, 495
Summary of Size and Weight Limits, 338
Supplementary Report of the Highway Cost Allocation Study, 489, 492, 500
Swaine, H. H., 374

T

Taff, C. A., 235, 239, 251, 483
Task Force Report on Regulatory Commissions, 277, 533
Taylor, F. M., 131
Technology, effects of changing
  dominant type of carrier, 67
  effects on traffic, 67, 68
  improved transportation, 66
  issue of public ownership, 70
  pervasive competition, 68
  role of common carrier, 70
  structure of transport, 66
Terminal Railroad Association of St. Louis, 585

Terminals, transport; *see also* Airports; Motor terminals; Port of New York Authority; Railroads, terminals; Services, terminals; Urban transport; Water, terminals
  intercity and urban transport, 578
  problem, 412, 579–81
Through Routes and Joint Rates between Ohio and Mississippi Transit Company and Other Common Carriers, 249
To Rob Our Youth, 498
Traffic routes
  air, 89
  highway, 89
  maps, 86, 90, 91, 92, 93, 94, 95, 96, 97, 99, 100, 101, 102, 103
Transcontinental and Western Air, North-South California Service, 371
Transport
  concentration and decentralization, 7
  economic structure
    differences in, 129
    group of industries, 127
    products substitutable, 128
  economical system of, 18
  efficiency principle, 19
  engineering versus economic aspects, 5
  function of, 4
  geography
    implications, 77
    railroad districts, 81
    resources for traffic flows, 80
    topography of the United States, 78–79
    traffic sources, 82; *see also* Traffic routes
  group of industries, 21
  limitations on competition, 21
  location
    basis of traffic routes, 7
    urban centers, 8
  meaning of cheap transport, 19
  mixed system of ownership, 20
  nature of, 3
  object of consumption, 4
  part of production, 5
  political basis
    common carrier obligations, 17
    eminent domain, 16
    Interstate Commerce Act, 17
    national defense, 16
    political unity, 15
  and prices
    price policies, meaning, functions of, and strategy, 8
    price policies in transport, 9–10
      incidence of freight rates, 10
      limitations on competition, 9

Transport—*Cont.*
  and prices—*Cont.*
    price policies in transport—*Cont.*
      unique problem of discrimination, 10
    pricing theory; *see also* Railroads, rate-making theory
      ascertain precise costs, 177
      reflection of costs, 176
      relevant costs, 178
    problem
      changing nature, 399
      formulation of policy, 400
      general objectives of public policy, 402
      national issues, 395
      public investigations, 400, 401
      uniqueness, 396, 399
    public investment, 22
    ruinous competition, 23
    scope of, 4
  services; *see also* Common carriers
    carrier groupings, 104
    private carriers, 105
  system
    multiplicity of agencies, 25
    multiplicity of ownership, 25
    ownership integration, 25
    principal groupings, 26
    relative importance of agencies, 26
    volume of intercity traffic, 26
  total investment, 45
  unique position of, 21
  and urban structure; *see also* Urban transport
    changing function of central city
      growing obsolescence, 557
      loss of population, 556
      shift of employment, 557
      Los Angeles industrial structure, 558–62
      Los Angeles residential structure, 562–67
    pattern of traffic movements, 567–68
    urban development
      decentralization, 556
      effect of railroads, 555
      new technologies, 555
Transportation
  development
    early transport, 48–49
      costs, 49
      traffic, 49
    significance of history, 47–48
  effects of improvement
    consumption and transport, 13
    development of technology, 11
    measuring the gains, 15
    mechanical power, 11

Transportation—*Cont.*
  effects of improvement—*Cont.*
    modern city life, 14
      transcontinental railroads, 14
    national defense, 14
    pervasive competition, 12
    political and social effects, 13
    production and transport, 13
  rise of modern; *see also* Railroads
    canals, 51
    coastwise shipping, 50
    domestic water transport, 50
    Great Lakes, 51–52
      traffic, 52
    value of commerce, 50
Transportation Act, 1920
  basis of new policy, 313
  car service, 320
  certificates of public convenience and necessity, 320
  consolidation of railroads, 318; *see also* Railroads, consolidation
  joint use of terminals, 321
  pooling, 319
  rule of rate making, 316
  transitional provisions, 316
Transportation Act, 1933
  consolidations, 326
  emergency provisions, 324
  rule of rate making, 325
Transportation Act, 1940; *see also* Regulation, water transportation
  Board of Investigation and Research, 329
  consolidation, 328
  declaration of national policy, 326
  land-grant rates, 328
  rate making, 327
Transportation Act, 1958, provisions
  discontinuance of train service, 331
  guaranteed loans, 330
  intrastate rates, 331
  rule of rate making, 332
    difficulties of, 332
Transportation in the Los Angeles Area, 576, 618
Transportation Plan for the National Capital Region, 572, 574, 606, 609
Turell, George, 51

U

Ullman, E. L., 80, 87, 98, 100
Unified and Coordinated Federal Program for Transportation (Sawyer Report), 400, 533
United Air Lines v. *Civil Aeronautics Board,* 376
United-Capital Merger Case, 382
United Parcel Service, 111

United Railways and Electric Company of Baltimore v. *H. E. West et al.,* 218
United States v. *Association of American Railroads,* 251
United States v. *Carolina Freight Carriers Corporation,* 347
United States v. *Champlin Refining Company,* 391
United States v. *Delaware and Hudson Railroad Company,* 302
United States v. *Drum,* 350
United States v. *Elgin, Joliet and Eastern Railway Company,* 302
United States v. *Reading Co.,* 302
United States v. *Rock Royal Co-operative, Inc.,* 264
United States v. *South-Eastern Underwriters Association,* 266
United States v. *Trans-Missouri Freight Association,* 251, 424
United States v. *Union Pacific Railroad Company,* 450
Urban transport; *see also* Commuter problem; Terminals, transport; Transport, and urban structure
  Chicago study, 612–13
  finance
    need for single authority, 576
    urban rapid transit, 576
  impact of technology, 548, 550
  industrialization and transport, 551
    rail facilities, 551
    street railway, 551
  inertia of the past, 554–55
    concentration of economic activity, 554
    vested interests, 555
  levels of government, 549
  Los Angeles program
    background of problem, 613–14
      population density, 614
    financing, 616–17
    Los Angeles Metropolitan Transit Authority
      Act of 1951, 615
      Act of 1957, 615–16
      Act of 1964, 617–18
  organization
    different means of transport, 575
    Los Angeles area, 575–76
    multiplicity of jurisdictions, 575
  President Kennedy's message
    emergency aid, 624
    Housing Act, 1954, 622
    Housing Act, 1961, 622
    interstate compacts, 625
    long-range program, 623
      eligibility, 623
      federal aid, 623
    mass transit research, 625

Urban transport—*Cont.*
President Kennedy's message—*Cont.*
relocation assistance, 624
role of the highways, 624
Urban Transportation, Joint Report, 622
pricing
aid to private automobiles, 573
electronic devices, 574
possible devices
free mass transportation, 573
parking facilities, 573
user taxes, 572
rationing of service, 571–72
need for, 572
problem of resource allocation, 549
proposed solutions
consulting reports, 632
Doyle Report; *see also* Doyle Report
conclusion, 605–6
federal legislative aid, 603
legal organization, 604
Metropolitan Transportation Authority, 605
urban transport problem, 602
problem of planning
effect of fares on transit, 630
need for planning, 627
roles of modes of transport, 629
technology running wild, 631
urban concentration, 631
revolution by automobile
cars per capita, 553
central business district, 553
city travel, 552
terminal facilities, 554
transport of goods, 553
urban passenger transport, 553
rise of the city, 550
San Francisco Bay area
Bay Area Rapid Transit District, 620–21
cost estimates, 621
financing the system, 620–21
powers, 620
rapid transit system, 620
geographical setting, 618
population growth, 619
Washington program
interstate compact, 612
Joint Committee, report, 608–12
proposals for action, 609–12
Mass Transportation Survey Report, 606–7
mass passenger transportation, 606
recommendations, 607
National Capital Transportation Act, 1960, 610

Urban transport—*Cont.*
Washington program—*Cont.*
National Capital Transportation Act, 1965, 611
National Capital Transportation Corporation, 611
Washington Metropolitan Area Transit Authority, 612
Urban Mass Transportation Act, 1964
Department of Housing and Urban Development, 625
Department of Transportation Act (1966), 625
federal funds, 625
report to the President, 626
Urban Transportation, 662

V

Valuation Act, 1913, provisions and purposes, 308
"Value of Service in Rate-Making," 232
van Metre, T. W., 383
Vernon, R., 557
Vickrey, W., 572, 629
Viner, Jacob, 165
Virginia—Norfolk and Western Merger, 452

W

Wabash, St. Louis and Pacific Railway Company v. *Illinois,* 268, 292
Walker, G. R., Jr., 499
Ward, E. S., 251
Water, terminals, Interchange facilities and port administration, 593
Water Resources Activities in the United States, 38, 40
Water transport, domestic
financing; *see* Financing, domestic water carriers
inland waterway system, 37
investment, 38
rate-making theory, 192
role of water transport, 39–40
advantages, 40
disadvantages, 39
traffic, 40
types of carriers, 36
waterways system, 36, 37
Watkins, Edgar, 246, 284
Watkins, M. W., 158, 169
Week's Report; *see Revision of Federal Transportation Policy*
Western Air Lines v. *Public Utilities Commission of California,* 369
Western Rail Grain Rates, 426
Westmeyer, R. E., 294, 474
Wilbur Smith and Associates, 573
Willcox v. *Consolidated Gas Company,* 217

Williams, E. W., Jr., 109, 110, 308, 332, 333, 401, 402, 500
Wilson, G. L., 26, 109
Wilson, G. W., 129, 183
Wilson v. *New,* 506
Windom Committee, 295
Wisconsin passenger fares case, 294
Wisehart, A. M., 516
Wohl, Martin, 556, 567
Wolbert, G. S., Jr., 390, 391
Wolff Packing Company v. *Industrial Court of Kansas,* 263

Wood, R. C., 601
Wright, C. W., 473
Wright brothers, 63

Y

Yakus v. *United States,* 201
Youngstown Sheet and Tube Company v. *Sawyer,* 256

Z

Zeppelin, Count Ferdinand von, 63
Zwick, C., 141, 142, 195, 196, 360

This book has been set in 12 point and 10 point Garamond #3, leaded 1 point. Part and chapter numbers and titles are in 18 point Spartan Medium. The size of the type page is 27 by 46½ picas.